CW00749839

MASTERS UNDER GOD

Makers of Empire: 1816–1884

A HISTORY OF THE BRITISH MERCHANT NAVY
VOLUME THREE

MASTERS UNDER GOD

Makers of Empire: 1816–1884

RICHARD WOODMAN

The History Press

'They mark our passage as a race of men,

Earth will not see such ships again.'

John Masefield.

First published 2009

The History Press
The Mill, Brimscombe Port
Stroud, Gloucestershire, GL5 2QG
www.thehistorypress.co.uk

© Richard Woodman, 2009

The right of Richard Woodman to be identified as the Author
of this work has been asserted in accordance with the
Copyrights, Designs and Patents Act 1988.

All rights reserved. No part of this book may be reprinted
or reproduced or utilised in any form or by any electronic,
mechanical or other means, now known or hereafter invented,
including photocopying and recording, or in any information
storage or retrieval system, without the permission in writing
from the Publishers.

British Library Cataloguing in Publication Data.
A catalogue record for this book is available from the British Library.

ISBN 978 0 7524 4820 6

Typesetting and origination by The History Press
Printed in Great Britain

CONTENTS

A first-class East Indiaman of 1,425-tons burthen, the HCS *Thames* was built by Barnard at Deptford in 1819. She made six voyages to the East before being sold to a succession of owners including Joseph Somes and Green & Co. She was broken up in 1843. She is shown here in an etching by E.W. Cooke. (Private Collection)

INTRODUCTION

Into the Eye of the Wind

The second volume of this work, *Britannia's Realm*, brought the history of the British merchant marine to the year 1816, three years after the East India Company had lost its monopoly to trade with India — though not with China, which was extended for twenty years — and within months of the defeat of Napoleonic France. With the ending of the long war, the political map of Europe had, it was thought, been settled under the now benign enlightenment of monarchy, and an explosion of industry, innovation and exploration seemed to usher in a modern age.

Thanks to the success of the Royal Navy, backed by a wealth-generating trade carried in merchant ships, Great Britain stood highest among the leading nations of the world, able to maintain and superintend a global *Pax Britannica*. But at home, post-war demobilisation and the adjustment to a peace-time economy brought wide-spread unemployment, social hardship and a long and difficult Tory administration under Robert Jenkinson, second Earl of Liverpool. Even after Liverpool's fall, he was succeeded by Tories: Canning, Lord Ripon briefly, and the Duke of Wellington, so that it was 1830 before the election of Charles, Earl Grey, initiated the reform of Parliament and the much needed social improvements which, in Britain at least, characterised the later nineteenth century. Elsewhere, the *Pax Britannica* was far from peaceful. Setting aside the social turmoil in Europe and the internecine suspicions that would culminate in the First World War, the imperial age would inflict the misery of what Kipling called 'the savage wars of peace' upon countless hapless people, and many of these one-sided conflicts involved the British mercantile marine. Indeed, it was the Opium Wars with China from which derived the *canaille* that 'trade followed the flag'. As I have previously argued, this was rarely the case, and the Opium Wars are the starkest example of 'trade' embroiling 'the flag' in the first place. Most obviously of direct benefit to British shipping were the Crimean and Boer Wars, in both of which troops had to be conveyed to a distant theatre of hostilities, but this was also true of other British military operations in South Africa, as well as in Burma, Sri Lanka, New Zealand, Canada, the West Indies and elsewhere, where either territorial aggrandise-ment or the suppression of rebellion were undertaken. All the while British India, with its mid-century 'Mutiny' and its long border disputes on the north-west frontier, kept shipping busy, while the least known of these 'bush-wars' — but of considerable importance to British seafarers in the Far East — was the extirpation of the *orang laut*, or the piratical 'sea-people' of Borneo, carried out during the 1840s. Perhaps more surprising is the effect of the American Civil War upon British shipping, since it temporarily removed the United States as a competitor.

A steady increase in the size of the British merchant fleet, attracting greater government and public interest during the nineteenth century, saw the introduction of the generic term 'Mercantile Marine' in place of the former 'merchant service', and it was this vague and sometimes unruly entity that the Board of Trade came to regulate. For shipping, the century between the end of the Napoleonic War and the outbreak of the First World War was indubitably 'British', and British ship-owners were eager to seize opportunities as they were offered. The opening up of the trade to India had, by 1816, attracted the attention of Thomas Brocklebank of Whitehaven. Loading the *Princess Charlotte* with a valuable cargo, he sent her under Captain McKean on a voyage to Calcutta, while at home the first coastal steamers were defying nature by proceeding 'against wind, waves and tide'.

The ability of steam-vessels to head into the eye of the wind would, in due course, shorten trans-oceanic passage time and quicken the heart-beat of humanity, but it is worth noting that the commercial sailing-vessel continued to develop throughout the nineteenth century, co-existing alongside the new-fangled steamer and even benefiting directly herself from the necessity to transport high-quality coal from British mines to the various bunkering ports of the world. Thus stocks of coal lay ready for both the merchant steamer and Britannia's new steam-powered men-of-war. Fascination with technical innovation and the promotion of progress as a primary historical theme has obscured this co-existence, and the fact that there were so many sailing ships. British mariners thus manned the sailing-vessel at the peak of her development, while others wrestled with the new technology of steam-propulsion, turning an innovation into a viable machine.

Indeed, it is clear that as steamers developed, they generated their own commerce, greatly expanding Britain's trade and carrying-capacity long before actually displacing the ocean-going sailing-vessel. Even in coastal waters the 1844 view of Brodie Wilcox, one of the founders of the Peninsular & Oriental Steam Navigation Co., was that: 'All the main articles conveyed coastwise are still left untouched to the sailing coasting vessels, such as iron, copper, lead, stone, lime, coals, timber.' In fact, Wilcox argued, 'coasting in steam vessels has taken existence from steam navigation, such as whole cargoes of cattle and dead meat, which never came by sailing-vessels.'

It was to be 1881 before steam supplanted sail on the long-haul deep-water routes of the world with the arrival of the *Aberdeen* in Australia, though the Western Ocean packet had given way to the ocean liner long before this. The period covered by this volume is therefore only partly one of transition, but more properly chronicles the twin development of the maturing steamer, alongside the continuing success of commercial sail.

To chronicle all these disparate activities across the globe is impossible; the challenge of cobbling anything resembling a conventional 'history' is problem enough, so it seems only fair to explain to the reader that if I have followed selected shipping enterprises, or a particular trade, or train of events, this has not been entirely arbitrary. As with the previous volumes, this work generally follows each theme to a conclusion before embarking upon another. Amid these strands there are the finer yarns of personal exploit. To some extent this uncouples the chronology, requiring an elasticity of chapter time-frames, but I hope that the interest inherent in each is worth unravelling, for it seems so to me. In this respect — and since this volume deals with the growth of South Africa, New Zealand and in particular Australia — I have, of necessity, wound the clock back a little, to recapitulate on the early transportation of convicts. Likewise, I have also exceeded the time-limit of 1884 in relating the development of the mail service to the Cape of Good Hope.

In covering the first half-century — 1816 to 1866 — I have treated 'sail' and 'steam' as distinct elements as they enjoyed their differing fortunes and were essentially separate in their operation. They converge tidily in the late 1860s with the coming-of-age of the steam-vessel and the opening of the Suez Canal, from which the final triumph of steam-propulsion flows naturally, though not quite seamlessly.

One significant event occurred in 1864, and that was the regulation of the use of British ensigns. Hitherto merchant ships had generally flown the red ensign of Great Britain, though the blue and white were occasionally and indiscriminately resorted to, usually upon a special occasion. At this time the red ensign was concurrently the senior naval ensign, the fleet's hierarchy having been organised in the reign of Charles II into three squadrons of descending seniority: red, white and blue. In 1864 the Admiralty retained the white ensign for its own exclusive use, though yachts of the Royal Yacht Squadron were privileged to wear it on the assumption that, being then generally substantial vessels, they would be offered for service in time of war. The blue ensign was reserved for official craft and naval auxiliaries, appearing either plain or defaced with some appropriate device, a measure also extended to select yacht clubs. The Union flag was also reserved as a jack for men-of-war or the personal flag of an admiral-of-the-fleet when hoisted to the main truck. Union flags were forbidden to merchant ships unless bordered in white, in which case they could be used as a jack,[1] hoisted at the bow, or as a flag for a British pilot to replace the former use of the Union flag. Most shipping companies tended to favour a diminutive form of their own house-flag as a jack, while the signals for pilots, distress and so forth, were gradually codified into what would eventually, in 1897, be ratified as the International Code of Signals. Much of this was developed from Captain Frederick Marryat's code for merchant ships, helped half-heartedly by the first Board of Trade code of 1857, by which every vessel on the British registry was allocated with identifying signal letters, confusingly known as her 'numbers' and much beloved by pier-head artists.[2]

Finally, a few technical points: although I have not greatly troubled the reader with the history of the development of ships, a subject which I have dealt with elsewhere, an occasional reference to technicalities is necessary.[3] Where I have used contemporaneous terminology, particularly place names — not least because it was the common nautical argot of the day — the modern equivalent appears in parenthesis at least once in the text. I have also retained certain contemporary collective nouns which are now regarded as pejorative, such as 'coolie' and 'lascar', as no suitable synonym offers. No offence is intended and, I hope, none taken, as I hope none will be taken from my last confession: quite unapologetically, I have used the female pronoun for ships, even when they are named after males. It is an old and perhaps an odd tradition, but one I refuse to abandon, for I have, in my way, loved them. And finally, I take my title 'Masters under God' from an ancient insertion in bills of lading and other documentation concerning a ship and her cargo being placed under the charge of a master-mariner, the traditional title for the commanding officer of a merchant ship. The phrase does not appear to be legally defined by case-law, but was enshrined by underwriters in Lloyd's 'Ship-and-Goods' insurance policies from 1779. Sadly, 'after frequent instances of judicial criticism' – one of which as early as 1791 called it 'absurd and incoherent' – it was finally removed from Lloyd's Form of Marine Policy in 1983. However, even then it was not entirely moribund. As late as 1990 it was stated in the Admiralty Division of the Supreme Court of New South Wales that:

> whereas the old concept of 'the Master under God' had disappeared, and more egalitarian attitudes were now to be found on merchant ships, nevertheless, there had always to be one person on board a ship who had overall command and bore overall responsibility. No ship could safely put to sea without such a commander. Under normal circumstances the office of master carried with it great responsibility and it demanded special personal, training, experience and skill.[4]

How true; and how much the more-so when those circumstances strayed from the normal.

INTRODUCTION NOTES:

1. Properly a 'jack' is a flag flown at the bow of a vessel. Although the fashions of flag-etiquette have changed over time, a jack is normally taken down when the vessel is under way, though there are certain exceptions to this. An ensign is 'worn' in the after part of a ship and denotes its nationality, an important factor in establishing and maintaining the principle that a ship is an extension of that nation's territory.
2. Marryat's original identification signals were numerical, which accounts for the fact that the four-letter flag signals seen on so many ship-portraits were known as a ship's 'numbers'. Today a combination of both is used in alphanumeric form.
3. See Woodman, R., *The History of the Ship*, Conway Maritime, 1997.
4. Supreme Court of New South Wales, Admiralty Division, Carruthers, J., 15 June 1990. I am most grateful to Douglas Potter, William LacLachlan and Philip Roche for drawing my attention to this, the fact that the phrase 'Master under God' appears in the Admiralty Court Act Book of 1650 on a bill of lading; and that it is to be found in an insurance policy recorded in the Admiralty Assignation Book in 1692. To this erudition David Squire kindly ferreted out additional references to the term being used in the Netherlands in 1663, and in colonial Connecticut in 1745.

ACKNOWLEDGEMENTS

I would like to express my gratitude to the following who have helped in the preparation of this volume: Captain Peter Adams; Mr Alexander Aiken; Mr Rupert Baker of the Royal Society; Sir Michael Bibby; Captain Aris Finiefs; Captain Joshua Garner; Mr Michael Grey; Mr Gwilym Hodge; Mr William MacLachlan; Mr David Mole; Professor Sarah Palmer; Captain Graham Pepper; Mr Douglas Potter; Mr Paul Ridgway; Mr Philip Roche; Dr Ann Savours-Shirley; Mr Colin Singleton; Mr Michael Stammers; Commodore David Squire; Mr Adrian Vaughan; Mr Richard Walsh; Ms Sarah Williams; and Mr Harry Wright. All have offered time, advice, information, guidance, suggestions, resources or permission to use material in their possession, and I am most grateful for their interest and assistance. My thanks go to the staff of the National Maritime Museum's Picture Library, especially Mr Douglas McCarthy and Julie Cochrane; Nathan Pendlebury of Liverpool Museums and Matthew Bailey at the National Portrait Gallery. Finally, Mr Michael Charles, proprietor of the British Mercantile Marine Collection; Mr Richard Joslin of the N.R. Omell Gallery; Ms Susan Morris and Mr Richard Green of the Richard Green Gallery; Ms Barbara Jones of *Lloyd's Register of Shipping* and Ms Susie Cox, Curator of the P&O Heritage Collection, must have especial mention for their kindness and generosity in providing illustrations free of charge.

I must also express my gratitude to the Master and Wardens of the Honourable Company of Master Mariners and the staff aboard the HQS *Wellington* for help in sourcing some illustrations, logs and so forth. Although I have endeavoured to determine the origins of all images, I have been unable to discover the whereabouts of a few.

Richard Woodman
Harwich, 2009

ONE

'A COMPLETE DISGRACE TO THE BRITISH NATION'

British Shipping, Regulation and Redemption, 1816–1850

Napoleon Bonaparte once contemptuously remarked that the British were a nation of shop-keepers. Later, contemplating the ruins of his ambition along with the deep swells of the South Atlantic Ocean from the lofty isolation of St Helena, he also observed that wherever it was possible to float a vessel, there the French were certain to find a British ship. During the long wars of the French Revolution and Empire, Great Britain's Royal Navy had been compelled to adopt an all-weather world-strategy in order both to defeat France and her allies and to protect Britain's immense trade. This was essential not only for the preservation of Britain and the funding of her own war-effort, but for the subsidies she paid to her allies. The legacy of this was to leave Britain supreme at sea until the outbreak of war with Germany in 1914. According to Lord Roseberry, the exiled Napoleon added: 'You English can dictate to the World.'

So indeed it seemed, for, despite losses, the British mercantile marine had greatly increased in size during the war, from 16,079 to 24,418 vessels. In terms of capacity, the rise had been almost double from 1,540,000 tons in 1792 to 2,616,000 in 1814. Moreover, the only trade into which the war had made serious inroads was the near-continental traffic with France and the Low Countries, much else being conducted by hook-or-by-crook in defiance of edicts and economic blockade, as has been recounted in *Britannia's Realm*. The effects of war upon the Arctic and Pacific whale-fisheries were rapidly erased in the decade after the war, although the latter was not to endure.

Elsewhere matters looked favourable. In 1816 the highly restrictive Navigation Acts remained in force as a protection to British shipping and the Honourable East

India Company still enjoyed the greater part of its monopoly on trade with China – though it now shared that with India. These benefits, however, proved illusory. It was soon apparent that the British merchant fleet was too large, much of its tonnage was worn-out, and too many ships were chasing insufficient cargoes. Freight rates fell and hardship set in, mirroring what was occurring ashore as foreign competition from recovering economies elsewhere in Europe began to bite. Although the full repeal of the British Navigation Acts did not take place until 1849 and followed a period of erosion during which a policy of reciprocal removal of preferential duties had been adopted with those countries which would co-operate, Great Britain had of necessity virtually abandoned the principle of protecting her merchant shipping by reserving the carriage of colonial goods to British bottoms. The United States, which had gone to war with Great Britain between 1812 and 1814 over the principal of 'Free Trade,' was not slow to take advantage of the privilege of reciprocity; American ships were soon carrying cargoes between American and British ports, and to ports within the British Empire. Despite the short and bitter conflict, the United States had carried British trade by default, owing to the volume of British tonnage chartered by the Transport Board for trooping and supplying the British and Portuguese Army in Portugal and Spain during the Peninsular War.

Merchant seamen.
(Author's Collection)

Much of this trade was thereby permanently lost to British ships while the exigencies of war had produced in the Baltimore clipper a new hull-form, unconstrained by the archaic tonnage measurement regulations which hindered the development of British mercantile naval architecture, bound as it was throughout the long struggle with France between 1793 and 1815 to the restrictions of keeping in convoy. The fast American hulls, with hollow entrances and slim runs in their after-bodies, were designed as privateers to overtake their prey and out-run pursuing British cruisers. In this they had been successful, and on the rare occasions they were themselves captured, they spawned imitation. Seized in December 1814, the *Prince de Neuchâtel*'s lines were taken off at Portsmouth with consequences which will become clear presently.[1]

The clipper hull-form rapidly converted in peace to smart Yankee packets which had soon captured the post-war North American passenger and mail traffic, challenging notions of British maritime superiority. This Yankee enterprise was initiated by Jeremiah Thompson, a Yorkshire Quaker who had emigrated at the turn of the century. In 1818 he put the ship *Pacific* on the North Atlantic route, distinguishing her by a large black disc on her fore-topsail and thereby founding the American Black Ball Line. Thompson soon had four ships on the service, and they became the epitome of Yankee seamanship: fast, crack vessels whose masters were drivers and whose crews considered themselves without equal. Thompson expected his commanders to make a down-wind easterly crossing in under twenty-two days and a westbound one to windward in fewer than thirty-five, for which he rewarded them with a new coat, their wives receiving a new gown. The success of the Black Ball Line excited competition from other firms, and rivals rapidly appeared. The Red Star, Black Cross and Blue Swallowtail Packet companies, each with their own device on their fore-topsails, sped back and forth across the Atlantic, cocking-a-snook at post-war British complacency, picking up British passengers and mails and, at the same time, attracting a large number of British seamen who 'deserted' to the American flag. In 1839 Lieutenant Maury of the United States Navy remarked of the packets that: 'For strength, safety, fleetness and beauty; and for a combination of all the requisites of a good ship, in such admirable proportions, no nation can boast of vessels, public or private, comparable to them.'

Despite two serious disasters – the sinking of Black Ball's *Albion* off Ireland in 1822, with the loss of forty-four lives, and the disappearance of the Black Cross's *Crisis* in 1826 – far heavier losses were occurring among the British Admiralty brigs run by the Royal Navy as mail-packets on behalf of the General Post Office. These had become known among British seamen as 'coffin-brigs', and a Parliamentary Commission concluded in 1836 that American vessels were better-built than their British counterparts. Herein lay the genesis of British admiration for all things American.

Of lesser immediate impact than the domination of the North American packet-route, but of serious long-term effect, was the war-time system of licenses which had enabled trade to continue between Britain and Europe despite the constraints of Napoleonic exclusion. Such provisions, generously supported by British gold, British exports and British markets, provided opportunities and awakened ambition in foreign mercantile houses from which serious competition arose during the next sixty years. Traders resisted relinquishing what they had gained thereby, while a further complication was caused by the adoption of foreign-flags — most notably that of Austria as the sometime sovereign-power of the Port of Ostend — by British merchants and ship-owners wishing to break the East India Company's monopoly. Such a device created nothing less than a flag-of-convenience, and although long before the term itself had been coined, its benefits were realised.

Furthermore, the newly independent republics of South America were flooding the markets of the world with produce, under-cutting the exports of the British West Indies and directly attacking what had become a traditional British source of relatively stable-priced commodities. In home waters smuggling remained rife and was exacerbated by the economic depression at the end of the war, partly attributable to the rapid industrialisation of the country in the preceding thirty years and which had resulted in the forced migration of working people from their traditional rural way of life to toil as wage-slaves in the growing manufacturing towns.

To this social upheaval was added the rapid demobilization of the Royal Navy. Begun the instant Napoleon was exiled to Elba in 1814 and long before his final defeat on the field of Waterloo, this flooded the ports with thousands of unemployed seamen whose fates, having been decided by the harshness of the Government's Impress Service and its brutal press-gangs, were now at the mercy of market-forces.[2] This all added to the social unrest and economic stagnation that confronted Liverpool's Government, and only the throwing open of Indian trade to the 'free-traders' who had, under the East India Company's monopoly been considered 'interlopers', absorbed some of this redundant man-power. This was to the greater advantage of the ship-owner, rather than the common sailor.

While matters grew increasingly depressed in the general world of British commercial shipping, the ten years following the war were not entirely without merit or highlight. Nor were all seamen drink-sodden wrecks: seafarers suffered then, as they always have, from the taint of a bad name. While probity was not guaranteed in any class or rank of sailor, it was something expected of a member of the Religious Society of Friends, and there were many at sea who came from Quaker stock. One such was Edward Beck, and his service at sea in the 1820s warrants examination from the variety of experience he enjoyed. Beck was engaged as apprentice and cabin boy to Captain William Moyse — also a Quaker — of the brig *Constantia* of Liverpool, which he joined there in May 1823. Beck's early experiences in a small vessel were of discomfort and deprivation. Cleaning Moyse's accommodation was a job he 'soon learned to detest. There was too little of the sailor in it to please me, and in order that I might the sooner escape from it, I made myself useful on deck and to get all the information I could.'

The *Constantia* traded to Ireland, carrying a crew of master, mate, 'a sort of Second Mate' who was Moyse's son, a carpenter, one able-seaman 'and six apprentices — some of them as good as men, and indeed, but for their wages, the same six of us were Friends [Quakers], had received good educations…' As for his Quaker sensibilities, Ned Beck soon discovered that: 'Oaths, alas, I soon found at sea more plentiful than oakum', and in respect of a day of religious observance, even aboard a vessel so stiffened with sober Friends, he found that: 'There's no Sunday for sailors in seven fathoms of water.' The *Constantia* bore foodstuffs to Ireland, entering Waterford where Beck discovered the metamorphosis that transfigures a ship-master:

> With a rattling breeze we soon ran up into the King's Channel, which is a very deep and dangerous passage on account of some rocks, to avoid one of which (the Golden Rock) a boat had to carry out a thick rope to haul the ship from striking it. It required quickness and quietness, but our skipper set up such a roaring that he frightened everybody about him. It was the first specimen I had heard of his abilities in this way, and if anyone had told me that the gentle, inoffensive man that sat so quietly in the corner [of the Quaker Meeting House]…could have raised such a storm of words and with such astonishing volubility, I do not think…I could have given credit to it, and I often smiled…at the difference between his voice at a Friend's tea-table and aboard the *Constantia*.

Of their victuals, Beck records their daily allowances whilst in port and in a fresh-water river:

> We had, one pound of meat including bone, as much bread [biscuit]…as we chose to eat, an ounce of butter, one teaspoonful of coffee…and one ounce of sugar. The meat was always salt, except on Sundays, and alternately pork and beef, with at times…frequently though not always, potatoes. For drink we had as much water as we pleased to draw up from alongside, but nothing else. For plates each used his biscuit, cutting his meat upon it till…by this means they were fairly equally consumed.

However, there was no regular cook, and this duty was undertaken by one of the ship's boys. For homeward cargo they took aboard 380 pigs, first loading ballast and then 'hoisting them in (by hooking a rope round just behind their forelegs and walking them up to the yardarm) then, pushing them over the hatchway, lowered them into the hold where they were regaled with potatoes'. Some pig-men embarked to tend the cargo while the *Constantia* proceeded to the River Avon and afterwards to Swansea. Here they went into a graving dock where 'the old brig showed some dropsical symptoms'. Then:

> rather late one evening when we were loaded with coals for Waterford, our head ropes broke and we swung across the river, one end of the vessel lying very awkwardly pointed across, instead of facing, a strong ebb tide…considerably swollen by some heavy rain… She laid so, for some hours, in a position that subjected her to a very great strain, and to it we attributed all the misfortunes that befell us on the following passage.

Anchored in Swansea Bay awaiting the arrival of Moyse, who was still ashore, the mate discovered the brig was making water. All hands turned-to to pump, but when

Moyse rejoined he ordered the *Constantia* to proceed, and they 'left the Mumbles — as beautiful a moonlight evening…to match so fine a preceding day'. The *Constantia* reached Waterford safely and, having discharged her coals, loaded flour for London. It was now that they found the pump choked with mud and eventually traced the leak to the failure of the shipwrights at Swansea to caulk a seam. This was a fortunate discovery and while it necessitated a delay in 'seeing the ship ashore at the building yard', it was even more timely as 'we had [as] rough [a] passage up the English Channel as ever poor weather-beaten rogues need desire'. With the wind in the east, we:

> placed the brig under double-reefed topsails and kept tacking incessantly for ten days and nights, on one of which latter we were neatly run down by an East Indiaman, who was sailing in stately order before the breeze. It was very dark and rained very heavily, and cold… Fancy a little vessel…loaded so deeply that in the smoothest river we could dip a pail of water from alongside, and then imagine a noble large ship…with high and lofty sails, moving majestically, like a huge castle, over the waves, and some idea may be formed of our situation…she passed so close that we distinctly heard the order to move the helm…

Recalling the sight of the East Indiaman led the reminiscing Beck to contrast the hardships in vessels employed in the coastal and home trades with 'the youngsters brought up in the East India and foreign trades'. He had by now begun to tire of the *Constantia*: 'we were too little at sea, and too much in harbour', and in August the ambitious Beck joined the *Lady Frances*, Captain Robert Barry, then lying in the Pool of London, discharging coal from Sunderland whither the vessel returned. Here she loaded another cargo of coal from the 'keels', which brought the freight down the River Wear from the pits in 21-ton loads.

The *Lady Frances* was employed carrying coal to London in the winter, sailing for America or the Baltic in the summer. Beck's observations on Sunderland are of interest:

> The place owes its advancement completely to the spirit of its inhabitants. The harbour was good for nothing until they ran out, at a great expense, two piers a great distance into the sea, which makes a fine appearance; they each have a lighthouse, one is a landmark, the other to inform ships the height of the water on the bar — on which, with a gale of wind from the eastward, the sea breaks with a heavy swell at the entrance, which causes vessels frequently to miss it…, they are inevitably lost — and their crews with them, were it not for the admirable invention of the lifeboat…

The lifeboats of Henry Greathead which had entered service shortly before 1800 had provoked a general interest. A series of rescues made off the Isle of Man in 1823 brought a Bill before Parliament in the following year by which a voluntary body was formed; the precursor of the Royal National Lifeboat Institution.

Among the other wonders Beck observed at Sunderland was the iron bridge which 'was sufficiently high to admit laden ships of 400 tons' burthen sailing under it — but, when light, they are obliged to strike their topgallant masts'. Going ashore, Beck rode aboard one of 'the hinder wagon of eighteen empty ones drawn by a steam engine…' which were used to bring coals from the mines to the riverside. Here, early mechanisation was causing hardship:

> At the bottom of the hill the wagons are drawn over a kind of platform, where the bottoms of them are knocked out and, by means of a large chute, the coals are conveyed to the hold of the vessel loading, but there are engines for lifting them over the hatchway and then letting them [the coals] drop out…these engines are the means of preventing the poor from finding employment and cause great decrease in manual labour, and frequent attempts are made to injure them and their machinery.

In addition to coal, the *Lady Frances* loaded a large quantity of locally manufactured glassware and, having signed the crew on articles for a foreign voyage, she embarked her passengers. These consisted of 'an old man, his wife and one daughter, going in search of a land with no King to oppress them…' Beck remarked later that the fellow's expectations were unrealistic and fermented by the rather disparaged notions of William Cobbett. As an early example of a migrant family, this sailor's-eye view is informative. Beck supposed the man's 'enemies [to be] the King and the rich, for whom he fancies he is slaving. He is what is called a *leveller*, or one who believes the days are at hand when everything will be equally shared out to the beggars as well as the princes'.

Upon his ship's departure, Captain Barry 'cleared out at the Custom House to go Northward (on account of the expense of lights and harbours incurred by going by the English Channel)…' When they reached Ronaldsway a strong north-westerly wind compelled them to anchor. After a wait of three days for a fair wind, the *Lady Frances* sailed for Quebec. Captain Barry proved to be:

> an exceedingly agreeable, kind man and is much liked by all the crew; he is very desirous of giving me all the instruction in his power, both as to practice and theory, and I think we shall agree very well, because there is a mutual desire of being happy together. I am very satisfied with the change from coasting to foreign trade.

The passage was marked by strong winds and calms when the blowing of the Fin Whales 'disturbed the breathless silence… [and] very much resembles the noise made by a large puff of steam escaping from an engine…' Beck also observed the beneficial effects of the Bethel Seaman's Society which issued bibles and prayer books, abjured seafarers to observe the Lord's day and hoped that by this means 'many a profligate sailor [may be made] a sincere Christian'.

A waterspout, dolphins and porpoises beguiled him, the latter because they gamboled at night in a 'milk-sea' full of the bioluminescence caused by dinoflagellates, though Beck and his shipmates had a more portentous explanation:

One of our steady fellows told me the world was destroyed by a flood formerly, but when it is again so, it will be by fire; the rainbow when it rains is the assuring proof that the Lord will no more destroy it with water, but the fire there in the sea is to remind us that the days are approaching when all the ocean will be one flood of fire and will consume the earth we live upon.

As they ran out of food and Beck experimented with oatmeal and treacle — or burgoo — which he did not like, they ran into fog on the Grand Banks, taking in sail for fear of hitting the coast, especially the low-lying cay of Sable Island. They eventually sighted Cape Breton Island where they fell in with the *Harvest* of Sunderland, which had left Orkney at the same time as the *Lady Frances*. They also saw something less encouraging: 'the *Royal Edward* of and bound to Liverpool, a barque that I would not venture across the Western Ocean in…although she had very little sail upon her at the time, her gunwale was in the water. I really wonder how men will sail in such vessels…' Soon afterwards they embarked their pilot from 'a fine large boat… with three sprit sails…they [the pilot and his apprentice] live entirely in it, from the time they leave Quebec till they meet with a ship…' and entered the St Lawrence River. Four days later they lay 'anchored under Quebec', which loomed on the heights above, and here they discharged their passengers who proceeded upstream to Montreal by 'steamboat'.

Having discharged her cargo of glass and coal, the *Lady Frances* began to load 'deals' for home, moving first to Wolfe's, and then to Sillery Cove. Having filled the lower hold and the ''twixt decks' they topped-off their lading with a deck-cargo of sawn timber and 'announced the glad tidings to the rest of the ships in the cove with three loud hurrahs, which were all answered'. It had taken four weeks in all, but they were now penned in the St Laurence by easterly winds. Finally, on their way downstream, they 'encountered a tremendous squall with very heavy rain, in which we lost our main topgallant mast, broke the yard in two, and were in great danger of losing our topmasts'. With all made-good, they passed into the Gulf of St Lawrence and observed the splendours of the *Aurora Borealis* as they ran before a north-westerly wind under all plain sail plus 'top-mast and lower studding sails'. Next morning they sighted the *Harrisons* of London, then 'the largest ship trading to Quebec', which soon ran far ahead of the *Lady Frances*.

Once clear of the fog and the Grand Banks, Captain Barry proved something of a driver, keeping sail on the ship and running when opinion on board favoured heaving-to. Beck spent:

two as anxious hours as I ever recollect to have done; the safety of the ship and crew depend entirely on the helmsman — a mistake would very likely prove fatal to [all], so that the utmost care and vigilance is requisite for their preservation; we have not been much washed at present, except by one enormous sea which, breaking in by the main rigging, compelled us to take to it to get out of its way… Rather less wind last night, but as much this morning; obliged to set more sail, to make her run clear of the sea, which has a wicked appearance. Noon, in topgallant sails and took two reefs in the topsails, thick weather and much wind...

A week later they had a strong northerly gale, which was 'as bitterly cold as ever I felt in my life, I am sure it has come from Greenland...'They passed another ship hove-to and out-ran the gale, finding fairer weather, though this did not last:

> We were obliged to take in reef after reef, until we got her under the two double-reefed topsails... At 7 we were pooped by a heavy sea which did much damage, washing away the round house, paint locker...it was a mercy the poor fellow at the helm was not washed over the quarter....The sea broke all the panes in the sky-light...all away from the breakfast table in the cabin...

Two days later they saw land, finally identified through the murk as the Butt of Lewis. A course was laid for the Pentland Firth and the *Lady Frances* had a hard beat down the coast:

> All our hopes are now gone of getting into port for another week. It is a bad job, as all our tea and sugar is gone, all our beef spoilt, and our water growing short; the rigging is also getting bad and needs much repair, and all this within 30 miles of our harbour, it is truly mortifying...

However, after an absence of four months and a week, they arrived to pay-off in Sunderland.

Beck was just twenty years old, but his indentured time was far from over. He made a second transatlantic voyage in the *Lady Frances*, this time under a Captain Read who was a more nervous and less admirable man than Robert Barry. His position on board is unclear; although still an apprentice, he was no longer the menial cabin boy he had been when his indentures were new. In addition to her cargo of 'nine Keels of coal, one Keel of glass bottles, and one of earthen pots', the vessel embarked forty-seven passengers, all emigrants, and some livestock, including a gravid jenny-ass.Their passage was beset by the usual Western Ocean weather, but their real enemy was smallpox, which had been brought aboard by one of the passengers and killed several of them. One of the male passengers was buried – presumably so as not to upset the ladies – at two in the morning.

> [T]he body, sewed up in a blanket and rug with a great weight at the feet, was brought upon deck and laid upon one of the main hatches, which was rested upon the bulwark, the inner ends held by two men. At the mainmast stood the Captain and the crew, with a few of the male passengers, a lanthorn in one of their hands, by whose glimmering light the service for the dead was read that did credit to the Captain's feelings; when he came to the part 'ashes to ashes' etc., the inner end of the hatch [board] was raised and the body, sliding off, was deposited in its watery grave...

The proximity of sudden death was an ever-present danger, particularly in merchant ships with small crews. One blustery morning:

> the southerly wind freshened upon us, took in the m[ain] topgallant sail. The boy that helped the man stow it was very nearly lost, being pulled over the yard by the sail blowing over his head, but he held fast and the other man helped him into safety.

Both the close relationships that existed between the seafaring community and the problems of fixing their position under the usual overcast gloom of the Western Ocean is exemplified by an entry in Beck's diaries when, homeward from Quebec and approaching a landfall of the north-west coast of Scotland, they encountered another ship:

> After a fine run all night, at day break we discovered a sail upon the wind right ahead, apparently outward-bound; the sight of her gave us great satisfaction, as we felt sure of knowing where we were. 11 p.m., we spoke her, she proved to be the *Prince of Orange* of Sunderland, from Archangel bound to Chepstow [on the River Wye in Monmouthshire], Captain Cooke the Captain's brother-in-law; as it fell less wind just as we met, we had plenty of time to know of each other what cheer. They had experienced all fine westerly weather for a long time, and had not had any of the easterly gales which we have [had]. A relation of the [*Prince of Orange's*] Captain, of a fine brig called the *Robsons* which sailed on the 4th month 1st [i.e. 1 April — the style being Quaker] for Quebec, and which is no doubt entirely lost, learnt the melancholy tidings from us; he hopes, he says, to hear in time of the crew being saved. They saw the island of St Kilda at 3 this morning.

Such brief exchanges, with both vessels hove-to, were sometimes accompanied by the lowering of a boat and an exchange of stores or letters. This sort of thing was sometimes to a crew's disadvantage, as occurred to the *Lady Frances* when foul winds again prevented her fetching her destination quickly, for their food ran very low:

> What makes the case more aggravating for our Captain is that, thinking from what we had consumed on the passage out, we should have more than sufficient for home consumption, he spared two casks to one or two ships in Quebec who were in want.

On completion of this voyage his apprenticeship was over, so Beck took himself south and found a berth as third mate in the former East Indiaman *Woodford*, owned by Chapman & Co., whose senior partner, Captain Abel Chapman, stood high in the East India Company's inner circle. His son Alfred commanded the ship, his brother Edward serving as chief mate. The *Woodford* had actually been built at Bristol in 1819 to the account of Aaron Chapman, another member of the family who had originally chartered her for one voyage to the East India Company. Old Abel came aboard before the *Woodford* left the Thames, and Beck was 'gratified' by his 'kind attentions' and his 'enquiring of me after our mutual friends and giving me his good, sound, wholesome advice'.[3] Despite the private nature of the voyage, the *Woodford* was bound for Madras and Calcutta with a number of passengers, including East India Company servants and military officers, together with their families. Beck formed a good opinion of the crew:

> At noon Captain C. came on board, mustered our crew, and signed articles for the voyage. Wages for seamen two pounds five shillings; I have been agreeably disappointed in them, as I had quite expected to see a vile, drunken set of fellows, but our men have to this time behaved with the greatest propriety, altho' they have had part of their advance [of pay].

This was praise indeed for the somewhat priggish Beck, but he was soon induced to change his mind, for though his previous shipmates had been rough men, a few days later he found 'the inferiority of our sailors to those I have been accustomed to for the last two years in the coal trade – there are some good smart seamen, but the most part of them are quite middling'. It was not long before they showed other signs:

> This morning, from one of the men being insolent to the 2nd Officer, he was confined on the poop until half past ten, when, previously to the church service beginning, the hands were all mustered aft and then told by the Captain, surrounded by us [officers], that as this was the first instance of insubordination that had occurred he wished to let them know that, if anything of the kind occurred again, the individual so offending should most certainly be flogged, for he was determined that, before he would suffer anything of the kind, he would lay down his life on the quarterdeck. It had the desired effect; the man was turned to his duty, and all the men united in blaming him, as having behaved in an unseamanlike manner.

The ship's routine was strict, with the decks holystoned at 05.00 and an hour later 'two hands and the junior officers of the watch go into the fore hold and pump off 6 pints of fresh water to every man and boy on the ship'. At 07.30 the hammocks were piped up and aired in the nettings above the bulwarks, whereupon the hands went to breakfast, the passengers following suit at 08.30. At this point the watch was piped on deck and given maintenance tasks in the rigging, about the decks or assisting the sailmaker or carpenter. These duties ended at 11.30 when the ship was pumped dry, and in the meanwhile the officers assembled on the poop with their sextants to observe the meridian altitude of the sun and calculate the vessel's latitude at noon. As the sun culminated in the commander's horizon mirror, he called out, 'Strike the bell eight! Boatswain, pipe to dinner! Boatswain's mates, pipe to grog!' The deck then became the scene of lively activity with 'the cook of each mess getting the dinner ready, the caterers with their pots to receive the grog, the boys going backwards and forwards from the coppers, altogether make a bustling scene'.

Beck was among the sun's observers on the poop, confessing that he was 'exceed-
ingly gratified with the opportunities…of increasing my stock of naval theoretical
experience, and after being used to five, I do not know how I should like to be again
in a ship without one chronometer'. Later:

> As a proof of the clearness of the atmosphere, it is worth remarking that Venus could
> be seen this day at 11 o'clock [in the forenoon]…and the distance between the sun
> and moon's lines, taken for the purpose of ascertaining the Longitude, was to be
> observed with beautiful exactness; it afforded me the finest opportunity of taking a
> lunar distance I have yet had, and was not neglected.

The ability to determine longitude by lunar observation, combined here with longitude by chronometer and possibly by the Sumner Line just then being promulgated
as a means of fixing position, is evidence of both Beck's competence and of Captain
Chapman's diligence. Chapman promoted Beck acting second mate owing to the
indisposition of Mr Duncan Lard. 'Altho' an arduous task,' Beck writes, 'it gives me
the situation I want to fill'. He was not long left in this post and before leaving
Calcutta, where a new officer was engaged, Beck was reverted to his former rank
of third mate, a move he considered a demotion and one which may have led him
to abandon his journal. The *Woodford* returned to London on 23 May 1826 and was
taken up by the Transport Board to carry convicts to Australia, thanks to the 'very fair
height in her 'tween decks'. Already provided with twenty-seven cabins for the Indian
trade, accommodation for the felons was provided at the Government's expense from:

> the fore part of the main hatchway to the fore part of the fore one; from there to the
> bows was appropriated as an hospital for their sick and fitted up accordingly. Abreast
> the main hatchway, to fore part of the after hatchway of the starboard side, was fitted
> up for the soldiers or guard, and on the larboard side was the part appropriated to
> the seamen, etc. belonging to the ship; from the bulkhead, including the…spaces
> right aft, where the [eight] cabins for the officers and the passengers… the poor
> accommodation for the Captain, Surgeon, Commander of the troops and part of
> the colonial secretary's family, remained the same…
>
> The lower deck or prison is divided into bed places, each for four men… Before
> each row of bed cabins is a seat fore and aft for them to sit on, they not being
> allowed to get into their sleeping places during the day.

The transport of convicts to Australia had begun with the sailing of the First Fleet in
1787. The Second Fleet had left Portsmouth in January 1790 and consisted of fewer
ships among which the *Surprize, Neptune* and *Scarborough* had been chartered from
Camden, Calvert, King & Co., a firm having had close connections with slaving, the
East India Company and Trinity House. The Company was contracted to ship 1,006
felons for £17 per head, but the voyage proved disastrous for the ships were over-
crowded and the mortality rate was severe, with 267 prisoners dying at sea. Indeed,

although the *Neptune* landed 341 convicts, only seventy-two were healthy, and her hold was so foul that the stench drove back an Anglican chaplain who boarded the ship on arrival, and one man was found with thousands of lice on his body. The measures taken to confine the convicts had been heartless, the ankle-irons being more restrictive than the 'basils' and chains used in slavers, with the wretched felons denied exercise and proper food. One, Thomas Milburn, wrote to his family in Liverpool that he had been 'chained two and two together and confined in the hold during the whole course of our long voyage'. Such was their hunger that they were driven to desperate measures:

> we were scarcely allowed a sufficient quantity of victuals to keep us alive, and scarcely any water... when any of our comrades that were chained to us died, we kept it a secret as long as we could for the smell of the dead body, in order to get their allowance of provision, and many a time have I been glad to eat the poultice that was put to my leg for perfect hunger. I was chained to Humphrey Davies who died when we were about half way, and I lay beside his corpse about a week and got his allowance.

Captain Donald Traill, master of the *Neptune*, and Captain Nicholas Anstis of the *Scarborough*, were both guilty of what one of the junior officers of the New South Wales Corps sailing in the Second Fleet called 'villainy, oppression and shameful peculation' for, having delivered what remained of their convicts, they set up stalls to sell off the surplus food and slops that Camden, Calvert, King & Co. had provided. Some of the *Neptune*'s prisoners died after landing at Sydney Cove while others 'were not able to walk, to stand or stir themselves... Some creeped (sic) upon their hands and knees, and some were carried on the backs of others'. The only satisfaction in all this misery was the death on the outward voyage of the charterer's agent, Thomas Shapcote.

Although Governor Phillips collected evidence and sent it to London, the outcome was unsatisfactory. Anstis escaped scot-free of any penalty and although Traill was eventually brought to trial with his chief mate, both men were acquitted. Conditions were therefore little better on the departure of the Third Fleet in 1791, and of 1,869 men and 172 women who were taken aboard at Spithead, 173 men and nine women died, with a further 576 needing medical attention on arrival. Again, peculation had been rife and the convicts kept on half-rations, a fact that ended the contract with Camden, Calvert, King & Co.

The attraction of the trade for old ships and incompetent masters was a recipe for such abuses, given the state subsidies and the distractions of the war which began in 1793, but greater Government regulation was a welcome if tardy outcome. A system of deferred payments and the introduction of naval surgeons appointed by the Transport Board was brought in, the first sailing in the *Royal Admiral* in May 1792, initiating a slow improvement. But real reform was some way off, and it is shameful to record that vicious regimes of flogging were maintained in transports like the *Britannia* under

Captain Thomas Dennott, who terrorized his unstable surgeon, Augustus Beyer, and ordered one convict named James Brannon to receive 800 lashes, from which – after several days of agony – Brannon died. In all Dennott gave out 7,900 lashes and killed six of the Irish political prisoners he was responsible for conveying to the Antipodes. The subsequent enquiry ruled that Dennott had been 'over-zealous' and Beyer 'negligent', and, although neither served in a convict transport again, such punishments were far from condign. For the most part, however, the abuse of prisoners, though fatal to their well-being, consisted of the vile practice of with-holding a measure of food. This occurred aboard the *Queen*, whose second mate weighed out less than half the daily allotment of beef. Similarly, in 1798, Captain Hingston of the *Hillsborough* denied rations and double-ironed his convicts at night, refusing to exercise them and consequently losing a third during the voyage. Captain Brooks of the *Atlas* in 1801 ran a private cargo of 2,200 gallons of rum in anticipation of a ready market in Sydney Cove, indifferent to the fact that sixty of his charges expired on the voyage. Although he was forbidden to land his illegal cargo, Brooks was not removed from his command and, as Robert Hughes points out in his sorry tale of the penal colony, *The Fatal Shore*, Brooks commanded 'several more convict voyages and died, a respectable old salt, as a justice of the peace at Sydney'.

On embarking, the convicts were often in a dire condition following their confinement aboard the prison-hulks used to hold all felons awaiting transportation. Here they were made to labour at useless and deleterious tasks. The tempting opportunity for the convicts to mutiny and take-over the ship will have influenced many heartless masters to institute regimes so harsh as to be crushing, and in 1801 fourteen such mutineers were shot aboard the *Hercules* while thirty more died of disease and maltreatment. There is little doubt that during the long war the transportation of convicts attracted the dregs of the mercantile marine in both ships and men. However, the numbers of felons conveyed were limited and it would be 1814 before more than 1,000 arrived alive in a single year. With the coming of the peace and the consequent social upheaval, the number rose rapidly, by which time something of a more compassionate regime emerged. In 1814 the relatively liberal Governor Lachlan Macquarie ordered his personal surgeon, a convicted criminal named William Redfern, to conduct an enquiry into the deaths aboard the *Surry*, *Three Bees* and *General Hewitt* – an Indiaman trading as a private vessel under Captain Walter Campbell – which had just then arrived. Trusted by Macquarie, Redfern's position and background enabled him to access information from both convicts and crews, and to sift truth, falsehood and exaggeration. Redfern recommended the introduction of a strict regime of cleanliness and ventilation, the appointment of surgeon-superintendents 'as Officers with full power to exercise their Judgement, without being liable to the Control of the Masters of the Transports', and an inspection at the end of the outward passage. Three years later Macquarie had the master and officers of the transport *Chapman* arraigned for killing or wounding twenty-two alleged mutinous convicts with small-arms. He rightly anticipated he would fail to secure a conviction, but considered the case would 'protect the persons of the convicts…from the cruelties and violence to which they have heretofore been exposed'. Poor Macquarie brought official disapprobation upon himself, but he had succeeded in easing the convicts' conditions as Redfern's recommendations found favour in London and produced an immediately beneficial effect.

This was timely, for while only forty-two transports had left Britain between 1797 and 1800, each averaging about 200 souls, and between 1811 and 1816 only another 3,850 had arrived in Australia in twenty-three vessels, in the period 1816 to 1820 seventy-eight ships transported 13,221 convicts. Moreover, after Redfern's recommended regime became standard practice, the death-rate dropped from roughly one in thirty, to around one in 100. Most outward voyages took about 110 days, with a stop at Rio de Janeiro, although four vessels managed it in fewer than 100, the *Eliza I* in 1820, the *Guildford* in 1822, the *Norfolk* in 1829 and the *Emma Eugenia* which accomplished it in ninety-eight days in 1838. This then was the situation when Edward Beck was engaged in the *Woodford* which, like the *Guilford*, was an ex-East Indiaman chartered by the Transport Board for a voyage to Van Dieman's Land.

The *Woodford* had lost Alfred Chapman as her master. She was now commanded by her former chief mate, Edward Chapman, and a new mate named Rybot was engaged in his place. She proceeded to Spithead where she embarked 100 convicts who were under the direct supervision of the surgeon-superintendent, a Dr Dickson. This individual immediately showed his mettle by pinioning a man who complained about the rations, and it is interesting to note that although the crew was forbidden to talk to the felons, the *Woodford* was not the same well-ordered ship she had been on her previous voyage. There was quite obviously bad-blood between the officers who variously fell out as time passed, and Edward Chapman was not of the same calibre as his elder brother. Worse, the numerous floggings are reminiscent of a naval man-of-war, while even the apprentices gained access to grog, one being beaten for the offence of drunkenness, lashed incommunicado to the mizzen mast and put on bread and water for three days. On repeating the offence a few days later, the feckless youth was seized up and 'punished with the cat, with half a dozen [lashes each] from the other six apprentices'. Any infringement of good order among the convicts was met with a loss of privileges – of which there was really only one, being without leg-irons – plus a flogging administered by a hearty boatswain.

For the most part Dr Dickson's strict regime seems to have been not merely necessary but largely beneficial, given the confinement inherent in a 550-ton ship. Thirty-eight days out Beck records:

All going on well, several convicts ill of a low fever, the rest in good health, our own ship's company and soldiers quite well, excepting an ordinary seaman, who has been ill all the passage. The cleanliness preserved among the prisoners must have a very salutary effect, their clothes are scrubbed twice a week regularly and, as they all pass before...[the Surgeon Superintendent] as they receive their pint of lime juice, wine and water... and he is in the habit of not giving it them if dirty in their person, he is quite certain of their being washed once a day – for they would think nothing of being hand-cuffed a week, but stop their punch, and they are immediately punished to a desirable extent. It is a melancholy sight and I cannot accustom myself to see it without indifference, the degradation of so many fellow creatures who, hobbling about the decks with their irons rattling at their heels, seem to be quite indifferent to it.

However, this scene must have been transformed when the *Woodford* reached the higher southern latitudes and began to run her easting down. Now she laboured under:

> Very strong breezes from the westward [which soon] continued heavy squalls, some of them…enough to tear the masts out of her, at 5 o'clock the main topsail gave way, hauled it up and repaired it, double-reefed and set it again. Split the fore topsail…unbent it and got a new one out… We have had a good deal of hail with some of the squalls, and bitterly cold air. Got the dead lights on the lower after windows, the ladies all abed and frightened out of their wits. Midnight, double-reefed the fore topsail, reefed and furled the mainsail, squalls coming one after the other, strong and heavy, with lightning to the westward, indeed I thought several times the topmast[s] would have gone over the sides. Glass rising but no improvement…

Beck had proved himself with a chronometer, which he found unreliable, but he nevertheless:

> Obtained a victory, observed three sets of lunar observations, each within five degrees of the Captain's… It is certainly the most gratifying thing imaginable, to be able to determine without any other aid than a sextant our position upon the globe within a few miles.

Although he omits reference to the ephemeris also requisite to this accomplishment, it is clear that Beck's diligence was unremitting and that he took satisfaction from his auto-didacticism. This may have engendered certain smugness and been the root cause of the animus felt for him by Mr Rybot, the mate, but he was by now a mature officer with a keen sense of responsibility and the relief that goes with it when the weight was lifted from his shoulders. He was also challenging his commander's sea-sense, while recording the anxiety common to sea-officers navigating through waters still uncharted and where much was taken on trust:

> I have never been better pleased in my life than when I was relieved last night; the anxiety I felt under the press of sail we were carrying I cannot describe. I am sure no one can be easier than myself when, in my judgement, the canvas is equal to the breeze, and no one can be more miserable than I when I think the ship is carrying too much sail…in my humble opinion it is in the end a folly, as this ship loses in bad steering what she gains in her speed, besides the additional wear and tear. I should just notice that, when at dinner yesterday we felt the same motion as if the ship was touching the bottom slightly, the Captain immediately jumped in deck, as we have

laid down in the charts as very doubtful lots of shoals etc., but there was no appearance whatever of shoal water, and we concluded it must be the rudder.

On their arrival off Hobart the official persons came on board and took the height and particular marks of the prisoners, asked them their place of birth and about their crimes, how many times they had been convicted, whether they were married and what family, if they had relations here and where, asked them whether they had received their rations and if they had been humanely treated by the Surgeon, Captain, officers, people of the ship, and took all their answers down. They at the same time asked the Surgeon about their behaviour, and he told them about their characters from gaol in England, hulks, and on passage...

A few days later the convicts were landed and 'in this place of their exiles, they seemed very low-spirited and lost a good deal of the assurance they always possessed in so large a degree'. Once the human element of the *Woodford*'s lading was ashore, the crew turned their attention to the cargo proper and 'Broke bulk and began discharging government stores'. Here Rybot, having been both duplicitous and argumentative, was discharged by Chapman, and Beck found himself promoted in his place. From Hobart they loaded 800 sheep and 'thirteen most notorious prisoners... who are going to pass the rest of their days at Norfolk Island, where they are treated with the greatest rigour and work very hard; they are all ironed, and we have therefore that horrid jail-clanking in our ears'. The *Woodford* then sailed for Port Jackson:

> but whilst reefing our fore topsail in Storm Bay in a very heavy breeze of wind, Douglas Graham, a seaman working his passage to Sydney, a quiet, well-disposed man, fell head foremost from the topsail yard overboard and never rose again. We lowered the cutter immediately and the boatswain, a sailor and myself went immediately astern, but could not find him. It blew so hard that we could not fetch the ship again. The Captain wore ship and took us in tow, whilst they again wore on the larboard tack; I though we should have lost...[the cutter] whilst hooking on [the davit falls], the ship pitching a good deal...however we got the cutter hoisted up and secured again to the quarter...

When the weather eased they made for Sydney Cove and anchored in:

> the finest harbour in the world, with delightful scenery and the best accommodation for shipping, being just the same, where we lie, as if in a dock. We found here the *Warspite*, 74[-guns], *Success* and *Volage* frigates... The merchantmen are about seven ships, some with prisoners and some loading for London; we all be within hail of each other without any inconvenience...

Having embarked a detachment of troops, their equipment and stores, the *Woodford* sailed for Calcutta, laying a westwards course across the Great Australian Bight. Here they endured:

heavy seas, tremendous squalls, split sails, sever contusions, leaky decks, wet beds, no appetites, dinners spoilt, milk capsized, bad water, sprays flying over and wetting thro' thick clothing, lee lurches, weather rolls, cot-screens drawing, hammock lashings stranding, shelves falling, Captain grumbling, mates echoing, boatswain swearing, sailmaker drinking...

But a week later:

Weathered Cape Leeuwin after an absence from SW extremity of Van Dieman's Land of four weeks, of which I may safely say, we have had three weeks of continued gales of wind with heavy seas...

Heading north into the tropics, a routine of:

Gymnastic exercises among the troops seem[s] now to be the order of the evenings; some feats of agility I have witnessed among them that were quite astonishing...our tars, not liking to be left in the background, last evening took the shine out of the red coats...

At Calcutta there arose a rather obscure disagreement over the survey Beck and Second Mate Govey had made of the *Woodford*'s stock of fresh water for which Beck was confined to his cabin. Captain Edward Chapman's conduct at this point, based entirely on his victim's evidence, seems oddly irrational and, having humiliated Beck – who described his commander as a 'fickle young man' – normal relations were shortly afterwards restored, suggesting a temporary breakdown in the *Woodford*'s master. Certainly, whilst clearly a competent enough sea-officer, Chapman seems to have suffered a nervous collapse owing to the strain of the voyage and the heat in Bengal, which at this time drove the officers' steward to lose his reason and run amok while the crew was hit hard by malaria. Referring to Captain Chapman, from whose house he must perforce seek advancement, Beck – with Quaker forbearance – bore 'testimony to his general kindness to me' but also obtained a voluntary written testimonial from the military officers who witnessed his confinement. By the mediation of the surgeon, the difference – whatever it was, and Beck seems unclear of it himself – was patched up and put right, but Beck's journal ends abruptly shortly afterwards, in May 1827, at Calcutta. However, its 'Introduction', written much later, gives a clue as to the conclusion:

There was much to make me devoted to my profession, I was led on by the ambition of one day being the commander of an India ship, which I hoped to attain by my own exertions and which I fully believed would make my fortune. It seemed a long ladder when I began at the bottom, but I always endeavoured to think myself destined for the top. I persevered, rose step by step in a manner that gratified and incited me, reached the summit, stood there four days in the long wished-for command – was sold out – and am now a landsman – writing with the same moon shining through my window that has often been my pleasant watch companion on wide seas.

Beck's accounts of four routes followed by merchant shipping – the coasting, North Atlantic and Indian trades, and the carriage of convicts to the Antipodes – are invaluable both for their general and their personal insights. As for his last ship, the *Woodford*, she foundered off Madagascar on her way from Batavia to Amsterdam on 18 February 1829.

The incidence of such losses of merchant ships was of increasing public interest, as was much else in the merchant marine, and the 1830s saw a number of parliamentary enquiries set in motion, the details of which follow. One, which connects with Beck's remarks on the *Royal Edward* and his own experience in the *Lady Frances*, was the Royal Commission ordered to examine the numerous casualties suffered by vessels in the North American timber trade. Reporting in 1839, the Commission deplored the practice of carrying excessive deck-cargoes, but also drew attention to what the *Aberdeen Herald* of 13 July called 'the proved defect in the model of our mercantile marine…borne out to the very letter by…Parliamentary evidence…'

That matters remained far from satisfactory even *after* much official deliberation may be gleamed from the memoirs of a young Guernseyman, Hilary Marquand, who went to sea aged fourteen in November 1839 in the brig *Nancy*. Like Beck, Marquand's evidence of the general contemporary scene is best examined before reviewing the measures Government took to address the imperfections his story reveals. It is also worth mentioning that this period also marked great changes in hull-form – that 'model' to which the *Aberdeen Herald* referred with reference to the launch of the schooner *Scottish Maid*, which we shall come to presently.

Marquand left St Peter Port in the *Nancy*, bound for Havana to load coffee and sugar for Trieste, enduring such heavy weather that after her arrival in the Austrian port her repairs required the services of 'forty or more carpenters'. She then loaded beans for London, avoided a boat-load of pirates off the Barbary Coast and arrived off Gibraltar where her master, Captain Le Cheminant, was declared insane. This proved a ticklish business for the naval authorities. Le Cheminant declared his crew to be in a state of mutiny, and they were more inclined to favour the word of the *Nancy*'s master than heed the protestations of innocence made by Mr Cohu, her mate, supported by all her hands. From what Marquand reveals, however, it is probable that Le Cheminant's mental breakdown was caused by tertiary syphilis.

The *Nancy* returned to Havana 'with a part cargo of potatoes' before proceeding again to Trieste with coffee and sugar. She was now commanded by Captain Moses Reeves, a tall, balding muscular man in his early fifties and an inveterate tobacco chewer. Marquand leaves an unflattering portrait:

He wore large whiskers which…when left unshaven for a week or two resembled… the back of an old badger. His forehead was low and protruding, his eyes large and of the same colour as his beard, and with a large pair of eye-brows coarse and long, rather darker than grey… His nose formed a conspicuous part of his physiognomy, it could not have been less than six inches long…and at the base it was an immense width, perforated by two wide opened nostrils from which a bunch of hair hung.

No cargo was offered at Trieste, so the *Nancy* returned to Havana in ballast, and there found yellow fever raging. In the epidemic of 1841 'seven cases out of ten proved fatal', and Marquand himself was infected, spending thirty-nine days in the hospital where 'several hundreds were laying upon their stretchers in double rows in each ward, and at an average one every hour taken away to the grave prepared for them… This was a large pit…half filled with lime'. Marquand survived, but in doing so he 'endured many sufferings…'

> The repeated cuppings on my neck, shoulders and abdomen…left me literally weltering in my own blood, my hair which had grown long became clotted with gore…and…I was not allowed a drop of water to wash myself once during my illness. Wounds were inflicted on my thighs in thirty-two places on one and twenty-seven on the other… but that was not the worst part pertaining thereto, they had been inflicted for some particular purpose and therefore were not allowed to heal but must be kept open… Consequently every morning one of the assistant doctors (Mr Hayes)…by picking and probing…[removed] the scab…then taking some ointment…he would rub it in the raw flesh… Oh, it was a cruel pain to bear…

Marquand contracted gangrene in his right foot and amputation was in prospect until Reeves interposed and a Spanish doctor recommended the insertion of a silver tube in Marquand's knee by which means 'the putrid blood' was drawn off. In due course Marquand made a remarkably full recovery. The voyage, however, was a commercial disaster and the *Nancy* returned empty to Guernsey.

Marquand next shipped aboard the brig *Adelaide*, Captain Robert Taylor, as an ordinary seaman at a monthly wage of £1 15s. Having loaded codfish in Jersey, the *Adelaide* sailed for Rio de Janeiro, but not before Marquand had encountered Taylor's fist. The passage took forty-two days and there followed over two years of voyaging, from Rio to Trieste, on to Sète and back to Rio with a return cargo to Trieste and from thence to Cagliari in Sicily before returning again to Rio de Janeiro. The *Adelaide* now loaded a cargo for the Isle of Wight and Hamburg, where she was caught in the frozen Elbe and obliged to over-winter. 'It was a miserable time!' lamented Marquand, as was the voyage, for he fought the tyrannical Taylor when the master denied him grease to clean his hands. From the Elbe the brig carried a cargo to Newcastle before returning to St Peter Port after an absence of over two years.

In the spring of 1844 Marquand was invited to sail as second mate aboard the *Duke of Gloucester*, but protested he was unqualified, whereupon the owner declared him to have 'qualifications enough… I am satisfied by what I have heard of you that you will do'. The relevance of this casual appointment will shortly become clear, but it was unofficial, an acting rank, Marquand being selected as second mate from among the most able of the seamen. Captain John Touzeau appears to have been satisfied with Marquand's performance, for Marquand obtained a 'certificate of service' shortly afterwards, and it was this that thereafter established his 'qualifications'. The *Duke of Gloucester's* voyage, however, was not a success. She was bound for Ichaboe, an island off what is now Namibia, to load guano. Unlike the diggings off Peru, mentioned later, these deposits of some 300,000 tons were ravaged by February of the following year, having attracted hundreds of ships eager for cargo during a bad slump. A group of French seamen from a Nantes barque elected an Irishman named Ryan as president of a new republic, in an echo of the buccaneering days on the Campeachy Coast, but that too was short-lived. As for the *Duke of Gloucester*, she lost all her anchors in a heavy swell off the Skeleton Coast and Touzeau was obliged to run across to Rio de Janeiro where he obtained replacement anchors — from a British man-of-war — and a homeward cargo.

A year later, in March 1845, Marquand joined the *Swift*, Captain John David, a small, 95-ton brig then lying in London's West India Docks, which sailed for St Kitts in the West Indies. The *Swift's* crew was minimal; besides her master and second mate, she carried a chief mate, carpenter, five seamen, a cook and one poor apprentice. Marquand's wage was £2 10s per month and the voyage, about which he reveals nothing, lasted four months. On her next trip the *Swift* carried coal from Newport, Monmouthshire, to Malaga, there loading a ground tier of lead ingots before filling up with a cargo of raisins, almonds, grapes and nuts which, upon their discharge in London, added a mere 'handful to the already innumerable quantities stored in the vast magazines of Lower Thames Street'. Having been fortunate to survive a fall into the *Swift's* hold, Marquand made several voyages in her between Europe and the West Indies, principally to St Kitt's, Nevis, Trinidad and Jamaica, hauling cargoes of sugar and other commodities such as coffee and 'cocoa-nuts'. Between each voyage the *Swift* returned to St Peter Port to refit and give her crew a brief leave. By October 1847 Marquand, still only twenty-two, had risen to chief mate at £3 5s a month, sailing for Newport where the *Swift* took in coal and, after riding out westerly headwinds in Penarth Road, made for Cadiz, a passage taking three weeks. Loading salt, the *Swift* set off south for 'Bahia' in 'the Brazils'. On the passage the foremast carried away and, although temporarily repaired, needed more proper attention at Bahia (Salvador) where she arrived after forty-three days. Here Captain David found a cargo of sugar consigned to Stettin (Szczecin), then in Prussia, the *Swift* sailing on 11 March 1848. After a seventy-day passage she entered the Øresund only to learn that Prussia and Denmark were at war and Stettin was in a state of blockade. Captain David accordingly made for the Pomeranian Port of Stralsund where the *Swift's* sugar was unloaded and where he found a full load of wheat for Guernsey. The passage home was extremely rough, the *Swift* suffered severe damage and her fourteen-year-old cabin boy, John Brouard, fell overboard in the short, steep seas of the Øresund.

After repairs, the *Swift* left on 7 August in ballast for Pernambuco (Recife) to load sugar for London. She arrived in the Thames on 3 December, afterwards returning to Guernsey where Captain David was transferred into another of his owners' vessels and, on David's recommendation, Marquand found himself appointed master of the *Swift*. Having:

> gone through all the grades of my profession with more or less credit, and here I am now but twenty-three, chosen by a Committee of competent judges of qualifications to take charge of their property to the value thousands and thousands and not only as in charge of that property, but as that agent to execute with that property whatever transaction my own judgement might enable me to think fit for the promotion of their interest. It is no small charge, that of master of a ship trading around the world...

It is clear that Marquand's promotion had everything to do with trust and commercial acumen, and in this sense was typical of what might be called 'the old method'. His 'Committee of competent judges of qualifications' made no attempt to verify his skill as a navigator or seaman, though we may presume that David had reassured them on both scores. Even in reminiscence it is his business skill that Marquand chiefly self-eulogies. A master, he says:

> must be able to combine at once the essential qualities of merchant, and broker, to that of ship master, and I feel no reluctance to add that no man in whatever situation he may be, is surrounded by a greater set of disguised enemies in the mercantile world. From the tradesmen and the ship broker who present their cards with extreme professed civility on arrival, to the merchant in whose hand you place the consignment of your ship, and who receives you generally with all the courtesy imaginable, there is that avaricious feeling of imposition which if not wisely guarded against proves in the sequel [to be] of material consequence.

He goes on to rail against the rake-offs, fiddles and extortionate devices used by the 'gentle and affable dealer, who is always ready to treat you with a cigar at any hour of the day or with a small drop of brandy and water at eleven o'clock to give tone to the stomach'. He particularly inveighs against:

> The broker who generally acts in concert with the merchant, and who has a freight to offer not really worth accepting, will not scruple in calling falsehood to his assistance, to assure the...ship master that it is really the best freight in the market, that he had better accept it at once, as he is aware by secret channels that there is going to be a crisis in the freight market, and nothing will be done for five or six weeks. He commences by computing what the ship will carry, and in spite of your knowing the carrying capacities of your vessel, he will insist upon her carrying much more, showing reasons...why he is right, and you are wrong...

What with 'Custom House Charges', commissions and brokerage, plus deductions on sums advanced to the ship for her expenses in port, Marquand's rant continues:

[T]hese handsome remunerations, say on a cargo of wine value, or rather sold for, £30 per pipe, number of pipes we'll admit to be 350, the amount at once presents itself at £10,500, on which we will first charge the five per cent as commission which gives us £525, then five percent guarantee, which adds to the former an additional £525. Afterwards comes the discount of one per cent per month which swells to the vast amount of £1,890. The brokerage of two and a half per cent of course is not the merchant's but independent of that, we at once show a balance in favour of the merchant of £2,940.

A pretty fair transaction, certainly, considering that this is besides their 'Wine & cigar' money and other advantageous prerequisites. Is it any wonder if these princes of the mercantile world keep house as they do in foreign countries especially, and lavish such sums of money upon their numerous wives, and display in general such independence...

Apart from the sharks ashore, his lot at sea is little better. While his opinion of himself is high and that of many of his own cloth correspondingly low, Marquand's general comments on the ship-master's situation are not without honest insight:

It is true [he says] that the master of a ship has his officers with whom to associate, but oftentimes it will happen that they are such that a respectable and intelligent ship's master cannot make companions of them. Or if perchance they possess those qualities which will enable a companionship to exist...there is the urgent necessity of a master to prevent too much familiarity which entirely precludes the possibility of his officers to take the place of confidential friends. Thus without remedy is he left alone to brood over his misery, to brave the howling of the tempest, the roar of the mighty ocean dashing in milk white spray...over his tiny bark throughout the awful gloom of night...the whole imposing upon the mind a heavy burden... I do not wonder, nor can it be wondered by any, that many of my brother ship masters in their solitude fly to the recourse of stimulants to alleviate their gloom. But it is a great folly, as well as a great sin to do so, for while that remedy cheers the spirits for the time being, it ultimately causes a reaction which is distressingly depressing and sinks the mind into a brutal state of morbidness... It robs him of that energy which God has given him to overcome the trials that lay (sic) in his path... I have invariably found in the monotony of a seafaring life that there is nothing better adapted to disturb it than exercise; and I have had considerable share of trial, for I have had some officers...whom it was not only impossible to associate [with], but...who tried by all the well devised means in their wicked compositions to make me as unhappy as they possibly could, but I can assure my readers they have invariably fallen short of their desires, and have ultimately found themselves wounded with their own weapons. Exercise has been my remedy against all evil. Exercise has made me proof against their railings and back-bitings. Exercise had made me proof against the dangers of the tempest, and against the dreadful stillness of the calm...

There is a good deal more, and the chief interest in the foregoing is its evocation of conditions in small, deep-water merchantmen of the era. Marquand's life at sea was relatively unregulated by anything other than his principals' commercial interest. He married in 1851, becoming a ship-owner in his Sarnian home port, later moving to Cardiff where, ironically, he took up ship-broking himself, dying there in 1872.

In 1866, however, he was at Mangalore on the Malabar Coast in the ship *Channel Queen* in what was probably his last voyage. The details are sketchy, but the *Channel Queen* had been first to Adelaide, then on to Ceylon and Rangoon, and was loading coffee when he wrote to his wife, relating the capsizing of his gig on the bar and the loss of his 'hat, umbrella, and 21 pieces of clothing' which he was taking ashore to be laundered. Although still only forty-one years of age, he complains he is 'a martyr to rheumatism in the right arm and shoulder' from which he suffered 'so much at times that I could cry with pain. This does not affect my appetite or my spirits and hence do I call my health good'. But Captain Hilary Marquand, despite his relative youth, belonged to a past age. His career had begun as the fine-lined *Scottish Maid* ran down the slipways of Alexander Hood's Aberdeen yard and ended as Alfred Holt's steamer *Agamemnon* reached China. Both were epochal events, but, during the intervening three decades, Marquand, among hundreds of other British seafarers, had pottered about the globe in out-of-date ships, doing the world's work as adequately as he could.

While the traditional global trades prospered and those to the Orient were soon to greatly increase, the lure of oil had already taken hold. Until the discovery of mineral oils and the near contemporaneous demands of the internal combustion engine coincided, heat had been provided by coal and a plastic coating by natural tars. Lubrication and other requirements were obtained from a variety of sources, notably vegetable oils, such as rape- and linseed, while whales were the prime source of white oil. One consequence of the hunt for the Northern Right Whale was the lit streets of Whitby on the North Yorkshire coast, long before any other town in Britain boasted illumination greater than an ensconced torch, or the flares of the link-boys. As noted earlier, by 1790 the quest for whale-oil had led British whalers into the South Pacific. To the rendered blubber of the Right Whale — later to yield the baleen that was commonly called 'whale-bone' and made excellent corseting — could now be added the finer-quality oil of the sperm whale, with an occasional fortuitous bonus of ambergris. In addition to the risky hunting of the great whales, the whaling-vessels went in pursuit of the seal, walrus and sea lion, quarries that lured the most adventurous seamen towards both poles.

During the late war the northern fishery had suffered from the raids of French cruisers, but it recovered quickly thereafter, with Hull whalers dominating the national fleet. In 1816 fifty-five ships sailed north from the Humber, against London's nineteen, Aberdeen's fourteen and Leith's ten. Peterhead and Dundee both dispatched eight, Newcastle six, Montrose four, with Liverpool, Berwick, and Banff sending two apiece. Single ships went from King's Lynn, Grimsby, Greenock, Kirkwall and Kirkaldy, with the Whitby fleet — formerly the major component — sending eleven. The Banff ship, the *Earl of Fyffe*, was lost on the bar on 12 March, and a few others were disabled, but it was a sizeable showing. Once on the whaling grounds a number got into difficulties, especially the junior Captain Scoresby's *Esk* of Whitby. A successful whale-hunter, Scoresby had about 120 tons of blubber in the *Esk*'s hold when the ship ran foul of a submerged ice-shelf which tore off most of her keel, and she began to founder. Thanks to Scoresby's superb seamanship and assistance from other whalers, especially Captain Jackson and the crew of the *John*, the *Esk* was moored to a floe, her boats, stores and cargo of casked blubber were landed on the ice, her upper yards and masts were struck and she was hove-down. Scoresby, his carpenter and crew, with help from the crew of the *John*, repaired her as best they could, then reloaded her with half her lading and put the balance aboard the *John*. Jackson, who was Scoresby's brother-in-law, agreed to abandon his cruise and took the *Esk* in tow back to Whitby.

Captain Munroe — 'a most intelligent, experienced and successful whale fisher' — had that same year headed the *Neptune* north of Spitsbergen to reach 82° 15' North, but while the sea had been ice-free it had also been devoid of whales. It was increasingly clear that the Davis Strait offered better yields than the traditional Greenland and Spitsbergen grounds. Nevertheless, Jackson and Scoresby, who now commanded the *Mars*, returned to the Greenland coast in 1817 and, with Captain Bennett of the Hull-whaler *Venerable*, landed on Jan Mayen Island, climbed Smeerenburg Volcano and descended into the crater. From the Davis Strait the *Larkins* of Leith and the Aberdeen ship *Elizabeth* crossed Baffin Bay and encountered numerous whales on the seventy-seventh parallel, but in the strait itself at even higher latitude, on 5 May, a heavy gale wrecked four whalers in the ice. These were the *Dauntless*, Captain Bruce, and the *Fortitude*, Captain Galloway, both of London; the Liverpool ship *Lion*, Captain Nesbitt, and the *Leviathan* of Newcastle commanded by Captain Preswick. Fortunately their crews were rescued from their boats by other whalers, but Scoresby's *Mars*, which had doubled Cape Farewell in quest of whales, came across the water-logged *Dauntless* drifting derelict a fortnight after her abandoning 182 miles to the south-west. That year the greatest haul was made by the *William and Ann* of Hull, which killed twenty-two whales and made 200 tons of oil.

The reports of the whaling masters began to rekindle the interest of the Admiralty in the North-West Passage and Lieutenant John Franklin, whom we last met as a midshipman aboard an Indiaman in the action with Linois off Pulo Aur in *Britannia's Realm*, was put in command of the *Trent*, one of four naval vessels sent north in 1818. That season marked an increase in Scottish interest in the northern fishery, with a decline in fleets from all English ports except Hull, which sent no less than sixty-four ships. In the Davis Strait the whalers encountered the naval expedition and both helped each other when one of the latter, Ross's *Isabella*, briefly ran aground. In reciprocation, Ross was able to lend his surgeon to assist Captain Hawkins of the *Everthorpe* who had been in pursuit of a whale when he was attacked by a polar bear and dragged from his boat. Caught by the thigh, Hawkins was held until the bear had been run through with three whale-lances. He survived the mauling.

The vicissitudes of the whalers were many and various, not least the separation of the whale-boats from their ship in 'thick and calm weather'. Losses occurred every

year as they penetrated further north into what they called 'the North Water', lying
beyond Disco Island where ships were occasionally beset. The year 1819 was poor,
but the following season yielded an immense profit, sixty ships earning £318,000,
although several were wrecked. In the following year the younger Scoresby, who had
transferred to the *Fame* in 1819, took command of the *Baffin*, which had been ordered
to his own specification and was the first custom-built whaler laid down on the banks
of the Mersey, handing the *Fame* over to his father.

Many of the exploits of the younger Captain William Scoresby have been related
in *Britannia's Realm*. He was the doyen of the scientific breed of whaling officer and
a Fellow of the Royal Society. In 1820 he shipped Captain George Manby with him
in the *Baffin*, and with a Lieutenant Colquhoun of the Royal Artillery in the *Fame*,
the Scoresbys, along with several other whaling masters with connections to them,
experimented with ways of killing the whales that were less risky for the boats' crews
and quicker for their quarry. Colquhoun was an advocate of Congreve rockets and
Manby was the inventor of the line-throwing life-saving apparatus, and these men
undertook a number of trials with a harpoon gun. Of 8 June Manby, with the fresh
and impressionable observation of the tyro, wrote:

> I went in the boat… We were ordered to go beyond a point of ice belonging to an
> extensive field upwards of a mile from the ship; as we were going to our destination
> the blast of a whale was heard among the ice. Presently it was repeated, and about
> 150 yards from us we saw the vapour of its breath issue from a small opening in the
> ice. Like smoke from a chimney it rose until it mingled with and was lost in the
> atmosphere, and immediately afterwards we beheld the object of our pursuit… The
> boat was instantly brought to the edge of the ice, and the harpooner being armed
> with his weapon whilst the boat's crew and myself conveyed the line, we all raced to
> the spot where the fish was lying. It appeared much above the surface of the water
> and had a harpoon already attached to it; our harpooner soon drove his weapon into
> its mountainous back, when the fish instantly went under the ice, and ran out two
> lines with a velocity truly astonishing, for its friction in running round the bollard
> enveloped us in smoke. The fish rose to breathe in a small opening about half a mile
> distant, and the contrast of its black arched back rising above the surface of the ice,
> which was covered with the purest white, had a most extraordinary appearance.
>
>   The crew of a[nother] boat…pursuing a similar plan…struck it again, but it
> swam off with equal rapidity until it rose about a quarter of a mile from us. Though
> I now hastened with two lines towards the spot, it went down tail foremost before
> I arrived, and therefore I returned to the boat and found it had not only run out our
> complement of six lines but also three others belonging to the boat that had been
> sent to our assistance.
>
>   I now observed the boat from which the second harpoon had been struck
> moving rapidly along the ice, over large hummocks, whilst its crew were exerting
> their utmost strength to impede its progress… Determined…not to give more line,
> we put over the stern a heavy grapnel and long tow line to which every man held

on with his utmost strength, while I, having got into the boat to travel in this unusual manner, was drawn with great speed...

Fortunately the whale quitted the ice and came up in open water, where we had soon the pleasure of seeing a jack displayed from another of the boats to announce that a third harpoon had struck the prey. About a quarter of an hour after this, we heard the welcome shout which follows the death of a whale...after three hours' labour...we returned to the ship where, perhaps, the most beautiful whale ever beheld was lying with its belly uppermost ready for flinching (sic)... [B]esides 15 lines of 240 yards each, which it had taken from our own boats, it had fast to it six similar lines, a harpoon, and a boat belonging to the *Trafalgar* of Hull.

The younger Scoresby made his last voyage into the Arctic in 1822, his father the following year, as related in the preceding volume of this work. Their retirement coincided with the beginnings of a slow decline in catches and a series of severe winters which culminated in 1830-31 with the loss of several whalers — including the splendid *Neptune* — from becoming so beset in the ice that their extrication proved impossible. In the winter of 1835-36 several ships wintered in the ice, and another bad year followed in 1835. Although the fishery was to survive and to enjoy a renaissance later in the century, demand for oil declined following an increase in imports of better quality sperm whale oil, the taking of which was by this time chiefly in the hands of the Americans. In 1832 the British northern whale-fishery consisted of eighty-one vessels, employing 4,000 seamen whose efforts realised 12,578 tons of oil and a quantity of baleen used largely in corsetry and the fashion-industry as 'whale-bone' stiffening, though other items were manufactured from it. The United States sent ten times as many vessels a-whaling to the benigner waters of the Pacific, employed 10,000 seamen who tried-out 227,960 tons of the superior sperm-oil with a value of $4 million, to which must be added the products of thousands of seals. The losses of whale-ships in the Arctic, owing to the dangers of the extreme environment, had no equivalent in the southern fishery.

Nevertheless, the observations submitted by the Scoresbys, Monroe, and other whaling masters, made an invaluable contribution to navigation and meteorology. On his last voyage in the *Baffin*, the younger Scoresby, in addition to taking whales and reaching within 570 miles of the North Pole, made close observations of several phenomena, in particular the effects of iron within a ship and that of high latitude upon a magnetic compass. He also recorded the effect of refraction on visibility, the creation of mirages and collected specimens of small aquatic life forms.

Far away in the southern Atlantic, the Falkland Islands and South Georgia had become refuges for vessels mauled by the Southern Ocean as well as bases for forays into Antarctic waters. Such was the rapacity of the sealers that between 1772 and 1822 the fur seal — hunted for its pelt — was almost exterminated, while the oil-producing sea elephant was in a similar plight. The ferocity of the competition between rival sealers was such as to cloak the original discovery of Antarctica itself in secrecy. The whaling firm of Enderby & Co. of London had sent exploratory expeditions into the southern seas before the war, their *Emilia* pioneering British sperm-whaling in the Pacific in 1788, and by 1791 the company had an office in Port Jackson. Having obtained a license to hunt sperm whales in the Pacific, with the coming of peace they began to expand their operations in the eutrophic waters of the sub-Antarctic. It became common for Enderby's whalers to carry convicts on their outward voyages, and this association with the Transport Board also led the company to employ a number of former naval officers.

In February 1819 Captain William Smith, a Northumbrian from Blyth with experience of sealing, was on a trading voyage from the Rio de la Plata to Valparaiso in his brig, the *Williams*, when he encountered heavy weather off the Horn. Driven to leeward, he fell in with islands to the south of Drake's Passage, fixing their latitude by meridian altitude and their longitude by chronometer. At Valparaiso, HMS *Andromache* lay at anchor and Smith reported his findings to Captain William Shirreff, who ignored them, thinking that Smith had seen nothing but ice. Stung by this rejection, Smith returned to the islands in October and claimed them for Great Britain, naming them the South Shetlands before returning to Valparaiso where Shirreff took the master-mariner more seriously. Chartering the *Williams*, Shirreff put his own sailing master into her as charter-party, with instructions to survey the archipelago Smith claimed to have taken possession of. This man was Edward Bransfield, and he and Smith surveyed the South Shetlands in January 1820.

The two then decided to head further south and touched the Antarctic Peninsula on the 30th after crossing the strait now named after Bransfield. Continuing their running survey, Bransfield named the passing coast Trinity Land, claiming two of the islands lying off its extremity as King George and Clarence Islands. Rounding the northern tip of the peninsula, the *Williams* turned south again, crossing the Antarctic Circle to work along what was later called the Larsen Ice-Shelf before putting about to the north, a cruise which fully vindicated Smith but ensured Bransfield – the naval warrant officer – was better remembered for the exploit.[4]

A few months later the American sealer Captain Nathaniel Palmer in the *Hero* also fell in with the continental coast of Antarctica that had eluded Cook. In the Austral summer of 1821–22 Palmer was back sealing in Antarctic waters, discovering the South Orkney Islands in company with a British sealer under Captain George Powell. Meanwhile the American sealer Captain John Davis in the *Cecilia* actually landed on the Antarctic Peninsula in Hughes Bay on 7 February 1821.[5]

Another British commercial expedition left Leith in 1822 led by Captain James Weddell in the brig *Jane*, with the small cutter *Beaufoy* as tender under Matthew Brisbane. Weddell, the eponym of the great bight of the Antarctic continent, had had a chequered career. He appears to have served briefly in the navy as a seaman and was later in a coasting vessel, probably a collier, in which he had an altercation with the master, whom he struck. Condemned to serve in the navy as a punishment, Weddell's abilities soon attracted notice and he was rated midshipman. Aged twenty-two, a commission was out of his reach, so he gained a warrant as acting master in HM Schooner *Firefly*. Thereafter Weddell served as sailing-master in several men-of-war, one commanding officer describing him as 'one of the most efficient and trustworthy officers I have met', and he afterwards proved to be a man of scientific and enquiring, rather than commercial, mind. After the war Weddell finally found employment in the sealing-vessels owned by Strachan & Gavin of Leith, and in 1820, in command of the *Jane,* he visited the South Shetlands in Smith's wake, hunting seals throughout the Antarctic summer. During this time he may also have touched the South Orkneys, but the voyage made no profit. Despite this, Weddell's discoveries and the prospect of finding fur seals persuaded James Strachan to refit the *Jane.* Weddell sailed south again on 17 September 1822.

Late that year he began a systematic survey of the South Shetland Islands, turning south from Clarence Island, the most northerly of the group, and then penetrating deep into the great coastal indentation that now bears his name. Finding the sea clear of anything other than loose pack-ice, Weddel reached a latitude of 75° 15' South – roughly in longitude 23° West and not far from the mainland of Antarctica near Halley Bay. It was by then February 1823 and the *Jane* and the *Beaufoy* were obliged to head north to refit in Indian Cove, Tierra del Fuego, before returning home the following year. Weddell's *A Voyage Towards the South Pole, performed in the years 1822–24, containing an Examination of the Antarctic Sea,* was published in 1825, and two years later he was elected a Fellow of the Royal Society of Edinburgh. It was the high-point of his life.

For a few years British sealers were content with their findings, but Messrs Samuel Enderby & Co.[6] decided upon another speculative southern voyage, dispatching Captain John Biscoe in the brig *Tula,* attended by the cutter *Lively.* Biscoe's career was similar to Weddell's, for he too had served in the Royal Navy's smaller cruisers, initially volunteering to avoid impressment, which suggests that he had originally gone to sea in the merchant service. Biscoe was midshipman and acting master in the 16-gun sloop *Moselle,* earning a commendation from his captain as able, attentive and promising. After the war he obtained employment with Enderby & Co., although he clearly retained his reputation at the Navy Board, for the expedition was under-written by the Admiralty in recompense for which Their Lordships would receive all the surveys carried out by Biscoe. The *Tula* and her consort – the *Lively,* under George Avery – left the Thames on 10 July 1830, taking-in wood and water in the Falklands that autumn. From the middle to the end of December the two little vessels surveyed the South Sandwich Islands before heading south. On 28 February 1831 Biscoe saw 'several hummocks to the southward which much resembled tops of mountains, and at 6 p.m. clearly distinguished it to be land, and to a considerable extent…the black tops of mountains showing themselves through the snow on the lower land.'

These were the *Nunataks* of Antarctica and, as the *Tula* and *Lively* worked east through the pack for mile after mile, Biscoe rightly concluded that he had fallen in with 'a large continent'. Biscoe named it Enderby Land, in honour of his employers, and persisted in trying to carry out a running survey of the coastline. After 300 miles, badly affected by scurvy, Biscoe and Avery turned north and made for Hobart where they arrived in a poor condition. Of the twenty-nine men and boys in the two vessels' complements all but four, including Biscoe, were seriously ill. Here Biscoe proved lucky, for at Hobart lay the *Eliza*, a convict ship commanded by James Weddell.

Poor Weddell had lost the *Jane* on her way home from a commercial voyage to Buenos Aires in 1829 when, off the Azores, she was found to be making more water than the pumps could cope with and was abandoned. Weddell and his crew embarked in another homeward-bound British vessel, surviving *her* wrecking on the way. In 1830 he gained command of the *Eliza*, hence his presence in Hobart when the distressed *Tula* and *Lively* arrived, whereupon Weddell and his men generously helped Biscoe refit his vessels.

Undaunted, Biscoe sailed for New Zealand, the Auckland Islands — where the *Lively* was wrecked - and Chatham Island before setting off across the Southern Ocean for the South Shetlands. On 15 February 1832 he discovered a large island off the Antarctic Peninsula which he named after King William IV's consort, Queen Adelaide. He then surveyed the archipelago strung to the north, which now bear his own name, before calling at the South Shetlands and arriving home on 30 January 1833. Biscoe's charts — surrendered to the Admiralty — were of a high standard, and he was honoured by both the British and the French Geographical Societies, the former accepting him as 'an ordinary member without payment of fees'. Despite these achievements, however, the Navy Office denied him the warrant as master that would have secured him permanent employment in the Royal Navy.

In 1833 Captain Peter Kemp of the sealer *Magnet* sighted what was probably Heard Island, deep in the Southern Ocean. Continuing south Kemp saw what was later called the Kemp Coast (east of Enderby Land), and Cape Borley in longitude 67° South. That same year the Enderby brothers appointed Biscoe to command another expedition consisting of the *Hopefull* and the *Rose*, but on discovering that he would be appointed to the smaller tender *Rose* and falling out with the Admiralty's appointee, Henry Rea, Biscoe resigned. Rea — who was Biscoe's junior in both a naval and a mercantile sense — had assumed an attitude of superintendence from the start, which Biscoe deeply resented.[7] Biscoe next made a trading voyage as master to the West Indies before commanding the *Superb*, a vessel twice the size of the *Tula* and in which he ran out to Hobart in 1837. Here he transferred into the sealing-brig *Emma* and appears to have worked out of Tasmania, for it is 1838 before we hear of him again.[8] Off Campbell Island to the east of New Zealand that southern summer, Biscoe fell in with Captain John Balleny in the *Eliza Scott* and Captain Thomas Freeman in the *Sabrina*. Balleny left his name to an island and the name of Freeman's ship — which disappeared soon after they left Campbell Island — to 'an appearance of land'. Biscoe reached the seventy-fifth parallel and struck soundings on what was later named the Pennell Bank when James Clark Ross was credited with the discovery of the sea that today bears *his* name. Biscoe was denied this last claim to fame, and for a few years he commanded the *Marian Watson* and then the *Trugenina*, trading out of Sydney.

In failing health, Biscoe sailed for Britain aboard the *Janet Izatt* in the spring of 1843, but died at sea during the voyage. He was about fifty, and he left his wife and children in extreme poverty. Sir John Franklin and Queen Adelaide were among those who subscribed for their relief.

Weddell also died in poverty, ruined by a lawsuit brought against him by a man named Richard Brown whom Weddell had carried out to Hobart as an alleged escaped and convicted criminal. Brown later cleared his name and sued the wretched Weddell for wrongfully transporting him against his will. Weddell's fortune, never great, had been lost with the *Jane*, and his command of the *Eliza* seems to have been a condescension, probably the result of memorialising the Transport Board. The artist P.G. Dodd recorded that his 'bold features' when in repose bore 'an appearance of melancholy…indicating that he had experienced disappointments', while a friend said that Weddel had been 'more wrapped up in the ambition to follow up his brilliant naval adventures than to look out for and realise the fruits of commercial industry in the ships entrusted to his command'. He died in abject penury in September 1834 at his lodgings in the Strand and was buried in St Clement Dane's.[9]

The pitiful ends of these two ship-masters were typical of the time as the challenge of British polar exploration was taken up by the Royal Navy, yet it was they who were the true pioneers. Neither Weddell nor Biscoe had been commissioned officers and the important phases of their lives had been spent in the merchant service. While one of Biscoe's sons was granted a charity place at the Greenwich Hospital School, it was 1901 before his surviving daughter Emily was given a civil-list pension of £30 'for her father's service to geography'. The achievements of both men were outside the limelight of national-flagged expeditions, at a time when the merchant service had reached a nadir – not only in the opinion of the Admiralty's influential Arctic Council which was busy resuscitating that old chestnut, the North West Passage, and preparing to send James Clark Ross south – but in the shocked eyes of the entire nation. Indeed the British Pacific whale-fishery itself was slowly failing, despite early post-war promise.

In addition to sending ships south after the war, Enderby & Co. also returned to the Pacific in 1819, their *Syren* discovering the 'teeming' whaling-ground off the coast of Japan, the waters of which yielded 'for many years an average annual catch of 40,000 barrels of [sperm] oil…at the average price of £8' each. With their agency at Port Jackson, Enderby based their Pacific operations there and began hunting whales off Tasmania and New Zealand. Typical of the whaling voyages made at this time was that of the *Sarah* under Captain James Choyce. He left home on 1 September 1820 and took five sperm whales off the Cape Verdes before heading for the Pacific, taking twenty-seven days to double Cape Horn in heavy headwinds. Stopping for water at Juan Fernandez, he disturbed a nest of American, English and Spanish pirates, but escaped any ill effects from the encounter. While off the Galapagos the *Sarah* met the British whalers *Sir Andrew Hammond* and the *Offy*, learning that the *Offy*'s master, Captain Hales, and five of his boat's crew had been killed by the pirates when going ashore in search of fresh fruit. The pirates, a product of the general revolt through-out the Spanish colonies against Madrid's rule, had also captured the *Perseverance* of London. They were later apprehended and their leader, one Benevedo, 'was afterwards taken prisoner, and his head cut off and stuck up on a pole at Concepcion as a warning to others'.

The colonial revolt encouraged some of Choyce's men to desert and join the rebel armies, which were full of Britons. Otherwise the scarcity of whales drove the *Sarah* further west. The spirit of rebellion seemed endemic, for the *Sarah's* crew refused to lower the boats to chase whales unless Choyce gave them more salt meat:

> I had allowed them more than a pound a day since leaving England, with as much good bread as they chose, and coffee night and morning, with plenty of flour four days, and peas three days a week, besides a fair proportion of pickles, grog, &c, enough to satisfy any reasonable man – but sailors are difficult to please. As I had no remedy I was forced to yield, for I could get no redress without sacrificing my voyage, and to do that to get revenged on a parcel of unruly sailors would be of no benefit to myself or my owner.

Choyce managed to fill his casks with oil but had to return to the Galapagos Islands to catch terrapin to eat as his salt meat was running out, 'owing to my unruly crew using it wastefully'. The *Sarah* then headed for home, arriving at Gravesend on 13 June 1822 after a 'long and tedious voyage' which had lasted 'two years and nine months, of which only forty-five days had been passed at anchor.'

Although a considerable number of whalers occupied their business in these waters, the sperm whale was deserting the Galapagos Grounds favoured by British masters. The Pacific fishery was therefore relatively short-lived, and by the 1830s disaster was beginning to exceed success. In June 1830 the whaler *Betsey and Sophia*, owned by Messrs Barkworth & Co., left London. Her master, Thomas Fotheringham, had a bad fall and died off the African coast, whereupon the mate, Peter Paterson, assumed command. For some months the *Betsey and Sophia* prosecuted a successful hunt for sea elephant oil among the islands of the Southern Ocean, arriving at Kerguelen – better known then to the British as Desolation Island – in the spring of 1831. On their fifth attempt to beat out of Rocky Bay on 16 March, the whaler drove into a thick bed of kelp, missed stays and lost her rudder. Paterson lowered the whale-boats in an attempt to pull the ship clear, but the wind drove her between two rocks where she remained for three days being pounded to pieces by the heavy seas. During this period the crew frantically took as much gear and supplies out of her as they could, but they lost the oil upon which they depended for their livelihoods. Having consumed their stores and despaired of rescue, they set-to constructing a boat large enough to attempt to reach safety, subsisting on birds, shellfish and sea elephants. On 22 October, after 'unequalled perseverance they at last succeeded in completing their little bark' which was duly launched as the *Liberty* and in which fourteen men departed on 6 December, five men electing to remain on the island. Astonishingly the *Liberty* fetched the west coast of Tasmania on 18 January 1832, and two days later, 'being reduced…to the last extremity…they entered Macquarie Harbour' where the commander of the penal settlement succoured them. A year later, thanks to the good offices of Lieutenant-Governor Arthur, Paterson took command of the former 90-ton Government schooner *Adelaide* which was sold and fitted out for a commercial sealing voyage, the primary purpose of which was to finance the rescue of the five beleaguered men at Kerguelen. Paterson arrived there on 25 January 1833, but there was no sign of his seamen and he was obliged to hunt seals to pay for the voyage. While doing so they were joined by another vessel, the *Sarah Barry*, whose master, Captain Alexander Distant, informed Paterson that on 5 March he had been in command of the *Ocean* and had picked up the five survivors, carrying them to St Helena. The *Adelaide's* later voyage back to Tasmania was not without incident, but Paterson, who continued to command ships sailing from Hobart, had accomplished something of a minor epic in the *Liberty*. As the polar scholar Ann Savours points out, this was 'a voyage to equal Shackleton's in the *James Caird*', but was obscured amid a series of losses.

In December 1832 the *Coquette* of London, Captain Thornton, had disappeared on the Japan Grounds; the *Duke of York* was wrecked off Queensland in September 1837 and the *Lucinda*, Captain James, went ashore on New Caledonia in the January following. She had been two years out from London and filled 1,500 barrels with sperm-oil, but this was abandoned as the crew took to the boats. Two men died and one was murdered before the survivors were picked up by Captain Dixon in the *Success* of Sydney. In December 1838 Captain Lee of the whaler *Achilles* had two of his boat-crews massacred by Solomon islanders at Tucopia, and in January 1842 the *Conservative*, Captain Cristall, was wrecked and plundered off Bali, though Cristall's oil was afterwards salved. The islanders of the eastern archipelago were frequently hostile; in late 1840, the *Mary* sent her boats ashore to Lombok for water, whereupon her seamen were attacked, one man was killed and the remainder had to be ransomed by Captain Blosse. The *Sarah and Elizabeth* of London was seized by the *orang laut* off Timor at the end of 1843, her second mate being wounded and taken prisoner after the pirates had plundered the vessel. Timor, the traditional watering-place of passing English ships ever since the early days of Pacific exploration, was, despite its Dutch colonial government, a dangerous place. A few years earlier Captain William Simmons of the *Kingsdown* was killed in an altercation while trading with the islanders. His chief mate, Mr Edwards, assumed command, but the crew refused duty and Edwards was obliged to make for Sydney where, it appears, matters were straightened out and the *Kingsdown* resumed her cruise. Unfortunately Edwards was later killed by a whale and the ship was brought home by her original second mate, a man named Jenkins. Another whaler to lose men at Timor was the *Zephyr*, two of whose seamen seem to have been poisoned while Captain Richardson died after an accident while flensing a whale alongside his ship. The mate, a Mr Kitching, brought the ship into Sydney where he confessed to be incapable of navigating the *Zephyr*, so her agents, although they confirmed Kitching in command, entrusted the navigation to an apprentice named James Knight on the grounds that the youth claimed some expertise. This unlikely duo seem to have managed for some time until, perhaps unsurprisingly, the *Zephyr* was wrecked off Borneo on All Fool's Day, April 1840.

The manner of payment by shares made whalers' crews susceptible to indiscipline, particularly if things were not going well. Consequently, 'refusal of duty' – or striking – rather than malicious mutiny was not infrequent, particularly if it was felt by the men forward that those aft were incompetent. In mid-1838 Captain Darling brought the *Guiana* into Sydney flying the fever flag. The vessel was quarantined and, before she put to sea again, eighteen of her seamen refused duty. Having the presence of a naval guardship nearby, Darling charged his refractory sailors with mutiny and they were brought to trial. However, the 'mutineers' produced the *Guiana's* surgeon who in turn provided evidence that Darling was a useless drunkard, and the charges were dismissed. Such a happy conclusion was not always the case; when Captain Bunker brought the *Harriet* into Port Jackson 'to refresh' his men 'especially in consequence of the mutinous conduct of the greater part of the crew', he probably acted wisely, but the move was insufficient to save the ship, and the *Harriet* was subsequently lost to seizure by the inhabitants of Strong's Island, her crew massacred to a man and the vessel burned. On the other hand, Captain Brooks of the *Jane Eliza* arrived in Sydney in 1838 and had eight of his men arrested, tried and remanded for mutiny, firm action that saved his ship from the fate of the *Kent* nine years later, almost at the end of the fishery. Captain King's crew had been so reduced by desertions that the remainder had refused duty. King thought he could make up his numbers in Sydney but found this impossible and was obliged to abandon his voyage and sail for London.

By this time the fishery had passed its peak, and in 1838 only a dozen whalers left London for the Pacific. Despite this gloom, it was as late as May 1842 when the *Active* returned to the Thames with a record haul of 3,859 barrels of sperm oil. Nevertheless, four years later only 400 tons was imported by four vessels, a loss of £20,000 to their owners who declared they had no intention of refitting the ships for further whaling. With the Government uninterested in reviving the business, the consumer was obliged to rely entirely upon American imports, although the repeal of the Navigation Acts provoked a brief attempt to resuscitate the fishery and Thomas Baring headed a consortium intending to raise £250,000. Enderby & Co. proposed the establishment of a whaling station on 'Lord Auckland's Islands', the remote archipelago to the south of New Zealand which had first been visited in 1806 by one of Enderby's masters, Captain Abraham Bristow, in the whaler *Ocean*. Bristow had returned the following year in the *Sarah* and thereafter several British and American sealing vessels had collected immense quantities of furs from the seal colonies scattered about the islands. It was here that Briscoe called in 1831 and where he lost the *Lively*, for the Aucklands were acquiring a reputation as a graveyard of ships, particularly for those whose masters, leaving South Australia for Cape Horn, took a wide sweep south of New Zealand's south-west cape and Snare's Island. Balleny and Freeman called at the Aucklands in the *Eliza Scott* and *Sabrina*, shortly before the disappearance of the latter and after their encounter with Biscoe off Campbell Island, and Ross's Antarctic-bound naval expedition put into one of the inlets in 1840. Here the *Erebus* and *Terror* passed most of November, naming the anchorage Port Ross, releasing sheep, rabbits and poultry and planting vegetables. The following year about

150 Maoris were landed, followed by more in October 1842 who were transferred from Chatham Island by the whaler *Hannah*.

Matters stood thus until December 1849 when the Enderby brothers sent out the last of their commercial expeditions in the *Samuel Enderby*, *Brisk* and *Fancy*. With Baring and others, the Enderbys had formed the British Southern Whale Fishery, an entity incorporated by royal charter. Appointed lieutenant-governor, Charles Enderby led about 150 British colonists with a view to establishing a whaling station. Few whales were caught and although there were a handful of weddings, births and deaths, Charles Enderby proved a poor governor and the little colony was riven by discontent. In late 1852, after two years and nine months, the shortest-lived British colony was abandoned, although a refuge was erected on Enderby Island which saved the lives of some of the seafarers and passengers wrecked on the islands in the succeeding decades, a relief vessel being sent periodically from New Zealand. So, with their company bankrupt, the Enderbys and their partners withdrew from these waters. Notwithstanding this final failure, as H.R. Mill remarks: 'There is perhaps no other instance of a private mercantile firm undertaking so extensive a series of voyages of discovery without much encouragement in the way of pecuniary returns.'

Enderby's masters Weddell and Biscoe had gone south at a time when it looked as though trade and shipping were emerging from the post-war economic slump, thanks to the reciprocity policy of the President of the Board of Trade, William Huskisson.[10] Huskisson's policy – which, once introduced in 1825, began to reverse the trend of depression – was, in the long term, helped by advances in the efficient performance of sailing ships, itself a consequence of the 'New Measurement' tonnage regulations of 1836. But progress was not smooth. In an age of social ferment the forces of reaction collided with those of aspiration, nowhere more so at sea than in the ships of the East India Company which staggered into the new century relying largely upon a business model perfected in the previous one. It was now to be shorn of the last protections of monopoly. By 1820, although building fine-quality ships, these were increasingly out of date and unable to compete with interloping 'free-traders'. What was more disturbing; they were rife with indiscipline, and in this they were not alone.

While a degree of disorder, insobriety and unreliability had long characterised the personae of British merchant jacks, the rigid, naval-style regime prevalent in the ships of John Company had elevated them to a status quite separate from the generality of merchant shipping. Similarly the company's officer corps remained as professionally competent as its naval counterpart.[11] However, a loosening of the social bonds during the post-war era combined with an increasing self-awareness among seamen, as among other working men, of their economic muscle, and they began to argue the toss, something many East India officers were ill-prepared for. Legal challenges to authority in merchant ships – though possessed of all the dignity of common sense, precedent and usage – increased. What the masters and mates considered 'mutiny', but the 'mutineers' called striking, caused innumerable confrontations, so-much-so that one East India commander, Captain Christopher Biden, wrote an exposé of the evil, published in 1830, in which he draws upon a number of examples, most of which – though by no means all – occurred in the ships of the East India Company. To summarise Biden's standpoint one need only quote his assertion that:

> Scarcely an Indiaman arrives in the port of London but some disgraceful scene ensues, the crew imagining the sight of the British shore to be the herald for revolt. The influence of inflamed passions [largely by the importation of alcohol by boats running alongside an incoming merchantman], excited by Jew[ish] crimps, land-sharks, and pettifogging lawyers, who crowd alongside, and, at times steal on board, the moment a ship is at anchor or within the port of London, produces this terrible effect. [12]

It was not only in home waters that merchant jack disgraced himself. Disorder was frequent abroad, especially in China where the severe restrictions placed upon the seamen in an Indiamen only provoked trouble. Notwithstanding this, it must be emphasised that most seamen behaved well at sea, especially when the ship was in any danger. One factor in this general disaffection was a direct consequence of the post-war situation: many of the better class of sailor had defected to the American flag, the quality of whose mercantile marine – and especially those crack Western Ocean packets – was regarded with some envy at this time. These men were simply continuing a trend established by deserters during the late war and presaging the mass migration that would shortly follow. Thus, not only did British mercantile houses benefit from commercial alliances with the English-speaking and quondam colonists, but the common working-sailor also enjoyed benefits of this distant kinship.

While the character of most ship-masters was such that they would brook no interference with their authority, an increasingly litigious climate often caught them between the devil and the deep blue sea. Biden quotes his friend Captain Driver who, 'like many other brave officers (he has served with great credit as a master in the navy) would rather run his guns out for action…than *engage* in a court of law.' Driver's dilemma in command of a free-trading interloper was given in detail:

> When I commanded the *Clyde*, in the free-trade [to India], one of the seamen stabbed my chief mate. I considered myself fully justified in flogging him; but one of the [other] rascals attempted to rescue this blood-thirsty villain. To preserve any-thing like discipline, I flogged him also, but only inflicted eight lashes. However, on my arrival in England, I had one of those hornets after me, called proctors. I employed another; who said, if I gained the suit, the expenses would be heavy; and, by his advice, I gave the informer ten pounds; this I did, which, in reality, is paying a man for behaving ill, and rewarding a fellow for attempting to rescue an assassin.

Quoting such incidents, Biden's testimonial is depressing, a catalogue of infamy from which few emerge with credit. In an era in which the well-being of the mercantile fleet was understood by the governing classes not only to maintain that trade essential for the economic prosperity of the nation, but also as a reserve of man-power for the navy, the condition and quality of seamen was of some importance and caused anxiety at a high level. In the twenty-five years following the publication of Biden's book, the state was to take a greater interest in the regulation of the mercantile marine. Its two agents were Trinity House and the Board of Trade and Plantations, the former of which had been a form of consultancy to the Navy Board for centuries, and had, since time immemorial, examined and certificated the Royal Navy's sailing masters. The opinion of the Court of Elder Brethren was well regarded, all but the honorary members having served at sea, many of them in the East India Company. Several remained managing-owners and some were ship-owners entirely on their own account. However, in due course the lion's share of regulation passed to the Board of Trade and Plantations, which, once it had dropped the latter part of its title, became the great department of state responsible – among other matters – for merchant shipping.

Although the Navigation Acts had protected British maritime commerce, other legislation could inhibit trade and cloud the issue. Acts granting powers and monopolies to the ancient joint-stock concerns, in particular the East India and South Sea companies, had to be formally set aside in an Act of 1802 to allow the hunting of whales in the South Pacific, the consequences of which have already been related.[13] After the peace, the first Act governing shipping was to protect passengers from the evils of over-loading, the numbers of persons on board a ship, including crew, being limited in a Bill of 1817 to one for every 1.5 registered tons. This Act also provided for proper provision of food and water, and the landing of passengers at the place specified at the time of ticket-purchase. Amendments followed in 1825 and 1826 which enacted that if no 'tween-deck was available to accommodate passengers, a wooden platform had to be laid over the cargo in the lower hold, such legislation being 'itself a proof of what had been going on – viz., that the unfortunates had been tumbled down below, treated as so much more cargo, and left to shift for themselves'. The passing of the 1825 Bill repealed all previous marine legislation and incorporated the entirety in the new Act which retained the ruling that three-quarters of a crew must be of British nationality, though if one British seaman was carried for every 20 registered tons, the remainder might be foreigners.[14] Ten years later two shipping Acts were passed, the substance of which was to reassert and restrict 'the qualification for a British ship-master to the natural born subjects of the Empire, or to persons naturalised by process according to law'. This, as will be seen, had been practically abandoned long before the end of the century. A further Act provided for the establishing of a formal running Register of Seamen, which identified the man-power available to the Royal Navy in time of war. The same Act made another important provision for the 'regulation and binding of apprentices' which obliged a ship-owner to train for the future by ensuring that he carried apprentices on a scale related to tonnage. This ranged from two in a vessel of between 80 and 200 tons, to five in a ship of more than 700 tons, while failure to comply attracted a fine of £10 for every missing apprentice, making – for the first time – the carriage of apprentices compulsory.

The importance of apprentices and other young men who aspired to be future ship-masters cannot be overlooked and, before considering the officers proper, a diversion is necessary. According to William Spavens, writing in the late eighteenth century:

> Young gentlemen who have learned the theoretical part of navigation in a good school, and have opulent parents who wish them to be taken into…posts of prefer- ment, without submitting to an apprenticeship, or the drudgery of a boy serving before the mast, if such wish to be in the service of the united East India Company, their initiation…is in the capacity of a guinea-pig, as they term it. Their parents or guardians give a premium with them to the owners or the ship's husband (for the company have no ships of their own except their own men-of-war and grabs, with a few packets) and if such premium…be about 50 guineas, the boy is put to mess in the steerage with the third, fourth and inferior Mates; and such youths are some- times put to assist them and the Midshipmen in their respective duties; but where a premium of 100 guineas or more is given, the young gentleman messes in the coach or great cabin with the Captain, Super-Cargo, Chief and Second Mates, and Purser: Such are treated entirely as gentlemen; and so acquiring the art of seamanship, together with the practical part of navigation, are often made Mates of the lower order; from then they may rise either by their own merit or the interest of friends to fifth, fourth, third, second, or Chief Mates, and from thence to be Captains, whose pay is £30 per month, and that of a Chief Mate £20.

Despite this career path for the sons of 'opulent parents', Spavens points out its great disadvantage by comparison with the Royal Navy:

> [W]hen a ship in the merchants' service is cast away (i.e. is wrecked or founders), the men and officers lose their pay, except they can save as much of the cargo as will pay them; and if she is taken by an enemy, their property, pay and liberty are lost together, until they recover the latter…

The element of patronage, though most extreme in the East India Company's service, was nevertheless present in less grand vessels, reflecting wider contemporary social practice. Its worst excesses provided for the promotion of the incompetent, a fact not unrelated to the loss of shipping through lack of technical skill, if not in seamanship, than in faulty or deficient navigation. Spavens remarks that some:

> Captains belonging to the ports of London, Bristol and Liverpool, will often take sprightly lads on monthly pay at their first going to sea, and if such prove diligent and obliging, they often get to be good seamen; nevertheless those who serve an apprenticeship are in general most esteemed; and some lads…willing to learn navi- gation, are frequently put in by their Masters as Second Mates, Boatswains, &c. a year or two before they are out of their times (i.e. their indentures), particularly so in vessels employed in the coal trade.

Before examining the parlous state to which a large section of the British merchant marine had been reduced by the post-war slump and foreign competition, it is important to establish the means by which training standards were set in better days. The chief 'nursery of seamen' — that recurrent phrase which concealed the state's essential role of procurer for the Royal Navy — was the coal-trade down the east coast of England and its summer extension into the Baltic. This harsh school maintained an early form of trade union, not so much for securing better wages but to maintain a high quality of seamanship so that:

> before a man was allowed to serve as an able seaman he had to pass a *viva voce* examination in seamanship before a Committee of experts... Not only had the candidate to answer questions on how to handle a ship in any given circumstances (even to 'club-hauling' off a lee shore), but he had to be able to demonstrate the sail-maker's art and carry out numerous tasks to his interlocutors' satisfaction.[15]

This was the system that unlocked the genius of James Cook. Such a restrained but practical nepotism often worked to advantage, whereby a hand-picked youth familiar with a master's *modus operandi* was promoted in a ship, as was the case with Beck and Marquand who had begun as mere cabin boys. The apprenticeship system lasted until the last half of the twentieth century, although displaced in some liner companies by cadetships, a distinction that was more bureaucratic than otherwise.[16] The differences between the systems mattered little since the significant qualification for sitting an examination for a Certificate of Competency was — besides a good, sober character-reference — that the requisite sea-time had been served. But these measures lay in the future, as we shall see.

For those apprentices not employed in Indiamen in the first four decades of the nineteenth century, the quality of their training rested entirely with their master and mates, irrespective of the trade their ships were engaged in. If these men were minded to encourage an intelligent youth and pass on what they knew of navigation, he would prosper. Unfortunately, war had drawn many of the most able ship-masters into the Royal Navy as sailing masters — warrant masters RN — and the standard of mercantile ship-masters and mates declined elsewhere as a consequence. To some extent this was mitigated at the end of the war when not only the redundant Masters RN returned to their original avocation but they were joined by a number of young naval lieutenants whose careers were ruined by peace and who understood no other calling. Notwithstanding this, many owners required submissive masters, an atmosphere not conducive to ambition and therefore encouraging of laxity and inefficiency. Former naval officers proved quite unsuited to this, and most therefore went into steam. Unfortunately for the apprentice, an ignorant master was not likely to reveal his lack of knowledge to a callow youth, would keep the apprentice at a distance and — since the boy could do nothing about it — use him as cheap labour.

Throughout the entire history of the British merchant marine the quality of British ship-masters was to be varied. Although it would be unjust to regard it as an exercise

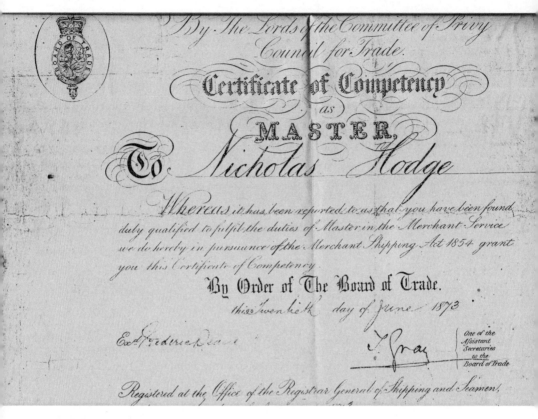

A Certificate of Competency as Master, issued in June 1873 by the Lords of the Committee of Privy Council for Trade to Nicholas Hodge. The document is franked by the common name of this grandiloquent body, the Board of Trade, acting under the provisions of the Merchant Shipping Act of 1854. (© Courtesy of Mr Gwilym Hodge)

in exculpation, Biden's book told only one side of this story, reinforced by the significantly woeful voices of under-writers complaining about 'increasing and abnormal losses, which they attributed to the incompetency and reckless carelessness of those in charge'. The stagnant decade that followed Waterloo was one of the low points in the history of British merchant shipping, faced as it was by the meteoric and energetic rise of its American counterpart. As Captain Edward Blackmore wrote retrospectively in 1897, 'it appeared as if we were to be beaten upon what we proudly conceived was our own ground', and while Biden and his fellows complained at the loss of prime seamen to the American flag and the ship-owners railed against state-intervention, loss of trade and unfair competition from foreigners, seamen had horrid tales of 'ill-usage, bad-food, and miserable quarters'. While every man blamed the next in the pecking order, so that the charges were circular within the industry, they were also vociferous from without.

There was a philanthropic spirit abroad which slowly turned its attention from the evils of slavery to the state and condition of ships and seamen. Although the carriage of slaves had been abolished in 1807, this neither ended the trade nor slavery itself. While the Royal Navy pursued slavers on the high seas, Parliament had to exert itself further, for its sanction against slave-trading had been no more than a heavy fine. In 1811 slave-trading was made a felony punishable by fourteen years transportation or imprisonment with hard-labour. Faced with the sight of other nations merrily continuing to enjoy the profits of the abhorrent traffic, even this deterrent was insufficient, and in 1825 a further Act pronounced slave-trading an act of piracy, thus making it a capital offence if committed within the jurisdiction of the Admiralty Court. This effectively terminated all residual involvement under the British flag, but it wanted until 1834 before the owning and working of slaves was an offence throughout the possessions of the British Crown. Sadly, as we shall observe, even this act of assumed enlightenment did not entirely liberate the black plantation slaves who now themselves discovered the hunger of individual liberty in an over-crowded labour-market.

But, on the passing of the 1834 Act, the focus of national philanthropy shifted to the means by which this pernicious trade had been carried-on and from this to the wider mercantile marine. Thus, at its darkest hour for two centuries, under economic threat from a vigorous competitor, actually shrinking in terms of tonnage and opportunity and deprived or inhibited by its own Government, British shipping received intense investigation. What was found – though subject to the over-emphasis of exaggeration by virtue of its worst cases – was alarming.

The extent of the scrutiny and its subsequent agitation was widespread, fed by newspaper articles reporting shipwrecks and the brutality of masters and mates:

> indeed, the whole of the British maritime world was in a state of complete unrest, and the minds of ship-owners, mariners, and the benevolent public was alike exercised to find a remedy. Public meetings were held throughout the country, notably in Edinburgh, and Parliament was inundated with petitions to inquire into the causes of such increased loss of life.

Other concerns emerged: over-loading, the unseaworthiness of ships, the inadequacy of crews and – most significantly – the incompetence of masters and mates. The nub of this issue was placed openly in the public domain by a Captain Hyland who announced in the City of London, before the assembled Royal Humane Society, that 'great loss of life at sea [was] caused by the ignorance of ship-masters'. Hyland went on to vilify these men, enumerating insufficient knowledge in many cases of the use of the sextant and chronometer to find a ship's position, highlighting the failure in the generality of British shipping – with certain notable exceptions – to have adopted a professional training scheme for master and mates. Many of these men were superb seamen and ship-handlers, even in confined waters, so long as they knew where they were. The deficiency came when poor visibility, high winds and heavy weather made the exact knowledge of the precise whereabouts of their vessels a matter of life-and-death. Recriminations as to how this state of affairs arose, so contrary to the public's original notion of its tars, flew back and forth. All were to blame: the ship-owner 'for buying…imperfectly built ships and carelessness of loss being protected by over insurance'; the underwriter for 'slackness of survey and gambling insurance, the greater the premium,' and the masters for 'ignorance, carelessness, and insobriety'. In consequence of this upheaval, a Royal Commission was set up in 1833 to examine the state of the nation's mercantile marine.

Armed with assertions that losses of British ships and seamen were increasing; that foreign ships were better built, found, commanded and manned; that when 'on the berth' and open for cargo they were therefore favoured by shippers and obtained higher freight rates than their British counterparts, the Commission set to work. It reported three years later, and its conclusions were as comprehensive as they were disturbing. The loss of ships and life were due to a bad system of classification which depended upon age and not worth; foreign owners succeeded in running their ships more cheaply; masters and mates were in many cases incompetent; they and the seamen they commanded were frequently drunk; there was a lack of safe refuges; the system of marine insurance encouraged risk-taking, if not outright malfeasance; the quantity of charts was inadequate, the quality poor; and too few chronometers were in use. Moreover, the form of British ships was bad owing to the restrictions of an archaic tonnage-measurement system. It was a damning indictment which, while it did not include the British mercantile marine in its entirety, was true to such an extent as to have raised the matter to a scandalous disgrace of national importance.

Many reasons were adduced for these various ills: the increasing abilities of other nations while the British system slumbered beneath the Navigation Acts; the tardy acceptance by the world's foremost exponents of maritime sea-power to adopt a proper hydrographic policy; and the long-deleterious effects of a war of national survival. This last had seriously impacted upon both ships and men, upon the former by a combination of innate conservatism retarding innovative ship-design and a tonnage-measurement system that blocked any such initiative. As for the state of the merchant seafarer himself, it chose not to condemn the state's constant plundering of seamen and the excoriating but often subtle consequences of impressment, preferring to point out as a superior cause 'the low state of education then existing throughout England, and the fact that too many took to a sea life to escape [it]…imposed upon by the idea that, for a sailor, book learning was unnecessary'. For all the considerable skills in seamanship that might be learned about the decks of a ship:

> the deeper parts of a navigator's art, and a thorough knowledge of the sciences upon
> which it is founded, as also general courtesy of behaviour and sobriety of conduct,
> are seldom attained without polite education and literary ability, the want of which
> had stamped the British sailor in the eyes of foreign nations with contempt and gave
> rise to the terrible revelations of his conduct as displayed in the reports of consular
> agents in foreign ports. The consequence of this was said to be shown in the fact
> that the good name of the British ship was lost… The position and character of the
> British sailor was the result of [a lack of] training rather than deliberate choice, and

the immediate question which the Commissioners answered was, how were these to be improved?

The Royal Commission's recommendations included the formation of a 'Mercantile Board' to regulate the affairs of the 'Mercantile Marine', chief among which would be the establishment a 'standard of acquirement' for masters and mates by means of examinations. To this end, nautical schools should be set up while courts of enquiry convene to investigate shipwrecks, empowered with powers of censure and reward. New regulations for measuring tonnage should better reflect the capacity of a hull, but incidentally liberate ship-design and spark a slow improvement in hull-form in order to minimise tax liabilities. Thus in January 1836 there came into being what was called 'New Measurement'.

To ameliorate the perceived abuses in the system under which seamen were engaged and employed, a savings bank was set up and an asylum of refuge founded for those worn-out by long service. The Seamen's Register and its administrative officers were to keep records of a seaman's character; tribunals were to be established to settle disputes arising on board ship; and, insofar as it was possible, alcohol was to be discouraged aboard ship. Finally, as an enlivening flourish, the Commissioners called to the nation's attention 'the vast superiority in officers, crews and equipment, and consequent superior success and growth of American shipping'.

Some of these provisions were not new. Nautical schools already existed in some numbers; almshouses were already provided, along with charitable funds for 'decayed mariners' by the Corporation of Trinity House, among others; examinations were undertaken in some quarters and high standards in navigation prevailed throughout many shipping concerns. Indeed some powers to regulate seamen had been vested in Trinity House, but the means by which they could be enforced combined with challenges to the corporation's authority beyond the Thames Estuary rendered these increasingly useless once Glasgow and Liverpool became large-scale centres of ship-owning.[17] So much had been hitherto hit-and-miss, particularly the lack of charts, sextants and chronometers. Poorly paid masters and mates were unable to afford what were regarded as luxuries, largely because of their prices. What was lacking was the rigor of a national system.

A Bill was therefore brought before the Commons by James Silk Buckingham, the chairman of the Commissioners and a former ship-master, and Robert Fitzroy, late the commander of HMS *Beagle*. It sparked off a lively debate in which Buckingham and Fitzroy were supported by the reformer Joseph Hume — himself the son of a ship-master — and Admiral Sir Edward Codrington. Sadly the Bill itself was wrecked by the entrenched shipping interests in the House, 'especially the member for Sunderland, notwithstanding the petition of the mariners of that port, and their friends in favour of its principle'. This followed the lead of the arch rejecter of the Bill, Mr Poulett Thompson, then President of the Board of Trade. Thompson was not hostile to the concept of the proposal, only to the badness of its detail. In his view it was impractical. Instead, Thompson 'threw out a hint' that 'he thought it might serve a good purpose if the authorities of the Trinity House…would institute voluntary examinations for ship-masters and officers'. On division the Bill failed by 176 votes to a miserable twenty-eight.

Moves were made to revive the Bill in 1839 and 1843, and, consequent upon the latter, a letter was sent out from the Foreign Office to enquire of all British consuls in foreign ports 'as to the qualities and conduct of British ship-masters…especially in regard to their comparison with foreign ship-masters'. More Marine Acts followed in 1844, but none addressed the specific issues raised by the Royal Commission, most merely reprising earlier legislation largely in respect of manning and apprentices whose underlying purpose had nothing to do with the mercantile marine but sought to secure a man-power source for the Royal Navy in time of war. Part of this lack of activity had arisen from a slow but steady amelioration of conditions and improvement in standards that was market-driven, although one Act did seek to regulate victualling standards and scales in British merchant ships. For the time being the merchant seaman remained exploited, as Charles Dickens wrote after observing him ashore at first-hand: 'Ill lodged, ill-fed, ill-used, hocused, entrapped, anticipated, cleaned-out…[to be] tempest-tossed till…drowned!'[18]

Notwithstanding these wholesale perjorations, change was abroad both ashore and afloat. In that same year of 1836 an Act had passed through Parliament empowering Trinity House to buy-out the remaining leases of all private lighthouses in England and Wales where the archaic proprietorial system had persisted for far too long.[19] Shortly thereafter the adoption of steam-vessels in their service enabled the Elder Brethren to thoroughly modernise the system of seamarks and bring them into line with the arrangements in Scotland and Ireland. Although unable to entirely prevent shipwreck, the ensuing programme of lighthouse-building and the provision of other aids-to-navigation such as an increasing number of lightvessels and buoys, greatly contributed to safer coastwise passage-making. The mood caught the imagination of a significant number of masters and mates, and not just those involved in extreme trades such as the whale-fisheries. Individual self-improvement, based upon the several educational texts such as those by Hamilton Moore, D'Arcy Lever, Charles Wilson and others were complemented at sea by practicing mariners. These men were individually improving the standards of everyday navigation, adding slowly but cumulatively to the common store of hydrographical knowledge, and cultivating a following in their officers and − occasionally − their apprentices or midshipmen. Much of this had come out of the experience of war and the additional demands it made upon personal competence among a number of able mariners.

Moreover, the ship-owners and ship-masters of the Port of Sunderland had of their own initiative instituted examinations 'and enforced regulations which had been utterly opposed by their own member in Parliament'. True, the examinations were seen by others as nothing more than 'a mere pilot[age] board' for the east coast of England rather than a test of the examinee's skill in the higher navigational arts, but that was where most of the port's ships traded. Private firms did rather better. Messrs Daniel & Co., of Mincing Lane, who − it is important to note amid this deluge of death and doom – had lost only one ship in twenty years owing to having implemented a system of examining their officers. Finally, in 1845, the Lords of the Privy Council for Trade issued orders for a voluntary system of examinations for masters and mates.

Such examinations, encouraging a proper, professional understanding of the higher aspects of navigation, had long been submitted to by the officers of the East India Company. Nor was the greater mercantile service devoid of expertise – an impression easily formed from the plethora of evidence brought before Buckingham and his fellow Commissioners. The problem arose in small merchantmen in which the shipmaster was often appointed by the nepotism of the ship-owner, having risen from before the mast where discipline 'was paternal rather than military, and the rope's end as frequently used on refractory sailors as the father's rod or the schoolmaster's birch'. In this way the common sailor was often kept in an almost childlike state of submission, psychologically, notwithstanding the prodigies of valour he was capable of performing at war with the elements or an enemy:

> As a race…[such ship-masters] were not the best educated of men, although many by sheer force of character and self-education raised themselves above the crowd. It was the ignorant and careless among them who, by their vicious life and conduct, brought such shame upon the whole race of sailors as was displayed in consul's letters from abroad…

'Such,' continues Edward Blackmore:

> was the position…up to the termination of the [East India] Company's Charter and exclusive trade to India. When the London passenger trade to the East fell into the hands of private owners whose ships were termed 'Free Traders' in contradistinction to those of the East India Company, many of which were commanded and officered by men who had previously served in the chartered ['Extra' and 'Licensed'] ships of the Company and also by naval officers, thrown adrift at the end of the war in 1815, the traditionary (sic) discipline of the Company was maintained…

Though not always as perfectly as hitherto, as Biden complained. Nevertheless, while the poor quality of service had lost the North Atlantic trade to the crack Yankee Western Ocean packets, comparison with other European nations shows that the British attitude of *laissez faire* stood in stark contrast to the measures taken in all Scandinavian nations, Russia and Prussia. In these countries, in addition to submission to an examination in which a candidate had to demonstrate a thorough knowledge of seamanship, 'a knowledge of astronomy, and the motions of the sun, moon, and stars, and how to find their positions…[and] a knowledge of tides and currents', candidates also had to master English and French. The Dutch demanded strict qualities, and consequently 'Gentlemen of good families and superior education entered the Merchant Service of that country…'

France had gone beyond all other countries in this respect. The combination of her naval and mercantile services is very complete, as the officers and masters of her foreign-going ships not only pass the same examinations as the lieutenants and sub-lieutenants in the Government service, but also thereby acquire substantially the same rank, a course of action which required an officer to attend at least six months at a Naval College, and not until then might he become a 'Capitaine de long cours'… In the face of such educational advantages, was it any wonder that the foreign merchant sailor was a better educated man than the British, who was dependent entirely upon his own resources, and left to pick up his knowledge as best he could, unless indeed he, as sometimes happened, was a fairly well educated young man before he had ever thought of going to sea? [20]

The formal change in this dire situation was occasioned by an Order in Council of 19 August 1845 which authorised the Board of Trade to institute voluntary examinations. Certificates of competency were to be issued under certain graduation, allotted to the various classes of vessel in which an officer was to serve. Masters showing higher attainments than were demanded for the first-class were awarded a superior category of 'Extra-Master'. Examination boards were to be constituted of voluntary examiners drawn from the Trinity House at London, the other Trinity Houses at Hull, Newcastle and Leith, and various pilotage boards, sub-Commissioners of pilots and, in certain cases, such as Shields and Dundee, 'competent persons'. The comprehensive curriculum was centrally laid down under the provisions of the Order in Council, the first of which was that a candidate 'must be able to write a legible hand and understand the first five rules of arithmetic'. The age of a candidate for master had to exceed twenty-one years and certain minima of sea-time had to be proved, but it was up to the individual authorities to determine the manner of examination, and a consequent variation in standard inevitably ensued.

Probably the most rigorous board was that of Trinity House in London who, in addition to appointing four master-mariners of their fraternity to their examining board, added a Mr Boulter Bell, 'a very able mathematician' as 'scientific examiner'. They also required all candidates to demonstrate a thorough knowledge of the pilotage of the English and St George's Channels, 'as had been customary in the examination of officers in the Honourable East India Company's service'.

An analysis of the Younger Brethren, from whom the examining Elder Brethren were drawn, shows the wide variety of experience the Trinity House could call upon and which these men possessed. Since with election to the status of a Younger Brother went an implicit confidence in a man's competence in command, and since many of these individuals were distinguished in their profession, it goes some way to offset the otherwise universal impression that the entire British merchant marine was populated by drunken and incompetent ship-masters. Of the 167 masters elected Younger Brethren between 1800 and 1825, fifty-seven were in the service of the East India Company, thirteen were either employed in the Company's Indian Marine (its armed wing, formerly the Bombay Marine), the Indian Country-trade, or were free-traders trafficking with India following the removal of the Company's monopoly. Sixty-six commanded ships engaged in the West Indies trade; six were in the Government's Packet or Transport Services; nine commanded ships in the Baltic, Hamburg, North European coal and coastal trades, with seven in the Mediterranean and 'Turkey' trades. One served on the Newfoundland route, one in the Greenland whale-fishery, three traded to South America, one to South Africa and three remained unspecified.[21]

Nevertheless, the introduction of certification was not welcomed everywhere. The ship-owners resented the appointment of masters being removed from their exclusive patronage, while the bluff jack-my-hearties considered with contempt the notion that a seaman could be proved by examination! Needless to say, neither objection could support the full weight of the fact, but as late as June 1848 the *Nautical Magazine*, published in Glasgow then as now, recorded a lengthy letter which quotes amid the consular damnations: 'That it has been observed that the masters of vessels *under* 300 tons are in no manner superior to their men, who are as good seamen, and in many instances, as good navigators!' The correspondent runs down the voluntary quality of the measure, stating that:

> The art of navigation, or of merely conducting a ship from one place to another, and even that of seamanship, to a certain extent, may soon be acquired; but how far short are such acquirements of those regular habits of temperance, and morality, necessary for the establishment and preservation of discipline in a ship?

He also defends the professional standards of many of those:

> who are daily improving the charts for their brother seamen; who are communicating their observations to your journal [the *Nautical Magazine*]; few numbers of which have appeared without some useful contribution of the kind gathered in the different parts of the world which they have visited. The reports which have been collected by Government, shew (sic) the general incompetency of the former class, to which I have alluded, those vessels under 300 tons especially.

Thus wrote the unknown '*B.C.*'

As a model of the consular disapprobation teased from the four corners of the globe by the Foreign Office, that of Mr Winyard, British consul at Riga, will suffice: 'I have no hesitation in affirming broadly, that the merchant seaman's service, as it is now constituted, and especially that part of it visiting the Baltic, is a complete disgrace to the British nation.'

The question has to be asked what manner of owner possessed such ships? The answer is that in many cases ownership remained fragmented into shares. This practice, much in evidence in earlier years, was beginning to break down, though the practice of dividing a ship into sixty-fourths remained – and would remain – in force. Commodity merchants, importers and processors often became ship-owners because it suited their business, but it did not guarantee close interest in their ships and it was these smaller vessels of 'under 300 tons' that still made up the bulk of British tonnage. Owners of such craft were often content to leave the nautical side of things to their ship's-husbands, ex-masters mostly, which was one reason why appointment as master often owed more to a nepotistic relationship with the owner than a demonstrable competence.

Men like the flax-importer David Landale of Kirkaldy, on the east coast of Scotland, acquired a few shares in a ship or two, but improving industrial practices such as enabled him to engage in processing the fibres, spinning the yarns and weaving cloth, provided him with a greater incentive to better regulate the shipment of his finished material. Of such quality was the bleached and finished linen, transformed from the brown cloth produced by the first process, that it 'could grace a bed or a dining table – or be turned into the famous "Kirkaldy stripes" that working men wore on their backs throughout England.'[22] The value added to his imported flax therefore drew him into ship-owning of a grander sort, and in October 1818 he extended his business by founding the Kirkaldy & Leith Shipping Co. While this greatly assisted his importation of flax from Riga, it also allowed him to ship cargoes of Kirkaldy stripes south and to further his business by the carrying of passengers to Dundee, Edinburgh and even London.

One must bear in mind that the reforming legislation enacted in this period preceded the introduction of steam-vessels on all but coastal and short-sea routes, while many of those steamers then in service were commanded by men eager to embrace the new technology, some of whom were the redundant naval officers alluded to earlier. All such men possessed intellectual qualities and abilities that distinguished them from the rough tarpaulin ship-master inveighed against. Some of the new steam-navigation companies insisted their officers submitted to examination not least because under-writers, nervous of the new-fangled 'steam-kettles', were terrified of placing them in the hands of traditionalists. Predictably, however, voluntary examination had a poor take-up. By the end of 1846 fewer than 200 candidates had obtained their certificates, the majority in London. Compulsion was clearly necessary. Early moves towards this emanated from the Admiralty who refused to permit the Transport Board from chartering vessels as troop- or convict-transports after 23 March 1847 'unless the master and mates have obtained the required certificates'. This coercive ruling spread rapidly to cover all vessels carrying mails or in any other way coming under state influence, so that in the following year 400 passed their certificates. Thereafter the number steadily increased.

Many other influences now began to lift the greater part of the mercantile marine out of the slough into which it had subsided. It was never to entirely fling off charges of drunkenness, if not incompetence – though the one led inevitably to the other – and because of its growth and extent it was always to be divided by distinctions of class and education, maintaining a basic standard of examination with archaic reasoning until too late in the day. But the beneficial influences which initiated a period of slow change began with William Huskisson's Reciprocity Act of 1825, and this was followed by the repeal of the Corn Laws in 1846 which, in order to keep down wages in the manufacturing centres, had been the result of lobbying by powerful industrialists intent on lowering the cost of bread – that index upon which the humble wage was based. The success of this ruthless policy now persuaded the industrial barons to press for the repeal of the Navigation Acts, entirely freeing-up trade and introducing cheap freight-rates for the export of their manufactures and import of the raw-materials – principally cotton – for their factories.

The hitherto powerful parliamentary ship-owning lobby now found itself out-manoeuvred. It pleaded the importance of protection, quoting the discrepancies in ship-building costs between Dantzig at £10 per ton, Canada at £11 and the United States at £12, against the price in Britain of not less than £25 per ton. This was a serious matter. After an increase in overall tonnage in 1825, there was a decline between 1835 and 1845, with no less than forty ship-builders failing in Sunderland on Wearside between 1841 and 1847. It was not until iron replaced wood that any revival in Sunderland's fortunes occurred. Matters came to a head in the years 1848 and 1849. The former, known throughout Europe as the Year of Revolution, was marked in Britain by the contemplation by Parliament of the Foreign Office's report on the consular responses by Mr Murray:

> What was wanted was not merely a study of navigation and seamanship but a thorough knowledge of ship's husbandry, and of the stowage of cargoes, of exchanges, and other commercial information which would qualify the master to act if necessary as the representative of his employer in the character of merchant; the commander of a ship being in law, considered the representative of the owners of the property on board.

Murray's conclusions were objected to by the ship-owners who again considered measures taken by the state to ameliorate anxieties an unwarranted intrusion into their private affairs. The contemporary ship-owner W.S. Lindsay, author of a monumental tome on merchant shipping, a contemporary of the debate, and a man who had raised himself by his own efforts from a cabin boy, summarised the ship-owners' point of view anecdotally thus:

> In my own time I remember a ship-owner saying to me that he never would have a 'scholar' in command of any of his vessels, because education taught him how to make up false accounts and the art of cheating; while another whom I knew only retained one 'educated' master in his service, because he was flattered by being invariably addressed as Mr Joseph Perkins, Esquire!

However, Lindsay concluded that:

> It was, nevertheless, but too evident that, however much British ship-owners might deprecate the assistance or interference of Government, a large proportion of their ships were commanded and navigated in a manner reflecting discredit on our national intelligence, and injurious to the interests of Great Britain...[23]

Lindsay raises the curtain upon the final act, for the impact of the consular reports —
so graphically drawn and touching so closely upon national honour — made common
sense prevail. There is no doubt that a significant proportion of merchant ship-masters and mates fitted the dismal and drunken model that Murray's exposé revealed,
and while many did not, those that did must needs be extirpated. So a majority in
Parliament thought, and passed an Act making examination for masters and mates
compulsory after 1 January 1851. All extant certificates were recalled and reissued
under the auspices of the Board of Trade, while a few senior men with unblemished
records were issued with 'certificates of service'. Instead of basing the classification
of certificates between ships of differing types, the new system was based upon rank:
second mate, first mate and master; with the 'extra-master' qualification remaining
voluntary and available to officers wishing to progress ashore to positions as surveyors,
examiners of masters and mates, and similar positions of regulatory importance rather
than active sea-service. All candidates had to prove age, experience and sea-time, and
the formal record that was held by the Registrar-General of Seamen, to whom it
was furnished by the ship-masters with whom a candidate served, had to attest to the
candidate's conduct and sobriety.[24]

All this had been given impetus in 1846 when Robert Peel's repeal of the Corn
Laws introduced the concept of universal free trade. Within two years legislation
had been set in train which culminated in the revocation of the Navigation Acts.
The President of the Board of Trade, Henry Labouchere (afterwards Lord Taunton),
responded to a question by a Select Committee member that he proposed to establish
a regulating Committee. This would be composed of unpaid officers, of which:

> the members shall be the President and Vice-President of the Board of Trade, one of
> the Naval Lords of the Admiralty…one or two persons connected with merchant
> shipping…a Board [which]…would be most valuable in dealing with all questions
> that relate to the mercantile marine of the country. The want of it is very much felt.

Thus the Merchant Shipping Act of 1850 finally established the Board of Trade's
Mercantile Marine Office to 'undertake the superintendence of matters relating to
the British mercantile marine…', entrusting it with carrying out the reforms. Some
responsibility was taken by the subsidiary Local Marine Boards, which were set up in
the major ports for the welfare of seamen, though this was rudimentary. These Boards
consisted of nominees of the state and of local ship-owners, setting aside the former
examining bodies of Trinity House, the Pilotage and Ballast Boards, and so forth. There
is evidence that this depreciated the quality of some examinations and it was but the
first move necessary to reinvigorate a depressed shipping industry, but such steps as
were subsequently taken, important though they were, occurred later in the century.

The wider world of commerce went on in spite of parliamentary deliberation. We
shall have reason to return to the West Indies later in respect of one aspect of the final
abolition of slavery throughout the British Empire in 1834, but the most obviously
consequential effect was to alter the character of West Indian shipping, since one leg

The *Thetis*, Captain Barton, was among the smarter ships engaged in the West India trade. She is shown here, her topsails aback and her fore-yards braced to throw her head to starboard as she gets under weigh off the Isle of Wight. This was the ship command of which Captain William Pixley declined. Etching by Edward William Cooke. (Private Collection)

of the infamous triangular trade had been kicked away – at least for British vessels. This was to encourage a new shipping route to trade directly with the west coast of Africa and, with the formation of the West India Association in Liverpool, the West India trade took on a new lease of life. Stealing a march from the prestigious East Indiamen, ships on the sugar, molasses and rum route to Jamaica and the islands of the Antilles were known as West Indiamen and run on smart, quasi-naval lines. One such was the *Thetis*, a ship of some 800 tons commanded by a Captain Barton, and which seduced the eye of the artist Edward William Cooke when she was lying in the Thames. The elevation from a 'Guineaman' to a West Indiaman was an unsubtle one, but one which marked a change of century: slaving was an activity of the eighteenth century, utterly reprehended in the nineteenth and left to 'foreigners', most notably the old colonial powers of Portugal and Spain that were, even then, in the process of losing their Central and South American possessions.[25]

It was a period of enormous change and upheaval, both socially and commercially. In 1843 there occurred the first major shipping slump which was fortuitously ended by the discovery by the British ship-master Captain Andrew Livingston of huge guano deposits upon the Chincha Islands off the Chilean coast, not far from Pisco and some ninety miles south of Callao, the port for Lima. Here the cold, northward sweep of the Humboldt Current brought plankton and their predator, the anchovy, close inshore to provide a perfect food chain for the Guanay cormorant, the Peruvian booby and the brown pelican. The excrement of these birds, dropped over thousands of years, covered the barren islands in fields over 30m deep, and contained a blend of nitrates, phosphates and potassium which, cured by the Chinchas' uniquely low moisture levels, made the finest imaginable fertiliser. Although the indigent Peruvians had appreciated the engendering properties of guano, it was largely ignored by the gold-seeking conquistadors, and it was Alexander von Humboldt who first drew European attention to its properties. A licence to dig it was granted to a Lima businessman, Don Francisco Quirós, by the newly independent Peruvian Government, and it was not long before Captain Livingston pioneered its export as a commercial cargo. In 1841 some nineteen vessels had landed about 8,000 tons at Southampton, initiating an immense boom. Within a short period all idle ships were employed in loading this valuable fertiliser, which had the added 'benefit' of being a constituent ingredient of explosives, and lay conveniently close to immense quantities of another, potassium nitrate.[26] Guano, and later nitrates, were to become a staple cargo for sailing-vessels for the next sixty years, only ended abruptly in about 1910 after Fritz Haber devised a method for making both fertilizer and explosives from an industrial process.[27]

Between 1841 and its peak in 1872, the guano boom was thought to have removed some 10 million tons from the Chincha Islands, initially dug out by convicts and later by indentured Chinese labour, as we shall note in a later chapter. Guano exports had an estimated value of about US$25 million, which made up three quarters of the Peruvian Government's income. For shipping, for the Americans in particular, guano provided a paying cargo for vessels homeward from the gold fields. For British vessels leaving Australia it also offered a homeward lading, though the Pacific had to be crossed in ballast unless a grain cargo – or later an Australian coal cargo – could be secured for a South American market. By 1850, upwards of 100 vessels of all nations would be anchored close to the Chinchas themselves, for the water was deep enough close-in. The local launches ferried guano out to them as they lay at anchor or, thanks to the deep water, actually secured to the rugged coast 'with their yards cock-billed, and rolling their royal masts almost against the face of the rock, all covered with guano [dust]...' Here the bagged guano was received on board down long canvas chutes. Its value as a cargo was tremendous, attracting many of the world's best known sailing ships, then becoming increasingly desperate to find a cargo. In October 1853 no less than 200 vessels and well over 3,000 men lay off the archipelago waiting a turn to load.

The uptake of guano cargoes was adversely affected by the American Civil War, which left Great Britain both the principal market and the principal carrier. The shortage of labour to dig the stuff led to all manner of abuses, including illegal 'black-birding', and the Chinchas were briefly the scene of Spanish occupation in 1864, while British investment – which had largely financed Peru's war of independence against Spain in the 1820s – placed much of the country's infrastructure in British hands. By the 1880s the guano trade, though carried on for many years, was giving ground to the carriage of nitrates from neighbouring Chile – which fought a war with Peru between 1879 and 1883 over the rich potassium deposits of the Tarapacá.

Another cargo brought away by British ships from this region was copper ore. This too was lifted in huge quantities and sustained the Welsh port of Swansea where massive deposits of coal were available for its smelting. Native British sources of copper-ore, largely from Cornwall and North Wales, were rapidly exhausted at the onset of the industrial age, but the smelting works and local coal supplies attracted the import of the ore from Chile in a fleet of fine sailing-vessels from the Welsh port, which, by mid-century, was producing 60 per cent of the world's copper.

However, other consequential events which would affect British mercantile shipping were occurring, chief among which were the launching of the American ship *Rainbow* in New York in 1845, the discovery of gold in California in 1849 and the Irish Potato Famine of 1850. The *Rainbow*, and successive ships like the Baltimore-built *Ann McKim* of 1850, took the hollow-lined hull of the small 'Baltimore clipper' and scaled it up for the deep-water merchantman. The *Rainbow* is generally regarded as the first 'true clipper' though, to some extent, these distinctions are meaningless since fast hulls were being designed and built in the Far East for the opium trade, as we shall presently observe. However, the immediate impact of these larger, faster, full-rigged ships coincided with the Californian gold rush and the onset of a busy emigrant trade which would increase steadily in the following sixty years, driving the development of other mercantile marines. The Irish Potato Famine was one of the prime initiators of mass emigration, though Ireland was not the only country to be affected by high food prices for the poor. The social upheavals of 1848 produced other migrant movements from central Europe, Italy and Russia. These were initially directed towards the United States but, following the discovery of gold in Australia and then New Zealand, new destinations beckoned.

Many of the new American ships – known as 'Down-Easters' – were built for the mass carriage of passengers, taking speculators out to California and the fabulous diggings where, it was affirmed, a man might make his fortune in a trice. They made astonishingly fast passages, most remarkably in their impressive west-bound doublings of Cape Horn against the prevailing winds, showing that, despite the presence of the new paddle-steamer on the North Atlantic, there remained plenty of work for new sailing-vessels.

Once again Great Britain found herself in a state of immediate competition in which its ships compared badly with other nations', especially those of the 'damned Yankees'. It was cold consolation to learn that by the following year San Francisco Bay was filled with idle, anchored ships, all of them deserted by their crews who had left for the diggings at Sutter's Hill on the American River. What was worse, the feeling of inferiority was brought to the British public's attention when a black-hulled schooner – odd-looking to British eyes – scooped the honours at Cowes on 22 August 1851 after a race round the Isle of Wight. John Stevens, commodore of the New York Yacht Club, had had the yacht *America* specially built to humble the British, and the cup he won that day has borne his schooner's name ever since. This was not the only national humiliation but came hard on the heels of another, the consequences of which were more serious, touching as they did a matter of grave economical and national concern: tea.

The year before the *America* took the cup home from the Royal Yacht Squadron, the American clipper *Oriental* arrived in London from Hong Kong. She was the first foreign ship to do so since the repeal of the Navigation Laws and she created a sensation, for not only did she carry tea — a commodity that had more than once upset relations between Great Britain and North America — but she accomplished the passage in only ninety-one days. Her arrival provoked a deep gloom in British ship-owning circles, for the *Oriental* represented a real threat to the carrying trade, and she was just one of a swiftly growing fleet of brand-new, fast sailing ships. The year she flaunted the stars-and-stripes over the grey waters of the Thames, 1850, the first 'extreme clipper' — a further refinement in hull design — was launched by Donald McKay at East Boston and named *Staghound*.

The apparent rapid ascendancy of American maritime culture was backed by more than clipper ships. In 1850 the relatively junior Lieutenant Matthew Fontaine Maury of the United States Navy published several works to help passage-making in sailing ships. Having accompanied Charles Wilkes as navigation officer in the USS *Vincennes* during the United States' exploratory circumnavigation between 1838 and 1842, Maury had produced a comprehensive study of the global wind system, taking Dampier's seventeenth-century pioneering but partial work to its logical conclusion.[28] In 1853 Maury addressed the members of Lloyd's of London and greatly impressed his audience. It had long since become clear that something must be done to check this perceived insolence on the part of Cousin Jonathan who, it was feared, might yet wrest Neptune's trident from Britannia's grasp. Hardly had the *Oriental* astounded the ship-owners of London than they responded, determined to fight fire with fire.

Despite the gloom, British ship design was not as far astern of the Americans as the jeremiahs claimed. Stretching the new measurement regulations, a long overhanging bow had appeared from Alexander Hall's Yard at Aberdeen in 1839 on the opium-clipper *Scottish Lass*. Christened the 'Aberdeen bow', it marked a departure from the apple-cheeked entrance of the traditional hull and echoed the sharp entrance of the Baltimore schooners and clippers of the late war. But the more prominent counter-blast must necessarily come from London's river, where the insult had been most keenly felt.

At a dinner in the City of London, given for the benefit of a marine charity, the ship-owner and builder Richard Green made a speech intended to rouse the British spirit to meet the challenge from across the Atlantic and to counter the doubts among his colleagues as to the wisdom of repealing the Navigation Acts, a move Green himself had advocated. Green's speech was in response to a hectoring from a 'young gentleman' then serving as 'Secretary to the American Legation' in London. It initiated a rivalry that was given added piquancy by the then construction of a large 2,600-ton ship named the *Challenge* at New York. In the following year this was fur-

Richard, better known as 'Dickie', Green, the ship-builder and ship-owner who responded to the Americans and built the *Challenger* in 1851. (Whereabouts of original unknown)

ther spiced up by a stake of £10,000 being put up by the American Navigation Club for a straight race between a British and American clipper, though no such race was ever held.

In the event Green was obliged to take the lead himself, and as a consequence the keel of a new ship was laid down at Messrs R. & H. Green's Blackwall Yard, from whence had issued many of Britain's finest merchantmen. She was named *Challenger* and was to be commanded by Captain James Killick, a man who had first gone to sea in 1833 in the 262-ton brig *Ganges*, a type of vessel instantly recognisable to James Cook two generations earlier. The *Ganges* had been commanded by a part-owner, Captain George Bowlby, and had been engaged in the Baltic trade. Killick was one of two apprentices, for the rest of the crew consisted of Bowlby, a mate, six seamen and a cook. The general utility and commonplace nature of these vessels and their mundane voyages has excited little attention and much of the detail is lost, but the trade in a variety of commodities from tar to iron ore, flax and other materials essential to the shipping industry, including hull- and mast-timber, soft iron, turpentine and rosin were added to dried fish and pressed oils. The *Ganges*, later commanded by a Captain John Sinclair, made several voyages to St Petersburg during Killick's four years of indentured service, which ended in 1837. After this his movements are obscure until he surfaces in command of the barque *Arun* in Chinese waters, running between Whampoa and Singapore in 1842. Hints are given by his biographer, David MacGregor, that Killick served briefly in command of the opium-clipper *Mischief*, which is a possibility supported by Basil Lubbock, but three years later he took command of the *John Dugdale*, named after a partner or shareholder in the Liverpool firm of Little & Co. who, in 1848, acquired the ship entirely for himself. Killick had risen to command without formal qualification, and it was 1849 before he obtained a master's certificate. As this was issued from the Liverpool Custom House it was probably a certificate of service, his abilities having been impressed upon his owners by his achievements, thus his acquisition of a Board of Trade certificate as master was simply one of exchange. In January 1851 Killick gave up command of the *John Dugdale*, but his reputation was such that he was selected by Dicky Green to command the new *Challenger*. A contemporary, Captain Andrew Shewan of the *Norman Court*, remarked of the new ship and her commander:

> This vessel had the advantage of having a most energetic commander, Captain Killick, and I am inclined to think she was, all round, the fastest ship in the China trade…until…1859… The *Challenger* loaded in Hankow in 1864, making her thirteenth passage home with teas, thus she must have been a well-built vessel… The *Challenger* was of a different type from the Aberdeen clippers, not so sharp forward, more of the 'dolphin head and mackerel tail' type, and consequently faster in light winds.

The *Challenger's* first owner was Hugh Lindsay, who seems to have bought her on the stocks. Thanks to Killick, she would live up to her builder's expectations and initiate a new period in British shipping, the brief but exciting era of the tea-clipper when the sailing ship reached a high-point of splendour.

CHAPTER NOTES:

1. American-owned, the *Prince de Neuchâtel* was named for Napoleon's chief of staff, Marshal Berthier, Prince of Neuchâtel, and manned initially in Cherbourg. She was a very successful privateer and was only later captured in heavy weather by a British frigate squadron.
2. For the impact and detailed depredations of the press gangs, see *Neptune's Trident* and *Britannia's Realm*.
3. Abel Chapman was an Elder Brother of Trinity House and the longest serving until his record was broken in 2007 by the corporation's present master, HRH Prince Philip, Duke of Edinburgh. Aaron Chapman was also an Elder Brother. He sat as a Conservative MP for Whitby between 1832 and 1847.
4. Shortly afterwards a Russian naval expedition commanded by Captain Thaddeus Bellingshausen in the *Vostok*, with Captain Lazarev in the *Mirnyy*, was in the same waters.
5. Another American master, Captain Edmund Fanning, the intellectual equal of Weddell, was also active in these waters at this time. Fanning wrote of South Georgia: 'The brightness of a clear sun shining on these islands, and on the sea as it broke against their base, formed a view, which for grandeur and beauty, is seldom or ever surpassed.'

6. Originally founded by Samuel Enderby in the mid-eighteenth century. Enderby had connections with the East India Company and had manned some of his London-registered whalers with Nantucketers to avoid their being pressed into the Royal Navy. By 1830 the firm was run by the partners and brothers Charles, Henry, George and Gordon Enderby, all of whom are immortalised on the map of Antarctica. An Enderby sister was mother to General Gordon who fought the Taiping rebels in China and died at Khartoum.

7. The voyage of the 129-ton brig *Hopefull* of Ipswich and her tender, the 100-ton 'yawl' *Rose*, was a confused affair. Enderby's first appointee to command was Captain William Lyle, a successful South Seas whaling master who had made profitable voyages in the *Lady Amherst* and was afterwards appointed to the *Samuel Enderby* — which makes a fictional appearance in the conclusion of Hermann Melville's novel *Moby Dick*. Rea pushed too far into the pack and lost the *Rose* in ice off Clarence Island, turning back to the Falklands where, incidentally, he fell in with HMS *Beagle* under Robert Fitzroy on her circumnavigation with Charles Darwin on board. Later in Paris, Biscoe — who spoke French — told the great French explorer Dumont D'Urville that the disaster had been caused by Rea's lack of experience, but was otherwise tight-lipped about whatever he knew. Undoubtedly there had been trouble between Rea and those he perceived as his subordinates. Rea had passed the examination for lieutenant but had never been commissioned and remained at the age of twenty-nine either a master's mate or midshipman. He seems to have assumed that the expedition, though carried out entirely in Enderby's vessels and with an experienced sealing master, Captain Edward Prior, in attendance, was a naval expedition and that he, Rea, had the charge of it. In fact the Admiralty had only under-written part of the expense and provided Rea with instruments, etc, while it was Prior's task to make the voyage a *commercial* success. Moreover, the actual command of the *Hopefull* seems to have resided with another merchant master, possibly a Captain Leslie, although the twenty-two-year-old ex-naval master's mate, John Foxton, aboard the *Rose*, seems also to have exercised some control under Rea, though he was actually Rea's surveying assistant. The *Rose* continued under the command of John Mallows, her master in the South African trade from whence Enderby's had recalled and diverted her. It was all rather messy and there was certainly bad blood between Rea and the others, particularly the mercantile crew who would have been relying upon sea-pelts for their pay-off, and would have had little truck for the exploratory aspect of the voyage. Rea, like so many of his ilk, undoubtedly saw the expedition as his chance to prove himself as a surveyor and win the coveted commission as lieutenant with its security blanket of half-pay. Enderby's experienced masters and their ships' companies were in no doubt that the voyage was commercial, with discovery and hydrographic surveying a secondary sideline. The experience ended the Admiralty's appetite for joint-ventures. Enderby & Co. tried to interest the Admiralty in another in 1839, but by that time preparations were in hand to send James Clark Ross south in *Erebus* and *Terror*. Instead, Enderby's appointee to command the next intended expedition, Henry Mapleton, another Master RN, joined Bellany in the *Eliza Scott*. Mapleton had been with Ross in the *Cove* during the search for the whalers beset in the ice in Baffin Bay in 1835-36. See *The Mariner's Mirror*, Volume 51, No.3, p233 *et seq* (1964).

8. There was a thriving colonial whaling business in Tasmanian coastal waters, but in 1841 what was called 'Bay-whaling' began to fail owing to the success of the hunters. From this date Tasmanians began whaling offshore, penetrating deeper and deeper into Pacific and Antarctic waters. In 1849 Hobart's locally owned fleet of whalers numbered thirty-eight vessels, a reminder that the Antipodes, as well as Canada and India, possessed a colonial merchant fleet which was part of the greater 'British' mercantile marine, all wearing the British red ensign.

9. There was a last flourish of commercial daring by Enderby & Co. in the Southern Ocean when in 1850 Captain Tapsell of Enderby's *Brisk* penetrated Antarctic waters further than the United States expedition under Lieutenant Charles Wilkes in the USS *Vincennes* had done ten years earlier.

10. Huskisson is better known for being the first fatality caused by a railway accident, but his speech in the House of Commons in May 1826 set out the Government's new policy, it being 'thought more prudent and more dignified to enter into amicable arrangements with other powers, founded on the basis of mutual interest and entire reciprocity of advantages, rather than embark on a contest of commercial hostility and reciprocal exclusion'. While the consequences of this are generally held to be enlightened, its long-term effect on British shipping may not, in the long run, prove to have been so.

11. The Royal Navy was less careful that its commissioned officers were adequate navigators than the Honourable East India Company, and tended to rely upon warrant sailing masters to conduct their ships and carry out the daily tasks of dead-reckoning and navigation. These warrant officers were generally drawn from the merchant service and never commissioned, though in 1805 Masters RN — a rank not to be confused with the master of a merchant ship, who was her commander — were admitted by Admiralty order to the status of wardroom-officers. All Masters RN became commissioned as staff-commanders in about 1840. Popular fiction has obfuscated this, but masters had to pass a more rigorous test of their navigational skills than lieutenants throughout the Age of Nelson.

12. Biden's book has the succinct title of *Naval Discipline. Subordination contrasted with Insubordination; or, a View of the Passing a Law establishing an Efficient Naval Discipline on board ships in the Merchant Service; comprising a Valuable Record of Occurrences on board Various Ships; evincing the Advantages arising from Good Order on the one hand, and the Disasters attending the want of it on the other.* A copy in my possession has annotations in soft pencil which, if not the amendments of Biden himself, are clearly those of a well-informed and contemporary person, presumably a sea-officer in the Company's service.

13. See *Britannia's Realm*.

14. These Acts were respectively Act 6, Geo.IV. c.109; Acts 3 & 4, Will.IV. c.54; Acts 5 & 6, Will.IV. c.19.

15. See Northcote Parkinson (Ed.) *The Trade Winds*, p111. See also *Neptune's Trident*, Chapter 3.

16. An apprentice, having signed an indenture with his master, or later, his shipping company, was obliged to serve the term, or 'time', stipulated by the indenture, whereas a cadet signed articles on a voyage basis. Moreover, whereas the apprentice was regarded as a young seaman metamorphosing into an officer, the cadet was assumed to be an embryonic officer from the start, and often — to the neighbouring apprentice's chagrin — allowed a small alcohol allowance once over eighteen years of age! Several ship-owners, from the East India Company and Blackwallers to Elder Dempster & Co. and Alfred Holt's Blue Funnel and Glen Lines, called their aspirants midshipmen, further muddying the waters of clarity.

17. Trinity House secured a dominant position with regard to all shipping entering or leaving the Thames where its writ, under the authority of several royal charters, ran from London Bridge to 'the main sea to the Eastward'. This conferred on it greater powers than the other Trinity Houses at Hull, Newcastle and Leith, but its failure to provide decent lighthouses on the west coast of England and Wales until about 1830, and the desire for the ship-owning merchants of Glasgow and Liverpool to run their own affairs, made any attempts to regard Trinity House in London as a national regulator of seafarers a non-starter.

18. See 'Poor Mercantile Jack' in *The Uncommercial Traveller*, which first appeared as late as 1860.

19. With the west coast of England and that of Wales poorly lit, when the increasingly powerful lobby of ship-owners from Liverpool wished for better lights in the Irish Sea they refused to countenance the 'English' system of private lighthouses licensed by Trinity House and petitioned Parliament to have lights erected on the Isle of Man by the Commissioners for Northern Lights. This was approved and to this day these lighthouses remain under Scots supervision. Elsewhere the Mersey Docks and Harbour Board established lighthouses while the cost of buying-out some of the private proprietors was considerable, Trinity House being obliged to compensate the owner of the Skerries lighthouse off Holyhead to the tune of £444,000.

20. See Edward Blackmore, *The British Mercantile Marine*, Chas. Griffin & Co., 1897, Chapters VII and VIII.

21. From data collected by Captain William Chaplin, Elder Brother, and drawn to my attention by Paul Ridgway.

22. Landale, J., *Duel, A True Story of Death and Honour*, Canongate, Edinburgh, 2005, p21.

23. R.H. Thorton says that in 1837 'there was little to be proud of in the British Mercantile Marine'.

24. At this time the minimum age a candidate might pass for a second-mate was seventeen years old, which meant that he must have gone to sea aged thirteen – still a young age for a lad to have first acquired anything other than a rudimentary education.

25. Although slavery was not abolished in the United States of America until after the Civil War, the Congress outlawed the slave-trade in 1808, emulating the abolition of the British Parliament.

26. So valuable were guano deposits to the over-farmed tobacco and cotton plantations of the American South that the United States of America passed a law in 1851 enabling any island where an American citizen discovered guano to be automatically claimed on behalf of the United States. Six islands were acquired in this way, though often clashing with other states also claiming sovereignty. This legislation, known colloquially as 'the bird-shit law', only added fuel to the flames of paranoia over American intentions that grew after the Monroe Doctrine of 1822, the most recent modification of which had been made by President Polk in 1845.

27. Haber's part in the industrial production of fertiliser ended the guano trade overnight, ruining many companies and destroying the means of earning a livelihood for thousands of workers, afloat and ashore. His work on explosives and chlorine, both of which were used for the destruction of British, French and American forces in the First World War, earned him the Nobel Prize for Chemistry. In 1919 the Allies demanded he be handed over as a war-criminal, but he received the prestigious prize instead, though his wife Clara shot herself as a consequence. After the war Haber sailed aboard the *Hansa* and *Württemberg* on expeditions determined to obtain gold from sea-water. Perhaps fortunately this was not a success. Forced to resign by the Nazis owing to his Jewish roots – remarkably he had converted to Christianity! – Haber died whilst emigrating. His life seems to have been dedicated to either denying others a living, or applying a more direct approach and simply depriving them of life itself.

28. For references to William Dampier, see *Neptune's Trident*, Chapter Three.

TWO

'THE ETERNAL GAME OF EXTORTION'

End-Game, Opium and Aftermath in the Far East, 1816–1842

The arrival of the *Oriental* in the Thames marked a final change in trading conditions begun by the removal of the East India Company's monopoly on Indian trade in 1813. Twelve years later, in 1825, it lost its right to wear its distinguishing colours – John Company's 'grid-iron' ensign.[1] Simultaneously, the charter of the ancient Levant Company was revoked, the British Government taking over all the company's Middle Eastern consulates. During the first three decades of the nineteenth century the East India Company had remained the dominant though fading enterprise command- ing eastern trade, especially that with China, because it provided the infrastructure through which all commerce was handled, even when not directly connected with it. Such was the Company's grip on its routes that even in its last years, despite the erosion of its monopolies and the increased competition, East Indiaman maintained their lordly pretensions. They even occasionally still bore a commission against 'such Pirates, Freebooters and Sea Rovers' that might be encountered on 'the Coasts and Seas of India and any other Seas whatsoever.'[2] Importantly, they remained the slender but reliable rein by which London controlled the Company's Indian possessions.

Passengers bound for Calcutta hired a cabin or part thereof void of fittings, pro- viding their own bedding, washing facilities and furniture, paying up to £300 for a good stern cabin. Dinner consisted of three courses plus dessert, no fish being served. Wine and beer were provided at dinner, and there was champagne twice a week. Most Indiamen carried a 'good milking cow' and also bore sheep, pigs, ducks, and fowls for the passengers' and officers' benefit. A calf, which invariably accompanied the cow, was butchered for the table when in the Southern Ocean. The midshipmen, who were in the charge of a fourth or fifth mate, lived in the 'somewhat dismal hole' of the steerage, the other junior mates and surgeon sharing double-berthed cabins, while the first mate and commander each had a cabin of their own. It was customary to issue grog whenever all hands were called out at night to reef topsails or shorten sail after the duty had been performed, otherwise it was served out to the seamen at dinner time and on Saturday nights when the toast 'sweethearts and wives' was drunk. The ceremony of crossing-the-line was encouraged, as were concerts, theatricals and dances, otherwise daily routine was man-of-style, with hammocks being piped up and down.

The East India Company, although continuing to charter ships from the Marine Interest and its Court of Directors, built new tonnage, even though their design was increasingly archaic. Typical of this last generation of Indiamen was the 1,325-ton *Edinburgh*, a splendid ship built by Wigram at Blackwall for Henry Bonham and launched amid much pomp on 9 November 1825.[3] The *Edinburgh* was commanded by Captain Henry Bonham Bax, whose middle name gives some clue to the close connections enjoyed by these men.[4] Bax, an accomplished water-colourist, would later become an Elder Brother of Trinity House.

Earlier that year the Company had suffered one of it worst disasters in the loss of its latest *Kent*, an unlucky name in the Company's service. Built in 1820 by Wigram and Green at Blackwall to the order of Stewart Marjoribanks she sailed on her maiden voyage for Bombay and China on 14 March 1821 under an experienced commander, Henry Cobb, who had been at sea almost twenty years when appointed to the *Kent*. She was the sixth ship in the Company's service to bear the name and she sailed on her third voyage on 19 February 1825, bound for Calcutta and Canton. As well as the usual crop of passengers, she bore a detachment of the 31st Foot under Lieutenant Colonel Robert Fearon, who had with him his wife and several daughters. The *Kent* ran into a gale in the Bay of Biscay and on 1 March a cask of spirits which had been brought up out of the hold broke loose and shattered, over-setting a lantern which ignited the vapourising spirits. In an instant the fire had taken a firm hold. Cobb immediately threw out a signal of distress with little hope in the high sea running, but a small 200-ton brig named the *Cambria*, commanded by a Captain W. Cook, performed prodigies in successfully rescuing 547 souls. The *Cambria* was carrying a number of Cornish tin-miners who were desperately seeking work and were bound for Vera Cruz where employment awaited them, and they assisted Cook's small crew in their desperate task. Despite the large number saved, eighty-two lost their lives, most − if not all − members of the *Kent*'s crew. Displays of such seamanship must be set against the complaints against British masters mentioned previously, for Cook commanded a vessel included in that category of 'under 300 tons' so vilified by the *Nautical Magazine*'s correspondent, 'B.C.'[5]

By 1833 the East India Company had had its day as a shipping enterprise and on 28 August an Act passed through Parliament abrogating the Company's monopoly of trade with China. It took effect from 1 April 1834, after which the Company retained the armed-cruisers of the Indian Marine, while it continued to govern India under a Government-appointed Board of Control until direct rule by London, was undertaken during the Indian Mutiny in 1857.[6] Matters swiftly thereafter came to a head; the Company was finally disbanded under the Government of India Act a year later, and its armed-vessels became the new Royal Indian Navy, part of the greater Royal Navy.[7] As John Keay summarises:

> A maritime empire based on free-trade was an improbable legacy from a mercantil-ist and monopolistic entity like the Honourable Company. But perhaps no more so than the vast continental empire that was the Raj. With a few exceptions...the Company's servants had seldom craved political supremacy. Some form of com-mercial dominion had ever been closer to their ideals. Had James Lancaster or Jack Saris...been vouchsafed a glimpse of the future, they would scarcely have found the Raj enviable or comprehensible; but in the off-shore metropolises like Penang, [and] Singapore...they must have rejoiced.[8]

We shall come to the last homeward sailings from the Pearl River — and to Singapore — in due course, but the last outward voyage of an East Indiaman under the Company's auspices was that of the *Elizabeth* which, built in 1816 for Gilmore & Co. of Calcutta, traded to India until 1833 as a private Licensed-ship. In July 1833, however, she was formally chartered by the Company and, under Captain John Craigie, sailed from the Thames on a final voyage to China with orders to proceed from Canton to Halifax. A relatively small Indiaman of only 544 tons, the *Elizabeth* arrived back in the Thames in December 1834, several months after the Company's 'Maritime Service' had been wound-up. No doubt Craigie added his name to the memorial the redundant com-manders presented to the Court of Directors requesting compensation for the loss of income, prospects and perquisites. They claimed, with some accuracy if little natural justice, that the East India Company's Maritime Service — that is to say its cargo and passenger carrying ships — had existed for over 200 years during which they as a class had been 'in a great degree instrumental in acquiring and securing the now vast ter-ritories of British India for the Company and in advancing its commercial success'. The supplication was fruitless and many continued much as before, though the nature of their business was undergoing far from subtle changes.

From the moment the East Indiaman ceased to exist officially a number of them retained the title and style under their private owners. Others were sold off, and in their place arose a new, crack cargo-passenger sailing ship generically known as a 'Blackwall frigate' and usually commanded by former Company commanders, run on identical quasi-naval lines and commonly, also confusingly, referred to as 'East Indiamen' on the grounds that they carried out the same function as their pred-ecessors. In 'a period of growing energy and vitality' which is a counterpoint to the lugubrious deliberations of Parliament upon the drunkenness of the British merchant jack elsewhere, the Blackwallers regarded themselves as separate from the 'ordinary Mercantile Marine' in precisely the same way that the old Company ships used to, notwithstanding the evidence presented by Captain Biden.[9] These owners not only took up the old routes of the Indiamen but also opened the passenger traffic to

Australia that was soon augmenting the depressing export of convicts with an invigorating flow of emigrants, and therein creating a renaissance in British shipping.

Nevertheless, the economy of British India remained reliant upon a trade route extending further east, beyond the Dutch East Indies, to the vast, misunderstood empire of China. The domination of the China trade by British shipping houses, whilst owing everything to the eventual acquisition of Hong Kong and the vacuum left by the ending of the East India Company's archaic monopoly, would not have been possible without the prior establishment of a British base nearer to the China Seas which could circumvent the Dutch sphere of influence in the eastern archipelago. This was accomplished by the founding of the Port of Singapore which, while not being an intended product of the East India Company's policy, grew directly from its long desire to outwit the Dutch. Attempts to establish an entrepôt further east than Calcutta had long preoccupied the Company's Court of Directors. The island of Balambangan, ceded by the Sultan of Sulu in 1762, was colonised ten years later, but proved 'a short-lived and abject fiasco'.[10] The best that had been achieved was the acquisition of the island of Penang at the northern end of the Malacca Strait, while the old pepper-growing station at Benkulen on the west coast of Sumatra (Sumatera), remained important in name only.

The Napoleonic War had dramatically changed things, making Penang a subordinate Company Presidency under Calcutta in 1805. With the appointment of a new governor went an assistant to the chief secretary, a young man named Thomas Stamford Raffles. Raffles had been born at sea in July 1781, aboard the 260-ton West Indiaman *Ann*, of 4-guns, of which his father Benjamin was master. The *Ann* was four days out from Jamaica, part of a large convoy heading for Britain during the final phase of the American War of Independence when control of the Atlantic passed briefly but crucially to the French. In Britain's loss of the American colonies Benjamin Raffles's fortune was compromised. The old ship-master fell into debt and his fourteen-year-old son was found an appointment as a clerk to the Honourable East India Company. Two years later his father died and Thomas Raffles found himself the family breadwinner responsible for his widowed mother and several sisters on an annual salary of £70. At East India House in Leadenhall Street Raffles not only found himself sitting in the copy-room with the future essayist Charles Lamb, but rubbing shoulders with the Company's librarian, the great Orientalist Charles Wilkins. Wilkins was to inspire Raffles's passion for knowledge and focus it on the Far East. He also noted the youth's diligence, seriousness and precocious grasp of matters beyond the direct business of a mere clerk. Thus, after a decade's service at his desk, Raffles found himself promoted – at a salary of £1,500 – to assist the chief secretary being sent out to Penang on the staff of the new governor, the Hon. Philip Dundas. The elevation of Penang to the status of a Presidency was a mark of the island's growing importance as a trading post. Not only did it stand at the northern end of the Malacca Strait, offering a safe anchorage and watering-place, but it lay not far from the independent Muslim state of Achin on Sumatra with which Indian-owned 'Country-ships' had traded for generations under the British ensign.

Marrying the beautiful Olivia Fancourt, the widow of a Company surgeon ten years his senior, Raffles embraced his new task with enthusiasm. A man of rare ability, he learned Malay, became fascinated by the history and ethnology of the Malay peninsula and the East Indies, and met another influential Orientalist and polymath, Dr John Leyden, the brilliant son of a Scots shepherd. They became firm friends, and Raffles continued to attract the notice of his superiors, but excited the jealousy of his peers. Although personally an unassuming young fellow, by March 1807 Raffles had been made chief secretary to Dundas at a salary of £2,000. When Leyden was in Calcutta he recommended Raffles's abilities to the new Governor-General, Lord Minto, a kindly man for whom much of the pomp of office was distasteful but who had previously held the post of chairman of the Board of Control.

Raffles and Minto met in Calcutta in June 1810, the two men striking a rapport in consequence of which Raffles was sent back to Malacca with the Indian Marine brig *Ariel* at his disposal, as agent to the Governor-General in Malaya. This was a confidential appointment, for Minto had charged him with discovering the attitudes of the Malay princes and their peoples to Dutch rule. The situation in the Indian Ocean had, by 1810, become critical and, as was related in *Britannia's Realm*, Minto eventually authorised the taking of the East Indies from the Dutch. With the Dutch dislodged from Java and their eastern possessions in the hands of the British, Minto appointed Raffles lieutenant-governor at Batavia. Raffles at once instituted reforms in the colonial administration, sweeping away the repressive Dutch mercantilist regime in which the peasants were obliged to grow specific produce, sell it at a low fixed price to their colonial masters and buy imports through the Dutch East India Company. With his flair for Malay and his charmingly easy manner augmented by Olivia's talents, Raffles soon suppressed remaining resistance to the British, won over the bulk of the Javanese and all but the most intransigent among the Dutch settlers. While his enlightened administration began to benefit the indigenous population, it disappointed his principals in London. Minto, pursuing war objectives, had in reality exceeded his instructions and saddled the Company with a territorial burden they did not want. In compensation London required the new territory to turn-in an immediate profit, but because Raffles's reforms needed an injection of specie to redeem the economy and compensate for the devalued Dutch paper-currency, the distant Court of Directors 'took the view that Raffles was an amateur philanthropist and gave him no time to prove that his policy was financially sound'. At this point Minto was recalled and Lord Moira appointed to succeed him. A distinguished soldier, Moira was obliged to campaign against the Mahrattas, and was not much interested in events in far away Java. He was, moreover, poisonously misinformed about Raffles, to the extent that he did not hold the young man in the same esteem as Minto. Thanks to this malice of a disappointed colleague, Raffles was recalled and sent as lieutenant-governor to the back-water of Benkulen, where Olivia shortly afterwards died.

Raffles now suffered a further blow. Following the final defeat of Napoleon the negotiated settlement of the Congress of Vienna returned to the Dutch the islands so lately taken from them. It was imperative for the British to have a friendly power dominating the Schelde, the principal reason for going to war with the French in 1793 having been that country's occupation of Antwerp, the great port which, in the hands of the enemy, was perceived as a 'pistol pointing at London'. Britain also required a friendly Netherlands to restore the balance of power in Europe, and consequently the Dutch regained all their eastern colonies. Unfortunately, neither Britain's power nor her friendship — whatever its reception in The Hague — was considered conciliatory by the Dutch colonial officials who guarded 'their' archipelago jealously. Moreover, despite the East India Company's well-established right to sail through the Indonesian seas, the Colonial Dutch pursued a policy not so much of *mare nostrum*, but of *mare clausum*.

Thus, in the immediate post-war period, the situation in the East Indies was restored to its pre-war status, with one important exception; the frequently referred-to abolition of the East India Company's monopoly on Indian trade, relinquished in 1813. With this went administrative control of the lands ceded to it under successive agreements with Indian princes, which now resided with the political appointees who made up the Board of Control, an important distinction in view of what was about to happen.

A disappointed and bereaved Raffles returned to London. Here, for a while, the self-confessed restless spirit worked on his book, the *History of Java*, which was soon published to critical acclaim, stimulating interest in both subject and author. Elected a Fellow of the Royal Society, Raffles began to move in high social circles and, in consequence, remarried. Finally he was cheered by a knighthood conferred by the Prince Regent, taking his second name for his title. Sir Stamford Raffles also met George Canning, then head of the Board of Control overseeing the administration of India, and in the course of their discussions he submitted a paper to Canning concerning eastern trade. He also met Henry Ellis, lately returned from the latest British diplomatic fiasco at the hands of the Chinese.

In an attempt to loosen the shackles on trade with China and open her markets to the increasing output of British industry, the British had determined to send another embassy to China. The fate of Lord Macartney's mission of 1797 has already been recounted in some detail, and it is only necessary to relate that Lord Amherst's was no more successful; indeed it was a great deal less so, since HM Frigate *Alceste*, Captain George Murray, was wrecked on a reef in the Gaspar Strait on her way home in 1817.[11] The ship's company landed on Pulo Leat, Amherst made Batavia in the ship's barge and persuaded the Dutch governor to send the Dutch East Indiaman *Ternate* to rescue the *Alceste*'s people, whose safety had been threatened by Malay pirates. Thereafter, Messrs Brocklebank's *Princess Charlotte*, under Captain McKean, conveyed Lord Amherst, his suite and the ship's company back to Calcutta. Almost the only significant feature of the *Alceste*'s mission for the humiliated British was that between the evening of 10 July 1816 until the 13th, the frigate and her consorts, the sloop-of-war *Lyra* and the Company's hired ship *General Hewitt*, lay in 'Hongkong Bay'. For the Chinese, however, the attempt to open trade only increased the Manchu Emperor's resolve to keep the 'Red Barbarians' at a distance. This mixture of contempt and fear, the latter generated by the rather shaky hold the dynasty had upon its vast possessions, was to have dreadful consequences for China within a generation.

However, the publication of Ellis's account of Amherst's mission touched Raffles in that Ellis complimented Raffles's administration of Java where the *Alceste* had called upon her outward passage. In due course Raffles returned to Benkulen and, after a tour of the hinterland in which he sought the opinion of the native princes of Sumatra on various matters affecting trade and colonialism, he presented Moira — now elevated to the dignity of the Marquess Hastings — with an address urging the necessity of restraining the Dutch from reimposing their exclusive trade restrictions on the region. Clearly the Dutch had no intention of being so obliging, so it seemed to Raffles that their intransigence could be avoided by the British acquiring a post at the southern end of the Malacca Strait which, backed by the power of the Royal Navy, would prove of immediate benefit to British-Indian trade with China, and of ultimate benefit to the neighbouring Malay states. Raffles and Hastings finally met, the latter immediately revising his previous opinion of the former and concerting with him a plan to seek such a British post.[12]

It was initially intended to approach the local sultan in the Rhio Islands, but in the event Raffles, acting on discretionary instructions from Hastings, intervened in a local dispute over the succession of the Sultanate of Johore. Before leaving the Hughli, Raffles had revealed in a letter to a friend:

> We are now on our way to the Eastward in the hope of doing something, but I much fear the Dutch have hardly left us an inch of ground to stand upon. My inten-tion is principally directed to Johore and you must not be surprised if my next letter to you is dated from the site of the ancient city of Singapura.

Raffles was prescient, but the Dutch were no less so, for they had rumbled the plan. On arriving at Penang on the last day of 1818, Raffles learned that they had occu-pied Rhio. He also encountered the hostility of the governor of Penang, now a Colonel Bannerman, who considered Raffles a meddler. Telling his friend Marsden of Bannerman's attitude, Raffles confessed he was relying upon Hastings's support: 'his last words to me were — "Sir Stamford, you may depend on me." '

In the end Raffles was obliged to outwit Bannerman, sending him on ahead with troops before following in the merchantman *Indiana* with a handful of Company infantry. On 26 January 1819 a detachment of sepoy infantry under Major Farquhar embarked aboard the Company's cruisers *Investigator* and *Discovery* at Malacca to join Raffles. The various parties combined off the Kariman Islands, 'but, finding them unsuitable, they then, on the suggestion of Captain Ross [of the *Investigator*], went to Singapoora Island. There they found a good anchorage with mud holding ground...'

It was now imperative to move quickly to outwit the Dutch at Rhio. The ships brought-up off the low-lying wooded shoreline on the afternoon of 28 January 1819. The island was part of the Sultanate of Johore but had once been the site of a walled city which, until the dissolution of the Sri-Vijayan Empire in the late fourteenth century, had been an important place rendered in Sanskrit as *Singha–Pura*, the Lion City, or holy city of Lord Vishnu. Since that time the island had become sparsely populated by a mixed number of native Malays and industrious Chinese. It had also been an occasional refuge of the *orang laut*, the piratical and rapacious 'sea-people', or Sea-Dyaks, the remnants of which fished from their rickety *kampongs*, and several accounts tell of passing European seamen seeing the shore-line dotted with skulls. Whatever fanciful notions attached to the place, the Dutch had hitherto neglected it while generations of British Indiamen had sailed blithely past, keeping a good offing, for the island was but the largest of a reef-strewn archipelago. Only a few people, for Raffles was not alone in his enthusiasm, had realised its potential.[13] On 19 February Raffles and a small suite attended the sultan's representative, the *Temenggong*, who welcomed them. Raffles proposed leasing the island for a fair rent and persuaded the *Temenggong* to pass word to the rightful sultan, *Tunku* Long, then on an outlying island in some fear of his life, having had his throne usurped by his younger brother. As a Malay admirer of Raffles known only as Abdullah wrote in his account of the event (known as the *Hikayat*), the *Tunku* was to be persuaded to come 'by hook or by crook even if he had only one shirt on his back'. In the meanwhile Raffles set the seamen and 340 sepoys to work making an encampment and, with the agreement of the *Temenggong*, erecting a 12-gun fortified battery. *Tunku* Long arrived on 1 February and was received by Raffles. '[S]miling with infinite charm...his words sweet as a sea of honey...' Raffles rekindled the *Tunku*'s ambition in his rightful inheritance. 'The very stones would have melted on hearing his words,' Abdullah recorded, and on 6 February, in one of the tents, the *Tunku* was installed as sultan. The occasion was as grand as possible: about thirty of the Company's officers turned out in full dress, the sepoys paraded in close order, their bayonets glinting in the sunshine. Offshore the ships were dressed with flags and, as the *Tunku*, at the head of his suite of Malay nobles and a *kris*-bearing guard, was led up to the main tent on a red carpet, the sepoys crisply presented arms.

The *Tunku*, who at the time had little more to his name beyond the figurative shirt Abdullah had referred to, was to receive an annual grant of 5,000 Spanish silver dollars – the common trading currency throughout the East Indies – the *Temenggong* was to receive 3,000, and the *Tunku* and his throne were guaranteed British protection. In return the *Tunku* granted the British the right to establish a settlement on the island exclusive to them, no other nation being allowed to occupy territory in the sultan's dominions as long as the British wished to retain Singapore. The costs of the settlement and its administration would all be borne by the British, while any attempt, implicitly by the Dutch, to force the issue was to be met by armed resistance. On the treaty being signed and sealed, the ships fired a salute and the Union Flag was hoisted before the entire party retired to a convivial celebration. There had been not one jot of coercion or contest, and the only losers were the Dutch.

The Dutch claim to much of the East Indies, as the Indonesian archipelago was then called by Europeans, was tenuous; they possessed innumerable trading-posts but had, for the most part, neglected to secure title by treaty, a matter in which the

fair-minded Raffles was punctilious.[14] While the Dutch claimed a vague, putative sovereignty over the Sultanate of Johore, Raffles had established a proper leasehold over
the island, leaving the Dutch to grind their teeth impotently. Having accomplished
his master-stroke, within a week Raffles appointed Farquar as lieutenant-governor
and departed for Benkulen.

Although Raffles was accused of exceeding his instructions, he did not lose
Hastings's support, and this was reinforced by the swift approbation of the merchants in
Calcutta who perceived the genius of his action and by praising Hastings for his sagacity and boldness, cementing the Marquess's confidence in Raffles. Within four months
'a population of about five thousand souls has collected under our flag...' Raffles
wrote as the new factory attracted Chinese from Malacca and the archipelagoes of
Rhio, Carimon and Linga to the southwards, 'The harbour is filled with shipping from
all quarters... Everyone is comfortably housed, provisions are in abundance.'

It was to be a year before the reaction of the Court of Directors was known. While
unwilling to annul Raffles's treaty, they were not pleased. Once again the acquisition of territory presented a threat to their profits, notwithstanding the long-standing
want of a strategic staging-post between India and China capable of neutralising
Dutch power and influence. They accepted the gift without reward, and as Hastings
skilfully turned aside the wrath of the Dutch governor at Batavia, Raffles found himself condescendingly referred to by Lord Bathurst, the secretary of the colonies in the
House of Lords, 'as a mere trade agent'. Learning 'with much regret the prejudice and
malignity by which I am attacked at home...', Raffles was philosophical. He had outwitted the Dutch who could do nothing about the *coup* except complain, and:

> If the controversy drags on a while, so much the better. In two or three years' time
> Singapore will have become an indispensable British settlement. To give it up now
> would be idiotic; to give it up then would be a disgraceful humiliation to which the
> great British public would never submit.

He was right. Raffles returned to Singapore from Benkulen on 10 October 1822.
'Here all is life and activity,' he wrote to the Duchess of Somerset.

> It would be difficult to name a place on the face of the globe with brighter pros-
> pects or more present satisfaction. In little more than three years it has risen from an
> insignificant fishing village to a large and prosperous town of over 10,000 inhabit-
> ants, actively engaged in commercial pursuits.

Land prices and buildings were rising; in two and a half years 2,839 vessels had entered
and cleared the port, 383 of which were owned and commanded by Europeans – the
others being Indian-owned Country-ships commanded by ex-patriate Britons or
Indian *nacodas* – and the turnover was some 8 million Spanish dollars. In the single
year of Raffles's visit the figures exceeded this combined total, the value of the trade
being calculated at 8,568,172 dollars, more that that of Penang and Malacca com-

bined. In addition to the Anglo-Indian shipping, Chinese junks and *lorchas*, and Malay trading *praus*, lay at anchor, while business houses owned by Chinese, Siamese (Thai) and Indians were being set up weekly.

Raffles himself gained little from 'the great blow' that he had struck. His health was wrecked and he sought retirement, eventually taking passage from Benkulen with Lady Raffles on 2 February 1824 in the East Indiaman *Fame*, Captain Samuel Remington. Besides his papers and possessions, Raffles had shipped his collection of specimens and a live tapir. That evening a fire was reported to have broken out in the cargo of saltpetre and within minutes the vessel was ablaze. All escaped in the boats and landed safely next day having been swept south of Benkulen by the coastal current. While awaiting another ship Raffles received a warm letter of commendation and good wishes from the new Governor-General at Calcutta, Lord Amherst. Raffles and his wife finally left Benkulen on 10 April in the Licensed-ship *Mariner*, owned by Abel Chapman & Son, reaching Plymouth on 24 August. Here they learned that an agreement had been concluded with the Dutch in which they retained all possessions south of the equator, the British retaining those to the north. Malacca, which had been returned to the Dutch in 1816, was exchanged for Benkulen, and Singapore was safely part of the East India Company's 'Straits Settlements'.

Unlike Java under Raffles, the Lion City was already remitting specie to Calcutta, but the Court of Directors pursued Raffles for a refund of what they claimed were not legitimate expenses. A complex matter, it was more a vindictive act than an exercise in fiscal propriety. The Court of Directors never commended Raffles nor pressed for the peerage he half expected; instead they hounded him beyond his few years of retirement on his estate at Mill Hill, a village to the north-west of London, finally securing what they wanted from his widow. Unruffled to the end, Sir Stamford Raffles died of a brain tumour and stroke on 5 July 1826. He was only forty-five. Often lionised as a great imperialist – for Singapore would soon transcend a mere commercial entrepôt – Raffles was essentially a man for whom trade was the prime mover of men. His respect for the indigenous peoples he came in contact with, his reforms and benign authority, his fascination with ethnography, owed nothing to racial superiority or imperial ambition. It was his misfortune to live in an age of transition, perceiving the new, but shackled to the old in the shape of the so-called 'Honourable' East India Company. Raffles saw the dead hand of tradition strangling innovation, of men tenaciously holding a position ever more untenable, lacking the energy of their forebears, content to count their profits, reap their dividends and ripe for take-over. 'The Directors,' he wrote after a meeting with the chairman of their court, William Astell, 'are a large heavy body and move slowly'. Characteristically, he bore them no malice: 'I shall not be the first public servant to be neglected by the higher powers,' which was a pity, for Raffles was an exemplar of an age already passing into history. His precocity had attached him to the Age of Reason, not the Age of Revolution and certainly not that of imperial aggression yet to come.

Nevertheless, as a servant of the East India Company, Raffles was not an advocate of free trade as it is now understood. His liberal management of the Javanese economy had been that of controlled monopolism, and his declaration of Singapore as a 'free-port' was not intended to weaken the Company but to provide it with that eastern depot that it had so long required. In fact Singapore became a free-port in the fullest sense of the words because, with the lifting of the Company's monopoly on trade with India, British manufactures could be shipped directly to Singapore by private merchants. Here it was legally trans-shipped and carried onwards to China in traditional Country-*wallahs* as part of their coastwise traffic, an expedient which, in John Keay's phrase, 'soon became a mere formality of documentation and thus by 1830 non-Company shipping had already captured a sizeable slice of the China trade'. Cargoes were shipped home in similar fashion, of course, excepting tea on which the East India Company retained its monopolistic grip to the end.[15]

The means by which he acquired Singapore for British trading interests — bearing in mind that these drew in almost every other trading partner in the hemisphere except the jealous Dutch — was a model of scrupulous propriety. The bargain was not at gun-point; it solved a political crisis in Johore, and transformed a low, swampy island into a great and prosperous port which would, in due time, become a city-state of almost fabulous wealth. Such was an act of extraordinary far-sightedness which there seems little doubt Raffles possessed.

In the manner of its founding, Singapore remains a stark contrast with the acquisition of the forthcoming ports whose annexation by the growing British Empire would shortly occur. All, however, would have proved impossible without the existence of Singapore, from where the British could now smash open the gates of the Celestial Kingdom.

The demise of the East India Company owed much to the rise of industrial Britain which had as its power-base the unenfranchised heartlands of northern England and Scotland. Here whirring machinery churned out manufactures of all descriptions, fuelled in some part by imported sugar as much as iron ore and coal, yet the greatest trading company the world had ever seen was unable to sell them in the greatest market the world possessed: China. That this inability to trade with China arose from perceived incompetence in London only added fuel to the flames of opposition in Parliament and unrest in the rising industrial towns, catching fire from the general discontent and reforming zeal of northern iron-masters, mill-owners, ship-owners and politicians *manqué*. As the production of manufactures rose, new markets were sought, engendering a political discontent that would eventually accomplish the destruction of the Company's monopoly in 1833/4. Ironically this was aided by an application by the Court of Directors — itself divided — for a large loan from the Government. Now, however, in the wake of the Reform Act, votes depended upon a greater popularity of Government policy than hitherto, and this was the first time the needs of British workers had a major effect upon foreign policy. As John Keay points out, jobs began to matter:

> However eloquent the Company's defence of its loyal Indian artisans, there was no political mileage in protecting Bengali weavers from being overwhelmed by a con-

tinuous roll of mass-produced, duty free [cotton] prints. Against the need for full
employment in Manchester, Midnapur stood not a chance. After all, what was the use
of subject territories if they did not afford a market for the imperial manufacturer?[16]

Subject to the Board of Control, the East India Company directors were emasculated
and all was swept away. The effect this was to have on India was profound enough,
but the impact on China was to be tragic – as it would ultimately prove to Great
Britain because, for all its faults, the East India Company had never sought an imperial mantle, whereas Great Britain herself was an altogether different entity. In the
final days of its last monopoly, the Company's auditors had remarked that 'India does
entirely depend upon the profits of the China trade', and, in addition to the account-
books at Fort William in Calcutta, the duties raised upon imports of China tea were
annually putting £3 million in the British Exchequer at home, about a tenth of the
revenue receipts from England itself. With the Company gone, matters began to
unravel in China where the business of maintaining trade had been delicate, and the
Company's servants at Macao and Whampoa had managed affairs against the odds
by a skilfully long-winded policy of appeasement and side-stepping. Chinese suspicion, xenophobia and contempt for the *fan–kwai*, or foreign-devils, had engendered
a complex pattern of bi-national negotiation which worked, more-or-less. A gradual
erosion of the Company's authority had been taking place since the late eighteenth
century, caused mainly by the Country-traders from India who had slowly metamor-
phosed into powerful interlopers, but also by tactless interventions by Royal Naval
officers during the war, for whom such subtle pragmatism as was practiced by the
Company's Selectmen smacked too much of submission.[17] The British ship-owners
who had run out under the Austrian colours of Ostend and traded with British merchants who masqueraded as the consular officials for Prussia, now mushroomed as
Singapore made it all so much easier. In the period immediately following the end of
the war, in addition to Portuguese, British and Indian trading houses at Macao, there
were – besides the supposed Ostenders and Prussians – suddenly nominal Poles,
Sicilians, Genoese and Sardinians, as well as perfectly legitimate Americans. The trading firms often combined, so that Daniel Beale who acted under Prussian authority,
and Henry Cox representing Sweden, became business partners. In 1827 they turned
their firm over to the son of a Scottish baronet, James Matheson, who was, notionally
at least, a Dane![18]

On the other hand, the Chinese were no less complex in their own arrangements.
They too were driven to adopt expedient measures to out-manoeuvre the edicts from
the Peacock throne that sought to restrict all intercourse with the Red Barbarians by
confining trade to Canton under the Eight Regulations. While the common ethnic
Han Chinese sought to trade, the Manchu civil and military administrations carried
out the imperial will of the Son of Heaven in far-away Peking (Beijing), articulated
in the Regulations. At the same time, partly as a weapon to curb trade, they imposed
every conceivable difficulty, including setting a tariff of bribes that raised extortion to
new heights. Almost nowhere in the imperial system were there proper regulated tar-

iffs; instead, from the imperial Viceroy and military governor at Canton to the lower administrators of the mandarinate, all wanted their rake-off, or *cumshaw*.

So much for the facilitators of commerce; but what about the commodities trafficked? Indian cottons, so long a staple of the trade, were of declining interest to the Chinese, as were the English woollens that never found much favour in the warmer south of China, though they might have done well had commerce been allowed further north. By the end of the war the East India Company's Court of Directors had already 'resumed the practice of sending silver coin to the Committee at Canton, and supplies came from both London and Bengal' in order to buy tea, silk and porcelain. The peace with both France and America immediately brought an influx of vessels, particularly American, with the Dutch, Portuguese and Swedes close behind. These, seeking advantages, joined the Indian merchants representing the interests of the Country-trade, so much so that a protest was made by six English and fifteen Indian firms from Bombay about the continuing irksome controls exerted by the Company's Selectmen, which were increasingly resented. It was only through the Select Committee that the Chinese officially recognized British trade, and they were often rendered as helpless as their direct counterparts, the Chinese merchants of the Co-Hong, who handled all business on the Chinese side. This commercial aggression on the part of what until 1834 were regarded as interlopers — though they had always styled themselves as 'free-traders' — began to effect a slow change in the balance of trade. British manufactures, long resisted by the Chinese, except for a few clocks and gimcrack items, began to be sought-after, so that the traditional flow of silver from Calcutta to Canton slowed and then began to reverse. Moreover, previously the occasional drain of Bengal silver had been offset by shipping opium into China where it was sold for *sycee* silver.

The opium trade had long been prohibited both by the Chinese authorities and by the East India Company whose ships were expressly forbidden to carry it. But the Company controlled the production of opium poppies in India, oversaw the auction of the harvested crop and ignored the carriage of chests of opium to the Pearl River in Country-ships. In China the traffic was managed to the private profit of the mandarins by the discharge of the opium into 'Receiving-ships', hulks which lay outside territorial waters at moorings off Lintin Island in the outer estuary of the Pearl River to the south of the Bocca Tigris, the Tiger's mouth, or the Bogue. Beyond these narrows, access was gained to the international anchorage at Whampoa and the great city of Canton, thirteen miles further upstream. The opium was transferred from the Receiving-ships either into local craft, the 'scrambling-dragons' and 'swift crab boats' manned by ferocious Tanka river-pirates who 'fought or bribed their way' upstream to link up with the Triad members who distributed the drug, or into junks which carried it along the coast of Kwantung province where it was eagerly purchased with silver. This was now paid to the Company and remitted in bills of exchange, or shipped to Calcutta, thus allowing the Company to purchase the next season's Patna and Benares opium for export. It was a complex and lucrative trade, and, although 'illegal', was accomplished with little risk, for while the ordinary Chinese were eager to buy, the authorities were no less eager to participate through back-handers, maintaining sham disapproval on behalf of Peking. However, as the East India Company slowly lost what grip it retained in the early 1830s, there were an increasing number of traders eager to capitalise on the opportunity provided by the approaching lacuna, for in the previous decade they had been slowly gaining the upper hand.

The tacit approval of the East India Company's officials in India, encouraging Indian ship-owners to carry more and more of the opium crop that the Company's ships were forbidden to load, had been facilitated by the anchoring of the Receiving-ship *Mentor* off Lintin Island in 1819. This ran counter to the wishes of the Selectmen at Macao who felt the situation was running out of control. In October 1820:

> the President [of the Selectmen] took occasion to notice to the Board [of Control in Calcutta] the great influx of British Subjects, Europeans as well as Natives of India, that of late years resorted to China, by the Country Ships from India, for the purpose of prosecuting their mercantile pursuits, many of who resided in China, beyond the limited period prescribed by the Hon'ble Court [of Directors in London], in defiance of our repeated Notifications, and the Indentures entered into by the Captains or Owners of Ships bringing them. [19]

Among these was Thomas Dent, who held power of attorney for two merchants acting as consul for 'His Prussian Majesty', and also William Jardine and James Matheson, whose personal histories we shall come to shortly. The participation of Parsee companies in the opium trade alluded to in the President's remonstrance increased in 1820 when the cotton crop failed in Gujarat and they sought alternative lading for their ships. [20]

There were also others involved: the import of Malwa opium in Portuguese ships and Turkish opium in American vessels had begun to create a serious competitive trade from which the British were theoretically self-excluded. The notion that others profited while they did not excited a form of cupidity such that lengths were gone to to bring in opium from any source whatsoever, and in January 1817 the ship *Pitt*, from London, had trans-shipped Turkish opium at Madeira into the HCS *Vansittart* 'bound to Bombay and China. These chests, thirty-one in all, had been brought from Smyrna by the *Hember Hodge*.' It is usually asserted that these thirty-one chests mark the first importation of opium in a Company's ship into China which, if true, was unofficial, illegal and clandestine, for there is no record 'of their having provided funds for the Company's treasury' at Canton, and they may well have been discharged at Bombay, and then put aboard a Country-ship.

A further incident occurred in October 1819 when a boat from the HCS *Essex* was stopped by a Chinese customs galley and a pot containing 12lb weight of opium was discovered. The Hong merchant acting as agent for the *Essex* was distraught, as well he might be, for the Chinese authorities controlled the Red Barbarians indirectly by the effective method of squeezing their agents. In this case the Hong merchant Manhop had to bribe the mandarins to save his liberty, relying upon Captain Nisbet of the *Essex* to refund 6,000 dollars. This imbroglio was finally settled by an accommodation which involved the beneficial owners of the *Essex*, and was the traditional way of smoothing over any disagreements, whether the traded commodity was legal or otherwise. This was ultimately in the interests of all parties, and it explains the high cost of silk and tea on the other side of the world in Britain. As a member of the Co-Hong, the trade association consisting of immensely rich merchants who alone were licensed to deal directly with the Westerners, Manhop was much more vulnerable to the wrath – real or otherwise – of the Viceroy and his chief customs officer, the Hoppo. Maintaining relationships with their counterparts in the Co-Hong was vital to the Select Committee of East India Company Supra-cargoes, for they were based at Macao and only allowed in their factories at Canton during the trading season in the cool of the year. While the Selectmen maintained their power, matters remained under some sort of control, but the aggressive attitudes of merchants like Jardine, Matheson and Davidson of Dent & Co. grew more demanding as it became increasingly apparent that the East India Company's powers were waning.

Manhop seems to have acted in support of the maintenance of the brig *Mentor* as Receiving-ship at Whampoa, and the affair of the *Essex* was but the precursor of worse to come for all concerned, for soon afterwards, prompted by Peking's insistence that the opium trade was ended, proceedings were brought against three British Country-ships, the *Merope*, *Hooghly* and *Eugenia*, among the lading of which were 470 chests of Bengali opium consigned to James Matheson. Once again the matter was smoothed over with bribes, but an incident involving a confrontation with a party of seamen from HM Frigate *Topaze* resulting in Chinese deaths, and another involving the HCS *Scaleby Castle*, marked a general souring of relations which included obstructions placed in the way of payment to the 'native merchants of Bombay'. The Viceroy, outraged at the effrontery of foreign men-of-war entering Chinese territorial waters, declared that since the European war had ended and piracy had been stamped out along the China coast, the convoying of men-of-war was unnecessary. He insisted once again, and quite reasonably, that men-of-war were to remain outside the Bogue forts.[21]

There were other problems too:

> The private trade of the junior officers in the Company's ships was jealously protected against the encroachments of the commanders, who were always trying to take it by fair means – purchase – or by foul – the tyrannous exercise of their authority. In one such case [in 1822]…the Committee intervened and ordered a commander to allow to his fourth officer the privilege which was his by rights…

Of much more significance, however, was the shipping of opium from Calcutta to Singapore in the HCSs *Dunira* and *Castle Huntly*. Although under 'a stringent bond to discharge them there', this was a tacit and stealthy advance whose consequences were only too obvious. Country-ships were, meanwhile, constantly 'hovering about the Coast' with a view to illegal trans-shipment into smuggling junks. But the many mostly insignificant incidents that occurred between the members of the merchant ships' companies and the Chinese excited all sorts of disagreements. Sampans that persisted in lying alongside, either begging or touting for business, were often warned off by blank gunshots, or the throwing of missiles, mostly quite ineffectually, but occasionally with fatal result when they caused a Chinese to fall overboard and drown. The practice of liquidating such deaths in fines led to extreme and ingenious methods of extortion, such as that attempted on the *Earl Balcarres* on the morning of 5 January 1823. A sampan deliberately lay alongside the ship until ordered off by both the ship's officers and the Chinese in the comprador's boat. An exasperated midshipman 'took a small piece of wood…which he threw upon the Cover of the boat, and which immediately fell into the water without touching anyone'. The two men in the boat, however, claimed it had killed a third man lying under the canopy, and the ship's assistant surgeon boarded the sampan to find the 'dead' man 'in a dying state', not from a missile but from syphilis. Whatever the truth of this, the matter was referred as high as the Viceroy before it was dropped.

Amid this man-made wrangling, nature now took a hand. On 1 November 1822 a fire in Canton had spread south under a strong northerly wind. Urged to create a firebreak by demolishing houses between the fire and the factories, the Viceroy refused. In the meantime messages had been sent down to Whampoa for assistance from the ships' crews, but nothing could be done and attempts at salvaging what merchandise lay in store were largely unavailing, and the consequent losses were enormous. The seamen did, however, succeed in guarding the treasure, some 760,000 Spanish dollars worth, and an abject petition by the Committee secured the remission of the import duties levied on the destroyed goods.

The factories were swiftly rebuilt, although not without convoluted wrangling with the Co-Hong merchants over freehold, but the times were changing rapidly and they, like the Company's representatives, were losing influence as the loss of monopoly allowed others to force the cautiously opened door of free trade. The difficulties made for the Bombay Parsees to participate were now being nicely circumvented not merely by dealing with the consuls of other European countries – conveniences of which Dent acting for Sardinia and James Matheson for Denmark took full advantage as commission agents – but by a plethora of 'outside merchants'. These, usually British and led by Dent, Jardine and Matheson acting for themselves, were actually acting illegally by their residence on Chinese soil and in defiance of the Company's prohibitions. The Selectmen's constant admonitions were 'an empty menace' that fell on deaf ears, so much so that their own servants defected. The attraction of setting up as a 'commission agent' was so seductive that Mr James Walker, third officer of the HCS *Farquharson*, deserted when his ship left on 12 January 1828. The Committeemen sent to Captain Robert Dalrymple, the senior commander aboard the *Vansittart*, who proceeded upstream to arrest Walker and order him conveyed home aboard the HCS *Windsor* where he would be 'allowed to leave the ship without further orders' – a euphemism for dismissal.

In general the conduct of maverick traders disturbed the whole balance of the system – the practice of measurement and the granting of the Chop that secured homeward clearance from the imperial customs – and were led mainly by the Americans with the private 'British' merchants a close second. Among the latter must be included Indians who, since the arrival of Homranjee Dorabjee and Eduljee Cowasjee Patel in the early 1800s, had multiplied to some fifteen trading-houses by about 1830. Their vessels, usually officered by British masters and mates, though also commanded by Indian *nacodas*, flew the British ensign and constituted the almost distinct second eastern British mercantile marine mentioned earlier. Faced with this volume of non-Company shipping, the power of the Select Committee waned and was still further weakened by floods in northern China reducing the demand for woollens. This in turn increased the level of 'squeeze' applied by the Viceroy to mitigate the flood-damage, and the heavy cost of repaying the loans – largely from the chief Hong merchant Howqua – for rebuilding the burnt-out factories. A request for 1 million dollars in specie was sent to Calcutta, and 21 *lakhs* of silver were dispatched, a significant reversal of the flow of bullion which would have dire consequences.

With the *Merope* and other Country-ships again buzznacking off the coast – the *Merope* was in fact 'three years stationary in the neighbourhood' as a Receiving-ship – in anticipation of landing consignments of opium, it was clear that any major drain on treasure from India could be offset by forcing the drug-trade. This expedient continued to be winked at and although imports in Company ships remained officially proscribed, it was a growing traffic for the Country-*wallahs*. The *Sullimany*, owned by Framjee Cowasjee, passed up to Whampoa where, after a quick verbal agreement of the price, she was 'hastily unloaded'. With cotton freighting close to a loss, the necessity for shipping such a paying cargo became ever more necessary, and some ships were now going no further west than Singapore to load opium brought from India. All this was facilitated by the now well-established use of Receiving-ships as floating warehouses. In 1822 the *Eugenia* and the *Merope* had been joined by another Receiving-ship, the *Samarang*, owned by Remington Crawford and commanded by Captain Gover. Referring to these vessels, the Committee recognized that since they had not been 'noticed' by the Chinese authorities then the Chinese Government 'will suffer the Opium trade to relapse into that system of connivance which has hitherto marked the conduct of this extraordinary Traffick'. In addition to Crawford, other Country-owners involved included Jamsetjee Jejeebhoy whose *Good Success* bore Malwa opium to China, while he shipped Patna opium in his partner Motichand Amichand's ship, the *Cornwallis*. Apart from its obvious advantages in releasing the ships bringing opium to China for further carrying, the practice of trans-shipping opium into moored Receiving-ships also avoided the tiresome business of undergoing inward 'measurement' and its consequent levy. This therefore encouraged the depositing of a ship's entire cargo in the Receiving-ships, further undermining the status, power and revenue-generating abilities of the Hoppo as well as the Hong merchants, whilst at the same time depriving the imperial mandarins – including the Viceroy – of their *cumshaw*. It was an added irony that this increase in the availability of opium reduced its price on the open market, stoking growth in demand among the populous addicts as it became more and more accessible, all of which opened up voracious possibilities for both consumer and supplier.

Prices were highest at the beginning of the season, a fact which encouraged the introduction of fast specialist 'opium-clippers' whose owners were beginning to abandon mixed cargoes in favour of the immensely high-value, small volume consignments of opium alone.[22] In this new development the partners William Jardine and James Matheson played a major role.

William Jardine had come east as an East India Company surgeon, serving in the HCSs *Brunswick*, *Glatton* and *Windham*, in which he took full advantage of the space allowed for private trade, bought up the allotments of his shipmates and proved a most efficient private trafficker. Resigning his post in the *Windham*, Jardine decided to go into partnership with Thomas Weeding, another former Company surgeon who had served in the *Glatton* and whom Jardine had met in Canton in 1802 when Weeding had acted as Jardine's agent in selling his private trade-goods. In late 1818, through a new Company director, John Thornhill, Weeding obtained for Jardine the necessary indenture to permit him to represent their interests in Macao. Engaging a further partner in Framjee Cowasjee to handle the Bombay end of their business, the three men floated a venture in the *Sarah* which was actually the first 'free-ship' to leave Whampoa with a cargo of tea consigned openly for London. On arrival at Macao, Jardine met James Matheson for the first time. Thereafter an obscure period of four years intervenes during which one presumes these men consolidated their positions. By 1822 Jardine was at Canton during the trading season, as was then the practice, and imported 649 bales of Malwa opium, selling them for 813,000 Spanish dollars and making about £20 profit on each 150lb bale. Three years later Jardine, having joined Magniac & Co., took over the mantle of the ageing Charles Magniac and, as head of a mercantile house, became a *taipan*.

James Matheson, having graduated from Edinburgh University as a keen disciple of Adam Smith, went east in 1815 with the necessary sanction from the East India Company to trade from Calcutta. Here he joined his uncle's firm of Mackintosh & Co., but the association did not last long, perhaps due to youthful high-jinks, and in June 1818 Matheson teamed up with an ex-Indiaman purser, Robert Taylor. Taylor asserted that 'opium is like gold, I can sell it at any time', and in the following year they began shipping the drug to China. However, their complicated dealings and the sudden and often catastrophic fluctuations in the sale-price of opium resulted in the foreclosure of loans and the indebtedness of the partners. In August 1820 Taylor died, leaving Matheson's affairs on the edge of ruin. He was saved by a sudden rise in the price of opium which entirely changed his fortune; he travelled to Canton where he acted as Danish consul, and in July 1821 he went into partnership with Xavier Yrissari, a Spanish merchant with whom he had been dealing. For a while all went well. Yrissari & Co. purchased a vast quantity of Patna opium to ride the rising tide of prices, but this again plummeted in the spring of 1823 and Matheson, fearful of a second disaster, decided to avoid the conventional intermediary facilities of trans-shipment from the Receiving-ships into junks. Instead, in June he engaged the services of his cousin, John McKay, an experienced seaman, and purchased the Receiving-ship *Eugenia*. Re-rigged as a brig and – since she traded in the Yrissari name – recommissioned under the Spanish flag as the *San Sebastian*, Matheson and McKay had her loaded with bales of opium.[23] Taking passage with McKay, Matheson sailed east, putting in at Amoy where the Chinese allowed trade with the Spanish from the Philippines. Spanish colours notwithstanding, the discharge of a contraband cargo proved difficult and the *San Sebastian* departed to coast north to Chinchew where the opium was disposed of for a healthy profit of 80,000 Spanish dollars. Encouraged, Matheson made a second voyage from Canton in the autumn, but bad weather forced McKay to shelter the *San Sebastian* in an obscure bay some thirty miles west of Amoy. Quite fortuitously, the brig had anchored in the very spot used by the Chinese smugglers themselves, and the sale of her cargo yielded $132,000.

Word of this success leaked out and other firms cashed-in, most notably that of Dent & Co. whose two partners, Thomas Dent and George Beale, chartered the American brig *Nile*, Captain Robert Forbes, for the purpose. However, this activity caused a fall in the price and Matheson, having off-loaded the surplus Patna, returned to conventional trading for a while.[24] An intellectual as well as a merchant, Matheson took more interest in Chinese culture than the average trader hopping annually from Macao to Canton. He owned copies of Robert Morrison's Chinese grammar and dictionary, and would later – in 1827 – print and publish the *Canton Register*, a local business newspaper produced on a hand-press in which he disregarded the sensibilities of the Chinese, not only blatantly advertising the price of opium in defiance of the official Chinese embargo against it, but anathematising the Chinese attitude to trade. This, he declared, was due to 'imbecility and avarice, conceit and obstinacy'.[25] That October Yrissari died whilst on a visit to Calcutta, and Matheson was obliged to sail thither and wind up his partner's effects. Before leaving Macao in March 1827, Matheson placed the day to day affairs of his company in the hands of his cousin Alexander and the newcomer William Jardine. On his return to Macao from Calcutta in September, Matheson announced that henceforth Yrissari & Co. would trade under his own name. However, Matheson and Jardine had by now become friends and decided to merge their businesses, and consequently Matheson joined Magniac, Jardine & Co., bringing $60,000 with him. Charles Magniac had by now died, but one member of the family remained as a sleeping partner so the old name was retained for some time, partly so as not to dislocate business, but also to wind up the Magniac family's connections. On 30 June 1832 Magniac, Jardine & Co. closed its doors to further business, and on 1 July they opened again, trading as Jardine, Matheson & Co.

Jardine was already a rich man, calm and impassive, celebrated by the Chinese who referred to him as the 'Old Iron-Headed Rat', for he had been unmoved when struck on the head in Canton while awaiting an opportunity to present a petition at the Petition Gate of the Viceroy's Yamen. He was well known for his firm business methods and the fact that he had only one chair in his office for himself, all others having to stand in order to hasten their business. In Magniac's name he had profited from the variable nature of the sale-price of opium, but he largely dealt on commission, preferring to spread his risks and confident that a series of modest gains would survive the volatility of the market. These fluctuations were almost entirely due to the sporadic attempts by the Chinese Viceroy to enforce the imperial laws with fierce edicts, though this did not tame official corruption. Under prodding from Peking, officialdom apparently bristled with indignation against the infamy of the foreign-devils, and although a low-level of trade usually remained constant, occasionally obedience and more rarely virtue infused the mandarins. To enforce the laws of the distant Emperor, the Viceroy and the Hoppo increased their squeezing of the Co-Hong merchants, an expedient they themselves could scarcely fail to profit from.

Usually, once the pressure had eased, the mandarins relaxed and the trade, which closely involved not only a handful of corrupt Chinese officials but hundreds of Tanka smugglers and Triad couriers, resumed as before. This apparent caprice no doubt inspired Matheson's contempt, but it could also catch a cargo on the high-seas, bought in India at a higher price than it realised on the unofficial market at Lintin. The ruin to which this exposed the European merchants was not to be borne, and the history of the opium trade is the tale of sporadic Chinese enforcement running concurrently with a gross rake-off, and Euro-American – but largely British-Indian – resistance to interruption. This, unlike the often supine appeasement of the Selectmen which invariably avoided open rupture, was bound eventually to lead to confrontation. Indeed, the prescient, Jardine among them, connived to precipitate a crisis. It had been long in coming.

The first of the series of imperial enforcements had occurred in 1820 when the Co-Hong merchants, although acting as agents for a specific ship of the East India Company or the Country-traders from India, were each held in surety for the ships in his charge and obliged to search for contraband cargoes of opium. Using the Chinese merchants in this manner, part of the policy of 'squeeze', was the most efficient way of enforcing the law since the foreign-devils were difficult to bring to justice, whereas the Viceroy held power of life and death over the Emperor's subjects. The *fan–kwai*, on the other hand, could do nothing without the intermediary assistance of the Co-Hong and, as a result of the 1820 embargo, Dent & Co. were compelled to remove a shipment from the anchorage at Whampoa, a decree 'which no money could reverse'.

In the following year, when no relaxation on the part of the mandarins appeared likely, a Macao merchant named Asee sent copies of his account-books to Peking, thereby revealing the extent to which the mandarins, the servants of imperial governance under the Viceroy, military governor and Hoppo at Canton, had previously been implicated in breaking the imperial laws. Revelation of the scale of this facilitating *cumshaw* only provoked the severest reaction from the accused, who were now even more eager to prove their rectitude to the Emperor, applying what Charles Magniac anathematised as 'the hottest persecution' he could recall. The Hong merchants, in fear of their lives, absolutely refused to countenance the smallest quantity of the illegal drug being brought in, and it was the 'discovery' of 470 chests of Bengali opium among the holds of the *Merope*, *Hooghly* and *Eugenia* which implicated

James Matheson. Despite the fearful misgivings of the wretched Hong merchants, no charges were pressed, with substantial bribes stopping rumours and for a while soothing all concerned. However, these difficulties and the rising level of *cumshaw* persuaded the merchants to devise an alternative method.

The anchorage increasingly favoured for the congregating of incoming laden ships was that off Lintin, in the vicinity of the Receiving-ships. The success of the new mode of traffic had not only increased the ambition of the free-traders but had greatly discomfited the Selectmen. No longer was it a matter for them to communicate with the Hoppo and Viceroy, affecting a remote hauteur to match that of the Chinese dignitaries towards the free-traders. Now avoidance of the formalities of measurement at Whampoa reduced a voyage's expenses considerably, and while it likewise lowered the imperial customs dues, sufficient import and export duties were still honoured to a degree, sufficient to maintain imperial connivance at the vice-regal level, and prevent outright ejection. Thus, by sweeping aside the prevarications inherent in the Chinese customs system and emasculating the Selectmen, the private speculators could see a bright future. This was all very well until a ship got into trouble, when a reciprocal indifference — always endemic along the coast where an over-burdened peasantry found the accommodation of hungry foreign mouths an often insupportable burden — now became the norm, as the crew of the Country-ship *Lackassar* found when wrecked on the coast of Hainan.[26] When such cases arose, the Selectmen were obliged to act in the interests of the castaways, even when the ship from which they came had no attachments to, and was probably working against, the interests of the East India Company. Altogether there was little in the situation that could be tolerated by any of the parties.

To add to the Selectmen's woes, further upheavals in Macao made their dependence upon the Portuguese enclave increasingly irksome. On 25 November 1825 the Company's chartered ship *Royal George*, Captain Charles Timins, caught fire when lying at moorings at Whampoa. Although her people escaped in the clothes they stood in, she and her partly loaded cargo of tea were consumed. The Hoppo remitted the duties on the lost cargo but: 'This was, however, the last act of grace; from this time [onwards] the Committee were constantly subjected to petty annoyances'.[27] This was unsurprising, for the Viceroy was himself moving against the assembled shipping off Lintin and had appointed a new naval commander to the squadron of war-junks off Macao. In late May 1826 these showed:

> a disposition to interfere with and embarrass the Opium trade at Lintin by preventing the smuggling boats from going alongside the ships, which have in consequence been obliged to disperse… As the War vessels are at all times prevented from attacking the smuggling boats from the latter being manned by desperate people, who if apprehended in offering resistance would probably be put to death, while the crews of the former are persons hired at low wages and often very ignorant of all seafaring matters, it is not probable that any violent measures will be adopted or that the interruption will be of long continuance.

The tone of this minute betrays a shift of attitude on the part of the Selectmen, driven by exasperation at their impotence to do anything about this consequence of the deregulation of the trade in general and the increase in the traffic of opium in particular. But while the easy-going attitude fed inactivity on the European side, the increasing 'problem' for the Chinese demanded stronger action, and five months later a new Viceroy was condemning the actions of the native *Fai-hai-ting*, recognised by the Selectmen as 'swift crab-boats' which, 'when smuggling fails them, they become pirates'. But such potentially rich pickings usually proved too much for the venality of officials, while half-hearted and inadequate suppression only spread the points of import, roping in others along the coast, both smugglers and officials, happy to turn a blind eye at a rake-off in what Hosea Morse aptly calls 'the eternal game of extortion'.

The Company dissimulated over the opium trade. It maintained and enforced its prohibition in its own vessels, 'even in the smallest quantities...but, because of the Indian revenue, it was nonetheless keenly interested in its transport and sale by others', sending regular reports to the Governor-General in council at Fort William, Calcutta, and even commenting upon the deficiencies in quality, particularly when this depressed the price. Crucially, of course, opium paid for 'the greater part of the specie exchanged for the Company's bills, thus providing the additional funds by which the investment of tea for London was paid for'.

And so, embroiled with this dubious commerce, the export of tea from China went on unremittingly, and with tea went an amount of silk limited to the allowances of the private trade of the Indiamen's officers, along with porcelain and cheaper 'china' pottery. Woven calicoes from Manchester were now added to the import of English woollens, Indian cottons and shipments of lead, iron and so forth, and this first profitable 'footing' of industrially manufactured cloth in the volatile Chinese market of 1827 is a marker of the rise of Great Britain as the workshop of the world. Nevertheless, the vicissitudes of the trade continued to plague the Indiamen. In August 1829, when inwards for Whampoa, the HCS *Bridgewater*, Captain John Manderson, anchored for the night off Lintin. To Manderson's annoyance the best holding ground was occupied by a number of Country-ships and, mindful of orders not to associate with 'the opium fleet', he was obliged to bring-up in a place not entirely of his own choosing. Here the *Bridgewater* was struck by the onset of a typhoon, dismasted and driven ashore on the island. She was got off and, after struggling up to Whampoa to refit, eventually reached Calcutta where she was condemned for breaking-up. The *Bridgewater's* enforced sojourn at Whampoa not only came at a bad time but was aggravated by it. The Selectmen were in dispute with the Chinese authorities over numerous grievances arising from difficulties in obtaining credit at Canton, a failing market for imports, and the long-established but expensive obligation to trade through the Hong merchants. Some of these were in financial trouble and their collapse was not in the Company's interest since it was itself among their creditors. These burdens were in large part caused by the interlopers and free-traders remaining outside the river, hovering along the coast and, wherever and whenever possible, avoiding imperial duties. While they adequately supplied the market, they failed to fill the imperial coffers. Although some Selectmen objected on the grounds of 'Policy, and Courtesy to the Viceroy', the Committee ordered the incoming Indiamen in 1829 to remain outside the Bogue and take up anchorages 'between the Island of Toon Koo and Castle Peak, or at your discretion to any part of the Cap-sing-moon Passage'. It was this circumstance that obliged Manderson to expose the *Bridgewater* to the typhoon and, in the continuing wrangling, it also compelled the Selectmen to order her down to join the other ships as soon as a jury rig had been fabricated at Whampoa.

While the dispute rumbled on the season passed and anxiety arose as to the safety of the anchorage upon the onset of the south-west monsoon. An alternative to the Cap-sing-moon Passage was found 'within the north-west point of the island of Hongkong proceeding in an easterly direction towards the Lyeemoon Passage' – that of modern Hong Kong Harbour – and here, over the succeeding months, six Indiamen lay at anchor. To no one's satisfaction trade slowly resumed, the ships again working up to Whampoa. For their own part the Chinese nursed greater anxieties over the import of opium and the steady export of *sycee* silver, which had now begun to concern the Viceroy. In an attempt to reduce the quantity of the drug on the market, its cultivation within the borders of China had been forbidden, but the consequences of this are obvious, despite the concluding imperial prohibitive injunction to 'Tremble at this [proscription] and respect it'.

With Singapore's influence now felt as a trans-shipment entrepôt, the free-traders had frequently offered to continue consignments shipped thither in their vessels onwards to London beyond, but this had been denied officially and the terms of the Company's charter revision of 1813 were enforced. But by 1830 this twenty-year extension of monopoly was coming to the end of its term and few in the east thought that it would be renewed. The free-traders began to shove against these constraints, Matheson's Country-ship *Dhaulle* sailing from Lintin to Manila to trans-ship cargo into a vessel proceeding directly to London. The *Dhaulle* had been especially constructed in the United States at Baltimore to take advantage of the then new American hull-form 'for the purpose of smuggling on the coast of China,' reported Lieutenant Fitzgerald De Roos of the Royal Navy, who saw her on the stocks in 1826. 'Everything was sacrificed to swiftness and I think she was the most lovely vessel I ever saw.'[28]

For all the disadvantages and perceived affronts it threw up, the Chinese authorities favoured the control exerted over the so-called 'English-trade' by the East India Company and its Selectmen to any alternative. It produced satisfactory results locally, and results that could be presented as satisfactory to the Emperor. The Viceroy, governor, Hoppo and the mandarinate were rightly fearful of the free-for-all which would follow the Company's disintegration, rumours of which were now circulating in Canton. To reassert his powers of control, the Hoppo refused issue of the Grand Chop to the HCS *Berwickshire*. Captain H.L. Thomas's vessel was under no cloud other than the disgruntlement of the Hoppo who, entertaining some malice against the 'Security Merchant Fatqua' of the Co-Hong, and fearful of losing income, decided on his arbitrary action in the hope of wringing greater extortion from Thomas. The Selectmen determined to order the ship to sea as:

> It becomes absolutely necessary to resist by every available means the system which is now adopted by the Hoppo of making the Company's trade answerable for the duties due by Hong Merchants in affairs extrinsic from it, and for every exaction which his rapacity may dictate.

The Chop was quickly issued and the *Berwickshire* sailed, but a similar performance attended the sailing of the HCS *Reliance* a month later. Not before time, the Hoppo raised his sights to include the ships lying at Lintin, fixing upon the moored Receiving-ship *Hercules*. The Hoppo's problem was that contact through the Selectmen only brought a firmly worded denial of any Company interest in a vessel trading in opium, which was true in the absolute sense.

The continual aggravation of the opium trade now set the foreign devils at loggerheads, for in addition to the dispossessed Chinese officials, the transfer of trade to an illegal open roadstead at Lintin also inflicted losses upon the Portuguese, whose hospitality towards the British and Americans was being abused by both parties through the 'Lintin System'. When British subjects were attacked by Chinese in Macao, the Portuguese authorities did little about it. Such occurrences usually followed a refusal to pay extortionate levies, such as that by Captain Durant of the Country-ship *Good Success*. In late January 1829 Durant, his comprador and wife, were at the Praya Grande, about to embark in their boat to return to their ship. The Chinese manning the customs post demanded twice the embarkation fee, which Durant refused, whereupon he and the comprador were badly beaten. Such unpleasant incidents only dissuaded masters from treating with Macao which, in turn, only further encouraged the trade through Lintin. Even Portuguese ships were arriving off the coast of China to discharge cargoes and load homeward consignments without troubling to enter Macao.

Lisbon now insisted that Macao *was* sovereign Portuguese territory, 'acquired by right of conquest' 300 years earlier. Whatever the rights and wrongs of this assertion, and the Chinese certainly did not concede, it was clear that the only thing to do was for the British to follow suit and establish a port of their own which, if they wished, they might make a free-port. With Singapore in mind, the desire for a trading-post on the frontiers of China soon gripped the imagination of the British merchants making the annual trek up to Canton for the season. Many reasons were adduced in its favour, not least the matter of women. Although at least one wife – Mrs Whiteman – was accepted in Canton without voluble protests, any wholesale influx of white women would invoke enforcement of the official prohibition against the presence of foreign females, whatever their status, whereas a British possession would be a different matter.

While circumstances were not yet ripe for this culmination, the opening incidents of an almost inevitable train of events had already passed. Much else was happening by 1832 for, with the Company's monopoly collapsing, the evidence of its displace-

ment by the extemporised and illegal Lintin System demonstrated to Jardine and
Matheson that a solution to the remaining problem of distribution lay as much in
operating from a 'British' port as in circumventing the Pearl River altogether by
reviving Matheson's project of coastwise delivery. By this time the export of opium
from India resided largely in the hands of Indian trading houses. Jardine, as the head
of Magniac & Co., had a long-standing arrangement with Jamsetjee Jejeebhoy, as
the company's 'chief Bombay correspondent, client and associate in the trade' and, as
noted earlier, he already enjoyed links with Framjee Cowasjee.[29] Thus the traffic had
become sophisticated. The high-value, low-bulk cargo, comprising bales or chests of
opium that had once made up part of the several commodities consigned from India
to China in the Indian-owned Country-ships had by now become almost entirely
a specialist cargo.[30] This was carried in the new opium-clippers, few of which were
capable of loading more than 250 tons deadweight, and which relied upon their speed
to fill up with the drug at the conclusion of the crop's harvest and subsequent auction, rush it to China and catch a premium market-price.

Such was the demand for opium and the importance of its prompt delivery that
several of the early opium-clippers were former slavers, many of which had adopted
the then new lines of the American Baltimore clippers and some, like Matheson's
Dhaulle, were direct copies, from whence the generic noun derived. Among the ex-
slavers were the brig *Ann* and the schooner *Nymph*; another was the 190-ton schooner
Syed Khan, a slaver captured in 1831 and sold to and commanded by Captain John
McKinnon. Built on the Baltimore model, she in turn was copied by the shipyards of
the Hughli, while in 1835, at Magazon, the Bombay Dockyard built the smart 240-ton
brig *Lady Grant* for the Jain merchant Kemchund Motichand. She was commanded
by William Jeffrey and mounted six guns, but her fine lines and tall rig provoked
speculation that she would be incapable of surviving a typhoon.

Fruit schooners of good reputation, such as were owned by MacAndrew and
built for the carriage of perishable oranges and other fruits grown in Spain and the
Canaries, were also purchased for the opium trade, while the British yards of Hall of
Aberdeen and John White of Cowes were building opium-clippers to order, after the
success of several fast vessels purchased especially for the trade. Chief among these
were the Earl of Yarborough's two successive yachts named *Falcon*. The second, a
beautiful full-rigged ship of 350 tons, had been built at Fishbourne on the Isle of
White in 1826 and became the senior clipper in Jardine, Matheson's fleet. Later on, in
1843, the *Royalist*, formerly owned by James Brooke – the Rajah of Sarawak – but
by then owned by Boustead & Co., was another among the several opium-clippers
which had formerly worn the white ensign of the Royal Yacht Squadron. Even the
Royal Navy sold a few of its redundant small cruisers into the trade, the 382-ton
sloop-of-war *Curlew* being bought by Jardine, then of Magniac & Co., to become the
Jamesina; while HM Brig-sloop *Pelorus* was purchased by Joseph Pybus about 1842,
retaining her own name.[31]

Indeed, such was the quest for a first-class design that in 1830 the Admiralty's chief
naval architect, or surveyor to the navy, Sir Robert Seppings, accepted a private com-

mission to design the barque *Sylph* for a partnership of Rustomjee Cowasjee, James Cullen, Robert Browne and Alexander Robertson, all of Calcutta. The ownership of the *Sylph* was as typically complicated as that of many of these smart little ships, for she seems to have been bare-boat chartered to James Matheson on occasions. Cowasjee retained an interest in the *Sylph* when his partners sold out in 1833, and he was joined by Thomas da Souza & Co., Brightman & Co. and the vessel's commander, Robert Wallace. Cowasjee bought her outright from his partners in 1841, only to sell her on to John Lyall of Calcutta, who altered her rig to that of a ship before selling her in 1846 to another Calcutta owner, John Johnstone.

Complex ownership was often further confused by convoluted chartering arrangements. To those of the *Sylph*, two further examples will confirm the point. In 1831 the 363-ton opium-clipper *Waterwitch* was built by J. Kyd & Co. at Kidderpore, near Calcutta. She was charged to the joint account of her first owners Dwarkanant Tagore, a partner in Carr, Tagore & Co., a merchant named William Storm and her first master, Captain Andrew Henderson, who was also her designer and perhaps merits more plaudits thereby than Captain William Clifton, of which more shortly.[32] By 1841, Dent & Co. had acquired half the shares in the *Waterwitch* from Storm and Henderson, and by 1848 Lancelot and John Dent had also bought out Tagore. The second *Falcon*, like the first, flew Jardine, Matheson's blue and white St Andrew's saltire as a house-flag, but she seems to have been on a long-term bare-boat charter from her actual owner, one of the Cowasjee dynasty, an arrangement that conveniently left the freighting and manning of the vessel to the Indian end of the trade.[33]

Rustomjee Cowasjee had been prompted to commission Seppings on observing the success of the *Red Rover*, a vessel which, although not in herself seminal, is often regarded as the 'first' of the opium-clippers. The *Red Rover* was the brain-child of Captain William Clifton, who had entered the Royal Navy as a fourteen-year-old midshipman in 1809. Although the exceptionally able Clifton passed for lieutenant, the onset of peace and the consideration that 'he might do something better' than languish on half-pay, prompted him to consider the East India Company. He gained an appointment as third mate in a vessel named the *Royal George*, owned by Alexander & Co., only to discover both the uniform and the mess-bills far higher than in the navy.[34] However, his naval patron came to his rescue and by 1825, after nine years in the Indian trade, the young Clifton was actually commanding the *Royal George* with £15,000 to his name. Later that year he is thought to have been master of Lord Yarborough's first yacht *Falcon* on her sale and delivery voyage to Calcutta, though whether he afterwards remained in her is unclear. He did, however, become interested in the difficulties the *Falcon* and all the vessels making up for the Pearl River encountered when faced with the north-east monsoon, and soon after his marriage to Anna Vrignon, the daughter of the Calcutta ship-builder François Vrignon, he heard of the success of the schooner-rigged *Dhaulle* in making a good passage against the contrary monsoon.

At the same time, Clifton had taken delivery of a small brig, the *Louisa*, from his father-in-law, in which he began trafficking in opium and saltpetre to Canton. Outward bound on one such voyage on the late evening of 26 July 1829, the *Louisa* was towing down the Hughli astern of the steam-tug *Forbes*. Between Kedgeree and Saugor Road the *Forbes* struck the Mizen Sand at full speed and the *Louisa* ran up astern of the tug, holed herself with her own anchor, rode over the *Forbes's* stern and stuck fast. With her bow wrecked, and despite the assistance of Fifth Mate Stewart and a boat's crew from the Indiaman *Duke of York* anchored nearby, the *Louisa* was a total loss. A crest-fallen Clifton returned to Calcutta in the *Forbes*, which had succeeded in getting herself off the shoal. One imagines that on his tedious way up-river, his fertile mind turned itself to recovering his fortunes.

The *Louisa* had been one of several vessels carrying opium to China that year, among which was the *Jamesina*, consigned to Magniac & Co., whose master disdained to put up the customary bond on clearing outwards on the grounds that the *Jamesina* would not be discharging at Whampoa, so therefore the Company's Selectmen could not 'take any cognisance of me or my ship, being expressly prohibited by the orders of the Honourable Court of Directors from acknowledging in any way the existence of the opium trade'. Apart from the 233 chests of opium lost in the *Louisa* and about 452 landed at Macao, upwards of 10,000 were put aboard the Receiving-ships at Lintin that season.

Meanwhile, Clifton had stolen a march upon his rivals. Immediately upon his return from the wreck of the *Louisa*, he sought an interview with the Governor-General, Lord Bentinck. Betting upon his intention of emulating the *Dhaulle's* performance and beating the north-east monsoon, Clifton argued the Bengal treasury would be greatly enhanced if a vessel could carry three cargoes annually to the Pearl River instead of the customary two. Short of *sycee* silver, Bentinck took heed and agreed to advance Clifton funds to back his experiment while Clifton sought a joint-ownership with his old employers Alexander & Co. Within days of his return from the *Louisa*, Clifton had ordered a new vessel from the Howrah Dock Co. She was laid down 'in early September, 1829,' and launched by Lady Bentinck on 12 December.

> Her ladyship having christened the vessel, the dog shores were struck away, and… the *Red Rover* glided majestically into her new element amid deafening shouts of applause and a salute of thirteen guns from the beach, which was answered from on board. This beautiful little vessel [of 254 tons and barely 100ft in length]…is, of her kind, perfect in every respect.

Mindful of the *Dhaulle's* origins, Clifton had hedged his bets, for the *Red Rover*, carrying a name and figurehead inspired by William Cowper's piratical character, and although barque-rigged, was otherwise a copy of the former Baltimore privateer the *Prince de Neufchâtel*, mentioned earlier. Quite how Clifton obtained the lines which had been taken off the captured Yankee schooner by the Royal Navy's surveyors is something of a mystery, though he had had the ear of several senior officers, including his old patron Vice Admiral Lord Torrington.[35] By the end of December 1829 the *Red Rover* was fitted out and, loading 800 chests of Bengali opium, Clifton left Calcutta on the 28th, clearing the Sandheads on 4 January 1830 with the north-east monsoon at its height and in company with the first *Falcon*. Clifton was denied early success, for the *Falcon* arrived at Singapore a few hours ahead of the *Red Rover* on 20th, departing on the 23rd. The *Red Rover* could not get away until the 26th owing to the necessity of overhauling her standing rigging and relacing her new sails, all of which had stretched. Having set-up the barque's rigging to his satisfaction, however, Clifton resumed his interrupted passage, aware that the telling part lay ahead with the north-east monsoon fresh in the South China Sea. He accomplished 1,400 miles to windward in record time, far faster than the *Dhaulle*. Ten days later, on 27 February, Clifton set off for the Hughli, his outward cargo discharged into the hands of Dent & Co., who were then his agents. To his intense delight the *Falcon* had yet to arrive. The *Red Rover* was back off the Sandheads signalling for a pilot eighty-six days after her departure, and the news, when learned about in Fort William and along the Calcutta waterfront, caused a sensation.

Rumours of Clifton's daring project excited envy and competition. Some thought his pretty new barque unfit for the trade; others took him seriously and considered what they might do in response. With the *Red Rover*'s cargo consigned to their great rivals, Jardine and Matheson sought a way to beat Dent & Co. As will be seen later, steamers were already making their presence felt in Indian waters, and the *Forbes* was much in demand, towing vessels up and down the Hughli. On the return of the *Red Rover*, the *Forbes* was chartered by James Matheson to take the *Jamesina* in charge for an ocean tow, both tug and tow being loaded with coal. The *Jamesina* carried 840 chests of opium, and they left Diamond Harbour at dawn on 14 March, making directly for Singapore. Taking in more coal, they were away again on the 31st, butting into the monsoon. On the windward passage frequent stops had to be made to clean the *Forbes*'s boilers and to trans-ship coal, but on 14 March, with little coal left and still far short of Lintin, the *Forbes*, under Captain Henderson, was obliged to cast off her charge and set her own sails. Thus, under auxiliary power, the *Forbes* arrived at Lintin on the 19th with the *Jamesina* coming in under sail alone on the 21st. Although the passage had taken only thirty-eight days, it earned a mere $5,000 and, with awkward stops at sea for transferring fuel, it was hardly practicable. Besides, within a few months the *Red Rover* had excelled it.

A year after his first voyage in the *Red Rover*, and, having fulfilled his bargain with Bentinck by making three round voyages in twelve months with 'unprecedented speed', Clifton was dined-out by the Calcutta Chamber of Commerce. At the conclusion of the meal Bentinck delivered himself of a panegyric on the benefits Captain Clifton had conferred upon the commerce of India and China, and presented Clifton, still only thirty-five years of age, with a *lakh* of rupees – some £10,000 – together with an elegant filigreed silver cup.[36] Imitation being the sincerest form of flattery, and indispensable when so much was at stake, a number of racy schooners and barques followed the *Red Rover*, one of which was Cowasjee's *Sylph*. Although these were inspired by the speed of the *Red Rover* and the returns consequent on fast passages in this trade, there remained one difficulty that barred them enjoying the enormous profits which they knew awaited them: the limitations of trading either formally through the Co-Hong and Whampoa, or by way of the Receiving-ships of the Lintin System, which largely tied them to the estuary of the Pearl River and the co-operation of the Tanka pirates who distributed the drug along the coast. It was to this that William Jardine now turned his formidable attention.

In addition to the triple passages of the *Red Rover* in 1832, the *Waterwitch, Sylph* and *Lady of the Lake* made two. The *Sylph* accomplished 'an extraordinary passage of 18 days from Bengal', and on her arrival she was chartered by the then newly constituted firm of Jardine, Matheson & Co. The notion of breaking into the Chinese markets other than through Canton was not new. The East India Company had made discreet periodic attempts without any success, and it will be recalled that James Matheson had, ten years earlier, made a coastwise voyage in the *San Sebastian/Eugenia*. Clearly the matter was in great debate throughout the disparate trading community assembling about the great estuary of the Pearl River in the winter of 1831-32. A tentative venture was made in January 1832 by Rustomjee Cowasjee's *Agnes*, which sailed along the coast and anchored off a small walled town to await contact from the shore. Such was the fear of the consequences of defying the imperial edict against smuggling that her master could obtain only fresh vegetables and returned to Macao with his opium cargo intact. That spring the East India Company revived the idea, despite the fact that there had been the latest in a series of infringements of the Chinese ruling that neither men-of-war nor their boats must proceed up the Pearl River beyond the Bogue forts, when Captain Fremantle of HMS *Challenger* and Captain Harris of the Company's cruiser *Clive* were alleged to have offended the Viceroy's sensibilities. Notwithstanding official watchfulness, and eager to test markets along the coast, the Selectmen dispatched Mr Hugh Lindsay, 'a senior supercargo below the Committee [in status]... in a chartered ship'.

Lindsay took passage in the 350-ton *Lord Amherst*, a Blackwall-built ship hired from Whiteman & Co. Loaded with 'presents', consisting of small quantities of broadcloth, camlets, cotton yarn, Indian raw cotton and British calicoes, the *Lord Amherst* was forbidden to traffic in opium and Lindsay was left to exercise his own 'Enterprise, Discretion and Judgement' in prosecuting his mission. Commanded by a Captain Rees, the *Lord Amherst* left Lintin on 26 February and proceeded to Namoa, Amoy, Foochow, Ningpo and, passing inside the Chusan Islands, she entered the Shanghai River where she lay between 20 June and 8 July, before heading first for Wei-Hai-Wei and then Korea. Lindsay, who was accompanied by the Reverend Karl Gützlaff as interpreter, of whom more later, knew of the imperial edicts forbidding his progress, but by ignoring these – which were never pressed by force and only ever expressed formally – found a not unfriendly reception in most ports. However, Lindsay sold little in the way of trade-goods, and the venture was a flop. As the *Lord Amherst* had made her way up the coast, however, the chief activity that alarmed the mandarins was not so much the party's attempts to trade, but the practice of surveying, which was constantly carried out and was to be a feature of all commercial ventures in Chinese waters in the coming years. 'We are afraid of you; you are too clever... no sooner does a ship of yours arrive,' one mandarin explained through Gützlaff, 'than you take to your boats in all directions, you take soundings and make charts, and in a week know the whole place as well as we do'.

The *Lord Amherst* was not the only vessel to explore the possibilities of expanding trade along the coast. Jardine, Matheson's *Jamesina* and *Sylph*, along with one Dutch and two Danish opium ships, including the *Danebrog*, were also probing the Chinese coastline, [37] and they too bore small consignments of cotton piece-goods to cloak their true trade in opium. The *Jamesina*, which, since her arrival with the *Forbes*, had been anchored off Lintin as a Receiving-ship, made a discreet passage to Chinchew Bay, Amoy and Foochow. She brought back $300,000 in silver along with her super-cargo's report that he was of the opinion that: 'the only chance of pushing English manufactures on this coast is by having them as a small item in an opium cargo; at the same time it must be stated that the population of the country are most anxious to trade if they could escape mandarin vengeance.'

The voyage of the *Sylph* was an altogether different undertaking; there was nothing discreet about it, and the blatant hoisting of flags and colours, the firing of gun-salutes — nominally in honour of the provincial mandarins — was clearly intended to provoke the issue, since neither Captain Robert Wallace nor his supercargo Alexander Robertson would have done so without the instructions of the Old Iron-Headed Rat himself. Jardine had awaited the return of the *Lord Amherst* from which he quickly winkled out Lindsay's interpreter. The pidgin-English that had sufficed for communications in the Pearl River since time immemorial was inappropriate for the contemplated expedition, and Jardine, with characteristic cunning, secured the services of the Reverend Karl Frederick August Gützlaff. Gützlaff had been born in Prussian Pomerania, but was, in addition to being a Lutheran cleric, both an ardent Anglophile and a distinguished Sinologist who commanded several Chinese dia-lects, including that of Fukien, considered the most difficult of the coastal provincial tongues.[38] Gützlaff soothed whatever conscience he may have had over facilitating the expansion of the opium trade with the consolation that it was the only means by which Christianity might be brought to the Chinese; an opinion augmented by other churchmen who righteously considered the opium trade God's medium, because 'God in His loving mercy ever delights to bring good out of evil'. Buoyed-up by this pious oxymoron, Gützlaff received his instructions from Jardine who made no secret that the voyage was intended to seek alternative openings for selling opium and establish a coastal trade. Nor did Jardine seek to disguise its iniquity:

> it is our earnest wish that you should not in any way injure the grand object you have in view by appearing interested in what, by many, is considered an immoral traffic, yet such traffic is so absolutely necessary to give any vessel a reasonable chance of defraying her expenses, that we trust you will have no objection to inter-pret on every occasion when your service may be requested...

Echoing his partners' frustration with the attitudes of the Chinese, he went on with something of an air of exculpation by absolute accuracy:

in the state of our intercourse with the coast of China no other cargo holds out
a prospect of gain… From all we can learn opium appears to be the only article
through…which we are likely to be able to gratify the cupidity of the authorities
on the coast…

'After much consultation…and a conflict in my own mind,' Gützlaff embarked, and
the *Sylph* proceeded on her voyage, leaving Lintin on 20 October 1832 and heading
north, manned by a crew of some seventy lascars. Doubling the Shantung peninsula
and braving the bitter winter cold of the enclosed Gulf of Pechi-li (Po Hai), the *Sylph*
attempted to anchor off Tientsin but was unable to find good holding ground as a
furious northerly gale swept out of the freezing wastes of Manchuria. Captain Wallace
beat up to windward to seek shelter under the Dairen peninsula, but the *Sylph* ran
aground on a shoal 'which was entirely unknown to us'. According to Gützlaff she
was only got off with divine intervention:

> The next morning, a fierce north wind blew from the ice-fields…the water
> decreased, the ship fell over on her beam-ends and all our lascars were disabled by
> cold… While we were on shore endeavouring to hire some lighters, the ship got off
> by the interposition of God, who had ordered the south wind to blow, thus driving
> more water on the bank… After several hours…we succeeded in getting up the
> anchor and took a speedy farewell of these dismal regions.

The interposition of the Almighty did not prevent one lascar from freezing to death
in the cold, and while Gützlaff considered 'Manchu Tartary' a 'hopeful field' for proselytising, the survival of the *Sylph* owed much to the new and robust construction
method of her designer. (Seppings, faced with a shortage of timber for naval construction, had devised a method of utilising shorter lengths of wood than were traditionally
employed, and strengthening them with diagonal braces, for she seems not to have
suffered from her ordeal.) Wallace and Alexander decided the poverty of the peasantry
and the inhospitable nature of the locality was unpromising, so the *Sylph* headed
south. They traded a little near Shanghai, at Chapu in the Chusan Islands and on the
Fukien coast, arriving back at Lintin on 29 April 1833 after an absence of six months.

Although the voyages of the *Jamesina* and the *Sylph* provoked imperial protests,
the Viceroy being obliged – from lack of other channels – to make these to the
Select Committee, who had nothing to do with either vessel, they did not deter
Jardine or Matheson. With their fingers in another pie, they had gleaned information
from the impetuous James Innes, who had acted as supercargo for the owners of the
brig *Danebrog*, mentioned above. The Danish vessel had anchored for three weeks
off Ningpo during which the local Chinese had been keen to buy both opium and
British manufactures. Moreover, even armed imperial war-junks had slunk alongside
to traffic quietly with the Red Barbarians. Armed with Innes's intelligence, the following year the partners sent the brig *Colonel Young* to lie at anchor in Chinchew Bay
as a Receiving-ship. In order to convey goods to and from the *Colonel Young*, Jardine

and Matheson decided to use the new 160-ton brig-rigged *Fairy*, which arrived at Lintin from Singapore on 6 January. She had been built to their order in Liverpool and had brought out from Britain by Jardine's nephew, but the acquisition of a substantial interest in the *Red Rover* rendered her superfluous to her original purpose of running to India. Instead the partners put her to trafficking between Lintin and the *Colonel Young* as the first regular British coaster on the China coast.

Thus emboldened, the opium smugglers began to acquire their own ships. Early in 1833 Clifton had met Jardine and suggested he bought shares in the *Red Rover*, and between 1833 and 1846 the barque passed entirely under the control of Jardine, Matheson & Co. and out of Dent's. Clifton, having made upwards of £40,000, sold his own shares and retired. The firm of Jardine, Matheson & Co. had rapidly become one of the most influential on the coast, but they did not have things all their own way. The *Samarang*, one of their Receiving-ships, lay off Macao at Kum-sing-moon, and in August 1833 it was found necessary to ground her to scrape her bottom. While the trade with England was seasonal, and carried out in the winter months of the north-east monsoon, between November and April, the opium trade continued all year, exposing the ships engaged in it to the south-west monsoon from May to October, and the typhoon season between July and October. During bad weather the *Samarang* dragged from her inshore anchorage and ran aground, shortly afterwards being broken up. The company had another Receiving-ship, the *Hercules*, whose master, Captain Grant, fell into dispute with the Selectmen over an accusation of his having opened a mail bag brought from India by the *Sylph*. The *Hercules* lay:

> in the Kumsingmoon harbour on the mainland of China, a few miles only from Macao, and so immediately under the observation of the local Authorities of the District as to render it we believe very disagreeable to them. We cannot but bear in mind that Captain Grant has appeared before us under a great variety of implications of disorderly conduct and we are aware that his ship is notorious among the Chinese for acts of violence.

Gone are the inherent courtesies of the late century. Grant's conduct — brash, swaggering and opportunist — marks the true beginnings of the eastern adventurer, cast in a maritime mould, for he was more than the master of a moored hulk, being the custodian of Jardine's and Matheson's floating stock of opium. Faced with all this, the frustration and weariness of the Committee's comments indicate a weakening of resolve. Grant and his firm were assuming the upper hand: the partners — not the Selectmen — were now the chief *taipans*. When the *Samarang* drove ashore, she was plundered by the local Chinese for her copper fastenings, even while Grant's men were breaking her up. One wretched Chinaman was caught in the act by the English gunner from a Portuguese ship, and locked up aboard the *Hercules*. The local villagers retaliated by abducting an Indian *tindal* from the *Hercules* and, in mounting his rescue, a *seacunny* was captured. When Grant learned of this on his return from a business visit to Macao, he decided a show of force was necessary, but judged it inexpedient to take part himself. An appeal was sent to all the ships in the anchorage to send armed boats. Captain Hector of the *Lady Hughes* was to command, but no one was to open fire unless met by armed opposition; intimidation being the watchword. As the boats approached the village they were shot at by cannon. A desultory fire was returned and one villager was reported wounded as the boats withdrew. The unfortunate *seacunny* was never heard of again.

The Committee, having protested its policy of professing themselves ignorant of all that went on in the offshore anchorages, opined that Grant had pursued 'a series of unjustifiable acts amounting we might almost say to piratical conduct which render him altogether unworthy of the command of any British Vessel'. They ordered him to shift his ship. Grant refuted the piratical charge. These were, he wrote:

> all comprised in the present occasion and one former case when a thief (likewise taken in the fact) was confined on board for a few days. In adopting this, our only mode of checking plunder in a country where there is no appeal to the laws, but thro' the intervention of a body which declines intervention [the Committee], or only interferes against us [the free-traders], I was as I conceive, performing a simple duty to the owners of the property committed to my care.

At this point the wounded Chinese villager died, provoking a demand from the Viceroy for the surrender of the murderers. The Committee denied any responsibility, bolstering this by the argument that the attack had been conducted by ships' companies of several nations. As with such previous affairs, the demand for a reciprocal life met a refusal, and the matter ground to stalemate with a charade of scapegoats being proposed. As the Selectmen's control finally came to an end, it blew over. That year of 1833 saw the last sailing of a 'fleet' of Indiamen, some twenty-two including the 1,500-ton *Lowther Castle*, owned by Joseph Somes and commanded by Captain Henry Harris, the splendid 1,400-ton *Thames*, also owned by Somes and commanded by John Rhodes, and the *Farquharson*, Captain John Cruickshank, which Somes would shortly purchase as a hulk. It also included Sir Robert Wigram's *Lady Melville*, Captain Thomas Shepherd, the *Marquis of Huntley*, Captain John Hine, and the East India Company's own *Buckinghamshire*, Captain Richard Glasspoole, which would soon be sold to Cowasjee & Co. It was truly the end of an era, for they were displaced in influence not so much by their fellow travellers – the three dozen private ships that had arrived with general cargo and rice – but by the mere handful of dangerous little opium-clippers: the *Jamesina* and *Sylph*, the *Falcon*, *Red Rover*, *Waterwitch*, *Lady of the Lake* and *Fairy*; along with their moored Receiving-ships: Jardine, Matheson's *Hercules*, Dent & Co.'s *Jane* and *Charles Forbes*, and Russell's *Lintin* with her own covey of American opium smugglers.

This portentous departure could not be marked by a quiet withdrawal, for the importance of the China trade and the refusal of the Imperial Court at Peking to accept a formal ambassador required a British presence 'in China' to replace that of the Selectmen. Lord Grey's foreign secretary, Palmerston, chose William John, Eighth

Baron Napier, a man from a distinguished Scots family who had joined the navy in 1803 and by 1814 had risen to post rank. Retiring to live the life of a country gentlemen, Napier had published a manual on sheep-farming and, in 1823, succeeded to his father's peerage. In anticipation of the removal of the Selectmen, Lord Napier was appointed chief superintendent of British trade in China, and embarked aboard HM Frigate *Andromache* with HMS *Imogene* in company. The appointment was unwise; Napier knew nothing of the extreme and subtle peculiarities attached to commercial intercourse with the Chinese and, while he had two former Selectmen, John Davis and Sir George Robertson, attached to his suite as advisors, along with the sinologist and linguist Dr Robert Morrison, he was of neither temperament nor character to play a long or subtle game, regarding himself as an ambassador in all but name. Moreover, Napier's instructions which, as a naval officer, he felt bound to obey to the letter, ordered him to take up residence 'at Canton'. Whatever the long-term folly of the appointment or the unsuitable character of Napier's instructions, the arrival of so puissant a personage in two men-of-war was widely welcomed by the aggressive traders glad to see the backs of the Selectmen whom they regarded as debased milk-and-water characters who had never successfully obtained any remittance of the Eight Regulations constraining trade imposed by the mandarinate except one, that governing pleasure boating!

The long agitations in favour of free and unrestricted trade now burst forth in defiance of the Chinese policy of sufferance, and with the added prospect of removing from all trade – legal and illegal – the corrupt impositions of the Chinese administration. In an article widely considered to have been written by Jardine, the *Canton Repository* of December 1833 railed about the many abuses suffered by the British trading community, resurrecting old grievances in purple prose and proclaiming the energetic virtues of British entrepreneurship as 'patient, thrifty, [and full of] dexterous assiduity of private and untrammeled enterprise'. While opium was the current leading commodity and its traffic the inevitable consequence of Chinese intransigence, there was a little more to all this than a simple, amoral and avaricious desire to push the drug, for the article had a wider appeal and combined political persuasion with commercial argument:

> It is well known that the Tartar Manchu dynasty floats upon a smooth but dangerous sea, and that its authority rests upon the habit of tranquil obedience to its authority. Sensible of this, the high authorities view with abhorrence anything that savours of perturbation. But the rallying shout was that 'our capital, our manufacturing interest. Our power-looms...cry out "Obtain for us but a sale for our goods, and we will supply any quantity" '.

What the merchants wanted was a show of force, a push to the point of war, but that stopping short of destabilising the regime and ruining all prospects of free trade – and certainly not war itself. It was unfortunate therefore that in the spring of 1834 a curious incident occurred in which the Viceroy, Lu K'un, and the senior members of the Imperial Government in Canton paid a visit to the Company's old factory. Beset by protocol, the affair was protracted and the hauteur and status of the guests prevented them from meeting – let alone thanking – their hosts. Although conforming to Chinese practice, this was, in a sense, a last straw to the men of Jardine's stamp. With the constraints of the Company removed, they had had enough of what they perceived as unreasonable humiliations, and it was into this charged atmosphere that Lord Napier sailed. Anchoring at Macao, he went directly upstream, in a cutter provided by the East India Company, to the English factory where he was met by Jardine. Shortly afterwards, all trade having been stopped by the Viceroy's edict, the Hong merchants arrived to pass the Viceroy's order that Napier should await the imperial pleasure at Macao and that he had no permission to be in Canton. Napier, mindful of his status, imagined or otherwise, demurred. Instead of adopting the expected policy of establishing himself at Macao and embarking upon the lengthy process of opening negotiations with Peking, he sent his secretary, Mr Astell, to present his credentials to Lu K'un. Waiting at Macao was not consonant with his lordship's dignity, and although it had been done by Macartney in 1793, Amherst had not bothered in 1816. Nor did it suit the influential Jardine, with whom Napier dined. The wretched Astell paid for his master's precipitation, for he was obliged to wait for hours at the city's Petition Gate with a letter, the superscription of which made it plain that it was not a formal petition – and only a petition was acceptable. Astell was rebuffed by a series of mandarins, all the while subject to the taunts of the population with a consequent loss of face. This and the inevitable formal refusal to permit the men-of-war to pass beyond the forts of the Bocca Tigris – along with other communications in which a veiled insult was concealed – brought his lordship's blood to the boil.[39] Napier now lost the one man who might have restrained his impetuosity, Dr Morrison, who sickened and shortly afterwards died of age-related illness. Davis and Robertson, the Selectmen, were sidelined, and although the to-ings and fro-ings went on, they could have only one outcome: from the Viceroy's humiliating rejection of Napier and the Chinese refusal to conform to the international practice of exchanging ambassadors rose the confrontation that Jardine and his fellow free-traders had so devoutly hoped and so assiduously worked for.

Napier sent word to Captains Chads and Blackwood, in their warships anchored at Chuenpi, to force the passage of the Bogue, and on the afternoon of 7 September 1834 they did so, reaching Tiger Island, well short of Whampoa, before the wind failed in the hot sunshine. There were dead and wounded on both sides, though far fewer aboard the *Andromache* and *Imogene* than in the forts ashore. With the men-of-war went a small cutter belonging to the East India Company aboard which Captain Elliot of the Royal Navy sat under an umbrella. Once above the Bogue, Lu K'un ordered the men-of-war blockaded: an awkward stalemate from which Napier was forced to climb down. Obliged to retire to Macao and await events, he was not permitted to travel downstream in a man-of-war's boat, but compelled to do so in a sampan; he already had a fever and the bureaucratic prevarications, fireworks and gong-beating that was deemed necessary to accompany his progress and announce his humiliation, extended the trip to a gruelling week. Napier rejoined his wife and daughters at Macao on 26 September. Three weeks later he was dead. Captain Elliot was made his successor.

While these events had been brewing to boiling-point in far away China, a change of moral tone had overcome the British. Ever since the suppression of the slave-trade, what the future prime minister Lord Melbourne would call 'this damned morality' had been on the rise. Governmental obfuscations necessary to conceal the trafficking of opium from the wider public were considerable. Some success had been achieved by emphasising the useful conversion work being done by missionaries like Gützlaff, but nothing could conceal the plain fact that, unlike the slave-trade prior to 1807, the opium trade was illegal — and illegal on both sides. Without further digression into the ramifications of policy by both the British and Chinese, the situation was much as was summed up by another future prime minister, then the foreign secretary in a short-lived Tory ministry, no less a personage than the Duke of Wellington. After a meeting with James Matheson, who had undertaken to escort the widowed Lady Napier and her family home, and to explain matters to the Government, Wellington noted succinctly: 'That which we require now is not to lose the enjoyment of what we have got.'[40]

As for his own summing up, Matheson — who thought Wellington 'a cold-blooded fellow' — wrote to his partner:

> The fact is, Jardine, people appear to be so comfortable in this magnificent country, so entirely satisfied in all their desires, that so long as domestic affairs, including markets, go right, they cannot really be brought to think of us... Until therefore there is a stoppage of trade, or something to touch the pockets of the merchants and ship-owners, expect no sympathy here.

Within weeks of Matheson's encounter with Wellington, Palmerston had replaced him as foreign secretary. Palmerston was a man who misunderstood the world — especially the Orient — to the extent of regarding all men as similar in their fundamental reasonableness. Unfortunately this was increasingly mixed with that demand for respect which, in combination with dealings with the Manchu administration, could only lead to a trial of strength. With whatever misgivings and disappointments Matheson returned to Canton, he need not have worried. The tide had turned in his and Jardine's favour, though it would want five years before push came finally to shove. In the meantime the opium trade thrived. New ships joined 'the fleet' in 1835: the *Syed Khan*, the *Lady Grant*, the *Sir Herbert Compton* and the *Cowasjee Family*, all of which were owned by Parsee firms, with half a dozen more the following year. Other events occurred: on 30 January 1835 Wallace grounded the *Sylph* on an uncharted reef off Pulo Bintang at the eastern end of the Singapore Strait. Battered by the north-east monsoon seas, the *Sylph* beat her rudder and stern-post off and much of her cargo was spoiled as water poured into the split hull, but the timely arrival of the Indian Marine's cruiser *Clive* enabled Wallace to salvage most of his cargo. Lightening the *Sylph*, he subsequently succeeded in patching her, refloating her and returning to Singapore where she was repaired, a tribute to her design and build. Wallace suffered nothing from this disaster, being appointed by Rustomjee Cowasjee to his new Seppings-designed and Currie-built *Cowasjee Family*. This barque was superbly fitted out, her fine-lined hull built of teak, copper-fastened and capable of lifting 1,500 chests of opium:

> The carving and gilding are…exceedingly well done. In the centre of the stern is a sun — *splendens micante auro* — in a cerulean-blue field with cornucopias of the right and left, and a wheat-sheaf below, over which the God of Day sheds his genial influence. At either side of the stern-frame is a shell richly gilt, emblematic of the… wealth of Neptune's empire…the [figure] head is the bust of a male — pater-familias of the Cowasjee…well carved and richly gilt.

The *Cowasjee Family* was launched by Lady Grant to flags and fanfares which culminated in a grand reception for three hundred guests given by Rustomjee at his country house. After various changes of ownerships she, like the *Sylph* and *Sir Herbert Compton*, ended their working lives as full-rigged ships. In the following year, 1836, the *Lady Grant* was attacked by Malay pirates in the Singapore Strait. On the evening of 2 February, having outrun pursuit earlier in the day, the *Lady Grant* became becalmed and the *praus* closed in. Captain William Jeffrey dropped his kedge anchor, clapped a spring on the cable and hove-in until his broadside commanded the approaching boats. He opened fire without apparent effect, then:

> Finding they closed in with us very fast, we gave them a second broadside which checked their ardour a little. They were by this time within half a cable's length of us…determined to board, but a well directed fire of grape and canister made them sheer off…

That summer the *Fairy*, having carried a cargo of opium to Chinchew Bay and put it aboard the *Colonel Young*, was on her way back to Lintin when the crew rose against the master and mate, the mutiny being precipitated by the criticisms of the chief mate, a man named Guthrie. The nature of the trade and its basis on India and, in many cases, Indian ship-owners, generally guaranteed the excellent services of loyal lascar seamen and petty-officers. However, the delivery crew of the *Fairy*, all Liverpool men, declined to serve on the China coast, having heard stories of typhoons, extreme cold and piracy. Their commander for the voyage, James Innes, was 'surprised to see well-behaved men quit such a service', but quit they did, and Jardine and Matheson were obliged to crew their new tender with whatever manpower they could round-up along the waterfront at Macao.

Most of the commanders and officers of the opium-clippers were recruited from the younger men made redundant from the East India Company, or junior naval-officers on half-pay. All were active and intelligent men for whom the making of money was a priority. They were, wrote one of their number:

for the most part the younger sons of good families at home… Some acquaintance with nautical astronomy and the physical sciences, with a taste for Eastern languages, and a tongue and turn for Eastern colloquials; approved physique; steadiness and courage; reliability of temper; with the higher moral gifts of coolness and patience under trial and provocation — all these were essentials.[41]

Owing to their large sail-plans, the need to drive their ships and the possibility of having to defend them, opium-clippers carried large crews. These imperatives required willing and skilful seamen, while their commanders, used to the habit of command, found in the devoted lascar the perfect complement to their own skills in seamanship and navigation. When, however, it proved necessary to find a scratch-crew, the lack of symbiosis could be telling, and this appears to have been the case aboard the *Fairy* in August 1836. Captain McKay had 70,000 Spanish dollars-worth of gold and silver in his charge as he headed the *Fairy* back towards Lintin when Mr Guthrie was set upon by a clique of seamen from Manila. It was before dawn, the weather was wet and blustery and Guthrie's orders were not met with the promptness he required. The mate had for some time hazed the Filipinos, knocking them about when they failed his exacting standards, and upon the morning in question they attacked and killed him. They next burst into the after accommodation and killed McKay, the second mate and the gunner, all of whom were thrown overboard before the mutineers woke their shipmates in the watch-below. These men, a mixture of Portuguese, lascars and Chinese, were turned out of the *Fairy* into her boat and luckily reached the shore, though in the heavy surf the boat capsized and several were drowned. In due course the fourteen survivors appeared before the district magistrate, who extracted an account of the affair before sending them back to Macao. The *Fairy*, meanwhile, headed for Luzon with her treasure and was believed to have been scuttled by the mutineers, for she disappeared.

Among the young opium-clipper commanders were Joseph and Henry Pybus. The brothers came from a seafaring family and both had served in Licensed-ships, Henry having at the age of only twenty-two secured command of the *Windsor Castle*, originally the frigate *Porcupine* but bought by J. Short & Co. in 1816. Whether he was master when she put into Mauritius in June 1825, leaking so badly that she had to be condemned, is unclear, but, at an auction of captured slavers held in the Captain's Room at Lloyd's in 1835, he is supposed to have bought the former Spanish brigantine *Tangador*.[42] Renaming her the *Ann*, Pybus sailed for the Pearl River, determined to try his luck. At about the same time Joseph Pybus purchased a small schooner named *Time*. She had been employed in the Mediterranean fruit-trade and, taking command, Joseph made two voyages in quest of fruit before having her sides raised and re-rigging her as a topsail-schooner. Fitting a brass 12-pounder long gun *en barbette* amidships and six 4-pounder broadside guns, Joseph signed-on a crew of two dozen and left for the Orient. The *Time* made Cape Town in fifty-four days, and picked up a series of charters that delayed Joseph from joining Henry for over a year. Henry, meanwhile, had ordered a 350-ton barque at Moulmein, the *Sir Edward Ryan*, which was taken into the opium trade by a Captain McGowan, though the two masters afterwards exchanged vessels. Eventually, however, the two brothers went into partnership.

In 1838 there occurred a first disquieting among those merchants and ship-owners the touching of whose pockets Matheson had informed Jardine was a necessary pre-requisite to fundamental change in China. Three mercantile houses in London failed; Messrs Thomas Wilson, George Wildes and Timothy Wiggin all traded with China for tea and other commodities, including woollens. At first the opium trade seemed unaffected. General uncertainties in commerce elsewhere attracted others into the apparent certainties of the drug-traffic for which new ships were being built every year. McKinnon left the *Syed Khan* to take command of the new *Rob Roy*, owned by Da Souza & Co., while Edmond, Bibby & Co. built the brigantine *Pearl*, which was soon afterwards bought by Cowasjee, for she proved very fast, and the clippers were now racing each other regularly to secure 'top-dollar' for their illicit freight. But that year the very speed and capacity of the clippers caused a glut of opium: 19,000 chests of Benares and Patna, and 22,000 of Malwa opium lay in the holds of the Receiving-ships and the anchored clippers. That year, too, a number of casualties occurred. The *Antonio Pereira* and *Waterwitch* weathered typhoons and cyclones only with the great-est difficulty, but the brand-new *Ariel* and the *Cowasjee Family* were demasted and the *Rob Roy* struck off her false keel on a rock, though without serious damage. Then, in addition to the glut of opium, the market for English woollens dried up.

That November Dr William Jardine retired after being lionised at a grand dinner held in the old Company factory at Canton and attended by all the principal mer-chants, British, Indian and American. The partners were making an annual profit of £100,000 from opium alone, and the old *taipan* was reputed to have made himself over a million. Back home, Jardine purchased an estate at Lanrick in Perthshire and a house in London. He was elected Member of Parliament for Ashburton in Devon, a town that relied upon the export of woollens, and was briefly an advocate of free trade and an opponent of tariffs in the Commons. Events in China, however, called him back to public life.

While Jardine had been engaged on parliamentary and constituency affairs, mat-ters in the Far East had come to the head both he and Matheson had intrigued for. The glut of 1838 was followed by rumours of outrageous interference by the British superintendent of trade and then, in March 1839, by disturbing news brought to Calcutta by Henry Pybus in the *Sir Edward Ryan*: Pybus had heard that notices dis-played in the streets of Canton expressly forbade the traffic in opium. Ship-building came to an abrupt stop along the banks of the Hughli and opium-clippers were put up for sale. Then, on 24 June, McKinnon arrived in the *Rob Roy* with news that quan-tities of opium had been seized in Canton and burned on the orders of a new official, an especially appointed imperial Commissioner named Lin.

The Chinese point of view exactly mirrored the anxiety of the British in Calcutta a generation earlier: 'that foreign-mud,' as the Chinese euphemistically called opium, 'was always coming in, and pure silver was always going out'. For years the policy of soothing western traffickers and of bending with the wind had failed, for the

Red Barbarians always wished for more. Something of a moralistic attitude seems to have overcome the Imperial Court at Peking, which owed much to the energising of Lin Tsê-hsü, an able and intelligent mandarin of the first-rank who stood high in the Emperor's favour and who had displaced Lu K'un as the Emperor's voice in Canton. Lin's representations consequent upon Napier's conduct in 1834 had persuaded Emperor Tao Kwang – he of 'Glorious Rectitude' – to assert his authority and stem the out-flow of silver. Lin travelled south, invested with plenipotentiary powers. While Jardine, Matheson, Dent and Russell had all wanted a firm show of strength in 1834 and considered the forcing of the Bocca Tigris a necessary demonstration thereof, Lin had seen matters differently. The temporary confinement of the two British men-of-war between the Bogue and the Second Bar, and the expulsion of Napier in a humiliating descent of the Pearl River in great discomfort, after which he had expired, encouraged Lin.

Napier's death was not merely convenient, it was portentous; but it was also misleading. Lin's ignorance of British sea-power was to have terrible consequences for China, although it was not without foundation if seen from his perspective. Despite their xenophobic provocations, the Chinese had never witnessed extreme naked aggression by the British during the East India Company's long monopoly. Quite the contrary, for the Selectmen had always squirmed, ducked and dived, avoiding confrontation, mindful that their duty was to keep commerce open. There had been some awkward moments during the Napoleonic War and they had struggled with flag-officers like Admiral William Drury, but even when a boat attack was made by the Royal Navy up the Pearl River it had ended in débâcle, the withdrawal being seen and celebrated by the Chinese as a great military victory.[43]

Lin also drew comfort from the attitude of Captain Charles Elliot, now superintendent of trade in the wake of the last of the Company's Selectmen. Elliot, an essentially decent man, but one with a fashionable contempt for trade and a lack of understanding of the subtleties of Sino-British commercial relations, was literally a fish out of water. As a commissioned naval officer he not only disapproved of the illegality of the opium trade but deplored the 'frequent conflicts with firearms' in the hands of merchant seafarers. For some time his representations to Palmerston brought no response, but eventually the foreign secretary admitted that 'Her Majesty's Government could not interfere for the purpose of enabling British subjects to violate the laws of the country to which they trade'. Naïvely, Elliot published these words in the *Canton Register*, provoking an outraged response from the *taipans* not so much that London failed to support their interests but that Palmerston's perfectly logical statement 'committed the Government to a knowledge of the opium trade'! As if this public admission was not enough, on 28 December 1838 Elliot gave three days notice of a prohibition of 'all British owned schooners, cutters and otherwise rigged small craft...engaged in the illicit opium traffic within the Bocca Tigris...' He also warned that if any British subject caused the death of a Chinese citizen, 'by any wound feloniously inflicted', they would be liable to capital punishment as if such crime had been committed within the jurisdiction of Her Majesty, Queen Victoria.

Moreover, Elliot gave notice that in the event of any British vessels being seized within the Bocca Tigris by the Chinese Government, 'Her Majesty's Government will in no way interfere...'

These British injunctions coincided with Commissioner Lin's proscription of the smoking of opium that had appeared on the streets of Canton and news of which Henry Pybus had borne to Calcutta. Lin had also publicly executed a Chinese opium smuggler in the vicinity of the foreign factories, on ground leased to the *fan kwai*, and when a second execution on 26 January was interrupted by the factors who regarded the ground as subject to their own jurisdiction, a riot ensued, fuelled by a party of British seamen on a jolly run ashore from the *Orwell* who thought they would join in.[44] The riot soon turned into a full-scale attack on the go-downs and factories of the foreigners, and only a sally over the roof-tops and across the gully of Hog Lane to reach Howqua's residence brought the magistrates and soldiers bearing whips to restore order among the howling mob of Chinese. Although Commissioner Lin, whose authority over-rode that of the Viceroy, had chastised the Chinese rioters, he now inflicted a condign punishment upon the foreigners. Having first carried out the executions of more smugglers in front of the factories during the hours the foreigners were walking out, Lin made a most impressive and pompous entrance into Canton by way of the Pearl River on 10 March. In response to the insult of the execution on neutral soil, the *taipans* ordered their national flags lowered. A week later Lin summoned the members of the Co-Hong, ordered all trade suspended and then issued an edict to the factors informing them that all opium then in their go-downs must be surrendered upon pain of death. He also invested the factories, bricking up some of the alleys and making all intercourse impossible.

Next morning Matheson, Dent, Dadabhoy Rustomjee and the other *taipans* met an anxious Howqua and the other Co-Hong merchants, seeking a compromise and agreeing to surrender a substantial quantity of opium to placate Lin. After conducting an audit that revealed a quantity amounting to 20,000 chests, valued at $12 million, lay in the various Receiving-ships, the Europeans offered Lin 1,034 chests with a value of $725,000. The offer was rejected: Lin meant business. Having delivered himself of a remonstrance to Queen Victoria as a vassal of the Son of Heaven, Lin ordered all Chinese citizens in the employment of the Red Barbarians to desert their masters before besieging the factories. This was more serious than at first appears, for, apart from armies of servants and menials who earned their daily rice in the employment of the Barbarians, there were many Chinese whose part in the trade — and in commerce generally — was crucial. Every opium-clipper, for instance, carried a *schroff*, a treasurer-cum-interpreter, who handled the dealing when making sales, while there were others, tally-clerks and go-betweens, who materially assisted in all aspects of trafficking.

Matters were now serious for the men inside the factories, though they were clandestinely supplied with essentials by the ever resourceful Hong members. On the 24th Captain Elliot came upstream in the launch of HMS *Larne*, shoved through the cordon of sampans in the river, strode ashore and ordered the Union Flag restored over the British factory. Commissioner Lin was equal to this bluster and ordered Howqua and Mowqua into the disputed territory of the Factory Square with chains about their necks. To see their only allies in this sorry business executed before their eyes was beyond the resistance of the *taipans* and Elliot now offered the factors full compensation if all opium was surrendered to Lin, an arrangement to which Lin graciously consented having secured the moral victory. The *taipans* were no less enthusiastic, for the embargo holding the distribution of the stored opium would mean a glut when the new season's crop arrived. To avoid a consequent depression of the market price, the wholesale destruction of what lay in store would create such a demand for the new crop that its price would be sky-high. Characteristically, Matheson, taking the long view, sent his nephew to Manila to await events and from where, if the trade was utterly finished from Lintin, he could resume sailings to the China coast. To add to these universally happy circumstances, Captain Elliot assured the *taipans* that the British tax-payer would indemnify them for their losses. This assurance of reimbursement in an illegal trade was one of the more curious aspects of this affair, but was most encouraging for the importers. Matheson and Dent each yielded up about 7,000 chests, Dadabhoy Rustomjee relinquished 1,000 and Russell about 1,500, held in the name of British subjects — for this company had suspended the trade in opium on behalf of American interests some time earlier. All Receiving-ships and clippers were ordered to the anchorage at Chuenpi to surrender their contents. Accordingly, all obeyed, except Joseph Pybus of the *Time* who, just then arriving and hearing the news, slipped away. Some of the merchants agreed to sign a bond giving up the traffic to retire, but the remainder were held in the factories as Lin and the Viceroy made certain of the business of destruction. After careful preparations and the mustering of several hundred coolies, the opium was burnt in trenches dug within fenced ground bordering the Bogue at Chuenpi, beginning on 3 May and lasting for three weeks.

Meanwhile Pybus arrived at Singapore with the publicly aired news of the collapse of the market and secret instructions to his agent to buy as much opium as he could lay his hands on. He got 700 chests to add to the thirty aboard the *Time* and, after disappearing for a few weeks, Pybus returned to Calcutta, refitted the *Time* and departed for China. He made straight for the east coast and swiftly off-loaded his cargo at ten times what he had paid for it in Singapore.

In Canton, after the destruction of the opium, the siege of the factories was raised on condition that the factors and their staffs left forthwith. The Americans at Russell's remained, carrying all the trade except opium in their old Receiving-ship *Lintin*, while the British followed Elliot downstream, uncertain of the future but bearing their superintendent no apparent real ill-will, consoled with his assurances of compensation for their losses. As they did so, on 29 March, HMS *Larne* sailed with despatches, leaving Elliot alone in Macao with no force to back him up.

Evicted from Whampoa and unwilling to linger at Lintin, the British merchantmen made for another anchorage: Hong Kong, the 'Fragrant Harbour' hitherto only occasionally visited. With British shipping largely immobilised, the Americans made hay. Captain Philip Dumaresq's *Akbar* carried two tea cargoes to Calcutta and brought 5,000 bales of cotton to Whampoa while other opportunists moved in: 'Even the little opium–clipper brigantine *Rose* went up the [Pearl] river with her hold full of East India goods, cotton piled on her deck three tiers deep, and casks and her spare spars lashed alongside to prevent her capsizing.'

Other American ships brought tea downstream and transferred it into waiting British ships, while the opium-barques *Ariel* and *Waterwitch* were commissioned by the Governor-General at Fort William, Calcutta, to take the mails to Suez, working alongside the steamer *Zenobia* (see Chapter Four). Elliot's despatches left Macao on 30 May aboard the *Ariel* and were then forwarded to Suez. Captain Warden was obliged to beat the length of the Red Sea, then heave-to for three days in a northerly gale off Tor in the Gulf of Suez.

In China, Lin paraded Chinese opium-smugglers through Canton in chains. Meanwhile, the chancers lying offshore probed the Celestial Empire's defences. The Pybus Brother's *Ann* was attacked by imperial war-junks at Tienpak as Captain Grey attempted to land a cargo well to the eastward of Macao. Grey retreated to Hong Kong and then sailed to sell his opium at Manila. Captain Wright's *Red Rover* and Henry Pybus's *Sir Edward Ryan* appear to have discharged their opium on the China coast, but on their next voyages went direct to Manila.[45] Thus, with a few rare exceptions, Lin had succeeded in raising the coast against the Red Barbarians, denying them their markets and depriving them of the all-important 'face'.

Meanwhile at Kowloon, the mainland peninsula opposite Hong Kong Island that divides the harbour, there grew up a shanty-town to minister to the needs of the idle British seamen. It was Whampoa all over again; poisonous alcohol and cheap women caused several affrays in which a Chinaman was killed and an attack was made on the *Black Joke* in which several of the schooner's crew, including her master and mates, were killed.[46] Emboldened, Lin ordered that all Britons caught on Chinese soil were to be put to death, while a price of $5,000 was put upon Elliot's head and other rewards were offered for British masters, seamen and ships, including British men-of-war. The commander of the opium-schooner *Psyche* was fortunate to escape with his life when abducted, owing his deliverance to the timely appearance of HMS *Volage*, 26-guns, whose captain, Henry Smith, blockaded the Pearl River until the ship-master was released. There were other confrontations: an exchange of fire between naval boats and imperial junks initiating a game of brinkmanship being played out by Elliot and his naval colleagues, who now wished the trade's suspension to work against Commissioner Lin. Meanwhile the assembled fleet of merchantmen in Hong Kong road grew daily until numbering sixty idle vessels.

Into the middle of this crisis Joseph Somes's former Indiaman *Thomas Coutts* arrived, sweeping up from the south under a cloud of sail as if times had not changed. Dismissing Elliot's warnings and armed with legal opinion of his own, her master, Captain Robert Warner, took her directly up the Pearl River, securing the usual permit and bond, braving the Bogue forts to anchor at Whampoa. A few weeks later she emerged loaded with tea, secured from Russell & Co., and in her wake provoked a vociferous clamour from the ship-masters of the idle vessels at Hong Kong who remonstrated with Elliot and demanded action. Compelled to attempt to reopen trade, Elliot sent a letter to Lin which, after much parleying, was returned. Elliot then boarded *Volage* and conferred with Smith, the upshot of which was that Smith weighed anchor and, on 29 October 1839, with the sloop *Hyacinth* in support, the two men-of-war proceeded towards the Bogue forts to deliver the message. Here Lin had assembled his own blockade: twenty-nine war-junks with orders to arrest the British warships. Flying their pendants, beating gongs and letting off fire-crackers, the junks lay at anchor, and as the *Volage* and *Hyacinth* approached to pass them, the incendiary devices known as 'stink-pots' were hurled at the British warships. Smith and his colleague, Commander William Warren, returned fire with devastating broadsides: five junks were destroyed; others were swept by grape and small-arms fire. Elliot was sickened by the sight and ordered a cease-fire, but full of admiration for the 'gallantry of the Chinese admiral' Kuan T'ien-p'ei. Although hostilities were not declared between Great Britain and China until 6 December, the First Opium War had begun.

On Christmas Day a second abduction occurred. Captain Gribble of the *Thames* was returning from a social visit to Captain Robert Towns of the *Royal Saxon*, just arrived from Sydney and anchored not far from the Bogue. Gribble's hired sampan was over-taken and he was taken prisoner when on his way back to the *Thames*. Conducted to Canton, Gribble was charged with smuggling opium at an interrogation on 2 January, and it took all the persuasive powers of Towns and the Hong merchants to obtain his release. Such uncertainties persuaded the owners of some opium-clippers to guard against attacks and treachery by signing-on all-British crews. Determined to force matters at gun-point, if need be, the *Waterwitch* and *Lady Hayes* both fought their way through a blockading squadron of seventeen war-junks to land cargoes of opium at Macao for onward carriage into China. In early May the *Sylph* and *Cowasjee Family* attempted to run a cargo north of Amoy. They were attacked by several junks and Captains Viall and Wallace were obliged to beat off their assailants. Within days the *Omega* suffered a similar onslaught, while at the end of May one of Jardine, Matheson's coasting schooners, the *Hellas*, was set upon to the north of Namoa. Captain Jauncey and his crew met very determined opposition and, after firing a number of broadsides, fought hand-to-hand in a furious and bloody engagement in which a number of the *Hellas*' crew, including Jauncey himself, were wounded before fighting clear.

It would appear that the *Hellas* had been met with a pirate squadron whose leaders were aware of the vulnerability of solitary British vessels and determined to earn some of Commissioner Lin's bounties for captures. Jauncey had been attempting to land a cargo on the east coast, well away from Lin's influence, as Matheson sought to outwit the Commissioner's proscriptions and to better his rivals, the Pybus brothers, who repeatedly defied the coastal mandarins. Nor were the smugglers averse to retaliating by seizing their would-be attackers and, in order to intimidate their leaders and keep the coast clear for opium deliveries, they ran them ashore later, humiliatingly shorn of their pig-tails. Such a loss of face was almost unsupportable for a poor Chinese, and such high-handed arrogance earned the Pybus brothers a fortune. They built several new vessels at Moulmein on the *Time*'s lines and chartered them to run

The opium schooner *Hellas* hove-to and picking up her boat. Note the use of the white ensign to convey a quasi-naval legitimacy, a practice forbidden after the reorganisation of ensigns in 1864 when the white ensign was reserved exclusively for the Royal Navy and the Royal Yacht Squadron. Artist and origin unknown. (Private Collection)

the mails between Calcutta, Penang and Singapore while they awaited events on the South China coast.

It was now that Jardine, Matheson & Co. – the firm retaining the old name despite William Jardine's retirement – acquired the services of the second *Falcon*. Built on the lines of a sharp 22-gun corvette, she had been sold by the ageing Lord Yarborough after he had suffered a serious fall at sea. She was actually purchased by Captain William Clifton, with money raised by Thomas Baring on behalf of Rustomjee & Co. Fitted with steam-engines and paddles, she made awkward progress to Calcutta where it was decided to remove her steam-plant and charter her to Jardine, Matheson. Hoisting a version of the company's house-flag in the form of a commodore's swallow-tailed pendant, the beautiful *Falcon* became the senior ship of the Jardine, Matheson fleet. She was not immediately risked in the prevailing uncertainties of the opium trade, but was sent back to London with a cargo of tea. Superbly built for Yarborough, as commodore of the Royal Yacht Squadron, deliberately designed for speed and beautifully appointed, the *Falcon* was an exceptionally smart little full-rigged ship, as a panegyric thought to be by Captain Jauncey, who commanded her, makes plain:

> With a bow round and full above the waterline, she was as sharp as a wedge in her entrance below. Her midship sections gave her a long flat floor; whence commenced a clean run aft… Her breadth of beam…enabled her to stand up under a more than ordinary press of canvas, while it afforded quarters for a small battery of

guns, including a long brass piece amidships and some pivot and swivels over [the] bows, counter and quarter[s], that made her a wholesome terror...

In all cases of bad weather...there were times when the whole armament was dismounted and out under hatches, so that nothing should encumber the spacious white flush deck beyond the neat coils of running gear placed in tubs... The *Falcon* was a full-rigged ship, heavily but beautifully masted, as to rake and proportion. Her yards and spars were of dimensions equal to a ship of, perhaps, twice her size in actual carrying power in the ordinary Mercantile Marine...

In summer-like weather we sent up topgallant and royal masts on one, but during the strength of the monsoons and in all passages to the Northward – and we sometimes went very far North – short topgallant masts were fidded. We trusted more to spread than hoist; and in going free [that is with the wind astern] the show of canvas...[was] further extended by lengthy stunsail booms – in the rigging out of which our topmen had few compeers.....[W]here metal was employed it was mostly of copper or brass, even to the belaying pins; and that toprails, stanchions, skylights and coamings were of mahogany, whilst the accommodation below for the officers and crew was extravagantly luxurious... She was easy, handy and smart in every evolution. She swam like a duck and steered like a fish. She was fast, yet dry; lively, yet stiff. Sensitive and responsive to every yard of canvas that could be judiciously spread, as to every touch of the braces, tacks and sheets, and to every spoke of the wheel... 'She can do everything but speak,' was a common remark among the crew.

Matheson and his younger Jardine partners manned her with a picked crew, and such was their loyalty that they stuck with her for years as, once on the China coast, she was employed to seek out new landing spots and anchorages, her officers and crews becoming skilled hydrographic surveyors. However, her charterers were wise not to despatch her immediately, for the Chinese had embarked on more serious hostilities, sending incendiary junks and sampans of poisoned tea amid the anchored shipping at Cap-Sing-Moon to smoke out their enemy. The idle British crews welcomed the diversion, manning their own boats, securing lines to the burning junks, which were chained together in pairs, and towing them out of harm's way. After the junks had burnt out or exploded, the remnant timber was eagerly snapped up as firewood for the ships' galleys. Through the long summer nights sporadic attacks were made on individual vessels, and on one occasion an imperial junk seized from their sampan two Tankas who had been attending the opium-schooner *Mavis*. In response to the men's shouts for help, the *Mavis*'s Malay crew led by a British mate tumbled into their own boat and went in pursuit. They caught up with the imperial party on the beach and, after a sharp scrap, succeeded in setting the Tankas free.

But such a hiatus could not last. Once news of the siege of the factories, the destruction of the opium and the inactivity of British shipping reached Britain, it created at first a sense of outrage and then one of vengeance. Now touched in their pockets, the merchants and ship-owners not only began to lobby Government as

Matheson had predicted they would to Jardine, but did so with Old Iron-Headed Rat as their leader. Emerging from retirement, he led a delegation which had collected a war-chest of £20,000, and was able to play on national sensibilities: the investment of the Canton factories was another Black Hole of Calcutta; the seizure of British 'property' was an attack on free trade and a grave and unendurable insult to the British flag. Jardine had sufficient funds to secure, 'at a high price, the services of some leading advocates to advocate the cause', and the nation was minded to exact revenge and restore trade, along with 'the most cringing and humiliating concessions'. The future historian Thomas Macaulay harangued Parliament that the *taipans*:

> belonged to a country unaccustomed to defeat, to submission or to shame; to a country which had exacted such reparation…as had made the ears of all who heard it to tingle…to a country which had avenged the victims of the Black Hole on the field of Plassey… They knew that, surrounded as they were by enemies, and separated by great oceans and continents from all help, not a hair of their heads would be harmed with impunity.

Meanwhile, an equally young William Gladstone, the son of a Liverpool ship-owner grown rich on slaving, aware the root-cause lay in an illegal and unsupportable commerce, attempted to rein-in the contemplated folly:

> A war more unjust in its origin, a war more calculated to cover this country with disgrace, I do not know. The right honourable gentleman opposite spoke of the British flag waving in glory at Canton. That flag is hoisted to protect contraband traffic; and if it were never hoisted except as it is now hoisted on the coast of China, we should recoil from its sight with horror.

Neither the ramifications of this lobbying nor the details of the naval and military operations that it spawned need detain us long. Jardine had roused Palmerston and set in front of him the objectives of the proposed expeditionary force, and they included the acquisition of Hong Kong and the opening of four Chinese ports to free trade. By 22 June 1840 a potent force consisting of one 74-gun line-of-battle ship, HMS *Wellesley*, several frigates and sloops of war had joined HM Ships *Volage*, *Druid* and *Hyacinth* off Macao. With them were two of the East India Company's armed-steamers and twenty troop-transports, all sailing merchantmen, many of which were Country-ships. Besides the warships' marine detachments, they bore hither infantry from four line regiments, a detachment of sappers and miners, the sepoys of the Madras Native Infantry, the Bengal Volunteers and the Madras Artillery. With them, from the Hughli, 'came a swarm of opium craft, ready to take advantage of every opportunity'.

Leaving the three men-of-war already at Macao to blockade the Pearl River, Rear Admiral George Elliot, a cousin of Charles Elliot's, ordered his squadron north. Not without difficulties, in formally uncharted waters, the squadron anchored in the Chusan archipelago and took the principal town while Charles Elliot went even farther north in a steamer to deliver Palmerston's demands. Faced with this insult to his territorial integrity, the Emperor dismissed and exiled the loyal Lin, for whom the actions of the British were as shocking as they were unprecedented. Soon afterwards the British ships anchored on the Taku Bar, a move that persuaded an essentially weak Peking to negotiate. A new plenipotentiary, Commissioner Kishen, was appointed, and a truce was arranged, both parties agreeing it was more congenial to resolve matters at Canton. By November the British men-of-war were therefore back off Macao. However, on 21 November, bearing a flag of truce, the Indian Marine's steamer *Queen* attempted to land a despatch at the Bogue only to be met by cannon fire. Kishen arrived at Canton at the end of the month and there followed weeks of the usual prevarications without any prospect of a solution, all of which cultivated a conviction on the British side that they were being made fools of. Matters came to a head on 7 January 1841 when, after giving forty-eight hours' notice — a circumstance which persuaded a large number of the curious merchant ships to follow the squadron as observers — the British naval commanders resolved to bring the matter to a speedy conclusion.

The combined warships of the Royal Navy and the Indian Marine went into action, but it was the prospect of the Indian Marine's small paddle-steamer *Nemesis*, hitherto occupied with running the mails from Bombay to Suez (as described in Chapter Four), which caused a panic among the Chinese. Supported by small paddle-steamers *Madagascar* and the *Enterprize*, their paddles thrashing, their tall funnels belching smoke, and devoid of sails, they first landed troops and then made their way up the Bogue in support of the conventional men-of-war with all the appearance of the dragons that featured so much in Chinese mythology. It seemed to the watching Manchu mandarins, their bannermen and credulous troops, that the old prophecy that the Peacock throne would fall to strangers with grey eyes was coming true before them. Not only did the passing steamers throw explosive shells into the Chuenpi fort but, led by the *Nemesis*, they proceeded north and fell upon the assembled warjunks of Admiral Kwan. The *Nemesis* fired a Congreve rocket into a junk causing her powder magazine to explode, upon which Chinese resistance fizzled out.

On 23 January a treaty was signed, the first clause of which was the cession of Hong Kong. As one merchant remarked, 'the lion's paw' had been 'set down upon China'. The little *Enterprize* of the Indian Marine, whose previous history appears in a later chapter, was sent to Fort William with the news, and on the 26th a detachment of seamen and marines under Captain Belcher of HMS *Sulphur* landed and took possession of the island.

However, Kishen was still under orders to prosecute the war, and had concluded the treaty without imperial sanction. Charles Elliot, now the chief negotiator in the absence of his cousin, who had been taken ill, fretted that he still awaited the agreed formalities that would re-open trade. Although orders had gone to Chusan to evacuate the island, it was clear that the affair was far from settled, and reluctantly Elliot realised Kishen had outwitted him. British ships with despatches for Kishen at Canton were again fired upon, so Elliot ordered a forcing of the Pearl River and an advance upon Canton.

By 18 March the British appeared before the city and within hours a brisk traffic in souvenirs was under way! Kishen had left six days earlier in chains and, although sentenced to death, he was, like his predecessor, humiliatingly banished. A truce was reached but substantive negotiations dragged on under a new Commissioner. The Chinese reinforced the city, and on 20 May attacked the British fleet at anchor while shortly afterwards a mob looted the factories. On 25 May a full-scale attack on Canton was mounted and the Chinese gave way. Elliot ransomed the city and withdrew, but he too was now dismissed as reinforcements arrived, sent out by a frustrated Ministry which set aside the Treaty of Chuenpi.

More Company steamers arrived with more senior officers. The British force, beset by sickness, was reorganised, reinforced and left Hong Kong on 21 August. Instead of making for the Bocca Tigris it headed east, and on the 26th took Amoy, where an 'excellent harbour made it…one of the most important markets of Asia'. The Reverend Gützlaff went on: 'Vessels can sail up close to the houses, load and unload with the greatest facility, have shelter from all winds and in entering or leaving the port experience no danger of getting ashore.' After Amoy, Chusan was again taken after a fight lasting three days. Then on 10 October the steamers forced the forts of Chen-hai at the river's mouth and ascended the Yung River to anchor off Ningpo. The Chinese garrison fled on 13 October, and here the expeditionary force went into winter quarters.

In the meantime, in July of the summer of 1841, while both men-of-war and merchantmen lay off Hong Kong, the harbour was struck by a fierce typhoon which caused great damage among the anchored shipping, injured the new 'Government Jetty' and blew down the shanties ashore.

The Chinese re-opened hostilities in 1842 with an attack on Ningpo, but were driven back and pursued upstream before the war degenerated into 'a sordid affair of small scale atrocities and reprisals…'[47] Then the British resumed their offensive, burning Ningpo as they left for the main thrust against the Yang-tze River. They met furious resistance at Chepu, and followed this by looting and raping. The fighting raged up the great river and its tributary, the Huang-pu, which led to Shanghai. The ferocity and violence was appalling, and reached a culmination before the city of Chinkiang on 21 July 1842. The British then moved on Nanking, but the governor reported the city could not be held, and the Emperor sued for peace.

The Treaty of Nanking, confirming Hong Kong as a British possession, was signed aboard HMS *Cornwallis* on 29 August. In addition, the other 'cringing and humiliating concessions' included reparations of $21 million over three years, an amnesty for all Chinese serving the British, a diplomatic intercourse between equals – and with it a tacit agreement for Peking to conform with international law – and, most importantly for the *taipans* awaiting news of success:

> the ports of Canton, Amoy, Foochow-foo, Ningpo and Shanghai to be thrown open to British merchants. Consular officers [were] to be appointed to reside in them, and regular and just tariffs of imports and exports, as well as transit duties, to be established and published.

On receipt of the first $6 million of reparations and the Emperor's ratification, British forces would withdraw, though a garrison would remain on Chusan until all arrangements establishing the treaty-ports were concluded. The ink was scarcely dry upon the treaty before notices appeared advertising cheap opium. Like a flock of camp-followers, a large number of opium-clippers had trailed the progress of the British squadron, squatting under the guns of Chusan, lying in the creeks and inlets of the coasts of Chekiang and Fukien to deal with the locals. They had not had it entirely their own way. Although the opium trade had revived in the wake of military operations, Captain Stead of the Country-ship *Pestonjee Bomanjee* had been captured, tied to a stake and flayed alive, while one of the *Lyra's* officers, a Mr Wainwright, and a seaman, having gone ashore to sell opium, were also murdered. The British brig *Ann*, Captain Denham, had run aground on the coast of Taiwan and her crew were appallingly treated before all but a handful, including Denham, were beheaded. Only nine survivors, six British and three Indians, were finally released under the terms of the Treaty of Nanking. Undeterred by all this, over forty vessels were engaged in trafficking, and by early 1841 the quantity of opium either already secured in the Receiving-ships or on the high seas in transit to China exceeded that seized and burnt months earlier on the orders of Lin Tsê-hsü.

The acquisition of Hong Kong was, of course, the glittering prize of this obnoxious affair. Hardly had the news of the Treaty of Nanking reached Macao than Alexander Matheson arrived at Hong Kong to buy up all of East Point, rapidly filling it with houses and go-downs, while the army and navy set up cantonments and a proto-dockyard at West Point. Unsurprisingly, the new colonial city whose foundations were thereby laid was called Victoria, and the harbour was soon full of shipping. Jardine, Matheson's flagship, the *Falcon*, finally arrived to take up her new duties, though she did so with a cargo of saltpetre, not opium. Nevertheless, she dropped anchor within sight of the rising bamboo scaffolding surrounding her owners' new headquarters. In buying land at Hong Kong, Alexander Matheson had acted on the orders of his uncle, and now James, handing over the reins to his nephew, went home himself to call on his old partner. The Old Iron-Headed Rat was near the end of his life, and he died in February 1843 of 'a long of painful illness'.

Matheson succeeded Jardine as Liberal MP for Ashburton and from 1847 to 1868 sat as member for Ross and Cromarty. He married, acquired large estates in Scotland, including the Isle of Lewis, was awarded a baronetcy in 1850 and reorganised the London banking firm of Magniac, Jardine which became Matheson & Co. Among his achievements, and besides the setting up of the *Canton Register* in 1827, in which Jardine had written his grand remonstrance, Matheson and his partner had founded the Medical Missionary Society in Canton and built and staffed a hospital in Macao. Such apparently contradictory philanthropy built on a trade in opium was less of a paradox to the two men who, had the Chinese opened their trade properly, would have trafficked in legitimate commodities and were, in any case, largely commission agents rather than out-right racketeers in the drug. Despite the retention of the name, no member of the Matheson clan subsequently had an interest in the firm which, at least colloquially, became known as 'Jardines', although James Matheson was himself some time the chairman of the Peninsular & Oriental Steam Navigation Company.

Matheson's departure made no whit of difference to the prosecution of the opium trade which now enjoyed a boom. The Pybus brothers were still acquiring vessels, and in January 1842 they purchased the former New York pilot schooner *Flying Fish*, which had been commissioned as a United States warship for the purpose of joining the Wilkes's exploratory expedition and which he sold off in Singapore as the cost of her repair was considered exorbitant. Joseph Pybus had her sheathed with teak and renamed her *Spec*, since she was a speculation, though she was sold-on the following year. Jardine, Matheson & Co. acquired new tonnage, some of it in partnership with Jejeebhoy, who was now Sir Jamsetjee. The former brig-yacht *Anonyma*, and the specially built *Lanrick*, were two of their new vessels, both of which were put on the India to China run. The first craft to be built at Hong Kong was the schooner *Celestial*, launched on 12 February 1843, and in the summer of that year Edward Boustead & Co. brought onto the coast Rajah Brooke's *Royalist*.

Some idea of service in the secretive opium trade is gained from the memoirs of Thomas Gerard. In July 1842 Gerard had been second officer in the opium-clipper *Wild Irish Girl*, owned by J.A. Durran, earning $40 per month, more than thrice that earned by Marquand. He had left the Country-ship *Futtay Salaam* 'and joined a very fine vessel…in the opium trade which is considered by far superior to the Transport Service in which the *Futtay Salaam* was employed'. Gerard had followed Captain Gillet from one ship to the other, but in due course, and particularly when Gillet moved on, Gerard became disenchanted with the opium trade. The *Wild Irish Girl* spent five months anchored off Lintin Island in the estuary of the Pearl River, in company with many other vessels 'selling opium'. By 1846 the fast American opium-clippers were set fair to undermine the British, so the Aberdonian ship-builder, Alexander Hall, built the schooner *Torrington* for Jardine, Matheson, and in 1855 John White of Cowes built the schooner *Wild Dayrell* for Dent, but the trade was nevertheless increasingly dominated by the Americans. Not that this cut out the British, for the most prominent among the American companies employing fast schooners in the trade, Russell & Co. of New York, secured alliances with both Howqua in China and the British bankers Baring Bros in London. Among the expert American ship-masters employed in this trade was one Captain Warren Delano, great-uncle of President Franklin Delano Roosevelt. The period 1845–55 saw this rivalry intensify, with bets being laid upon individual clippers.

Despite the booming times, profits in the opium trade were by no means assured, owing to the fickle fluctuation in the drug's price: Durran failed, along with Stewart Marjoribanks, of whom we have heard and of whom we shall encounter again. 'Nobody is sure of his life in China today,' remarked Thomas Gerard, who was in Dent's service, though Jardine, Matheson & Co., with the *Falcon* scouting under Jauncey for new markets, continued to profit as commission agents. The Pybus's *Sir Edward Ryan*, armed with fifteen guns and manned by seventy men, made a net profit of £15,000 on a single opium voyage, and the trade continued to attract a certain type of adventurer of which Captain Lindsay Anderson is a good example. Initially intent upon a military life, he settled — as so many socially disadvantaged Britons were to do — for a life in the merchant marine. 'For myself,' he lamented, 'if I could have had the exciting and adventurous life, which was born of the opium trade, in any other way of life, I should have preferred it, but the fighting services in England are only for the rich and aristocratically born.' However, Anderson later abandoned the traffic on the grounds that: 'A thinking man has only to see the shrivelled carcases of the inveterate opium-smokers, to give him an everlasting disgust against the use of this pernicious drug.' Anderson's opinion was echoed by Thomas Gerard who, notwithstanding that he had remained some time in the trade and made at the very least a decent competence out of it, wrote on 4 August 1847 that it 'is certainly a disgusting profession and one that I would not advise anyone to send a person into for whom they have any regard'. Nevertheless, five years later Gerard was still involved, as chief mate of a Receiving-ship moored off the Chinese coast at Namoa, near Swatow.

In 1834 there had been sixty-six 'private English' merchants in Canton; three years later it was 156. The number of opium-clippers rose in proportion; there were only half a dozen up to 1832, when the coastwise distribution was extended. By 1837 the number had doubled, and went on increasing until 1860 when a small number transferred to the equally obnoxious trade known as 'black-birding', enslaving islanders from Fiji and enrolling them as indentured labourers in Queensland, Australia.

As for the new jewel in the crown, Hong Kong initially attracted armies of thieves from Canton who in April 1843 burgled Government House and the new establishments of Jardine, Matheson & Co., Dent & Co., and Gillespie & Co. Jardine, Matheson immediately recruited and armed a dozen Indian *chokidars*, or watchmen, and worked towards lighting the streets. The Morrison Institution, which sought to proselytize a Christian mission and to cross the cultural divide, was also attacked. Along with the thieves came a myriad of vendors, laundry-girls, sew-sew women and 'flower-girls' to pander and cater to the seamen rollicking ashore. Disreputable repetitions of the scenes of debauchery and affray that had so disfigured Dane's Island at Whampoa soon made of the Kowloon and Hong Kong waterfront a colourful, dangerous, diseased and occasionally fatal environment. That summer the first naval guard-ship, HM Sloop *Dido*, arrived under the command of Henry Keppel who, with his friend Joseph Pybus, suppressed several disorderly riots. Both of the Pybus brothers retired that year and their fleet was sold. The smart little *Time* that had seduced Joseph ended her days as a Receiving-ship at Woosung, near Shanghai, where she was eventually driven ashore in a typhoon. Henry Pybus, who was one of the few Europeans who indulged in opium, died at Madras on his way home, his health wrecked by addiction. It was the end of an amoral era, for the new treaty ports were opening to foreign trade, and that November Shanghai, which would in time become an extraordinary western enclave, first admitted the Red Barbarians. Landing opium in a Chinese city remained illegal, and little was smuggled into Shanghai. Instead it was transferred into the Receiving-ships that lay at Woosung at the confluence of the Huang-Pu with the Yangtze-kiang. Within a short space of time there were six of them — including

the *Time* – and Jardine, Matheson & Co., Dent, Rustomjee and Russell were among
their owners.

Although the staple India-bound cargo was specie, the ships leaving China now
carried many other commodities. Tea and alum were the chief exports, with sago
and camphor running them a close second. Smaller consignments of silk, musk,
fans, carvings of ivory and wood, snuff boxes and human hair added to the cargoes
of pottery held in the new go-downs rising along the shoreline at Hong Kong.
'Three years after its foundation,' Captain Ponsonby of Brocklebank's *Patna* wrote,
'Hong Kong is becoming a wonderful place, considering the short time that has
elapsed since it was ceded to England.' In 1845 the newly appointed governor,
Sir John Davis, legalised the opium trade, but he had little need to, for the traffic
throve and the finest of the opium ships picked up their cargoes in Hong Kong
from those coming from India and braved the piracy that the trade in turn revived
and kept going all along the coast of South China. In 1847, following a series of
attacks on Receiving-ships in Chimmoo Bay – during which all the crews were
massacred – and on the opium-clippers *Omega* and *Caroline*, at anchor off Amoy,
in which several men were killed, the Legislative Council of Hong Kong issued
an Ordinance against piracy. The Receiving-ships were moved to Chinchew Bay
and the Royal Navy was urged to suppress the scourge. Now it was not only the
Chinese who were caught; a number of European and American rogues were
involved, and in 1856 a handsome young man named Eli Boggs was convicted of
piracy and transported for life.

From time to time the opium ships got into trouble and were cast ashore, to be
looted by the local peasants, as occurred to Captain Bell's *Warlock* in Mirs Bay in
September 1847. Bell and his crew were obliged to abandon their vessel to plunder
and walk eight miles until they were picked up by boats from the Receiving-ships
at Chinchew. Uncharted rocks, typhoons and pirates challenged the masters, mates
and crews of these smart little vessels and, notwithstanding the amorality of the
pernicious trade, they were handled with exceptional boldness by commanders and seamen whom greed, necessity and expedience made highly competent.
But they were not always the winners, and in 1849 no less than nine vessels were
lost on the coast. Seven were opium-clippers: the *Coquette, Kelpie, Greyhound, Don
Juan, Mischief, Anna Eliza* and the *Sylph*. Jardine, Matheson & Co., getting wind
of a rumour that the *Sylph* had been taken by pirates off Hainan, persuaded the
senior naval officer at Hong Kong to send the steam-sloop HMS *Medea* to search
for her, but no trace could be found. Likewise Russell & Co., the owners of the
American-flagged *Coquette*, chartered the P&O steamer *Canton* to search for her in
the aftermath of a typhoon which the *Gazelle, Poppy* and *Ariel* survived, but she too
had to be posted missing.

By the late 1840s the British had come to dominate trade in the Far East. With
Singapore and Hong Kong both free ports, an era of consolidation could begin. In
1847 the decision was taken, 'after years of arguing and the death of countless seamen,'
to build a lighthouse at the eastern end of the Singapore Strait and to name it after

one of the East India Company's pioneering surveyors, James Horsburgh. Such things were incremental, but were evidence of the store Great Britain now put in her eastern enclaves. As Robert Blake points out:

> Of the various regions of the globe where the British traded, The Far East was by no means at the top in terms of volume. North and South America counted for much more. So did India. But the peculiar three-cornered trade between Britain, India and China in terms of tea, opium and bullion gave the Far East in an importance to the British Government finances which outweighed the trade statistics. It was enough to pull Britain into two wars, the morality of which has been disputed ever since... The events which led to the acquisition of Hong Kong and the establishment of the Treaty Ports [with their self-governing extra-territoriality] are an extraordinary compound of idealism and greed, piety and contraband, cut-throat competition and political intrigue.[48]

Further aggrandisements were to come at Chinese expense.[49] Another war was to be fought with China within fifteen years, before which China herself was to be plunged into the bizarre and bloody quasi-Christian Taiping Rebellion, in which the fomentations of the Reverend Karl Gützlaff played a part and which followed hard upon the death of the Emperor Tao Kwang in 1850. The First Opium War had kicked down the doors by which the Ching Emperors had sought to keep the rest of the world at bay, and the British brought much opprobrium upon their heads for doing it, both at home and abroad.[50] Napoleon remarked that China should be left to her slumbers, for once she awoke 'the world will tremble'. That is not entirely impossible; certainly what was started by the intrigues of the Old Iron-Headed Rat and his fellow *taipans* is still being played out today.

Contemporary opinion and justification took another tack, for it was in 1848 that Lord Palmerston, the foreign secretary, made his famous remark that Great Britain was 'at the head of moral, social and political civilisation', with which came a concomitant obligation 'to lead the way and direct the march of other nations.' This publicly uttered seizure of the moral summit, though counter-intuitive to the nation's real fiscal interests, and never embraced by the pragmatists at the Colonial Office or the *taipans* in Hong Kong, nevertheless articulates the manifesto of British imperialism from which great ills are said to have flowed. This may be so, but it is only part of the story. Western exploitation of China is undeniable, but commerce was not entirely unbeneficial to the Chinese, nor were the Treaty Ports without some merit. Kwang-Ching Liu is trenchant in his observations on:

> those enclaves of Western influence where Europeans and Americans once enjoyed an extraordinary status. It is neither possible nor necessary for historians to justify the entire Western record in the era of the treaty ports. But whatever the final balance of good and evil, there were nevertheless elements of treaty-port life that represented the best in Western civilisation and of which the West can well be proud.[51]

There were other mitigations, less subtle but no less true. The Co-Hong merchants, held responsible for every real or imaginary infraction perpetrated by the *fan kwai*, were themselves squeezed so much by the imperial authorities that they amassed a common fund from which to buy off their masters. This insurance was called the Consoo Fund and it was raised by their own extortions on the Company, the free-traders and all those despicable foreigners with whom they had dealings, being ultimately funded by the purchasers of tea and silk in Britain. It was from the Consoo Fund that the Chinese paid the huge sum in reparations demanded by the British at the conclusion of the First Opium War, so, in a sense, the British Government received what the British consumer had paid for.[52] Had the Chinese not placed every conceivable barrier in the way of an open and honest commerce, it is unlikely that Jardine, Matheson or Dent would have turned to opium to profit by eliminating a trade-balance the East India Company could not cope with. And, having done so, the profits made by those who controlled the trade — British, Parsee, American and Chinese — could not end it without renouncing avarice. The preposterous assumption by the Emperor at Peking, the Viceroy and governor at Canton and the Manchu administration in general, that Britain was a barbaric but vassal outpost of the Celestial Empire was ultimately fatal to the Ching dynasty.

Nevertheless, while the story is not ended, the founding of Hong Kong by the brutality of British bayonets signals the increasing engagement of the British state in imperial governance, and marks the initiation of that *canard* that trade follows the flag.

CHAPTER NOTES:

1. The surveying vessels of the Indian (Bengal) Marine continued to wear the striped grid-iron ensign until that service was abolished and transformed into the Royal Indian Navy in the 1860s.
2. A commission on parchment dated 1823 is made out 'To our trusty and Wellbeloved William Hunter' who commanded the Honourable Company's Ship *Sir David Scott* under the sign manual of King George IV. It is in the Guildhall Library, London, Ms 30379. Nor were the 'Indian Seas' the only place where pirates might be encountered. The pursuit and apprehension of slavers by the Royal Navy had created a new threat by those dispossessed of their traditional trade, and on a voyage from Hull to Tasmania in 1827 Rosalie Hare, the young wife of Captain Robert Lind Hare of the *Caroline*, a Calcutta-built teak brig owned by Chapman & Co. of London and on charter to the Van Dieman's Land Company, was brought-to in mid-Atlantic about 180 miles north of the Equator by a Spanish pirate masquerading under French colours on 9 September 1827. A Mr Drybrough, the *Caroline*'s first officer, was summoned aboard the Spanish vessel with his own ship's papers. On the pirates discovering there was nothing worth plundering, the *Caroline* was suffered to proceed. See Rosalie Hare, *The Voyage of the* Caroline*, from England to Van Dieman's land and Batavia in 1827-28*, p14 *et seq.*
3. The launching ceremony of the *Edinburgh* is indistinguishable from that of a first-rate man-of-war and was celebrated by the marine artist William Huggins who had himself been a purser in the East India Co.'s service. A print of the event was made and shows the yacht of the Elder Brethren of Trinity House at its right-hand margin and the mast-house of the East India Dock in the background. It is reproduced as a plate.

4. For a full explanation of the complexities of ship-ownership and the marine interest of the East India Company, see *Neptune's Trident*.

5 This is probably Captain William Cook, by 1829 master of the *Highbury*, who had been 'master of other ships in the West India trade,' and was sworn-in as a Younger Brother of Trinity House in August 1829 after such a distinguished service brought him to national attention. The rescue was celebrated by a medal and two paintings by William Daniell, both of which were exhibited at the Royal Academy.

6. The Board of Control had been imposed by Pitt's India Act of 1784.

7. It was not until 1877, however, that Queen Victoria was proclaimed Empress of India at a Grand Durbar at Delhi. The officers of the Company's Indian Marine were commissioned into the Royal Indian Navy, which existed as such until independence in 1947 when it was disfigured by a series of mutinies.

8. Keay, J., *The Honourable Company*, p456.

9. Nor had they ever been, as readers of *Neptune's Trident* and *Britannia's Realm* will recall.

10. See *Neptune's Trident*.

11. Among the reasons for Amherst's failure was his refusal to *kow-tow* in the Emperor's presence. Amherst felt greater empowerment than Macartney, given Great Britain's success in the late war, while the Chinese, ignorant of such matters, streadfastly refused to acknowledge Westerners as anything other than hirsutely primitive, if clever, barbarian subjects of the Emperor. Such dangers to navigation as caused the loss of the *Alceste* equally plagued the East Indiamen. On 28 November 1821 the HCS *Inglis* ran aground in the Banka Strait and, to get her off, her guns, spare spars, water and 5,000 chests of tea, were jettisoned, the latter at a loss of £50,000. On his way home Amherst visited the exiled Napoleon on St Helena.

12. In London Hastings had been one of the Holland House set and a confidant of the Prince Regent. During Raffles's absence in London, Hastings had become aware that he had been deceived about Raffles and the fact that Raffles had been knighted and had become intimate with the Regent's short-lived but lively daughter, Princess Charlotte, would have further mellowed any earlier disapprobation. See Maurice Collis's biography, *Raffles*, from which I have drawn several quotations.

13. Another was William Farquar, an associate of Bannerman and servant of the East India Company who had previously visited the island and was present when the treaty was signed. He and Bannerman afterwards intrigued against Raffles, who had left Farquar as governor of the Straits Settlement, subordinate to Raffles himself at Benkulen. The island had in fact been considered earlier, and readers of *Neptune's Trident* may recall Captain Alexander Hamilton of the Bombay Marine. In 1703 Hamilton claimed that the then Sultan of Johore 'treated me very kindly and made me a present of the island of Singapore; but I told him that it could be of no use to a private person, though a proper place for a Company to settle a colony on, lying in the centre of trade…' Certainly Raffles was not the only advocate of the island's acquisition, but he was its most influential, and it was he who negotiated the settlement.

14. During his brief rule in Java, the inquisitive Raffles had sent out surveying expeditions, one of which uncovered the great ruin of Borobudur, 'of which the Dutch knew nothing'.

15. See Keay, J., p454. For a discussion of Country-*wallahs* and the 'Country-trade', see *Neptune's Trident*.

16. Keay, J., p451 *et seq.*

17. The complicated background of trade with China is fully covered in *Neptune's Trident* and *Britannia's Realm*.

18. These commercial houses were collectively known as 'the Private English', though many of them were Scottish, as were many of the masters commanding the 'Indian' Country-ships from Bombay, most of which were beneficially owned by Parsees.

19. The Indentures referred to in this case were the necessary trading licenses which a Country-merchant — that is to say one working in the interests of a commercial house based in India — irrespective of whether he was British or Indian, was required to obtain from the East India Company before he could proceed to China and set up shop. Such companies were not infrequently unions of British — commonly Scottish — and Indian — commonly Parsee — partners, reflecting the commercial firms ashore.

20. Bulley, A., *The Bombay Country Ships*, p153.

21. News of Napoleon's death reached Canton on 17 September 1821.

22. As a snap-shot taken in 1823 the acknowledged imports of Malwa opium amounted to 4,650 chests, of Patna opium 1,850 chests and of Turkish opium (largely in American vessels). Morse, Volume IV, p85.

23. Lubbock states the name of this vessel was the Country-ship *Eugenia* but not that she was under Spanish colours. The change of name mentioned elsewhere allowed her to be registered under the Spanish ensign.

24. As one of the long established houses, Dent & Co. would become chief rival to Jardine and Matheson. Thomas Dent, the father of the company, acted as Sardinian consul. Robert Bennet Forbes was then about twenty-three years old and in the employ of his uncles, J. & T.H. Perkins. He was later to go ashore to head the firm of Russell & Co., the agent acting for the majority of the American opium ships.

25. Matheson recorded this opinion later in a pamphlet entitled *Present Position and Future Prospects of Trade in China*, published in 1836, a significant date in the history of Sino-British trade.

26. A further problem arose from this — and other vessels arriving with women — in that the chief mate's wife, Mrs Morley, was among the survivors, and her arrival at Whampoa, where the presence of any white women was forbidden, only added to the diplomatic tangle. Similar complications occasionally arose when female passengers embarked in India for a homeward passage via China.

27. Morse, H.B., *The East India Company Trading to China, 1635–1834*, Oxford University Press, Undated (*circa* 1860) IV, p131.

28. Quoted by Howard Chappelle, *The Search for Speed Under Sail*, p317.

29. For a full explanation of the part played by Indian merchants and their ships, the reader is recommended to Anne Bulley's fascinating *The Bombay Country Ships, 1790–1833*. Jamsetjee Jejeebhoy shipped opium in ships other than Jardine's or his own, landing a consignment at Macao from the Portuguese-flagged *Angelica*, Captain Fernandes da Silva, and Remington Crawford's *Samarang*.

30. The Country-*wallahs* were often very superior ships. One of their masters, writing in 1836, says 'they were kept so clean, were so well ordered and navigated — heavy, ugly teak vessels, very true…but their condition on board was admirable with their *sea-cunnies*, *tindals* and Lascars — obedient and good sailors in those days. The only Europeans on board were the captain and his three mates. All the duty was carried on in the Hindoostanee (sic) language…[which] most of us lads picked up…'

31. Both *Curlew* and *Pelorus* were 18-gun brig-sloops of the *Cruizer*-class. About 100ft in length with a tonnage of 382, they were extremely successful small cruisers.

32. In 1854 Henderson read a paper to the British Association in which he said that: 'The term "clipper ship" is applicable to all vessels in which speed is made the primary object… the *Waterwitch* [was built] so sharp and shallow, as to stow a cargo of only one-half the 380 tons registered; while carrying the sails of a 500-ton ship, having a numerous crew to man her efficiently, experience proved her very long masts and square yards were within the limits of safety.'

33. Dr William Jardine enjoyed a close business relationship with Jamsetjee Jejeebhoy who was later knighted and afterwards made a baronet. Among the scions of the Cowasjee

family were Dadabhoy Rustomjee, Rustonjee Cowasjee's son, who arrived in Canton in
1830 at the age of nineteen to manage the Chinese agency. He was joined in 1831 by his
younger brother, the sixteen-year-old Manockjee, and in 1834 the two set up the firm
of D. & M. Rustomjee & Co. in Canton. Rustomjee Cowasjee was a lineal descendant
of Banajee Limjee, and he and his two sons were major owners of opium-clippers. The
other Parsee opium-clipper owners were the three Cama brothers. See Lubbock, B., *The
Opium-clippers*, p93.

34. Lubbock claims the *Royal George* was the smaller of two East Indiamen of this name, but
neither was in service in 1816 nor owned by Alexander & Co. Clifton's *Royal George* − a
popular name − was probably an entirely free-trader run on Indiamen lines by her owners,
as there is no such ship listed as either an Extra-ship or a Licensed-ship, and no William
Clifton of the appropriate age appears in the List of the East India Company's officers.

35. According to Basil Lubbock, due to incompetence in undocking the *Prince de Neufchâtel*,
the 'Dockyard officials allowed her to get across the dock sill so that her back was
broken, and she was thereupon sold for a song'. Perhaps a copy of her lines was treated
with equal indifference. See *The Opium-clippers*, p77.

36. The *Red Rover* cup remains in the possession of the Honourable Company of Master
Mariners.

37. The Danish vessels were the *Danebrog* and *Kronbourg*, the Dutch the *Carlotta*. The
Danebrog had on board as supercargo the maverick James Innes, an independent merchant
who had burned down the house of the Hong merchant Howqua when that worthy
took no notice of a complaint by Innes that the storage of combustible materials near
the Canton warehouses would result one day in a fire. Such frictions, literal or otherwise,
constantly jarred the relations between the foreigners − chiefly the British − and
their hosts. Howqua's attitude was not so much fatalistic as detached and Confucian, a
procrastination that had led him to absent himself to his country dwelling and postpone
heeding Innes's advice. Such apparent indifference was beyond the patience or the
understanding of James Innes. In 1834 Howqua − whose Chinese name was Wu Bingjian
− estimated his personal fortune at 26 million Spanish dollars, making him probably the
richest merchant in the world, some recompense for his many humiliations at the hands
of the imperial Chinese system.

38. In his portrait of Gützlaff, George Chinnery depicts him in the costume of a Fukien
seaman. Gützlaff successively married three English wives, the first of whom, Maria
Newell, was a member of the London Missionary Society. They married in 1829, but the
unfortunate woman died in 1831. Gützlaff's second wife was the independent missionary
named Mary Wanstall, whom he married in Malacca in 1834, but she died in 1849. After
his service to the British during and following the Opium Wars, he left China in 1849.
His third wife, Dorothy Gabriel, whom he married at Bristol in 1850, outlived him, for
he died of dropsy soon after returning to Hong Kong in 1851.

39. In his response, the Viceroy caused Napier's name to be represented by two ideograms
which, while they made pretence at phonetically expressing Napier's name, could be
interpreted as a pun meaning 'Laboriously Vile'. When the same terminology was used in
a letter from Howqua, the senior Hong merchant, Morrison was obliged to translate the
pun literally to Napier.

40. Matheson thought Wellington was 'a strenuous advocate of submissiveness and servility',
but in fact the inscrutable duke also recommended to the Admiralty that 'till the trade
has taken its regular course, particularly considering what has passed recently, there
should always be within the Superintendent [of Trade]'s reach a stout Frigate and a
smaller vessel of war'.

41 The writer added the ironical comment that 'among the officers were many sons of
clergymen, who, after a period of active service afloat, would retire to succeed ultimately

to their fathers' livings or to practice at the bar, not a few finding their way into Parliament.'

42. Lubbock claims the Pybus brothers were in the Maritime Service of the East India Company, but there is no record of them in the list of officers, whereas two of the vessels Lubbock states they served in are recorded as Licensed-ships – 'East Indiamen' by extended courtesy but not in fact, an imprecision common to the parlance of the day. Selling of ex-slavers was forbidden by Act of Parliament the following year when there were still two dozen lying arrested at Sierra Leone.

43. See *Britannia's Realm*.

44. The *Orwell* was a former East Indiaman bought out by Larkins & Co., formerly a member of the Company's inner circle, and commanded by Captain Thomas Larkins.

45. Three other opium-clippers went missing, overwhelmed by heavy weather, the jeremiahs who had proclaimed their rigs too lofty, their hulls too shallow and their ballast inadequate, being proved correct.

46. The name *Black Joke* was common, and in this case should not be confused with the pirate vessel mentioned earlier. This schooner was the former Portuguese slaver *Esperanza*. In 1839 she was owned by Rustomjee & Co.

47. See Ian Hernon's *Britain's Forgotten Wars* for a fuller account of the campaign. For a personal account, illustrated by its author, *The Cree Journals*, by Edward Cree, Surgeon RN, Webb & Bower, Exeter, 1981, edited by Michael Lieven, cannot be bettered.

48. Blake, R., *Jardine Matheson, Traders of the Far East*, p254 *et seq.*

49 Another more modest aggrandisement occurred in 1845 when the British bought the Danish Indian trading-post at Tranquebar, leased in 1620 and traded with intermittently in the interim.

50. The most ironic of which were the condemnations of the Americans who were quietly able to make a great deal of money out of opium after the British had done all the dirty work.

51. Kwang-Ching, L., *Anglo–American Steamship Rivalry in China, 1862–1874*, 'Introduction'.

52. The complexities of this clash of cultures are brilliantly evoked in Maurice Collis's *Foreign Mud*, Faber and Faber, 1946.

THREE

'ROUNDING THE CAPE IS ROUGH WORK'

Making the Modern World Under Sail, 1834–1884

That great benchmark in British history, the Parliamentary Reform Act of 1832, obscures two near contemporaneous Acts which would impact upon world history. These, when combined with a subsequent series of disasters, political upheavals and discoveries, accelerated the impetus of global change by their influence on British shipping. We have followed the first of these Bills, the abrogation of the East India Company's monopoly on the trade with China, to the year 1842, insofar as the Far East was concerned. However, there was another effect touching the carriage of passengers, mail and cargo to India. This is partly dealt with in this chapter insofar as sailing-vessels were involved, and is continued in the history of the development of steam-vessels in that which follows.

The second influential Bill was that which finally ended slavery throughout the British Empire, an Act of arguably greater importance than the abolition of the slave-trade almost thirty years earlier. This was to create a mass movement of Indian and Chinese labourers and their families, which was just one part – but an often forgotten part – of a growing movement of migrants which had begun in the seventeenth century as a quest for political and religious freedom. This was subsequently augmented by enforced migration, or transportation – both tools of the British nation-state to rid itself of political misfits, rebels and criminals – first to North America and later to Australia. The evictions, clearances and resettlements of the early eighteenth century, which developed into the transport of convicts to Australia, was later transformed by perceived opportunities such as appealed to the passengers that Edward Beck carried across the North Atlantic in the early post-Napoleonic period. By the early 1850s the movement of people was to gather momentum, following the Irish Potato Famine and the discoveries of gold in California, Australia, New Zealand and South Africa.

Insofar as it concerned British shipping, the impact of the gold-finds in California in 1849 resulted chiefly in the mass desertions of crews from British ships calling at San Francisco, and this in turn was followed by later gold-strikes such as that on the Klondyke, which did nothing to ameliorate this. On their ship's arrival, prudent masters often had their entire crews arrested on trumped-up charges of insubordination to preserve them for the homeward voyage, once cargo had been worked. For the opportunistic sailor, the reality of dreams of instant wealth was rarely realised on the gold-fields. Their common fate was to be deceived on arrival by crimps boarding their ships, before being fleeced by bar-flies, pimps and whores ashore, overwhelmed with spiked drinks and 'sold' to a ship-master desperate for a crew the following morning. The activities of the crimps in this *demi-monde* of abduction frequently dispossessed a seaman of his money and his sea-kit, to 'shanghai' him aboard a vessel — usually a hard Yankee Down-Easter in want of a crew — within a few hours of his arrival. That the men deserted, abandoning their meagre but earned wages in prospect of far greater riches, saved the ship-owner money and led to a general indifference, as long as the distracted ship-master mustered another crew — from any source — and carried on with a profitable voyage. The appearance of San Francisco Bay was consequently full of idle, unmanned ships, a sight that can only be described as fantastic.

The discoveries of gold in Australia in 1851, in Canada in 1858, and at Otago in New Zealand in 1861, while seducing many seamen, also created a tremendous demand for shipping. The growth of adjacent colonial settlements grew rapidly. Numerous 'diggers' were followed by dependants, small-traders, opportunists, regulators, soldiers and civil servants, all of whom in turn demanded the trappings of civilisation, from tin-pots to double beds, and from mirrors to grand pianos. In due course the uncertain quest for gold revealed alternative mineral deposits of copper, iron and coal, while sheep-farming and wheat-growing grew apace. Within a few years quantities of raw materials and foodstuffs, predominantly grain, wool and — before the end of the nineteenth century — frozen meat, were exported to an eager market in the 'Mother-Country'. For the emigrants themselves, whether gold prospectors or jobbing carpenters, one sustaining truth held true. As a settler in Taranaki in New Zealand, who had secured the agency for the importation and sale of Sydney-manufactured boot-polish, summarised: 'The labouring class is as well off here as the nobs are at home… A person has a little chance to do something in this part of the world, and that is more than you can do at home'. Such modest ambition impelled people to up-root themselves and submit to an uncomfortable journey half-way round the world, but it required ships and seamen to accomplish.

Of the effects of the dissolution of the East India Company as a ship-charterer, only one was examined in the previous chapter. In 1834 all its ships were disposed of to a

number of new companies, most of which derived from connections with the dissolved Court of Directors. Redundant Indiamen were bought or, having 'lost' their
charterer — the Company — were retained in the oriental trade entirely on their
owner's account. Thus, what appeared to be new ship-owners came into being alongside genuinely new investors, including Smith of Newcastle and Somes of London.
Joseph Somes was one of the promoters of Lloyd's Register and acquired a number of
East Indiamen, giving extended life to first-class ships like the *Thomas Coutts*, the *Earl
Balcarres* and the *Edinburgh*.

The *Thomas Coutts* we observed last in the Pearl River under Somes' house-flag,
and she was to trade with China until being broken up in 1845. The *Earl Balcarres*,
built in Bombay to the Company's account in 1811, was a large ship of 1,418 tons
burthen. Commanded by James Jameson and later by Peter Cameron, she made nine
voyages to India and China before her sale in 1834. Bought by Thomas Shuter, she
continued in the now free trade with India, being bought by Somes Brothers in 1848
and sold again in 1863 when she became a coal-hulk on the African coast owned by
the African Steam Shipping Co., a testimony to her fine, teak hull and the skill of her
Indian builders. The *Edinburgh's* life was shorter; after four voyages to the Far East
she was sold on 2 July 1834 for £7,500 to James Gardner who, in 1839, resold her to
Tomlin & Co. She was broken up in 1844, the British oak-built Indiamen not possessing the longevity of their teak-built Indian cousins.

The very last survivor of these ships is of passing interest and demonstrates the
somewhat chaotic history of many. The *Java* had been built of teak in about 1812
by Anthony Blackmore of Calcutta for Paxton & Co., Country-ship-owners with
offices in London and Calcutta. She carried thirty guns and bore a fine figurehead of
a beautiful Javanese girl which owed its inspiration to a romantic rescue in Java by a
member of the owner's family. Commanded by Captain Thomas Driver, the *Java* was
busy in the Indian coastal trade under charter to the Company, but in 1825 she was
sold to Joseph Hare of London and put into the Bengal to China service. Two years
later Hare sold her to Fairlie & Co., another London and Calcutta firm, who brought
her home and loaded her in London. For almost forty years she sailed back and forth
between London, India, China and Australia under a succession of owners including Joseph Somes — who had her briefly in 1841 when she conveyed 750 soldiers to
Hobart in a long passage of 138 days. In 1866 she was sold as a coal-hulk to Smith
Imossi & Co. who moored her in Gibraltar until, on the eve of war in 1939, she was
towed away for breaking up.[1]

Immediately following the Company's demise, all manner of shipping sought cargoes to and from India and China. One early ship into the free China trade was the
Premier, commanded by a former East India Company officer, Thomas Narramore
Were, who came from Quaker ship-owning stock.[2] Were's career demonstrates the
fortunes of a merchant officer in this era of change, for he had first gone to sea as
a midshipman in the Honourable Company's Ship *Somerset* in 1822, at the age of
sixteen. Thereafter Were served in four further East Indiamen until, in May 1834, he
joined the *Broxbournebury* as chief officer. In his memoirs Were continues to refer to

the *Broxbournebury* as one of the 'Honourable Company's Ships' – or HCS – which was a conceit, for in 1813, when the Company lost the monopoly on Indian trade, she was sold to Andrew Chapman, a regular charterer of ships into the Company's service, by which they gained the designation of 'HCS'. This was a device to employ the ship as before, for the *Broxbournebury* continued trading to India as a 'Licensed-ship,' that is, a ship sailing under a Company license, carrying cargo both for the Company and her private owners, but able to make full use of all the Company's considerable infrastructure – agents, chandlers, repair facilities, and so forth – in India.

When Were joined in May 1834 the *Broxbournebury* was under a new commander, Captain Alfred Chapman, who was not merely a relative of the owner but part of the powerful maritime family we met in connection with Edward Beck's career, related to several Elder Brethren of Trinity House and himself a Younger Brother. The *Broxbournebury* sailed for Calcutta on 28 May. On 8 September she arrived at Madras, embarking a council member with a salute of fifteen guns before leaving on the 23rd. On arrival she anchored off Colvin Ghaut until 1 February 1835, loading and discharging. Were served several voyages in this ship before being asked to call upon some tea merchants who wished to acquire a medium-sized ship to enter in the China trade, and offered her to Were. In due course he located a suitable vessel in Liverpool of around 550 tons, called the *Premier*, and she was purchased for £4,000, a further £13,000 being spent on coppering and refitting her. The *Premier* was jointly owned by Messrs Sanderson, Fry, Fox & Co., and Messrs Morrison, Cryder & Co., the latter acting as managing owners, who contracted with Messrs Tyrer of Liverpool to load the ship – or, as it was termed, 'put her on the berth'. She was to arrive at Canton in early December 1837, calling outwards at ports in South America. To this end agents had to be appointed. Maxwell, Wight & Co. were to manage matters in Brazil, with Alsop & Co. appointed at Valparaiso, Coquimbo and other ports in Chile. Elsewhere a number of American companies were asked to act. The *Premier* was to load Chilean copper, call at Callao and Lima for specie (100,000 silver dollars), and at Santos for 400 tons of white sugar, before crossing the Pacific to pass through Torres Strait and discharge at Calcutta. Here Ferguson & Co. acted as agents and the *Premier* was to load cotton and opium for Canton where Wetmore & Co. were the consignees. Here a cargo of tea and 'other goods' would be loaded for London.

A problem arose in making these arrangements; Sanderson, Fry and Fox were Quakers – indeed the Fry brothers' sister was the reformer Elizabeth Fry – and they made an objection to the ship being armed. Were pleaded the necessity of a gun because the intended voyage across the Pacific and through the eastern archipelago exposed the vessel to possible attack. 'I was,' wrote Were, revealing his own financial interest in the ship:

> although captain, [also] part owner of the ship, and the insurance companies would
> have objected if the vessel was not protected from the pirates, cannibal and hostile
> natives that infest those regions. So after some remonstrance on my part, and demur
> on the part of my friends, I got their sanction to provide a gun, which was at that

time the only signal for a pilot, or being in distress. It was possible then, too, that this gun might burst, or otherwise prove inefficient, so I persuaded them to allow me a second. My own experience further told me that I might be in such a position among these isles as to require a boat armed, and to effect this I adopted the plan of purchasing some cutlasses, boarding pikes, pistols and muskets. My co-owners would neither have admitted the necessity nor sanctioned the purchase, so I had to resort to the system of increasing my bills for ironmongery and hardware.

Narramore Were would himself become an Elder Brother of Trinity House, joining not only Henry Bonham Bax, but also William Pixley (whom we met in *Britannia's Realm* as a prisoner of the French, dancing with the Empress Josephine). Having in the summer of 1814 obtained command of the West Indiaman *Orestes*, owned by a Mr Briggs of Ipswich, Pixley had married. His wife accompanied him to sea and bore him a daughter before the voyage ended in July 1816. Pixley thereafter took the *Orestes* back and forth to Jamaica, his wife with him producing a succession of children, until in 1827 he transferred into the *Princess Charlotte* – not to be confused with a ship of the same name owned by Brocklebank – owned by Mr James Ruston. Pixley was unfortunate, for:

full of supplies and passengers for Jamaica, a furious gale came on off Beachy Head, and she was driven on shore near Hastings. The passengers I endeavoured to comfort with the assurance of perfect safety of their lives and property. On the news of a large ship being wrecked, by 7 o'clock there were a large number of waggons (sic) and carts alongside. My first duty was to see the passengers and their effects safely landed and well cared for on shore. I then landed as much cargo as possible, until the [incoming] tide prevented our working longer. We continued floating all stores that would float for 48 hours, when the ship took fire and defied all our efforts to extinguish it.

In the mean time, the owner, Mr Ruston, arrived in post-chaise and four and comforted me exonerating me from all blame, and after having all the cargo lotted and sold by auction, I repaired to London the 1st May 1828.

Pixley was immediately given another ship, made a successful passage to Jamaica in thirty-two days and, on return to London, was 'gratified to find a splendid ship called the *Thetis* built for me'. However, Pixley turned this offer down, and the *Thetis* went to a Captain Barton, while he accepted an appointment as ship's husband – or marine superintendent – to the East Indiamen owned by Stewart Marjoribanks, a member of the Company's Court of Directors and ship-owner who, it will be recalled, we met earlier. Pixley moved his family to Poplar, relieving a predecessor who 'had made in 19 years £98,000 from nothing but plunder'. The honest Pixley was soon 'on the most friendly terms with the captains and officers of these splendid vessels', and so impressed his employer that in 1835, 'with the sanction of Mr Marjoribanks', he joined the board of Joad & Curling, who were 'large rope manufacturers'. At this time Pixley was sworn-in as a Younger Brother of Trinity House.

Several years earlier, in 1825, it will be recalled, Marjoribanks had lost the *Kent*
to fire, and during Pixley's time as ship's husband for him, Majoribanks also lost
the *Duke of York*, which was caught at anchor in the Hughli by a furious cyclone
and driven ashore at Hidgelli in 1833. Although she was refloated, she was declared
a constructive total loss and sold at Calcutta for breaking up. Pixley continued as
ship's husband for Marjoribanks, superintending his ships as they continued their
regular trading, but there was no longer any cushioning against the vagaries of the
market, and this began to tell. After making eight voyages for Marjoribanks in the
Company's interest, the *Thomas Coutts* continued under his private colours for several years until, in 1839, she made a poor return, with heavy losses owing to the
depressed price of tea. The first shipment of Indian tea to London had occurred the
previous year, and Marjoribanks held stocks of increasingly valueless China tea in his
warehouses.[3] He wound up his business in good time and, paying 20s in the pound
and having 'a large balance' left, sold the *Thomas Coutts* to Joseph Somes. Pixley was
not thrown entirely on his own resources, as he claims, for on the death of his two
partners, Joad and Curling, in 1839, he had taken over their rope-making business
himself. However, Marjoribanks commended Pixley to Sir Henry Pelly, an Elder
Brother of Trinity House, and Pixley was himself elected an Elder Brother, relinquishing his rope-walk to two friends.[4]

Although many well-built East Indiamen lingered on, the now open trade attracted
other private ships. The fortunes acquired in previous decades by interlopers who
had exploited loopholes, worn dubious ensigns and connived with the Indo-British
Country-traders to out-wit the Company's monopoly, had excited sufficient jealousy
to prompt others to join in. Joseph Somes and his competitors – Messrs Wigram,
Green, Dunbar, Smith, Tindall and their ilk – were soon, therefore, building new
ships, as the increased competition created the need for faster vessels. In 1837 the
former East India Company shipyard at Blackwall, having been taken over by Richard
Green and Money Wigram, laid down the first of a new type of merchantman, the
Seringapatam, to Green's own account. Although most came to be called 'Blackwall
frigates', in consequence of their construction in or near the old Blackwall Yard on
the Thames, others were built elsewhere. The generic noun 'frigate' was applied as a
compliment, a recognition that this new breed of merchantmen were 'cracks', lineal
and legitimate descendants of a proud tradition, as they took-over the Indiamen's task
of carrying passengers and cargo to 'British India'. Accordingly, they continued to
be decorated with false painted gun-ports, although they carried a small number of
broadside guns.

Despite being regarded as an innovation, the *Seringapatam* did not adopt the hollow
lines favoured by the Americans and was no proto-clipper. Instead she may be considered as a final mercantile refinement of the fast frigate of the late wars, so that her
colloquial classification was apt. She bore simplified but traditional stern windows
and was decorated with a figurehead of a be-turbanned Tippoo Sahib. Under the
command of Captain George Denny, she soon became noted for making good passages, and her form was followed in successive Blackwallers. A description of her at

anchor in the Hughli conveys the rather confused terminology of the day, as well as the admiration these vessels invoked:

> we came in sight of a noble Indiaman, with sides like a frigate's, canvas stowed on the yards and anchor down...the *Seringapatam* of 1,200 tons. She had troops on board, and the sounds of a military band, playing for dinner-time, floated to us across the water in the well-known notes of 'Rule Britannia'. While we glided slowly by, her numerous crew greeted our ship with a hearty three cheers, which was responded to from the *Westminster*.

The Greens and the Wigrams who built her were prominent in shipping and commercial business circles, the rise of the latter having been outlined in a previous volume. Between 1788 and 1813 Sir Robert Wigram owned twenty-one Indiamen, all of which were chartered to the East India Company, but after the end of the Indian monopoly, his ships traded under Wigram colours. In 1824 a George Green had acquired the *Sir Edward Paget* and placed her under the command of a former naval officer, Captain Geary.[5] He is said to have adopted St George's cross as his house-flag, the flying of which at the mainmast-head was challenged by the port admiral at Portsmouth when, on her maiden voyage, the *Sir Edward Paget* arrived at Spithead. That his house-flag corresponded to that of a full admiral would have been well known to Geary, and it is alleged that on being peremptorily ordered to strike this illegal device, the *Sir Edward Paget*'s chief mate ordered the flag down and had a blue handkerchief sewn over the centre of the red cross.

The two families, having already merged their interests in the Blackwall shipyard, constructed the *Edinburgh* for the East India Company's interest — as has already been mentioned as being owned by Henry Bonham — and her sister-ship, the *Abercrombie*. In the same period, around the later 1820s, they were building a smaller vessel for the Hudson's Bay Company called the *Prince Rupert*, and two whalers intended for the Pacific sperm whale fishery, the *Harpoon* and the *Matilda*. Also on the stocks was the *Roxburgh Castle* of 565 tons, for their own account, which was to be chartered to the Company. In 1829 George Green's son Richard was taken into partnership and the company was renamed Green, Wigram & Green, but was almost immediately crippled by a shipwrights' strike during which grass sprang up on the slipways and the yard was only kept ticking-over by the labour of the foremen and trade-apprentices. When at last the strike ended in the shipwrights' victory, the Blackwall Yard began to turn out a number of ships which were usually built in pairs for the profit of the independent shipping concerns of both families, though the *Roxburgh Castle* and the *Pyramus* remained co-owned until a final schism in the firm in 1844.[6] When this occurred, the enterprise was divided, as was the Blackwall Yard, Money Wigram & Co. taking the western portion and R. & H. Green the eastern. Richard, better known as 'Dicky', Green was the senior of the two brothers and was a great philanthropist, founding a Sailor's Home and other charitable institutions; Henry had been trained as a shipwright before serving at sea, and both were conservatives, refusing to countenance either the introduction of iron hulls or steam-vessels in their Blackwall Line.

Money Wigram on the other hand, was less hidebound. In 1837 he perceived the increasing trade with Australia and built the small 293-ton barque *Emu* as a speculation. Although never owning such a large number of ships as his rival and former partner, Wigram adopted steam and his sailing fleet declined when he switched his ships to the Australian service as gold-fever created a sudden demand for passenger shipping.

The dignified outward façade maintained by the East India Company's inner-circle of owner-managers vanished as they now found themselves in open competition. Former Company colleagues rapidly realized that as British shipping was transformed, a good reputation was a magnet for money. Ship-owners assumed a more prominent character than hitherto, a counter-point to the newly emerging race of steam-engineers, all forerunners of the shipping-magnates of a later generation. Besides Wigram and Green, there were other strong-minded individuals like Joseph Somes who had also been a ship's husband to East Indiamen and became a more eclectic owner of ships than either Wigram or Green. We have already noted his acquisition of several Indiamen, but Somes also owned South Seas whalers, West Indiamen and at least six convict-ships on long charter to the Government's Transport Service. He too flew a variant of St George's cross, its upper hoist canton emblazoned with a gold anchor on a blue ground in cheeky emulation of the Royal Navy's white ensign. With his two sons in partnership, his ships were collectively known as the Merchant Shipping Company, and when he died in 1845, Somes left a fortune of £434,000.[7]

Two other 'Blackwall' frigate-owners of distinction were Duncan Dunbar and T. & W. Smith, neither of whom built their ships on the Thames. Many of Dunbar's vessels were teak-built at his own yard at Brema, near Moulmein, from where they first breasted the waters of the Irrawaddy. Duncan Dunbar inherited a modest ship-owning business and a thriving trade in beer, wine and spirits from his father, but raised his shipping-company into a crack line. The family had settled in Limehouse where they owned a wharf in Narrow Street and from where Dunbar took over the business at the age of twenty-one on the untimely death of his father. Perhaps it was his youth that attracted him to building fast ships, but he had noted the lack-lustre speeds of the East Indiamen and rightly reckoned on a ship earning her living at sea. Consequently he encouraged his masters to invest in their ships and to minimise the time they spent in port.

Most of his ships were named after battles – the *Cressy* (sic), *Agincourt*, *Poictiers*, *Trafalgar*, *Hougomont*, *Blenheim*, *Ramilles*, *Vittoria*, *Vimiera* (sic), *Lincelles*, *Copenhagen*, *Camperdown*, *Nile*, *Alumbagh* and the crack *La Hogue* – though there were exceptions, usually those built at Moulmein. Such names were often common to other owners: both Green and Dunbar owned a *Trafalgar*, an *Agincourt* and a *Blenheim*; there were two named *Agamemnon* and no less than thee ships called *Star of India*, though only one was a Blackwall-frigate, while there was both a *Dunbar* and a *Duncan Dunbar*. Thus far the Registry did not forbid the practice because each individual vessel had her string of unique signal flags, or 'numbers', which were flown when passing Lloyd's

Owner of 40,000 tons of shipping, the great Blackwall frigate owner, Duncan Dunbar. (Whereabouts of original unknown)

signal stations at places as distant as the Lizard in Cornwall and Anjer Point in the Sunda Strait.

In addition to his Indian Blackwallers — in which he shipped quantities of India Pale Ale from an adjacent brewery in which he had a financial interest — Dunbar was soon into the Australian emigrant trade. He later joined the Smiths in ordering ships from Wearside yards, favouring James Laing's slipways. Many 'Blackwallers' were built on the Wear; besides Laing's there were other yards in the vicinity of Sunderland such as Marshall's, Doxford's, Reed's, Haswell's and Pile's. London owners of these ships also placed orders further afield, being attracted to Scottish yards.

Although Dunbar was a London owner, Thomas and William Smith were a Newcastle partnership that emerged from the happy conjunction of a master rope-maker marrying his proprietor's daughter. Thomas inherited the rope-walk while William became an apprentice-shipwright to William Rowe, then the largest ship-builder on the Tyne. In 1810 the brothers' father and architect of the family's fortunes bought Rowe out and shortly afterwards built the *Duke of Roxburgh* for Wigram & Green. Impressed with the quality of the Smith's building, Wigram & Green ordered a second ship, but she was lost on her way south from the Tyne to the Thames, and a third was laid down. This was the 600-ton *Duke of Northumberland* which, at the time of her launch in 1831, was considered the finest passenger ship in the Calcutta service. When Smith senior died in 1836, the two brothers went into ship-owning in a major way and moved part of their main-line operation south to the Thames, to which they were soon running a fleet of colliers. To support their operations, T. & W. Smith owned coal-hulks at Gravesend, a warehouse in the East India Dock and a sail-loft at Blackwall itself. As will be seen from the following, their ships earned a reputation of high standing:

> Before Government built the special transports for the Indian service this new breed of Indiamen did nearly all the trooping; and in the pre-canal days, when the P&O was the only steam passenger line to India, all but the rich and those in a hurry went out round the Cape, so that they were always full of passengers. The ships built for the Eastern service after 1833 were of the highest class, and the best examples were found between 1850 and 1870. The finest vessels of all were those of T. & W. Smith. These ships were built at Newcastle-on-Tyne.

Although the improvements in standards in the British merchant marine mentioned earlier were slow, delayed in part by the parliamentary process, the Blackwall frigates marked a continuation of what was best-practice, revitalised by the opening up of the trade to the east. Despite being considered a considerable departure from the East Indiamen, the Blackwall frigates remained relatively conventional, having apple-bows, a tall narrow rig with deep single topsails, man-of-war fashion, and they relied upon setting studding sails in fair weather. Such a traditional ship-rig required not only a high standard of skill on the part of all hands, but a large crew. With their customary painted – and not always *faux* – gun-ports, they were handsome vessels and capable of good days' runs, but they were expensive to run, narrowing the margin of difference in costs with the new-fangled steamer which, by the 1860s, had began to threaten their existence:

> All the ships were of wood and all were, for merchant vessels, heavily manned. A thousand-ton ship would have a crew, all told, of seventy. In. this number, besides the seamen, were butchers, cooks and cuddy servants. The watch on deck would number twenty-five seamen, besides midshipmen and the officer. These midshipmen came from families where £400 or so could be spared for a boy's sea career; they were, therefore, of a better class socially than the general run of merchant officers. From these youngsters the mates were picked, and a stranger from outside was a rarity. The seamen were as good as Britain ever possessed; fine, able men… A Dutchman,' as all foreigners were known, was a rarity, though there were always some West Indian Negroes… The ships were frigate-built and copper fastened throughout; a ship of 1,100 tons, in 1860, cost close on £40,000. Smith's ships were pierced for guns, having regulation gun ports and ring and eye bolts for the breechings. The *Blenheim* and *Marlborough* of their fleet were built exactly in design and scantlings, as the 40-gun frigate of their date (1848); they were submitted to a special Government survey and reported fit to carry armaments. In 1851 they were judged to be the finest merchant ships afloat. Smith's smaller vessels, such as *Hotspur* and

Saint Lawrence, were equal to the large naval corvette class, but were not true corvettes, inasmuch as they had poop and forecastle. The ships of Green and Wigram of the same date were not pierced for guns, though they had square windows in their poops for lighting the passengers' cabins; they were more graceful models than the bluff frigates of Smith.

Under her first commander, Sir Allen Young, a 'kind, gentlemanly' man, the *Marlborough*, like her sister, was employed carrying passengers, troops and cargo between London, Madras and Calcutta, but in 1853 both ships were diverted to run passengers to Australia, such was the volume of speculators anxious to reach the diggings of Ballarat and Bendigo in quest of gold. To prevent the desertions common among European crews, Smiths took the then unusual step of manning the *Marlborough* with a permanent crew of lascars. Carrying 325 passengers, the *Marlborough* reached Port Philip after a passage of seventy-eight days from signalling Lloyd's station at the Lizard. On her return passage, by way of Cape Horn, carrying sixty passengers and 72,000 ounces of gold dust valued at £288,000, she broached-to and lay on her beam ends in the trough of a heavy sea. Fortunately her main topsail blew out, she righted herself and continued on her way, only to run perilously close to a large iceberg before she had doubled Cape Horn, arriving off Start Point eighty-four days from Hobson's Bay.[8]

So highly regarded were the *Blenheim* and *Marlborough*, both of which grossed a little under 1,400 tons, that they were judged the finest British merchant ships afloat at the Great Exhibition of 1851 and presented with red ensigns and house-flags of silk. But as early as the mid-'50s, despite their many creditable passages: 'Their style and hull form made them anachronisms in an age hastening towards mechanisation, and the trappings of past grandeurs contrasted strangely with the sleeker lines of ships being sent afloat as their competitors.'[9]

The Smiths had adopted a white flag intersected by a blue cross, and in consequence their vessels were known as the Blue Cross Line, the noun 'line' being increasingly applied to smart companies who ran a regular service.[10]

These ships obtained all the choicest freight, out and homeward, and, always being full of troops and passengers, they paid so well that unless they made 40 per cent they were thought to be doing badly. Considering their build, for they were not clippers... they made wonderful passages; this was due to the fact that owing to their large crews they could make and shorten sail quickly, and, could 'carry on'; and that they could run out a gale without heaving to. It used to be said that, in contrast to their predecessors which hove-to during darkness, they made their passages at night; no matter what the hour, as soon as there was the least decrease in wind, sail was made instantly. Again, sail was never shortened until absolutely necessary. In tropical squalls, when by the wind, the ships were luffed and shaken through them, instead of lowering royals and skysails; and topmast and square lower studding sails were often hung on to when the royals and first reef of topsails were taken in; they were, in fact, carried on for all they were worth, but, legitimately it was considered bad seamanship to lose a sail or spar, other than a studding sail boom.

An average passage was 90 days, but often such runs as 70 to 80 days 'from pilot to pilot' were made, and when in 1857 some of the celebrated clippers were engaged to carry troops to India, they were beaten by the slower but better sailed 'Blackwallers'.[11]

The Smiths moved into steam early. Upon the opening of the Suez Canal they combined with another Tyneside company, and one of their steamers was among the first ships to use the canal. The other Blackwall companies rapidly lost trade to the P&O steamer service — which is described later — and as freight-rates plummeted, withdrew from the Indian trade in favour of the colonial run to Australia. By 1871 scarcely a passenger to India other than consumptive convalescents went round the Cape, while all trooping went by way of the canal.

Command of such ships in their hey-day was at a premium, for it was possible to earn colossal sums, occasionally as much as £5,000 *per annum*. By convention their masters continued the tradition of using the quasi-naval title 'commander', and their professional accomplishments, particularly in the technical matter of determining longitude by lunar observation — which dispensed with the chronometer, mastery of which was considered the apogee of the art of navigation, as we saw with Ned Beck — were remarkable. By the 1840s, in quest of fast passages, they were running their easting down from the Cape of Good Hope towards Australia, not along the conventional rhumb-line of the 38th Parallel, but by sailing on the great-circle and stretching down beyond 60° South latitude to cut 400 miles off the distance. In so doing they were encouraged to submit their observations on meteorology and natural phenomena to the newly established Meteorological Office, headed by Admiral Robert Fitzroy, whose interest in the betterment of the mercantile marine was mentioned earlier. Fitzroy persuaded the Board of Trade to supply selected masters with the necessary recording instruments, and he issued commendations accordingly. Such diligence earned not a few of these men Fellowships of the Royal Society.

One such was Captain Henry Toynbee of the *Hotspur* who regularly used a dredge-net to recover specimens from the sea and who had an oceanographical laboratory in his cabin. Toynbee was popular with both his crew and his passengers, circumstances that guaranteed a full saloon on the *Hotspur*'s several voyages to Calcutta under T. & W. Smith's house-flag. The son of a gentleman farmer from Lancashire, Henry Toynbee had sailed as midshipman in the last year of the East India Company's monopoly before transferring into the free-trading barque *Eleanor* for a voyage to China. He was next third mate in T. & W. Smith's *Duke of Argyle* under Captain John Sydney Webb.[12] Remaining in Smith's service, Toynbee was promoted master of the *Ellenborough* and, after commanding several other of the company's ships, was appointed to the *Hotspur*. Upon the suicide of Admiral Fitzroy in 1865, Toynbee succeeded him as the Marine Superintendent of the Meteorological Office, retiring in 1888.

The reports of bad weather, meteorological phenomena — the more pleasingly logical term atmosphereology had been abandoned — and other natural observations submitted by the masters of these ships improved a general understanding of the natural world. They were published in periodicals and journals such as the *Nautical Magazine* and *Philosophical Transactions* and would lead, in due course, to the world's first oceanographical circumnavigation by HMS *Challenger* in 1872-76. Of Toynbee himself, Midshipman Downie of Green's *Trafalgar* wrote in 1863:

> Our captain was a thorough gentleman and a fine sailor, far more scientific than the general run of skippers of his day, and had dived deeply into the law of storms, on which subject, I believe, he had written a book. He was one of the few seamen I have met who habitually wore an eyeglass, and I can see him now screwing it into his eye preparatory to asking you some very straight question you would very much rather not have to answer. He was very kind-hearted, but a strict disciplinarian.[13]

Downie describes the *Trafalgar*'s officers as: 'Good fellows and good seamen, very much alive to their own dignity, and inclined to be just a trifle hard on the junior members of the [midshipmen's] mess...' He added that, 'you must have a certain amount of go in an officer,' while 'the crew were picked men who had sailed from their boyhood in East Indiamen or Blackwall ships, a splendid crowd...' That said, Downie admits that on leaving the moorings at Blackwall they dropped down to Gravesend where the *Trafalgar* anchored for twenty-four hours:

> a course which always had to be adopted in those days, in order to let the crew get sober, and to facilitate the process, a cask of porter, strongly impregnated with jalap (a purgative drug obtained from the resin in the tuber of a Mexican convolvulus), was placed in the forecastle. Amongst a crew of forty or fifty men it was, of course, soon empty; but the medicinal effect was superb, and clearer heads than they had known for some weeks soon enabled the seamen to set about their respective duties in a satisfactory manner.

Truly, the *Trafalgar* was blessed with a scientific commander.

Such young aspirants as Downie rose from being midshipmen rather than indentured apprentices, and berths were secured not by a single, four-year premium, but on a voyage basis, as much as £60 being demanded for a first trip in Green's ships. This was followed by a payment of £50 for the second, £40 for the third, the fourth being free of premium and the fifth as fifth mate on £1 per month. In contrast, T. & W. Smith charged a single premium of £150 plus £10 mess-money, and no indentures were signed. Blackwall frigates carried about ten midshipmen as against about six in smaller cargo ships bound for Calcutta, and such was the prestige attaching to these cracks that they became refuges for wards of court and finishing-schools for the more wayward sons of the well-to-do. As well as learning their craft as seamen and navigators, the presence of passengers — including a considerable number of women — had a beneficial moral effect, divine service being observed when the weather permitted. The wilder instincts of young men were curbed by the risks they took in their work and the routines of the ship, which required them to undergo the grim initiation of crossing-the-line.

It was not at all unusual throughout the nineteenth century for the wives of ship-masters to accompany their husbands to sea. Downie recalled:

> a little lady who seemed to spend her time between settling the quarrels of certain lady passengers and bossing her husband… she gave orders when to shorten sail, or, at any rate, we thought so… [Her husband was] a fiery little man, who slanged everyone on board except his better half. She ruled him with a rod of iron. He was that *rara avis* in those days — a staunch teetotaller. With his temper, perhaps, it was as well he was.

There was, Downie assures us, a distinct difference between the regimes aboard Blackwallers bound for India and those heading towards Australia. On the former route discipline was strict, reflecting the prestigious connections of the ships in Indian waters where they lay at their moorings 'with yards squared with mathematical precision, and swinging booms rigged out, with the boats fast to them, [so that] we might have been a Royal Navy frigate by our looks'. On the other hand, matters were more casual in the Australia-bound ships, for the Antipode was no longer a destination only for convicts:

> One found a much greater variety among the Australian passengers than in the people going to India. Society in the great Dependency [of India] had been more or less stereotyped for decades, whereas in the newer colonies, there was room waiting for all sorts and conditions of men… I have taken young fellows out third-class one voyage, and on the next found them well on the road to success…

On the other hand, however, whereas the Blackwall midshipmen could enjoy the delights of being waited on hand-and-foot in Calcutta, they often had to fight for their lives against 'the larrikins' looking for trouble in the vicinity of Circular Quay, Sydney.

In Calcutta the Blackwallers were towed to the Esplanade Reach by steam-tugs and always with a Hughli pilot — the epitome of the white *pukkah–wallah*, with his several uniforms to be changed into as they became grubby, his leadsman and his 'boy' to attend to his several wants. Once brought to a running or standing moor with her own anchors, or secured to the mooring buoys that oscillated in the brown stream that bore the melt-waters of the distant Himalayas to the Bay of Bengal, their commanders enjoyed a gay social life ashore, while their crews toiled. The outward cargo was usually discharged into lighters by the crew, the midshipmen — when they were not manning the commander's gig — tallying the cargo out, sling-by-sling. Loading was undertaken by contracted gangs of coolies, while the crew painted ship and prepared for the homeward voyage. The tiers of moorings were congested with ships and vulnerable to the occasional onslaught of a Bay of Bengal cyclone, such as had stranded Marjoribanks's *Duke of York* in 1833. Another followed in 1842 and a third caused devastation in the Hughli in 1864.

This struck the crowded reaches on 5 October, a relatively small local disturbance rather than the great tropical revolving storm of the Bay of Bengal or the *taifun* of the South China Sea. Nevertheless, it did immense damage, the anchors of only two ships – Dunbar's *Alumbagh* and *Sir Robert Lees* – failed to drag, while all but four sets of stream-moorings parted or started from the riverbed. In all, about 200 vessels of all descriptions were driven onto the banks; three foundered in the river and a Country-*wallah*, the *Ally*, capsized and drowned 300 lascars and coolies who were on board. One steamer, the *Thunder*, drove across the wreck of an American vessel; two others, torn adrift, collided with each other and sank off the Custom House. Among the big deep-water merchantmen, Green's *Newcastle* and *Renown*, and Dunbar's *Camperdown*, were stranded and damaged, while the P&O steamers *Hindoostan*, *Bengal* and *Nubia*, together with the Indian Marine steam-vessel *Nemesis* – she who had awed the Chinese – were also driven ashore, unable to use their engines to ease the strain on their cables and moorings since their boilers were 'blown-down'. The devastation caused among the native craft, lighters and steam-tugs, was immense, and the loss of life incalculable as the driving rain, wind and storm surge in the river caused havoc ashore. Downstream at Saugor Island and Diamond Harbour the scene was repeated, but the material damage to shipping was worst in Esplanade Reach and its environs. As a consequence of this disaster, standing orders were issued that anchored sailing-vessels must strike their upper yards and topgallant masts during the cyclone season.

Within three weeks another cyclone struck, the full force being felt off the Sandheads where Captain Henry Toynbee had just brought the *Hotspur* to her anchor on the evening of 21 October. At about 22.30 Toynbee struck his topgallant yards and veered out his full scope of port cable as the wind rose 'with heavy squalls and tremendous rain'.

> A cyclone was manifestly passing over us. The lightning was beyond description. The rain fell in a sheet rather than in drops, and one may truly say that the darkness could be felt except when the red glare of the lightning made all visible. 2 a.m. wind began to shift to south, and round to N.W. The hardest gusts from S.W. lay the ship over as if she had been carrying a heavy press of canvas, and it must have been then that our topgallants masts blew over the side. Considering...the yards were down on deck, one could hardly have believed it possible that it could blow hard enough to carry them away; the sound of their fall was not heard on deck.

Tonybee, the prudent ship-master, had already given orders for the topgallant masts to come down, but had sent the hands for coffee before beginning the task, and, in the hiatus, nature struck. Midshipman Whall was aloft in the mizen top, the after mast being the especial charge of the midshipmen.

[T]he fearful force of the wind made any kind of work impossible, we lay clinging where we were, between sea and sky, and watched the awful spectacle. At the mast-heads sat three globes of flame — which sailors call corposants — and the flashes of lightning came down in a way I never saw but once before or since, in straight lines from sky to sea... Suddenly the middy by my side, having happened to look aloft during a lightning flash, roared out:– 'The topgallant masts are gone!' I looked up. Yes, they were hanging in the rigging, having broken off short at the topmast caps, and though we lay not 20 feet from the broken [mizen] mast we did not hear its fall in the roar of the storm.

'Jolly good job,' cried I. 'Let's get down out of this.' And down we went. [14]

Green's *Alnwick Castle*, with troops on board, was even more battered than the *Hotspur*, which she joined in the anchorage at the height of the storm. She 'had her topmasts blown clean out of her,' taking with them her fore and main lower mastheads, half the lower mizen and her long jib-boom.

Sadly the *Hotspur* was to be lost in similar circumstances off Madras in 1872, under the command of Toynbee's former first officer, Captain T.L. Porteous. She had been lying at anchor in the exposed road when, on 1 May, the anchor-age was swept by a cyclone. Several of the ships in company parted their cables, 'but the *Hotspur* was too close in,' drove ashore and broke up. Open to the east, Madras Roads were a graveyard of shipping, and in November of the previous year another of Smith's ships, the *St Lawrence*, had a lucky escape in the same vicinity. Once again Whall was a witness as the *St Lawrence* beat up for the anchorage in a heavy sea and strong north-easterly gale with vicious squalls which, at the crucial moment, caused her to miss stays. She stuck at this for two whole days, and on the 6th, after experiencing some odd atmospheric phenomena, felt the murderous force of the cyclone:

a red brick dust glare...very severe squall with strong sulphurous smell accompa-nying it and heavy rain... Moderate gale and thick dirty weather... Dirty leaden appearance to eastward and sea still getting up...wind N.N.W. increasing fast and sea rising very quickly to a tremendous height. Sent down fore and mizen topgal-lant yards. Got up mast-rope for main but were obliged to call the hands down... ship labouring fearfully and awful sea running, hove-to on port tack... Noon... blowing a hurricane... Ship lay-to very well, lee side of main deck in the water... blowing furiously... 3 p.m. (about), a tremendous gust from W.S.W. which laid the lee side of the poop in the water, starboard cutter and the main rail washed away: jib-boom went in the cap taking with it fore topgallant mast... wind at greatest force between 3 and 3.30. By 3.30 wind began to decrease and to haul rapidly to southward... 5 p.m., called all hands to clear the wreck...

It took three more days for the wounded ship to regain lost ground, and only on 9 November could Whall write:'Came to anchor in Madras Roads.'

George Thompson's *Aberdeen* of 1881 was built by Robert Napier at Glasgow and was the first ocean-going steamer to be fitted with a triple-expansion engine. Put into the Aberdeen Line's Australian service, she was to be sold to the Ottoman Turkish Government and sunk by a British submarine in 1915. Painting by C. Kennington. (© Courtesy of The British Mercantile Marine Memorial Collection)

The history of these ships is complicated by the several trades and occasional wars which offered them employment. Owners switched them to meet shifts in demand and, as steam-vessels increasingly took over the ebb and flow of the civil and military servants of the Indian Government, the Blackwallers were transferred to carry the growing traffic in emigrants. Others, indistinguishable in appearance, were built especially for the Australian trade. In a short period shipping was required to convey troops to the Black Sea during the Crimean War (1854−56), out to Calcutta for the suppression of the Indian Mutiny (1857−58), and to China during the Second Opium War (1856−60). There was also a campaign in Persia between 1856 and '57 and two military expeditions in 1867, one to the Andaman Islands, the other to Ethiopia. Of these, the first two had the greatest effect upon British shipping, while opportunities were scooped up during the American Civil War of the 1860s.

In short, the period between 1834 and 1881 produced a magnificent coda to the development of the sailing ship. At this latter date, the long-haul passenger traffic was eventually captured by the steam-vessel following George Thompson's decision to inaugurate a forty-day service to Australia with his new *Aberdeen* of the Aberdeen White Star Line. That this period roughly coincided with the better known but short-lived era of the China tea-clipper further confuses the picture. So does the transfer of many fine sailing-vessels, whose names had been made in the tea and other trades, to end their working lives under the British ensign by running the annual wool-clip from Australia to Britain. This then is the turbulent background against which the fleets of Dunbar, Smith, Willis, Devitt & Moore, Thompson, Pilkington & Wilson and James Baines earned their keep, and from which would emerge the smart lines of steam-vessels under the house-flags of the White Star, Federal Steam Navigation Co., the New Zealand Shipping Co., Shaw, Savill and Albion, among others.

Among the best known of Duncan Dunbar's Blackwallers was *La Hogue*, the largest and finest passenger ship produced by James Laing's Wearside Yard. Completed in 1855, with a length of 226ft, a beam of 35ft and an initial gross tonnage of 1,478 tons under the measurement rules introduced in the Merchant Shipping Act of the previous year (it was later reduced to 1,331), *La Hogue* was a fine full-rigged ship. She set double topsails from which, according to Captain David Bone, 'the [falling] statistics of our sea-fatalities give a definite date to their introduction' of 1854. *La Hogue* was strongly constructed with massive iron bracing inside and outside her futtocks, giving her immense strength. She had a long saloon below a poop almost 100ft in length, roomy cabins for all three classes, generously provided with water-closets, proper ventilation and a sophisticated lighting system of oil lamps. Altogether she could accommodate 150 passengers, the first and second classes aft and the intermediate forward 'where two large rooms were provided for single men'. The cabins, including eighteen first-class state-rooms, led out of the saloon that ran down the centre of the vessel under the poop, with tables and settee seating.

Under Captain Henry Neatby, *La Hogue* joined Dunbar's fleet at a time when this merchant prince owned 40,000 tons of shipping and had engaged in a great competition with Liverpool owners. These were not content with dominating the transatlantic trade to North America and wished to wrest the rapidly expanding emigrant trade to Australia from the London firms, of which Dunbar was one. We shall presently come in greater detail to the Australian trade and the *arriviste* Black Ball and White Star Lines, but Dunbar's response to Liverpudlian pressure was to build the *Dunbar* and then *La Hogue*. Despite being named after a naval battle of the war of the English Succession in 1692, *La Hogue* bore as a figurehead the Scottish lion rampant, motif of the Dunbar house-flag. She maintained a regular service to Sydney for some thirty years, carrying mail, general cargo and passengers, making one voyage to New Zealand when, in 1874, she carried 443 emigrants thither. Her loading brokers were the firm of Devitt & Moore, originally two shipping clerks who had left an established firm to set up on their own, securing the contract for loading eleven Blackwallers on the Australia run in 1836. When Dunbar took them up as his own agents in 1840, the partners were loading agents for thirty-nine vessels.

La Hogue owed her great popularity to her second commander, Captain John Williams, who joined her in 1858 and was 'a careful, fatherly man…to whom the *La Hogue's* reputation as a happy family ship was greatly due. It is said that intending passengers often waited months in order to secure a berth' in her, for Williams's first consideration was for the comfort of his passengers:

> He would not, like the captains of the Black Ball Line, take his ship down south, amongst the floe ice and icebergs of the sixty latitudes, to shorten his passage, or to

attempt to crack on with more sail set than his ship should be asked to stagger under and have the decks almost continuously under water. He spared his passengers the discomfort of the uneasy jerking roll and pitch of a ship carrying too much sail, and gave them as comfortable a time as was possible when his ship was running her easting down in the roaring forties. Yet Captain Williams made consistent passages to Sydney of from eighty to ninety days − a fortnight longer than the Liverpool clippers, but at least he had happy, contented passengers.[15]

Typically, Dunbar gave him a free hand, issuing him with only two instructions, the first of which was that he was not to take risks but to treat the ship as his own, without a penny of insurance on her. Secondly he was to remember that he was trusted as the man in charge, and it was his duty to report on the agents. It was not expected that the agents need to report on Dunbar's commanders, so that 'the Masters of their ships were Master not only in name but in reality'.

Of the *Dunbar*, also built by James Laing, something must be said. Constructed of oak timbers and 'planked, decked and even masted with teak', copper-fastened and strengthened with iron knees, her accommodation, saloon and internal fittings were beautifully appointed and her cost of over £30,000 reflected this. She was launched on 30 November 1853, at the end of the Australian gold rush, but when the emigrant passenger trade was settling into a steady stride. She rapidly became a favourite on her regular run to Sydney under the command of Captain Green. Early in 1857 she left the Thames with thirty cabin and thirty-three steerage passengers, a crew of fifty-nine and a general cargo valued at £22,000. She rapidly overtook Dunbar's newest ship, the *Duncan Dunbar*, and late on the afternoon of 20 August she was approaching the entrance to Sydney in lowering weather, with heavy rain and a rising onshore south-easterly gale. The *Dunbar* was reported to the Sydney Post Office from the South Head Signal Station as it appeared that Green's intention was to get into the shelter of the great harbour before night, but it was already dark as the *Dunbar* made her final approach, her passengers below turned-in for the night. Green apparently sent his chief and second mates, with three sharp-eyed able-seamen forward to keep a lookout and sing-out when they could see the Sow and Pigs lighthouse on a reef within the Bluff Heads that flanked the narrow entrance; all hands were on deck ready to attend any order that might suddenly be given. By some mistake, however, the ship stood in for a notch in the cliffs known as The Gap, entirely missing the entrance in the vile conditions, and when the second mate bellowed out 'Breakers ahead!' it was too late. The *Dunbar* drove ashore on rocks and took only an hour to disintegrate as the breaking seas smashed her and those aboard her to pieces. Only one man was found alive, twenty-three-year-old Able-Seaman James Johnstone, who clung to the rocks for thirty-six hours. As the news came in and the ghastly remains of the 122 people on board washed ashore, every ship in Sydney lowered her colours to half-mast, minute guns were fired and the city mourned, for among the *Dunbar*'s passengers were several people coming home after a trip to Britain. As for Johnstone; he settled in Australia and became the principal lighthouse keeper at Newcastle, New South Wales.

When Dunbar dropped dead on 6 March 1862 at the age of only fifty-eight, Neatby
bought up sixteen of Dunbar's shares, selling them on to Joseph Moore, whose firm
rapidly acquired the ownership of *La Hogue*, and it was therefore under Devitt &
Moore's house-flag that she prospered.[16] Captain Williams's methods were carried
on by his successor, William Goddard, who had been chief officer under Williams.
Goddard was master until 1874 when he transferred to the *Parramatta*, and *La Hogue*
was briefly commanded by David Corvasso until taken over in 1876 by Captain F.
Wagstaff. Wagstaff took his wife to sea with him and the pair were renowned for
making an evening promenade up and down *La Hogue's* long poop, even during her
homeward passages across the Southern Ocean and round Cape Horn. One 'fact'
alleged to *La Hogue* is that she is supposed to have been the ship responsible for introducing rabbits to Australia. On her homeward passage in 1886 she developed a serious
leak which was to dog her for the rest of her life as she defied all efforts to stop it
completely. Sold to Thomas Hick of London in 1887, she was employed in the Baltic
timber trade under a Captain Nicholson and had her hull frapped by chains, but was
soon afterwards sold again, to end as a coal-hulk at Funchal, Madeira.[17]

While the loss of spars and occasional storm-damage to deck fittings was an
accepted risk, most of the considerable number of sailing ships running regularly to
the Antipodes and back did so without serious mishap. A number, like the *Dunbar*,
came to tragic endings, and among these were a few other losses of some significance.
The first of these to be considered is the *Cospatrick*, a 1,200-ton full-rigged ship built
of teak at Moulmein for Duncan Dunbar as late as 1856 when the iron frame of composite construction was beginning to displace heavy timber futtocks. Intended for the
Indian passenger trade, the *Cospatrick's* early life was spent trooping to India during the
sepoy 'Mutiny' after which, with *The Tweed*, she was chartered to lay a telegraph cable
on the sea-bed of the Persian Gulf. Dunbar died during this task and the *Cospatrick*
resumed work on the India run in 1864 under the Fleming house-flag until her purchase by Shaw, Savill & Co. for the sum of £10,000 in 1873, whereupon she was put
onto their booming New Zealand emigrant service. She left London for Auckland
on 11 September 1874 for her second voyage with emigrants, 429 of whom joined a
crew of forty-four men under Captain Elmslie. Two months later, in the small hours
of 17 November, as she ran east before a light north-westerly breeze somewhere south
of the Cape of Good Hope, fire broke out. All hands were called, hoses were rigged
and the emigrants roused out before the seat of the fire was discovered in the paint-
locker forward. Elmslie ran off before the wind and the men plied the pump-handles
so that for a while the fire seemed contained and the smoke was blown ahead of the
Cospatrick. What happened next is unclear, but the vessel was suddenly taken aback.
The unfortunate vessel rounded up into the wind, the smoke poured aft in a dense and
impenetrable cloud, driving the men gasping from the pumps and, at a stroke, dissolved
discipline among crew and passengers alike. Within seconds the fire had taken a greater
hold, roaring through the 'tween decks and up the rigging. The oil that gave teak its
longevity added to the tarred hemp to feed the conflagration and, within ninety minutes of the first shout of 'fire!', the *Cospatrick* was ablaze from end to end.

Elmslie ordered the boats lowered but hardly had the starboard quarter-boat hit the water than a great number of jumping emigrants swamped and capsized her. With the longboat burning on deck, Elmslie's men succeeded in launching only two unprovisioned boats in which eighty-one persons got clear. The survivors were in nightclothes and Second Mate Hector MacDonald's had only a single oar available. These boats lay-to and watched as the *Cospatrick* was slowly consumed, those left aboard finally jumping into the sea, shrieking with fear, as the fire reached the poop and blew out the glass in the stern windows. Last to leave was the captain who 'was seen to throw his wife overboard and spring after her himself'. The two boats lay adrift until the wind strengthened on the night of the 21st when they lost contact despite MacDonald whistling and shouting across the wave crests next morning. In MacDonald's boat they made the best of it, rigging a sea-anchor to keep them head to wind, but a rough sea, strong wind and the tortures of thirst, hunger and hypothermia took their toll. Despite a ship passing within yards of them in the early hours of the 26th, no one heard their feeble screams. Although the weather was squally, they 'never caught a drop of water' and instead 'kept on sucking the blood of those who died'. On the 27th two more expired, one of whom they threw overboard, but they 'were too weak to lift the other'. There were now only five people left alive; 'two able seamen, one ordinary, myself and one passenger,' MacDonald testified afterwards.

> The passenger was out of his mind. All had drunk salt-water. We were all dozing when the madman bit my foot and I woke up. We then saw a ship bearing down upon us. She proved to be the *British Sceptre*, from Calcutta to Dundee. We were then taken on board and treated very kindly… I was very nigh at death's door. We were not recovered when we got to St Helena.

The passenger and ordinary seamen died aboard the *British Sceptre*, so there were but three survivors from the *Cospatrick* when they landed from their jute-laden saviour.

Fire was a constant hazard. The fate of the Black Ball Line's *Fiery Star* on 19 April 1865, shortly after leaving Moreton Bay for London with a cargo of oily wool, being a case in point. It was thought that the wool had ignited spontaneously, and initially the crew battened down and appeared to be containing the fire, but this burst forth again on the 20th. Captain Yule consequently ordered four of her boats away immediately, two others having been smashed a few days earlier by a heavy sea. The chief mate, Mr Sergeant, along with four able-seamen and thirteen apprentices, volunteered to stand-by the ship and continued to fight the fire for three weeks before their efforts seemed fruitless. They were, however, rewarded by the appearance of another vessel which answered their distress call and picked them up. This was the *Dauntless* which had herself endured a long outward passage of 135 days during which the crew had been in a constant state of unrest and near-mutiny on account of the lack of food and poor accommodation. In this they were abetted by a discontented caucus of emigrants. The *Dauntless* was making her only voyage with a human lading, and it is clear that she was unfit for a task for which her people were equally unprepared.

Captain Moore had been threatened with death off the Cape of Good Hope and, having clapped three men in irons, he and his mates had remained armed while running their easting down. Some notion of the turbulence and fractiousness that could disturb such voyages may be gained from the fact that, in addition to picking up Sergeant and his gallant band, Captain Moore had logged seventeen births and two marriages.[18] Of Captain Yule and his boats, nothing further was ever heard.

The ability with which a perfectly undistinguished crew could tackle a fire was commented on by Joseph Conrad, the novelist. Describing the crew of the wooden barque *Palestine* of which he was second mate and which caught fire in the Banka Strait, Conrad said of the men that despite being 'without the drilled-in habit of obedience' and having the appearance of 'a lot of profane scallywags without a redeeming point' in their favour, their performance when their ship caught fire had something 'inborn and subtle and everlasting,' and seemed 'solid like a principle and masterful like an instinct'.

Since the fate of the *Palestine* was not uncommon, and Conrad was a witness, it is worth recounting. The *Palestine* had been built at Sunderland in 1857 and, prior to the voyage in question, had been laid-up for some time. She loaded a cargo of 557 tons of Hartlepool coal but on sailing from England she had been in a collision which delayed her departure for three weeks. Then, while beating down Channel, she encountered heavy weather and developed a leak which obliged Captain Beard to put into Falmouth to seek repairs. This took nine long months to accomplish and required the discharge of her cargo. However, she finally got away and by 11 March 1883 was sailing north through the Banka Strait, when:

> a strong smell resembling paraffin oil was perceived... Next day smoke was discovered issuing from the coals on the port side of the main hatch. Water was thrown over them until the smoke abated, the boats were lowered, water placed in them. On the 13th some coals were thrown overboard, almost 4 tons, and more water poured down the hold. On the 14th, the hatches being on but not battened down, the decks blew up fore and aft as far as the poop...

As the *Palestine* broke up, Captain Beard, First Mate Mahon, Second Mate Korzeniowski (Conrad) and her crew took to the boats. The damp coal had caught fire by spontaneous combustion and had probably been smouldering for weeks. The boats arrived at Muntok, a small tin-exporting port on Pulo Banka, and Beard and his men eventually reached Singapore where a Court of Inquiry was held on 2 April 1883 on the loss of the barque.[19]

Just as the *Cospatrick* had begun her career trooping during the Indian Mutiny, another of Dunbar's ships, the *Northfleet*, began hers trooping to the Black Sea in the Crimean War. Named after the place of her building on the Thames, she was launched in 1853, a man being killed during the celebration. Although a first-class passenger ship, she lacked the sophisticated fitments of the later *La Hogue*, but under Captain Benjamin Freeman, who took over the *Northfleet* in 1856, she continued her military service by carrying out troops to Hong Kong for several voyages, bringing a cargo of tea home from Whampoa in between. Freeman made fast passages in her, and Dunbar rightly claimed afterwards that his ships' running costs when trooping at £17 per head were favourable to the public purse when compared with steamers. Freeman was a distinguished master who had evacuated the *Pyrenees* under the fire of Cossack cavalry when she had been a hospital ship in the Crimea. Later, in the *Northfleet*, he carried out a daring rescue of the crew of a water-logged brig, the *Hebe*, Captain Stratton, in the North Atlantic in November 1858.[20] Heaving-to, to windward of the derelict, the *Northfleet*'s long-boat was veered down on a line and the *Hebe*'s people plucked out of her. Second mate Arthur Knight, in charge of the boat, was presented with a handsome telescope by the Board of Trade for this, and each of the boat's crew earned a bonus of £2.

When Dunbar died, Freeman bought the *Northfleet* from his executors, Gellatly & Co. Retiring himself, he put his chief officer, William Symington, in command, and she continued to bring tea home during the early tea-races of the 1860s. Outward-bound with a general cargo in May 1866, Symington nursed her through a typhoon and this event seemed to mark a change in the *Northfleet*'s fortunes. In 1868 she was sold, then sold again in 1871, to a J. Patton, who placed her under the command of a Captain T. Oates and then a Captain Knowles, who engaged her in the emigrant trade. In January 1873, full of passengers mainly consisting of 'railway navvies and their wives and families,' she sailed from the Thames for Tasmania. Running into heavy westerly weather and mindful of his charges who would have suffered severely from sea-sickness so soon after departure, Knowles tucked her under the lee of Dungeness and anchored. Although windy, the night was clear and the *Northfleet* burned her regulation anchor light, but at 22.30 and before the anchor-watch could do much about it, a steamer ran into the *Northfleet* at speed, almost cutting her in two. Instead of remaining in the gash and reducing the ingress of water, the steamer went astern to escape into the darkness, leaving the sea to pour into the stricken ship. The terri-fied emigrants rushed the boats and compelled Knowles to fire his revolver to restore order and evacuate the women and children, while the mate and crew tried to stem the inflow with a collision mat made from spare sails. Knowles managed to get one boat away containing his wife and several other women, but within fifteen minutes of the collision the *Northfleet*'s deck was awash and five minutes later she was on the sea-bed, her topgallant masts and yards above water the only refuge for survivors. There were only a dozen of these, all members of the ship's crew; Knowles and 292 other souls – men, women and children – all drowned. Mrs Knowles received a state pension while, in a pitiless sequel, a handful of the *Northfleet*'s penniless crew were put on stage in a music-hall act in which their individual survival stories were told by a posturing orator. The offending steamer was tracked down in a European port with damaged bows. She was the Spanish-flagged *Murillo* which, as a consequence of having no name upon her bow, as was then quite common, prompted the Board of Trade to issue a regulation under which all vessels under the British merchant flag must display their name on either bow.

Other losses by collision, fire, stranding and foundering occurred – and Duncan Dunbar was unfortunate in this respect – but by far the oddest loss was the disappearance of the *Madagascar* in 1853. Like her sister-ship the *Seringapatam*, the *Madagascar* was one of Green's fastest and most popular ships but, unlike her sister, the *Madagascar's* history culminates in the greatest mystery among those ships 'posted-missing' at Lloyd's. The facts are few, far-between and connected only by speculation, but they are as follows. In July 1853 the *Madagascar* lay in Port Phillip with the blue and white signal flag for departure – the 'Blue Peter' – at the fore-truck. On board were a large number of passengers, some of whom had made good at the gold-diggings, and Captain Fortescue Harris had 68,390 ounces of pure gold secured in his lazarette. As the ship awaited her pilot, a boat full of police came alongside. They bore warrants for the arrest of two passengers suspected of having taken part in a recent armed-robbery. After a search, a quantity of gold dust was discovered in the suspects' baggage and the *Madagascar's* sailing was delayed while she waited upon events.

While the law took its time, most of Harris's crew deserted and he was obliged to resort to the usual scouring of the waterfront bars, brothels and hotels for likely seamen. While he was doing so, the *Roxburgh Castle* arrived from London on the 21st, having on board a Mrs de Cartaret, her three children and – it is thought – their nurse, all on their way to join Mr de Cartaret, an emigrant lawyer. On boarding the *Roxburgh Castle* her pilot brought the customary bundle of newspapers in which the unfortunate Mrs de Cartaret discovered herself a widow. Without means of support, she arranged to return home immediately and she, her family and baggage, transferred to the *Madagascar*. Having manned his ship a few days later, Captain Harris and the *Madagascar* departed and thereafter vanished.

Such tragedies were not unknown; ships occasionally disappeared without trace, overwhelmed by heavy weather or holed by ice. Normally, after a period of being 'posted-missing', she would have been forgotten, as were so many, except that odd rumours fuelled speculation as to her fate. The presence of gold on board added to the possibility that ill-disposed persons – and Harris was known to have signed-on some ne'er-do-wells – had wrecked the ship and escaped with the treasure, but it was not until many years later that a possible explanation surfaced. Towards the end of the century an elderly woman on her death-bed in New Zealand requested the presence of a clergyman to whom she confided she had been a nurse aboard the *Madagascar*. She had, she said, witnessed a mutinous seizure of the ship off the coast of Brazil by a handful of the crew and passengers. Harris and his officers had been murdered, the loyal seamen and passengers confined below. Boats had then been lowered and provisioned, and a number of the younger women sufficient to pair-off with the conspirators put in them, whereupon the *Madagascar* was set on fire. According to the woman's testimony, only one boat containing six survivors reached the coast where it capsized in the surf and the gold dust was lost. When the party reached a small village they found that yellow fever was rife and only the woman and two of the men were left after a few weeks. How the supposed survivor reached New Zealand is unclear, though not impossible, and dark doings are hinted by her claim that one of the men who degraded her was later hanged in San Francisco for murder.

Such tragedies must be offset by the huge numbers of voyages that were accomplished without incident, or at least incident worth recalling. That matters did not always go smoothly may be gleaned from a curious paper given to Captain Thomas Mitchell of the Aberdeen White Star ship *Queen of Nations* by his passengers on a voyage from Sydney to London. This accompanied the customary vote of thanks signed by several passengers in which they desired to 'express our grateful thanks to you…for the skill and care with which, under God's providence, you have conducted us over so many thousands of miles of ocean…' In the second document the signatories also wished to 'certify that the behaviour… of Mr and Mrs Holliday throughout the passage has been most unbecoming, disgraceful and offensive to Captain Mitchell and ourselves'. Adding that Mitchell had been 'most forbearing towards them under circumstances which would have justified severe measures', they concluded that they fully concurred 'in the course pursued by Captain Mitchell throughout the unpleasant and trying circumstances connected with the ill conduct of Mr Charles Jones and Miss Allerton'. Such were among the manifold concerns of a passenger-ship commander in the 1860s.

Among the best-known full-rigged ships active in the mid-nineteenth century was *The Tweed* — the definite article included in her name to distinguish her from other ships named after the river. This big full-rigger links the history of the East India Company with the wider mercantile marine, for she was built as the *Punjaub* by Curtsetjee Rustomjee, the master ship-builder of the Wadia dynasty of Bombay, as a steam paddle-frigate for the Indian Marine. She was designed by Oliver Lang and only the finest Malabar teak was selected for her construction, making *The Tweed*, according to legend, among the most expensive wooden vessels ever constructed. With a length of 285ft in length, a beam of almost 40ft and a tonnage of 1,745, she was launched on 21 April 1854, armed with ten 68-pounder guns and powered by 700hp paddle-engines sent out from Britain. She was not commissioned until 2 January following, but was immediately ordered to fit out for trooping. Embarking two squadrons of the 10th Prince of Wales's Hussars, she sailed for Suez from Bombay under Commander John Young on 9 January 1855, immediately proving herself a fast ship, even under power. Having delivered the hussars on their way to the Crimea, she joined the expeditionary force sent up the Persian Gulf from Bombay that November under Commander A. Foulerton. She was in action against shore batteries and cruised in the Gulf before returning to Bombay in time to be sent to Calcutta where the sepoy rebellion had broken out. Here she remained as a guardship for some time, again seeing action against the insurgents, and after a brief hiatus ended her service in the Indian Marine in 1860 off Zanzibar. From here the *Punjaub* and her sister-ship the *Assaye* were ordered to Britain to be fitted as screw-steamers, but on their arrival the absorption of the Indian Marine into the Royal Navy rendered them redundant.

Both *Punjaub* and *Assaye* were purchased by a London-based ship-owner named John Willis. The Willis family hailed from Berwickshire, retaining a strong affinity

with the Border Country and deriving their ships' names from Scotland. Owing to
his sporting a tall top-hat made of white felt, John junior was known as 'White-Hat'
Willis, and he took the engines out of the two vessels, renamed the *Punjaub* as *The
Tweed*, fitted her with a fine figurehead of Tam o' Shanter, and appointed a Scot named
William Stuart as master. Having secured a Government contract and converted the
vessels accordingly, *The Tweed* and the *Assaye* then joined Dunbar's *Cospatrick* in laying
the telegraph cable between Bombay and Basra in 1863. Following this, they returned
to Bombay to be restored to serviceable passenger ships. After bringing home the
Seaforth Highlanders, Willis sold the *Assaye* but retained *The Tweed* in the Indian service in which she successfully brought home sick troops for whom it was feared the
overland route via Suez would prove fatal.

The Tweed was, by now, well known as Willis's flagship. On her outward voyages she
often went first to Sydney or Calcutta, occasionally going to China and, like other
fine sailing-vessels in the right conditions, could overtake a steamer. When Willis
switched her to the Australian run, she came home from Melbourne in eighty-three
days, thereafter consistently making outward and homewards runs in similar times. In
June 1874 *The Tweed* embarked emigrants for New Zealand and continued a popular
ship under Stuart's successor, Captain Byce. Stuart had been appointed to command
the new *Loch Etive*, and Byce was followed in *The Tweed* by Captain J.M. Whyte, who
customarily took her to Hong Kong from Sydney to load tea for the homeward passage. 'Gentleman' Whyte succeeded in getting caught aback in the Southern Ocean
and lost spars, though this did not prevent *The Tweed* reaching Sydney in ninety-three
days. In 1885 *The Tweed* was taken over by Captain Moore, who had served as chief
mate under Stuart. Moore had been the *Cutty Sark*'s first master and disappointed
Willis in failing to drive the specially built tea-clipper, as we shall note in due course,
but loyalty to his officers was characteristic of Willis. Moore's performance in *The
Tweed* was no better, but she continued to earn her owner good freights, bringing
home from Australia mixed cargoes of 30,000 dried bullock hides, thousands of cases
of tallow and canned meat in her lower holds, while her 'tween decks were tightly
packed with bales of wool. On 18 July 1888, having sailed to China for a homeward
cargo for New York, she was east-bound and off Algoa Bay, South Africa, when she
was dismasted. A passing steamer got a line aboard and towed her into port but she
was leaking badly and the decision was made to sell her for breaking-up. Some of her
heavy futtocks were incorporated in the roof of a church in Port Elizabeth.

It is clear that while an outstanding ship like *The Tweed* owed much to her design,
the happier conjunction of a fine ship with a highly competent master was crucial to
fast passage-making under sail. This will become most apparent when considering the
tea-races, for which speed was of the utmost importance in securing the greatest profit
from a voyage, but smart passages were invariably to be aimed at, and a reputable captain could command his pick of ships. One of these was William Stuart who, as noted
above, left the teak *The Tweed* for the iron *Loch Etive*, built by J. & A. Inglis in 1877.
Stuart, who left Willis's employment to take the *Loch Etive* from her builders – she was
owned by the Glasgow-based Loch Line of Aitken, Lilburn & Co. – was not only a

great seaman, he was also a shrewd businessman and ideal for the new, heavily sparred, 1,235-ton full-rigged ship. The *Loch Etive* was put on the berth for Sydney and usually came home with wool or wheat, but on the ship's maiden voyage Stuart secured a cargo of jute from Calcutta and went thither in ballast. A hard-driving sailor who did not suffer fools, Stuart was apt to over-awe his junior officers, one of whom left a vivid picture of him. 'I am sure he meant well, and I am certain that never, not even at the time, could I bear him malice for his extraordinary gift of incisive criticism', one recalled, but it was 'often a stormy process'. Stuart left the deck to his young third mate, Joseph Conrad, with two contradictory instructions, the first of which was not to take sail off the ship, and the second, not to carry anything away. He must have been a hard task-master, but Conrad's anecdote of shortening down when the wind shifted suddenly is revealing as to the constant anxieties of a sailing ship master, of relying upon less experienced men to stand their watch and look after the vessel, and the mental and physical toughness, judgement and endurance required to accomplish it all successfully. It was significant that Stuart had not come up on deck and interfered, but after shortening sail and at the end of his watch, Conrad was summoned to the captain's cabin where Stuart lay in his bunk reading. Entering, Conrad was asked what had happened. The *Loch Etive*'s third mate explained the wind had flown round onto the lee quarter. Could Conrad not see the wind-shift coming? Stuart asked. 'Yes, sir, I thought it wasn't very far off,' he admitted. Then why, Stuart pressed him 'in a tone that ought to have made my blood run cold, did you not have the courses hauled up at once?'

> But this was my chance and I did not let it slip. 'Well, sir,' I said in an apologetic tone, 'she was going eleven knots very nicely, and I thought she would do for another half-hour or so.' He gazed at me darkly out of his head, lying very still on the white pillow, for a time. 'Ah, yes, another half-hour. That's the way ships get dismasted.' And that was all I got in the way of a wigging.

Such insights are all too rare, and so, one suspects, was Stuart himself. He died aboard the *Loch Etive*, five days after leaving Glasgow on 16 September 1894. It was his sixty-third birthday and he had been a ship-master for forty-three years, during which time he had never lost a man or a mast overboard. Mr Wade, the chief mate, took the ship over and reached Adelaide in ninety-eight days where command was taken over by the mate of the *Loch Garry* who was senior to Wade.[21] Captain Fishwick commanded her until he shifted into the *Loch Torridon* in 1909, overseeing the reduction of her rig to a barque in 1904 and being followed by Captain Anderson, late of the *Loch Katrine*, who held the command until the *Loch Etive* was sold to the French in 1911.

As for Conrad, he felt that conflict of vocational tug and economic self-interest common to many a hopeful but frustrated young officer. In receipt of a small but useful allowance from his uncle, Conrad wrote to his friend Spiridon Kliszczewski in November 1885 that he wished to work for himself and that he was 'sick and tired of sailing about for little money and less consideration. But I love the sea: and if I could just clear my bare living…I should be comparatively happy.'

Unhappily, even in a crack-ship at this late date, not all subordinate officers were competent, as Captain Mitchell, commanding Thompson's *Centurion* at the time, complains to a friend, Captain Edward:

> I am not at all pleased with my mate. He is, without exception, the greatest booby I ever saw on a ship's quarterdeck. He has never been able to work a chronometer sight for me, and not even a course and distance....and there is a man who comes around to me from the Noble Board of Trade (of which by the bye, you are a Noble Member) with a Master's Certificate... My Second Mate cannot work a sight, or a course and distance either. He has a 2nd Mate's Certificate...although no Navigator [he] is a good sailor. I have the best crew on board that I ever sailed with, but I am afraid this blockhead of a mate will soon spoil them.

Mitchell tried tutoring them both, but it is clear from subsequent correspondence that while the second mate improved, the chief mate suffered from some sort of personality disorder.

Among the smaller ships serving the *Raj*, those of the London ship-owners, W.H. Tindall & Co., were notable in their day for their smartness. As representative of similar shipping houses they are worthy of closer examination. By the 1860s the Tindalls owned several full-rigged ships, notably the *Avon*, *Severn*, *Tweed*, *Teviot*, *Thames*, *Wynand* and the largest, the *Nimrod* of about 700 tons, most of which were fitted with Cunningham's patent reefing topsails, an attempt to manage the traditional deep topsail prior to its division into two. Tindall owned coffee plantations in Ceylon and his ships, originally registered in Scarborough but later in London, carried an outward general cargo of 'Manchester goods' consisting of machinery, cotton cloth and other manufactures, bringing coffee home. Like many other ship-owners, the Tindall family were strict Quakers and, as was common among them as we noted in the case of Captain Were, had originally forbidden their masters to carry arms until the *Morning Star* was taken by pirates.[22]

This ship, a slow-sailer, had been homeward bound from Ceylon in 1832 with a number of sick soldiers among a handful of passengers – which included some females – when off Ascension on 21 February she fell in with the notorious Benito de Soto. De Soto was a Portuguese slaver-turned-pirate who had seized his brigantine, the *Defensor de Pedro*, and renamed her *Black Joke*. Ranging up alongside the *Morning Star* with his boarders ready and loaded guns trained on his quarry, De Soto ordered Captain Souley aboard with his papers, but a gentleman passenger offered to go across in the boat in his stead and sue for terms. In this the volunteer was disappointed, receiving blows for his trouble and returned to the *Morning Star* to repeat the pirate's demand for Souley's presence. Having gained the *Black Joke*'s deck, Captain Souley, with his second mate and a small escort of the fitter soldiers, confronted the fearsome De Soto, who drew his sword and cleft Souley's skull. His chief mate struck the *Morning Star*'s second mate dead and the *Black Joke* fired a hail of grape into the waist of the *Morning Star* under her lee.

Boarding their prize and tumbling both the crew and the sick soldiers into the hold, from which one officer died directly, the pirates looted the *Morning Star*, cleared her out of liquor and raped the women before slashing the rigging and boring some holes through her bottom with an auger. They then abandoned her to her fate. Meanwhile the men in the hold contrived to work themselves free and came on deck at sunset to find a scene of utter devastation and the ship settling under them. Plugging the holes and effecting repairs, they obtained assistance from another vessel which they encountered next day. In due course the *Morning Star* reached the Thames to cause 'a great sensation'. Some time later, having wrecked the *Black Joke* near Cadiz, De Soto was actually recognised by one of the soldiers from the *Morning Star* who, on his way to Malta, had gone ashore at Gibraltar. Spotting the pirate, the soldier laid evidence against him and De Soto was found with stolen goods directly traceable to the *Morning Star*, including Souley's pocket-book. He was tried, condemned and hanged.

As a consequence of this foul act, Tindall's ship bore arms, and even thirty years later, in 1864, as was common in most merchantmen, the *Avon* carried:

> two four-pounder and two one-pounder swivels fixed aft, one on each quarter, 12 muskets, 12 pistols, and the same number of cutlasses and boarding pikes, with suitable ammunition for all carried in two copper tanks, padlocked and stowed aft in the lazarette. The small arms were all placed in racks in the saloon and under the break of the poop.

It was one of the apprentice's duties 'to keep those under the poop properly cleaned and greased,' recalled Captain N.G. Hatch in 1926. Built for cargo and passengers, the *Avon*:

> was practically all poop and fo'c's'le, as the former reached to the mainmast, with an overhang break of quite six feet, under which on each side were the cabins of the first and second mates. There was accommodation for ten first-class passengers besides two cabins with a small messroom for a few second class. The fo'c's'le came well abaft the foremast, the galley being under the fo'c's'le deck, abaft the mast, with a door on each side. We boys berthed in the fo'c's'le on the starboard side, a bulkhead going fore and aft, as far as the windlass, separating us from the men. Abaft our berth and divided by a bulkhead was the halfdeck (as it was called), accommodating the carpenter, boatswain and cook.

Hatch was an apprentice aboard the *Avon* when she sailed from the West India Docks on the Thames for Colombo in late May 1864 under Captain John Edmonds. Her first-class accommodation was full, which obliged her to carry a doctor, her passengers having paid £150 for the passage, which included wines and spirits. Livestock was taken aboard from a lighter off Erith and the last passengers embarked at Gravesend where the river-pilot was relieved by the sea-pilot. The *Avon*'s deck was encumbered by a large boiler on its way to Ceylon, and its securing was supervised by the mate, a

Mr Somerville, who 'was not liked by anyone' and was fond of striking the apprentices with a piece of line. The second mate was a man named Smith and the third,
an anomalous lad named Read, was 'an apprentice who held a second mate's ticket'.
Read may have been too young and awaiting a birthday before his qualifications
became valid, but he was a protégé of Edmonds. In addition to her apprentices, she
carried a boatswain, carpenter, cook and twelve able-seamen. These were:

> a fine lot of chaps…mostly hailing from London; a few were up in years, but still as
> active as the youngest. They were of a type which I fear is no more, growling occa-
> sionally, of course, but the first on deck when all hands were called out to shorten
> sail, and taking as much, if not more, interest in keeping the ship clean and doing
> work properly as did the after-guard.

Hatch recorded later that his:

> first attempt to stow the mizen royal was severely criticised by the second mate, in
> whose watch I was, but Captain Edmonds, hearing him calling me a young lubber,
> quietly enquired whether he had shown me the way to stow a sail. Mr Smith reply-
> ing in the negative, the captain sent me aloft to loose the sail and, to my surprise,
> mounted up after me, and standing on the topgallant yard [immediately below]
> directed me in every detail how to gather up and furl the sail, remarking emphati-
> cally when I had finished, 'Mind, I never have to tell you this again'.

The line-crossing ceremony persecuted the two first-trip apprentices, of whom
Hatch was one, largely for the amusement of the passengers. As the *Avon* was running
her easting down off the Cape of Good Hope she was 'nearly caught by the lee, and
the captain and the second mate, rushing to the wheel and starboarding hard, just
saved the old ship from disaster. As it was we shipped some heavy water…' The *Avon*
arrived at Colombo after a long passage of 131 days and fired two guns in salute, to
which another of Tindall's ships, the *Wynand*, dipped her ensign. There was then no
breakwater to provide refuge off Colombo and the prevailing south-west monsoon
caused a steady rolling of the anchored ship. This made the disembarkation of the
passengers difficult and greatly complicated the discharge of the heavy-lift cargo of
the boiler lashed on her main-deck. This was hoisted out and lowered onto a lighter
by rigging a special derrick, the crew having first unshipped the mainyard and cleared
the ship's side. This done, the crew were assisted by coolie labour to discharge the rest
of the *Avon*'s cargo.

The *Wynand*'s master, a Welshman named Jones, flew 'the Bethel flag' on Sundays
and held a chapel service to which all were thereby invited. When her homeward
lading was completed, Captain Edmonds, his second mate and some of the seamen
were pulled over to the *Wynand* in the boats and helped Jones and his people get
her under way, a co-operation common to the times after a vessel had lain off a
port for some time and dug her anchor well-in. The *Avon* herself loaded about 150

three-quarter-ton casks of coconut oil as a ground tier in her lower hold on the top of which were laid casks of coffee, graphite (then commonly called plumbago) and rolls of coir, the fibrous by-product of coconuts. The work of loading was hard on her crew and Edmonds issued tots of rum by way of encouragement. The last sling was brought aboard with a seaman sitting astride it waving his cap to the cheering of all hands, after which, as the hatches were put on, a tot was doled out. With the Blue Peter hoisted to the *Avon*'s fore-truck, the crew of the iron barque *Palestine* (the same which Conrad later abandoned) came aboard to help weigh the anchor. A few passengers were embarked, 'mostly invalids…suffering from fever; but in less than a month most of them were quite well…' One, an army major, did not recover and Edmonds was obliged to put in to Simon's Bay to land him and his wife. The *Avon* next called at St Helena, 'anchoring there for a short time to give the passengers a run on shore.'

Edmonds took considerable trouble to exercise his apprentices in taking in and making sail, even when they were on watch below, making them masters of their chosen craft. The lads were taught the rudiments of navigation by the junior officers and they assisted the boatswain and three able-seamen to shift a new fore lower mast when rot was discovered in this heavy spar in London at the end of the next voyage. Such experience stood an aspiring officer in good stead. Edmonds must have taken a dim view of the unpopular Mr Somerville, who was discharged on arrival at London, Hatch records with more than a hint of glee. He appears not to have harboured any grudge, though time may have dimmed any resentment, for he wrote long afterwards: 'The captain and officers treated us fairly, taught us our work and made us practical sailors… If we got punished, as we often did, it was our own look-out…'

Unlike the Blackwall frigates with their regular service, Tindall's ships, though designed to support their owner's distant coffee plantations, might be chartered to others, particularly in later years when a leaf-disease destroyed the coffee shrubs and the planters switched to tea. On a subsequent voyage, the *Avon* was chartered by Hong Kong Chinese and shipped a Chinese supercargo to supervise the acquisition of a cargo of bean-cake at Xnau Da Bunglam in Cochin China. No charts existed of the place so Edmonds anchored and lowered a boat. Mr Read – the third mate of the earlier voyage who had now been promoted to chief officer – took charge and, with the apprentices at the oars, sounded his way in, marking a passage with buoys made from cork fenders and life-preservers, 'attached to which for moorings were pigs of kentledge'. Once the passage had been marked, the *Avon* was brought inshore and safely anchored. Here, during two months of hard labour, the *Avon*'s crew took out the ballast and loaded the compressed, cartwheel-sized bean-cake from native canoes, to be used in southern China for fertilizer in the cultivation of fruit and vegetables. The *Avon*'s 'tween decks were filled with a malodorous cargo of bales of dried shark's fin, garlic and large wooden tanks full of bean-oil, work that was very demanding on the British crew in the airless climate. The bean-cake was usually made from the soya bean after it had been pressed for oil, and the loose or baled cakes filled the lower-hold where it was liable to heat and ignite by spontaneous combustion.

Once loaded, the *Avon* sailed for Foochow where she was to discharge her cargo and, having fulfilled her charter and disembarked the Chinese supercargo, she loaded tea for London. Although this was the era of the crack clippers, the *Avon* was not loading the first of the harvest, sharing the lading of the residual crop with Brocklebank's *Maiden Queen*, Captain Ray, her consort in this hum-drum traffic.

We must now return to 1833 to consider the consequences of the other great reforming Act that affected British shipping, the final abolition of slavery throughout the British Empire. The Act of Parliament which declared slavery illegal in all British colonies was accompanied by a disbursement of some £20 million sterling by way of compensation to their former owners. No such compensation was offered to the former slaves but, to preserve the economies of the West Indian sugar islands, they were required to continue working on their plantations as indentured labour for three quarters of every week until August 1838. Understandably, if hopelessly optimistic, the black population of about 770,000 expected a rise in their fortunes, but their liberation coincided with a fall in the market price of sugar and a decline in the plantation system to which their own manumission contributed. Most abandoned the sugar-cane fields and followed a path outside the scope of this work, but one which consigned them to an economic servility in which their only dignity was that they had at least become 'the sellers of labour'. Conditions in the various islands varied, but plantation bosses accustomed to a docile and biddable labour force or, failing this, one which could be beaten into submission, shied away from employing former slaves. Despite having received enormous sums in compensation for the loss of their 'property', they again sought cheap labour.

Although an illegal slave-trade continued, particularly to the Spanish island of Cuba, both Spain and France followed the British lead in the liberation of the black workers, causing a similar demand for tractable, inexpensive workers in their own islands. This requirement was met by what became known as 'the Coolie trade': the shipping-in of indentured labour from two sources, the Indian sub-continent and China.

The wholesale shipping of vast numbers of people across the world is a marked feature of the nineteenth century:

> Immigration was in keeping with the spirit of the age. The eighteenth century had seen the movement under compulsion of vast numbers of people from West Africa to the Americas. The nineteenth…saw an even greater free movement of people from Europe and Asia. In the sixty years after Waterloo some 7,000,000 people went from the United Kingdom alone to the [British] colonies. In the ten years immediately after 1815 the population of Canada rose from 80,000 to 150,000. At the same time, in the East, the Chinese were making their way down through Indo-China to Java and the islands of the Pacific. The emigration of Indian labour on a large scale began in 1830 when a French merchant took 130 Indian artisans to [the Île de] Bourbon. By 1847 there were 7,000 Indians in Mauritius and the movement of Indians into Africa had also begun.[23]

Set against the vast shifts of white populations under the influences of such events as the Irish Potato Famine and the several gold strikes occurring some years later, the lifting of numerous indigent and unfortunate people from India and China (and other places such as Madeira) has been forgotten. The numbers were not as great, nor the outcomes as positive, as the European migrations, yet the trade persisted for about seventy years, was hugely influential and accounts for the rich ethnic mix in the destination countries today. In the troubled West Indian islands of the late 1830s, and soon afterwards in South Africa and Mauritius, the labour market cried out for cheap workers. The notion of shipping people from the east had been exploited for some time, especially to remote spots like St Helena, where tasks requiring labour were not unknown. Indeed, the confinement of Napoleon on the island in 1816 – leased from the East India Company for the purpose – increased emigration to St Helena, whose governor, General Sir Hudson Lowe, wished for 'a few Chinese [to be]...sent in each [East India] ship', and this was to be continued until about 350 were settled in the island, masons and carpenters being much in demand.

The opportunities offered to ship-owners to facilitate this diaspora even further were swiftly recognised, but: 'The British Government was not unnaturally suspicious of any scheme that might conceivably lead to a revival of slavery...', until John Gladstone, father of a later and Liberal Prime Minister and then himself a prominent Liverpool ship-owner, secured permission to ship Indian labourers into Guiana under the terms of a five year contract. British ship-owners, especially those of Liverpool, had grown accustomed to the transportation of human cargoes, that of slaves having long been their particular maritime expertise, but since the departure of the First Fleet for Van Dieman's Land with its lading of miserable convicts, Government had had a regulatory hand in the matter, as we have noted. This was not immediately the case with the new trade, which got off to a bad start both in terms of losses of life on passage and resistance to Government intervention by the Colonial Office. It was not until 1847 that the Imperial Government passed a Coolie Immigration Act which initiated a series of regulations, subject from time-to-time to revision both by Parliament in London and by the colonial administrations, that the Crown Agents for the colonies did in the end supervise the trade, supplied and fixed the appropriate scale of necessary stores for the carriage of emigrants and appointed the surgeon-superintendents in the same way as aboard convict ships.

In essence the regulations laid down conditions of carriage which in turn influenced the design or modification of the sailing ships which undertook this work. Registered tonnage being a measure of capacity, at 100-cubic-ft per registered ton, a vessel's ability to embark coolies was on the basis of 1.5 registered tons per coolie, though later this was subject to a formula based on covered deck space. Lessons of basic hygiene had been learned in the transportation of convicts, along with the doctrine of cleanliness being next to godliness. Ventilation and exercise were practised where possible, though bad weather put a terrible strain on all concerned, and several ships and their unfortunate human cargoes suffered typhoons. Welfare of the human cargo was vested in the surgeon-superintendent whose writ, in all things other than the handling and navigation of the ship, ran higher than the master's. It was his responsibility to examine those coming aboard, particularly for symptoms of contagious diseases such as measles, scarlet fever, smallpox, typhoid and typhus. Perhaps most dreaded of all was cholera which, in January of 1860, was discovered aboard the *Thomas Hamlin*. The disease did not manifest itself until the ship was clear of the Hughli and she was obliged to put in to Table Bay with fifty-eight of her 400 coolies dead. By the time she arrived at the bar of the Demerara River in Guiana, she had lost another two dozen.

The surgeon-superintendent also had to ensure the vessel had a deck-house available as a hospital, that the 'tween decks were adequately ventilated in good weather and watertight in bad, that 'native' cooking arrangements were adequate and safe and awnings were spread in very hot sunshine. The surgeon was appointed and verified by a colonial Government officer known as the Protector of Immigrants who acted on behalf of the Crown Agents and instructed his appointee to: 'watch over the conduct of the master and officers of the ship in all that relates to the emigrants... [This] will require the exercise of as much discretion and firmness as your relations with the emigrants...' Surgeons were not on the ship's articles, nor were they paid a salary, but they received an allowance based on head-money of 10s per emigrant (rising by the end of the century to one guinea). The sum was liable to forfeiture in part or in whole if a surgeon-superintendent was guilty of dereliction of duty, and was based upon the emigrants arriving in good health. To prevent them being influenced by a ship's master, surgeons were conveyed out to India as passengers on P&O steamers and repatriated from the West Indies by the Royal Mail Steam Packet Co., sailing in their appointed transport only when she carried coolies.

A coolie ship's third mate also received a capitation allowance since he acted as a quasi-purser. With a half-a-crown payment for every labourer safely landed, a third mate could expect to make about £300 per year for his work supervising the distribution of Government stores put aboard for the feeding and welfare of the coolies, matters that were taken out of the ship-master's hands. Another key man was the engineer, a surprising rank to find on a sailing-vessel, but whose duty was to tend the auxiliary steam machinery, chief of which was the condensing plant providing about 800 gallons of water daily. He too earned a gratuity, conditional upon the surgeon's favourable report.

Most of these ships had Indian crews, a circumstance that to some extent put the apprehensive emigrants at ease, and trusted crew-members were appointed to liaise with them and pass instructions. Chief among these intermediaries were two 'compounders', or *baboos*.[24] There were also the *bandarries*, or storekeepers, who doled out the rations of salt fish and rice, soap and so forth, and the lowly *topazes*, or sweepers, who ensured the emigrants' messes were kept clean.

Most of these economically displaced Indian emigrants came from the central northern and north-eastern parts of the Indian sub-continent, though others came from the desperately poor areas of Travancore and the Carnatic. They undertook to serve a five-year indentured 'apprenticeship', an arrangement that guaranteed them low wages but ensured they were fed and housed. The exploitative nature of this wholesale trans-shipment of human beings has to be set against the conditions which most seemed content enough to leave. For the ship-owners, ship-masters and even their 'native' crews, the 'coolie-trade' simply answered the laws of demand-and-supply. Business was business and the white man had, he thought at the time, a burden to assume.

Chief among the owners serving Mauritius was the fleet of John Allan of London, who employed about a dozen wooden sailing ships, most built in Sunderland but others which were constructed of teak in the shipyards of Bombay and Moulmein. He also picked up bargains such as the *Lincelles* sold after the death of Duncan Dunbar in 1862. Ships other than Allan's took part, and it was aboard the *Shah Jehan* that there occurred an incident which, at the time, was briefly notorious. Bound from Calcutta to Mauritius under a Captain J. Bentham with a crew of seventy-five, the *Shah Jehan* bore 410 Indian emigrants, including women and children. On the morning of 27 June 1859, about 1,100 miles short of her destination, a fire broke out on board. Although Bentham and some of his crew hove the ship to and began to fight the fire, it took a firm hold of the ship, and at noon Bentham had no option but to abandon her. With the four ship's boats inadequate to the task of rescuing all on board, the hands not employed in fire-fighting had constructed three substantial rafts from the spare and studding-sail spars.

By now, however, the sea was rough. Nevertheless, not without a struggle, the rafts were got overboard, the boats lowered and provisioned and Bentham ordered everyone off the ship. Many of the Indians were terrified. None had seen the sea before taking passage, but all understood the danger of fire. Most clambered onto the rafts while some thirty refused to budge. In the panic and confusion about seventy were lost overboard and drowned, and with them went the *Shah Jehan*'s third mate, her doctor, gunner and twelve of her sailors.

Bentham and about sixty of his crew escaped in two of the boats. The ship burned for three days before sinking, but by then the boats and rafts had become separated and Bentham set a course for Mauritius, being 'obliged to leave the rafts to their fate'. The boats made about sixty miles a day and after five days were picked up by the French ship *Vasco da Gama*. Any pleas to search for others made by Bentham to her master fell on deaf ears, for the *Vasco da Gama* made directly for La Reunion, without returning to the last known position of the *Shah Jehan*. Although Bentham and his officers were exonerated of any blame at the Court of Inquiry, the fact remains that only one coolie was ever rescued.

The first ship to land emigrants in Trinidad was the *Australia*, Captain Noble, owned by the Liverpool house of Charles Moore & Co., which delivered 443 Chinese coolies in March 1853. She was unusual among these early coolie-carriers in being built of Canadian soft-wood. Most 'coolie-ships' were either oak or teak, and no longer young. A number of Wigram Green's Blackwall frigates, made redundant from their original occupations, proved relatively comfortable carriers. At this period the complement of emigrants varied from between some 270 to 480 souls, though the numbers increased later. The first transportation of Chinese was not to the West

Indies but to the Straits Settlements, notably Penang and the rapidly expanding port-city of Singapore.

The trans-shipment of several thousand Chinese coolies to the West Indies was not considered particularly successful since they were insufficiently obedient to their masters' requirements. Moreover, it was a less popular task with the ships' companies concerned, being regarded as a more dangerous occupation than the carriage of Indians. The Chinese often proved rebellious, particularly in bad weather when terror, confinement and squabbling could spark trouble. Violence broke out aboard the *Sophia Fraser*, Captain McKellar, in November 1846, a few weeks before the introduction of proper regulation, a surgeon and condensed fresh water. The ship was three days out of Amoy and bound for Penang when she ran into a typhoon in the South China Sea. McKellar hove-to and hoped to ride out the tropical revolving storm, but heavy seas came aboard and tore at the ship's fabric so that: 'The Chinese passengers were helpless, and in a most deplorable condition.' Although McKellar tried to get the ship before the wind, as it shifted, he was frustrated and his anxiety for his passengers increased. While it was necessary to prevent water from getting below, battened hatches were not merely claustrophobic, they excluded fresh air. In order to ventilate his 'tween-decks, a tented arrangement was tried with limited success, though it denied access to the upper deck. Hours passed while McKellar and his crew struggled to save their ship, then terrible noises emanated from below. Those on deck 'had no means of ascertaining the cause…without opening the covering of the hatches which would have allowed the sea to enter.'

The disturbance below demanded investigation despite the weather. A corner of the main hatch was lifted, whereupon it was discovered:

> that there had been a severe fight among the Chinese, a number of whom, about thirty, were found dead in a heap dreadfully bruised and mangled, several others were severely wounded… [I]n the height of their affray, [they had] stove in seven casks containing 250 gallons of water. The supercargo [Koo Hang Leng the Chinese agent responsible for the coolies and at this time the precursor of the surgeon-superintendent] had the dead bodies removed and the captain dressed the wounded…

The inquiry at Singapore decided that only four of the thirty-five dead expired from natural causes. Some were the victims in a panic-induced fight in which billets of firewood had become weapons. Others had been cut from broken crockery flung about by the violent motion of the *Sophia Fraser*. Another witness, Lin Jun, gave suffocation and exhaustion as the cause of many of the deaths which, he claimed, were double that stated by Koo. For four days the poor coolies had been mewed up in conditions terrifying to simple peasants unused to such an environment. Koo Hang Leng, by his own admission, had spent the entire period clinging to a leg of the saloon table.

Occasionally the distraught Chinese took steps to obtain their freedom, particularly when the ship was in sight of land as she made her way through the straits of the East Indian archipelago and sought the open waters of the Indian Ocean. To combat rebellion, arms and a gunner were carried, and sometimes a barricade was erected athwart the ship just forward of the poop. Often a seaman was detailed to stand sentry and watch for any rebellious symptoms, particularly at night. One was smoke, for it was not unknown for the Chinese to set fire to the ship in the mistaken belief that this would force the hated *fan kwai* to take them home.

A cautious and experienced commander of a 'coolie-ship' enjoined his crew to vigilance, which usually paid off. On 9 December 1852, 'while persevering to get the ship through the... Gaspar Straits during hard squalls, I received information that the coolies were then making arrangements to murder myself and crew,' wrote Captain John Hurst of the *Samuel Barrington*, which had left Amoy bound for Demerara. With great initiative and taking advantage of being in shallow water, Hurst 'let run sheets and halliards' and brought the *Samuel Barrington* smartly to anchor.

> I then put all hands under arms, and went to work to pick out the ring-leaders....
> And without shooting a man...secured [them]...on the poop, with the exception
> of six, who jumped overboard and perished. We then searched for arms, and found
> enough to arm 200 men...sharp-ground axes, Malay creeses (sic) dirks, knives and
> a variety of other murderous weapons. We have secured all, and no question this
> prompt step has saved the ship.

Hundreds of Chinese peasants were embarked at such ports as Amoy, Swatow and Shanghai, en route to the West Indies, while thousands more were transported, largely in American ships, to the Chincha Islands off Peru where they dug out guano in appalling conditions. Although then regarded as filthy in their habits, and requiring strict regulation in respect of defecation and expectoration, the Chinese were personally fastidious. However, their terms of employment, though identical to those pertaining in India, with a five-year indentured term of service, were often imposed upon them, and they exercised less individual free-will than their Indian counterparts, though that was little enough. Sold by unscrupulous relatives, often to half-caste brokers, the official regulation of the traffic by the regional mandarins was riddled with corruption, and the wretched peasants were herded like cattle into filthy baracoons prior to shipment. The result was a humiliating experience at the hands of the ship's crew in which the individual was forcibly washed and cleaned, an intervention from which he lost all-important face. The Chinese predilection for gambling may have sent many into this semi-slavery, and certainly once on board they would bet on anything, play *fan-tan* and *mah-jong*, or make music on drums, gongs, cymbals and single-stringed violins, so that the noise between decks was often appalling to the ears of the 'Red Barbarians' running the ship.

The strain on any master under sail was immense and many buckled under it. While a human cargo might, upon occasion, prove fractious and even rebellious, it was the weather that dominated a master's every waking moment. Vessels engaged in the coolie trade passed through four of the world's worst areas for tropical revolving storms. Running south from Amoy they ran the risk of encountering a typhoon in the

South China Sea, as occurred to McKellar in the *Sophia Fraser*. In the Bay of Bengal, south of the Sandheads, or in the south-western Indian Ocean, near Mauritius, they courted assault by a cyclone; while for those in the West Indies or off the coast of Florida a hurricane was a seasonal danger. Although an experienced master might divine the approach of such a disturbance, warning was often too little, too late.

Captain Upton's full-rigger *Hesperides* was on passage from Calcutta towards Demerara with 636 coolies in her 'tween deck. The ship was between Mauritius and the Cape of Good Hope one night; the moon was full in a cloudless sky when in the middle watch the second mate, Mr W.A.H. Mull, when writing up the log-slate, noticed a curious phenomenon which he described as 'lightning in the vacuum of the barometer'. Worried, he called the master. Upton and Mull watched as it happened again, and then both men stared as the mercury dropped before their eyes. All hands were instantly called and swarmed aloft to get every sail off the ship, Upton ordering extra gaskets passed to secure the canvas, 'and so we remained for forty-eight hours'. Losing time must have irked Upton, for at the first show of daylight two days later, and with a cheering rise in the glass, Upton decided to make sail again. 'All of a sudden,' Mull wrote afterwards:

> a squall as black as ink came, tearing up from the East. The barometer fell immediately…a moment later and a cyclone struck the *Hesperides*. In spite of all the precautions…in less than 10 minutes all ours sails were loose. We tried to save them, but it was impossible for our men to get up aloft. The braces carried away and the fore topmast came down, then the main topmast and the lifts of the mainyard, and, with the rolling of the vessel, the yard topped up and the sling and truss carried away. It came down crashing through the maindeck, and we naturally thought it was going through the bottom of the ship. Just at that moment the ship gave a heavy roll to port and tore up the starboard side of the deck. The coolies below were panic stricken, and we could not get them to order. We managed to get a sail along [from the sail-locker], trebled it, and nailed it over the broken deck; fortunately, it kept out the major portion of the water.

The cyclone blew for two days, after which 'it was quite calm, but a terrific confused sea was running.' Upton called Mull and the chief mate below to his cabin and, taking off his cap, asked: 'Is it possible that this is my own face?' The captain's brown hair 'had turned snow-white, and it remained so for the remainder of his life.' Five weeks later, lying in Table Bay, seventy-five coolies died suddenly and Upton was ordered not to land them for burial, being compelled to bury them at sea for fear of the plague, though they too might have suffered an extreme form of trauma.

Although initiated by the conveyance of Chinese, the coolie-trade to Trinidad and Guiana consisted mostly of Indian emigrants.[25] From 1853 a steadier but lesser number of Chinese arrived, some of whom occasionally undertook two or even three terms of indentured service, but their carriage was expensive, since it was run over a greater distance, and after 1843 the Chinese tended to be taken elsewhere, usually to the Chinchas off Peru. The carriage of Indian coolies became the specialised trade of two companies, one of which had originated in an eighteenth century West Indian trading house, Sandbach, Tinne & Co., who dealt in sugar, tobacco and general merchandise between Georgetown, Guiana, and Glasgow. They owned some small general trading vessels and did not enter the emigrant trade until the 1840s, building their last emigrant carrier, the *Genista* of 1,852 gross tons, in 1882. Although some ships in this trade were known for their fast passages, it was generally observed that in a well regulated ship the emigrants disembarked in a better state of health and well-being than on embarkation. For this reason, and the comparatively low cost of running sailing-vessels during this period, sail maintained a hold in the trade. When occasionally employed on the long-haul routes, steamers appeared to deliver emigrants in a poorer state of health than those 'benefiting' from a sea-cure under sail. Only during the shipment of Indians to South Africa later in the century did the steam-vessels of Bullard, King's Natal Line carry the majority of emigrants.[26]

In addition to Sandbach, Tinne & Co., the other major coolie-carrier was James Nourse.[26] Born near Dublin in 1828, Nourse went to sea and in 1851 passed for master, being appointed to command the *Token*, owned by W.N. Lindsay of London. In the following year he transferred his services to another London firm, Foley, Aikman & Co., taking command of their *Aberfoyle*. In August 1855 the *Aberfoyle* caught fire in Calcutta and had to be sunk to extinguish the blaze, being afterwards refloated and sold. No blame seems to have attached to Nourse, who moved to the passenger ship *Tasmania* which had been launched in 1853 at the height of the Californian and Australian gold rushes. He remained in the *Tasmania* until 1861 when, with a partner named Sword, he went into ship-owning himself and bought the 839-ton iron full-rigged ship *Ganges* from the Sunderland shipyard of Messrs Pile & Hay.

Nourse was both the majority shareholder in the *Ganges* and her master. Loading a general cargo for Calcutta, the *Ganges* went on to Australia where Nourse made contact with Sandbach, Tinne & Co. and was encouraged to enter the coolie trade of which he was already aware. On the return of the *Ganges* to the London River in 1864, Nourse appointed another master and set up offices in Fenchurch Street. Sword sold out his shares in the *Ganges* and Nourse was joined by some other backers, including J.R. Foley of his former employers. To carry coolies, Nourse had first to secure a contract with the Crown Agents, agreeing to transport emigrants from Calcutta to Mauritius, the West Indies and Fiji, after which he bought the iron barque *India* from Cowie & Co. of Liverpool (later owners of the Knight Line) and chartered a second iron barque, the *Adamant*, from T.O. Harrison of London. With these two vessels in service, Nourse began to expand. Between 1866 and 1869 he placed orders with several yards for four iron ships built to his own specification for the carriage of coolies. These, the *Indus, Jumna, Neva* and *Syria*, were joined three years later by the *Stockbridge* and the bare-boat-chartered *Jorawur*, whereupon the *Adamant* was given up, to be sold to Shaw, Savill & Co.

Nourse was to run a large fleet of some three dozen sailing-vessels in the emigrant trade before going into steam. His ships sailed from London, completing a general cargo in Hamburg, Rotterdam or Antwerp, before taking the Cape route to Calcutta and mooring in Esplanade Reach to discharge. After preparing the ship, loading a cargo of rice in the lower holds and embarking some 600–700 coolies, she would then clear outwards and be towed down the river in charge of the steam tug *Hughli* which Nourse bought for the purpose. Meanwhile the surgeon-superintendent anxiously scanned his charges for late symptoms of disease. Should he discover anything amiss, the infected coolies were landed in their family group before the ship reached the Sandheads. The ship would call at St Helena on her way to Trinidad or Demerera, where they would land the coolies and sail north. Somewhere on the eastern seaboard of the United States, a cargo of case-oil would be loaded for Europe and, in due course, the ship would return to the Thames after a round voyage of about a year. Vessels with coolies for Mauritius or Fiji, having delivered their cargoes of rice and humanity, would sail in ballast for Australia to load coal, usually returning to Calcutta where, among other purposes, the coal was used for the bunkers of steam-ships.

Although he retained the original names of some of his second-hand vessels, most of Nourse's ships were, like Tindall's, named after rivers. Nourse was relentless in his acquisition of tonnage, which reflects the volume of coolies being transported, augmenting his fleet as demand increased, even though he borrowed heavily and most of the ships flying his diagonally crossed house-flag carried mortgages or were transferred to backers as a form of equity-release. Nevertheless, his enterprise was not without tragic consequences. He lost the *Ganges*, which had been lengthened, when she was wrecked in October 1881, and owned one vessel with a bad reputation, the *Boyne*, which suffered a run of ill-luck. The company's worst disaster was the loss of the *Indus* which sailed from the Hughli on 7 January 1873 with coolies and a cargo of rice in her lower hold. Bound for Demerara, she was expected at St Helena but went missing with all hands.[27]

In 1874 Nourse ordered five larger ships grossing around 1,600 tons: *Bann, Boyne, Foyle, Liffey* and *Lee*. These were followed in the 1880s by the purchase of four second-hand vessels, *Allanshaw, British Peer, The Bruce* and the *Rhone*, to which were added from the famous Clyde Yard of Russell & Co. seven 1,700-ton iron sister-ships, the *Main, Moy, Erne, Rhine, Elbe, Volga* and the ill-fated *Avoca*. He also retained the name of his first ship with the second *Ganges* of 1882, built by Osbourne, Graham & Co. at Sunderland. She remained in the trade until 1904 when, like other ships of the company, she was sold to Norwegian owners and, in her case, sunk by a U-boat in 1917.

Nourse's ships did not always carry a human cargo, occasionally returning to Britain from the Hughli River with wheat, jute, linseed and saltpetre, having carried case-oil out to Calcutta. Jute was usually carried home for the jute-mills of Dundee, but was a dangerous cargo. In 1895 the *Avoca* loaded a full cargo at the Esplanade moorings, Calcutta, bound for Boulogne. South of the equator the jute caught fire by spontaneous combustion. Captain W.H. Millichip, who had his wife on board, ordered all ventilators plugged in an attempt to deny the fire oxygen, but this proved useless and in the end he ordered the hatches lifted and the cargo jettisoned. Despite dense clouds of suffocating smoke, the crew of the *Avoca* dug out the cargo until the seat of the fire was revealed in the forward 'tween deck. A little while afterwards, however, flames roared out of the lower hold and leapt high into the air. Millichip ordered the *Avoca* abandoned and her crew took to the three boats.

Like many former ship-masters turned owner, Nourse was known for his 'hustling' and tight-fisted management style. His ships were under-capitalised but well-known for their smartness. He did not modernise his rigs, as was increasingly the fashion, but kept them fully ship-rigged, his employment of cheap lascar crews enabling him to avoid the economies forced on other sailing-vessel managers. Although he cut costs in other ways, Nourse retained in most of his ships the handsome, traditional painted-ports, and even carried studding sails – with their extra gear and demands on seamanship – well into the twentieth century.

In 1854 the various Acts regulating shipping had been consolidated under a new Merchant Shipping Act. In the following years the Government was preoccupied with the conduct of the Crimean War and revelations of inefficiency in the British Army, and then with the suppression of the Indian Mutiny. As will be seen in the following chapter, steamers had proliferated and, since they increasingly undertook international voyages, notice had to be taken of the competence of their engineers, examinations for which were introduced on a similar model as those for masters and mates, by another Act of 1862. The increasing popularity of iron in ship construction also created problems which exposed further deficiencies in the management of ships. The composite hull using an iron frame and wooden planking was a compromise, a partial setting aside of ancient prejudice which, although it produced some of the loveliest clippers, was soon displaced in favour of iron hulls which proved thinner, lighter and with greater internal capacity than in a wooden hull of similar dimensions. Initial difficulties were found in deterring the growth of weed and barnacles – solved by the application of copper-based anti-fouling paints – but greater menace lurked in the compass-influencing properties inherent in the soft iron of the hull. This had been anticipated in the early 1800s, particularly by the naval officer Matthew Flinders who devised a method of reducing this unwanted magnetic interference, but the extent to which a ship's compasses could deviate was not generally appreciated, nor was much done about it until loss of life occurred. The most prominently influential incident was the disastrous end of a very early and large iron ship of 1,750 tons built by Charles Tayleur & Co. at Warrington on the Mersey in 1853. Named *Tayleur* after her builders and owners, she was put into the emigrant trade, but her compasses were unadjusted and no allowance had been made for the compass deviation caused by her hull. Two days out of Liverpool on her maiden voyage she was wrecked on the Irish coast with the loss of over 300 people. As a consequence, a rigorous study of the effects of shipboard magnetic influences was undertaken. These fluctuated for a number of reasons, not least of which was the attitude of a ship to magnetic north, the movements of magnetic components in her fabric and the ferrous contents of her constantly varying cargoes. Consequently, a demonstrably proper understanding of compass and course-correction was incorporated in the syllabus of the Board of Trade examinations for certificates of competency for masters and mates.

The state's bureaucracy proliferated by way of the Board of Trade's 'shipping offices' established at all the major ports where 'shipping-masters' regularly presided over the formal contractual rite of 'signing-on' when a ship's articles were 'opened' with her master's signature prior to her 'going foreign'. Here, too, the examinations for masters, mates and engineers were regularly conducted, and nearby grew up the crammers, or navigation-schools, which honed the examinees' skills in nautical astronomy, mathematics and the other 'nautical sciences' necessary to master before taking the examinations – and especially its oral component – in order to obtain the coveted 'ticket'. To be 'passed for master' guaranteed nothing in itself, but it was a pre-requisite before one could be considered for promotion and ultimate command.

This, too, was the period in which an immense expansion of the nation's wet-dock system was under way. The entire coast of Great Britain is subject to tidal variation, that at Bristol being second only to the tidal range in the Bay of Fundy in Canada, so that to keep an ocean-going merchant ship afloat throughout her cycle of loading and discharging meant that enclosed basins of constantly deep water had to be provided. This also avoided a hull undergoing strain when it went aground at low water, the ship did not list, and – apart from a sinking or rising owing to the movement of her cargo – a constant relationship was maintained between ship and quayside, greatly facilitating the handling of cargo. Nor, in this final period of the sailing-vessel's dominance, must we ignore the great contribution of the lowly steam-tug whose skippers ventured far down Channel, particularly in long periods of easterly winds when sailing ships were either awaiting a slant in Falmouth or Plymouth or beating 'off-and-on' in the 'Chops of the Channel'. A more usual cruising ground for a tug was off Dungeness, near the Trinity House Pilot Station, and the services of such vessels were often crucial, particularly in the arrival time of a tea-cargo from China.[28]

While the prosperity of great port-cities like Liverpool and Glasgow could be linked with general trade, ship-building and the supporting infrastructure which ranged from broking to tailoring, others became closely linked with certain specific trades or commodities. The conjunction of coal and copper in the case of Swansea has already been mentioned; another is that of jute and whale-oil in Dundee. The Scottish port had for many years supported a trade with Russia in timber and flax, along with other 'naval stores' from Baltic ports, but the vacillations of Tsarist policy during the Napoleonic War and the increase of British hegemony in India suggested the sub-continent as a more reliable source of sail-cloth and cordage for the Royal Navy and the mercantile marine. Hitherto, jute had been discounted on the grounds of its brittle fibres, but around 1830 it was discovered that these could be made into a fine yarn by saturation with right whale oil at the initial process of combing the hank as it was torn from the bale. The consequences of this were to be manifold: Dundee rapidly industrialised, capitalising on its own whaling fleet which hunted on the Arctic grounds. Native Scots-grown and imported Russian flax diminished in importance and the cottage weaving industry withered as venture capital established large collectivised and mechanised weaving mills. The women and children of the city provided the cheap labour required by the rapidly enriched 'jute-barons', and many men were unemployed, acquiring the half-pitying, half-derisory title of 'kettle-boilers' while Dundee, when not proudly trumpeted as 'Juteopolis', was known as 'the city of women'. In the dominant position of wage-earners, the city's women quickly picked up the attributes of men elsewhere, the incidents of female drunkenness becoming excessive, forming fertile ground for the temperance movement. Limited male employment could be found in the foundries and machine shops which produced the plant required to process the jute, carding, spinning and weaving it into sail-cloth, hatch-tarpaulins and sacks.

With the steady expansion of world trade throughout the nineteenth century, jute products increased so that the conversion of the Royal Navy to steam power had little effect upon the wealth of Juteopolis. The Crimean War, which again choked off the supply of Russian flax, simply increased the imports of jute. Dundee also benefited from the American Civil War which so badly affected the Lancashire cotton industry by cutting off imports of cotton from the Confederate states, but increased the demand for substitute materials. The importance of so sustainable and versatile a raw material as jute during the whole of the Victorian age can scarcely be over-emphasised, and, ironically, war benefited the city of women. Jute products varied from burlap sacks, in which hundreds of commodities from Arabica beans to zircon sand were carried in the holds of thousands of ships, to the tilts that covered the wagons of settlers migrating across the American west or the Australian outback. The tent-canvas under which the ill-disciplined camps of gold-prospectors made their homes on the diggings in Kimberley, California, Ballarat, Bendigo and Otago, came from the mills of Dundee, as did the contrastingly regular cantonments of the British and Indian armies in the Crimea or across the vast sub-continent of India. The universal spread of jute-derivatives was remarkable, gracing not only these rugged outposts of entrepreneurial greed and Victorian military adventure, but the homes of Her Majesty's subjects. Jute backed the linoleum appearing on the floors of ordinary citizens of modest wealth, just as it did the carpets of the more affluent who were able to afford the products of the new Axminster process.

Dundee's trade had, of course, long since established ship-building as a Tayside industry and, owing to a curiosity of the jute-manufactories, timber ship-construction was to co-exist longer here than elsewhere. Many fine wood and iron sailing ships were designed and built to bring home Indian jute from Bengal, and to make the trade viable these were mostly engaged in the outward carriage of emigrants to Australia and New Zealand, after which they made a passage in ballast to Calcutta to load a full cargo consisting of 400lb (200kg) bales of jute fibre. These so-called 'jute-clippers', among which were some fine ships, often made fast homeward passages of around ninety days, and one bore her home-port's soubriquet, *Juteopolis*.

To Glasgow and her elegant iron and steel sailing-vessels we shall return in a later chapter, but it is now necessary to consider the position of Liverpool, which had long seen herself as London's rival and now seized the opportunities offered by emigration. We shall come to Liverpool's attachment to the history of steam navigation shortly but, amid the innovation and adoption of new technology, the banks of the Mersey took a full part in the last days of fast wooden sailing ships, assuming a position as the hub of the emigrant trade. In this way Liverpool inexorably elevated herself into a place of imperial prominence and importance, having long since eclipsed Bristol as the second port in the land, and leading Glasgow in her domination of the North Atlantic. Recalling the Liverpool of his youth, the ship-owner Sir William Forwood wrote:

> The inspiring and wonderful sight of the Liverpool docks, a forest of the masts of English and American clippers; the river Mersey at high water, alive with splendid sailing vessels leaving or entering our docks, and at anchor in a line extending from the Sloyne to New Brighton, or towing out to sea, or may be sailing in from sea under their own canvas − all was activity and full of life and motion. I remember seeing one of Brocklebank's ships − the *Martaban*, of 600 tons − sailing into the George's Dock Basin under full canvas; her halliards were let go, and sails were clewed up so smartly that the ship as she passed the Pierhead was able to throw a line on shore and make fast. It is difficult in these days to realise such a thing being possible. It was skill supported by discipline…
>
> The old-fashioned sailing ship was handicapped by her inability to contend successfully with strong head winds. After the continuance of a succession of north-west gales the river Mersey and our docks became crowded and congested with outward-bound ships waiting for a shift of wind to enable them to get away, and when this took place the river was a wonderful sight. I remember, as a boy, standing on the shore at Seaforth and counting over three hundred sailing vessels of all sorts and sizes working their way out to sea on the ebb tide between the Rock Light and the Formby Light ship, and interspersed among them were also a number of sailing ships towing out to sea…
>
> The most trying winds, however, were the easterly gales, which prevailed in November and December, and also in the spring. With easterly gales blowing I have known Liverpool to be a closed port for weeks together, few or no vessels entering it; and more than once this blockade of our port by easterly gales had a serious effect upon our stocks of cotton and produce. The inward-bound fleet was caught in the chops of the Channel, and. was there detained until the wind changed.

The brokers and under-writers, the stevedores, wharfies, riggers, sail and rope-makers, tailors, crimps, boarding-house and brothel-owners, whores and, of course, the seamen that swelled this teeming port owed their existence to the ship-owners whose grand houses began to adorn the leafier suburbs of the higher ground that rose from the broad sweep of the Mersey. Many of these had long since established shipping companies, men like MacAndrew, Bibby and the Brocklebanks.

William MacAndrew had, in 1770, begun importing fruit from Iberia into Liverpool. By the time of his death in 1819 he had been succeeded by his sons, and these admitted new partners. In due course disagreements between the brothers led, in 1853, to Robert MacAndrew migrating further, to London's Lombard Street, leaving William to continue in Liverpool as an importer. Robert established the shipping business known as MacAndrew & Co., and before his death saw the reunification of the two sides of the family with two sons of brother William joining the board in London. The MacAndrew's first steam-vessel was the 315-ton *Acor*, built in Glasgow in 1857, and the company registered many of its ships under the Spanish ensign.[29]

The Brocklebanks had moved to Liverpool in 1819 following the success of Captain John McKean's eastern voyage in the *Princess Charlotte*. On arrival at Calcutta, McKean had offered his ship to the Indian Government and carried out a short trooping charter. Having shrewdly thereby obtained the approval of the East India Company, he put the *Princess Charlotte* in the Country-trade, made a voyage through the Dutch East Indies and assisted in the rescue of the survivors of HMS *Alceste*, referred to earlier. On 2 October 1816 McKean left the Hughli for home with a cargo of cotton, sugar, saltpetre, rice and ginger, all of which was insured for £26,000 and yielded a handsome profit of £10,650. This persuaded Thomas Brocklebank to hasten the construction of his new *Perseverance* while, after a refit which added a new deck to his *Hercules*, he placed her in the North Atlantic passenger trade to St John's Newfoundland. Increased state interest in the shipping of passengers had, in 1816, produced a Bill linking passenger numbers with capacity tonnage, and at one passenger per 5 tons, the potential in the *Hercules* was unviable. This regulation applied to the United States, not the colonies, hence Brocklebank's decision to try for Newfoundland, whither Irish migrants were going at £10 per head. Carrying coal in her lower hold and emigrants in the 'tween decks, the *Hercules* made little profit.

At this time Thomas moved the business to Liverpool, his brother John remaining at Whitehaven supervising their shipyard. By 1820 no less than fifty Liverpool-registered ships had cleared outwards for India in the wake of the *Princess Charlotte*. After fifty years of being in shipping, in 1820 Thomas managed a dozen or so ships, of which the three largest, *Princess Charlotte*, Captain McKean, *London*, Captain Wise, and *Perseverance*, Captain Mounsey, traded to India. The *Ariel*, Captain Cragg, went out to Valparaiso, being joined the following year by the *Crown*, Captain Craig; the *Cossack*, Captain Poole; the *Prince Leopold*, Captain Jackson; the *Candidate*, Captain Bacon; the *Caroline*, Captain Brown; the *Westmoreland*, Captain Warner and the *Duke of Wellington*, which was wrecked on the voyage. These served ports in Brazil and the Argentine, while the *Mary*, Captain Wilson, and the *Hercules*, Captain Kneale, persisted in the Newfoundland emigrant traffic, with the *West Indian* running back and forth between Liverpool and the West Indies. Such routes were varied as markets shifted and cargoes offered; losses were not uncommon. In addition to the 140-ton brig *Duke of Wellington*, wrecked near Bahia in 1821, the *Candidate* was lost by grounding on the Ortez Bank in the Rio de la Plata in June 1823, and the *Cossack* suffered the same fate the following year. The old *Hercules* was run down by a schooner off the Smalls lighthouse off Pembrokeshire in November 1825, and the *Mary* was lost on the Hoyle Bank off Liverpool in 1825 with heavy loss of life, there being only one survivor. In March 1829 the *Perseverance* went to the bottom off Madras, that graveyard of shipping, though the news took five months to reach Liverpool. As if to emphasise the diversity of the company's business, the schooner *Bransty*, Captain Dixon, was wrecked on the coast of Yucatan whilst on a voyage to Tampico.

The Brocklebank brothers and their family owned shares in other vessels in the old-fashioned manner, but they were beginning to establish a worldwide web of services, with ships painted a distinctive colour – black hulls with a broad white band – and an identifiable blue and white house-flag flown, by order of Thomas Brocklebank, in defiance of the custom of the day, at the foremast-head.[30] They had yet to adopt a convention of linked names for their ships – eventually they would all begin with 'M' and have eastern connections – but their operations were assuming a cohesion that would, in time, establish a cargo-liner service with regular sailings. Although the Brocklebanks dabbled in investing in steam, having shares in the Whitehaven Steam Navigation Co., and built the 240-ton paddle-steamer *Countess of Lonsdale* in 1827 for that company's Irish Sea route, it would be 1879 before they built steamers for their own deep-sea services.

All the time their ship-masters were building up knowledge and experience in trades once denied them. The *Andes*, a 216-ton brig built in 1823, under Captain King, extended the company's writ by sailing from Callao to Calcutta, while the chartered *Superior* sailed to the new Port of Singapore in 1829. Although shipping vast quantities of cotton from the southern United States and opening up a service to both the Atlantic and Pacific coasts of South America, the Brocklebanks' business began to coalesce round the Indian trade. To support all this, the senior management brought in men outside their family, Daniel Bird taking over the shipyard in 1831 after the death of John Brocklebank from a fall from his horse, and Captain Joseph Pinder coming ashore in 1836 to take up the new post of marine superintendent for the company's entire fleet, a replacement of the old, individual ship's husbands.

Pinder had served his time as apprentice, first in the *Hercules* in 1814 under Captain Caffrey while she was employed as a Government transport running either to Malta or the Cape of Good Hope. By 1821 Pinder was master of the *Caroline*, and a year later took over the *Globe*. In 1832 he was placed in command of the brand-new *Hindoo*, a 266-ton barque which would spend the next quarter-century running to Calcutta before ending her days with a further decade in the South American trade. Pinder was not long in her, however, taking over the new *Jumna* in 1833. A celebrated full-rigged ship of 364 tons, Pinder made her and himself famous with fast runs to and from Calcutta, a trade in which Brocklebank already had the *Hindoo*, the *Crown*, the *Patriot King*, the *Lord Althorp* and the faithful *Princess Charlotte*. With an outward time of 104 days from the Mersey to the Hughli, Pinder now discharged his cargo of lead, iron, 'Manchester goods', wine, tar, beer, woollens, earthenware and cheese – a variety soon to be better known as 'general cargo' – and in five weeks had loaded rice, sugar, hides, indigo, silk and oil for Liverpool. Some was consigned to Brocklebanks, but much else was destined for other consignees, among them John Gladstone. Pinder passed the Sandheads on 16 November, hove-to briefly to exchange news with another vessel and exchange mails, stopped to replenish water at St Helena and, on 22 February 1834, noted in the *Jumna's* log that they were: 'Anchored in [the] River

Mersey at 8 p.m. completing the voyage out and home in the shortest time on record, eight months and two days.'

On 14 May following, Pinder reboarded the *Jumna* in the Prince's Dock for a voyage believed to have been the first direct from the Mersey to China. Sixty-four days later she was off the Cape of Good Hope and heading east, as Pinder kept her going until 600 miles west of Cape Leeuwin, when he hauled up for the Sunda Strait. On 16 August, the *Jumna* was brought to an anchor off Anjer to take on water; twenty-two hours later Pinder hoisted in his boats. A few days later, negotiating the Gaspar Strait in light winds, he loaded his guns as the *praus* of the *orang laut* hovered in the offing. On 1 September the *Jumna* anchored off Lintin Island and awaited her pilot up to Whampoa, 16,241 miles from home in 110 days. Whilst this would be considered undistinguished thirty years later, it was a creditable passage for the time. More important was the rapid turn-round that impresses perhaps more than Pinder's passage-times, for, of the three months that elapsed before her departure on 1 December, two were lost 'owing to the dispute with the Lord Napier and the Chinese'. Having completed her lading of silk, ivory, fans, preserved ginger and tea — 2,625 chests on Brocklebanks' account and 3,897 for other consignees — the *Jumna* weighed anchor and ran south. She passed Anjer on 17 December, was at St Helena on 4 February 1835, and arrived in the Mersey on 13 March after a passage of 102 days, then considered, notwithstanding the delays occasioned by the pre-amble to the Opium War, as 'the quickest voyage to China and back ever known'.[31] Pinder was to make one more voyage to the Pearl River before taking up his post as marine superintendent where he remained until his death in 1850. His sea-going career was relatively short for the time, only twenty-two years, fifteen of which had been as master, with only two as a mate; he was clearly a man who both attracted and deserved his employer's advancement, and one who returned their confidence in full.

By this time, with their ships trading worldwide, the Brocklebanks were beginning to co-operate with other owners. After difficult beginnings, the traffic with Newfoundland had picked up and they began operating in conjunction with Benjamin Bowring & Son who, in addition to coastal vessels, were beginning to exploit the sea populations of Labrador. In 1832 the *Westmoreland*, *Manchester* and *Ariel* all made outward voyages to St John's, picking up seal-blubber, seal-oil and seal-skins, in addition to fish, before sailing south to Bahia to complete their lading. This was always a risky route, the prevalence of icebergs in the spring melt combined with fog to entrap many small ships. In May 1837 the Liverpool-registered *Hope* was crushed in the ice off Newfoundland and, a few days later, a ship's long-boat was found adrift off the coast. In it were nine dead bodies, and later discoveries confirmed that it belonged to the Brocklebanks' *Swallow*.

Contemporary with Thomas Brocklebank, John Bibby and John Highfield had founded another Liverpool shipping house in 1807, a subject mentioned in the previous volume. By 1821 Bibby had shed Highfield and was trading as John Bibby & Co., running a line of four packets to Lisbon, the *Lancashire Witch*, the *Bootle*, the *Hardware* and the *Ellen Jenkinson*. As packets, Bibby's vessels were obliged to sail regularly, in his case 'on the 1st of every month,' irrespective of whether they were 'full or near full'. Described as 'first-class, Liverpool-built under inspection of the owners, expressly for despatch', Bibby assured his consigners and prospective passengers that his ships were coppered 'and well-known for making quick passages', to which end 'the period of sailing will be strictly adhered to'. It is worth noting this advertising of both speed and a schedule, for it was a well-established feature of shipping long before steam-vessels actually made it reliably possible. Beyond Lisbon, Bibby's ships ran mainly into the Mediterranean, though they also ventured to South America, but it was not long before they too were following their rivals to Calcutta and Canton. Outward lading consisted of the standard 'general cargo' of the day: 'Manchester manufactures', textiles from the mills of Lancashire, pottery from the Black Country and quantities of machinery of all kinds, from lathes to steam-plant. From the Mediterranean and Iberia they returned with fresh fruit, raisins and wine, while sugar, wood, raw cotton, molasses and rum came home from Demerara, and hides arrived from Bahia. An out-ward cargo to Rio de Janeiro consisted of copper sheets, shot, cast-iron wheels, glass, rope cables and, surprisingly, dried beef. In 1836, taking advantage of the East India Company's commercial demise, the *Mary Bibby* brought home from Canton 3,462 chests of tea and a quantity of silk. Named for Bibby's wealthy wife, this vessel was, with the *George IV*, larger than Bibby's earlier vessels. Launched in 1825, she measured 290 tons and, at the time of her China voyage, she was one of eighteen vessels of which all but three had been built specifically for Bibby's services. The eponymous Mary Bibby left her husband a widower for some years before his mysterious death in July 1840. John Bibby's body was dragged from a pond near Aintree, and evidence suggested he had been robbed, for he died a wealthy man, his estate being valued at £25,000, owning, besides his ships, much property on Merseyside and a large house named Mount Pleasant at Linacre Marsh, from where he commanded a fine view of the estuary of the river that had brought him his fortune.

John Bibby's business was taken over by his two sons John and James, of whom the former withdrew from the shipping enterprise in 1864. During the 1840s the fleet was increased with the purchase of second-hand tonnage, one the *Hannibal* at 821 tons, a large sailing-vessel for her day. In 1853 James Bibby purchased his last sailing-vessel, the *Pizarro*, and by 1856 the eighteen-strong fleet he managed included only five sailing-vessels, two of which — the *Hannibal* and the *England* — were already reduced to coal-hulks. Finally, the 1,212-ton *Melbourne* was acquired in 1858, but eight years earlier the Bibby brothers had not only invested in steam but in iron steamers. Nevertheless, the company's sailing-vessels had affected Bibby's more dis-tant ambitions. In 1844 the *Jessie Miller* had carried two small demountable steamers and steam-plant out to Bombay, the *Hannibal* following with a similar cargo in 1850, bringing a homeward lading of cotton for the Liverpool cotton-brokers Rathbone & Co. and in 1854 the *Pizarro* had ventured as far as Valparaiso, but Bibby's commitment to steamers was now paramount, and is followed in the following chapter.

Brocklebanks, however, remained committed to sail and were making tentative steps to open a trade with New South Wales, with an interest in, but not outright purchase of, two barques, the *Avoca* and *Helvellyn*, in the 1830s. These, under the command of two brothers named Boadle who owned the majority shares, made a number of voyages thither, returning by way of Singapore or Bombay, but it was not until gold was discovered in Australia that firms like the Brocklebanks were elbowed aside. For some years other Liverpool owners had been increasingly turning their attention to distant waters and the opportunities that awaited enterprise beyond the traditional routes to the West Indies, North America, West Africa, even South America and China. Envious eyes were cast south and east towards London where the rapid expansion of the emigrant trade was driving maritime enterprise. This was, in part, equally spurred by envy of the domination of the North Atlantic by the Yankee packets, particularly those of the Black Ball Line, while the sudden lure of wealth by the mid-nineteenth-century succession of gold rushes created a remarkable collateral effect.

Among the men who emerged to dominate the new passenger traffic from Liverpool was James Baines who was born in 1823 over the shop of his parents' confectionery business at 85 Duke Street. While his father refined sugar, his mother made and sold sweetmeats, presenting one of her cakes to the young Princess Victoria. Later Mrs Baines was appointed confectioner to Her Royal Highness. Indeed, from his mother, Baines inherited a streak of commercial opportunism so successful that it has eclipsed his parents and his partners, Thomas MacKay, Joseph Greaves, John Taylor and Thomas Marwood. One contemporary wrote of him that he 'never appeared to be able to buy a hat sufficiently large to contain his big head. With his henchman, Mr Graves,[32] he was always active and pushing, and kept [his own]...Black Ball Line of Australian packets well to the fore'.

Of short stature, Baines was to become a controversial figure, regarded by some as an upstart, by others as a man of kindness and generosity. Such paradoxical characteristics would adorn the reputations of a number of British ship-owners in the century that followed, the truth of which is that they were all of these things to different people. Baines appears to have done little more than dabble in ship-broking until 1848, living as a self-proclaimed gentleman with his mother, and sponging off her for his first investment in shipping. In this year, however, he married, and thereafter his business dealings become complex, for he was several times a bankrupt before his death of cirrhosis of the liver in 1889.

Little is known of the British Black Ball Line's other architect, Thomas MacKay. He was a ship-builder – not to be confused with the Nova Scotian Donald McKay who supplied the firm with ships – and would become in time a member of the then new Mersey Dock and Harbour Board. The son of a soldier, sometime corn-merchant and later partner in a successful ship-building business, MacKay & Miller, Thomas MacKay's union with Baines took place in September 1851 when both men took equal shares in the brig *Vesta*, MacKay in the name of MacKay & Miller. This firm had been share-holding ship-owners on their own account for some time, possessing complimentary experience to that of the broking Baines, so that it was MacKay who became 'the active manager of the Black Ball Australian Line assisted by James Baines and Joseph Greaves'. It was also MacKay who usually presided over departure

dinners and had the honour of escorting Queen Victoria round the Black Ball liners
James Baines and *Champion of the Seas* when they lay at Spithead waiting to embark
troops for the suppression of the Indian Mutiny. The complexities of the business
arrangements that entangled these men need not detain us, for although MacKay was,
as it were, front of house, it was Baines's name that became better established in the
public's imagination.

Suffice it to say that Baines had ridden a rising tide of good fortune in the ship-
broking business, linking consigner (the shipper of a cargo or part thereof) with the
carrier (or ship-owner), and drafting the contract for the services of a ship, in whole
or part, known as the charter-party. A ship-broker might also charter a ship in his
own interest and then solicit among potential shippers for a suitable cargo. In this way
he might appear to 'own' a ship – even to the extent of flying his own house-flag
– without actually doing so: such men could be persuasive enough to 'talk a corpse
back to life again'. There were other associated activities and an energetic man like
Baines could make himself useful in ancillary businesses like insurance, placing contracts for ship-construction and the sale of vessels. In all such transactions the broker
acted on commission, amassing capital for additional speculative investment, and it
is exactly this – with a start-up sum from his mother – that Baines appears to have
done. In this he was not alone; as Michael Stammers points out in his history of the
Black Ball Line, *The Passage Makers*. Thomas Ismay began in this way,[33] taking over
the ailing Liverpool White Star Line in 1867 and transforming it into the great rival
of Cunard, with his own passenger liners on the North Atlantic. Another such was Sir
Alfred Jones who started life as a mere cabin boy and who would later dominate the
coast of West Africa.

By the time he was twenty-two, Baines was part of a partnership acting as agents for
several ships and, at his marriage, he became a ship-owner. Among his vessels was the
421-ton, Nova Scotian-built brig *Cleopatra*, in which he had half-shares, and a larger
barque, the 624-ton *Deborah*, of which he owned an eighth. The master of the *Cleopatra*
was named James Nicol Forbes while the master of the *Deborah* was James Liston, and
it was Forbes who handled the purchase of the Quebec-built *Maria*, of 1,014 tons, on
behalf of Baines, MacKay and Miller, thereafter assuming command of her.

In 1852 these men initiated what on the surface was simply called the Black Ball
Line, but below the bright red swallow-tailed house-flag with its black disc there
was a veritable entanglement of complex inter-related interests. To start with, the
company picked up the name from the most popular and therefore most familiar of
the Yankee Packet companies. The American Black Ball Line had a good reputation,
and there was then no brand copyright. The advantage of a good name, however,
was well-appreciated but, in addition, ships that had actually made their own reputations under the stars-and-stripes were often chartered by Baines & Co., or by T.M.
MacKay & Co., and placed on the British registry. This had several advantages, not
least because many were built by the Americans, then the world-leaders as builders of fast ships, the doyen of which was the Nova Scotian Donald McKay, himself
descended from a British Army officer of Loyalist persuasion who had settled in the

Canadian maritime province rather than the United States. Donald, however, moved his successful ship-building business along the coast, setting up his yard in east Boston, from where he almost single-handedly redefined the underwater form of the sailing ship. As William Forwood points out, these soft-wood ships were short-lived, becoming water-logged with time, and they left McKay's yard neither fully fitted in their cabins nor coppered on their hulls. The former was better executed by the skilled joiners of Liverpool, and supplies of copper were to be had cheaper closer to the great copper-smelting works of Swansea in South Wales. Such inter-dependence made close commercial links easier.

Baines worked on credit and, thus, of the 600 sailings reputedly under the Black Ball house-flag between 1852 and 1871, one-third were carried out by 'bare-boat' charters, that is ships hired from their owners and treated as though the charterers owned them, while the other two-thirds were in fact the property of either Baines & Co. or T.M. MacKay & Co.[34] Most of the chartered ships were the products of United States and Canadian yards, large – much more so than many contemporary British general traders where 1,000 tons was considered big – at around 1,800 tons.[35]

In addition Baines and MacKay chartered their own ships to the Emigration Commissioners under-writing sponsored voyages, in which case the ships did not carry Black Ball colours, though they would certainly bear the company's reputation. Moreover, in order to supply the boom, it made commercial sense for the partners to offer their own tonnage to the Commissioners and charter-in the shortfall this created in the sailings of the line itself. As a further, but far from final, complication; in 1866 the ships had to be sold on Baines's first bankruptcy. However, they were immediately chartered back to the line.[36]

In all this it is clear that passage-speed became critical, not least to minimise the risk of losing passengers during a voyage through illness or injury. Consequently, the Liverpool ships – in contrast to the London Blackwallers transferred into the Australian emigrant traffic – acquired a reputation for fast runs. Indeed, any not proving fast enough were quickly dropped and others sought in their place in an almost frenetic quest that included the calibre of their masters as 'drivers'. Among these was Captain James Nicol Forbes, known to history as 'Bully' Forbes.

There is a tradition that Baines's Black Ball Line burst on the world's consciousness when Forbes brought the *Marco Polo* across the Atlantic from her builder's yard in New Brunswick in record time, but this is – as is so much attached to Baines – a simplification. In fact the line began work with the *Deborah*, *Vesta*, *Cleopatra* and *Maria*, together with one of MacKay and Miller's ships, the *David McIver*. But the *Marco Polo* was bought almost new, James Smith of St John, New Brunswick (her builders) having run her across to Liverpool, then out to Mobile for cotton, returning to the Mersey where Baines bought her for £9,000. At 1,625 tons, with high freeboard and 'tween decks, she was admirably suited to carry emigrants, in some ways compensating them for the discomfort they would endure being hard-driven by Forbes. With her success the line, having sent out a number of small vessels to handle a perceived demand for coasters on the Australian coast, sold off its residual small-fry and began buying and chartering much larger North American-built ships, eleven in 1860 and another fifty-five before 1863. These were mostly former American Down-Easters built for the Californian gold rush, then petering out. Baines's Black Ball Line also benefited from the tonnage sold in desperation by Yankee owners on the outbreak of the American Civil War, when Confederate cruisers began a *guerre en course* against Union shipping. Canadian tonnage built on speculation was also purchased, and by 1863 the company had begun ordering iron ships and had acquired a second-hand steamer, the *Great Victoria*, which they re-engined. This expansion was curtailed by the crash of 1866, but their old ships were chartered back from their new owners, many of whom had close connections with the partners, so that, by-and-large, the Black Ball Line ended as it had begun, with chartered tonnage.

From among these ships, many of which enjoyed high reputations, it is only possible to view a sample, of which further mention must be made of the *Marco Polo*. A fine, powerful, full-rigged ship with the old-fashioned deep single topsails, she was high sided and dry with a flared bow; very deep-draughted, flat-bottomed but sharp in her entrance and long in the lower sections of the run of her after-body. She could stand an immense spread of canvas, and Captain Forbes made the most of her. She left Liverpool on 4 July 1852 and arrived off Melbourne on 16 September, being seventy-four days on passage with a best day's run of 364 miles — a contrast to Captain Pinder's 180-odd and a credit to her crew of fifty-nine. Forbes had achieved his remarkable run by sailing deep into the Southern Ocean along the great-circle route which took her into icy seas. But of the 930 emigrants she carried, two adults and fifty-one children — mainly infants — died on the voyage, despite the attentions of a surgeon, assistant surgeon and a matron. To offset this, there were nine births and the ship was reported clean and orderly on arrival, the practice of inspecting incoming vessels being carried over from the transportation of convicts.

Forbes's ship was also met by boats full of crimps eager to seduce and fleece his seamen by spicing the lure of sex and alcohol ashore by throwing 'gold' nuggets aboard as additional temptation. To outwit these parasites Forbes had the entire crew arrested on a trumped-up charge and they languished in gaol until, loaded with wool, the *Marco Polo*, handled by her mates and apprentices, was actually under way and homeward-bound before a boat brought them back alongside. Thus did Forbes — a commander who clearly considered himself 'Master under God' — acquire the soubriquet 'Bully'. The *Marco Polo* came home in seventy-six days, bringing the news of her own outward and record passage with her, announcing her arrival with the discharge of a gun, and netting Baines £13,000.

On her next voyage, her outward passage was a couple of days longer and her homeward voyage took ninety-seven, five of which were spent among icebergs in the high latitude of 60° South. Forbes then left her to take over the *Lightning*, and the *Marco Polo*'s third voyage was under her promoted mate, Captain Charles MacDonnell. Towed by two steam tugs directly to Cork to embark emigrants, MacDonnell sailed on 16 November 1853 to reach Port Phillip Heads sixty-nine days later. The *Marco Polo* then went round to Melbourne before heading for home. Such passages secured the mail contract for Baines, a circumstance that only made the Black Ball masters drive their ships even harder, for they were required to deliver the mail in sixty-five days. This was all but impossible and cannot have been much fun for the emigrants. Their wants were catered for to a degree by the provision of a ship's band, some milking cows and livestock for fresh meat and eggs, including 360 chickens, fowl, game, rabbits, hares and thirty each of sheep and pigs. A small printing press and photographic equipment provided for the production of a newspaper in which the passengers were encouraged to participate by way of diversion.

The success of the *Marco Polo* led Baines to order four large emigrant-carriers from Donald McKay when the master ship-builder visited Liverpool in the summer of 1853. These were the *Lightning*, the *Champion of the Seas*, *James Baines* and *Donald McKay*. The speeds and best days' runs of these ships has been much debated, claims exceeding 20 knots with day's runs of over 400 miles being extant. The *Champion of the Seas* boasted 465 miles between noon on 11 and noon on 12 December 1854. As the late David MacGregor was keen to point out, although American-built:

> Many of the ships obtaining these speeds were British-owned at the time with British masters; they were large ships, designed for speed and carrying cargoes considerably less in tonnage than their register. Many of the large iron and steel ships of later years attained high speeds in knots and big 24-hour runs in the 380-mile range, but they were primarily designed to carry huge bulk cargoes. So what could not a large ship, designed for speed achieve? [37]

Among these fast vessels must be counted Forbes's *Lightning*, which was not only capable of day's runs, noon-to-noon, of 430 miles with average speeds of some 18 knots throughout, but carried a press of sail even in strong winds. On 27 February 1855 her log records that she ran under a 'Fresh gale with heavy squalls and occasional showers of hail and snow, the sea running high,' but nevertheless: 'During six hours in the morning the ship logged 18 knots with royals, main skysail and topgallant studding sails set.' Even when reefed down in a 'Fresh gale', under 'single reefed topsails, foresail, trysail and foretopsail' with the 'wind abeam' she was 'going 17 knots' on 11 March. Forbes assembled a formidable crew for the aptly named *Lightning*, his chief mate being known as 'Bully' Bragg, but after a couple of voyages Baines transferred Forbes to his next new ship and put Captain Anthony Enright into the *Lightning*, he having just made a name for himself in the China tea-clipper *Chrysolite*. Enright had chosen the *Lightning* in preference to a command in the Black Ball Line's rival company, the White Star Line. He must have been a hard nut, for he is said to have demanded, and got, the then unprecedented salary of £1,000 *per annum*!

Enright made the *Lightning* a popular as well as a fast ship, unlike Forbes who did not trouble himself over the comfort of his passengers whom he tended to frighten with his sail-carrying and bombast, circumstances further justifying his nickname. With the *James Baines* and *Champion of the Seas*, the *Lightning* was chartered for trooping to India at the time of the Mutiny. The *Lightning* went round to the Thames and,

on the eve of her departure for Calcutta, a dinner was given on board in honour of
Enright at which Benjamin Disraeli delivered a panegyric on him 'as one of the most
respected master-mariners under the Red Ensign'. Owing to his wife falling sick,
Enright gave up the command in August 1857 after four voyages, and the *Lightning*
was taken over by a Captain Byrne.

Byrne returned the *Lightning* to her old trade and she ran regularly to Melbourne
for twelve years, mostly under Byrne's successors, Captain Thomas Robertson and
finally Captain Henry Jones, her soft timber gradually becoming water-logged.[38] As the
hatches were put on, the tarpaulins battened down and the crew prepared to haul off
the wharf at Geelong on 31 October 1869, smoke was seen pouring out of the forehold.
In minutes the ship was on fire. Despite the best efforts of her company, the local fire-
engines and the crews of the *Argo*, *Aboukir* and *Lanarkshire*, there was no saving her. She
was towed clear and anchored while attempts were made to scuttle her and extinguish
the blaze, but the falling of the masts ended her life. Two guns were fired into her from
the wharf, but it was not until Jones and a party of carpenters got back alongside that
they succeeded in sinking her at her anchors in four fathoms of water.

Although the chartered Black Ball Liner *Sovereign of the Seas* managed to reach
Australia in sixty-five days, this was a record and almost the only time the mail-
charter was actually fulfilled under sail – though another follows below. Amid the
turmoil of poor capitalisation and the failure of Baines's bankers, the severe competition of other emigrant carriers and the encroachment of the steam-ship forced
Baines's Black Ball Line into decline. The company's apogee was Queen Victoria's
visit to the *James Baines* at Portsmouth in 1857, where the ship was embarking the
97th Regiment for India. The Queen was reputed to have 'declared that she did not
know her Mercantile Marine possessed such a fine ship'; she was also alleged to have
taken Captain MacDonnell to one side and expressed her anxiety over the outbreak
of the sepoy mutiny and offered him £100 for every day that he cut off the contract
length of the voyage – though the anecdote is probably apocryphal. Sadly it was to be
the *James Baines*'s last voyage, for she too caught fire, having brought home from India
a cargo of rice, jute, linseed and cow-hides. On opening the hatches in the Huskisson
Dock, a fire was discovered, and although scuttled in the dock, her falling masts damaged the dockside sheds and she proved too badly affected to be saved. In a few hours
a fine ship and cargo worth £170,000 had been reduced to a wreck, though she was
afterwards raised and sold for £1,000, becoming a coal-hulk in Galway and afterwards in Alexandria, whither she was towed. As for her master, MacDonnell retired to
Glengarrif where he assisted in the rescue of the crew of a brig that had run ashore,
contracted pneumonia and died.[39]

Among other Liverpool ship-owners rising to prominence at this time, some entered
Parliament while others achieved varying degrees of fame and notoriety. Among the
first was Sir Arthur Forwood – father of Sir William, who is quoted elsewhere –

The Great Agitator and Seaman's
Friend, Samuel Plimsoll MP.
(Private Collection)

who founded the West India & Pacific Co. in 1865, becoming its managing-director
until he became an MP. Forwood senior was 'A man of striking ability and power
of organisation... endowed with enormous energy', and became Parliamentary
Secretary to the Admiralty. In contrast, Edward Bates, whose ships traded to Bombay
and bore family names, was among the notorious category. He was not only an MP
but became the thorn in the flesh of Samuel Plimsoll, being a ship-owner 'who came
to represent the worst aspect of the heartless, ship-owning capitalist', and as such we
shall encounter him in a later chapter. Others, however, did embrace at least a degree
of philanthropy. James Beazeley founded the Seamen's Orphanage, and Balfour,
Williamson & Co., who owned small, sturdy barques trading to the west coast of
South America 'made a noteworthy departure in providing a home in Duke Street for
their masters and [their] apprentices when in port'.

The second most notable Liverpool shipping house in the 1850s was that of
Pilkington & Wilson, chief rivals of Baines and MacKay, who's Liverpool-based
White Star Line shared the mail contracts to Australia. Since this was only once delivered within the stipulated time, the companies paid a forfeit for every day the mails
were late, although their crack ships made impressive day's runs. Among these was
the *Red Jacket*, built at Rockland, Maine, in 1853 by George Taylor to a design by
a well-respected Bostonian naval architect named Samuel A. Pook. She was huge
for her day at 2,006 tons with a length of 260ft and a beam of 44ft, a good-looking
ship with a figurehead representing 'Red Jacket', a noted Seneca chieftain whose

adherence to the Loyalist cause during the American Rebellion had earned him the commission, gorget and red-coat of a British officer. Initially she was half-owned by her builder and a partner but at the end of 1853 she was brought across the Atlantic under American colours making the passage in thirteen days and one hour, logging 417 miles in one day's run. Her fitting-out was completed in Liverpool whereupon she was chartered by Pilkington & Wilson for £30,000 for their White Star Line of Australian packets, just as Baines had taken-up the *Lightning*.

Under British colours and a new master, Captain Reid, the *Red Jacket* sailed from Liverpool on 4 May 1854. She had several classes of passenger, but none in the steerage, and was therefore catering for the upper end of the market. On her homeward voyage Reid was entrusted with gold dust and specie worth £208,044, and the *Red Jacket* made the Horn in twenty days, only to be beaten two weeks later by the *Lightning* who made it in nineteen. Three days after passing Cape Horn the *Red Jacket* was surrounded by ice which 'seemed to extend on every side in solid fields as far as the eye could reach, without any prospect of getting out…' Obliged to run along a *polynya*:

> All sail was clewed up except the topsails, and as there was a good breeze we proceeded along at about 4 or 5 knots. Our situation at this time seemed most appalling, as we appeared to be getting further into the ice… About noon the captain and 2nd mate, who had been on the fore topsail yard all the morning, discovered clear sea again, to gain which we had to force a passage through dense masses of ice. It was here she sustained the principal damage to her stem and copper… We soon got clear, and the rest of the day we saw no trace of ice and were very thankful… But to our dismay, at 8 p.m. we again fell in with it… At daybreak sail was made… At first it was only large pans… Afterwards large masses of icebergs presented themselves. In grinding the ship through these, great difficulty was experienced…we cleared it again about noon. Icebergs were still…seen both near and in the distance; their appearance was most grand… We hove to again at night. Next day…there was not a breath of wind; a clear sky and beautiful weather, only the air sharp. The next day, Sunday, we passed a number more, which were the last ice seen.

As a homeward account by a passenger, the foregoing is unusual. Since large numbers of passengers were conveyed 'down-under' in these ships, it is unsurprising that we have a number of accounts of emigrant voyages, some from London, others from Liverpool. Many record the privations of being crowded aboard ship, of the misery below decks when the ship ran her easting down in high southern latitudes, and heavy weather that had to be endured day after wearisome day; in short the *mis en scene* of life largely below decks, though their pages are enlivened by accounts of concerts, amateur dramatics and the crossing-the-line ceremonies. Few capture the experiences of the ship's crew and the sense of passage-making over vast distances in wind-driven ships, but that of the young Sir William Forwood is a vivid and ebullient reminiscence of a passage to Australia in *Red Jacket* in 1857, just after Pilkington and

Wilson had placed her under the command of Captain M.H. O'Halloran. Forwood had a genuine interest in the handling of the vessel, so he is quoted at length:

Some account of the first few days of my voyage may be of interest, and bring into contrast the ease and luxury enjoyed on board an Atlantic liner, with the hard life on board a first-class clipper ship. It is not too much to say that on board an Atlantic liner the weather does not count; on board an old sailing ship the weather meant everything... On the morning of the 20th November, 1857, I embarked by a tender from the Liverpool Pierhead. It was nearly the top of high water. The crew were mustered on the forecastle, under the 1st Mate, Mr. Taylor. An order comes from the quarter-deck, 'Heave up the anchor and get under way.'

'Aye, aye, sir. Now then, my boys, man the windlass,' shouts the Mate, and to a merry shanty, [*Paddy Murphy*, the crew manned the bars]... A good shanty man is a great help in a ship's crew. A song with a bright topical chorus takes half the weight off a long or a heavy haul. The chain cable comes in with a click, click of the windlass... 'The anchor is away, sir,' shouts the Chief Officer.

'Heave it a-peak and cathead it,' comes from the quarter-deck, and the tug *Retriever* forges ahead, and tightens the towrope as we gather way. Bang, bang, went the guns, and twice more, for we were carrying the mails, and good-bye to old Liverpool, and the crowds which lined the Pierhead cheered, for the *Red Jacket* was already a famous ship, and it was hoped she would make a record passage.

Next morning we were off Holyhead, with a fresh westerly breeze and southerly swell. We were making but poor headway, and shortly the hawser parted. 'All hands on deck!' shouted Captain O'Halloran, and a crew of eighty men promptly appeared on deck, for we carried a double crew.

'Loose sails fore and aft; hands in the tops and cross-trees to see that all is clear and to overhaul gear; let royals and skysails alone!' The boatswain's whistle sounded...as the men quickly took their positions and laid hold of the halliards and braces. 'Mr. Taylor, loose the head-sails!'

'Aye, aye, sir!' The top-sails, courses, and top-gallant sails were all loose and gaskets made up.

'Sheet, home your topsails!'

'Aye, aye. Now, then, my men, lead your topsail halyards fore and aft, and up with them.' Away the crew walk along with the halliards, and then with a long pull and a pull all together the topsail yards are mastheaded to the shanty *Whiskey, Johnny.*

'Vast heaving! Belay there! Now brace up the yards, all hands on the lee fore braces.'

'So handy my boys, so handy,' sang the shanty man.

'Pass along the watch tackle, and have another pull. That will do. Belay there, and man the main braces. Down tacks.'

The jibs are run up and the spanker hauled out, and the good ship *Red Jacket* like a hound released from the leash, bounds forward, and runs the knots off the log reel.

Captain O'Halloran was hanging on to the rail to windward, munching, not smoking, his cigar, with an anxious eye to windward, asking himself, 'Dare I do it?

Will she carry them? Yes, I think she will.'

'Mr. Taylor, stand by the royals, haul on the weather braces, steady the yard
while the youngsters lay aloft, up [you go] boys'; and half a dozen or so youngsters scampered up the rigging, over the tops, and through the cross-trees, and
quickly were the royals loosed and sheeted home. 'Well done lads. Tie up the
gaskets-clear the clew lines and come down.' But we not only wanted all sails,
but every sail well set, for we were close on the wind. Jibs and staysails, courses
and topsails, topgallant sails and royals must be braced sharp up at the same angle
to the wind, and every tack and sheet pulling doing its work. The good ship felt
that she had the bit in her mouth, and bounded along, throwing the seas in spar-
kling cascades to port and starboard. The man at the wheel kept his eyes upon
the weather-luff of the fore royal, and kept the sail just on the tremble, so as not
to lose an inch to windward. As evening approached, the wind increased with
squalls, the Captain looked anxious, and shouted to Mr. Taylor, 'See that all the
halyards are clear, run life-lines fore and aft, sand the decks, and see that the lee
scuppers are free.'

So the good ship plunged along, occasionally taking a sea over the bows, and in
some of her lurches pushing her lee rail under water and throwing spray fore and
aft; she was just flirting with the weather, romping along, seemingly enjoying every
moment, and revelling in her element.

'Keep her going!' shouted the Captain to the man at the wheel, 'full and bye; just
ease her a few spokes when the squall strikes her.' A loud report like a cannon [and]
the second jib is blown clear out of the bolt ropes.

'Hands forward-bend a new jib!' – Not an easy matter with seas coming over
the forecastle; but with [the shanty] *Haul in the bowline, the bowline haul!* the sail was
mastheaded.

'Mr. Taylor, heave the log.'

'Aye, aye, sir.'

'What is she doing?'

'Eighteen knots, sir, on the taffrail.'

'Good, we shall make over 400 knots by noon to-morrow.' And we did.

We need not say that passengers under these conditions were not at home, or,
indeed, wanted on deck, and the fifty saloon passengers and 600 steerage were
on such days kept below in an atmosphere which was stifling; but this was rather
an exceptional day. We had also soft, bright, sunny days, when life was a delight, a
luxury, a dream, and the sea heavenly, but we had something exciting almost every
day: sails split, spars and gear carried away, albatross circling overhead, Cape pigeons,
icebergs off Kerguelen Land, and finally we made Port Philip Heads in sixty-four
days – the record passage. Bravo, *Red Jacket*.

Unfortunately a smart passage like this could never be relied upon in a sailing vessel,
even when it was within grasp. On returning from Sydney, Forwood came home in
the *Queen of Avon*, a small barque of 400 tons:

I was the only passenger, and selected this little ship purposely that I might learn something of the practical working of a ship at sea. I told the Captain of my wish, and found him quite sympathetic, and he offered to teach me navigation; but when I showed him the log I had kept on the *Red Jacket*, and the many observations I had taken and worked out, he said he felt he could not teach me much. He, however, agreed to my taking my trick at the wheel, and going aloft when reefing or making sail.

When the ship was ready for sea the police brought off our crew, for, in consequence of the lure of the goldfields, it was only possible for a ship to keep her crew by interning them with the police while she was in port — in other words, placing them in gaol. The police and the crew soon set our topsails and foresail, and with a fair wind we quickly passed down Sydney's beautiful harbour. When we reached the entrance the police, getting into their boat, left us, and we started upon our long voyage to Valparaiso. From Valparaiso we proceeded to Guayaquil, where we loaded a cargo of cocoa for Falmouth for orders.

Our voyage was uneventful. I obtained the knowledge of seamanship I desired, for we were fortunate in having in our small crew an old man-of-war's man named Amos. Amos was a splendid man, a stalwart in physique, and most estimable in character. He quickly took the lead in the forecastle, and exercised great moral influence. No swear word was heard when old Amos was present. When reefing he had the post of honour at the weather ear-ring, and when he got astride the yardarm the weather ear-ring was bound to come home. He taught me my knots, bends, and splices, and looked after me when aloft.

At the end of ninety days we sighted the Wolf Rock off the Land's End. In the afternoon we were off the Lizard, and stood off shore to clear the Manacle Rocks. The crew were busy hauling up the cables from the chain locker, for we expected to be in Falmouth before sunset, and all hands were bright and gay at the early prospect of being on shore once more. The wind, however, became more easterly, and when we again tacked we failed to clear the Manacles. Standing out again we were blown off the land, and thirty days elapsed before we again made the Manacles, during which time we battled day after day with a succession of easterly gales. We were blown off as far west as the meridian of the Fastnet; then we got a slant, and crawled up as far as the Scillies, only to be blown off again.

It was monotonous and weary work; standing inshore during the day and off-shore at night, mostly under double-reefed or close-reefed topsails, or hove to with a heavy sea running.

Indeed, we met many ships which apparently had given up the contest, and remained hove-to waiting for a change of wind. We had some bright sunny days, but mostly drab grey Atlantic days, and an easterly wind always. At the end of ten days HMS *Valorus*, a paddle sloop, came within hailing distance, and offered to supply us with fresh provisions. This offer our skipper declined, much to the disappointment of his crew, for our hencoops had been empty for weeks, and our one sheep and two pigs had been consumed long ago, and we were living upon hard biscuit and salt tack, boiled salt beef and plum duff one day and roast pork and pea soup the next. There was no variation; our food had become distinctly monotonous.

The crowd of ships thus weather-bound increased day by day — ships from Calcutta and Bombay, deeply-laden rice ships from Rangoon, and large heavily-laden American ships with guano from the Chinchas. Some we met almost daily; others came upon the scene now and again, and we welcomed them as old friends. The only vessels that got through to their port of destination in spite of the easterly gales were the fruit schooners conveying cargoes of Oranges from the Azores. They were smart brigantines — perfect witches of the sea — well handled, and they never missed a chance. They seemed to have the power of sailing right into the teeth of the wind. At the end of a further ten days another relief ship hailed us, but our Captain again declined any supplies, arguing with himself that the east winds could not last much longer; but another ten days had to pass before a gentle westerly swell told us that westerly winds were not far away, and before twenty-four hours had elapsed we squared away before a westerly breeze. We soon passed the Lizard, and the Manacles, and dropped our anchor in Falmouth, making the passage in 120 days, of which we had spent thirty in the chops of the Channel.

The frustrating persistence of a contrary wind could utterly blight a voyage, particularly when it occurred on the threshold of her destination.

More typical is the account of a passenger named Edward Lacey who sailed to Adelaide aboard the *Orient* in 1862. The *Orient* was owned by James Thompson who ran a small fleet of merchantmen to the West Indies and, in 1853, had a new vessel built especially for breaking into the Australian trade. Thompson ordered his new ship from Anderson, Anderson & Co., proprietors of the Nelson Dock at Rotherhithe where a talented naval architect named Thomas Bilbe and an elderly but energetic former ship-master named Perry ran their graving dock and building slip.[40] Bilbe and Perry built one of the earliest iron hulls in 1855, that of the *White Eagle*, but the crippling ship-wright's strike, which paralysed the Thames at the time, did not encourage ventures into the new material and the business was lost to the Clyde, the Wear, the Tyne and the Mersey. Instead, to maintain their innovative edge, Bilbe & Perry produced a very early composite ship in the *Red Riding Hood* of 1857, and, indeed, built one of the last on the Thames in 1866 when the *Argonaut* was launched. The *Orient*, however, was to be a conventional wooden passenger ship, with a long poop that sheltered her saloon and cabins below and gave her passengers a promenade-deck. On completion, however, she was taken up for trooping to the Crimea, becoming Transport No.78 and carrying the 88th Foot — the Connaught Rangers — to Balaclava. Here she survived the enormous loss of life caused by the great gale of 14 November 1854, during which thirty-four ships were wrecked, including Captain Freeman's *Pyrenees*.

Having served as a hospital ship off Odessa, the *Orient* took up her proper trade in the summer of 1856 and left for Adelaide under Captain A. Lawrence. While homeward-bound west-about on her sixth voyage and heading north in the South Atlantic, her cargo of wool caught fire. In addition to wool and copper, she carried 'several cases [of exhibits] for the Great Exhibition' held in London in 1862, and seventy passengers. Lawrence had the fire smothered, the boats lowered and towed astern; the carpenter drilled holes in the deck, through which water was poured, while the pumps were manned to lift it out of the well. In this way the blaze was subdued and the ship made for Ascension where the hatches were removed and the damage assessed, before the *Orient* sailed for London. It was on the next voyage, in late May 1862, when under a new master, Captain Harris, that Lacey joined her in Shadwell Basin.

Having endured 'Very dirty weather, cold wind and rain all day…and any amount of sickness on board,' passing Dover on Saturday 31 May, Lacey 'walked the poop for two hours before breakfast,' and, at sunset off Start Point, the passengers and crew were on deck:

> watching the sun go down, making a superb panorama view, while the ship is gliding along like a swan without any perceptible movement. The water is smooth and the sun setting behind the hills looks like a sheet of gold. It is a magnificent sight, as if England knew we were taking our last look at her…

It was not long, however, before they were crossing the Bay of Biscay, for on Sunday 9 June the weather was 'fearfully rough and the wind dead against us and blowing great guns'. The *Orient* rolled and pitched, taking green seas in her waist and suffering as: 'Three windows of the stern cabin were washed in, and the place filled with water; pumps were rigged to clear the cabin.' Nevertheless, 'Church Service was held at 10 a.m.' Next day was little better for the wind was 'still ahead and the ship close hauled; the sea is running mountains high. When the *Orient* lay in London Docks I little thought spray would fly over the main yard-arm, but now I am beginning to learn the power of the Atlantic'. The following night poor Lacey 'was pitched out of my bunk three times', but by mid-June the weather was 'getting very warm' and they were 'now shaking down to a settled mode of existence. Our ladies are appearing regularly every morning on the poop' and at the cuddy table. Heat and diarrhoea soon prostrated Lacey in his bunk where the doctor – Dr Nash, who was, unusually, a qualified physician rather than a surgeon – doused him with arrowroot and port so that he was soon up and taking daily baths in the canvas pool rigged-up amidships. The *Orient* impressed her passengers with her speed, particularly once she picked up the trade winds, but soon afterwards lay in the Doldrums awaiting a zephyr, with Lacey finding the heat intolerable. However, on 4 July she passed the equator, and the following day she carried away her main topgallant mast:

> [T]he mainmast was a wreck of ropes and spars; immediately all passengers were ordered below and both watches sent aloft to clear away the wreckage. [It turned into] the roughest day we have had for some time, blowing hard and continually shipping seas [and was followed by] a very stormy night and the crew, poor fellows, are all up aloft rigging a temporary main topgallant and royal.

They encountered more bad weather as they approached the Cape, and on the night of 14/15 July, Lacey was roused from his bunk on hearing the mate bellow for the helm to be put hard up, a-weather, and allowing the *Orient* to run off before the rising wind:

> I slipped on my clothes and went on deck; the sea was a sheet of foam, the wind came whistling like ten thousand arrows; a report like the discharge of a heavy piece of artillery came from for'd, and the jib flew away in a fleecy cloud to leeward; the vessel heeled over carrying everybody and everything into the lee scuppers; the lightning hissed and cracked as it exploded between the masts, making everything tremble from keel to the trucks, broad sheets of water were lifted up and dashed over the decks... As she struggled to lift herself against the tempest, the topsail halliards were let go, but the nearly horizontal position of the mast[s] prevented the sails from running down, and destruction threatened, when crack, away went the topmast over the side, the spanker sheet was cut away and the spanker followed the jib. The ship partially righted herself, and Captain Harris and the [other] officers rushed on deck, but the squall had passed; the moon shone again and the deceitful ocean was all smiles... All hands were called to clear away the wreck and the passengers were sent below...

They repaired the damage and ran on, logging 14 and 15 knots, as they swung south and east towards the Cape of Good Hope, and by the 19th were running under double-reefed topsails before a heavy sea and strong gale. It was cold again and the ladies remained below. On Sunday 20 July, after a 'very stormy night and shipping seas all the while; our cabins are drenched. Both watches were called on deck to work the pumps. I had no sleep and was pitched out of my bunk twice.' Later in the day the passengers were forbidden to go on deck as: 'The ship is lying over on her lee bulwarks', and by 10.00 the gale was 'driving us along at 15 knots with scarcely any canvas up'. The following night was equally rough:

> During the middle watch the two starboard guns on the quarter deck broke loose and crushed the left arm of one of the forecastle men; the poor fellow is now a cripple. The sea is mountains high and on the weather side the bulwarks are gone fore and aft; no passengers are allowed on deck... We are all beginning to feel very miserable having been confined below so long and smacked about like so many rats in a tub... [And between the 24th and the 31st] I am getting tired of this squally, gloomy and dirty weather as we are confined so much below, but to make up the wind is blowing us on the right course at a spanking rate. Today we have run 320 miles... Thick, rainy weather with squalls all day. I have been unwell again, the confinement below does not agree with me... Very ill today and could not eat. Overcast and raining... The ship is labouring very heavily through confused seas, and I feel very sick... A sudden squall has just torn our mizen topsail into ribbons... The ship is pitching very heavily, and the sky is dark and squally... Very squally and lightning in the south-east... Ugly dirty sky and lightning all over the horizon. The glass is

1 Sea-going paddle-steamers like the *Prince Llewellyn*, seen here in heavy weather off the Great Orme's Head, were by the early 1820s running coastal services which soon extended across the Irish Sea and English Channel. Painting by Samuel Walters. (© Courtesy of the N.R. Omell Gallery)

2 The HCS *Waterloo* was built in 1816 by Wigram at Blackwall for the East India Company and, after making nine voyages, was sold in 1834 when the Company lost its monopoly on the China trade. 'Taken on the spot', by W.J. Huggins, shows the view from Dane's Island, looking towards Canton and including Whampoa pagoda, other ships, junks and sampans. The *Waterloo* is flying the Company's gridiron ensign. (© Courtesy of the National Maritime Museum)

The **LAUNCH** of the Honble East India Comp.^{ys} Ship **EDINBURGH**, Captain Henry Bax ;
from the Dock Yard of MESS.^{rs} WIGRAMS & GREEN Blackwall, November 9.th 1825, with a view of the Ship ABERCROMBIE ROBINSON, Captain John James on the S.
To Henry Bonham Esqre M.C. the Managing Owner, this Picture is most respectfully Dedicated, by his Obedient humble Servant W. J. HUGGINS.

3 The launch of the HCS *Edinburgh* from Wigram & Green's Blackwall Yard on
11 November 1825. The sense of occasion is obvious and the presence of the Elder
Brethren in their yacht (on the right) emphasises the close links between John Company
and Trinity House. The *Edinburgh*'s commander, Henry Bonham Bax, was later an Elder
Brother. (© Courtesy of Trinity House)

4 Named after John Bibby's wife, the *Mary Bibby* of 1825 was the largest of his ships. She is depicted here twice by Joseph Heard, weighing and setting sail as she leaves Liverpool. The small craft on the extreme left is a Mersey Flat – a local sailing barge. (© Courtesy of Sir Michael Bibby)

SINGAPORE

5 Singapore in about 1845. Painting by an unknown Chinese artist. (© Courtesy of the Bridgeman Art Library)

6 Instrumental in the founding of Singapore, the enlightened Sir Stamford Raffles was far from the 'empire-builder' he is reputed to have been. Portrait by G.F. Joseph. (© The National Portrait Gallery)

7 The *Sovereign*, probably of Glasgow, by an unknown artist, *c.*1836. She is an early example of a barque with no yards on her mizzen and the spanker surmounted by smaller fore-and-aft top and top-gallant sails spread by monkey-gaffs. The vessel in the background is an American brig. (From a Private Collection)

8 The 300-ton barque *Vere* in heavy seas off the South Stack Lighthouse, homeward bound from the West Indies with sugar and rum in 1833. The importance of lighthouses is vividly portrayed here as, with all hands on deck and her cables bent on to her anchors, the heavily beset vessel struggles to run before a gale that is in the process of rending her fore topmast staysail. Painting by Samuel Walters. (© Courtesy of N.R. Omell Gallery)

9 Master mariner, entrepreneur and opium-runner, Captain William Clifton, commander of the *Red Rover*. From a portrait by George Chinnery. (From a Private Collection)

10 A portrait by George Chinnery of an unknown master mariner, probably of an opium clipper. (© Courtesy of the National Maritime Museum)

11 Leader of the Co-Hong at Canton, Wu Bingjian was one of the richest men in the world. Known to the British as Howqua, he was the second so-named, following his father. Portrait by Chinnery. (From a Private Collection)

12 The Indian partner of Jardine and Matheson, Jamsetjee Jejeebhoy rose from poverty to be one of the great men of his age, a reminder of the importance of Indian ship-builders and ship-owners to British trade in the nineteenth century. The leading Parsee of his day, Jejeebhoy was knighted for his services and afterwards made a baronet. Portrait by Chinnery. (From a Private Collection)

13 A view of Hong Kong Harbour from East Point soon after its acquisition by the British. The anchorage, full of sailing ships, junks and steamers, marks the vigour of the port, while the early settlement of the city of Victoria sprawls along the shoreline beneath 'the Peak'. Artist unknown. (From a Private Collection)

14 Richard Green's 700-ton *Challenger* of 1851 is shown arriving at St Helena in December 1856 under a press of canvas, including weather studding sails, fore and main spencers and a ring-tail set on the spanker-gaff. She was commanded by Captain James Killick, who later bought the ship. Painting by Richard Dadd Skillett. (© Courtesy of the N.R. Omell Gallery)

15 Arthur Anderson of the Peninsular & Oriental Steam Navigation Co., founder of a commercial shipping empire which was to be integral and almost synonymous with the greater British Empire. Painting by T.F. Dicksee. (© Courtesy of P. & O. Heritage Collection – DP World)

Opposite: 16 Although built by Laing on the River Wear, Duncan Dunbar's *La Hogue* was among the finest of the London-owned ships known as 'Blackwall Frigates'. These crack ships replaced the East Indiamen and were run on quasi-naval methods. She is shown here in this painting by Jack Spurling at a mooring in the Thames, preparing to cast off and be towed to sea. She has Dunbar's house-flag at the mainmast-head below which men are casting loose her main topgallant. (Courtesy of The Honourable Company of Master Mariners)

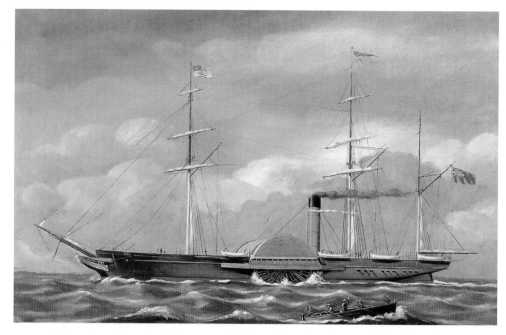

17 Cunard's paddle-steamer *Europa*, built at Port Glasgow in 1847, with the twin pendants flown by vessels of the then North American Royal Mail Steam Packet Co. The stars and stripes of the USA indicate her destination. Painting by George Napier. (© Courtesy of The British Mercantile Marine Memorial Collection)

18 The long and narrow Belfast-built iron screw steamer *Istrian* of 1867, a product of the Bibby – Harland & Wolff partnership, went to Leyland and later to Furness-Withy. From a painting by Samuel Walters. (© Courtesy of Sir Michael Bibby)

19 One of Alfred Holt's first trio of ground-breaking auxiliary screw-steamers, the *Ajax*
followed the *Agamemnon* and *Achilles* out to China in 1866, three years before the Suez
Canal opened. They carried cargoes of tea home at a higher freight-rate than the clippers.
Holt's monogrammed house-flag flies at the main-masthead with the flag of John Swire at
the mizzen. Swire had provided the homeward cargo and was appointed agent for Holt's
Blue Funnel Line. Painting by a Chinese artist. (© Courtesy of The British Mercantile
Marine Memorial Collection)

20 The Inman Line's *City of Brussels* iron auxiliary emigrant steamer entered service on the North Atlantic in 1869 and captured the record for the fastest passage from Cunard's *Russia*. She is shown here off Fastnet Rock Lighthouse after embarking Irish emigrants at Queenstown (Cobh). Painting by Richard Peterson Atkinson. (© Courtesy of N.R. Omell Gallery)

21 The Royal Mail liner *Medway* of 1877. Painting by R. Bennett. (© Courtesy of The British Mercantile Marine Memorial Collection)

22 When Bernard Waymouth designed the *Thermopylae* of 1868 for George Thompson's Aberdeen Line he incorporated the new double topgallants and double topsails to produce a lower but wider sail plan that, combined with a superb hull, made her arguably the finest of the tea-clippers. Painting by Jack Spurling. (Courtesy of The Honourable Company of Master Mariners)

23 The *Harbinger*, built by Steele for Anderson, Anderson & Co., was an exceptionally fine iron ship. She was later bought by Devitt & Moore who ran their ships 'Blackwall-fashion', and she is seen here under their colours about to depart with the Blue Peter aloft, the pilot flag flying below the ensign and a tug bustling up to assist her to sea. Painting by Jack Spurling. (Courtesy of The Honourable Company of Master Mariners)

24 The *William Hutt* was one of the first steam colliers to ply the east coast of England, displacing the old collier brigs. The huge uptake of tonnage to support the Crimean War finds her in the Bay of Naples. Owned by the General Iron Screw Collier Co. of London and Newcastle, this painting is attributed to Michele Funno of Naples and was executed about 1855. (© Courtesy of The British Mercantile Marine Memorial Collection)

falling and two whirlwinds passed us about noon travelling ENE carrying away our fore topsails and royals. No passengers allowed on deck today; all battened down below. Rounding the Cape is rough work!

We have been through a hurricane with squalls, rain and lightning all day. The ship behaves nobly, the only canvas we have aloft is the fore topsail... We lost the captain's gig; a...wave came rolling on top of us and washed it away; the last few days and nights have been...very uncomfortable. Continual storms...necessitate staying below, causing headaches and drowsiness, followed by *ennui*... however; we are progressing on our way.

August arrived with 'the worst storm we have had yet', with the waves 'running main yard high' and the two helmsmen 'lashed to the wheel to prevent them being washed overboard'. That afternoon Lacey 'watched the course of a whirlwind; happily we escaped its vortex, but felt its effects very severely in the gale which followed. A white squall would have been equally interesting had not its violence rendered a retreat below absolutely necessary'. They were now running their easting down in the Southern Ocean and passed close to several icebergs, with fog and continuous squalls of rain, each day passing as dismally as its predecessor. On Saturday 16 August, after going on deck and finding 'everything damp, dirty and unpleasant,' Lacey read a book in his bunk until that evening. Then 'a festive scene took place in the saloon, the birthday of a young lady on board being marked by some champagne presented by the unmarried gentlemen. I wish more of these interesting events had happened during the voyage as they produce much merriment.'

On the 18th the *Orient* passed Cape Leeuwin, having made a page across the Southern Ocean in eleven days. Lacey contemplated his fellow passengers, reflecting that although they would soon be 'scattered according to our respective vocations... yet those who have shared the dangers of the depths together will never be strangers...' Crossing the Great Australian Bight was little improvement on the previous weeks, but Captain Harris had put up two guineas for the first man to sight their landfall, and 'a man is perched like a bird at the masthead peering at the horizon to get a sight of mother earth'. A 'hard gale' like falling glass gave them a rough night before they heard the cry for land, and later in the day ran past Kangaroo Island at the entrance to Investigator Strait. But now the wind was from the north and they were obliged to tack back and forth, the passengers composing testimonials to Harris, his mates and Dr Nash. Eventually the wind allowed them to run up the Gulf of St Vincent, and by midnight on Sunday 24 August the *Orient* was 'safely at anchor at the lightship about nine miles from Port Adelaide'. Lacey disembarked next morning, under orders to report immediately to the chief secretary of the colony. His last tribute was to the ship which had carried him 'safely over 16,000 miles of angry sea and sheltered me through many a raging storm'.

The *Orient* was the first of a line of emigrant ships that, in due course and after the adoption of steam, would become the Orient Line, one of the great British shipping companies, until its amalgamation with P&O in 1961.

The Black Ball, Orient and White Star lines were not the only companies — indeed the Liverpool White Star Line was not the only White Star Line — carrying emigrants, and a handful of ships must here stand for the many others engaged in this trade and exemplify the alternative means by which passengers might reach the Antipodes. We have already met Devitt & Moore in connection with their acquisition of some of Duncan Dunbar's Blackwallers on his death in 1862, and in 1864 they launched the *City of Adelaide*, one of a pair of full-rigged composite ships built by William Pile, Hay & Co. at Sunderland. The other was the *South Australian*, launched into the Wear from the same yard four year later. Of the two, the *City of Adelaide* was the smaller, being 791 tons against 1,040, and therefore 24ft shorter than her half-sister at 177ft (her size encouraging her owners to carry the single topsails, though they were already ten years out of date). She sailed from London, and often picked up her first-class passengers at Plymouth, a contemporary poster advertising her as a:

> fine ship, built expressly for the Adelaide trade and noted for her quick passages… [with] a full Poop fitted with Bathrooms and every other comfort for the accommodation of Cabin Passengers; she also offers a desirable opportunity for a few Second Class and will carry an experienced Surgeon.[41]

The provision of a surgeon was essential, and on one occasion vital in limiting the number of deaths on board to eight when scarlet fever broke out in the emigrants' accommodation.

Loading 1,500 tons of general cargo, and embarking first- and second-class passengers, in addition to her emigrants, the *City of Adelaide* quickly made a reputation for herself. In 1867 she picked up the Adelaide pilot sixty-five days after dropping the Thames one. Both the *City of Adelaide* and the *South Australian* were commanded by members of the Bruce family, John Bruce being her first master and in command of her on the record voyage.[42] He was also in her when in 1872 she made an unusually long homeward run of 140 days round the Horn, caused by an extraordinary series of easterly winds and breathless calms. On 24 August 1874, under Captain L.W.E. Bowen, she had the misfortune to run aground near Adelaide, and it was necessary to discharge part of her cargo, lower her topgallant masts and charter tugs to carry out her anchors before Bowen and his crew were able to haul her off on 4 September, little the worse for her experience. It was customary for all these ships to bring home a cargo of wool from Australia, the *City of Adelaide* invariably loading at Port Augusta at the head of Spencer Gulf. After Bowen, Alexander Bruce was master until in 1876, and Captain Edward D. Alston took over and remained in her until she was sold in 1887. She had made twenty-three voyages to Australia, the last few as a cut down barque. After a brief period running coal from the Tyne to Dover, the *City of Adelaide* was bought by T. Dixon & Co. of Belfast, who put her in the North Atlantic timber trade under Captain J. McMurtry. In 1893 she was purchased by the city fathers of Southampton and moored in the River Test as a cholera isolation hospital, being sold to the Admiralty in 1923. Their Lordships had her renamed *Carrick* and con-

verted to a drill-ship at Greenock for the newly formed Royal Naval Volunteer
Reserve, where she was opened by the Marquess of Graham — afterwards the Duke
of Montrose — who, as a young man in 1899, had served in Devitt & Moore's *Hesperus*
and had subsequently accompanied Lord Brassey in his circumnavigation in the yacht
Sunbeam. After the Second World War the *Carrick* became the RNVR Club and lay
alongside the Broomielaw until the last quarter of the twentieth century when she
fell into a state of rotting neglect.

The *City of Adelaide*'s record passage was equalled by that of the Bilbe-designed
composite ship *Yatala*, owned by the Orient Line, and then exceeded by 'the wonderful *Torrens*'. Like the *City of Adelaide*, the *Torrens* was also a Wear-built ship, launched
from the yard of James Laing in October 1874, but she was considerably larger, at
1,276 tons and with a length of 221ft. Another composite hull with iron framing and
teak planking, she too had a long poop to accommodate her saloon and passengers'
cabin, and a tall sail plan which boasted a main sky-sail — then the hallmark of a
crack flyer — and she retained her studding sails until she was the only vessel on the
Australian run to bear their booms. Like many other legendary clippers, the *Torrens*
was capable of sustaining a good speed in both strong and light winds, frequently running well over 300 miles a day.

Although an Elder Liner in terms of operation and management, her first master,
Captain H.R. Angel, had ordered her to his own account. He remained the major
shareholder in her, and the *Torrens* was largely his brainchild. Angel was a luminary of
the line and regarded as its commodore, or senior master, to which end instead of the
red house-flag emblazoned with white stars and a crescent moon, the *Torrens* flew the
same device but in reversed colours. Angel lived up to his name, for he was 'thought-
ful for the comfort of all on board, passengers as well as sailors', and he held regular
concerts at which 'the sailors were not only invited, but expected to be present'. As
well as having his son Sydney as his second mate for part of his tenure of command,
Angel usually had his wife and the younger members of his family on board, despite
having lost his eldest son in a fall from the rigging in another ship. As mate, Angel had
Mr Moore, 'a hard man with the crew, but a fine sailor,' while in contrast the second
mate at the time was Archibald Flemyng, 'a delightful young Scotsman and a great
favourite with everybody on board'.

Consistently fast, the *Torrens* reduced the passage time between Plymouth and
Adelaide to sixty-four days, perhaps because Captain Angel always worked his ship
east of Kangaroo Island, eschewing Investigator Strait where odd, contrary winds
were often encountered, before heading up for the Gulf of St Vincent. Homeward-
bound he invariably headed west, avoiding the Horn and calling instead at Capetown,
St Helena and Ascension, all for the benefit of his passengers.

Between these two flyers, and running contemporaneously with them in the trade,
was the doyenne of all the emigrant clippers of this era, the *Sobraon*. At 2,131 tons, the
Sobraon was the largest composite clipper built and was laid down in Alexander Hall's
yard at Aberdeen in 1866 as an auxiliary screw steamer. She owed her name to a battle in
the Peninsular War and her figurehead of a lion bearing a shield depicting the flag of the

British union, to the fact that she was ordered by Gellatly, Hankey & Sewell, executors and successors to Duncan Dunbar. The firm soon abandoned the idea of a steamer, for the technology for long distance steam-ships resided just then in only one place, Scott's Greenock Yard, from which Alfred Holt's three revolutionary new steamers were just then emerging. Instead the space between her two stern posts intended to house her screw was filled in, adding to the length and slenderness of the run of her hull. Gellatly's also seem to have abandoned the *Sobraon* as a whole, for the bill of £44,000 for the ship was paid by Robert Smith & Co. of London, who shortly afterwards sold her on to another London house, Shaw, Lother & Maxton, better known for their tea-clippers. Teak on iron, with black hull and painted ports, she reflected all the attributes of a Blackwaller, though she had an unusually short poop, making up for this with a long forecastle. With lower masts of iron, and topmasts and lower yards of steel, she was an immensely powerful full-rigged ship, initially carrying skysail yards, though these were later removed.[43] Fitted with double topsails, she conformed with the fashion of 1883 when the single topgallants on her fore and main-masts were also divided into upper and lower. Capable in both strong and light winds and with fine sea-keeping qualities, she ran like a witch before a quartering gale and could also make 8 knots to windward with the wind six points on her bow, a by no means common achievement.

Despite Shaw, Lother & Maxton's ownership, the *Sobraon* had from the start been under the management of Devitt & Moore, whose house-flag she flew and who purchased her outright in 1872. She spent all twenty-five years of her life as a passenger sailing ship in the Australian trade, serving Sydney between 1866 and 1871. After Devitt & Moore took her over completely they put her on the berth for Melbourne, whither she ran between 1872 and 1891. Initially the *Sobraon* was commanded by Captain Kyle, but he only made one voyage and it was Captain James A. Elmslie – whose brother had been lost with the *Cospatrick* – who stamped his personality on her. Elmslie had gone to sea in 1842, sailing to India before joining a tea-clipper and then serving under Devitt & Moore's house-flag as an officer in the crack Blackwallers, *Parramatta* and *La Hogue*. He commanded the *Cospatrick* before his ill-fated brother and was made a Younger Brother of Trinity House in 1868, just after taking over the *Sobraon*. Captain Elmslie was one of the earliest members of the Royal Naval Reserve, the navy's professional reserve composed of merchant officers that had been established during the 1860s (of which further mention is made below). For most of his time as her master, Elmslie had one of his sons with him. Elmslie junior, having begun his career in the *Sobraon* as apprentice, later became her chief officer under his father, expressing a genuine affection for the ship:

> A glance at the perfect lines of the ship in dry-dock would be quite sufficient to show that there was nothing to stop her going through the water, and I can honestly say that during my eleven years I never saw any other sailing ship pass her...

In all but the most boisterous weather she was dry and, as with all emigrant ships, her master's reputation and competence underwrote her viability, attracting both passengers and cargo – as one might expect – but also retaining individual crew members for long periods. The foreman shipwright who oversaw *Sobraon*'s construction, James Cameron, signed on as her carpenter and remained so for her entire life under the red ensign, 1866–91. Her steward, Thomas Willoughby, was in her as long; Thomas Routledge served ten years as sail-maker and James Farrance began his own sixteen-year stint as able-seaman, but ended it as boatswain. In addition to her master, *Sobraon* carried four mates, eight apprentices, a carpenter, sail-maker, boatswain, two boatswain's mates, twenty-six able-seamen, four ordinary seamen with less than four years sea-service under their belts, two boys and an engineer for her auxiliary steam machinery. To look after the officers and passengers, she had sixteen stewards and two stewardesses. Of her eight apprentices for whom time in sail was mandatory, several became distinguished commanders in both sailing-vessels and steamers. Apprentice Robert Hoare, later in his career a commander in the Orient Line, became an Elder Brother in 1899; Apprentice A.E. Baker finally commanded P&O liners; and Apprentice F. Northey rose in the Devitt & Moore fleet to command the *John Rennie*, the *Collingwood*, the *Rodney* and the beautiful *Harbinger*. Two of Elmslie's sons served with him, one of whom has been quoted; his eldest, later Captain C.T. Elmslie, having served his 'time', left sail to join the P&O S.N. Co.

The *Sobraon* always hauled out from Devitt & Moore's berth in the West India Dock and departed from the Thames in September with about 3,200 tons of general cargo in her lower holds. Shortly before her departure she loaded her livestock of ninety sheep, three milking cows, three bullocks, fifty pigs, laying hens, ducks and geese numbering about 300. Pens were constructed on the main deck for the larger animals, between the boats on the skids for the smaller, while the poultry were kept in coops under the seats set alongside the skylights on the poop. These latter were supplied from Mr Moore's own West Country farm and brought to the docks by his own farm-labourers. From the same source came 'bales of hay, straw, sacks of Swedes, parsnips and corn, grit, pollard and bran, all…stowed on top of the deck-houses'. The *Sobraon*'s 'tween decks were entirely given over to her passengers: cabins, staterooms and a saloon, intended to accommodate 250 souls so that, with her crew, she carried 320 people. Although passenger numbers declined over time, even on her last voyage she carried eighty. Saloon passengers paid between £47 and £60 for the voyage, depending on the location of their cabins, the after-most being more expensive; second-class cost £18 to £25.

Although steamers were, by the mid-1880s, encroaching on the route, a voyage under sail was considered healthily beneficial, while a round-trip entirely avoided the Boreal winter. Consequently the *Sobraon* usually bore a quota of convalescents suffering from tuberculosis, neurasthenia, bronchial and nervous disorders, plus some suffering from 'anxiety' and even a few notorious somnambulists, one of whom fought manically with the officer-of-the-watch who prevented him from involuntarily climbing over the ship's side!

Although acknowledged as a fast ship, Elmslie rarely drove the *Sobraon* hard, for steam catered for the eager passenger and a certain quality of life was what made her well-liked. A fine all-rounder, even Elmslie could not escape the occasional dusting when running the easting down. His worst experience was in 1889 when the *Sobraon*, running along the 45th Parallel before a north-westerly gale, was passing north of the Crozet Islands. With a falling glass, Elmslie shortened down to fore course, fore lower topsail, reefed fore upper topsail, fore topmast staysail and main lower topsail. Such a configuration of sails was to keep the ship before the wind, prevent her from rounding to and broaching – hence the sail being carried well forward – and also of running ahead of the breaking seas. Sailing-vessels were vulnerable to being pooped, that is, suffering a heavy breaking sea over their after-part, and the finer lined they were in their after-body the more susceptible they were to this. It was therefore imperative to keep them moving ahead of breaking seas. With their steering right aft and the poop fitted with the binnacle, glass skylights and the after companionways, the dangers of a sea breaking on board may be readily appreciated. A moment's inattention on the part of the helmsmen could endanger a running ship, and they were expressly forbidden to look astern. Apart from out-running the seas, the only way to avoid being pooped was to turn into the wind and sea and heave-to, but there was a point-of-no-return beyond which the act of turning was far too hazardous, and on this occasion the *Sobraon* had already exceeded this.

With the wind blowing hard and squall succeeding squall, Elmslie was vigilant. Suddenly the wind chopped from north-west to south-west. The crew trimmed the yards, and just as they did so the foresail blew out of its bolt-ropes and flew ahead of the ship in tatters. The lack of the big sail slowed the *Sobraon*. Growling at the men at the wheel to keep their eyes on the compass, Elmslie called all hands, and thirty men spread out along the fore yard and bent on a new foresail. It took them four hours, during which several seas swept aboard into the waist, smashing the main saloon skylight and washing some of the passengers off their feet. James Cameron boarded-up the damaged skylight as quickly as possible, but the port bulwarks were carried away and one of the steel boat-davits along with the boat it served were utterly destroyed. While working on the foredeck in support of the men aloft, the chief officer and three able-seamen were washed from the main fife-rail to crash against the break of the poop. Meanwhile the forward deck-house, which contained the galley and the water condenser, was gutted. Once the new fore-course was bent-on, it was reefed and then sheeted home, whereupon the *Sobraon* leapt ahead again, but it was four days before the weather eased.

Given the risks run, accidents in sailing ships were comparatively rare. A fall from the rigging, if not fatal, was usually disabling and ended a seaman's career, but a few escaped serious injuries, as occurred twice on the *Sobraon*. An apprentice fell from the footrope of the main yard 58ft to the main-deck, but had the presence of mind to curl up with his arms over his head and escaped with a month on his back. On another occasion an able-seaman fell from the main upper topsail yard as the *Sobraon* approached Plymouth in 1886, but, by spreading out his arms and legs, his fall was broken by a succession of ratlines and he lived to tell the tale. However, if you fell overboard with the ship running fast in a heavy sea, you were irretrievably lost. It was in these circumstances, again near the Crozets, that the *Sobraon* suffered her only loss of a passenger overboard, a young lady occupying a first-class berth. It was four bells in the first watch, 10.00, and the helmsmen had just been relieved. The ship ran fast before a steady gale when the woman came up on the poop and sat on the grating just behind the helmsmen. It was assumed that she was taking the air when the cry went up that she had gone overboard and was clinging onto the rail. The third mate, Mr A.G. Elmslie, quoted earlier, ran aft, but she dropped into the sea before he could reach her. An apprentice threw two lifebuoys overboard and the fourth mate called all hands. Thanks to the large and competent crew, sail was shortened, the ship was hove-to and a boat was launched within five minutes – itself a shining achievement. But after a desperate search in appalling conditions, no sign of the suicide could be found.[44]

The *Sobraon* left Australia for home in February, always returning by way of the Cape of Good Hope, loaded with either wool or grain. Both outward and homeward passages were enlivened by, besides the inevitable 'dead-horse' and crossing-the-line ceremonies, amateur dramatics, formal debates, deck-quoit competitions, and ring-making, a curious hobby by which coins were beaten into rings using a marline spike as an anvil, after a hole had been made in them.[45] The dry-decked *Sobraon* was stable enough to play deck-cricket, even in the Southern Ocean. On the homeward passage, stops at Capetown and St Helena took in the tourist traps of the day: Napoleon's tomb – vacated by the late emperor on the return of his remains to France in 1840 – his residence at Longwood and Halley's Mount, from where Edmund Halley had observed the transit of Venus across the sun in 1676.

A famous ship, the *Sobraon*'s last voyage came in 1891. Having discharged her cargo at Melbourne she was sold for £12,500 to the Government of New South Wales, converted to a reformatory, towed to Sydney and moored off Cockatoo Island. In 1911 she was acquired by the Commonwealth Government of Australia, renamed HMAS *Tingara* – the Aboriginal for 'open sea' – and became a boys' naval training ship at Rose Bay until 1927 when she was moved to Berry's Bay. Here she lay until 1941 when she was broken up, some of her teak being used to build a yacht which retained her distinguished name.

Of the many other shipping lines running sailing-vessels between Britain and her colonial dependencies in the Southern Hemisphere, only a brief mention can be made. They supplemented and supplanted the convict transports, the last of whose 825 voyages was made in 1868 by the *Hougomont*, which discharged her prisoners – largely Irish Fenians – in Western Australia. After convict-labour had kick-started the most unpromising of economies, the tide of eager and hopeful emigrants flooding-in had sustained this growth. Moreover, there was also the new colony of New Zealand, to which emigrants were attracted in great numbers, especially following the discovery of gold at Otago in 1861. Settlement was encouraged by the colonial scheme of assisted migration initiated by Sir Julius Vogel, the colony's premier, and was catered for by two companies who would merge in 1882.[46] The first of these was Shaw, Savill & Co. which, like so many British shipping firms, was formed by two colleagues who began working for others. Shaw had been in the employ of Willis, Gann & Co., who sent 'two or three ships a year' out to New Zealand, while Savill had been a counting-house clerk. Both men seized the opportunity to capitalise on the expanding traffic thither, chartering rather indifferent vessels, including the *Edwin Fox* which had been built of teak and saul wood by William Henry Foster at Sulkeali on the Hughli in 1853 as a speculation for the Moulmein trade. Sheathed in Muntz-metal — a beaten mixture of copper and zinc — she was, in the event, purchased by Sir George Hodgkinson and sailed from Calcutta for London on 14 December with ten passengers and a mixed cargo of rice, jute, rape seed and castor oil. Damaged in a storm while anchored off Capetown, she did not reach London until 10 May 1854 where she was sold to Duncan Dunbar for £3,000. Dunbar chartered her as a trooper but, instead of the Crimea, the *Edwin Fox* first took French troops to the Baltic before settling into a regular run to Sebastopol. In 1856 she sailed to Melbourne before leaving for China where, at Swatow, she embarked 300 coolies for Havana and the sugar cane fields of Cuba. In 1858 she carried 280 convicts out to Fremantle, and thereafter bore cargoes in the cross-trade to India, often including Australian-brewed pale-ale, but also carrying rice, coir, cotton, coffee, graphite, cinnamon, general cargo and troops. When Dunbar died in 1862 she passed to Gellatly, Hankey & Co. who employed her trooping between Britain and India.

In 1873 she was purchased by Shaw and Savill, adding to their small fleet, and left for Port Lyttelton. The *Edwin Fox* ran into a gale in the Bay of Biscay during which her doctor died after accidentally impaling himself on a steel rod, a seaman was killed securing the boats, and an emigrant girl was swept overboard, then returned as the ship rolled her inboard again. Simultaneously, several of the crew got into the spirit-store and, disgracing themselves, obliged the emigrants to man the pumps as her master negotiated a tow into Brest from an American steamer. Before the *Edwin Fox* arrived in Lyttelton scarlatina had killed four emigrants, tuberculosis a fifth, and a child died of thrush, all of which resulted in the ship being quarantined after having to heave-to for a fortnight off the coast owing to the extremity of the weather.[47] Long before this disastrous voyage, Shaw, Savill & Co. had better ships among their fleet of some ten vessels, notably the *Wild Duck* which, between 1860 and 1873, made thirteen voyages to New Zealand under Captains Bishop and Baillie.

By this time Shaw and Savill were rivals of the Albion Line, which had been registered in November 1864 and had grown out of the Burma trade of Patrick Henderson which dated back several decades. The firm had originated with the purchase of a small brig, the *Tom & Jessie*, in 1829, by Captain George Henderson, her master. Henderson had several brothers, all in trade, one resident in Leghorn and another in Glasgow. Patrick, the father of the firm, was close to men like John Bibby. Henderson began to build up a modest fleet largely engaged with the trade to Leghorn, expanding in 1848 with the acquisition of the full-rigged ship *William Watson*, Captain Ebenezer Morrison, of Glasgow, which traded to the east, including Moulmein. In this year they engaged a fellow Scot named James Galbraith as a chartering clerk, and soon afterwards bought shares in another full-rigger, the *Ontario*, which was employed in worldwide general-trading. She carried a nitrate cargo from Chile, made several voyages from the Clyde to Bombay and bore sponsored emigrants to Natal. By 1860 only Galbraith and Robert Henderson survived of the original partners, and the company was restructured, nursing ambitions to go into steam to cater for the Californian gold rush. Robert Henderson's idea was to convey would-be gold prospectors to Panama, from where they could travel overland and pick up a ship for San Francisco. The Royal Mail Steam Packet Co., the only company running thither, was restricted by its mail contract from capitalising on this opportunity, leaving the field clear for others. However, when the two steamers intended for this were built, the Crimean War broke out and instead the new vessels transported French troops to the Black Sea. After the war the company became embroiled in a struggle for the mail contracts, of which more will be found in the following chapter, but Henderson was keen to set up steamers to run out to Alexandria and others to pick up the mails from Suez for Australia. The arrangements were complex and the project under-capitalised, with no repair facilities in Australia, so that, when the *Oneida's* machinery broke down and a Cunard steamer had to be chartered to cover the contract, she was badly damaged after running aground in the Red Sea and the company was nearly ruined. Henderson withdrew his ships to concentrate on New Zealand and Burma as destinations, abandoning all thoughts of mail contracts.

In 1856 he sent his first full-rigged ship, the *Lady Douglas*, to New Zealand, and in the following year the purpose-built *Robert Henderson* left Glasgow for Port Chalmers, proving a fast ship. Galbraith and Henderson soon built up a fleet which, like all their competitors running to the Antipodes, was part-owned and part-chartered, and included the *Jane Henderson* and the *Constance*. The business was given a boost by the Otago gold-strike in 1861, and concurrently grew its trade with Burma and China. In 1864, four years before Robert Henderson's death, the Albion Line was formally registered as an unlimited liability company. At the time it owned ten ships: the *Lady Douglas*, the *Lydia*, the *Robert Henderson, Jane Henderson, Viola, Wave Queen, Helenslee, Vicksburg, Edward P. Bouverie* and the *City of Dunedin*. While conditions aboard some of these attracted adverse criticism, the company gained major credit as pioneers in the frozen meat trade, their 1874-built full-rigged ship *Dunedin* of 1,250 tons being fitted with the Glasgow-developed Bell-Coleman refrigeration plant. The *Dunedin* sailed from the Clyde in August 1881 under Captain Whitson. At Port Chalmers she loaded 5,000 butchered sheep carcases, having first to freeze them down. Despite a dispiriting failure in her plant, at which her homeward passengers deserted her and the first lot of 500 carcases had to be discharged and sold while repairs were affected, the *Dunedin* finally brought a frozen cargo home. She was not the first vessel to carry refrigerated meat, but she was the first to bring home New Zealand mutton and, as the company's historian, Dorothy Laird, so elegantly summarises: 'The importance of the frozen meat trade in New Zealand's prosperity, and to Britain's larder can hardly be over-estimated. The feat of the...*Dunedin*...deserves to be set into its place in history'.[48] That year the Henderson's Antipodean enterprise merged with its chief rival to form the Shaw, Savill & Albion Line.

Nor were the colonial companies backward in taking their own initiatives. James Baines had recognised the potential of local trade early, as the Black Ball Line's small fleet of coasting vessels on the Australian coast testified, while the gold finds opened equal opportunities for the establishment of shipping companies native to Australia itself. One of these was set up by a William Howard Smith who formed a coastal cargo and passenger fleet, the Howard Smith Line. Other Australian coastal services followed as steamers began to proliferate, most notably the North Coast Steam Navigation Co., Sydney. Nor was colonial enterprise shy of establishing deep-water ship-owning firms such as The New Zealand Shipping Co., while in 1879 the world's first steel ocean steamship, the *Rotomahana*, was built for the Union Steam Ship Co. of New Zealand.

The New Zealand Shipping Co. was formed in Christchurch, New Zealand, in November 1872, a Mr Charles Wesley Turner being despatched to London 'to tender for the carriage of emigrants' at £15 per head with powers to offer discounts. This decision arose from dissatisfaction with the service provided by the British carriers, Shaw, Savill & Co. and the Albion Line, and within six months the chairman, John Lewis Coster, could report to a general meeting that the new company was 'from all parts of the colony receiving most encouraging promises of support...the public... generally taking a warm interest...considering it in the light of a national undertaking'. The company's first ship was a barque, the 883-ton iron *Punjaub*, built at Stockton-on-Tees in 1862 for Knevitt & Co., which sailed from Gravesend with 340 souls on board, of which twenty-eight died on the passage – twenty-one of whom were Danish and the remainder British.[49] The deaths among the eight adults and twenty children were caused by teething, measles, typhus and other unspecified causes, while a further eight died not long after landing. This was not a particularly auspicious start given the complaints against the British companies, but the *Punjaub* discharged a cargo that arrived 'in excellent order reflecting great credit on those engaged in the work'. However, the tide of emigration was relentless. Several further charters were taken up, and in November 1873 the company purchased two 'high class iron ships' and gave them Maori names, *Waitara* and *Mataura*, establishing a tradition that was to endure for its entire life. Two months after the *Dunedin*, the *Mataura* also carried a frozen cargo to Britain using 'Haslam's patent refrigerating engine'. At £6,000 the installation was expensive, with two-thirds being the cost of the plant, the balance paying for the insulation and Mr Haslam's royalty of 4½d a carcase (reducing to 2¼d in 1888).

In addition to these new vessels, the New Zealand Shipping Co. beefed-up its representatives in London and entered into a contract with the Sunderland shipbuilders, Blumer & Co. This was 'for building two 1,000-ton iron ships', the first of which would bear the name *Rakaia*, the second *Waikato*. Soon afterwards Turner cabled from London that he had purchased two more vessels whose names were changed to *Waimea* and *Rangitiki*. Before 1874 was out, the board was congratulating itself because:

the company has despatched no less than thirty-seven ships of very large tonnage from the United Kingdom to the colony, loaded with valuable cargoes; that it has sent six laden vessels from the colony and there are six more at present on the berth loading for London, [Coster adding that the charges for chartering were too high, for which] the real and only lasting cure is for the company to become possessors of its own vessels.

Besides the *Rakaia* and *Waikato*, both of which would 'be turned out completely ready for service at a very reasonable price' of £14,000 each, the *Rangitiki* would cost £25,000. Turner ordered two more vessels from Blumer's, the *Waitangi* and *Waimate*, each at £20,000, and consequently was obliged to appoint an overlooker, or marine superintendent, selecting a Captain Hodgson at a salary of £20 per month, 'upon the understanding that he devoted the whole of his time to the company's work'. Hodgson's salary was raised the following year, in 1875, to £25, to keep it in line with the salaries being paid to the company's masters. That year, of the 140 outward clearances of vessels from Britain to New Zealand, no less than fifty-four were under the house-flag of the New Zealand Shipping Co. This was the height of the emigration boom and the year in which the new company carried almost 11,500 passengers to New Zealand. In 1877 the company's outward sailings from the South West India Dock amounted to sixty-three, with thirty-seven homeward (reference being, of course, to London as the home-port) in which 92,652 bales of wool and 10,700 tons of wheat were carried. Although first-class passengers moved over to steam, as late as 1888 the company was advertising that its iron 'sailing ships...are of the highest class at Lloyd's. Most of them are full [i.e. long] pooped ships with commodious saloons, suitable for passengers seeking a long sea voyage for restoration of health'.

Unfortunately losses occurred, the worst for the New Zealand Shipping Co. being the collision between two of their ships, the *Waitara* and *Hurunui*, on the evening of 26 June 1883. Both had left London on the same tide and were beating down the Channel in misty weather when, off Portland, they both came in sight of each other on opposite tacks. The second officer of the *Waitara* – the 'give-way vessel' under the prevailing rule of the road – failed to alter course, and the *Hurunui* struck the *Waitara* on her starboard side. She sank in little more than two minutes, only sixteen of her twenty-eight strong crew and eight passengers being saved. Captain Webster of the *Waitara* was literally plucked from his own deck as he was caught in the tangled mess of the *Hurunui's* bowsprit, though he returned to the scene in one of the *Hurunui's* boats. He was, nevertheless, censured at the inquiry which placed the principal blame on the *Waitara's* dead second officer.

The defining moment, and that at which we take our departure, was the arrival in New South Wales of the *other* White Star Line's auxiliary steam-ship, *Aberdeen*. In 1825 George Thompson had founded the Aberdeen Line by acquiring the small, 116-ton *Child Harold*. Initially establishing a short-sea trading company, Thompson was soon building larger sailing-vessels, and by mid-century his ships were carrying cargoes to China, Australia and North America. About 1860 Thompson was employing the yard of Walter Hood & Co. to design and build extreme ship-rigged clippers for the China tea-trade, arguably the most beautiful and swiftest sailing-vessels under the British red ensign, of which the *Thermopylae* and *Salamis* were exemplary. But, unlike many other tea-clipper owners, Thompson soon adopted steam, and in 1881 his innovative 3,616-ton *Aberdeen* demonstrated the abilities of the triple-expansion engine and the low coal-consumption of her cylindrical, double-ended steel boilers by cracking the forty-day barrier for a passage to Australia.[50] Retaining the green hulls of his sailing ships and selecting a buff funnel colour, the Aberdeen White Star Line continued to build beautiful and useful ships in the true spirit of William Morris. As late as the turn of the century, Thompson's elegant steamers *Miltiades* and *Marathon* bore clipper bows and bowsprits, and in 1902 the *Miltiades* reached Melbourne from London by way of Capetown in the record time of thirty-five days.

From the foregoing, it is clear that British sailing-vessels played a major part in the creation of the modern world, from opening up new territories to laying telegraph cables and carrying frozen cargoes. Notwithstanding the frequent lapses in sobriety and occasional downright mutinous disorder into which their crews could lapse, their masters and mates were an astonishing breed. As well as ruling their often fractious crews with their fists, some resorted to intimidating displays of personal daring. The mate of Killick, Martin & Co.'s *Omba* over-awed his crew by going aloft 'via the main-tack and up the weather leaches [the vertical *edges* of the sails] to the main royal yard,' a trick by no means unique.

Unfortunately, men like Captain James A. Elsmlie of the *Sobraon* may have been regarded as fine and patriarchal commanders whose services were sought out by nervous and seasoned passengers alike, but they were not generally well-served by their owners. A master like Enright, who could click his fingers and demand £1,000 per annum, was exceptional, if not unique, the norm being the £300 paid to the New Zealand ship-masters, all of whom were home-grown. These men – the 'Masters under God' of the bills of lading – upon whom the prosperity and safety of many souls rested, by-and-large bore their anxieties well, discharged their responsibilities competently and earned their moiety. In the eyes of the state, however, they cut little mustard.

Even men like Elmslie could receive humiliations, for the experience of joining the Royal Naval Reserve could be far from pleasing, the Victorian navy never quite understanding how to treat a volunteer, let alone a mercantile officer:

> In the middle years of the century serious plans were tabled for the formation of a naval reserve from Merchant Navy officers. These overdue proposals revived old enmities dating from the days when His Majesty's captains exacted salutes from British merchantmen no less peremptorily than they did from Dutchmen. Relations had not improved in days of impressments, when captains of clippers (sic) in sight of home ports had been forced to stand by while cocky boys, sometimes not yet 16, had boarded them in the King's name and, with the barest of civilities, relieved them of some of their best men. The idea of making Merchant officers into naval

reservists was coldly received by some of the older admirals. Even the best of the mercantile officers, while mannerly enough, could not be expected (in the admirals' view) to absorb naval procedure and tradition in middle age… When the Royal Naval Reserve was eventually formed in the 1860s, veteran merchant officers who had sailed into every port in the world were granted the derisory rank of sub-lieutenant, which put them among the midshipmen. It was made clear to them that if war came they could expect no 'plum' commands.[51]

Captain Elmslie, as 'Master under God' of the full-rigged emigrant ship *Sobraon*, could rise no higher than a mere sub-lieutenant in the reserve. Captain Crutchley, commanding in the Union Line, sought an interview with Admiral Sir Augustus Phillimore, the admiral superintending reserves. Its outcome was unsatisfactory. The admiral:

> informed me that the rank of sub-lieutenant was ample for the master of a mail steamer, and with that I had to content myself, but when H.R.H. the late Duke of Edinburgh became admiral superintendent, I renewed my application in writing, and was promptly granted the rank of lieutenant.[52]

Although there were sound reasons for this limitation, even this modest commissioned rank did not play well with merchant officers. Another reservist, the well-connected Captain Ruthven of the Orient Line, used to hob-nobbing with Governors-General, resigned his commission as a consequence; and he was not alone:

> R.N.R. officers generally were at that time not at all too well pleased with their treatment and there were several other resignations besides mine… Although I had many friends in the Navy, I never met one of them through my connection with the Reserve, where I only saw warrant officers and instructors.[53]

This is echoed by the otherwise enthusiastic and intellectually hungry Crutchley who, in 1877, attended HMS *President*, the Reserve Drill-ship in London.

> [Crutchley found] that while the instructors were possibly the best that could be found in the Navy, and the teaching of the first order, there seemed always to be an under-current of indifference, so far as the [naval] officers were concerned. I was anxious to learn, and did not get nearly enough to satisfy me.[54]

More excoriating experiences awaited the younger aspirant. Afloat, a young mate might possess status and enjoy some self-esteem, but pay stopped when a seafarer – officer or seaman – was off articles and the business of seeking employment, of currying favour with a slick-haired shipping-clerk, could be a vile business. When searching for a ship, Joseph Conrad always experienced a 'sense of profound abase-ment'. Too often, however, the masters of merchant sailing ships were seen in their infrequent periods ashore in a less than flattering light. As the shipping-agent at Mauritius, Paul Langlois recalled, they 'usually dressed in white ducks, wearing caps or straw hats, their faces and hands tanned by the sun and salt-water…their language forceful and often coarse, [they] were not models of elegance and refinement'. Occasionally, however, one stuck out:

> In contrast to his colleagues, Captain Korzeniowski (Joseph Conrad) was always dressed like a dandy. I can still see him (and just because of his contrast with other sailors my memory is very precise) arriving almost every other day at my office dressed in a black or dark-coloured coat, a vest generally light in colour and fancy trousers, everything well cut and stylish; he wore a black or grey coloured derby [hat] slightly tilted to one side, always wore gloves and carried a cane with a gold knob.

Conrad, who arrived at Port Louis in the *Otago* on 30 October 1888, related that:

> In the British colonies of Hong Kong and Singapore there were a large number of adventurers who lived by their wits. For one reason or another, they had not found that royal road to fortune they had hoped to discover. Many of these had been to the Philippines, where they had failed in their undertakings.

According to another officer, Thomas Golding, Chinese-owned steamers in these ports:

> were at that date the last refuge of European officers who had fallen low owing either to misfortune or drink. They had no authority apart from their navigating duties, the virtual ruler of the vessel being the Chinese Supercargo or *Chinchew*, who was really a part owner.

But such men endured a life of unremitting responsibility, hardship and harshness. Even in the 'flying-fish' trades of Conrad's beloved East Indies, the sea-life could be precarious, as he had discovered when the *Palestine* caught fire in the Banka Strait. So too had a master-mariner who lent his name to a character in three of Conrad's novels. The fifty-one-year-old Captain William Lingard, master of the *West Indian*, whose brig was attacked by pirates as she lay anchored in the estuary of the Berau River on the coast of Kalimantam on 25 November 1875. Lingard had gone ashore in his steam launch, leaving his wife on board the brig. The two mates, a man named Avery and Lingard's nephew Joshua, had with them three Chinese quartermasters and about twenty lascars. The first attack occurred at about 03.00. Avery and Joshua Lingard opened fire with rifles while the Chinese seamen, wielding knives, bottles and axes, poured boiling water over the *praus* ranging alongside. For her part, Mrs Lingard shot one pirate attempting to damage the *West Indian*'s rudder. Having been driven off, the pirates renewed the attack at 08.00, but the crew again resisted. Lingard was by then returning and immediately waded in, opening a rapid fire until the pirates took flight and the *West Indian*, her sails already loose in their buntlines, let fall and escaped.

Although Captain Henry Keppel had largely cleared the *orang laut* out of the creeks of Borneo thirty years earlier and the White Rajah James Brooke had improved the civil government of Sarawak on the far side of the great island of Kalimantam, Dutch rule remained tenuous throughout 'their' eastern archipelago, and piracy would be a problem in the South China Sea until modern times. Men like Captain Lingard were precariously balanced between the old world of sail and seamanship, and the new world of technology. Were they, with their small fortunes sunk in half the shares in a small brig seeking cargoes of *gutta percha* in the Indonesian archipelago to sate the distant demand for the insulation of submarine telegraph cables, aware their days were numbered? Long before Lingard beat off his assailants in the Berau Estuary, and long before the *Dunedin* ran a cargo of frozen mutton to London under sail, the world had been turned upside down by capital and steam.

CHAPTER NOTES

1. The late Rowan Hackman in his *Ships of the East India Company*, World Ships Society, 2001, states that the *Java* was sunk by Italian limpet mines on 20 September 1940. This may well be the case, but an edition of *Sea Breezes* of 1939 has a photograph of her leaving her moorings in August, so she was probably in the hands of the breakers at the time of the Italian attack by human-torpedo a year later.

2. Later on, having to swear an oath of allegiance to the Honourable Company, and later to the Queen on entering the fraternity of Trinity House, Were was disowned by the Society of Friends, who refused to swear oaths but affirmed the truth of their intentions.

3. The sudden depression in what had hitherto been so valuable a commodity that it had been held in locked caddies by strict house-keepers gave rise to the expression 'Not for all the tea in China'.

4. Like Huddart, referred to in *Neptune's Trident*, who owned a chain-making plant and was, like Pixley, intimately connected with the Trinity House. Pixley was clearly a versatile businessman of some talent, as were so many of these former ship-masters.

5. I am unable to identify which of the naval dynasty of Gearys this was, but although he ran a very taut ship on man-of-war lines, the *Sir Edward Paget*'s maiden voyage was not a financial success, and Green replaced Geary with a new master at its end.

6. To differentiate their ships, Wigram retained the early house-flag worn by the *Sir Edward Paget* and her sisters, while the Greens adapted it, placing the blue rectangle *under* the intersection of the red cross. In consequence of this, Wigram's version of the house-flag – which was strictly speaking originally Green's – was retained throughout the subsequent history of the firm that became the Federal Steam Navigation Co. Ltd, where it was also borne as a device upon the company's red and black funnel.

7. Somes's convict ships in 1840 were the *Maitland*, *Eden*, *Mary Ann*, *Mexborough*, *Asia* and *Lord Lyndoch*, the last two of which had been East Indiamen. At the dissolution of the East India fleet Somes bought the *Earl of Balcarres*, the *Thomas Coutts*, *Abercrombie*, *Robinson*, *Lowther Castle*, *George the Fourth* and the *Java*, reference to some of which has been made earlier.

8. Like the old East Indiaman, *Java* and several other well-known ships such as the Blackwaller *True Briton*, the *Marlborough* ended her days as a coal-hulk in Gibraltar.

9. These are David MacGregor's concluding words in *Merchant Sailing Ships, 1815–1850*.

10. The lineal descendants of T. & W. Smith, Smith's Dock Co. Ltd, remained ship-builders and repairers on Teesside into the third quarter of the twentieth century and were famous in the Second World War for adapting the design of their standard whale-catcher to that of the Royal Navy's Flower-class corvettes. They also built the second *Patricia* for Trinity House in 1938, a vessel which was in service for over forty-two years and remains afloat in Stockholm as a restaurant. Their blue cross last appeared on the funnel of the plant shed in the ship-building and repair yard at Southbank-on-Tees.

11. See the article by Captain W.B. Whall in the first issue of *The Mariner's Mirror*, 'Journal of the Society for Nautical Research', published in 1911. Whall, who wrote a seamanship handbook and collected sea-shanties, began his career as a midshipman in Blackwall frigates.

12. Captain Webb, afterwards Sir Sydney Webb, was both an Elder Brother and, between 1883 and 1898, the Deputy Master of Trinity House. Henry Toynbee's brother Joseph was also a commander in Smith's Blue Cross Line, succeeding Sir Allen Young in the *Marlborough*.

13. Writing in 1912, Downie does not identify his commander in the *Trafalgar*, but he was probably Captain W.H. Rosser, whose *Law of Storms* was published by Charles Wilson in 1876.

14. Both quotations are from Basil Lubbock's *The Blackwall Frigates*, pp146–147.

15. See Course, A.G., *Painted Ports*, p12.

16. Devitt & Moore also bought Dunbar's *Vimiera*, which they retained until 1872, selling her on until she was eventually acquired by N. Olsen of Arendal, Norway, who cut her down to a barque and ran her until breaking her up in December 1903.

17. Basil Lubbock claims *La Hogue* was broken up in 1897 when still at Madeira. Captain Course says she was run down there by a steamer towards the end of the First World War.

18. The solemnising of marriages aboard ship was perfectly possible when a cleric was among the passengers. The idea that a ship-master had official sanction to marry couples under the laws of the Established Church of England is untrue, but it seems clear that, for the purposes of propriety aboard emigrant ships, when a man and a woman displayed public affection and a genuine desire to co-habit, a form of marriage service was conducted on condition that on arrival in Australia or New Zealand a proper service was conducted by an ordained priest.

19. Conrad was then Second Mate Josef Teodor Nalecz Korzeniowski and held a first mate's certificate of competency. He did not become naturalised until qualifying for master-mariner because, although British nationality was not then a pre-requisite for a master's certificate, his uncle wished him to remove himself from any possibility of military service under the Tsar, under whose rule Conrad had been born. The events aboard the *Palestine* – converted to the *Judea* for the purpose – form the basis of his novella, *Youth*.

20. The *Pyrenees*, lying in the crowded Port of Balaclava, had been forced from her anchors in bad weather when another vessel got athwart her hawse. Driven aground, she had come under fire and suffered one man killed. Freeman and his officers returned fire while evacuating the ship, for which he was – as a non-combatant in command of a hospital-ship – severely censured by a military court. However, the commander-in-chief of the British Army, the Duke of Cambridge, told him not to mind the sentence, and that men of his stamp were needed. Dunbar's favour came with the command of his newest ship, the *Northfleet*. Another master who distinguished himself was Captain Baynton of the Royal Mail Paddle-Steam Packet *Medway*, in which he towed the British flagship HMS *Britannia* into station for the bombardment of Sebastopol. During the bombardment Mrs Baynton and her companion were on board. The crew undertook this duty 'with the understanding that if fatalities occurred their families were to receive the same consideration financially as if they had been serving in corresponding rank in the Royal Navy'. See Crutchley, W.C., *My Life at Sea*, p123 *et seq.*

21. Wade afterwards commanded the *Loch Sloy*. The precedence of seniority was most important in many shipping companies and largely replaced the evils of nepotism, though it is clear that exceptional men like Stuart jumped fences and commanded salaries that were privately negotiated. As an indicator of the going rates of the day, the *Northfleet's* crew and their wage-bill are extant: She had four mates on monthly salaries of £9.5 for the first, descending to £2.5 for the fourth. The surgeon received £5 and the carpenters £6.5 – significantly 30s more than the second mate. A joiner was employed at £4, the steward at £5.5, the cook at £4.25 and the senior of two cuddy servants £2, his junior £1.5 and the pantry boy £1. There was also a butcher and a cook's mate, each on £3.5. On deck the boatswain received £5, the sail-maker £4.5 and the sixteen able-seamen £2.5 each. Of the seven ordinary seamen, the five seniors got £1.75 and the two juniors £1.5, with a solitary deck boy having the same as the pantry boy at £1 per month. There were also eight midshipmen who received allowances from the voyage premiums paid by their parents.

22. The number of ship-owners who were Quakers, both in Britain and the United States, is striking. It is clear that they tended to be more considerate of their employees than other owners, and generally ran better ships. They also seem to have made more professional masters and mates, as we have noted from Edward Beck's *Journal* quoted in Chapter One. The bestselling author Captain Frederick Marryat, a somewhat testy naval officer with a mordaunt eye for detail, remarks on page 96 of his novel *Newton Forster or The Merchant Service* that: 'Mr Berecroft…was very superior to the generality of masters of merchant vessels. His family, it was reported, were strict Quakers.' Coming from Marryat's acid pen, the remark can be regarded as telling.

23. Parry, J.H., and Sherlock, P.M., *A Short History of the West Indies*, Macmillan, 1971, p201. In 156 there were 134,271 Indian immigrants working on Mauritian plantations, and in 1859 no less than 825 ships entered Port Louis with labourers. Between 1853 and 1859 the revenue of Mauritius was doubled.

24. The etymology of many words used on board ship is of interest. *Baboo*, 'Properly a term of respect…and formerly in Hindustan applied to persons of distinction… [This] is now almost or altogether confined to Lower Bengal. …Among Anglo-Indians, it is often used with a slight savour of disparagement… And from the extensive employment of the class, to which the term was applied as a title, in the capacity of clerks in English offices, the word has come often to signify "a native clerk who writes English." '

    The word 'coolie' had gone through a similar change of meaning and seems originally to have referred to a tribe in western India known as the Koli. By the early 1800s it meant a hired labourer or burden-carrier and, while its origin was Indian, the word was increasingly applied to Chinese labourers, probably because they made up a greater number of emigrants and were ultimately more widespread. See *Hobson–Jobson, The Anglo–Indian Dictionary* of 1886 which treats with native tongues other than those of the Indian sub-continent and covers most of the words absorbed into the pidgin *patois* commonly used in British merchant ships east of Suez in the eighteenth, nineteenth and twentieth centuries.

25. In 1874, for example, Harrison's *Artist* delivered '383 men, 81 women, 17 boys, 16 girls, and 19 infants' to Demerara in Guiana. 'The Immigration-Agents General, and Medical Officer to the Department were much pleased with the appearance of the Immigrants, and pronounced them even a finer body of people than those introduced by the *Linguist*' (another Harrison ship).

26. Bullard, King & Co. had run sailing ships to Natal since about 1850, putting their first steamers into service in 1879 and providing a passenger service from African ports to Calcutta where transfer to the Far East services of other companies was available.

27. Such losses, although not common, were not unusual. The *Foyle* also disappeared
   with all hands when on a passage from Argentina to Antwerp in 1908, but by this
   time was in Norwegian hands and named *Jarlen*. The same fate awaited the *Arno*, also
   Norwegian owned at the time of her loss in 1913, as was the *Forth* when she sank in 1915
   after being damaged, though her crew survived.

28. There was one occasion, mentioned by Captain Andrew Shewan, in which so many
   sailing-vessels were caught in the entrance to the English Channel by a prolonged period
   of easterly gales that the Admiralty was prevailed upon to send a man-of-war down
   Channel with provisions.

29. The *Acor* arrived in Alicante from the Clyde on 18 August that year under the command
   of Captain Horatio Darling. Two years later, to obviate difficulties in the trade, she was
   transferred to the Spanish registry and renamed *Cervantes*, establishing the company's
   later tradition of adopting Spanish names. An auxiliary brigantine, her under-powered
   engines were replaced in 1868, six years after she had been lengthened. She served
   MacAndrew as a fruit-carrier for over forty years, being sold on in 1885 to be burnt-out
   in 1901. MacAndrew & Co. made a habit of registering their ships in Spain, making
   them somewhat ambivalent as 'British' merchantmen, but the practice demonstrated the
   commercial versatility both of merchant shipping and that of British owners who were,
   with their shareholders, the chief beneficiaries. In 1863 a subsidiary company, Miguel
   Saenz y Cia., was set up in Seville under the management of Juan Cunningham, 'a man
   of character, highly thought of in Seville where a street was named in his honour'. So
   too was one of the Spanish-flagged vessels, which all bore handsome clipper bows and
   long, yacht-like counter sterns. Cunningham had acquired orange groves from a local
   convent, and this in turn was acquired by MacAndrew & Co. Apart from oranges and
   other citrus fruits, liquorice was another import from Iberia.

   Extensive expansion took place in the last quarter of the century. The company lost
   the *Lopez de Vega*, reported missing in bad weather in 1891, and another vessel was
   sunk after a collision in the Mersey. A few of MacAndrew's ships were put under the
   red ensign, notably the iron steamers *Pelayo*, *Dante* and *Petrarch*, all built in 1872–73.
   In common with other companies, MacAndrew & Co. changed their ships' names as
   circumstances warranted, and it was as *Daoiz* that the *Dante* sank after a collision in 1892.
   Reorganisation of the Spanish company took place the same year and, as was so often
   the case, became complex and broken into separate subsidiaries.

   Technically at least these were not British ships, though MacAndrew & Co. retained a
   small number under the red ensign. These seem not to have been lucky, for the *Georgian*
   (acquired second-hand and retaining her original name) was lost off the Dutch coast
   in 1904 when under the command of Captain J.E. Taylor. Similarly the 1874 *Tasso*, on
   passage from Antwerp to the Rio de la Plata with general cargo, stranded off Cape
   Finisterre on 5 March 1886 and became a total loss. The second *Petrarch* suffered a similar
   fate. Some of the Spanish-registered vessels were transferred to the British flag. Typical
   of these was the 1,320-ton schooner-rigged *Campeador* (1894), originally operated by
   the Barcelona subsidiary Compania Maritima for four years, then transferred to Robert
   MacAndrew & Co. where she remained under the British flag until her breaking up in
   1932.

   The combined Hispano-British companies ran regular services from London,
   Liverpool and occasionally Antwerp or Hamburg to Barcelona, Bilbao, Seville, Cadiz
   and Alicante. When insufficieant outward cargoes offered, general cargo was taken up,
   or coal charters were picked up from Tyne and Wearside or South Wales. The company
   was not particularly innovative. Steel was not used until 1887, and fruit was carried
   without mechanical ventilation; nor was MacAndrew & Co. an early beneficiary of
   double-bottom tanks, though water ballast tanks were built in to their ships' hulls.

Enemy action and losses by misadventure, such as that of the new *Valdes* in November 1914 after running into the anchored Cunard liner *Andania*, were severe and led the partners to consider their position. In the end Robert MacAndrew & Co. Ltd was bought by Sir Owen Philipps, later Lord Kylsant. On 17 April 1917 the company was absorbed into Philipps's Royal Mail Group. Although owners of numerous ships since the company went into steam, only twenty-three had been British registered.

30. The convention for a house-flag was to fly it at the mainmast-head as a symbol of the owner's primacy. The Brocklebank Line retained the custom of flying their house-flag at the fore masthead until the end, although by the late twentieth century the accepted wisdom was that it was 'an honour' allowed them − by whom, no one could tell! − as the oldest British shipping company.

31. Gore's *Liverpool Advertiser*, 1835.

32. S.R. Graves was MP for Liverpool and a keen yachtsman, owner of the schooner *Ierne* and sometime commodore of the Royal Mersey Yacht Club. He was one of many ship-owners who rose to political prominence.

33. When Ismay took over the management of the Liverpool White Star Line he introduced iron hulls, so emigrant ships built for the company after 1867 were of iron construction. See Chapter Five. Sir Alfred Jones's career is given in Volume 4, *More Days, More Dollars*.

34. According to Michael Stammers, to who I am greatly indebted for the information garnered in his magnificent study of the Black Ball Line, *The Passage Makers*, Teredo Books, 1978, the actual number of vessels owned by Baines and MacKay between 1852 and 1871 was 151.

35. In 1853 Donald McKay launched the 4,555-ton *Great Republic*, then the largest sailing-vessel ever built and a proto four-masted barque.

36. Baines's bankruptcy was caused by the collapse of Barned's Bank, and it followed the crash of another Liverpool bank, Borough's, in 1857. The recapitalisation of the Black Ball Line was largely undertaken by Thomas MacKay's company through London, not Liverpool, investors, for Liverpool underwent a credit crisis and ship-owning became more modest, almost returning to the eighteenth-century practice of multiple share-holding for a while.

37. See MacGregor, *Fast Sailing Ships*, Conway, revised edition 1998, p190. MacGregor's thesis is drawn from *The Mariner's Mirror* of 1957 in which a lengthy correspondence initiated by an experienced sailing ship master, Captain James Learmont, was carried on by a variety of men who had experience in sail or who had compiled data relating to passage-making and may be regarded as authoritative and definitive.

38. Captain Tom Robertson was a very competent marine artist.

39. Lubbock calls him MacDonald, but the more reliable MacGregor refers to Charles MacDonnell, a fact confirmed by Stammers. Stammers also scuppers Lubbock's affirmation that the *James Baines* survived as the basis for Liverpool's Princes Landing Stage at the pierhead.

40. Captain Andrew Shewan refers to this man as Pirie in his memoirs, *The Great Days of Sail*.

41. To emphasise the *City of Adelaide*'s commitment to the place whose name she bore, she carried the arms of the city on her stern. In poor condition at the time of writing, the ship's fate is uncertain.

42. John Bruce's brother David was the first master of the *South Australian*, and John succeeded David in command of that ship when he left the *City of Adelaide*. David's son Alexander took over as master of the latter ship after Bowen. Most of these ship-masters owned shares in their ships, which made them careful. Members of the Bruce family settled in South Australia. About one third of the current population of South Australia is said to claim its ancestors emigrated in the *City of Adelaide*.

43. By the time of *Sobraon*'s composite construction, iron hulls were being built, but of significance in the later development of the sailing ship were the doubling of topsails and topgallants — which, by dividing sails, made their handling easier, reduced crew numbers and thereby increased voyage viability. Steel wire rigging and steel spars likewise reduced losses of rigging. The first ship to have lower masts, topmasts and lower yards of steel was the Liverpool ship *Seaforth* of 1863.

44. Deaths by falling overboard were not uncommon on this leg of the outward voyage to Australia. There was also the occasional loss of a master or mate, whose station on the poop left them more vulnerable than the helmsman who could be, and frequently was, lashed to his post. The Aberdeen White Star clipper *Queen of Nations* lost her master, Captain Archibald Donald, a noted driver, while running her easting down, though I am uncertain of the date.

45. The dead-horse ceremony celebrated the end of the first month at sea when the crew had worked off their advance of wages paid them at the time of their engagement, which they almost invariably disposed of before departure. The first month was therefore considered to have been worked 'for nothing', after which a sailor was in credit. The ceremony involved a number of characters, including constables, a jockey and a 'horse' consisting of an rough effigy made of old sail-cloth. It was often used as a fund-raising event among the passengers and, on ships like *Sobraon*, as well organised as the more familiar crossing-the-line ceremony. It concluded with the 'horse' going overboard to shanties and cheers. Funds raised by this and other events on board usually went to marine charities such as the Royal Merchant Seamen's Orphanage.

46. There was also the Wakefield Plan promulgated by Edward Gibbon Wakefield who advocated the state-under-written transportation of whole communities to preserve balance, stability and social cohesion in the new country which had been incorporated into the British Empire in 1840 after the Treaty of Waitangi with the fierce Maoris. Such ideas were encouraged by institutions such as the Free Church of Scotland so that local loyalties and affiliations linked would-be settlers with the shipping houses that would carry them overseas.

47. At the time of writing, the *Edwin Fox* is undergoing restoration in New Zealand. At the end of her working life she was used as refrigerated storage in London to serve Shaw, Savill & Albion's incoming mutton carriers. She then loaded a final cargo of coal and salt and in 1885 sailed to Port Chalmers, Dunedin, where she took up these duties, although afterwards moved to Picton. Her freezer capacity was 14,000 carcases. In 1902 the *Edwin Fox* was exchanged by Shaw, Savill & Albion with a local meat company for the contract to exclusive rights to carry frozen lamb and mutton to Great Britain. In 1905, her plant worn out, she was reduced to a coal-hulk and landing platform, duties which she performed until the 1960s.

48. Miss Dorothy Laird sailed round the Horn in the barque *Penang*, during which voyage the barque was dismasted. In the 1960s, she managed the Merchant Navy Hotel in Liverpool and showed the author the photographs she had taken of the catastrophe, for, with steel masts and spars, re-masting and re-rigging the twentieth-century square-rigged ship was not the relatively straight-forward matter of seamanship and skilled carpentry it had previously been with wooden-sparred ships.

49. Not to be confused with the Indian Marine's *Punjaub* which John Willis renamed *The Tweed*.

50. The introduction of the triple-expansion plant was the brain-child of Dr A.C. Kirk who installed it in W.H. Dixon's *Propontis* while he was manager of John Elder & Co. He afterwards joined Robert Napier's ship-building firm, of which mention is made in Chapter Four, and was responsible for its fitting in the *Aberdeen*. See the author's *History of the Ship*.

51. See Turner, E.S., *Gallant Gentlemen, A Portrait of the British Officer, 1600-1956*, p260 *et seq*. When war did come in 1914 and their own ships were taken up as commissioned armed merchant cruisers, the commanders of ocean liners were invariably retained as 'staff-captains', subordinate to the naval captain sent to take over, but responsible for ensuring that a shipping company's asset did not let the Royal Navy down. See *More Days, More Dollars* and *Fiddler's Green*, the final two volumes of this work. Nevertheless, a lieutenant could command a small warship.

52. See Crutchley, W.C., *My Life at Sea*, p225

53. See Ruthven, J.F., *Memoirs of Jocelyn Fitzgerald Ruthven, Master Mariner, 1849–1943*, p54. When commanding the *Chimborazo* Ruthven met Admiral Sir George Tryon several times in Sydney and was much impressed with him. It is significant in this context that Tryon 'told me amongst other things that he had had more to do with officers of the Merchant Navy than any other naval officer.' Tryon was to drown in the disastrous collision between HMSs *Victoria* and *Camperdown* nine years after these encounters.

54. See Crutchley, p163.

FOUR

'CAPITAL AND STEAM'

The Development of British Steam Navigation, 1816–1866

The tentative appearance of the steam-vessel offshore defied the experience of centuries, for at sea reliability was the touchstone of success and boiler-explosions, paddle-failures and reports of difficulties handling steamers in heavy weather counted against them. Nevertheless, the tide of progress was inexorable. The little *Comet's* debut on the Clyde in 1812 was soon matched by that of the Scots-built *Thames* and *Marjory* on the Thames. The *Marjory* was built at Dumbarton by Archibald Maclachlan, and fitted with a 14hp side-lever steam-engine by Cook of Tradeston. She steamed through the Forth and Clyde Canal to appear in the estuary of the London River in 1814. Belching smoke, she passed a squadron of men-of-war anchored at The Nore, to be hailed by some puzzled naval officers who wished to know what sort of vessel she was. 'A *steamer*, and from Scotland,' was the proud reply.

At the time there were only ten people brave enough to trust themselves to such a dangerous form of transport and willing to embark in her for her first advertised passage from London to Margate. This was unsurprising, for the newspapers, with their perennial preoccupation with disaster, broadcast the frequent boiler-explosions these early steamers suffered. As early as 1817 a Parliamentary Committee was set up to examine these failures but the products of Henry Cort's rolling mill, although used for making early boiler plating for Newcomen's mine-pumps in 1786, do not appear to have been adopted by ship-builders until much later. Without the rolling mill, the iron and steel ship would not have been possible, but at an earlier date marine boilers of rolled-plate would have reduced the risks of explosion so common in boilers of cast iron.

Notwithstanding this adverse publicity, it was not long before this diminutive vessel, all 63ft of her, was a popular attraction, and the *Marjory* remained in service on the Thames until her breaking up in 1858, earning distinction as the first British steamer to cross the Dover Strait to Calais. Within two years she had been joined by the *Thames*, originally built by Alexander Martin at Port Glasgow in 1814 as the *Duke of Argyle*, by which time paddle-steamers were rapidly becoming unremarkable.

Many of the factors governing the development of steamers had been known for years. As early as 1752 the Frenchman Daniel Bernoulli had proposed a propeller as a means of propulsion, and in 1794 the Englishman William Lyttelton had patented a screw-propeller, though this initially found little favour. The principle of compounding steam and transferring it from high to low-pressure cylinders, patented as early as 1781 by Jonathan Hornblower and Alfred Woolf, was set aside, to be resurrected in conjunction with the screw propeller much later in the nineteenth century. Iron as a ship-building material enjoyed a similar history. While wood prevailed as the building-material for sea-going hulls, canal barges were being built of iron by John Wilkinson of Ilkley by 1787, and in the following year, after some experiments in North America, the Scotsman Patrick Miller rigged a central paddle wheel between two hulls and made 5 knots.[1] William Symington's canal steamer *Charlotte Dundas* of 1802 is generally regarded as the first British steam-paddler, with the *Comet* raising the bar as she ventured down the Clyde below the Tail o' the Bank shoal. Abroad, in America in 1806, Robert Fulton – having paid a visit to William Symington, who took him on a special trip in the *Charlotte Dundas* – built the steamer *Clermont* for service on the Hudson River, and another commercial steamer, the *North River*, appeared in 1807. Fulton, who had touted his 'revolutionary' designs between the British Admiralty and the Ministry of the Marine in Paris at the height of the Napoleonic War, oversaw the construction of the first harbour defence steamer for the United States Navy, the *Demologos*, in 1812, just as the United States went to war with Great Britain.[2] India can boast an early steamer, William Trickett building a yacht for the Nawab of Oudh in 1819, powered by an 8hp engine manufactured at the Butterley Ironworks at Ripley in Derbyshire.

At this time sea-water was used in marine boilers. Heat and salt are prime causes of corrosion, and the frequent cleaning and scaling necessary to keep them working rapidly eroded their substance, and the slow development of the marine boiler was a major retardant in the pace at which steamers were adopted. The Parliamentary Commission of 1817, established to examine 'the means of preventing the mischief arising from explosions aboard steam-ships', recommended that boilers be made of wrought iron, fitted with safety valves and proof-tested to three times their working pressure; all steamers had to be registered and their boilers subjected to survey, introducing a measure of state control and interference into private enterprise resented by some ship-owners. In due course condensers introduced by Samuel Hall in 1834 enabled fresh water to be used and recycled. Boiler improvements – both in terms of higher-pressure output and fuel consumption – were finally achieved by Alfred Holt in 1866, as will presently be seen.

Besides compounding, Boulton & Watt's first two-cylinder slide-lever engine appeared in 1814, and fourteen years later John Maudslay fitted an oscillating steam engine to the paddle-steamer *Endeavour*. In the following year, 1829, Elijah Galloway's feathering paddle-wheel – which relied upon eccentric rods to keep the paddle-blades at right-angles as they passed through the submerged portion of their revolution – was modified by a Mr Morgan and became the industry-standard. One of the least known of the early pioneers was Charles Wye Williams who discovered that the introduction of air into a boiler above the fire as well as passing up through the grate from below greatly increased its thermal efficiency, burning off otherwise wasted gases and hugely decreasing the amount of smoke discharged from a natural-draft funnel. Wye Williams 'was a man of both science and industry' with wide accomplishments and interests in the City of Dublin Steam Navigation Co. This firm 'was admired in his day as the best and biggest short seas operator anywhere'[3] and was crucially supplying foodstuffs from the west of Ireland, by way of the River Shannon and associated canals, to the Irish steam-packets at Dublin, which conveyed them to the rapidly growing industrial conurbations of Lancashire. One of the paddlers operating on the Shannon was the *Garry Owen*, which was not only constructed of iron but incorporated un-pierced transverse bulkheads, as suggested to her builder, John Laird of Birkenhead, by Charles Wye Williams. These became a feature of Laird's ships and, soon afterwards, standard in all iron-vessels. Other influential figures such as David Elder, Robert Napier's works manager, made incremental improvements to both the steam-propulsion plant they manufactured and the tools used to do so. Many other mechanical problems were slowly resolved, notably the over-heating of metal shaft bearings, resolved by John Penn in 1840 with the introduction of self-lubricating bearings made of the oily hardwood *lignum vitae*.

But innovative genius alone was not enough. There were also numerous facilitators, the most obvious of which were the labourers of a score of trades who actually built the ships, the seamen who manned them and behind whom were the miners who dug ever deeper into the coal seams or the lodes of iron ore. Such raw materials, more readily available on the shores of the Clyde and other northern rivers than the Thames, ensured that ship-building grew in Scotland and northern England as it withered on London's river. This move was accelerated as first iron and then steel became commonplace for the construction of ship's hulls. However, the engineering skills that produced marine steam-engines grew up directly from works that had first produced pumping-engines for mines and – in particular – the cane-crushing mills exported to the sugar-plantations of the West Indies during the previous century. This kept some manufacturers in the south where a smaller steam-plant, such as was used for derrick engines, windlasses, steering gear and other auxiliary machinery, was produced in tandem with agricultural equipment.

From riverine and estuarial services, the paddle-steamer was soon common in the cross-Channel, coastal and short-sea trades. In 1818 Maclachlan's 90-ton, 7 knot *Rob Roy*, powered by David Napier's 30hp engines, initiated a steam-ferry between Glasgow and Belfast before operating a regular service between Dover and Calais as the *Henri Quatre*. In 1819 Napier's 150-ton, twin-engined *Talbot* began running between Holyhead and Dublin, with the *Prince Llewellyn* operating along the Welsh

An early 'leviathan', as paddle-steamers of 1,000-tons burthen were called, the *United Kingdom* lies at anchor, embarking passengers aft and loading cargo forward. The Blue Peter at her foremast announces imminent departure for Leith with a large number of passengers. She was acquired by the General Steam Navigation Co. Ltd. Etching by E.W. Cooke. (Private Collection)

coast so that, although the sea-sick misery of the short-sea passenger was far from over, he or she was no longer obliged to accept the exposure, uncertainties and privations of a sailing-packet. Passengers now began to enjoy – and soon learned to demand in an increasingly competitive market – a modest measure of comfort at sea, the beginnings of that luxury associated with first-class travel by steam-vessel.

The size and power of these early British steamers increased steadily. In 1822 Messrs John Wood of Port Glasgow built a steamer 146ft in length, measuring 448 tons, and powered by two Boulton & Watt engines which used the principle of compounding. This gave the *James Watt* a speed in still water of 10 knots, and she became the first steam-vessel to be entered in Lloyd's Register. In 1825 the first of what came to be called 'leviathans' – steamers exceeding 1,000 tons burthen – was built by Robert Steele of Greenock for Edinburgh owners. The *United Kingdom* had, besides her 200hp engines built by David Napier's cousin and brother-in-law Robert, elegant passenger accommodation far superior to the traditional Leith-smacks. Lying at anchor in the Thames flying the 'Blue Peter' as notification that her departure for the Forth was imminent, the *United Kingdom* was the largest passenger steam paddle-packet then in service, inspiring an etching by the marine artist Edward William Cooke.

Notwithstanding this progress in coastal waters, long international voyages remained problematical for several reasons. In the first place paddle-steamers were difficult to handle when rolling in a seaway, one paddle digging-in while the other thrashed in the air, so that keeping a paddler on course proved difficult. Use of auxiliary sails steadied the roll, but the consequent constant heel only aggravated matters, and, while sails made up for the shortfall in the power of early steam-engines and the quantities of coal their inefficient, low-pressure boilers consumed, nothing could compensate for the loss of cargo space taken up by engines, boilers and bunkers, still less generate additional revenue to pay for the extra engineers, firemen, greasers and coal-trimmers. As exponents of a new technology, these specialists — especially the engineers — tended to command relatively high wages. Such vessels could, therefore, only operate viably on routes with high freight-earning potential, and that meant essentially passenger-conveyance along the coasts or across the English Channel and the Irish Sea.[4] In time mail-contracts would enable ship-owners to underwrite these high overheads, and in 1821 the British Post Office commissioned two steam-packets for the Holyhead–Dublin service, but in the 1820s bold trail-blazers bent on long voyages were left to go-it-alone. In 1821 a steamer from Liverpool, the *Conde de Palmella*, which had been built in Britain for Portuguese owners, reached Lisbon, an early example of what in time would amount to thousands of vessels — both merchantmen and warships — constructed in the United Kingdom for foreign owners. Another such, the 428-ton *Rising Star*, built as a man-of-war though subsequently used as a merchantman, left her British builder's yard of David Brent on the Thames, bound for Valparaiso.[5]

The year of 1821 is better known for the first crossing of the Atlantic by an auxiliary paddle-steamer, the American *Savannah*, which not only used sails for most of the passage but which was sold on arrival and can in no way be regarded as having inaugurated a transatlantic service under steam. The Western Ocean remained dominated by the American sailing packets, so that it was the long run to India that attracted British interest. Even in its decline the East India Company encouraged initiative as, in 1824, a *lakh* of rupees — some £10,000 in silver — was offered as a prize for the first steamer to reach India within seventy days. The principal contender for this prize was the 470-ton *Enterprize*, then being built by Gordon & Co. at Deptford, which was acquired by a syndicate of interested London speculators. Launched on 23 February 1825, the *Enterprize* was fitted with engines constructed by Maudslay, Son & Field of Lambeth, which were fed by a corrosion-resistant copper boiler. The *Enterprize*'s paddles were capable of being raised when her sails were used, essential with a daily consumption of 11 tons of coal against a capacity of only 380 tons. Although she ran under power for about two-thirds of her passage-time, the *Enterprize* exceeded the limiting seventy days by forty-three, dropping anchor in Diamond Harbour in the Hughli that December. Although this was little better than an East Indiaman, the *Enterprize* proved that a long, sail-assisted passage was possible, for she had encountered severe weather and completed a passage of some 12,000 miles.

At the instigation of Captain Frederick Marryat,[6] the *Enterprize* went on to operate as a naval auxiliary during the Burma War before making some passages to Singapore, whither she carried the Bishop of Calcutta, within the limits of whose Anglican diocese the new port lay. Having become a tug on the Hughli, the *Enterprize* was rescued in 1829 by the Bombay Government and put into the then new Bombay to Suez mail service along with another auxiliary steamer, the *Hugh Lindsay*. This vessel, belonging to the Bombay Marine, was among the first steamers constructed in India, though her engines, built by Maudslay Son & Field, had to be shipped out to Bombay. However, the *Hugh Lindsay's* bunker capacity proved barely adequate and her voyage was nearly disastrous. Leaving Bombay on 20 March 1829, grossly over-laden with coal bunkers, she staggered into Aden on the 31st, almost devoid of fuel. After bunkering for six days she went on to top up at Mocha, repeated the process as Jeddah and finally reached Suez on the 22nd. It was an abysmal performance, despite the fact that she had been blessed with fair weather for sailing.

Things subsequently improved, but it was February 1835 before the company's steamers concerted operations with the arrival at Alexandria of the Admiralty's mail-packet from Malta. While the overland transit between Alexandria and Suez raised problems of its own, coaling stations were difficult to establish, Perim being selected as an initial staging-post at the southern entrance to the Red Sea, and although this was soon superseded by Aden, the changing monsoons further frustrated the precise scheduling of the mails. The Bombay to Suez service was intended to replace the traditional 'overland' route which went from Bombay through the Persian Gulf to Basra, up the Euphrates and overland by way of Aleppo to Antioch (Anatakya). It was never a great success.

By this time the *Enterprize* was worn out, though her engines were removed and fitted in a new vessel of the same name. The *Hugh Lindsay* was joined by a better-fitted vessel, the *Atalanta*. Built by Wigram & Green at Blackwall and fitted with Maudslay's engines, she left the Thames in mid-December 1829, reaching Bombay after 106 days, twenty-nine of which had been spent in port, mostly coaling. However, she had made her voyage largely under power, though at the cost of 989 tons of coal. The *Atalanta* was soon afterwards joined by the *Berenice*, built and powered by Robert Napier of Glasgow and superseding the *Hugh Lindsay*. By this time steam-tugs and steam-dredgers were as common on the Hughli as upon the Thames. The *Forbes*, mentioned earlier as towing the opium-barque *Jamesina* to Canton, was built at Howrah, opposite Calcutta, by Captain W.N. Forbes. Her 120hp engines were manufactured by Boulton & Watt and shipped out from Britain, and she was launched on 21 January 1829.

In addition to wooden vessels built at Bombay or on the Hughli, small iron steam-vessels were shipped out from Britain in prefabricated sections, with their engines, for construction in India. Although largely used as tugs, they made occasional forays down the Arakan coast to Cox's Bazaar, and up the Irrawaddy to Rangoon. By the mid-1830s mercantile steam-vessels, with a few Royal Naval or Company cruisers, were also operating on the Indus and in Mesopotamia (Iraq).[7] Among their advocates was Captain James Johnston, a former Royal Naval officer who, like others placed on half-pay at the end of the Napoleonic War, decided to embrace the new technology and brought the *Enterprize* to India from England. It was said that although the paddle-steamer herself had failed to earn the *lakh* of rupees, Johnston had been awarded a cash sum for his own enterprise.

Like Captain Clifton, Johnston had engaged the interest of the Governor-General, Lord Bentinck, whose enthusiasm lay beyond assisting the large East Indiamen up and down the Hughli and lightering their cargoes in 'flats' or barges, in military operations on the rivers of India and Burma, hence the involvement of the Company's Marine. After the first steamers[8] had demonstrated their capabilities, first on the Hughli and then during the Burma campaign, Bentinck sent Johnston back to London to seek out the latest developments in steam-plant. Johnston's London contact was the assistant examiner at East India House, a man better known as a poet than a force behind early steam navigation, Thomas Love Peacock.[9]

The two men co-operated in designing four new paddle-steamers which adopted the then new prefabrication techniques and were built by Maudslay, Son & Field. Hitherto engine-builders, this company now became the first shipyard to launch iron ships into the Thames from their works at Pedlar's Acre near Westminster Bridge. The vessels, the *Lord William Bentinck*, *Thames*, *Jumna* and *Megna*, were sent out to Calcutta in succession, the first being launched in July 1832 and, after satisfactory trials, dismantled and shipped east to arrive at Calcutta in August 1833. She was reassembled and re-launched in April 1834, the first of what were known as 'Peacock's iron chicks', intended to haul barges on the Hughli and further upstream to the greater Ganges – of which the Hughli was but one estuary.

At the same time as these ungainly vessels were gracing the Ganges, the Parsee builders of Bombay had not been idle, and in 1833 the Magazon Yard of Ardaseer Cursetjee launched a small teak steamer, the *Indus*, powered by a British-built plant and designed as a passenger ferry for the environs of Bombay.[10] After two years the *Indus* was acquired by other Bombay syndics who put her into commercial service running up to Scind – just then opened to trade, appointing another former Royal Naval lieutenant, John Wood, as her master. Wood ascended the Indus to Hyderabad, recording fulsomely that he had 'the proud satisfaction of unfurling our country's flag on the Indus from the first steamer that ever floated on its celebrated waters'.

Such pioneering spawned a series of steamers in the east, the iron, prefabricated hulls of William Laird & Son rapidly cornering the market and founding a great shipbuilding enterprise at Laird's Birkenhead Ironworks on the west bank of the Mersey.[11] While the riverine paddle-steamers of India made sorties into the open waters of the Bay of Bengal and, in the case of the *Forbes*, further afield, on the home coast steam-vessels were improving their sea-keeping abilities. Unconstrained by economics, the Royal Navy, though slow to adopt steamers as capital ships – largely because of the loss of broadside guns – were not tardy in making use of them in lesser roles. The yards that built for the navy were able to offer the small, incremental improvements in plant and boilers to commercial operators willing to accept greater risks.[12] By 1827 there were 225 steam-vessels registered in British ports, mostly small steam-tugs but including large vessels such as the 'leviathan' *United Kingdom*. Lloyd's Register, embracing mercantile bottoms, records eighty-one steamers by 1830, and 100 two years later.

One of the early 'steam navigation companies', the General Steam Navigation Co., announced its ambition by adopting a house-flag that showed the world encompassed, an ambition never actually realised. Although its mail venture to the Cape of Good Hope failed, it did become a short-sea trading company of distinction which was later absorbed into the huge P&O consortium. 'General Steam', as it became known, was formed in London by William Hall who owned steamers running coast-wise up to Hull, and Thomas Brockelbank (sic), a wealthy timber-merchant then running the steamer *Eagle* on the Margate route. On 11 June 1824 they were joined by others willing to invest in an enterprise conceived to establish:

> between the United Kingdom of Great Britain and such places as may be deemed advisable, a certain expeditious intercourse for the conveyance of passengers and merchandise, which the combined powers of capital and steam placed at their disposal will enable them under judicious management to accomplish.

Capital of £2 million was raised, and by the end of September a prospectus had been promulgated by numerous national and influential newspapers. In pursuit of their greater ambitions, the General Steam Navigation Co. gave out that their vessels would open services to India, North and South America, Portugal, Spain, France and Russia. Significantly, in addition to these destinations, the company magnanimously proposed:

> to station steam-vessels at those points on the British coast where most needed for the purpose of towing and assisting such vessels as may be detained by contrary winds or otherwise. Ships, [the directors asserted, meaning sailing-vessels] are enabled to enter and quit Harbours regardless of wind or tides, and it affords the most flattering prospects of connecting the remotest parts of the Globe by a more safe and rapid communication.

Established at 24 Crutched Friars in the City of London, the 'GSNC' purchased two steam-packets, the *Lord Melville* and the *Earl of Liverpool*, and ordered three 240-ton vessels, each with twin engines of 40hp. Its fleet of sixteen steamers began to provide a service between London and Great Yarmouth, Brighton and Dieppe, and London and Ostend. This was not the operational network vaunted in the prospectus, but at the first half-yearly meeting of the shareholders at the City of London Tavern on 11 August 1825, the chairman of the board, Mr Hylton Joliffe, was able to mollify any critics by declaring a dividend of 16 per cent.

The General Steam Navigation Co. was established in a mood of hope after a decade of post-war adversity. Heavy national debt, high taxation, excessive prices, a depreciated currency, the failure of some foreign markets and a continuing post-war slump all exacerbated high unemployment. This produced civil unrest, culminating in the suppression of legitimate complaint by such acts as the brutal 'Peterloo Massacre'.[13] Lord Liverpool's Tory Government picked its way through this quagmire with some difficulty and much public opprobrium. Despite its horrors, industrialisation brought wealth to an emerging middle-class, among which ship-builders, iron-masters, mine-owners and even steam-engineers were an expanding group. Seeking outlets for investment, many believed that innovation would produce the panaceas for society's ills, and while entrepreneurial activity may easily be portrayed as simple self-aggrandisement, particularly where ship-owning was concerned, the reality was more complex.

The influential economic and political ideas of the day, most notably those enshrined in Adam Smith's *Wealth of Nations*, published in 1776, Jeremy Bentham's governing principle of 'the greatest happiness for the greatest number' of people, David Ricardo's 'laws of rent' and of 'comparative cost' along with James Mill's *Analysis of the Human Mind* of 1829, hinted at the possibility of a system being discovered by which all mankind – or at least the inhabitants of the enlightened and fortunate nation-state of Great Britain – might prosper by free trade and democracy. Alongside and facilitating these abstractions it was confidently thought that much could be expected from advances such as canalised transport, macadamised roads and steam machinery, both at sea and ashore in the fields and on the new-fangled railways. The first of these opened in 1825, ran from Stockton to Darlington and was followed by the Monkland Railway in Scotland. Such notions, divinely inspired and combining the fruits of the earth with the God-given intellect of mankind, were designed to enable the enlightened to lift the labouring-poor from poverty. And so it seemed, at least for a while, for long before the demands and conditions of the Chartists and Parliamentary Reformers were addressed, the British economy began to emerge from stagnation.

By 1821 the post-war depression was over, wheat had fallen from over £20 per ton in 1816 to less than £10, bringing the price of bread down. Employment opportunities – harsh though they were – were in prospect, and two years later the President of the Board of Trade, William Huskisson, in the face of falling debt and taxation and a firmer currency, reduced import duties on sugar, cotton, linen, silk, woollens, paper, glass, iron, wine and coffee purchased from foreign markets as well as those coming from colonial sources. Finally Huskisson recognised the reality that the country had, under the stern imperatives of war, effectively abandoned the ancient Navigation Acts. This recognition was enshrined in the Reciprocity of Duties Act which concluded a number of treaties ensuring that foreign vessels were to be admitted to British ports on the same terms as British ships, always provided that British bottoms were, in turn, allowed into the ports of the foreign nations concerned.

This Act opened the door to free trade and such was the magnitude of British commerce and the mercantile marine which bore it that it seemed a very reasonable and proper thing to do, despite the manifest short-comings of British shipping outlined earlier. The Act was combined in 1824 with repeal of those passed in 1799 and 1800 prohibiting the combination of workmen which had threatened the stability of the state. Trade-unions became theoretically legitimate. However, this liberality was to produce a horrible reaction: 'strikes were called all over the country; employers were violently assailed; and some were murdered'. The consequence of this was to limit the unions' power, confining them by an Act of 1825 to the negotiation of wages, while the nascent labour movement was otherwise viciously suppressed, exemplified by the heartless deportation of the six Tolpuddle Martyrs in 1834 (though they were reprieved and repatriated two years later).

Other influences now came to bear upon the fortunes of the nation's commerce and its carrier. In South America the several revolts of the Spanish colonies had long since attracted British notice. A significant number of veterans of the Peninsular War had become mercenaries in the service of the newly independent republics.[14] Persons lacking military prowess but possessed of disposable income made loans to the new governments, seduced by exorbitant interest rates that proved quite impossible to meet. The collapse of private banks – over seventy of which stopped honouring demands for payment – and enormous pressure upon the Bank of England, precipitated a wave of unemployment, rioting, vandalism and renewed demands for the repeal of the Corn Laws which kept the price of bread beyond the reach of the indigent. It was against this desperate background that Joliffe made his next declaration of a dividend of only 10 per cent, to the fury of many shareholders in the General Steam Navigation Co.

But Hylton Joliffe and his fellow directors had more than an unstable international situation to cope with. They were to find, like successive generations of ship-owners, that this would only be part of their concern and that innovation would be resisted by an essentially conservative workforce. While technically minded officers of the Royal Navy and mercantile marine might ally themselves with exponents of steam-machinery, the steam-vessel was no more welcomed than the spinning-jenny. Luddites, in attitude if not in name, existed in the ports of the country, particularly the greatest; London. Steamers thrashing up and down the Thames not only took passengers away from the watermen in their wherries, they cut out the learnéd and ancient skills of the lightermen by towing numerous lighters, threatened the sailing bargemen's living by swamping their laden craft with their intemperate wash, and caused lighters and barges moored in the tiers to smash together, holing and occasionally sinking them. Moreover, they washed away the soft sand and mud riverbed upon which, at low tide, not only lighters, but sailing-vessels sat, damaging their bottoms. Such complaints as were made were drowned in the laughter and jollity of the vacationers, new to water-transport, over a million of whom annually tore down river towards The Nore and Margate beyond, taking advantage of the new service the General Steam Navigation Co. and the Margate Steam-Packet Co. offered in their newest steamers, the *Royal Sovereign* and *City of London*. Such horrific modernity annulled the rights of the watermen to carry people between Gravesend and London Bridge under Royal Privileges granted in 1401. A kind of war was declared, with watermen pulling provocatively under the bows of the steamers, forcing them to slow down; a dangerous tactic that provoked a select committee inquiry in 1831.

Set against the steady increase in London's home, near-continental and foreign trade, this apparent confrontation seems no more than a spat, but the extent to which this threatened the economic well-being of the port was not so lightly dismissed. The waterside population had long-since enriched themselves from pickings from

In between voyages a ship required refitting. The bustle of the process is illustrated here, with carpenters repairing the ship's boats in the foreground and seamen busy alongside scraping spars and aloft overhauling rigging. The port anchor cable, ranged ashore, indicates a date of about 1830, and the light spar whose inner end is triced-up in the fore-top is a lower studding sail boom. This view of the West India Docks was drawn by William Parrott in 1830. (Private Collection)

the barges and vessels lying in the tidal reaches of the Thames, from the Pool of London down to Gravesend. These euphemistically named 'Tier-Rangers' regularly plundered the many vessels moored to the buoys laid for them in midstream. Lying thus 'in tiers', their cargoes were trans-shipped into barges and swim-headed lighters but were thereby exposed to serious and extensive planned robbery. Even the casual pilferage of cargo by those who handled it was a daily abuse against which the river-police were conceived to act. As far as was possible, merchants trading in valuable rather than bulk goods sought to confine their shipping in secure docks. The walled East India Dock had long since provided the East India Company with a place from which cargoes could be loaded and discharged without loss, while other traders, lacking the homogeneity of John Company, were obliged to seek partners with capital to finance the digging of 'wet-docks'. These removed vessels not only from the worst excesses of the lawless riverside population but from the risks of collision with vessels working in the tideway and from frequent groundings at low water.

In 1802 London's wet-docks consisted of the East India Docks at Limehouse, the West India Docks on the Isle of Dogs and the Greenland Dock at Deptford. By 1824 the Howland Great Wet Dock, the London Dock, the Grand Surrey Basin, the Commercial Dock and the East Country Dock had been excavated, to which, in 1830, St Katherine's Dock had been added. Along with these were the ancient tidal berths provided by the 'legal quays' licensed by Elizabeth I in 1558 and the 'sufferance quays' that had grown opportunistically along the tidal littoral as trade demanded. The legal quays all lay in the Pool between the Tower and London Bridge where goods — except fish — could only be handled during daylight and where customs duties could be properly supervised by Crown officers. 'The legal quays speedily became a monopoly, extremely valuable to its owners, who strenuously opposed the development of the docks; and some of whom were bought out by the new dock companies'. Although no longer the only span across the Thames, it was between 1824 and 1831 that London's ancient, populated and antiquated bridge over the Thames was replaced by a modern structure.[15]

The social upheaval of these turbulent years encouraged Government policies in support of the emigration we have seen in respect of the Antipodes, with its effect upon shipping. In addition to Australia, Canada had provided a refuge for unemployed soldiers and seamen, slowly gaining popularity as a land of opportunity. In 1824 the Government offered grants to ease the appalling overcrowding of the slums in Britain's industrial towns. Five thousand colonists were shipped out and settled in Cape Colony at Port Elizabeth, and more went to Port Natal, later better known as Durban — the *rooineks* that would in due course upset the original Dutch Boer colonists. The sufferings endured by emigrants in sailing-vessels chartered for the purpose were soon well known. At this early period vessels offering for such traffic on the charter-market were usually unable to earn their living in other trades, among them the whalers and worn-out Indiamen mentioned earlier, whose owners sought the Government subsidies that kept them viable. It was in view of a betterment of conditions for their passengers, combined with a speedier and more predictable passage-time and the commercial opportunity thereby engendered, that the directors of the newly emerging steam-navigation companies launched their prospectuses with such global pretensions, and thus it was no accident that General Steam nursed an ambition to enter the trade with South Africa.

In this they were to be disappointed, an early proving voyage to St Petersburg founding a short-lived but loss-making enterprise. However, the directors were bullish. In addition to Brewers' Quay, one of the legal quays, the company purchased land adjoining Deptford Creek, formerly owned by the Honourable East India Company and known as The Stowage. Here ship-building and repair facilities were set up.[16] Meanwhile, by 1829 the company had moved from Crutched Friars to Lombard Street, and that year the company conveyed the Empress of Brazil from Ostend to London in their steamer *Superb*. In 1833 General Steam acquired its own 'leviathan', the 1,200 ton *Monarch*. The *Daily Mirror* described her as 'larger than any of His Majesty's frigates, and longer than our 84-gun ships...the accommodation below is so extensive that she will make up 140 beds and 100 persons may conveniently dine in her saloons'.

By 1830 General Steam was running services between London and Hamburg, Ostend, Boulogne, Rotterdam, Calais, Antwerp, Brighton, Newhaven and Dieppe, and had made a voyage to Lisbon. A year later it began swallowing its rivals; first the London & Edinburgh Steam-Packet Co., from which it obtained six steamers and warehouses at Newhaven; then the Margate Steam-Packet Co., which yielded more steam-vessels. By this means General Steam acquired the *City of Edinburgh*, built ten years earlier a little further downstream from The Stowage where, on the north bank, the building yard of Wigram & Green began turning out steamers alongside Blackwall frigates. The workshops of The Stowage also provided the engines for the new *John Bull* of 1835, the hull of which was built by Fletcher & Fearnall, while five other new vessels were ordered: the *Caledonia*, *Clarence*, *Ocean*, *Giraffe* and *Countess of Lonsdale*. The *James Watt*, purchased into the General Steam fleet at this time, carried to Spain the stores and equipment of the British Legion – raised to fight on behalf of the Spanish monarchy against the insurgency of Don Carlos.

By 1837, on the eve of the introduction of the screw propeller and iron-hulled sea-going vessels, General Steam had enlarged its works at Deptford and employed a fleet of forty paddle-steamers on routes that extended from London beyond the ports already mentioned, to Leith, Berwick, Newcastle and Ipswich. Besides this, they stationed a steamer at Falmouth to offer a mail service to wind-bound sailing ships. The following year the company's iron steamer *Rainbow*[17] was used by George Airy, the Astronomer-Royal, to conduct experiments on behalf of the Admiralty into the effects of iron hulls upon the magnetic compasses that all vessels relied upon.

Compass error had troubled navigators for some time and, while a knowledge of the vagaries of the earth's own magnetic field – known as 'variation' – was appreciated, quantified and allowed-for in laying a course or using a compass-bearing at an early stage, the variable effects of iron *within* a ship remained largely misunderstood. As mentioned earlier, Matthew Flinders had proposed one solution to part of this problem, but a hull constructed wholly of iron compounded the errors in the compass and, Airy discovered, varied according to the ship's heading and the degree to which she bore a cargo composed of magnetic metal. The complexities arising from this additional 'deviation' would not be resolved for some years – and would not save the *Tayleur*, whose loss in 1853 has been related – not until 1878 when Lord Kelvin had added to Flinders' soft-iron correcting bar, the two soft-iron spheres that to this day unkindly bear the name of 'Kelvin's balls'.

Competing rivals emerged as steam-navigation companies were formed to exploit the new technology and the opportunities in increasing foreign trade. Faced with this, the directors of General Steam abandoned their pretensions to distant destinations, concentrating on their established routes. The company would retain passenger paddle-steamers until the 1950s, while their smart coastal and short-sea fleet would adopt the names of birds and ply regular services from the Pool of London until the end of the Thames dock-system in the second half of the twentieth century. The early history of a company affectionately known as 'The Navvies' may be drawn to a fitting conclusion in 1842, the year that Green, Wigram & Green launched the *Princess Royal* and *Trident* to General Steam's account. Both were well-appointed, the latter being:

> one of the fastest steamships afloat. She carried three masts and a funnel amidships nearly as tall as the mainmast, and paddle wheels. Schooner-rigged, with her tall topgallant masts, high-steeved standing bowsprit, square overhanging carved stern,

and the long sheer of her bows, the *Trident*, Captain Richard Sharp, was the finest auxiliary steamship of her time.[18]

Learning of the young Queen Victoria's intention to visit Scotland in August 1842 in company with The Prince Consort, the company's directors offered one of their steamers to convey Her Majesty north, but this was politely declined. Instead Victoria embarked in the old, ship-rigged Royal Yacht *Royal George* at Woolwich, and was towed downstream by the tug *Monkey*. Off The Nore the *Royal George* was met by HM Steam-vessels *Shearwater, Black Eagle, Salamander, Lightning, Fearless* and *Rhadamanthus*, the first two of which relieved the *Monkey* of her charge amid a host of small craft 'displaying every manifestation of loyalty and affection'. Accompanied by the new Trinity House steamer *Vestal*, the squadron headed north.[19]

Sixty-six hours later the royal squadron was met off the Bass Rock by the General Steam Navigation Co.'s steamers *Monarch* and *Trident*. Captain Sharp had been instructed to 'hold himself in readiness at all times and to pay every attention to Her Majesty's royal wishes and commands should any such be expressed'. And, indeed, as may have been intimated by courtiers, they were. The old *Royal George* made little impression upon the young Queen, and even less upon her technologically minded husband who had eighteen months earlier been elected an honorary Elder Brother of Trinity House and must have watched his fellow brethren aboard their smart new steamer with some envy.[20] Prince Albert almost certainly influenced the outcome, for on the return journey Victoria decided to take passage aboard the *Trident*, much to the delight of Sharp and his principals.

Queen Victoria recorded the passage in her *Leaves from the Journal of our Life in the Highlands*. Writing on 15 September that the *Trident*'s 'accommodation for us was much larger and better than on board the *Royal George* and which was beautifully fitted up', she went on to say that:

> The *Rhadamanthus*, with some servants and carriages, set off last night, as well as the *Shearwater*... The *Salamander*... the *Fearless* and the *Royal George* Yacht set off at the same time with us, but the wind being against us, we soon lost sight of the yacht, and, not very long after, of all our steamers except the *Monarch*, which belongs to the General Steam Navigation Co., and had some of our horses on board. It started nearly at the same time [as the *Trident*], and was the only one which could keep up with us.

The Queen and her suite landed at Woolwich at 'ten past ten' on the morning of 17 September, the royal standard flying proudly from the *Trident*'s main-truck. Clearly the Queen's experience had not been off-putting, for she seems not to have agreed with Maria Edgeworth's assessment of a steamer-crossing to Ireland in 1820 that had proved 'like the shake felt in a carriage when a pig was scratching himself behind a back-wheel...' Not long after her passage in the *Trident*, the keel of the first of three steam-powered Royal Yachts to be named *Victoria and Albert* was laid-down.

The General Steam Navigation Co.'s early years exemplify the slow and limited ranges of the early commercial steamers. They were unviable without either a
passenger-base or a mail-contract but, where such elusive sources of revenue could
be found, British enterprise was not slow to seize the opportunity. Nevertheless, in
the imaginations of the visionaries and speculators, steam was the rage of the day,
even re-igniting that old chimera, the North East Passage. In 1829 the former naval
officer John Ross, with his nephew John Clark Ross, was financed by Sir Felix Booth,
magnate of the gin-distilling family, to take the steamer *Victory* to attempt a further
expedition in search of the elusive strait into the distant Pacific, in defiance of the
Admiralty's own efforts. It was not a success; the paddle-wheels proved vulnerable in
the ice and Ross reported 'our execrable machinery' unreliable and the *Victory* 'aught
but a sailing ship'.

But such setbacks were outside the thrust of commerce. Elsewhere other minds
were at work. One of the Dublin and London's Shannon steamers mentioned earlier,
the *Garry Owen*, had not only been constructed of iron and used — like the *Rainbow*
— for a series of experiments on the effects of an iron hull on a magnetic compass,
but in 1834 she also awakened interests in the possibilities of iron not just as an alternative for wood but a replacement. In bad weather, in which a number of wooden
vessels went to pieces, the *Garry Owen* proved durable. Moreover, it was on the very
deck of General Steam's *Rainbow*, a few months after George Airy had concluded
his magnetic experiments, that Christopher Claxton had ideas of his own. Claxton,
another former naval lieutenant, had found post-war employment as harbour-mas-
ter at Bristol. By 1834 he had also been appointed marine superintendent to the
Great Western Railway Co. whose directors were then considering building a ship
to extend their services across the Atlantic. Claxton was so impressed that he decided
that iron steamers were worth investing in, the consequences of which we shall come
to in due course.

While General Steam was swallowing its rivals, the mighty imperial company that
would one day consume it, was itself entering the world. The troubled history of the
Post-Office Packet Service and the taking over of its operations by the Royal Navy
has been dealt with in *Britannia's Realm*, and the eagerness of the Government to
contract the mails to Gibraltar and the Iberian Peninsula to a private company was
mentioned earlier in this chapter. To this end an agreement was concluded in 1837
with the Peninsular Steam Navigation Co., P&O in embryo, the genesis of which we
shall come to presently.

It was at this time, too, that the feasibility of a steam-powered transatlantic
crossing began to be debated. It had been sparked by the east-bound and stormy
crossing of the Canadian-built and financed, but Scots-engineered, paddle-steamer
Royal William. Leaving Quebec on 4 August 1833, she arrived in the Thames on
11 September but, like the *Savannah's*, her passage was no more than a steam-assisted
delivery voyage.[21] The *Royal William*, named for King William VI, had made several
coastal voyages carrying on her maiden trip twenty cabin and seventy steerage passengers, a quantify of cargo and 120 tons of coal. From Quebec she had proceeded to

Samuel Cunard, the 'Blue-Nosed' Nova Scotian whose name became synonymous with British transatlantic travel before the aeroplane. (Private Collection)

Halifax by way of New Brunswick where the *Acadian Recorder* declared her to possess a 'beautiful fast sailing appearance', adding that 'the powerful and graceful manner in which her paddles served to pace along, and the admirable command which her helmsman had over her, afforded a triumphant specimen of what steam-ships are'. Her commercial viability was threatened by high freight-rates and fares; moreover, when these were lowered, a cholera epidemic quarantined her. Unnecessary expenses had been incurred wintering in Quebec due to frozen pipe-work bursting, while her part-owners squabbled over the excessive expense-claims made by one of their number, Samuel Cunard of Halifax. The *Royal William* was therefore sold in 1832 for £5,000, less than a third of her cost, and set off for her new owners across the Atlantic.

Grossly overloaded with coal on the rueful admission of her master, Captain John MacDougall, she encountered a gale on the Grand Banks, sustaining damage to one engine cylinder, but pressed on. Every fourth day MacDougall was obliged to stop and shut down the *Royal William*'s boilers to scour out the salt deposits while the ship made sail, but after nineteen days they dropped anchor in Cowes Road, spruced the ship up and then made for the London River. Here the *Royal William* was sold to the Portuguese Government for £10,000, and while her crossing had been little more than an act of 'financial desperation', the fact that the passage had been accomplished even partially under power hinted at the possibilities inherent in steam-vessels on the North Atlantic. It was a subject intriguing the wayward Samuel Cunard back in Halifax.

It had also stimulated a debate in Britain where – largely in Scotland – steam-expertise resided. In London, Dr Dionysius Lardner famously declared an Atlantic transit impossible on the grounds that either a vessel could not carry a sufficient quantity of bunkers to ensure the voyage could be completed reliably, or that, if adequate coal was carried, no engine would prove sufficiently powerful to drive a vessel through turbulent seas against contrary winds.[22] The Great Western Railway Co.'s chief engineer, Mr Isambard Kingdom Brunel, demurred, arguing – quite correctly – that a long hull not only increased the capacity of a vessel but meant greater speed, an economy of scale which, Brunel argued, made the matter feasible.[23] As a consequence of this, Brunel began designing a new steamer specifically for the enterprise, securing backing on the rather grand grounds that it would extend the Great Western Railway from Bristol across the Atlantic. While Brunel found an ally in Christopher Claxton, he and his backers were not the only people willing to make the attempt.[24]

In November 1836 a newly constituted company, the British & American Steam Navigation Co., announced they had contracted with Messrs Curling & Young at Limehouse to construct 'the first of a line of steam-ships to run between London and New York...' The vessel, to be named *Victoria*, would be 220ft long with a tonnage of 1,700. She would be fitted with Hall's condensers and her consumption of 1.3 tons per hour, drawing from bunkers of 660 tons, would allow a passage time of fifteen days to be adequately covered. 'The capacity of the ship therefore to carry an abundant supply of coal is evident'. Mr Brunel was not alone in his thinking.

The two proposed ships, the *Victoria* and Brunel's *Great Western*, soon under construction in Bristol, were joined by a third, the *Liverpool*, then building on Merseyside to the order of Sir John Tobin's Transatlantic Steamship Co. While she alone would be the first twin-funnelled steamer, all three were wooden paddlers and were launched between 19 July 1837, when the *Great Western* slid into the water, and the 24 May 1838. By this time Princess Victoria had succeeded her uncle, William IV, and the British & American Steam Navigation Co.'s new vessel entered the Mersey as the *British Queen*. Thereafter her completion date was put back, and back again, while the other vessels, especially Brunel's *Great Western*, approached completion.

The British & American Steam Navigation Co. was a combination of British and American talent, the latter represented by Junius Smith, a Yale-educated Connecticut Yankee who had resided in London since 1805. Having conceived the idea of a steamship company running across the Atlantic, he pledged that he would 'not relinquish this project unless I find it absolutely impractical'. The greatest barrier to his ambition was prejudice. He wrote to a correspondent in New York that 'The patience and labor of forming a company in London is beyond all that you can imagine. It is the worst place in the whole world to bring out a new thing,' he bewailed, but admitted that it was 'the best when it was done'. The source of his opposition was clear, though: 'All the old sailing interest is against me'.

Undeterred, Smith took his ambitions north to Liverpool, acquiring an exceptionally able and practical company secretary in Macgregor Laird. Macgregor Laird was the son of William Laird of Greenock, the pioneering engineer who had moved south

Intended to beat the *Britannia* and the *Great Western* across the North Atlantic, the *British Queen* finally entered service in 1839. (© Courtesy of The British Mercantile Marine Memorial Collection)

and established his iron-works at Birkenhead. Here he was succeeded by his elder son John (born the year Smith arrived in London), who specialised, as we have remarked, in the construction of iron ships. Born in 1808, Macgregor Laird had involved himself in the exploration of the Niger which had been tentatively surveyed by John and Richard Lander. Following their report and in anticipation of opening the country to a commerce more beneficial to all concerned than the now illegal slave-trade, Laird had joined a syndicate of Liverpudlian merchants who, in 1832, sent the iron steamer *Alburkah* — built by the family firm — up the River Niger, in company with the *Quorra* under the amiable and engaging Richard Lander. The expedition was disastrous, most of the ships' crews perishing of fever. Macgregor Laird survived to involve himself with Smith's transatlantic project for which, following an announcement in *The Times* in November 1835, over £1 million was subscribed by investors. Many of these were Londoners who lobbied for the building contract to be placed on the Thames. In the end they had their way, Curling & Young's Limehouse Yard getting the job when Smith repudiated Laird's assertion that iron was superior to wood, arguing that the rigidity of iron — actually vital when embedding machinery — would prove fatal in the heavy seas and swells of a trans-oceanic passage. As for internal plant, the *British Queen*'s engines would be built in Scotland, although Robert Napier's bid of £20,000 was rejected in favour of a cheaper offer from the neighbouring workshops of Claude Girdwood at Greenock. This was to have grave consequences and result in seemingly interminable delays.

In seeking to man the first of his projected four new ships, delayed as she was, Macgregor Laird recruited Captain Richard Roberts, yet another ex-naval lieutenant who had for some years been commanding steamers owned by the St George Steam-Packet Co. of his native Cork. This company, founded in 1821, had long been running steamers to Glasgow, Bristol, London and Dublin, and Roberts was among the most experienced of its ship-masters. He was now to be paid twenty guineas per month, recruit his own officers and men − his first mate receiving £10, the second £7 and the third £5 a month − and to take up his appointment at the end of January 1838. Unfortunately the *British Queen* was nowhere near ready and, while the *Great Western* left Bristol and sailed round to the Thames to have Maudslay, Son & Field install her engines, the *British Queen*'s engine-builders had gone into liquidation. The *Great Western* was clearly going to leave that spring, long before the *British Queen* was completed.

To be trumped at this late stage by a rival was more than Junius Smith could bear; he was already considering himself 'the father of Atlantic steam-navigation', so he and Laird considered what to do. The solution was more remarkable for its success than history suggests, for Smith and his board were persuaded − quite by whom is uncertain, but Roberts probably had a hand in it − that the British & American Steam Navigation Co. should charter the steamer *Sirius* from the St George Steam-Packet Co.[25] The *Sirius* was not designed for the North Atlantic, her normal run being Cork to London, but she was a new wooden vessel from the Leith yard of Robert Menzies & Son. Her twin-cylinder engines were Scots too, made by J. Wingate & Co., of Glasgow; her boilers operated at 5psi and she was fitted with Samuel Hall's condenser, all of which plant was officially rated at 320hp, giving a service speed of 9 knots. Costing £27,000, the *Sirius* was 'schooner rigged with a standing bowsprit…square sterned, carvel built; with mock quarter galleries, and dog figurehead…' grossing 703 tons, large for a coasting steam-packet, but small for the North Atlantic, 55ft shorter than the *Great Western*'s length of 236ft and 1,320 tons, with engines of half the rated power of Brunel's ship.

On schedule the *Sirius* departed from London on 28 March. Her final departure from Cork was delayed until the 4 April, two days late, but she bore forty passengers. The eleven in first-class had paid thirty-five guineas for a cabin, inclusive of wine, the eight in second-class paying twenty guineas and the twenty-one in steerage accommodation, eight. St George's Co. sent their senior engineer, William Ramsden, to oversee the machinery while Roberts commanded a crew of thirty-six, including three mates, a boatswain and nine seamen, two engineers and a telling *twelve* firemen, two cooks, three stewards, an attendant, one stewardess named Margaret Linch and two boys. She lacked the 'surgeon, of high qualifications' appointed to her rival, the *Great Western*, which was herself about to depart. The third vessel, the *Liverpool*, had failed to make the common starting-line.

The *Sirius* completed her stores, coal and passengers lying at the St George's berth at Passage West in Cork Harbour. Here her master received his final orders − typical of their time and intent − from the hand of Macgregor Laird, who assured Roberts that it was:

the wish of the Charterers of the *Sirius* that you should be left entirely to your own judgement as to the course you may steer from Cork to New York, at the same time they would wish that, as abundance of good fuel is to be had at Halifax, Nova Scotia, you should keep as near that port as the weather permits, until you have passed... if after the first 1,500 miles of the passage is accomplished, you should apprehend your supply of fuel on board would fall short for the whole voyage, it would be advisable to make a direct course for that port, and I enclose you a Letter from Mr Cunard, the Agent in this country for the Coal Mines, there, which will ensure you an immediate supply.

On reaching New York, you will place yourself in communication with Wadsworth and Smith to whom the Vessel is consigned, and use your best exertions in conjunction with these gentlemen to procure passengers for the return voyage... I hope soon to congratulate you upon being the first transatlantic Steam Navigation, and can assure you that in this feeling I am joined by all concerned in this experimental voyage.

For his part, Roberts's report relates that:

The *Sirius* started from Passage, Port of Cork, on 4 April at 10.30am in company with the *Ocean*, another splendid steamer of the St George Steam-Packet Company. On leaving Passage we were loudly cheered by the inhabitants... Most of the gentlemen interested in our vessel proceeded with us as far as the Cove of Cork, where we stopped to let *Ocean* come alongside to take the above gentlemen out, which having been done, with three hearty cheers...we gallantly bent our way for New York.

We had now on board 450 tons of coal, 20 tons of water and 58 casks of resin, besides an incalculable stock of other stores, all of which I beg to be understood (with the exception of 90 tons of coal) was over and above what she was intended to carry as a dead weight, add to which her having 22 tons of water on deck and you may form some conjecture as to her probable fate had she not been an admirable sea boat and in every respect qualified for the most dangerous weather...

This was just as well, for within a few days the *Sirius* was reported as unflinchingly holding her westwardly course in defiance of a strong and adverse gale from the north-westward. The sea was running very high at the time, and the *Sirius* appeared to be manfully breasting the opposing waves dashing their spray at every plunge mast high.

A fortnight later, on 1 May, a second report from Captain Hore of the *Intrepid*, which had just arrived in London, appeared in the *Shipping Gazette*. Hore had:

spoke [to] the *Sirius* steamer on the 10th April in latitude 47° North, Longitude 24° West. At the time...the wind was blowing freshly from the southward and westward... The *Sirius* had been six days at sea; during that period in...defiance of one of the most severe, long continued and disastrous westerly gales, with which the fury of the Atlantic has ever been aroused, the steamer has succeeded in travelling a distance of 800 miles.

There is an element of journalistic exaggeration in all this, but from his own log Roberts undoubtedly encountered the Atlantic's usual 'fresh breezes…fresh gale and squalls, rain and heavy head sea…heavy gale and great swell'. On 12 April, in moderate weather and after a day's run of 190 miles, the *Sirius* was hove-to; her paddle-floats were resecured, having worked loose, and the stuffing boxes were also repacked. Her next noon-to-noon run was 220 miles, followed by 200 and 205 miles.[26] Finally, at 8.00 p.m. on 22 April 1838, Roberts's officers 'observed the high lands of Narranganset… [and] slowed the engines; at 9 p.m. fired signals for [a] Pilot; then hove-to for Pilot and anchored off the Battery at 10 p.m.' The engines had run at 15rpm and consumed all the coal, but without the need to divert for supplies from Halifax and without burning the cabin furniture or mast-timber that legend has attributed to this epochal passage. In any case, Roberts had worries enough, for unfortunately the *Sirius* briefly touched bottom on the shoals of Sandy Hook before the tardy pilot boarded. Nevertheless, Roberts had taken New York by surprise and allowed himself a rare moment of lyricism. As the *Sirius* made her way up to her berth, the sun set 'clear and resplendent' in the western sky, leaving behind the storm clouds of the open ocean 'in our rear like an impenetrable mass, tinged along the margin by other clouds of a snowy whiteness… a most beautiful sight'.

The *Great Western* had had no such luck. Leaving Blackwall at 6.10 a.m. on 31 March, bound initially for Bristol, her boiler insulation caught fire. On board with her master, James Hosken, another quondam naval officer, were Brunel and Claxton, the last named leading the fire-fighting with Chief Engineer Pearse. Hosken ran the new ship on the Chapman Shoal as a precaution. While playing a hose upon the fire, a man fell upon Claxton from a burnt ladder: it was Brunel, and he struck steelwork before Claxton broke his fall. He was landed on nearby Canvey Island as the *Great Western* was refloated on the tide and resumed her voyage, the fire extinguished. Brunel remained at Canvey for some time, missing his ship's final departure from Bristol on the forenoon of 8 April, mortified that news of the fire had deterred the *Great Western*'s passengers, only seven embarking with fifty-odd cancelling their bookings and demanding their money back. Four days behind the *Sirius* though she was, the *Great Western* made far better progress than her rival, steaming up the Hudson on the afternoon of 23 April, St George's Day.

The *Great Western* was destined to be the first steam-vessel to open a regular transatlantic service, had maintained a faster average speed than the *Sirius* and, while she had avoided much of the adverse weather encountered by her rival, she arrived with 200 tons of coal remaining in her bunkers. Unfortunately the significance of this was lost as her handful of passengers saw:

the *Sirius* lying in the North River, gay with flaming streamers and literally crammed with visitors, her decks, her paddle-boxes, her rigging… We passed around her, receiving and giving three hearty cheers, then turned towards the Battery. Her arrival was an achievement, we had been sharers in the chances of a noble effort and each of us felt the pride in the participation in the success of it and this was the crowning instant, experiment had ceased: certainty was attained.

The *New York Weekly Herald* added its journalistic hyperbole:

The approach of the *Great Western* to the harbour, and in front of the Battery was most magnificent. It was about four o'clock Monday afternoon. The sky was clear, the crowds immense…on the broad blue water, appeared the huge thing of life, with four masts and emitting volumes of smoke. She looked black and blackguard − as all the British steamers generally are − rakish, cool, reckless, fierce and forbidding in their sombre colours… As she neared the *Sirius*, she slackened her movements, and took a sweep around… At this moment the whole Battery sent forth a tumultuous shout of delight, at the revelation of her magnificent proportions. After making another turn towards Staten Island, she made another sweep, and shot towards the East River with extraordinary speed. The vast multitudes rent the air with their shouts…hurrahing to a very great degree. After showing herself thus, she took up her station at the foot of Market Street, at a slip assigned to her, and thus let the thousands rest in quiet.

The inherent superiority in his ship did not mollify Captain Hosken's disappointment, and he embarked upon a stupid public correspondence trying to claim his own ship's pre-eminence, which time alone would prove. Hosken's embitterment could not damn the torrent of public enthusiasm generated by the *Sirius* and volubly expressed in the New York press:

'The *Sirius*! The *Sirius*!' Nothing is talked of in New York now but the *Sirius*. She is the first steam-vessel that has arrived here from England; and a glorious boat she is. Every counter-skipper, merchant, loafer, deck-walloper and rowdy in New York went on board her yesterday. Nothing could exceed the kindness, the generosity, the hospitality of the officers on board of her, one and all, without exception.

As for the third vessel, the *Liverpool*, she was replaced by another Irish Sea paddler, the 720-ton *Royal William*. The Transatlantic Steamship Co.'s chartered substitute, not to be confused with the Canadian-built pioneer of 1833, left Liverpool on 5 July and arrived in New York with thirty-two passengers on the 24th. She soon afterwards returned to the regular employment of her owners, the City of Dublin Steam-Packet Co., as did the *Sirius* to St George's, but they had laid the foundations of a century of passenger sea-travel across the North Atlantic, refuting Dionysius Larder's jeremiad.

The British and American S.N. Co. had planned that two other steamers would join the *British Queen* on the transatlantic route and that Macgregor Laird's agents in New York, Wadsworth & Smith, agreed a joint-service with their own ships. Thus

Junius Smith's aspirations would unite the country of his birth with that of his adoption, the practicality of which combination was explained by Wadsworth & Smith:

> British ships, by Treaty of Commerce, are not permitted to take foreign and colonial goods from Britain to the United States; they must be shipped in American bottoms. On the other hand American ships are not permitted to carry colonial or foreign goods to Great Britain, except for exportation only; they must be shipped in British bottoms. By the union of the two, the whole trade is supplied and all descriptions of goods secured.

Moreover, the American company's prospectus also pointed out the advantages accruing to an efficient steam-service:

> Four steam-ships will make as many passages in twelve months as eight sailing ships, and the investment, while it will be more than equal [to] the cost of eight sailing ships of equal tonnage, will be more than made up, in the increased number of voyages and frequent returns of capital.

While steam-vessels would not fulfil this optimistic forecast for some time, they were attractive enough, and the returns sufficient enough, to deliver marginal profits substantial enough to maintain investment interest. While 1838 proved the possibility of transatlantic steam, steam could not avoid the dangers of sea-going. That spring a gale and thick mist had caused the War Office's steam-packet *Killarney*, laden with fifty passengers and 600 live pigs, to wreck herself on rocks west of Cork Harbour, while in an autumn gale the *Forfarshire*, bound north from Hull to Dundee with sixty-three souls on board, ran hard aground on the Harcar Rocks in the Outer Farne islands.[27]

The third vessel missing from the initial race, the *Liverpool*, finally entered service under Captain Nicholas Parker, who had been filched, like Roberts, from the St George Steam-Packet Co. She left the Mersey on 20 October with sixty passengers, making a long stop at Cork to repair heavy-weather damage. Leaving Cork on 6 November, she arrived at New York on the 23rd, having an average speed of just under 8 knots. She was never very successful and was soon afterwards chartered and then sold to the then newly reconstituted Peninsular & Oriental S.N. Co. where she became better known as the *Great Liverpool* for reasons explained later.

Meanwhile, the *Great Western*, bearing the scorch-marks of her boiler-room fire for the remainder of her life, was never a popular ship; Charles Dickens took passage in her and added to the constant complaints about 'dirt and mismanagement'. However, of the three contenders in that transatlantic competition of 1838, the *Great Western* not only lasted longest but had the most influence on the future, for Brunel, perceiving the weakness in her paddle-propulsion and her wooden hull, brought his formidable intellect to bear upon the problem and reached for his pencil and drawing-board. Despite her failings the *Great Western* made sixty-four transatlantic crossings until, in 1847, she was sold to the Royal Mail Steam-Packet Co. and ran between Southampton and the West Indies until her scrapping ten years later.

As for the little *Sirius*, she was to have an inglorious end. By January 1847 her owners had been reconstituted as the Cork Steamship Co. and the *Sirius* was employed on the Cork–Dublin–Glasgow route. Fog bedevilled the coast of Cork on Friday 15th and Saturday 16th, and by the end of the weekend it was known that the *Sirius* had been wrecked at Ware Cove, near Ballycotton. The wreck was sold by auction on 10 July, a few items – including the 'dog figurehead' – being saved for posterity.[28] It was a sad end for the little steamer.

Captain Richard Roberts was to suffer a similar fate. After the *Sirius*'s transatlantic success he continued in the employment of Junius Smith and Macgregor Laird, reverting to the *British Queen*, still languishing on the Clyde for want of engines. These were inexcusably delayed by their maker, Robert Napier, who had agreed to supply engines after the bankruptcy of Girdwood & Sons, but for an increased sum of £21,000. Napier prevaricated, constantly giving other contracts priority, and it was soon clear why. While a frustrated Roberts attempted to expedite his principals' interests during a year standing-by the incomplete ship, the British Government had invited tenders for a steam mail-contract to Halifax which was to begin in the spring of 1840. This was secured by the Nova Scotian Samuel Cunard, who had been watching events from the wings. As the rival companies strove to complete their transatlantic steam-vessels and prove the practicability of the project, he now astutely formed a partnership with the ship-owners George Burns and David and Charles MacIver. Hearing of this fly move and Napier's brokering part in it, an outraged Macgregor Laird wrote to Roberts on 11 March 1839 that 'Mr Cunard has, I hear, contracted with Mr Napier for three Vessels of 1,000 tons and 400hp for the Halifax Mail-contract...so our first opposition will issue from the shop which has so long delayed us.' And there was worse to come. On 27 April Laird wrote of Cunard to Roberts that: 'I hear from the Admiralty he has liberty to go on after touching at Halifax either to Boston or New York, I fancy he will run to the latter place – most probably in hot opposition...' It was during Roberts's tenure of command of the 2,000-ton steamer that Cunard began his own crossings, as will shortly be seen.

The *British Queen* finally left the Clyde on 30 June 1839, sailing on her maiden voyage shortly thereafter to enter a service fast becoming commonplace. Early in the following year of 1841 Roberts was transferred to the command of the new SS *President*. She was a large vessel of 2,360 tons, twice the size of Cunard's ships, and three-decked, allowing the passengers a long, uninterrupted promenade-deck, fitted out with some opulence and finished with a figurehead depicting George Washington, a respectful flourish complementing the *British Queen*'s image of Queen Victoria. Built by Curling & Young to a design by Laird, with engines by Fawcett & Preston of Liverpool, the *President* was internally subdivided 'so that the springing of a leak would be attended with comparatively little danger and would be readily overcome'. She was, nevertheless, made of wood, not the iron which would have better secured this claim. Although her steam-engine was rated at 540hp, then the largest on the North Atlantic, this was barely adequate for so large a hull. Her early voyages were slow, and she was overdue in November 1840. Two masters had been replaced prior to Roberts's appointment and much was expected of him in order that the *President* and the *British Queen* should maintain what was at the time – and pending the arrival of Samuel Cunard's enterprise – the first and only scheduled transatlantic steam-ship service.

That spring was unusually stormy in the North Atlantic. The *British Queen* suffered in heavy weather under Roberts's successor while in March Roberts and his new ship were reported missing. The *President* was presumed to have foundered in heavy weather, though her previous tardiness postponed anxiety for a while. On 14 May Smith wrote that he had not entirely given up the ship as lost, 'yet I fear there is but slight ground for hope'. In fact there was none. A board of inquiry convened in the office of the British consul in New York on 1 June 1841 and, consisting of the consul, Mr Buchanan, Rear Admiral Jacob Walton of the Royal Navy and the Lloyd's Agent, Thomas W. Moore, heard evidence of which that of Captain Cole of the packet *Orpheus* was the most telling. Cole had left New York in company with the *President* on the forenoon of the 11 March, and both vessels had remained in sight of each other until sunset on the 12th. By this time they were between Nantucket Shoals and St George's Bank, an area of convergence, where the Gulf Stream runs into shoaling water and where, in strong winds, heavy, breaking seas and overfalls may be encountered. When he had last seen the *President*, Cole related, she was pitching heavily into a head sea and appeared to him to be 'labouring tremendously'. The gale raged all night. Next morning 'the wind shifted suddenly [from] north-east to south-east, knocking up a still more tremendous sea, and that the gale continued with unabated fury till midnight of the 13th'. With his own ship 'labouring heavily and shipping large quantities of water on deck', Cole believed that the *President* had been overwhelmed and that the ingress of sea-water had extinguished the boiler fires or, worse still, caused an explosion. With such a catastrophic loss of power and damage, the vessel would have fallen into the trough of the sea and foundered.[29] The loss of the *President* ruined her owners, principally Junius Smith, and the British and American S.N. Co. went into liquidation.

Macgregor Laird returned to his first enthusiasm, West Africa, and in 1852 he founded the African Steamship Co. with Alexander Elder and John Dempster. Based in Liverpool, the company would be later better known as Elder Dempster Lines Ltd, and would become one of the major British shipping companies trading with West Africa. But Laird's early foray with the Landers had been one among several fascinated by this corner of the world, for 'Darkest Africa' had also attracted the interest of the newly founded Geographical Society after the publication by John Murray of Richard and John Lander's account of their ascent of the Niger.[30] The slave-trade had poured manufactured goods of one sort or another – though mostly low-quality arms, pots and pans and other utilitarian metal-work – into the eager markets of the 'Guinea coast'.[31] It was gold that had first lured Europeans to the west coast of Africa, and it was to gold, and the ivory that they had also found, to which they now

Robert Jamieson's paddle-steamer *Ethiope* of 1839 was designed to operate on coal or wood and built to penetrate the rivers of West Africa. Note the gun forward. (© Courtesy of National Museums, Liverpool, Merseyside Maritime Museum)

returned, bearing colonial aspirations and a quest for other useful commodities such as timber and vegetable oils. This was by no means a one-way exploitation, though the greater advantages always lay with the British and other European shipping entrepreneurs, such as the Hamburg merchant, Alfred Woermann.

Laird and his new partners were among many breaking into a new West African trade directly attributable to the advantages of steam-propulsion. Steamers were increasingly perceived as tools in their own right, enabling deeper penetration into hinterlands where new trade made fortunes. In 1839, galvanised by Richard Lander's expedition in which Macgregor Laird had participated, the Liverpool ship-owner Robert Jamieson had ordered from the Merseyside yard of Thomas Wilson a steam-schooner capable of burning wood or coal. Jamieson's *Ethiope* was intended to penetrate the Benin River in the hope of reaching the Niger River and thereby 'establish[ing] a commercial intercourse with the interior'. The germ of this idea seems to have come from John Beecroft.

Born in Whitby in 1790, Beecroft, like so many of his fellow townsmen, went to sea in coasters, and in 1805, at the age of fifteen, was captured by a French corsair and imprisoned until the peace of 1814. By 1821 Beecroft was master of the *Nautilus*, a transport chartered to accompany HM Ships *Fury* and *Hecla* on the first leg of William Parry's second voyage to the Arctic. This brief association with a Government expedition and his obvious capacity, recommended Beecroft in 1829 for the post of superintendent of works at Fernando Po. Although nominally Spanish, Fernando Po was being used by the Royal Navy as a base from which to suppress the slave-trade, and Beecroft's task was the establishment of a depot capable of supporting the navy's anti-slavery squadron. The British abolition of human trafficking was not welcomed by native rulers who had hitherto profited from it, yet the navy depended upon a supply of essentials from those whom it had dispossessed of their traditional economic power-base. A dispute among the chiefs of Old Calabar threatened these supplies and Beecroft successfully resolved this, displaying tact and sympathy which gained him respect both from the Africans and his political masters back home. In 1830 he was appointed acting governor, a post confirmed by the Spanish Government with a lieutenancy in the Spanish navy. British negotiations to acquire the island failed and the settlement was abandoned in 1833, but Beecroft stayed on as a partner in the trading firm of Dillon, Tennant & Co., which retained the shore facilities on a commercial basis for the next few years. In fact Beecroft remained the effective political power through his reputation and influence, and in 1843 he was confirmed officially as governor of Fernando Po.

Beecroft was now a significant power in the land, having undertaken exploration of the interior, but little-known because his expeditions were commercially inspired and mounted from Fernando Po. His commercial instincts had led Beecroft to consider the advantages of steam-power in trading on the coast, particularly ascending the major rivers to tap the markets and commodities of the interior, thus making up for the loss of income from slaves for the local economy as much as benefitting British merchants. To this end he had been corresponding with others of like mind, including Richard Lander, and in 1839 he had returned to Liverpool to take command of Jamieson's new steam-schooner.

The *Ethiope* left Liverpool in September 1839 and began her ascent of the Benin in the April following. Her crew consisted of 'fifteen Europeans…officers, medical men, an engineer, and seamen, with a full complement of blacks, or Kroo-men, besides interpreters'. Like most merchantmen of the time operating in potentially hostile waters, she was armed. The first attempt to reach the Niger failed, but the second, by way of the Warree, enabled the *Ethiope* to reach the Niger and steam more than 400 miles upstream. However, the toll taken by fever was horrific and Beecroft and Jamieson sensibly reported that 'commerce on the Niger can only be followed by means of steam-vessels manned entirely by Africans, under the direction of European officers and engineers inured to the climate'.

At this time the Government was also interested in the African interior and the *Ethiope*'s next task was to rescue the survivors of the official Niger Expedition and assist HMS *Albert* back to Fernando Po. Later exploratory-cum-surveying voyages were made up the Old Calabar River in 1841 and 1842 without significant result. Jamieson's attempts to sell the *Ethiope* failed and she made a further voyage to the Niger under Beecroft who took her to Rabba before returning to Liverpool in May 1847.[32]

Beecroft himself went back to West Africa where, in 1849, and in addition to his continuing Spanish governorship of Fernando Po, he was appointed British consul to Biafra and Benin by Lord Palmerston. Hitherto Great Britain had nursed no territorial ambitions in the region, but this now changed. As the senior and most influential British representative, Beecroft was behind the British occupation of Lagos in 1851 and the subsequent deposition of King Pepple of Bonny in 1854. That year, having been elected to the now *Royal* Geographical Society, John Beecroft was appointed to lead a new Niger expedition, but he died on 10 June at Fernando Po — of which he was still governor — and was buried there. From a man whose personality had charmed the Africans in the first twenty years of his residence on the coast, the final five of his life showed him to have become 'a forceful interventionist, determined to establish British paramountcy over what was eventually destined to become the colony of Nigeria'. The malarial coast and its hinterland, soon to be better known as 'the white-man's grave', was not invariably so, and between 1854 and 1857 Dr William Baikie,[33] in charge of a Government trading-settlement at the confluence of the Benue and Niger rivers at Lokoja, determined the prophylactic properties of quinine.

Samuel Cunard began his North Atlantic steam-service in March 1840. Cunard came from a family of German extraction; Mennonites turned Quakers who, as Loyalists, had at the Revolution migrated from America to settle in Nova Scotia. In 1825 Cunard had travelled to London to petition the East India Company and secure a tea-importing agency for the growing and increasingly sophisticated population of Canada's Maritime Provinces. Familiar with shipping and aware of the interest of the Assembly of Lower Canada in the encouragement of steam-navigation on the St Lawrence and the coastal waters of Lower Canada, Cunard had been involved in the joint Canadian-Scots venture that produced the first *Royal William*. Since then he had regularly visited Britain admitting that 'Altho' I am a colonist, I have many friends in this country' — chief of whom were his partners MacIver and Burns. Quietly, with a 'plan that was entirely my own,' he had secured the Government contract to provide a steam-packet service to Halifax with a cheaper tender than that of the opposition: the Great Western and the British & American Steam-Ship companies.

The five round voyages made by the *Great Western* in 1838 had induced the Government to seek a transatlantic operator not for the purpose of carrying passengers, though the operator might enjoy that subsidiary benefit, but to convey the all-important mails — the arterial medium by which policy, strategy and trade were promulgated and carried-out. The Admiralty, having subsumed the Post Office's responsibility in this matter, acted as agents and set a tight-schedule: Cunard, arriving in London early in 1839 in response to news of the proposed service, also discovered that the service had to begin the following spring.

Christopher Claxton now headed the Great Western S.S. Co., and, having signalled his interest in the Halifax mail-contract, requested more time to build proper new ships — smaller, more powerful and faster than the *Great Western*. Claxton proposed a sensible structured introduction of the service, offering monthly sailings each way for a seven year contract at an annual subsidy of £45,000. Claxton's tone in resetting the agenda struck the Admiralty Board as impertinent; he remained in their eyes only a lieutenant on half pay. Moreover, Claxton seemed to infer he knew more about steam-navigation than Their Lordships, a further impertinence, for they had already suffered at the hands of the Great Western Steamship Co. when another director,

Thomas Guppy, had declared at a meeting of the Liverpool Scientific Society in the autumn of 1837 that: 'Many of the Government [steam] vessels are of very bad forms; their power and size greatly disproportioned'. This was, under the circumstances and in contemplation of the crossing of the North Atlantic, a not unreasonable point-of-view, but Guppy, whose words and the laughter they produced would be faithfully recorded in the *Nautical Magazine*, had gone on to say:

> Whoever had seen the fine private steamers belonging to the ports of London, Liverpool, Glasgow and Bristol, and had then gone to view the Government ones in Woolwich Basin, must have been astonished at the extraordinary forms there collected; it would be well if a glass case could be constructed over the basin, to procure those curiosities of practical science, as exercised in our naval building yards.

Cunard's own experiences crossing from Halifax regularly in the Admiralty's sailing-packets had been equally disillusioning. Delays and a broken arm had enhanced the reputation of the packets for being killers in their commanders' relentless quest for speed in the face of Yankee competition, persuading Cunard that steam offered a decided improvement. Indeed, it was these losses, amounting 'almost every year [to] two or three hundred people,' that was urging the Admiralty to shed the task and find a private substitute. Nor did it help that the pragmatic merchants of Liverpool and Glasgow favoured the safer means of transmitting their bills of exchange, orders and documentation by the crack Yankee packets.

Personally, as far as Cunard was concerned, the colonial society of Halifax had become too limiting for a man of his ambition. His business deals had not always gone well and he was heavily mortgaged, all of which attracted him to the new project, experienced as he was with mining, tea-importing and the coastal mails. Within days of his arrival in London he had secured interviews with Admiralty and Treasury officials – largely Charles Wood and Francis Baring, both future First Lords – whom he persuaded that 'by going once a week the whole of the letters would be taken by our steamers, and the American packet ships that had previously carried the letters, would cease to carry them'. It was bold – too bold – and the final plan called for a fortnightly service, with a forwarding service from Halifax to Boston in smaller ships at an annual subsidy of £55,000. To outflank Claxton's Great Western S.S. Co. and Smith and Laird's British & American S.N. Co., Cunard took the advice of the East India Company for whose Bombay Marine John Wood's Yard on the Clyde had just built the steam frigate *Berenice*. Within three weeks of agreeing terms with the Admiralty on 11 February 1839, Cunard was in Glasgow, the consequences of which we already know.

Cunard's 800-ton, 300hp steamers would be built by Wood and powered by Robert Napier. Napier took him to the Vulcan Foundry – where 700 skilled men worked a six-day week – and introduced the manager, David Elder. Cunard wanted vessels 'of the very best description', able 'to pass a thorough inspection and examination by the Admiralty...plain and comfortable...but not the least unnecessary expense for show'. The contract price for the first two ships was agreed at £32,000 each, but Cunard had yet to secure a contract with the British Government. When Napier presented Cunard's first bill, he had some difficulty getting it honoured owing to a deal in Prince Edward Island compromising Cunard's liquidity in Britain. Suspicious, Napier confided in his Glaswegian banker, Robert Rodger, and behind the eponymous back of Cunard himself, the pair secured the future of the Cunard Line by inviting George Burns and David and Charles MacIver to join them. The three men were all sailing ship-owners, Burns's vessels operating between the Clyde and the Mersey where the MacIvers presided over their own coastal packets. A handful of other investors, including Napier himself, also joined in, and these syndics raised most of the necessary money. The association would, Napier assured Cunard, ensure that 'the [new steam-] vessels would be well and honestly managed, and save much trouble to all concerned and make money'. Faced with this shrewd and astute *fait accompli*, the otherwise solitary but cash-strapped Cunard concurred. He had had, he responded – somewhat condescendingly in the circumstances – 'several offers but am bound to no-one,' admitting nevertheless, and as Napier and Rodger knew he was bound to, that 'I should much like to have you and your friends with me'. In the event, besides Cunard, who chipped-in with the largest share at £55,000, these 'friends' turned out to be thirty-three investors from Glasgow, Liverpool and Manchester who raised between them £270,000 of working capital. Among them were the Glaswegian cotton-broker James Donaldson, who put in £16,000, eight other major backers who came in at £11,000 each and a number of lesser investors. Burns put in £5,500, the MacIver brothers £4,000 each. Napier contributed £6,100, but his greater investment was his expertise, which Cunard acknowledged, though he himself remained the manager. What was constituted and for long officially known as 'The British & North American Royal Mail Steam-Packet Co. Ltd' was from its inception named after Cunard.

In June 1839 Cunard, Burns and David MacIver signed a contract with the Admiralty as agents for the British Government to provide four steam-vessels, each of 400hp, measuring, on a length of 206ft, 1,120 tons. The contract would exist for seven years and the subsidy would be £60,000 *per annum*. While Halifax remained the principal western terminus – though Boston was now written-in as part of the main service, hence the increase in subsidy – the British departure port was altered. In recognition of its growing importance and the MacIver's place in this ascendancy, Liverpool would be the eastern terminus.

More pressing was the inaugural date of May 1840. Building the first four ships was such a matter of urgency that while Napier set up what amounted to a proto-production line for the power-plants, the hulls were laid-down in separate yards. John Wood built the *Arcadia*, his brother Charles the *Caledonia*, Robert Steele the *Columbia* and Robert Duncan the *Britannia*; each was carefully if classically named for the cardinal points of the new company's ambition. In the event, but unsurprisingly, the service was a little behind-hand when the *Britannia* dropped down the Mersey on 4 July 1840, outward-bound on her maiden voyage to Halifax and Boston. The readjusted timetable allowed for her departure on the 1st and although thought overdue, her

final arrivals at both ports were greeted with cheering crowds and fireworks. Samuel
Cunard took passage in her and, as the hero of the hour, eclipsed the *Britannia's*
Captain Henry Woodruff [34] to receive 1,800 dinner invitations on Sunday 19 July
from hospitable Boston society. The *Britannia* actually reached Halifax in eleven days
and four hours and Boston in fourteen days and eight hours, and besides her all-
important mails she bore sixty-three excited fare-paying passengers.

The four wooden sister-ships embraced some small but significant improvements:
heavy reinforcing and bracing of the hulls; lagged engine-rooms and tapered coal
bunkers that helped the firemen by 'feeding' coal to the boiler-room. As for their
plain appointments, this was achieved to a nicety. Taking passage in the *Britannia* in
3 January 1842, Charles Dickens wrote that the main saloon was:

> a long narrow apartment, not unlike a gigantic hearse with windows in the sides;
> having at the upper end a melancholy stove, at which three or four chilly stew-
> ards were warming their hands [while the state-room purchased by Dickens's ticket
> money proved an] utterly impracticable, thoroughly hopeless, and profoundly pre-
> posterous box, [its bed-place] a very flat quilt, covering a very thin mattress, spread
> like a surgical plaster on a most inaccessible shelf.

Shocked, Dickens sat down upon 'a kind of horsehair slab...of which there were two
within...' Elsewhere:

> There was a stewardess, too, actively engaged in producing clean sheets and table-
> cloths from the very entrails of the sofas... God bless that stewardess for her piously
> fraudulent account of January voyages! God bless her for her clear recollection of...
> last year, when nobody was ill, and everybody danced...and it was 'a run' of twelve
> days, and a piece of purest frolic, and delight and jollity! All happiness be with her
> for her bright face and the pleasant Scotch tongue...and for her predictions of fair
> winds and fine weather.

Another early passenger was the Bostonian Fanny Appleton who took passage in
the *Columbia* in May 1841 and missed, 'of course, the beautiful...exhilaration of a
sailing-vessel' but marvelled — in marked contrast to Dickens — at the near perfect
quiet: 'There is none of the constant bawling of orders' that had prevailed in the
American packet carrying her to Le Havre in May 1835. There was 'a slight trembling
of course, but not a sound from the machinery' which was generally a characteristic
of steam-propulsion. 'The only sounds are the bells every hour, the bugle to summon
us to meals, the slight sighing of the valves...' Miss Appleton was seduced by more
than the *Columbia*, being much favoured by the *Columbia's* master, Captain Charles
Judkins. A well-built fellow with strong, handsome features, then in his early thir-
ties and Fanny's senior by seven years, Judkins promenaded her, showing off his ship,
inviting her to his table and entertaining her with his guitar. Otherwise known for his
taciturnity, Fanny's good-looks melted him and he confided his firm conviction that

steam-navigation was the school of every future Nelson who would be 'the hero of a paddle-box'. Charmed and serenaded, Miss Appleton wrote of him as a 'right good fellow,' adding that 'there is a Mrs J. on shore to whom I must speedily resign him', but he devoted 'himself, heart and soul to the comfort of his passengers'. No wonder she wrote to a correspondent: 'We have no excuse for grumbling at anything.'

While the previously employed 10-gun brigs used by the Admiralty for the British mail service had proved crank and shown an alarming propensity to capsize — a Falmouth mail-packet having gone missing in the winter of 1838 as Cunard crossed the Atlantic in quest of his goal — many passengers found that the new 'steam-kettles,' as seamen in sail were calling them, did little to inspire confidence. 'How long is it, since the poor *President* went down?' enquired one of Dickens's eighty-six fellow passengers about to endure an ordeal for which they were ill-prepared. The *Britannia* ran into a gale and wallowed sickeningly for four days. Asking the cause of the ship's violent motion, a laconic steward told Dickens that there was:

'Rather a heavy sea on, sir, and a head wind.' Imagine the wind howling, the sea roaring, the rain beating: all in furious array against her [the *Britannia*, with 'her tall red funnel']. Picture the sky both dark and wild, and the clouds, in fearful sympathy with the waves, making another ocean in the air. Add to all this...the gurgling in and out of water through the scuppers; with, every now and then, the striking of a heavy sea upon the planks above, with the deep, dead, heavy sound of thunder heard within a vault — and there is that head wind of a January morning.... [W]hat the agitation of a steam-vessel is, on a bad winter's night in the wild Atlantic, it is impossible for the most vivid imagination to conceive.

Dickens, however, despite his queasiness and disappointment, perceived something of the new age:

The gloom through which the great black mass holds its direct and certain course, the rushing water, plainly heard, but dimly seen; the broad, white, glistening track that follows in the vessel's wake; the men on the lookout forward, who would be scarcely visible against the dark sky, but for their blotting out some score of...stars; the helmsman at the wheel, with the illuminated card before him, shining, a speck of light amidst the darkness... the melancholy sighing of the wind through block, and rope, and chain...

But, Dickens learned, it was within sight of the shore that real trouble could ambush a ship, even with a pilot embarked, for the voyage almost ended badly and ruined Cunard's enviable reputation for safety even before it was two years old. In the sudden fog for which Halifax is notorious they:

were running (as we thought) into Halifax Harbour, on the fifteenth night with little wind and a bright moon — indeed we had made the Light [on Chebucto

Head] at its outer entrance, and put the pilot in charge – when suddenly the ship struck upon a bank of sand. An immediate rush on deck took place…the sides were crowded in an instant; and for a few minutes we were in…a state of confusion… The passengers, and guns, and water-casks, and other heavy matters, being all huddled together aft, however, to lighten her in the head, she was soon got off; and after some driving on towards an uncomfortable line of objects (whose vicinity had been announced very early in the disaster by a loud cry of 'Breakers a-head!') and much backing of paddles, and heaving of the lead into a constantly decreasing depth of water, we dropped anchor in a strange outlandish-looking nook which nobody on board could recognise, although there was land all about us, and so close that we could plainly see the waving branches of the trees.

It was strange enough, in the silence of midnight, and the dead stillness …created by the sudden and unexpected stoppage of the engine which had been clanking and blasting in our ears incessantly for so many days, to watch the look of blank astonishment in every face; beginning with the officers…through all the passengers, and descending to the very stokers and furnace-men, who emerged from below…and clustered together in a smoky group about the hatch-way to the engine room… After throwing up a few rockets and firing signal-guns in the hope of being hailed from the land…it was determined to send a boat on shore. [Dickens observed]… how desperately unpopular the poor pilot became in one short minute. He had had his passage out from Liverpool, and during the voyage had been quite a notorious character, as a teller of anecdotes and cracker of jokes. Yet here were the very men who had laughed…at his jests, now flourishing their fists in his face…and defying him to his teeth as a villain!

[The boat returned] in less than an hour [with a young man who revealed that they were in] the Eastern Passage, 'about the last place in the world in which we had any business or reason to be, but a sudden fog, and some error on the pilot's part, were the cause. We were surrounded by banks, and rocks, and shoals of all kinds, but had happily drifted, it seemed, upon the only safe speck that was to be found thereabouts. Eased by this report, and by the assurance that the tide was past the ebb, we turned in at three o'clock in the morning.

I was dressing about half-past nine next day, when the noise above hurried me on deck. When I had left it over-night, it was dark, foggy and damp, and there were bleak hills all around us. Now, we were gliding down a smooth, broad stream, at the rate of eleven miles an hour: our colours flying gaily; our crew rigged out in their smartest clothes; our officers in uniform again, the sun shining… the land stretched out on either side, streaked with light patches of snow; white wooden houses; people at their doors; telegraphs working; flags hoisted; wharfs appearing; ships; quays crowded with people; distant noises; shouts; men and boys running down steep places towards the pier; all more bright and gay and fresh to our unused eyes than words can paint them. We came to a wharf, paved with uplifted faces; got alongside, and were made fast, after some shouting and straining of cables; darted, a score of us along the gangway, almost as soon as it was thrust out to meet us…

Dickens's account of the voyage in *American Notes* was 'written to kill time and tickle the reader,' the reviewer of the *Illustrated London News* claimed, conceived in a spirit of 'entire bad taste' and full of 'sneers, vituperations, [and] caustic sarcasms'. Perhaps a little exaggerated for effect, no doubt, but if the prose is over-blown, it rings true, grounding and all. In 1842 Dickens, not the *Illustrated London News's* reviewer, was still one of a minority who had experienced a winter passage across the North Atlantic in a steam-vessel. The author would return in the American sailing packet *George Washington*, which he appeared to find as delightful as Fanny Appleton had found it boisterous, but his voyage in the *Britannia* was to windward in winter, and hers in the *Colombia* was down-wind in spring. Moreover, her father and brother were business associates of Samuel Cunard, and she wrote for private consumption, not a public audience. Dickens marked the impact of steam when the *George Washington* lay becalmed awhile in mid-Atlantic. Inquiries made by the chief mate as to 'where he supposed the *Great Western* (which left New York a week after us) was *now*, and where he supposed the Cunard steam-packet was *now*, and what he thought of sailing-vessels as compared with steamships *now*...' only received a bad-tempered response.

The comings and goings of these steamers excited great interest for some time before becoming commonplace. On one occasion when due to sail, the *Britannia* was beset by ice in Boston Harbour, her vulnerable paddles dissuading her master from smashing his way out. To help despatch her, the citizens turned out to break-up the ice, creating a seven-mile *polynya* through which she escaped.

The four auxiliary paddle-wheeled 8.5-knot steamers *Britannia*, *Columbia*, *Acadia* and *Caledonia* were soon joined by the slightly faster *Cambria* and *Hibernia*. Sailings became weekly and Cunard's annual subsidy was raised to £81,000. By 1848 another four larger paddlers of greater tonnage and speed, the *America*, *Niagara*, *Canada* and *Europa*, were added to the fleet which bore both British and American mails and was picking up an increasing number of passengers. Such enterprise soon attracted fierce competition from American rivals, chief among which was the Collins Line which gained an American Government mail-contract. The Collins ships proved marginally faster, though the advantage was gained at crippling fuel and man-power costs, and the company found 'that to effect the saving of from a day to a day and a half in the run between New York and Liverpool was costing...nearly a million dollars a year'.

In response, Cunard built the sister-ships *Asia* and *Africa* in 1850. At 2,128 tons they were fitted with four boilers and a score of furnaces, requiring thirty-eight engineers and firemen and 900 tons of coal. They carried 180 passengers but were designed for ready conversion to steam-frigates, thus securing a continuing and generous Government subsidy. The even larger *Arabia* followed and the competition between the two companies was fierce, with Cunard losing business to Collins who boasted of 'defeating' Cunard. With freight-rates tumbling from £7.5 per ton to £4, MacIver grew anxious about his company's future and Burns considered retirement. Then, in September 1854, the Collins liner *Arctic* collided with the French steamer *Vesta*. Among the huge numbers of dead were Mrs Collins and two of her children. In the aftermath of this it also emerged that the sole surviving lifeboat contained only fourteen passengers, but thirty-eight of the ship's crew. Shortly afterwards the *Arctic*'s sister-ship the *Pacific* disappeared, followed by further losses which culminated in the demise of the American company in 1858.

Two years after the *Arctic* sank Cunard escaped a similar disaster only by having switched to iron hulls. In 1852, following the loss of the Royal Mail steamer *Amazon* – mentioned later – the Admiralty rescinded its increasingly archaic ruling that a mail-steamer must be constructed of wood. Despite Burns's personal misgivings, the board of Cunard ordered their first iron vessel from Robert Napier's new ship-building yard at Govan. In January 1856 the iron paddle-steamer *Persia*, at 3,600 tons and a length of 376ft, the largest merchant ship in the world, began her maiden outward voyage. Racing across the Grand Banks in thick weather at 11 knots, she struck an iceberg head-on. Her iron construction saved her, for, while rivets popped, seams opened and her paddle-wheels suffered damage, the sub-division of the hull by transverse bulkheads allowed her to limp into New York, Captain E.G. Lott a chastened but wiser man. While the nervous Burns retired, Napier was pleased with the strength of his large, elegant ship as she took back from the dying Collins Line the record for the fastest passage – a growing preoccupation that would, in time, be formalised as 'the Blue Riband'. The *Persia* reduced the west-bound passage to nine days, sixteen hours and sixteen minutes; the east-bound to eight days, twenty-three hours and nineteen minutes, but her coal consumption soared – 176 tons *per diem* – and while Charles MacIver fossicked over the extortion, passengers favoured her glamour and bought their tickets. Cunard was rewarded with a baronetcy in 1859: henceforth he was Sir Samuel.

By now new rivals appeared in the Western Ocean. The Inman Line was set up by William Inman and the Richardson brothers of Belfast in 1850, and the Guion Line followed in 1866. Both had an interest in the emigrant traffic which was growing in the wake of the Irish Potato Famine, the pogroms of the Tsars and social upheaval throughout Europe. The flood of emigrants seemed endless. In 1868 alone more than 150,000 Britons departed for the United States, stimulating more shipping companies, among them the Anchor Line.

The establishment of the Anchor Line was typical of the early years of major shipping firms, arising as it did from a small trading-house that initially chartered before purchasing vessels. Most, of course, started in sail, as was the case with Nicol and Robert Handyside, partners in ship-broking and trading in merchandise between Glasgow and Russia and the Baltic. In late 1852 the brothers began an association with Captain Thomas Henderson, a ship-master who had recently had the misfortune to lose his ship, the *Orion*, on the rocks off Portpatrick. Although exonerated at the subsequent inquiry – the *Orion*'s guilty second mate was sentenced to seven years' transportation – Henderson was obliged to seek employment ashore and began touting a scheme to establish a steam-vessel company, an idea adopted by the Handyside brothers who took Henderson as a partner. Quite why the new firm of Handysides & Co. first invested in sailing-vessels is unclear, but three were ordered from Sandeman & McLaurin at Whiteinch on the Clyde, and whilst awaiting the delivery of their new tonnage the firm chartered several vessels and loaded them with cargoes for Australia. In May 1854 they took delivery of their first ship, the *Phantom*, and advertised her as belonging to the 'Clyde Clipper Line of Australian packets for Melbourne direct'. This intention was frustrated and the *Phantom* and her new sister, the *Vision*, were subsequently sent out to India and then began a regular service between Glasgow and Valparaiso. Other ships followed, the Handysides investing in quarter-shares in two steamers of which they were appointed managers, and by 1856 they were handling four steam-vessels and three more fast sailing-vessels, all of which carried cargoes out to Bombay before entering the Glasgow to Valparaiso service.[35] One of these, the *Tempest*, was converted to a steamer, but the work was long delayed and despite announcements being made that a new firm to be called the Anchor Line would begin a North Atlantic service, it was some months before it did so. By 1859 a second converted sailing ship, the *John Bell*, which was owned by the Montreal Ocean Steam-ship Co., was signed-up for a joint-venture while a third steam-vessel, the *United Kingdom*, was being built.

Then disaster struck. On her homeward voyage from New York in February 1857 the *Tempest*, commanded by Captain James Morris, went missing. The following year the *Vision* was abandoned off Cape Horn. Relinquishing its transatlantic ambitions, the Anchor Line was rescued by the Indian Mutiny, both the *United Kingdom* and the *John Bell* being chartered by the Government for trooping. On returning from the east, the steamers were again put into the North Atlantic trade and, joined by the new steamer *United States*, initiated a regular emigrant service. Unfortunately such plans were premature, for the new vessel was lost in the Gulf of St Lawrence in April 1861 and in May the *Spectre* was also wrecked, after which the remaining sailing-vessels gave up the South American trade. The steamer service was now compromised by the '*Trent* Incident', mentioned elsewhere, despite the building of the *Caledonia* to replace the lost *United States*. But then the owners of the *John Bell* decided to sell her. To help maintain a footing on the Western Ocean emigrant run, the *Dalhousie* was adapted to carry passengers, and after two voyages to Canada and one to New York she too was converted to steam. However, the *Caledonia* ran aground on Cape Cod and broke her back 'with a report of a cannon', and although afterwards salvaged and put into service under the American flag as the *Concordia*, she too was lost to the Glasgow partners. The Anchor Line struggled with one ship until July 1863 when the *Britannia* was commissioned, and by the winter she had been joined by the second *Caledonia*.

The following year the steamers ran only to New York and Portland, but the flood of emigrants was such that the smaller steamers still venturing into the Mediterranean were diverted to Canada. The shortage of tonnage was made up by buying the *Iowa* from the London & New York Line in June 1866. She had spent some time aground in Dundrum Bay, but was repaired, refitted and put into the Anchor Line schedule, changing her name some years later to *Macedonia*. It is clear that, despite their run of misfortune, the Handysides and Hendersons (several of the latter – also brothers and ship-masters – having either joined as partners or commanding Anchor Line ships) survived only because of the steady flow of human cargo.

While Canada was also a beneficiary of emigration, the opportunism of the Anchor Line steamers indicates that the United States attracted the overwhelming majority of the aspiring and desperate migrants. Among the several lines then vying for their carriage across the Western Ocean was the White Star Line, which had been established in 1851 and consisted of the sailing ships serving Australia mentioned earlier. Its involvement with the North Atlantic passenger trade is related later.

Elsewhere, other pioneering voyages were in progress. In 1840, as Cunard initiated his famous line on the North Atlantic and almost twenty years after the despatch of the *Rising Star*, two small 700-ton paddle-steamers, the *Chile* and *Peru*, were despatched by way of the Strait of Magellan to serve the west coast of South America. From this enterprise sprang the Pacific Steam Navigation Co., or 'PSNC'. The two ships ran between London and Valparaiso until 1852 when they were put in the Chilean coastal service, being relieved on the international route by the sister-ships *Lima*, *Bogota*, *Quito* and *Santiago*, all of 1,125 tons and 425hp. By 1869 other ships such as the 1,000-ton steamer *Arequipa* further expanded the coastal services following the company's decision to extend the trade from Britain to Valparaiso by way of the Iberian Peninsula and the Straits of Magellan. Later on the company's services extended to Callao, a state of affairs that only ended with the dramatic transformation effected in 1914 by the opening of the Panama Canal.

Steam-vessels initiated profound changes in British ship-management. With steamer ownership centred in London, the ships serving the Atlantic sailed from Liverpool, thus delegating their management to the latter port. Ship-owners became detached from the daily contact that had been a feature of the dock-side life of the sailing ship, while the limited-liability shareholders increasingly supporting these brave new enterprises were even less interested in the daily handling of their investments, demanding only a return on capital. As the old 'sixty-fourths share-owner' disappeared, ship and ship-owner became separated. Competition produced a shipping tycoon who presided over a growing private empire as small firms were merged with larger 'lines'. 'The one was personal,' reminisced William Forwood in 1919, 'the other is remote.' But the change, howsoever inevitable, was slow. As Forwood pointed out, 'the wooden paddle-steamer was not a serious competitor [to the sailing-vessel] except in the conveyance of passengers and mail,' both of which attracted high rates of passage-money and Government contracts. The steamer could not be truly ascendant until she was viable in her own right, and in this neither Cunard nor his competitors were the true pioneers. Such work had to be left to the real risk-takers, men who ventured more than mere capital upon the great enterprise of shrinking the globe, who would lose much in order that others might gain; men like Isambard Kingdom Brunel and John Scott Russell.

Brunel had only a part in the building and design of the *Great Western*, a task in which Claxton was pre-eminent, but he became fascinated in the development of screw propulsion as a better means of driving a hull through the water. A number of practical proponents of the screw-propeller emerged in the later 1830s, and its inception need not detain us, but the properties of a helix had been known since ancient times and several small screw-steamers had been tried out without much success and no financial enthusiasm. Following some experimental models and a patent registered in 1836, the farmer Francis Pettit Smith found a number of backers – chiefly the banker and venture-capitalist John Wright – and formed the Ship Propeller Co., which three years later was incorporated by Act of Parliament. The company ordered a 200-ton auxiliary steamer to be propelled by Smith's device, a horizontally mounted helix of one full revolution, or 'single-thread'. The vessel was laid down and built at Limehouse by Henry Wimshurst and engined by George Rennie, being launched in 1838 with the appropriate name of *Archimedes*.

Simultaneously the British-domiciled Swede Johan Ericsson patented a differing helical device and found American backers, but it was Smith's company, helped by a promotional voyage made by the *Archimedes* round the British Isles in 1840, that attracted the interest of the Admiralty. Unfortunately, Rennie had boldly fitted a high-pressure boiler into the *Archimedes* and this exploded, killing several of the attending firemen, circumstances which, along with the failure to exceed 8 knots, cooled Their Lordships' enthusiasm, and the poor *Archimedes*'s last task in home waters was the ignominious duty of towing a new naval steam-sloop, HMS *Rattler*, from her builders' yard at Sheerness up the Thames to the East India Dock to receive her engines. The consequences of this would prove ironic. Thereafter the *Archimedes* was sent to haul cargoes of Australian coal to Chile, fading into obscurity like Smith himself as The Ship Propeller Co. folded and Wright's bank crashed.

But one of Ericsson's steamers – built by Laird at Birkenhead – had crossed the Atlantic to take up work in the United States, and before the *Archimedes* had completed her circumnavigation of Britain, her builder, Henry Wimshurst, had built a second screw-steamer largely on his own account, incorporating significant ideas of his own. These included placing the plant in the stern, minimising the run of shaft, and setting the screw in a 'banjo-frame' which allowed it to be lifted clear of the water when the vessel was under sail. Rennie's high-pressure locomotive boiler, which should have operated at 60psi, had to be dropped owing to a workers' strike and rejection by underwriters. Instead a 15psi boiler was fitted, though even this was considered risky. The detachable screw was, however – and in due course – taken into use by the Royal Navy.[36] Rejected by The Ship Propeller Co., Wimshurst found a charterer for his little-known vessel which he had named the *Novelty*, and she secured her niche in history when, in 1841, she carried coal out to Constantinople, the first screw-steamer to carry a commercial cargo. Wimshurst's subsequent attempts to sell the *Novelty* to the Admiralty failed. She was dismissed as 'entirely unsuitable', as were other projects, including the 'unshipping', or raising propeller. Only the relatively high-pressure boiler and steam plant was condescendingly admitted 'to show considerable ingenuity'.

Amid all this turmoil, the Admiralty ordered a formal trial to determine the screw-versus-paddle question. HM Steam-sloops *Alecto*, a paddler, and *Rattler*, a modified screw-powered vessel into whose new hull Brunel had himself supervised the installation of her engine, were coupled up, stern-to-stern. While popular opinion favoured the *Alecto's* speed, the *Rattler* developed more grip on the water and pulled her thrashing rival ignominiously stern-first.

Some time before this Brunel had been contracted to design a second large steam-vessel to enable the Great Western S.S.Co. to run a two-ship service. As matters progressed, Brunel took up the suggestion of Claxton — whose trip to Antwerp on the General Steam Navigation Co.'s iron steamer *Rainbow* has already been mentioned — to construct an iron hull. Claxton had been accompanied up the Schelde by the Bristol ship-builder William Patterson, whose yard would produce the new iron vessel. At 3,270 tons she was — for a while — the world's largest ship, and for that reason was constructed not on a slipway but in a dry dock. At the same time the *Archimedes* — which touched at Bristol during her round-Britain voyage — and the subsequent tug-of-war between the *Rattler* and *Alecto*, caused a second major change in the new ship's design. Observing the experience of early screw-steamers with interest, and considering their disappointing but demonstrable lack of speed when compared with paddlers, Brunel concluded that the after lines of a hull — that portion abaft the beam known as the 'run' and by which the flow of water was received by the driving screw — was fundamental to the efficiency of the propeller. He decided to dispense with paddles and to fit the new ship with a six-bladed propeller, a decision backed by Claxton and Patterson after long debate and experimentation. These men, allied to Thomas Guppy — who actually became the resident superintending engineer, with Brunel assisting from London — swung the company's board in favour of dispensing with the now well-established wooden paddle design in favour of this bold innovation. This, however, delayed the ship's completion date long after the 'most important' commissioning deadline of 'the early part of 1841'.

Brunel's genius was inimical to efficient ship-management; his ideas required seemingly endless, fussy modification and, with this, additional investment. As late as autumn 1842, when project costs had risen from £76,000 to £100,000, one stockholder inveighed against 'the continued demands…the system of making, altering, and remaking, which has been so long practiced to our cost, and of advantage to none but our salaried servants'. But the new ship had caught the mood of the age, *The Times* admitting her to be an 'experiment…of vast importance in a national point of view', and when she was finally floated out of her natal dock with the prestigious name *Great Britain* in July 1842, The Prince Consort was in attendance. Even then she took an age to fit-out; she cost £117,000 to build with a further £53,000 invested in her dry-dock and ancillary workshops. It was July 1845 before the *Great Britain* finally lay in Liverpool to embark her passengers for her maiden voyage, sailing for New York on 26th with only forty-five cabin-passengers, though she carried more in the steerage and had besides 600 tons of cargo. Significantly, however, she failed to impress with her heavy rolling and a speed of a mere 9.4 knots. On her return, with a small number of passengers and a cargo of cotton, the propeller blades were enhanced with riveted extensions, but on her second voyage in early October, with just over 100 passengers, she not only lost a mast in a severe squall but shed half her propeller blades, throwing the screw out of balance. After repairs in New York only twenty-three eastbound passengers could be found.

More modifications to her engines to increase her speed were carried out in Liverpool where bilge-keels were fitted to dampen her rolling motion. Public opinion, fickle as ever, now charged her inceptors as being guilty of 'a leviathanism which was wholly uncalled for'. Worse was to come. In September of the following year her master, Captain James Hosken (formerly of the *Great Western*), ran her aground in Dundrum Bay. A deviation of the compass was suspected, though Hosken denied this. No lives were lost and history records that this unfortunate event proved beyond peradventure the durability of an iron hull, for the *Great Britain* lay there until – after prodigious efforts – she was refloated in August 1847. If so, she nevertheless ruined the company, for her salvage cost a further £45,000 and she was sold to satisfy creditors. Notwithstanding all this, she was a remarkable ship and was yet to have a long and varied career, reduced eventually – as were many steam-ships unable to earn a viable existence – to a sailing-vessel. Before that extremity, however, having proved unsuccessful on the transatlantic run, her engines were replaced by her new owners, Gibbs, Bright & Co., who put her into the Australian trade in 1852 under a Captain Gray. On her first voyage to Melbourne she carried 630 emigrants but the passage took eighty-three days. Between 1855 and 1857 she was among hundreds of steam-vessels chartered by the Government to carry troops first to the Crimea and then to India, and although she returned to the Australian passenger trade for a few years, carrying out the first test cricket team in 1861, in due course her engines and boilers were removed and she was converted to sail. In 1885, homeward-bound with a cargo of wool, she suffered a battering off Cape Horn and limped to the Falklands Islands where she was reduced to a coal-hulk, a duty she carried out until 1937 when she was beached and abandoned in Sparrow Cove, near Port Stanley.[37]

The extraordinary sequel to this extraordinary story was the *Great Eastern*, not entirely Brunel's concept but a collaboration with the Glaswegian, John Scott Russell, a man of undoubted genius and the foremost naval architect of his day. Russell had moved his ship-building enterprise from Greenock to Millwall, on the Thames, where he took over an existing yard. He had conducted studies and tank experiments into wave formation and hull resistance to postulate a wave-line theory – later further developed by William Froude, with whom Russell frequently disagreed – for which he was awarded a gold medal by the Royal Society of Edinburgh in 1837. Russell had been approached by Sir Benjamin Hawes, Under Secretary of State for War, who enquired if he could construct two vessels capable of reaching Australia, where gold had just been discovered. The two ships were to be operated by the Australian Royal Mail Co., and Russell agreed, building two large 3,000-ton auxiliary steam-vessels in the short time of six months. In 1851 the two steamers, the *Adelaide* and *Victoria*, were put into service, the latter winning a prize for a fast passage outwards of sixty days.

The Australian Royal Mail Co. employed Brunel as a consultant chief engineer and, having persuaded Russell of the possibilities of a much larger vessel, he and Russell collaborated on a revolutionary new ship. She was to be a leviathan in every sense of the word, an iron monster of 18,914 tons, 693ft long with a beam of 82ft, designed to carry 4,000 passengers or 6,000 troops in addition to 6,000 tons deadweight of cargo: more than four or five times the size of any other contemporary steam-vessel. Fearful that she might not make the requisite 15 knots — which she never did — Brunel suggested she be fitted with both a horizontal direct-acting engine to drive a screw-propeller and an oscillating engine to power paddles which latter extended her extreme width to 120ft. Besides these relatively conventional appurtenances, she was the first ship to have a cellular double-bottom, an innovation for which Brunel is usually credited, though it was Russell's idea and it was Russell, not Brunel, who was contracted to 'design, build and launch' the new ship. She was also to have had a steam-powered steering engine to transmit power from her helm to her massive rudder, but this was not attended to until later in her life.[38] As an auxiliary steamer, however, she would set 6,500 square yards of sail; bear twenty boats, two of which were steam-tenders, and have internal gas-lighting and an electrical light on the mainmast to bathe 'the ship in perpetual moonlight'. Most significantly, her bunkers would hold 15,000 tons of 'navigation coal', giving her an unprecedented range, for she was conceived — at least on paper — to carry her own bunkers from London to Trincomalee by way of the Cape of Good Hope and back, a round voyage of 22,000 miles. This was a red-herring since Australia was her real target, however, insofar as her backers were concerned, she was to capture, dominate and possibly monopolise the very considerable traffic then in train between Great Britain and her Indian dominions, a market more readily comprehended by potential investors. Russell found finance — to the tune of £600,000 — and the keel was laid in 1853. Thereafter the project was beset by problems.

Firstly the shipyard suffered from an extensive fire, against which Russell was not fully insured; secondly the Crimean War with its demand for man-power had raised wages, and with Russell committed to several fixed-price contracts building men-of-war for the Royal Navy his cash-flow was compromised. Another fire, the death of his chief backer and problems arising from the new project itself, broke Russell's company. Although refinancing deals were done, Russell's relations with Brunel became strained. Brunel constantly interfered, insisting upon approving every detail and he was incapable of delegating, so valuable time was lost and plant such as the steering engine had to be abandoned.

Other standard shipyard practices were relinquished. The *Great Eastern* was neither built in a dock like the *Great Britain* nor on a conventional slipway 'end-on' to the river, but on a sideways-slip on the Isle of Dogs. Her immense size — she was to displace 22,500 tons when launched — attracted on the one hand wondrous panegyrics and on the other doom-laden predictions. Passing her as she rose above the huddled houses of Cubitt Town, the American Herman Melville thought her a 'Vast toy. No substance, Durable materials but perishable structure...' Others thought she would break up at sea, and it seems the gods did not smile for a riveter mysteriously disappeared and several men and boys were killed in her building. The details of her construction are complex and may be sought elsewhere, but, worst of all, she was reluctant to enter the Thames.[39] Russell's finances were strained and he fell out with Brunel who, sidelined by The Great Eastern S.S.Co., continued to supervise unpaid.

The *Royal Charter*, the ship that gave her name to a storm in 1859 when she was wrecked off Moelfre, Anglesey, with heavy loss of life. (© Courtesy of Whitby Museum)

Time dragged on but after many delays and technical problems the great ship was eventually launched at the fourth attempt on the spring tide of 31 January 1858. By this time she had become a 'monster' and a national nightmare. Fitted out, her hull was opened to visitors and impertinent cockneys squealed through her cavernous interior, marvelling at her engines and boiler rooms, the appointments of her vast saloon and smoking-rooms intended for only about 1,500 passengers. The artist Edward William Cooke sketched from her bridge, delineating the huge sweep of her upper deck and the long line of lifeboats in their davits swung out over her port side. Even Queen Victoria paid the ship a visit. In the end, with good money flung after bad in an attempt to redeem the initial investment, she was placed under the command of Captain William Harrison, one of 200 applicants – an indication that there were many mariners interested in her – and put into the North Atlantic passenger trade. Surprisingly, Harrison came from Cunard's line and received the ailing figure of Brunel who came aboard two days before the *Great Eastern*'s departure on 8 September 1859 to have his photograph taken. A broken man, Brunel died of a stroke a week later.[40]

The *Great Eastern* proceeded to Holyhead where she was assailed by a ferocious storm in which the winds along the coast of North Wales reached hurricane force. Thanks to Chief Engineer Alexander McLennan and Harrison's skill in manoeuvring her – a real feat, since no one had hitherto handled so large a vessel – the *Great Eastern* avoided the fate of several other ships. The great wind of 25 October 1859 was known as 'the *Royal Charter* storm' after the powerful steamer of that name that was its most notable casualty, but some 200 other vessels were wrecked, stranded or damaged that terrible night.

The *Royal Charter* had been built in 1855 by Messrs Sandycroft near Chester, a 2,719-ton auxiliary steamer of some 200-nominal-hp. Owned by the Bright brothers of Liverpool, forerunners of Gibbs, Bright & Co., and commanded by a Captain Taylor, she was a popular ship that had clipped a day off the *Victoria*'s record and reached Melbourne fifty-nine days out from Liverpool.[41] She had left Hobson's Bay, Victoria, on 26 August, homeward-bound with a cargo of wool. Among her 376 passengers were eleven riggers working their passage and – besides the usual crop of civil-servants and soldiers whose term of service in the colony had expired – a number of gold-miners and their families returning home with their fortunes, so that in her strong-room the *Royal Charter* carried about £500,000 of gold. Taylor ran his ship home by the traditional route, passing close to a large iceberg in the Southern Ocean and doubling Cape Horn, reaching the Cove of Cork on 24 October where 'all on board…were animated by the hope of arriving safe at Liverpool, from the circumstances of not a breath [of wind] disturbing the water'. During the following day, as the *Royal Charter* rounded Carnsore Point and headed towards the Skerries, the wind began to freshen and at nightfall 'burst with…fury over the devoted ship'. Passing the lighthouse on the Skerries, Taylor threw out a signal for a pilot, repeating it off Point Lynas, but no boat could venture out and Taylor sought shelter by rounding Point Lynas and making for Redwharf Bay to anchor and await moderation.

About midnight Taylor attempted to tack ship, but the vessel would not come up into the wind and he ordered the port anchor let go. One hundred fathoms of cable flew out through the hawse-pipe, but the *Royal Charter* still drove to leeward and the starboard bower was let go. The vessel was now perilously close to the rocks off Moelfre, and when the port cable parted at about 01.30, the starboard followed. A few minutes later the *Royal Charter* struck rocks and almost immediately began to break up. Her signals had attracted a small crowd gathered on the low cliff-top who watched with terrified excitement as, in the first light of dawn, they observed a man 'let himself down…by a rope into the midst of the breakers'. Joseph Rogers, a Maltese able-seaman, made three attempts to swim ashore and finally, with willing help from twenty-eight local men who ventured into the sea to assist, managed to rig-up a rope by which means – and with the help of Moelfre's menfolk – eighteen passengers, five of whom were riggers, and another eighteen of her crew were rescued. Neither Captain Taylor nor any of his officers, nor any more from the 100-strong crew survived as the stricken ship broke her back and shivered into pieces under the relentless pounding of a monstrous sea. The loss of the *Royal Charter* and, in particular, of her passengers, was to be one of many incidents that led to major reforms and increased Government regulation of merchant shipping referred to elsewhere.[42]

After this dreadful storm, the *Great Eastern* was ordered to winter in the shelter of Southampton Water as her shareholders rose in revolt against the directors. The ship had cost over £1 million, she was mortgaged and had yet to embark a single fare-paying passenger. Unsurprisingly, the Great Eastern S.S.Co. was all but bankrupt, having only £5,500 cash-in-hand. The directors, pleading the ship's value as a naval asset, appealed to William Gladstone, the Chancellor of the Exchequer, but the wily liberal was the son of a ship-owner and knew a bad investment when he saw one. There were no mails involved; this was a private speculation and literally sank or swam upon its achievements. Then personal tragedy struck. In January Captain Harrison, taking passage in his gig with the surgeon, the purser's nine-year-old son and seven seamen, was overset in a squall when the men could not douse the sail in time. Harrison, the boy and one seaman were drowned.

After this the board of directors resigned, Russell was dropped and the company was refinanced and renamed the Great Ship Co. The new board, led by the railway engineer, financier and former associate of Brunel, Daniel Gooch, continued to attempt the capture of the North Atlantic passenger trade. Despite everything, such was the anticipation in America that several ports vied for receiving the *Great Eastern*. Among these Portland, Maine, invested $125,000 in a pier designed for the huge ship, but its inhabitants were to be bitterly disappointed. New York sent Michael Murphy, a Sandy Hook pilot, across to England where he joined the *Great Eastern* for the sole purpose of piloting her through the Narrows and into the Hudson where the city had spent a paltry $3,000 to dredge out a berth alongside a timber wharf.

The *Great Eastern's* maiden voyage finally began from Southampton on 17 June 1860. Gooch and his wife sailed in her along with another company director and his spouse; there were a handful of naval and military officers, a few journalists and a mere thirty-five paying passengers. Her cargo was even more embarrassing, but her new master was a distinguished musician and astronomer, a man experienced in the East India trade and the first master-mariner to pass the new-fangled qualification for command of a steam-ship inaugurated by the Board of Trade. His name was John Vine Hall and he was supported by Alexander McLennan, the devoted chief engineer who had been in the ship since her building and had previously served in both the *Great Western* and the *Great Britain*. Thanks to Hall's sails and McLennan's engines the *Great Eastern* arrived off Sandy Hook on 28 June, coming up the harbour under the 'advice' of Murphy who awaited the full flood and enabled New York to assemble in admiration. Murphy passed the bar with only a churning of the mud, but the ship could scarcely be stopped as she came alongside the crowded wooden wharf, damaging both it and her own paddle sponson. Her gigantic size, however, impressed New York; the city went wild, as did the *Great Eastern's* crew, who got their hands on hard liquor. One of them assaulted the chief officer, Henry Machin, others fought each other and Fireman William Hicks killed fellow fireman Thomas O'Brien in a drunken brawl. One seaman drowned when he fell overboard examining a paddle, another because he was drunk, while a handful deserted. In the aftermath the board of the Victoria Pier Co. in Portland unsuccessfully sued the *Great Eastern's* owners for compensation.[43]

The *Great Eastern's* years of service in the North Atlantic were dismal; she carried passengers in a fiercely competitive and over-subscribed market, but was simply too big to pay her way and support her huge crew of 418. Her owners obdurately refused to put her into the then thriving emigrant trade, concentrating instead upon trying to out-Cunard Cunard. A slight advantage was had from picking up east-bound American passengers from among those young men eager to avoid being drafted into the ranks of the Union Army, but even with 400 first-class, 300 steerage passengers and 3,000 tons of cargo she remained uneconomic. Her sporadic ability to break even was offset by her occasional explosions and several collisions, both major and minor. All such incidents entailed significant charges, including spurious salvage claims, and even attracted a lawsuit served on Captain Hall alleging infringement of a United States patent on combined screw and paddle propulsion![44] After Hall had suffered a nervous collapse, he was followed by a succession of worthy masters, including Walter Paton, her sixth commander, whose conduct often enhanced her passenger list. Paton became among the first of the notably popular transatlantic liner commanders who briefly elevated the profession of merchant ship-master into a quasi-public office.

Few ships have had such a chequered career, yet the era was full of possibilities for British merchant ships. Although the Americans were increasing their steam-tonnage on the North Atlantic, the Civil War almost destroyed the United States' mercantile marine. More than 700 American merchant ships were re-registered as British to avoid the blockades imposed by the hostile factions, contributing to a rather spurious 80 per cent increase in British tonnage during the 1860s. In addition to ignoring the potential of shipping vast numbers of emigrants – 800,000 of whom arrived in the United States during the Civil War years – the Great Ship Co. failed to comprehend the importance of American wheat and serenely ignored other opportunities that might have rescued it. Although in 1861 the *Great Eastern* loaded the then largest-ever shipment of 5,000 tons of prairie-grown wheat at $25 a ton for discharge in Liverpool – thereby contributing to a collapse in the British agricultural economy – the ship never capitalised upon this bonanza. Even as demand drove-up standards and competition drove-down prices, creating an intermediate class of passenger, this and the emigrant trade was left to others, notably the Anchor Line, the Canadian Government-backed Allan Line and the enterprise of the newly unified Germans. Then in August 1862, concerned about the shallows off Sandy Hook, Captain Walter Paton, who was accompanied by his gravid wife, decided to take the *Great Eastern* to Flushing Bay by way of Long Island Sound, embarking a pilot for the purpose. Off Montauk Point the *Great Eastern* struck an uncharted rock – which now bears her name – and developed a significant list when she anchored and began to discharge her passengers into a tender and her cargo into lighters.

Again the *Great Eastern* became a sightseers' attraction as Paton wrestled with the problem of having a hole in his ship's bottom. There was no graving-dock on the planet capable of accepting her so, after much time, expense and the harnessing of American ingenuity, Paton secured the services of a diver, Peter Falcon, who donned Augustus Siebe's diving suit to discover a gash in the cellular double-bottom. Paton hired a consulting engineer, Edward S. Renwick, who designed and built what he called 'a caisson', which effectively placed a steel, clam-shaped blister against the wounded ship's bottom from which the water was pumped out and into which riveters then descended to secure new plates. This was less than straight-forward, for the seal between the ship's side was difficult to accomplish and, in addition to the natural claustrophobic horrors inherent in the job, an ashen-faced Falcon, sent down to check the caisson's seal against the hull, emerged to report hearing banging noises. Word spread that this was just one more manifestation of the ship's ghost, the riveter who had gone missing at Millwall during the ship's building, a report confirmed by a meddling spirit-medium among their ranks. To calm the workmen's fears Captain Paton went below, traversed the caisson from end to end and came up on deck to confide to Renwick that there *was* a noise. Soon afterwards, however, amid the tackle securing the caisson, a wire and shackle were found oscillating in the tide and knocking the hull. The ghost laid, the work was put in hand – a pioneering achievement – and the repaired ship finally headed for home. Paton was left with a bill for $350,000 and the prospect of an inquiry, along with the death of a passenger from natural causes. The only cheering news came when the *Great Eastern* was still west of Cape Clear fighting a strong easterly wind, when Mrs Paton was delivered of a fine boy named James.[45]

Paton was exonerated of any blame for the grounding, the accident being 'solely attributable to the ship striking on a sunken rock in the fairway channel, which is not laid down in (sic) the charts'. However, the *Great Eastern*'s underwriters refused to reimburse the Great Ship Co., which went deeper into debt over the survey of the repair. With no graving-dock available, a grid was built at New Ferry on the Mersey where the ship was grounded at high tide and beneath which, at low water, the riverbed was excavated. The muddy surveyor appeared to pronounce Renwick's patch satisfactory. Ironically, such vicissitudes as the *Great Eastern* endured earned her a grudging reputation for safety. In an era when shipping disasters were scandalously common and, with an increasing number of mostly indigent emigrant passengers, they made headlines. The *Great Eastern*'s durability began to impinge upon many. She had survived the *Royal Charter* storm, a disintegrating screw and a hole in her bottom, quietly plodding about the North Atlantic Ocean at a time when other vessels acquired notoriety of a more disastrous sort. Among these the emigrant-ship *Austria* had caught fire and was lost with all but sixty-seven of the 560 souls on board; and following the revelations about the crew of the Collins liner *Arctic* after her collision with the *Vesta*, there were further iniquities. When the American steamer *William Browne* struck an iceberg in 1841, the crew of the single lowered-boat threw out sixteen passengers to lighten her.

Not that the *Great Eastern* did not come close to disaster herself, but the point lies in the fact that she survived, as the ship-owner William Forwood, who took passage in the ship during the voyage preceding her encounter with the uncharted rock, relates. She was, despite her many faults, 'twenty years ahead of her time'.[46] But then Forwood puts his finger on her real weakness which was, despite her screw and paddles, a lack of power for her bulk and windage:

[I]f she had possessed sufficient engine power for her displacement, she would have revolutionized steamship travel across the Atlantic and hastened the era of large and swift Atlantic liners… [B]uilt in 1858 for the East India and Australian trades, for which routes a large coal carrying capacity was necessary…she never entered those trades. Her speed in smooth water was twelve to thirteen knots, but in a head sea she could do little more than hold her own, hence the cause of her troubles.

Not only was she a great advance in size, but she had many other novel points.
She was propelled by two sets of engines, oscillating paddle engines and horizontal
screw engines, which together developed 11,000hp. She was fitted with six masts
and four funnels. Her cabin accommodation was unusually capacious and lofty.
Speaking from memory, her saloon was 18 to 20 feet high. She had a smoking
room... but few deck houses, so that her decks were magnificently spacious.

Forwood's experience of her less impressive qualities makes him again worth quoting
at some length:

She sailed from Liverpool for New York on a beautiful afternoon in the early
autumn of 1861. We had on board about four hundred saloon passengers, and a
considerable number in the second cabin. She was commanded by an ex-Cunarder,
Captain [James] Walker. The dock quays in Liverpool, margining the river, were
lined with a vast concourse of people to see the great ship depart.

We had a splendid run down the [St George's] Channel, and on the following
evening we passed the Fastnet. Our people were having a gay time, singing and
dancing on deck, and greatly enjoying themselves. In the middle of this revelry we
passed the *Underwriter*, one of the Black Ball sailing-packets, also bound for New
York. She was under whole topsails, plunging into a head sea and throwing the spray
fore and aft.

We looked upon her with admiration, but with feelings of immense superiority. The old order had passed away, and the new had arrived in the *Great Eastern*.
Many were the congratulations expressed upon the advance in naval architecture,
and many indeed fancied that the perils and discomforts of the sea were things of
the past. The next day was one of those drab grey days so frequent upon the Atlantic.
The wind was increasing in force, and more northerly. The sea was getting up, but
the great ship, meeting it almost dead ahead, scarcely heeded it. 'She is as steady as
a rock,' and 'Wonderful!' were some of the remarks passed around as we took our
morning constitutional.

By noon the scene had changed. The wind had veered round to the north, bringing up a heavy beam sea. The big ship began to lurch and roll heavily, taking heavy
spray overall. Some of her movements were significant of danger [for] she hung
when thrown over by a sea, and recovered very slowly. A huge sea striking her
on the starboard bow swept her fore and aft, and carried away one of our paddle-
wheels and several boats. An ominous silence shortly prevailed, and it was whispered
that the rudder had been carried away. The great ship fell into the trough of the sea
and became unmanageable, lurching and rolling heavily and deeply. The seas, from
time to time, striking her with great force, made her quiver fore and aft. The second
paddle-wheel was soon swept away, and boat after boat was torn from the davits, the
wrecks in many instances being suspended by the falls. While destruction was being
wrought on deck, the damage in the saloons and state-rooms was appalling. They
were simply wrecked by the furniture getting loose and flying about, breaking the

large mirrors which adorned the saloon, and adding broken glass to the dangerous mass of debris. Many of our passengers were badly wounded.

The engineers were trying to repair the broken rudder-stock by coiling round it iron chains to form a drum, so as to be able to get a purchase upon it. That night was a night of much anxiety, but the behaviour of the passengers was exemplary. The ladies found a part of the saloon where they could sit on the deck in comparative safety, and here they knitted and sang hymns. There was a general effort to make the best of things.

The following morning the weather had slightly moderated, but the sea was still mountainous, and we rolled heavily. The chain cable stowed in one of the forward lower decks broke loose and burst through the outer plating and hung in a festoon overboard. The cow-house had been destroyed, and one of the cows was suspended head downwards in the skylight of the forward saloon, and a swan which had been in the cow-house was found in the saloon.

The Captain sent for some of the passengers he knew, and told them that, as the crew had broken into the liquor store, he wished to form special guards to patrol the ship. Some twenty or thirty volunteered, and for four hours each day we patrolled the ship, having a white handkerchief tied round our left arm as our badge of office.

Food had become a difficulty. All the crockery had been smashed, so the victuals were brought down in large stew pans, and taking pieces of broken dishes, we helped ourselves as best we could.

In the afternoon the *Scotia*, outward bound for New York, hove in sight. The great Cunarder looked stately and magnificent, and as she gracefully rode over the big seas without any effort, simply playing with them, she told us what design, knowledge and equipment could do. After sailing round us, she bore away on her voyage. Another miserable night followed, and it was obvious that the mental strain was beginning to tell upon some of our people.[47]

The following day the weather was much finer and the sea moderate, but we were still helpless, a derelict on the wide Atlantic. No success had attended the effort to repair the rudder-stock; nothing would hold it. In the afternoon a small Nova Scotian brig [the *Magnet*] hove in sight, and sailed round us, as we thought, within hailing distance. One of our passengers offered the Captain £100 per day if he would stand by us. No answer coming, an offer to buy both his ship and her cargo was conveyed to him, but still no answer came, and in the evening she sailed away. The Captain of the brig was apparently some time afterwards informed of what had taken place, and promptly claimed one day's demurrage, and was suitably rewarded.

It was now evident that our only hope was to hasten the repair of the rudder-stock. In our dire emergency a young American engineer, Mr. Towle, offered a new suggestion, to build a cross-head on to the broken stock, and to steer the ship with tackles attached to it. After some hours' work and the exercise of much ingenuity, he succeeded, to the great joy of everyone.

The screw engines were still in good order, and the big ship was soon on her way back to Queenstown, where we arrived five days after passing it on our outward voyage. The damage done to the ship was considerable, and some idea of the violence with which she had rolled can be formed from the fact that when the baggage room was opened, it was found that water having got into it, the baggage had been churned into a pulp, and was taken out in buckets.

After her repairs had been approved, Paton cleared Liverpool with 650 passengers and a cargo largely of tea; another voyage followed, the ship sank deeper into debt and the directors asked the shareholders for more money, at which they baulked. The game was up, 'the creditors foreclosed, the ship was bankrupted, and shorn of her army of one-pound stockholders'.

She was bought out by Daniel Gooch himself, along with two other directors one of which was Thomas Brassey, heir to the largest international railway constructor of the age, his father having built railways in Britain, Canada, the Crimea, India, Argentina and Australia. Gooch, Brassey and their associates had one last card to play, and it was to make the ship pay her way, for she was better suited to her new task than anything else, other perhaps than her original purpose of carrying the Indian trade. Gooch put her into the trans-oceanic telegraph-cable-laying business.

In 1843 a paper had been submitted to the Royal Society of Arts in London by Dr William Montgomerie, doctor to the Governor of Singapore. Montgomerie reported the virtues of a material used by the Malay people, a rubbery substance that became 'plastic in hot water and could [then] be moulded to any desired state...' This extraordinary material was *gutta percha*, gum from the tree of the same name, which grew throughout the East Indies. Visiting London, Montgomerie had called upon the agent of Charles Mackintosh, the eponymous manufacturer of waterproof clothing. The agent's brother, Charles Hancock, an inventor and artist, became interested in this substance as a potential replacement for cork bottle-stoppers. Hancock obtained a patent and went into partnership with a Dublin soda-water maker, Thomas Bewley, and in February 1843 the Gutta Percha Co. was formed. Also aware of the new substance, the electrical physicist Michael Faraday was recommending *gutta percha* as a cable insulator. This engaged Hancock's interest, but, in attempting to switch *gutta percha* from stopping bottles to insulating electrical cables, he fell out with his partner and set up a rival company. Following a price-war, this failed while the Gutta Percha Co. made articles which varied from children's dolls, by way of shoe soles to the machinery belting that drove the factory plant of Great Britain's workshops. Then, in 1848, the South Eastern Railway Co. ordered two miles of cable to be insulated with *gutta percha* and which was tested by laying a bight off Folkestone and running it out to a small vessel, the *Princess Clementine*, where a signal was received, thus proving that *gutta percha* not only insulated cable but did so under water.

The importance of this development is obvious; less obvious was the traffic it induced, many modest fortunes being made in shipping *gutta percha* from the rain forests of Malaya and Kalimantan to the growing entrepôt of Singapore where it was picked up by the equally growing numbers of cargo-ships loading colonial produce there.[48] The first international underwater telegraph cable was laid between Britain

John Scott Russell's *Great Eastern* on the Mersey, by Charles Dixon. Brunel has received more credit for this vessel than he deserved which, although not a commercial success, nevertheless pioneered the laying of trans-oceanic telegraph cables. (© Courtesy of the N.R. Omell Gallery)

and France by the Brett Brothers' Submarine Telegraph Co. in 1847 from the chartered tug *Goliath*. Three years later a gradual expansion of what would become an international telegraph cable network began, but until 1872 no specialised ships were built for the task. Instead the armoured cables – their interiors made by R.S. Newell & Co. and Glass, Elliot & Co., their exterior insulation made by the Gutta Percha Co. – were all laid by vessels chartered and modified for the job. Such was the potential that Glass, Elliot and the Gutta Percha companies amalgamated on 7 April 1864, the new firm becoming The Telegraph Construction & Maintenance Co.

In an age of bold innovation, a telegraph cable linking Europe and North America had been mooted some time earlier. In America Cyrus Field had formed the Submarine Telegraph Co. which had, in the face of a lack of investment from the United States, been largely funded from Britain. Field had corresponded widely, especially with Brunel and Gooch, and had even mounted an expedition in 1857 to lay a transatlantic cable using HMS *Agamemnon* and the USS *Niagara*, but this failed. A second attempt the following year laid a cable but this did not last, the transmissions mysteriously ending, suggesting a break. By now the project was being considered by several companies, one of which was the conjoined Telegraph Construction & Maintenance Co. upon whose board sat a new director, Daniel Gooch. Concerting matters with Field, Gooch offered the *Great Eastern*, chartering her to The Telegraph Construction & Maintenance Co.

Three enormous cable tanks were built in the ship's holds, necessitating the removal of one boiler room and the fourth funnel. This enabled the forward tank to receive a coil of cable 693 miles long, the main and after tanks each receiving 898 miles of cable. These were led from the tanks through sheaves, along a trough on deck, through a braking system and, by way of a laying drum, over the stern. Under the command of Captain James Anderson, her seventh master, and his chief officer Robert Halpin, the *Great Eastern* now entered upon the most productive phase of her life. In July 1865, assisted by accompanying men-of-war, HMSs *Sphinx* and *Terrible*, the former to sound ahead of the *Great Eastern*, the other to act as protective guardship and warn off any vessels approaching too close, the *Great Eastern* arrived off Valentia Island on the west coast of Ireland where a smaller vessel, the *Caroline*, brought off the shore-end of the cable. Once she had coupled this with the outer end in the *Great Eastern's* forward tank, the great ship began heading westwards. Accompanying Cyrus Field were a number of technicians, among them the physicist William Thomson, the future Lord Kelvin. Besides these men and the gangs of cable-handlers, there were a number of gentlemen-observers paying their passage, including *The Times's* war correspondent William Russell, a national icon after his exposure of British military incompetence in the Crimean War.

The project was truly heroic. As the *Great Eastern* paid out cable at the rate of up to 6mph, a device enabled the conductivity of the cable to be monitored. When this indicated a failure, the cable had to be recovered, an operation testing the seamanship of Anderson, his chief officer and the crew. The cable had to be brought to the bow by turning the ship slowly in whatever sea-state prevailed for fear of fouling her screw, with the paddles themselves constituting an obstacle in this ticklish task. They were obliged to undertake this operation on the very first night out, after the laying of eighty-four miles of cable. Having laboriously turned the ship round and, with the cable coming in over the bow, the *Great Eastern* slowly retraced her passage for ten miles before the fault was found. A 2in piece of copper had been driven through the outer covering of tarred hemp. It was, wrote Russell, 'flagrant evidence of mischief'. With the cable repaired they set off again; several days passed and they laid the cable over the summits of the Mid-Atlantic Range, called 'Telegraph Ridge', and on across the abyssal plain far below. At noon a week out they experienced their second dead earth. Again the cable was cut and taken forward; again they retraced their way and again they discovered the cause: sabotage. 'No man who saw it,' wrote Russell, 'could doubt that the [inserted] wire had been driven in by a skilful hand...it must have been done on purpose by someone in the [cable] tanks'. Captain Anderson concurred and turned the bibulous gentlemen-observers out of their smoking room and put them on watch as supervisors.

By 2 August they had lost contact with the *Sphinx* but were past the half-way point with 1,186 miles of cable laid-out astern of them. That dawn a shout went up from Cyrus Field himself, on watch in the cable tank: another wire was found sticking out of the cable and, upon examination, it was decided that it was not sabotage but carelessness that had left slivers of metal in the cable-tanks upon which the weight of the cable had pressed, enabling several to puncture the insulation. Once again it was cut and transferred to the bow, but now, in hauling in, chafe caused the messenger to disintegrate. With a splash, 'The cable parted, flew through the stoppers, and with one bound leaped over the intervening space and flashed into the sea. The cable gone!'

The decision was made to grapple and the *Great Eastern*'s engines were stopped. Under sail she approached Telegraph Ridge, lowering a large grappling iron on a succession of 100-fathom flexible wire ropes shackled together, dragging this across the rocky sea-bed far below. After grappling all night, early next morning they fouled the cable and began to lift it. After two hours of patient hauling the wire parted, but a cable-man – with great presence of mind – slammed on the winch-brake before the hitched cable-end, the grappling iron and retrieved cable were lost. Nevertheless, two men had their faces lacerated by the snaking wire as it ran out under enormous tension. They recommenced operations but that afternoon the recovery wire parted again. Anderson ordered Halpin to buoy it and, that done, they prepared to re-grapple. Night fell, and with it a dense fog. Sounding her siren and firing warning guns to notify the *Terrible*, the *Great Eastern*'s crew tried again, only to have the recovery gear part once more. As a gale rose that night they made ready for a third attempt; it was their last chance for they had run out of gear, and it too failed. As they headed east for home, it looked as though the *Great Eastern*'s ill-luck had not deserted her.

Not so. Gooch and Field recapitalised their cable company and the *Great Eastern* left on her second cable-laying attempt on 30 June 1866. On 22 July Valentia telegraphed London that: 'The *Great Eastern* has passed the place where the cable was lost last year and all is going well.' Then, on Friday 27 July, the cable was drawn ashore at – appropriately enough – Heart's Content, Newfoundland. Messages of congratulation flowed back and forth and were quickly followed by commercial messages at $25 a word, Gooch confiding to his diary that: 'Yesterday we had fifty messages, paying us, I suppose, not less than £1,200.'

But that was not all. Gooch and Anderson took their ship back to latitude 51° 24 North and Longitude 038° 59' West. Here they grappled thirty times before Halpin's men recovered the cable lost in 1865. Gooch described 'one of the most interesting scenes I have ever witnessed': because the recovered cable-end was live, a signal was sent to Valentia, and Gooch confessed himself moved to tears. They buoyed the cable, to be spliced and completed later, and went home. Captain Anderson, Thomson, Richard Glass and Samuel Canning of the cable company were all honoured with knighthoods, and Gooch and a fellow director, Curtis Lampson, were made baronets. There was, as James Dugan sadly points out, no honour for John Scott Russell.[49]

There being no immediate call for the *Great Eastern* as a cable-layer, she was chartered by the French Government of Napoleon III with the intention of bringing 4,000 rich American passengers to France to attend the Great Paris *Exposition Universelle*. An immense sum was spent on refitting her accommodation, replacing her missing funnel and – at last – fitting her with steam steering gear. Captain, now Sir James, Anderson, still with the faithful Halpin as his chief officer, was in command when the ship left Liverpool for New York on 23 March 1867. Among the 123 French passengers heading west was the young Jules Verne, but the day was marked by tragedy as, in a stiff breeze, the capstans could not haul the tremendous bulk of the *Great Eastern* up to her anchor; Halpin ordered seamen to the capstan to assist the steam-windlass and, when this failed, so did the capstan which, shearing its pawls, spun uncontrollably, expelling its capstan-bars like javelins. Of the five men cut down, four died. It was not a propitious start. Once again, even in the matter of auxiliary machinery, the vessel was grossly under-powered.

Out in the Atlantic they encountered heavy weather, the *Great Eastern's* huge, open decks were sluiced by green seas and her chief engineer, George Beckwith, estimated 2,000 tons of water had to be pumped out of her holds. Ironically when she anchored in New York harbour, the *Great Eastern's* anchor fouled one arm of the telegraph-cable: more expense, leaving Customs Inspector Herman Melville shaking his head, confirmed in his earlier jeremiad. For her return passage, instead of thousands of eager Francophile Yankees, the passenger list mustered just 191. The voyage lost about £25,000, some bills were unpaid by the French and, recalled to Liverpool, Anderson discharged his 300 crew without wages. With legal backing they demanded three months' pay, which Anderson could not, or would not pay. As a consequence of this obduracy, the Admiralty marshal arrested the ship.

In the meantime Gooch was negotiating to lay another transatlantic cable on behalf of the French. He was backed by Paul Reuter, eponymous father of the international news agency and, once again, Gooch, having bailed out his ship, offered the *Great Eastern* for the task. She was again converted, an even larger middle cable-tank being fitted where the original had been ripped out. Thus, in 1869, the ship laid another transatlantic cable from Brest to Miquelon, from where it was extended to the American mainland. On the eve of this expedition Anderson had retired and Halpin assumed command. One of his innovations was not to cut and transfer the cable to the bow when a dead-earth was discovered. Instead Halpin boldly went astern, on one occasion in heavy weather somewhat intemperately, whereupon the ship was pooped several times and the cable parted. By mid-July, however, it was done, and Halpin headed home to take up another task. Laying a new cable across the Arabian Sea from Bombay to Aden on behalf of the British-Indian Telegraph Co. dispensed with the unreliable land-line that ran through Ottoman territory. Besides her additional cable equipment – buoys, grappling irons, anchors, sinkers and recovery wires, and so forth – the *Great Eastern* loaded 3,600 miles of cable, weighing 5,512 tons. In addition she carried 10,323 tons of coal in her bunkers, all of which brought her displacement to an unprecedented 34,000 tons.

On his way out to Bombay by way of the Cape of Good Hope, Halpin had the *Great Eastern* painted white, and she attracted great interest, particularly among the Parsee ship-owning families, but the white-paint was besmirched by coaling, a filthy and prolonged procedure involving the ship's crew who supplemented the Indian 'untouchables'. This eastern operation included three other cable-laying vessels, the *Chiltern*, *Hawk* and *Hibernia*; all three converted merchantmen, the *Hibernia* having been an Anchor liner. The first pair named laid the cable from Malta to Alexandria while the *Chiltern*, Captain Edington, after accompanying the *Great Eastern* from Bombay, would take it onwards from Aden up the reef-strewn Red Sea to Suez.

This is almost the end of the *Great Eastern*'s history. In 1873 and '74 Halpin and the *Great Eastern* laid a further two transatlantic cables for the Anglo-American Telegraph Co. and repaired the original pair. In all Captain Halpin had been involved in the laying of 26,000 miles of telegraph cable, a remarkable achievement. A stocky man from County Wicklow, Halpin was described by Jules Verne as an 'active little man with a very sunburnt skin, a beard almost covering his face, and legs which defied every lurch of the vessel'. 'A skilful, energetic seaman... [who] gave his orders in a clear decided tone,' Halpin was a man of considerable personal courage to whom at least one seaman owed his life, willing to undertake tasks at which his sailors baulked. Besides his work in the North Atlantic and the Bombay to Aden link, Halpin laid cables between Madras and Singapore by way of Penang; between Australia, Java and Sumatra, plus another between Madeira and Brazil, though all these last were in ships other than the *Great Eastern*.[50] His chief engineer, George Beckwith, who had started as the *Great Eastern*'s second engineer, had been promoted to chief in succession to McLennan and remained with the ship throughout her career.

It is not inappropriate to conclude the story of the *Great Eastern* here. By 1885 the Telegraph Construction & Maintenance Co. had constructed their own vessel, yet another *Britannia*, by which time the Siemens Company had had built the world's first proper cable-layer, the *Faraday*. Many other liners were converted to cable-ships, notably Captain Judkins's *Scotia*, which was acquired by the Telegraph Construction & Maintenance Co. in 1879 and underwent extensive modifications including being re-engined and converted to twin-screws. As for the *Great Eastern*, she was to end her days as she had begun them, in indignity. Halpin took her on her final passage to Milford Haven and Sir Daniel Gooch accompanied him, writing that 'I do not know how we are going to employ her in the future. But...she is a noble ship and has done good service in the past'. Here, however, Gooch abandoned her to become an ugly tourist attraction and a base from which pile drivers constructed a graving-dock. So, with quiet irony, she helped build the only graving-dock capable of containing her and out of which she was floated – paddle-boxes removed – on its completion.

But what was to be done with her?

One extreme suggestion was to ship the entire aristocracy of Britain in her and sink the lot of them in the Atlantic, but in 1880 Gooch formally gave up the ship: Thomas Brassey's son Henry headed her owners and various schemes were floated, and then inevitably sank. In the end the weed and barnacle-encrusted hulk was acquired for the Liverpool Industrial and Maritime Exhibition of 1886. A Captain Comyn and a Welsh run-crew were shipped to take her to the Mersey. Chief Engineer Peter Jackson sent a telegram to Beckwith, who arrived from retirement in Swansea. The screw engine was coaxed into life and the *Great Eastern* struggled north, to be met by tugs off the Mersey Bar and towed up to New Ferry. Here the watching crowds were informed by the ship's charterers, who had had the side painted during the passage, that 'Ladies should visit Lewis's...Church Street' department store and that 'Lewis's are the friends of the people'. At New Ferry the *Great Eastern* was filled with curiosities and bizarre freaks, shooting galleries, a *camera obscura*, a photographic studio, the definitive and

Darwinian Bob — the 'Missing Link' of anthropological prurience — along with all
the varied fun of the fair, most too awful to recount.

Opened to the gaping public at 1s a head, she was a marked contrast to the three
training ships *Indefatigable*, *Clarence* and *Conway* — all old wooden walls — that lay
moored nearby. Between them, the *Indefatigable* trained orphans to become sailors,
the *Clarence* reclaimed the souls of recalcitrant Roman Catholic boys sent to her as
a reformatory, while the *Conway* was a public school aboard which were trained the
next generation of officers for the British merchant marine.

In the autumn of 1886 the *Great Eastern* and her exhibition were towed to Dublin
and the following year she was hauled to Greenock. Anchored on the Tail o' the
Bank in October 1887, she was put up for sale. The only taker was a put-up bid by
the owners. Finally she was acquired by the ship-breakers Henry Bath & Son who,
instead of scrapping her, decided that she would make an excellent petroleum tanker.
She was moved towards Liverpool under her own power with a tug in attendance.
Off Ailsa Craig the tug's help was summoned and she limped into the Mersey to sit
again on the New Ferry grid-iron. Popular opinion wished her blown-up and found
an advocate in James Paton, now a man of wealth and influence, whose birth-place
the old ship had been, but the agitation brought Henry Bath & Son to their senses.
They took the unprecedented step of auctioning her for scrap metal, her iron, copper,
brass, lead and gun-metal being secured by individual bidders. Her anchors, auxiliary
engines, panelling, officers' cabin desks, bells, tea-pots and other salvable items followed suit and — incredibly — stood to make Henry Bath & Sons a profit of 35 per
cent. Except that demolition had yet to begin, and when it started in May 1888, without the benefit of gas-cutting equipment the hull proved almost indestructible. Five
months later Gooch followed Russell and Brunel into the grave, yet still the old ship
defied the breakers until Henry Bath & Sons invented the breaker's iron ball which,
from its derrick, struck the plating below with a deafening impact heard far across the
Dee in Flintshire. Slowly the lines of rivets popped, prising Russell's well-wrought
hull apart. Even then the breakers went on strike; being on piece-work 'by the ton'
their pay dwindled as the cellular double-bottom proved indestructible. At last they
reached what was assumed to have been the cause of the *Great Eastern*'s misfortunes,
the dessicated corpse of the missing riveter, mewed up in her hull. It was a gruesome
end, and with it William Forwood concluded:

> The *Great Eastern*... was broken up on the New Ferry shore at Birkenhead. She had
> served, however, one great purpose which had borne good fruit — she taught us that
> to successfully fight the Atlantic on its days of storm and tempest, which are many,
> the design of the engine and its power should receive as much consideration as the
> design of the ship's hull.

But even Forwood ignored the real accomplishment of her existence, for, deprived
of that all-essential mail-contract which underwrote the operations of Cunard and
other steam navigation companies, the *Great Eastern* played a fundamental part in the

first chapter in the age of telecommunications which today has almost entirely super-seded conventional mail; and this she did rather well. Essentially, however, the story of the *Great Eastern* demonstrates that neither the prevailing conditions under which trade was conducted, nor the state of steam technology, were yet able to establish the steam-ship as a viable, global instrument.

In 1850 the sailing-vessel remained the world's carrier. In this year there were 168,474 tons of net-registered steam-tonnage under the British flag, but all were auxiliaries and they were outnumbered by 3,396,659 net-registered-tons still under sail alone. Moreover, in 1870, when the steam total had risen to 1,112,934, the ton-nage under sail had increased further to a prodigious 4,577,855 net-registered tons. Although this was the peak, it would still be the mid-1890s before the situation was reversed.[51]

Nevertheless, progress ground on. The Inman Line adopted the screw propeller and in 1862 the Cunard Line built its last paddler, the *Scotia*, which at 3,871 tons and 975-nominal-hp was larger than the *Persia* and, in crossing the Atlantic in eight days and twenty-two hours, smashed her predecessor's record. Cunard had been using screw-steamers on his Mediterranean routes for some time, and that same year the *China* was the first screw-steamer to run on the North Atlantic sporting Cunard's colours. She was followed by the *Cuba* of 1864 and the *Java* of 1865.

These events were in train as the Board of Trade gained a greater control over shipping with another Mercantile Marine Act in 1854, described more fully in the following chapter. Such a measure enabled the state to form a partial assumption of power over the manning, regulation and running of the mercantile marine, and – par-ticularly in the case of a ship's master – tended to split the loyalties of the officer corps so that, while they were paid by the owners of their ship, they were obligated to the state by the value they put upon their so-called 'tickets'. This was a subtle and probably unforeseen consequence of legislation, but went some way to sharpening perceptions of that amorphous mass of privately owned ships as a 'merchant *navy*', making the defection of the merchant marine to foreign flags in time of war less likely.

The more immediate consequences of this were to treble the staff of the Board of Trade within three years. The department of state assumed greater maritime responsibilities, supervising pilotage, wrecks, the wages of seafarers and, not least, an assumption of partial control over the United Kingdom's three general lighthouse authorities. These comprised the Commissioners for Northern Lighthouses, acting for Scotland and the Isle of Man; the Commissioners for Irish Lights, responsible for the island of Ireland; and Trinity House, whose writ ran round England, Wales and the Channel Islands, and south to Gibraltar. The last named had, following an Act of Parliament of 1836, bought-out all the residual private lighthouses on the English and Welsh coasts, and was, like its fellow boards in Edinburgh and Dublin, then embarking on a major lighthouse-building programme. The Board of Trade's chief task, which it had taken over from the ancient corporation, was as purse-keeper of the funding 'light dues', paid as a moiety of British port dues. Elsewhere in the Empire, respon-sibility for aids to navigation was usually vested with the colonial administration or, where these were small and could be geographically consolidated, were carried out by the Imperial Lighthouse Service.[52] Nevertheless, Trinity House assisted with light-house construction as far afield as Ceylon, the Falkland Islands and the West Indies.

With the great increases in commercial tonnage during the nineteenth century and the huge numbers of shipwrecks and loss of lives and property, the proper marking of all dangers to safe navigation was imperative. Just as steam-power had made possible the laying of international telegraph cables, it was to play a major part in this, not only in the manufacture and construction of buoys, beacons, lightvessels and light-houses, but in their placing on station, maintenance and manning. To this end all three home lighthouse authorities built small steam-vessels, the first constructed by Trinity House being the *Vestal*, mentioned earlier in connection with Queen Victoria's visit to Scotland. Superseded in the early 1850s, the *Vestal* was one of hundreds of British steam-vessels chartered to the Government in support of the British Army despatched to the Crimea. Having been sold by Trinity House, the *Vestal* was acquired by James Baines and sent out to the Black Sea where she acted as a tender for carrying the wounded to the military hospital at Scutari. Here too were steamers owned by Bibby and Cunard, among others, who provided chartered tonnage to act as hospital ships.

This was a rich source of income for steam-packet operators on the North Atlantic, occurring as it did at a time when fierce American competition was depressing freight-rates. With the end of the Crimean War in 1856 the gloom in many board-rooms over the consequent glut of shipping was swiftly lifted by news of another outbreak of hostilities with China, the Second Opium War. The following year it was further learned that the sepoy infantry who served the East India Company had mutinied and, with the Government seeking military transports and offering trooping contracts, many companies found new work for their ships as the insurrection escalated.[53]

Among those making profits from the Crimean War was the Union Steam Collier Co. of Southampton. Such were the tremendous demands on supplies of coal by industry and shipping, serious shortages arose on the domestic market. In September 1853 the price of coal reached a peak and the Port of Southampton was particularly affected. Once a flourishing medieval port, Southampton's fortunes had waned until around 1840 steamers, a railway and its proximity to London made it an 'embar-kation centre' for passengers and the imperial mails. With a newly dug dock and a revived local ship-building industry, Southampton attracted companies like General Steam, The Royal Mail Steam Packet Co. and P&O, but such customers dramatically increased Southampton's requirement for coal supplies, and in 1852 it was decided that the uncertainties inherent in relying upon the Geordie collier-brigs were insufferable. A small experimental steamer, the *John Bowes*, was constructed for the sole purpose of supplying the port with coal. The following year Arthur Anderson founded what shortly afterwards became the Union Steam Collier Co.

A Shetlander, Anderson had joined the Royal Navy during the Napoleonic War. Having become a captain's clerk, in which capacity he had learned Spanish, he found himself among the demobilised poor in 1815. After walking from Portsmouth to London, he found a job as clerk in a counting-house run by a man named Brodie

McGhie Willcox. Willcox, 'then a young man with no influence and but limited pecuniary means, [had] opened an office in Lime Street, London, and commenced business on his own account as a shipbroker and commission agent'.[54] By 1822 Anderson had so proved his business acumen and his thorough understanding of ship-management that he was invited by Willcox to join him as a partner, a change in fortune enabling Anderson to marry Miss Mary Ann Hill, the daughter of a Scarborough ship-owner. As we shall presently see, the two men had already founded what would become an immense shipping empire, the Peninsular & Oriental Steam Navigation Co., and his interest in the supply of coal, in which his father-in-law had a hand, was of vital importance to the survival of his new steam packet company, which was intended to run mails to the Iberian Peninsula.

While Anderson drew other men onto the board of the new coasting firm, which was to tender to the steam-packet companies, they would be overtaken by events. The initial plan called for five screw steamers, the *Union, Briton, Saxon, Norman* and *Dane,* each of which would carry 500 tons of coal from South Wales to Southampton. Although auxiliary steamers, the first three were designed with 'their engine works and funnels…placed near the stern, so as to leave the whole of the fore-part for cargo,' in what would become the classic layout of the steam-collier. But within a few months Russia and Turkey were at war, alliances were invoked and Britain was involved. In the spring of 1854 the *Hampshire Independent* was wailing that:

> There are but few ports, if any, which will feel the interference made in the mail service by the [Crimean] war more than the Port of Southampton. Our various large mail companies have been drained of nearly all their available ships by the Government, who have engaged them all in the transport service.

These circumstances threatened to undercut the very existence of the new Union Co. which was just then completing its first steamer. The *Union* loaded her cargo of coal at Cardiff and arrived to discharge it on 26 June. She began to be joined by the first of her sister-ships, but before the last of them, the *Dane,* came into service in March 1855 the failing demand of the steam-packets was replaced by a new opportunity. Several of the new colliers began running to Constantinople, Smyrna and the Levant, replacing a small number of Anderson's peninsular steam-packets engaged in a subsidiary service to the Ottoman Empire which had been chartered for trooping. It was an elegant solution enabled by Anderson's increasingly integrating shipping empire, but not all the new ships were thus employed. In December 1854 the brand-new *Norman* — chartered as a Government storeship — took out to the freezing hills of Balaclava 'The first shipment of wooden huts to provide for the comfort of our soldiers…100 of these habitations, each capable of accommodating 20 men'. This was in response to the heart-breaking accounts of incompetence then appearing in *The Times* as a result of the journalism of William Russell, whom we have already encountered. The *Norman* was joined on Government service by the *Union* and *Briton,* and such were the profits being made that the Union Co. ordered a sixth ship, the *Celt.*

At the war's end the coal situation had eased and the future for the Union steamers was uncertain. In defiance of one board member, a Captain Mangles who also sat on the board of the Royal Mail Steam Packet Co., Anderson and his fellow directors decided to open a service to Rio de Janeiro, all thoughts of coal-hauling forgotten. The directors abandoned the reference to colliers and reconstituted themselves as the Union Steamship Co., but the Brazilian venture did not turn out well and was given-up in 1857. Another service between the Mersey and the Elbe was equally unsuccessful while the *Briton*, outward-bound to Seville, foundered in the Bay of Biscay. The company was now in serious trouble, but at the eleventh hour was rescued by having a speculative bid for a new Government mail-contract accepted.

Whereas most mail-contracts guaranteed the profits of the successfully tendering company, early mail services to the Cape of Good Hope had failed, including that by General Steam's *Bosphorus* in 1851. A second attempt by William Lindsay was fore-closed after failing to deliver the mails in the prescribed thirty-six days, his auxiliary steamer the *Tynemouth* taking fifty-five. It was at this point that the Admiralty's Mail Packet Department opened Anderson's Union Co. tenders. Within eleven days of securing the contract for a monthly sailing, the *Dane* was heading south from Southampton. Although the hurried nature of her leaving raised only six passengers and a small cargo valued at a mere £102, the steamer's departure under the command of Captain William Strutt established what would become the longest running combined cargo, passenger and mail service in the history of the British merchant service. Thus, almost at a stroke, the company conceived to run colliers had been raised by an annual subvention of £30,000, and 'now found itself among the select fraternity of the world's great mail Steam Packet Companies'.[55]

Strutt had been poached from the Royal Mail S.P. Co. where his brother was superintendent, and on 31 October 1857 he steamed the *Dane* into a Table Bay crowded with shipping, mostly sailing-vessels, taking troops and military stores to suppress the sepoy insurgents in India. On 27 November the *Celt* arrived, and three days later the *Dane* sailed homeward, carrying 10,867 letters worth £325, a cargo worth £709 and a dozen passengers. One of these considered Strutt 'a famous fellow [who] fed us well [and] did everything to make us comfortable…' for, until the 1870s, victualling in the saloon was the master's direct responsibility.

The original three steamers employed on the Cape service, *Dane*, *Celt* and *Norman*, were soon joined by two purchased vessels which retained their original names, the *Phoebe* and *Athens*. As the new ships established a reputation, passengers grew in numbers and the cargoes swelled in bulk and value. Homeward freights consisted of Cape wines and brandy, aloes, ivory and horn, dried fruits, fashionable ostrich feathers, *buchu* leaves and occasional consignments of copper-ore from Namaqualand. The year 1860 saw improvements in Cape Colony as railways were laid down, the telegraph system was improved and the first harbour tug arrived. During the royal visit of Captain Prince Alfred, Duke of Edinburgh, in command of HM Frigate *Galatea*, the foundations of a breakwater were laid and the lighthouse at Cape Point was lit. That October the Union fleet was joined by the *Cambrian*, to which Strutt had been appointed, and was the first vessel specifically built for the company's long-haul mail service.

Old ships were scrapped and replaced as the Union Co. renewed its mail-contract and became part of the colonial tapestry, but the very success of the colony was breeding problems. The wool-producing colonists of the Eastern Cape began to complain of the delays inherent in moving goods and mail to Table Bay. A coastal service established by John Rennie's *Madagascar* and *Waldensian* ran from Natal to Capetown, calling at Algoa Bay, where it connected with the Union steamers, until, in 1862, both vessels were wrecked. In due course, the Union Co. took over the coastal link with their 'Inter-Colonial Service', using the *Norman* and *Dane* which had been made redundant from the main-line run by new tonnage, the *Briton*, *Saxon* and *Roman*. The service was gradually built-up as Port Elizabeth arose on Algoa Bay, East London transfigured the estuary of the Buffalo River and the hills of Natal were transformed by sugar cane, which joined wool and raw hides – the smell of which 'was a thing to remember' – as homeward cargoes. In October 1865 a mail-contract was secured with the Natal Government and a shallow-draught steamer, the *Anglian*, was built to pass the river bar at Durban, and she was succeeded by other small coastal steamers such as the *Natal*. The larger Union steamers calling there were obliged to resort to lighters which were hauled out on 'surf-lines' anchored outside the bar. As Captain Crutchley explained:

> the ship that had cargo or passengers to discharge, anchored as closely in as was prudent and then a warp to the buoyed end of the surf-line for the lighter to reach the ship by; the work was rough, very, and the boatmen in perfect keeping with their surroundings. I should not like to do the men an injustice, but they seemed to be the scourings of the roughness and rascality of the world. Their lives were mostly in their hands, and they did not attach much value either to them or the language with which they adorned them. It was no uncommon thing when there was a sea on the bar – and there mostly was – to see a breaker sweep a surf boat from end to end. The men generally managed to hold on, but fatal accidents were not infrequent. These boats would…land passengers, who were carefully battened down and in almost complete darkness while the passage was being accomplished. Both at this port and at Durban, passengers were put into the lighters in large baskets lowered by the cargo whips, and if the ship were rolling it would be no uncommon occurrence to see a basket containing perhaps three or four men and women hoisted half way out and held fast by derrick and stay until the roll had subsided. People got used to it, however…until…a wicker cage…with a door in the side would obviate the necessity for lifting the ladies into the basket. If the ladies were young and good-looking, there was never much difficulty noticeable in finding volunteers to take on this arduous duty.[56]

The Union Co. had been obliged to beat off rivals, most notably the Diamond Line of Port Elizabeth, and offered a rival 'private mail rate'. Competition between the ships of the two companies became intense, coming to a head in 1865 when the *Saxon*, Captain Hoffmann, made Capetown in a little over twenty-eight days, soundly beating her rival, the Diamond liner *Uitenhage*. The Diamond Line gradually lost ground; one of its ships was wrecked, the others 'were utterly wanting in punctuality' and in 1867 the company failed.

A further extension of the Union services to Mauritius was inaugurated by the *Athens*, Captain R.B. Davie, in November 1864. This was the longer 'Eastern Route' by which the mails at Mauritius were forwarded to Suez by a P&O steamer under a complex system of subsidies, but the main effect of this was to increasingly connect Cape Colony with India, Australia and the Far East. Some ex-patriate army and civil servants began to prefer a homeward journey that avoided the tedious, hot crossing of the Isthmus of Suez – a short-lived preference ended by the cutting of the Suez Canal.

Owing to want of expertise and the prejudice against steam among many sailing ship men, young officers making an early decision to transfer into steamers could rise quickly, William Crutchley becoming chief officer with a first mate's certificate – a state of affairs that would soon end. For Crutchley steam 'was a means of propulsion that would forever put in the background the manly management of masts, yards and sails', but he was in no doubt but that it meant 'the inevitable eclipse of a notable phase in a very noble calling'. The over-riding importance of the regularity of the mails bred efficiency and an opposition to competition that overcame most rivals – at least for the time being.

Such progress did not go untouched by tragedy. To the losses already mentioned has to be added that of the *Athens* which was one of the casualties of a strong gale that assailed the open roadstead of Table Bay in May 1865, and whose fate demonstrates a significant weakness of early steam-vessels. The *Dane*, *Briton* and *Athens* all lay at anchor as the wind rose. The *Athens*, due to sail for Mauritius on the 18th, began to drag her anchors, then her cables parted and Captain David Smith took her out to sea, clear of the dangerous lee-shore. As the *Athens* rounded Mouille Point she was overwhelmed by a tremendous green sea which swept aboard, poured down below and extinguished her boiler-fires. With the *Athens* not under command, Smith was helpless and his ship drove ashore and broke up with the loss of all twenty-nine souls then on board.

In June 1866 a further extension by the Union steamers carried the mails all the way to Galle, on the south-west tip of Ceylon. Although this was shortlived, the company negotiated a new ten-year contract, undertaking a fortnightly service to be supported by a new *Celt* and the *Norseman*. Two years later Arthur Anderson, the architect of the Union and the Peninsular & Oriental companies, died, but his legacy – the mail steamers of two great steam-ship companies – had become what Kipling called the 'shuttles of an Empire's loom'.

Frequent reference has been made in the foregoing pages to Anderson's other great shipping company whose name is embedded in the fabric and image of the British Empire and which he had founded with Willcox. Like Cunard's steam-ship company and the Union Co., the beginnings of the Peninsular & Oriental Steam Navigation

Co. were absolutely conditional upon a Government mail-contract's subsidy to iron out the fluctuations in world freight-rates which so bedevil shipping. Nevertheless, the future P&O conglomerate had a relatively modest birth when, on 22 August 1837, the partnership of Willcox and Anderson 'established a small but promising business in the running of little sailing-vessels to ports of the…Iberian Peninsula', in which it may be that Anderson's ship-owning father-in-law had a hand. This cosy arrangement was thrown into chaos by the political upheaval in Portugal. When civil war loomed, Anderson declared for the young Queen Maria da Glória's side, salvaged a schooner stranded near Dover, refitted her and shipped cargoes of arms into the country. Accompanying this gun-running foray himself as 'Mr Smith', Anderson brought back the Queen's envoys, disguised as his servants, and assisted in the raising of loans in Maria da Glória's favour. By 1832 the Queen's navy had attracted many former British sailors and was commanded by Sir Charles Napier who required more ships to act as troop transports. Consequently Willcox and Anderson chartered the *City of Waterford*, the *Leeds* and the *Birmingham* from the Dublin & London Steam-Packet Co., and the *Pembroke* and *William IV* from General Steam. Under Napier's influence, Queen Maria's fortunes were turned around and she re-entered Lisbon in 1833.

Almost immediately the Carlist insurrection followed in Spain, and again, faced with disruption of their trade, Willcox and Anderson favoured the reigning Queen Isabella. Meanwhile a force known as the British Legion embarked for Spain on the steamer *Royal Tar*, chartered again by Willcox and Anderson from Dublin and renamed *Reyna Gobernadera*. When Queen Isabella was also successfully restored to her throne, the Spanish ambassador in London was so impressed by the use of steamers that he sought to establish a regular service between London and San Sebastian. In consequence of their Iberian connections, Willcox and Anderson were given the contract to manage two steamers chartered from the Dublin & London Steam-Packet Co. These were the *Royal Tar*, whose services they had already contracted, and the *William Fawcett*, built in 1829 and three years older than her consort. These were afterwards joined by the *Liverpool* and the *City of Londonderry*. Anderson's frequent trips to Spain and Portugal, his contacts and his ability to write and speak Spanish, now paid dividends.

All this was in marked contrast with Anderson's first foray into mail shipments, for he was ever mindful of improving the lot of his fellow Shetlanders, setting up a scheme for them to migrate to Brazil, but his attempt to secure the mail-contract between Lerwick and Aberdeen failed, despite the fact that Anderson had the Aberdeen yard of John Duffus & Co. build a small steamer for the purpose.[57] This was the *Peninsula*, an ironic intimation that Iberia was central to Anderson's thinking.

The *William Fawcett*, built by Caleb Smith, bore engines made by Fawcett & Preston of Liverpool which were replaced when Willcox and Anderson decided to buy her outright. The partners then bought and re-engined the *Royal Tar* in 1838 at a cost of £16,000. It is clear that for some time before this the steamers managed by Willcox and Anderson supplemented the Admiralty-managed Post Office packets and that the partners were in a commanding position both home and abroad when the full operation of the mail service by private contractor came up for tender. The two men may well have connived at the acquisition of the contract, for the Admiralty's running of the mail service remained hide-bound and almost as inefficient as the preceding service run by the Post Office itself, which the naval takeover had been intended to better.[58] Only one steam-packet, the *Meteor*, was in use running the mails from Falmouth to Gibraltar, Malta and finally Alexandria, for overland carriage to Suez and transfer to the Bombay steamer. In short, the service was a muddle, and Willcox and Anderson, in chartering their own steamers, seem to have been intent upon wresting that part of the mail service that ran to Lisbon out of the dead hand of a Government department. It was a gamble, and they nearly lost.

Operating six steamers, often referred to as Peninsular and Mediterranean Steam-Packets, they were run under a management company variously known as Willcox and Anderson, Co., or the Peninsular Steam Navigation Co.[59] These maintained a service between London and Falmouth, and Oporto, Lisbon, Gibraltar and Malaga, with a seventh, the *Peninsula*, operating a 'branch line' to Cadiz and up the Guadalquivir River to Seville. At their main-truck they flew a banner diagonally quartering the red and gold of Aragon and Castile with the blue and silver of the Braganzas, the ruling house of Portugal, a distinctive and aspirational house-flag. The partners also took particular care of passenger comfort, displaying models of their ships' accommodation in their head office, maintaining a complaints book on board and offering during 'the Spring and Fall of the year' an extended facility for invalids to take passage for Madeira.

Supporting the main Government mail service had revealed the weaknesses of the Admiralty packets, but by itself Willcox and Anderson's service was ambitious, over-capitalised with a surplus of capacity and in danger of going under. The Admiralty's refusal to relinquish control was riposted by a vigorous lobbying, newspaper coverage contrasting the regularity of the partners' steam-vessel sailings with the vagaries of the wind-and-weather-dependent departures of the Admiralty brigs. This accurately predicted the steamer's ultimate and over-riding advantage over sail: she could be scheduled and relied upon. The policy paid off and public agitation, largely mercantile, pushed the matter to open tender. The aggressive tactics of Willcox and Anderson, which included an assurance that the postal rates would fall, had made enemies, and it looked as if a rival would secure the contract. Fortunately the British & Foreign Co. could not meet the standards demanded since it did not possess sufficient means. Almost by default, and with some help from the influence of the Spanish ambassador, Willcox and Anderson won the contract, signed on 22 August 1837, with an annual subvention of £29,600.

The new service used five of the original six steamers, each of which adopted the grandiloquent title 'Her Majesty's Peninsular Mail Packet'. These ran weekly from London every Friday and Falmouth every Monday, from 1 September, to Vigo, Oporto, Lisbon, Cadiz and Gibraltar. Thereafter, eastwards to Alexandria and India beyond, the mails remained in the Admiralty's hands and arrangements were made for passengers to travel in like style and speed. In the first year of operation all the steamers appear to have been chartered, the *William Fawcett* being largely employed on the

Madeira run. Amid all these shenanigans it is possible to lose sight of the fundamental part played in supplying tonnage by the Dublin & London Steam-Packet Co., the successor to the City of Dublin Steam Navigation Co., which was beneficially owned by Messrs Bourne, and included Charles Wye Williams on its board. Willcox and Anderson worked closely with the company's Captain Richard Bourne, a naval post-captain, who joined their own board, and brought with him one of the Dublin company's clerks, James Allan. Allan became secretary to the London partners and, having gained a seat on the new board, remained at his post until his death in 1874.

The support of the Bournes and their steamers suddenly became acute. Exactly two weeks after the first outward sailing, the *Don Juan* – homeward-bound from Gibraltar – ran aground on Tarifa Point, twenty miles west of The Rock, and became a total loss. The visibility had been poor and disaster loomed in the swirling fog: on board were the mails and $21,000. Moreover the ship had cost £40,000 and was not fully insured. Fortunately Anderson was on board with his wife, and he rose to the occasion. Hailing a Spanish fishing vessel, his fluency in Spanish swiftly secured help, the mails were transferred and Anderson set off in her to Gibraltar where the flag-officer in command offered a man-of-war to carry the mails and ordered her, in passing the *Don Juan*, to send a detachment of marines to secure the wreck against looting. Meanwhile the locals had gathered and began to steal items landed on the rocks as the *Don Juan*'s master, her officers and crew, strove to salve what they could, especially the specie, some of which was taken inside the walls of the fortified town. On arriving back at the wreck, Anderson and his party landed and entered the gate, recovered the boxes of specie but found their exit barred, the gate closed and guarded. The guard-commander declared he acted on the *gobernador*'s orders, but Anderson's fluent diplomacy failed to gain access to this official. An incident of international proportions, utterly fatal to the company, now loomed. Anderson readied his men for a struggle, and at this point the guard-commander relented. Having placed the specie in the charge of the marines, Anderson and his ship's master returned to iron out the matter, gaining an audience with the *gobernador*. The Spaniard began a tirade about the impropriety of landing uniformed and armed marines on Spanish soil, which Anderson countered with a charge that the *gobernador* had failed to protect distressed mariners on his doorstep. This was a matter for Her Majesty's Government, Anderson said, and the point, made in his own language, cooled the *gobernador*. Anderson's high-handed tone carried the day and all were shortly afterwards embarked in the man-of-war, the *Don Juan* being left to break up. The new company were obliged to absorb the loss, chartering another steamer – the *City of Londonderry* – from the Bournes, but the worst was over and the partners' service settled into a routine.

All the while the Indian Government had been increasingly troubled at the slowness and irregularity of the mails, and was joined in seeking some improvement by the merchants in Bombay and Calcutta. At this time the London to Bombay monthly mails took fifty-eight days via Suez, having cut down the time round the Cape of eighty days, but they remained uncertain. Government experiments to send the mail up the Euphrates by steamer in 1836 to reduce the time still further were a failure.

In 1839 an expedition led by the Bombay Marine seized Aden to extirpate the nest of Arab freebooters based there. British occupation followed, turning the great bay with its barren hinterland into another coaling station. To further secure the route, the following year the Indian Government acquired Karachi at the mouth of the Indus from Scind 'by cession'. In the same year the British Government had cut the time and distance between London and Calcutta by sending the mails overland by way of Marseilles, but Francophobia stirred and it was not thought commensurate with the dignity of a great-power that imperial communications should depend upon a state so lately hostile to its own interests. Lord Bentinck, the Governor-General of India, sought the advice of Anderson – who was now the dominant of the two partners – and the upshot was that in 1840 the British Government called for tenders for carrying the mails from London to Alexandria. This, with its subvention of £34,000 a year, was secured by Anderson.

Thus, in December 1840, the firm of Willcox and Anderson not only became the Peninsular & Oriental Steam Navigation Company – the 'P&O' of common parlance – with a capital of £1 million, but it was further dignified by Incorporation by Royal Charter. A service was opened that began as quarterly, then bi-monthly and finally monthly, attracting a subsidy from the East India Company of £20,000 a year. Within a decade it had become weekly, while within two years of the original contract it extended to India by way 'of a difficult and complicated overland route'. Besides P&O's own expansion, these services benefited others. The acquisition of Aden as a bunkering port, for example, created opportunities for British shipping, since charters were sought for carrying coal there.

In securing the extended mail-contract to Egypt, Willcox and Anderson had been exceptionally bold. The mail service to the Iberian Peninsula had, largely thanks to the loss of the *Don Juan*, cost them £30,000, and they had in effect staked all upon this further venture. Not only were the newly incorporated company's finances rocky but the East India Company's subsidy was inadequate to cover the Bombay to Suez route, a matter John Company knew well to his own cost. What sustained the two partners was a conviction – most unusual at the time – that if one put in place an infrastructure, in their case a shipping route, then trade would naturally flow along it. To the extent that this was a belief that 'trade followed the flag,' it was not the ensign of the Royal Navy which facilitated commercial intercourse, but the red ensign of the mercantile service.[60]

The Suez to Bombay leg of the Indian mails, then known as the 'Oriental' component, had long since been an objective of the British, as referred to earlier in this chapter. The Bombay Marine's service, initiated by the steamer *Hugh Lindsay*, had proved intermittent; apart from the intervention of the weather, the burning issues were reliability of carriage and regularity of schedule. Against the seasonal suspension of the Aden to Bombay leg of the East India Company's Bombay Marine mail service during the months of June, July, August and September, at the height of the south-west monsoon, had to be set the exemplary record of the scheduled services now being run between Britain and Iberia by the P&O steam-packets. That these private steamers regularly crossed the notorious Bay of Biscay attracted the attention of at least one officer of the increasingly discredited Bombay Marine.

Thomas Waghorn had joined the Royal Navy aged twelve as a midshipman in 1812. Following the end of the Napoleonic War he passed the examination for lieutenant but was not commissioned. Instead he sought employment as third mate of a free-trader sailing to India. Once in India he joined the Company's Bengal pilotage service and served as a Hughli pilot. On the outbreak of the Burmese War in 1824, on the grounds of his naval service, Waghorn was appointed to command the Bombay Marine's *Matchless*. He returned to the Hughli with five wounds, and on 13 December 1835 he boarded the little *Enterprize* when she arrived off the Sandheads and piloted Captain Johnston on his passage upstream to Calcutta. The experience focussed Waghorn's attention on the possibilities of steamers, and Johnston himself – although employed to pioneer a sea-route to India by way of Capetown – had an interest in the overland way across the Isthmus of Suez. In 1827 Waghorn had made himself so warm on the subject that Bentinck sent him to London with a view to soliciting investment. Waghorn's mission failed, as did a second, supported by capital raised in India, but Waghorn, backing his hunch, resigned from the East India Company's service to squander a fortune – in excess of £40,000 – inherited from a wealthy land-owning grandfather.

The hostility of the Egyptian Pasha, Mehmet Ali, and his Ottoman satraps offered little prospect of success for a regularly set-up overland route by way of Suez, but Waghorn persisted. In desperation he made his way to East India House and obtained a license to act as courier across the desert. After having made arrangements to be met by a steamer at Suez, he set off for Alexandria via Trieste. Passing through Cairo where Mehmet Ali, against the odds, proved cordial and conferred a *firman* on the Englishman, Waghorn reached Suez to discover the pioneering *Enterprize* had not arrived. He hired an Arab *sambuk* and sailed south to Kosseir, expecting to find the Bombay Marine's steamer coaling there. Again he drew a blank and set off across the Red Sea to Jeddah where he learned the *Enterprize*'s engine had failed. Soon afterwards, however, he was picked up by the Company's armed brig *Thetis*, which landed him at Bombay on 20 March 1829, one day after the overloaded *Hugh Lindsay* had left in order to meet him at Suez.

Since the Company was committed to the plan, Waghorn returned to London where he began preparations for a formal and regular crossing of the desert under the auspices of Mehmet Ali and which he was to maintain for four years. On one occasion he passed letters from Bombay to London in forty-six days 'by means of a fast French brig hired…from Alexandria, lying in ballast and ready to start at a moment's notice for Marseilles'. Waghorn built up this private venture with the aid of agents, among them Smith, Elder & Co. of London, and in 1835 he was advertising it in London by a circular addressed to all mercantile-houses trading to India. Waghorn stated he would 'take charge of any letters given me, at Five Shillings each…once a year you can count on rapid communication with India'. For some years the *Hugh Lindsay* kept up a faltering service, but it was unsatisfactory and out-classed by Waghorn. In November

1836 Waghorn had written that 'in July last, unaided, [I] accomplish[ed] the transit of H.M. Mails between Falmouth and Bombay in 63 days, personally taking it myself from Cairo to Mocha (without solicitation or recompense) on its way.'

Such was Waghorn's activity – the novelist Thackeray described him as 'bouncing' – that in 1837 the East India Company directors sent out two new steamers, the 617-ton *Atlanta* and the 765-ton *Berenice*. So highly were Waghorn's efforts regarded that they finally won him his long-coveted commission as lieutenant in the Royal Navy, but they cost him dear and he never reaped more material reward. As Waghorn exhausted his fortune, others were in on the game.

The East India Company was no longer what it was and the Bombay Marine appears to have lost much of its edge by the 1830s, for it was held in low esteem at this time. The *Berenice* was notorious, her:

> cabins were small and miserable, cockroaches abounded. Washing had to be done in a public room. Each passenger was expected to fit up his own stateroom... The rooms were hot and smelly, the servants lazy and indolent...Piles of coal soot invaded everything.

Among further ineptitudes was the acquisition of the steamer *Kilkenny* in 1839, sister-ship to the ill-fated *Killarney*. This pig-carrying coaster was quite unsuitable for running the mails and conveying passengers to Suez, despite a grand change of name to *Zenobia*. Although joined by the *Semiramis*, the Company's packets were dismal, unreliable and contemptible. More steamers intended to speed the mails arrived: the *Nemesis* in 1840 and the *Memnon* in 1842, but the Company's ways were out of date, unfitted to the new age. Others were more vigorous.

On obtaining the obligation to run the mails through to India, Anderson and his colleagues – including Charles Wye Williams – had to acquire steamers capable of operating during the stormy south-west monsoon. In order to extend their existing service through the Mediterranean they firstly took over the old Peninsular Co.'s *Tagus*, *Braganza*, *Royal Tar* and *Liverpool* for equity in the new company. They also chartered and later bought the Transatlantic S.S.Co.'s *Liverpool*, that unlucky third contender in the first transatlantic race mentioned earlier. In order to distinguish her from her smaller and synonymous consort, this ship became popularly known as the *Great Liverpool*.[61] She was joined by another acquisition of over 1,000 tons, the *Oriental*, and other large vessels followed, most notably the *Precursor*, *Hindostan* and *Bentinck*.

In India, the Peninsular & Oriental Steam Navigation Co. was regarded as *arriviste*. The East India Company's vested interest – at a last gasp – defended its perceived right to monopolise Bombay as the 'Gateway to India', while other investors had founded the East India S.N. Co., which wanted to disperse the mails from the hub of Ceylon. The subsequent negotiations need not detain us, but Bombay retained its pre-eminent position after persuasive arguments had been advanced by the P&O board who in due course bought out the East India S.N. Co.'s interest in the *Precursor*. Among the complexities of these arrangements there remained the problem of efficient overland transport between Alexandria and Suez. Although the necessary *firman* had been obtained from the Pasha, it was thought desirable that the passengers that would inevitably accompany the mail ought to be better provided for than on riding camels. Some of the journey at least could be by way of the Nile, and in order to acquire a river-steamer, negotiations were entered into with Waghorn. Among the agreements concluded was that Waghorn 'must rigidly abstain from forwarding any letter or despatches by private express'.

Waghorn fades from the picture — he was to die in 1850 — as the company's first large steamer was sent out to India. The *Hindostan* left Southampton on 24 September 1842, days before the mail-contract was actually signed and the subvention of £115,000 *per annum* secured. Both events ensured a rise in the company's share price and an explosion of persiflage on the new ship's 'elegant' and 'commodious' appointments (she contained 150 passenger berths); the first emergence of that short but meaningful word: 'posh'.[62] She killed a seaman removing paddle-boards off the African coast as the ship, then approaching Capetown, sought to eke out her dwindling coal stocks by making sail, and a nurse attending a passenger's baby lost her leg when one of the *Hindostan*'s guns was discharged to oblige some visiting naval officers at Mauritius, though she survived the amputation.[63]

The *Hindostan* was followed by the *Bentinck* in 1843, and the *Precursor* was bought from the East India S.N.Co. in 1844. All were large paddle-steamers and they were but the beginning of an enormous shipping enterprise that would in time subsume a score of subsidiary companies and include ships of all varieties. Soon afterwards P&O took the overland crossing under its own wing and made the ordeal palatable by diversions to the antiquities of the Pyramids south of Cairo where there was the additional 'attraction' of a slave-market specialising in females. The overland route was never satisfactory, but it drew attention to the narrow Isthmus, the consequences of which were to be immense and would, within thirty years, result in the Suez Canal.

In the meantime, however, the Peninsular & Oriental Steam Navigation Co. would push further east, passing Singapore, reaching Hong Kong and Shanghai, and inaugurating branch services such as that begun in 1848 between Hong Kong, Macao and Canton, where the little steamer *Canton* distinguished herself by towing a becalmed British man-of-war into action against Chinese pirate junks. Other branch routes appeared, and a main-line service to Australia followed. The instuition of Brodie Willcox and Arthur Anderson was fully justified. In the wake of the mails came a trickle and then a flood of passengers: Government civil servants, merchants, clerks, military officers, and their families. Eventually P&O ships would carry out to India the hopeful husband-seeking young women who were unkindly deemed 'the fishing fleet' by their intended quarry, the army subalterns in their cantonments whose sexual appetites had to be diverted from miscegenation.

In 1844 the Egyptian connection yielded the company another dividend, that of cruising. In that year it incorporated touring visits arranged from its steamers when in the ports of Egypt and the Levant. The novelist William Thackeray was among them, remarking in his published account that the excursion enabled him to see 'in the space of a couple of months, as many men and cities…as Ulysses surveyed and noted in ten years'. As for the firm in whose ships he travelled, Thackeray considered it to be a 'noble Company…whose fleet alone makes them a third-rate maritime Power in Europe'.

Mindful of consolidating what it had won, the P&O board set and demanded a high standard for its crews, mirroring the old East India Company in its heyday and in contradistinction to the contemporaneous poor standards elsewhere in the British mercantile marine. Rates of pay were high, a master receiving £20 per month, well in excess of his chief officer, the mate getting only £7, and of his chief engineer who was paid £12. The high value put on the services of the engineers is, however, obvious from others' pay. Against the chief officer's £7, his equivalent in the engine-room, the second engineer, was paid £8, while against an able-seaman receiving £2 10s and a quartermaster £3 per month, a fireman earned £3 5s.

Another beneficiary of the Government mail-contracts being touted for in 1839 was the Royal West Indian Mail Steam-Packet Co., established by James McQueen in order to carry mails to the West Indies. For this an enormous subsidy of £240,000 was put up and the company went about recruiting naval officers for their ships in the belief that such men were properly fitted for the new enterprise. The *Thames* left Falmouth on 3 January 1842, to be followed fourteen days later by the *Dee*, the *Medway*, the *Teviot* and the *Trent*. Their masters proved to be men 'who knew but little of steam, and nothing whatever of the requirements of a merchant ship…' Inexperience also reigned in the board room and, after a year's operation, 'the company's balance sheet showed a deficit of no less than £79,790'. Worse, it lost the *Isis* off Bermuda that year and the following April the *Solway* was wrecked near Coruña with the loss of her master and sixty souls, including passengers. In 1844 the *Medina* was wrecked off the Bahamas and on 12 February 1847 the *Tweed* was wrecked on the Alicranes Reef, Yucatan, again with many deaths. Almost exactly two years later the *Forth* struck the same reef. This was an inauspicious start, but it was to get worse with the *Actæon* wrecked off Carthagena in 1850 and then in 1852 the disastrous loss of the *Amazon*.

This 2,256-ton paddle steamer was, at 300ft in length, the largest wooden merchantman ever built, a product of R. & H. Green's Blackwall Yard. Surveyed by the Admiralty, she was certified for fourteen 32-pounders and two 10in calibre pivot guns, and she had cost £100,000. She sailed from Southampton on 2 January under Captain Symons with a ship's company of 110 souls and fifty passengers, bound first for St Thomas. On her first night at sea, in a south-westerly gale, her engine bearings overheated and she lay stopped several times, once for two and a half hours. Getting under way again, she was west of the Scillies by midnight of the 4th when a fire was discovered 'between the steam-chest and the galley, the flames at once rushing up…in front of the forward funnel'. Despite the best efforts of Symons and his officers and crew:

> the flames were…spread by the gale in every direction…far beyond anything that
> buckets of water or wet blankets could do to allay it. Unfortunately, it was some

little time before the fire-pumps could be rigged, and meanwhile the fury of the fire remained entirely unchecked.

What followed was a catastrophe. Distracted passengers massed on the upper decks, the fire drove the engine-room staff out on deck 'and the *Amazon* was dashing through the waves at full speed, which with the strong gale that was blowing, caused the fire to rage with additional fierceness'. All attempts to launch the boats were doomed, the several that were lowered being instantly swamped, their occupants drowned. Eventually the untended boilers caused the ship to slow and three boats were successfully launched, and of 161 people some forty-six were eventually picked up. The ship herself, blazing from end to end, her funnels glowing red hot, sank when her powder magazine exploded at about 5.00 a.m.

It was this appalling event which persuaded the Government to desist from their archaic insistence that mails must be carried in wooden ships. Henceforth iron and later steel hulls were to be used. Nevertheless, this did not prevent the further stranding of the *Demerara* off Bristol, which caused her to be declared a constructive total loss. Later, in 1886, the *Humber* sailed from Southampton only to be posted-missing. Despite this appalling tally of disaster the company retained its mail monopoly. On the undertaking of adding a Brazilian run and increasing the speed of the West Indian vessels by building five new steamers, it was granted a new contract and a subsidy of £270,000 in 1850. Although an outcry was raised in Parliament, a second charter was granted in 1852 extending the company's services 'to North and South America and such other foreign parts as to the said Company shall seem desirable...' This resulted in a change of name to the Royal Mail Steam-Packet Co. and the added responsibility to run passengers and cargo across the Isthmus of Panama, initially by mule and canoe on a scale similar to P&O's Alexandria to Suez transfer. Happily three years later a railway was built across the narrow neck of land, largely financed by the shipping company.

As touched upon in the previous chapter, the Bibbys had committed funds to steamers by the mid-1850s. This followed trials carried out in 1850 with the second-hand *Rattler*, owned by a subsidiary, the Liverpool & Mediterranean Steam Shipping Co. Signing-up shareholders, Bibbys made the jump directly into iron screw-steamers and ordered two larger vessels from J. Reid at Port Glasgow. Intended for the firm's Mediterranean services, they were named after Italian rivers, the *Arno* and *Tiber*, and entered service the following year. Of the eighteen ships Bibbys managed by 1856 on behalf of his fellow investors and himself, only five were sailing-vessels, of which two were already reduced to coal-hulks.[64] Of the thirteen steamers John Bibby & Sons and its associates owned, James Bibby himself was the majority shareholder in only four: the *Corinthian*, *Albania*, *Rhone* and *Danube*, an investment amounting to £135,100, eleven times the £12,000 valuation of the sailing-vessels. These steamers continued to work the routes long dominated by Bibby ships between Liverpool and the Western Mediterranean, specifically Gibraltar, Marseilles, Genoa, Leghorn (Livorno), Naples and Messina, but Bibby ships were now handling cargoes further afield, including Salonika in Greece, Constantinople and Smyrna (Izmir) in Ottoman

Turkey, and into the Black Sea as far as Trebizond and the Bulgarian ports of Varna and Kustenje. It was the Mediterranean that remained the key, being the western end of the direct trade-route to India which benefited from the completion of the railway from Alexandria to Suez in 1858. Here John Bibby & Sons made up the shortfall of tonnage being experienced by P&O on this section of their pre-canal Indian service. In 1866 the *Arno* was sold to General Steam, and more ships were ordered, this time from J. & G. Thomson's yard at Govan.[65]

By 1865 Bibby's ships were calling at most Iberian and Mediterranean ports, their outward cargoes of goods of every description drawn from the manufactories of Manchester and the English Midlands. On their return they arrived in the Mersey full of Turkish and Egyptian tobacco and grain, Syrian dates, Ionian wine, oil and fruit, Cretan wool and Palestinian hides. When these occasionally fell off, the ships began to specialise in the carriage of live cattle from the ports of Portugal and Spain, and so successful was the canny James Bibby that he was annually expanding his fleet by means of a partnership with Edward Harland begun in 1859, a connection made through one of the Bibby partners, the Liverpool merchant Gustav Schwabe.

Harland had originally advised Bibby on the purchase of the *Rattler* when he had been working in the Govan Shipyard of J. & G. Thomson where Bibby had ordered new tonnage.[66] Their relationship deepened and Bibby encouraged Harland to establish a shipyard on the Mersey. Even with Bibby's help this failed and Harland accepted the post of manager at Queen's Island, Belfast. In 1858 Harland purchased the yard, founding what would become Harland & Wolff, accepting an order from Bibby for three ships, the *Venetian*, *Sicilian* and *Syrian*. So pleased was Bibby with these vessels that he invested in Harland's new enterprise and ordered a further six steamers, *Grecian*, *Italian*, *Egyptian*, *Dalmatian* and *Arabian*. More followed, and of Harland's first twenty-one new vessels, eighteen were for Bibby.

Bibby's delight arose from Harland's new ideas. To compensate for the occupation of the hull's capacity for bunkers and consequent loss of stowage space, steam-ship design had, by 1860, produced a full-bodied hull without a deep keel. This came into its own after the introduction of iron, which lost less internal capacity to strengthening than wood. That year Edward Harland's three steamers for James Bibby had a length to beam ratio of 10:1, which increasingly became the norm elsewhere, marking Harland as a world-leader in his business. His new hulls for Bibby had 'a flatness of bottom and squareness of bilge' which attracted the nick-name of 'Belfast bottom' among Liverpool's ship-owners and characterised the three long Bibby steamers *Egyptian*, *Dalmatian* and *Arabian*. Harland also lengthened the *Calpe* and the *Tiber*, but his innovations were not greeted with universal acclaim. Less kindly waterfront-experts denominated them 'Bibby's coffins', a soubriquet apparently confirmed when in 1863 Harland launched the *Persian* for Bibby. She slid down the ways with neither figurehead nor bowsprit, but a straight, plum stem. Such heresies were only the beginning, as will be seen in the following chapter.

However, at this time a steamer with a speed of 8 or 9 knots was not of itself a serious competitor to the sailing-vessel, even when an Atlantic passage took an aver-

age of thirteen to seventeen days against the three weeks of a Yankee packet. Despite
the emerging realisation that the regularity of a steamer was its great advantage, until
Harland's innovation, steamers offered little in the way of comfort:

> Stuffy passenger saloons, placed right aft, with no seats except the long settees...
> [were] lit only by candles... The state-rooms were below the saloon...lit by oil
> lamps, one between every two rooms. These were religiously put out at ten o'clock
> every night.

Sir William Forwood recollected:

> There was no ventilation, and no hot water... There were no smoke rooms... the
> lee side of the funnel in fine weather, the fidlee (sic) at other times. Here sitting on
> coils of rope, and ready to lift our feet as the seas rolled in from the alleyways on
> either side, we smoked and spun our yarns. There was an abundance of food in the
> saloon in the shape of great huge joints of meat and dishes of vegetables...
>
> The conditions in the steerage were wretched. The sleeping berths were huddled
> together, the occupants climbing over each other; there was no privacy, no wash-
> ing accommodation except on the hatchways. The food was brought round in iron
> buckets, and hunks of beef and pork were forked out by the steward, and placed in
> the passengers' pannikin, and in a similar way potatoes and plum duff were served
> out.[67]

These were the conditions prevailing in the Liverpool passenger ships of the 1860s, of
which there were many run by men like James Moss who, following his father Miles,
pioneered steam traffic to Egypt and the Levant and founded the Moss, Hutchinson
Line. The city was a hot-bed of inter-related maritime interests and innovations. Moss
had business dealings with William James Lamport who, with George Holt, founded
Lamport & Holt. Notwithstanding the deficiencies of the early passenger accommodation aboard his ships, Lamport was 'a very able man and was the author of the
first Merchant Shipping Bill'. Other Liverpool ship-owners contented themselves
with largely cargo-carrying enterprises. Thomas and John Harrison, for example, had,
on the death of their partner George Brown in 1853, renamed their trading firm. It
had been engaged in a number of imports central among which was that of brandy
and wine from France. The treaty between France and Great Britain which was to
make them allies for the Crimean War persuaded the Harrisons that carrying their
own imports would improve their profits. In 1860 they 'owned a few iron ships in
the Calcutta trade and some small steamers in the Charente wine trade', but in the
succeeding years they purchased a variety of ships including screw-steamers and sailing-vessels of both iron and wood. Among the latter were two famous former vessels
of the American Black Ball Line, the *Lightning* and *Star of the Seas*, bought in 1865.
Harrisons rapidly extended their operations to South America and the West Indies,
but it was with the iron screw-steamer that the future of commerce lay. The passing

of the Limited Liabilities Act of 1862 freed up capital and revolutionised the financing of shipping, opening up opportunities for those willing to take risks, while others did not think bold ventures were necessarily risky.

Despite the incursion of P&O into the China Seas, there was no direct steam-vessel connection between Great Britain and the Far East. Up until 1865, long voyages had remained dominated by sail, and it was widely held that 'steamers may occupy the Mediterranean, may go to Brazil...but China at least is safe for sailing ships.' Although this was the great age of the tea-clipper, their days were already numbered and, while the Suez Canal has been blamed for their demise, it was actually preceded three years earlier when in 1866, even as the *Taeping*, *Ariel* and *Serica* raced home with their tea cargoes in the most exciting contest of the trade, nemesis was already smoking on the horizon.

The steamer, even the iron screw-steamer of the day, remained reliant upon relatively inefficient boilers and an excessive amount of the internal volume of their hulls being given over to propulsion-plant and fuel bunkers. The *Sirius* had steamed across the Atlantic with a boiler pressure of 5lb per square inch, and by the advent of the *Great Eastern* marine boilers had a working pressure of little more than 25psi. Small improvements were no longer capable of producing the major advance necessary to make the steamer properly ocean-going without the increased efficiency produced by a better fuel-to-power-ratio obtainable with higher working pressures. The problem was understood; many of the newer 'red-brick' universities with faculties for studying engineering were incorporating thermodynamics along with electrical theories in their curricula, but fear of explosions placed the surveyors of the Government's Board of Trade in alliance with the protection and indemnity clubs and classification societies – chief of which was Lloyd's – in opposing dangerous high-pressure boilers at sea, despite the fact that they were now common in railway locomotives.

The matter was resolved by Alfred Holt, a young engineer from a prosperous Unitarian background who had been apprenticed by his father to Edward Woods, chief engineer to the Liverpool & Manchester Railway Co. Holt matured into a consulting engineer, heading Lamport & Holt's engineering department, sailing as chief engineer in their *Orontes* in 1851 and assisting in the design of one of James Moss's steamers, the *Scamander* of 1854. Holt had so impressed one client that he was asked to manage a small steamer, the *Dumbarton Youth*, the success of which encouraged Holt and his backers to build another steamer, the *Cleator*. Although designed for the carriage of coal and minerals, the *Cleator* was immediately chartered to the French Government as the Crimean War broke out and a replacement, the *Saladin*, was laid down. The war was over by the time the *Saladin* was completed, so Holt and his brother Philip put her into the West Indian trade, soon afterwards adding the *Plantagenet*, *Talisman*, *Askalon* and *Crusader*. After initial success, however, the West Indies venture barely broke-even in the face of fierce competition, and in 1864 the Holt brothers sold their little fleet to the West India & Pacific S.S. Co. Disappointed in his first ship-owning foray, Alfred Holt mused on prospects of trading in steam in more distant waters, maturing ideas of his own in concert with a ship-master named

Steam-vessel master Captain Isaac Middleton was a friend, colleague and employee of Alfred Holt, and commanded Holt's Blue Funnel liner *Agamemnon*. (Private Collection)

Isaac Middleton. The two had met when Holt had been reconstructing Middleton's ship, the *Alpha*, in 1853, and they decided to experiment with the *Cleator*, fitting her with steam-plant of Holt's own design. Based upon a locomotive's, the braced and modified boiler raised steam at 60psi. Not content with this, Holt now addressed the excess volume problem of the engine and produced a tandem compound steam-engine in which a high-pressure cylinder was mounted *above* the lower-pressure one to produce a tall engine which used a relatively short connecting rod to throw the single crank. The main framework of the engine was, in fact, both low and light when compared with the norm, and it took up far less longitudinal space.

Holt re-engined the *Cleator* and the brothers dispatched Middleton on a risky proving voyage to France, Russia and South America, anticipating the cargo would recoup some of the costs. So confident were the Holts that they were onto something that without awaiting Middleton's return they ordered three identical iron screw-steamers from Scott's of Greenock at a combined cost of £156,000. They then wrote to contacts in the Far East establishing agencies and instructing them to solicit for homeward cargoes. In addition to Holt's boilers and tandem compound engine, the new ships would adopt Harland's plain, straight stem and a simple barque rig. Indeed the only vanity displayed was in painting the lower two-thirds of the tall funnels with a distinctive light blue paint, the hue of which was said to derive from a can of paint discovered in the *Dumbarton Youth*'s paint-locker, but was shared by Lamport and Holt. Before the new steamers were commissioned Middleton returned with the news that Holt's new plant effected savings in fuel of an astounding 40 per cent!

On 11 January 1865 the Holt brothers registered the Ocean Steam Ship Co., and on 19 April 1866 Middleton sailed from the Mersey in the auxiliary steam-vessel *Agamemnon* of 2,347 gross registered tons, a large vessel for her day and one which burned less coal than any other vessel afloat. The Holts' opportunistic adventure to China and the company's fortunes thereafter follow elsewhere, but the *Agamemon* and her sister-ships *Ajax* and *Achilles* could steam on only 20 tons of coal a day and Middleton reached Mauritius before he had to refuel, returning from China by way of the Cape of Good Hope in only sixty days, better than the fleetest of the tea-clippers.

The birth of what was popularly called The Blue Funnel Line was almost stifled when the collapse of the London banking firm of Overend Gurney in May 1866 precipitated a commercial crisis. This, following the previous crash of 1857, affected many shipping companies, both British and European. Along with the great China house of Dent & Co., who had long since traded in tea and opium, agencies like Mansfield went to the wall. This was unfortunate for the Holts who had appointed Mansfield as their agents in Singapore, but it was worse for others. Up to this time Dent, for example, had been considered 'as sure as the Bank of England' by its depositors, and this, the inroads of steamers, and the new Indian tea trade, caused the Dent brothers to wind-up their affairs in China and retire to their native Westmoreland.

Nothing, not even the collapse of Mansfields, could deter the Holts, nor wrest from them the advantages conferred by Alfred's revolutionary power-plant. Dionysius Lardner and his associates had been proved wrong again: China was no longer safe for sailing ships. Without Government subventions, Holt and Middleton had now brought the ocean-going iron screw-steamer to a state of unprecedented fitness-for-purpose. She was now in a position to seize the carriage of premium commodities from the sailing-vessel, and it would start with tea.

The impact of the American Civil War upon British shipping was complex. Hostilities between the northern states and the seceding confederacy of the south broke out in April 1861. On the one hand the war cut off the supply of American cotton, producing great hardship in Lancashire where the raw material was turned into cloth. This state of affairs encouraged British sympathies to align with the South and build – as Laird did – warships for the Confederate Navy. It was said then that 'Britain's bread hangs by Lancashire's thread', but the Union Government's embargo of Confederate exports of cotton had an immediate effect upon other areas of England. Two cotton mills in Hull were brought to a standstill and, while some British ship-owners sought to break the Union's blockade of the Confederacy's ports, many owners involved in the supply of the raw material to English mills were ruined. One of these, Zachariah Pearson of Hull, attempted to run the Union blockade with dire results: he lost ten ships and by 1864 was in debt to the tune of £640,000, whereupon he went bankrupt.

For most individual British ships the effects were minimal. Many steamers were armed, particularly after the affront to the British flag by a North American Union cruiser late in 1861. The British steam-vessel *Trent*, proceeding upon her lawful occasions but with two Confederate envoys, Messrs Mason and Slidell, on board, was stopped and boarded on the high seas by the Union warship *San Jacinto* and the two men were removed. 'The *Trent* Incident' was almost a *casus belli*, but British ire was cooled by the ailing Prince Consort. Meanwhile, President Lincoln ordered his secretary of state to release Mason and Slidell to resume their visit to London where their mission, intended to turn British sympathy for the Confederates into an alliance, was doomed.

Other 'incidents' occurred; in 1862 the British sailing-vessel *Emilie St Pierre*, commanded by a Captain William Wilson, was attempting to run the Union blockade into Charleston, South Carolina, when she was intercepted by the Northern cruiser *James Adger*. The vessel was seized and a prize-crew put aboard with orders to carry the *Emilie St Pierre* into Philadelphia. Most of the British ship's crew had been removed into the man-of-war, but Wilson with his steward and cook were kept on board. Wilson, however, was not relinquishing his ship so easily:

> By an amazing combination of stratagem and daring, the whole [of the prize] crew were made prisoners and put in irons by Wilson and his two assistants, who, unaided, navigated the ship and brought her in safety across the Atlantic into the Mersey, where she arrived on April 21st. As might naturally be expected, Wilson received quite an ovation. By a subscription amongst the merchants, he was presented with a gold chronometer, and a tea and coffee service. From the Mercantile Marine Association he received a gold medal, and from the owners the sum of £2,000. The cook and steward received £320 each.[68]

Ultimately the Americans were the losers because the war curtailed the rising fortunes of the United States' mercantile marine. 'Tariffs…killed her shipping,' it was said, and it took some years for the re-united States of America to make up the lost ground after Lee's surrender at Appomattox in April 1865. As mentioned earlier, however, many American ships were re-registered under the British flag and shrewd shipping agents and habitual charterers actually bought them outright at knock-down prices. Among such acquisitions was the full-rigged ship *Golden Horn*, bought by Edwin and Alfred Houlder in 1861, thereby establishing Houlder Brothers & Co. as ship-owners. As agents the brothers represented the London interests of the American Golden Line of sailing ships, putting the *Golden Horn* into the Australian trade. She was soon joined by the *Trebolgan*, but Houlders, although remaining sailing ship-owners for some time, also advertised for sailings in the steamer *Alhambra*, which reached Adelaide in less than sixty days.

While cotton played an important part in the entanglement of British shipping in the American Civil War, it was coal and iron that underpinned Britain as the world's workshop. The importance of native coal to smelt iron has already been mentioned, as has the competing demand for it at home, while its use as a fuel for steam-vessels is obvious. So too is its property to fuel other industrial processes of which copper-smelting, touched upon elsewhere, is a prime example. What is less obvious is the self-sustaining nature of steam-navigation in that coal from the north-east of England and the valleys of South Wales was exported as a freight-paying cargo to provide bunkers in foreign and colonial ports not only for mercantile steamers but the men-of-war of the Royal Navy. This bulky commodity filled out the lower holds of ships, both steam and sail, while manufactured goods were stowed in their 'tween decks. Eventually, as exported manufactured goods increased in volume, it was coal – along with bulk steel products such as railway lines – that gave sailing ships a last market for their outward-bound services. But the volume of this trade combined with a tremendous increase in imported raw materials to supply Britain's industry. By this time Britain could no longer feed her fast-growing, town-dwelling population and such was the demand for tonnage that, in addition to more sailing-vessels, the market also encouraged the construction of low-powered steamers. The iron screw-steamship with water-ballast tanks, based on Harland's 'easy convex waterlines' and with engines not only built on Holt's principles but adopting compounding engines, was soon encroaching directly upon the sailing-vessel's traditional trades. Such success gave birth to the British tramp-steamer, a low-cost 'good wholesome ship, a large carrier, with sufficient power to take care of herself in all weathers'. Thus, in the last quarter of the nineteenth century, all British merchantmen, steam and sail, had become indispensable, exporting manufactured products and bringing homeward cargoes of food for the British people and the raw materials with which they might labour.

Although steam had come of age, the lot of the seaman – whether he served in sail or steam – was very much the same: 'the pay of a sailor was small – £3 a month for an A.B. – and when they returned home from a voyage they were pounced upon by the boarding-house keepers [the notorious crimps], who did not let them out of their clutches while they had any money left.' Forwood, a Liverpool ship-owner himself, goes on to admit that Liverpool 'was a perfect hell, a scene of debauchery from morn to night'. London's waterfront was no better, though hidden downstream beyond London Bridge and the Pool. Glasgow, Newcastle and Shields were similar. Nevertheless, the standard of Britain's mercantile marine, though far from perfect and yet to be subjected to the measures to associated with the eponymous Plimsoll, was in better shape in 1866 than it had been fifty years earlier. It had beaten the Americans – at least for the time being – but had yet to face the challenge of the rising mercantile muscle of European nations. Moreover, insofar as steam navigation was concerned, it was about to benefit from a 'dismal but profitable ditch', the Suez Canal.

CHAPTER NOTES:

1. A conning and compass platform constructed across a paddle-steamer from one paddle-box to the other gave rise to the command position for the master and mates being removed from the poop of a sailing-vessel to this new-fangled 'bridge'. In tandem with these improvements in steam-propulsion went other advances useful to the operation of ships. In 1819, for instance, the German Augustus Siebe, working in England, invented the diving helmet supplied with air from a surface pump, and in 1830 he patented the enclosed diving suit with lead boots. This, coupled with the diving-bell invented in the previous century, greatly expedited repairs to ships, salvage and the clearing of fouled propellers.

2. R.H. Thornton unequivocally accuses Fulton of disingenuous motives for, having 'made copious notes and sketches, [Fulton] was full of compliments to Symington upon his ingenuity and there were even references to a partnership in the United States. Whereupon he departed with his note-book, and poor Symington never heard from him again.' See Thornton, p10.

3. See Paul Quinn, Charles, *Wye Williams, Boilers and Fuel, The Mariner's Mirror,* Volume 93, No.4, November 2007, p.450 *et seq.* Williams also experimented with peat-coke instead of coal which, because it was resin-bonded and burnt with a steadier heat-emission than coal which tended to damp-down a fire when first flung into the furnace causing a consequent loss of steam. Such arbitrary losses of power at perhaps a crucial moment, as an early steamer headed into a gale, could prove her undoing, and in certain circumstances could not be ameliorated by auxiliary sails.

4. Among the early coastal and short-sea runs was that between Bristol and Dublin, inaugurated by the *Palmerston*, built by Hillhouse at Bristol with engines by J. Dove of Liverpool; the Bristol to Bideford service maintained between 1835 and 1871 by the Appledore-built *Torridge*; and a Dublin to Bordeaux route opened by the Dublin and London Steam Marine Co.

5. Her side-valve engines, built by Maudslay, generated 70hp and gave her a service speed of 6 knots, although she used her sails for most of the voyage via the Strait of Magellan.

6. Advocacy of steam-vessels owes much to Captain Frederick Marryat RN who was later the bestselling novelist between Jane Austen and Charles Dickens.

7. The so-called Overland route had been used for many years, Nelson sending a lieutenant to India by way of Mesopotamia after his victory at Aboukir Bay in 1798 to warn the Governor-General of French forces in Egypt and their possible designs on India, an intention Napoleon later admitted. A regular route was surveyed down the Euphrates by a Colonel F.R. Chesney at considerable risk to himself, and afterwards two small iron steamers were built by Lairds on the Mersey to the account of the East India Company and shipped out to Antioch by HMS *Columbine*. From here teams of camels bore their prefabricated parts across the desert to the Euphrates at Mesken. The first, the *Euphrates*, went afloat in September 1835 and arrived at Basra in the following June. Her sister, the *Tigris*, was lost on the passage in a sudden storm, along with twenty of her crew. The *Euphrates* continued the East India Company's surveying of the Persian Gulf and the Company then ordered three more prefabricated steamers, the *Nimrod, Nitocris* and *Assyria*, all of which were assembled on the shores of the Shatt-al-Arab at the confluence of the Tigris and Euphrates. In 1841-42 the *Nimrod* and *Nitocris* ascended the Euphrates for 1,130 miles before all four vessels took part in the Scindian War. Thereafter the last survivor, the *Assyria*, having taken part in a campaign against Persia, ended her career surveying the Punjab rivers in 1860.

8. These were, besides Johnston's *Enterprize*, the Calcutta-built *Diana* whose engineer, John Anderson, commissioned Alexander & Co. at Kidderpore to build two small steam

passenger tug-tenders in 1825. These, engined by Maudslay and named *Comet* and *Firefly*, were not a success and were scrapped upon the winding-up of Alexander & Co. in 1831. There was also the *Pluto*, a dredger with steam-plant to drive a bucket chain but not the vessel. She too was Indian-built at Kidderpore with engines made by T. & W. Gladstone of Liverpool. During the Burma War she was requisitioned, her steam-plant modified to propel her, and made into a floating-battery.

9. Peacock's interest in steam-propulsion caused him to rename the Society for the Diffusion of Useful Knowledge, the less assonant Steam-Intellect Society.

10. Ardaseer Curstejee was a distinguished naval-architect. In addition to the *Indus* he also introduced gas street-lighting to Bombay, establishing a gas-works for the purpose. He visited London at his own expense in 1840–41 and secured the post of principal inspector of steam machinery to the East India Company. As a consequence, on 27 March 1841 Curtsejee's achievements were recognized by election as a Fellow to the Royal Society in London. Those who signed his citation included John Barrow, secretary to the Admiralty; Francis Beaufort, hydrographer to the navy; Sir Edward Sabine, general of artillery, arctic astronomer, associate of Herschel and scientific adviser to the Admiralty; James Walker, the lighthouse architect; Sir William Cubitt, inventor, civil engineer, chief of Ransome's Engineering Plant at Ipswich, railway, bridge and water-works builder; John Macneil, road-building associate of Telford; and Joshua Field, civil and marine engineer, partner with Joseph and Thomas Henry Maudslay in Maudslay, Son & Field, the great London marine steam engine manufacturers.

11. The first prefabricated hull seems to have been that of the *Aaron Manby*, built at Tipton near Birmingham in 1821. Taken to the Thames for assembly and then steamed to Le Havre, the little vessel served on the Seine for many years.

12. The Royal Navy scoop line-honours in this respect. It was a small auxiliary steam-sloop, HMS *Rhadamanthus* — that which escorted Queen Victoria on her visit to Scotland — which was the first British 'steamer' to cross the North Atlantic in 1833, and to the paddle-sloop HMS *Driver* goes the distinction of being the first steam-and-sail assisted vessel to circumnavigate the globe in the early 1840s.

13. The Chartists directly linked Britain's commercial success at sea with privation ashore, pointing out the contradictory comparison with *Rule Britannia* in an anthem of 1842, a verse of which said:
'Men of England, ye are slaves
Though ye rule the roaring waves.
Though ye shout, from sea to sea
Britons everywhere are free.'

14. Chief among these was, of course, Captain Lord Cochrane, whose dazzling career in the Royal Navy had been brought to an abrupt end by the taint of corruption by his alleged involvement in a stock-exchange fraud, but there were many others who served not only in the wars of independence against Spain and Portugal but in Greece with Lord Byron against the Turks and in the Carlist Wars in Spain itself. Many South American leaders solicited help in London and a statue of Miranda stands today on the corner of Fitzroy Square.

15. The London Bridge of 1831 was demolished in living memory for sale and re-erection in the Arizona Desert on *its* replacement.

16. See *Neptune's Trident* for a description of the establishment of the Blackwall ship-building yard.

17. The *Rainbow*, like the *Garry Owen* and other Laird hulls, incorporated transverse bulkheads intended initially to compensate for the lighter scantlings of an iron compared to a wooden keel, but which added the advantage of internal subdivision of an iron hull to which, later in the nineteenth century, John Scott Russell added the cellular double-bottom.

18. L. Cornford Cope, *A Century of Sea Trading, 1824–1924*, p42.

19. Under the direction of Captain John Woolmore, a former East India Company commander, ship's husband, member of the marine interest of the Court of Directors and then the Deputy Master of Trinity House, the corporation had commissioned the *Vestal* in 1835 and were to use steamers not only to lay buoys, tend beacons and supply lighthouses, but to build a remarkable series of lighthouses during the succeeding half-century. Steam was also quickly adopted for their tenders by the Commissioners for Northern Lights in Scotland, and the Commissioners for Irish Lighthouses in Dublin.

20. Prince Albert was to become the corporation's master in 1853, succeeding the Duke of Wellington, and establishing the tradition of the master being a royal prince.

21. For full details of the beginnings of steam-navigation on the North Atlantic and Samuel Cunard's part in it, see Stephen Fox, *The Ocean Railway*, Harper Collins, 2003.

22. There were other jeremiahs. Samuel Seaward, for instance, who was a business-associate of the engine-builder Maudslay, declared that no hull could carry sufficient coal to sustain a powered voyage in excess of twenty-one days.

23. Brunel realised that a hull has a theoretical maximum speed beyond which its forward progress causes an exponential demand for power, but that this depends upon waterline length, being one-and-a-half-times the square root of the waterline. He reasoned that: 'The tonnage increases as the cubes of their dimensions, while the resistance increases as their squares, so a vessel of double the tonnage of another capable of containing an engine of twice the power, does not meet with double the resistance. Speed will therefore be greater with the large vessel, or the proportionate power of the engine and consumption of fuel may be reduced.'

24. Claxton was aboard HMS *Leopard* in 1807 during the action and subsequent temporary surrender of the USS *Chesapeake*, was employed in land service during the Peninsular War and, after the peace, was the first naval officer to command a revenue-cutter, the *Tartar*, which he relinquished in 1819. Unemployed and on half-pay, he took up the appointment at Bristol and was promoted to commander in 1842. He is therefore sometimes referred to by that rank's courtesy title of 'captain', the rank in which he retired in June 1860. He died eight years later.

25. As a seaman, I cannot agree with Stephen Fox's almost solitary reference to the *Sirius* in his assessment on page 78 of *The Ocean Railway*. Fox states that: 'The voyage of the *Sirius* was just a heedless, dangerous publicity stunt, a desperate gambit by sore losers, and hardly worth the historical attention it has received ever since.' It might have been both desperate and dangerous, but it was not a publicity stunt and if nothing else it demonstrated the fundamental soundness of oceanic steam-power.

26. The 'Day's Run' or 'Day's Work' was calculated from noon-to-noon on the basis that at this period the optimum time for standing a chance of determining a ship's position was at mid-day by an observation of the sun, or 'meridian altitude'. The logged dates therefore also ran from 12.00 to 12.00.

27. It was in the rescue of the survivors clinging to the wreck of the *Forfarshire* that Grace Darling (with her father, who was keeper of the adjacent Longstone Lighthouse) earned immortality as the quintessential Victorian heroine.

28. The figurehead of a leaping hound clasping the dog-star Sirius is in the possession of the Town Dock Museum in Kingston-upon-Hull. I am indebted for several details concerning Roberts and the *Sirius* to Daphne D.C. Pochin Mould's *Captain Roberts of the Sirius*, Sirius Commemoration Committee, Cork, 1988.

29. The circumstances of the loss of the *President* gave rise to a number of myths. Relatives of Roberts claimed to have had prescient dreams and an old seaman on his death-bed years later claimed she had been taken by pirates. In 1841 the British marine artist William Leathern, who specialised in dramatic maritime events, exhibited

a picture entitled 'The *President* as last seen signalling with the brig *Pearl*'. It shows the paddle-steamer viewed from the port quarter, broached with a large sea breaking over her. The identity of the *Pearl* has never been established and the image is considered apocryphal. The painting is in the collection of the Merseyside Maritime Museum, Liverpool.

30. The humbly born Richard Lander was the son of a Cornish inn-keeper and began his exploring career as man-servant to Hugh Clapperton – whose overland expedition from Tripoli in 1822 discovered Lake Chad – received a parsimonious £100 reward for the expedition. He was the first to receive an award by the Geographical Society amounting to fifty guineas. His brother John received nothing and they were rescued by the publisher John Murray, then specialising in the new vogue for travel books, by an advance of £1,000.

31. For details of the slave-trade, see *Neptune's Trident*. The long established British firms trafficking with West Africa included Richard & William King, set up in 1695. The companies of W.B. MacIver of Glasgow, Thomas Harrison, and Hatton and Cookson of Liverpool, would combine in partnership to form Unilever and create Port Sunlight as the great Merseyside soap-manufactory.

32. Later sold on, the *Ethiope* had her engines removed and served various owners as a sailing-vessel. She was sold to Dutch owners in 1858, renamed *Biaffra* and broken up in 1867.

33. Baikie, who adopted local dress, took a local mistress by whom he sired several children, learnt several local languages, produced a Fuldi grammar and foisted a translation of the Book of Genesis into Hausa upon his neighbours. Though avoiding malaria by a regular dose of quinine, he died of dysentery.

34. Woodruff was another unemployed naval lieutenant who found work in steamers. He entered the Royal Navy in 1810, passed for lieutenant in 1816 but had to await a vacancy until receiving his commission in February 1830. This was given him in the Coastguard Service – which had been formed in 1822 – and he commanded a Coastguard station until 1836 when he was retired on half-pay. O'Byrne, in his *Naval Biographical Dictionary*, published by John Murray in 1849, asserts that after the maiden voyage of the *Britannia* Woodruff, like others of his unfortunate generation, 'has not been since employed', ignoring service at sea in merchantmen, even when in so prestigious a command as a 'Cunard steam-packet'.

35. The steamers were *Ignez de Castro*, *Vasco de Gama*, *Dom Alfonso* and *Dom Pedro* which traded to Portugal. The sailing ships were *Tempest*, *Spectre* and *Dream*, later followed by the *Dalhousie*.

36. Ironically, despite early disfavour by the Admiralty, the two fine examples of the lifting screw remaining extant are both fitted to Government-built ships: HMS *Warrior* and the RRS *Discovery*. The screws could be lifted in their banjo-frames either to improve their sailing qualities or, in the latter's case, to avoid damage from pack-ice.

37. The *Great Britain* was assisted off the sea-bed of Dundrum Bay by one of the Royal Navy's first iron paddle-frigates, HMS *Birkenhead*, built by Laird and famously lost while trooping to the Kaffir War in 1852. The *Great Britain* herself was brought home in the summer of 1970 and, after extensive refitting, restored to her original condition in the dry-dock in Bristol where she was built and may be seen today.

38. Among other abandoned features in the *Great Eastern* was the small pump which should have poured sea-water over a thermometer to give early warning of a drop in the temperature and the possible presence of icebergs. Masters like James Anderson were obliged therefore to have a man cast a bucket over the side to determine the sea-temperature.

39. The best account remains James Dugan's *The Great Iron Ship*, Harper Bros, New York, 1953, which also records her subsequent history in great detail.

40. Brunel had already had a brush with cholera, information for which I am indebted to Adrian Vaughan.

41. William Scoresby Junior had sailed in her as a passenger, as is mentioned in *Britannia's Realm*.

42. Charles Dickens wrote an account of the shipwreck's aftermath in the *Uncommercial Traveller*, the gloomy event being a national disaster. The incumbent of the local parish buried forty-four bodies in St Gallgo's churchyard after the church had been used as a mortuary and the details of each body carefully recorded by the Reverend Stephen Roose Hughes. Most of the gold was afterwards recovered.

43. What, asked the *New York Herald*, would the *Great Eastern* do in Portland, other than take away the entire population in two voyages and denude the 'entire State of Maine of all its products and manufactures'?

44. On the jacket of the first edition of his book *The Great Iron Ship*, James Dugan lists the *Great Eastern's* accomplishments thus: 'This is the ship that: killed her designer, drowned her first captain, logged four mutinies, killed thirty-five men, survived the Atlantic's weirdest storm, laid the Atlantic cable, sank four ships, made six knights, caused thirteen lawsuits, was six times at auction, boarded 2 million sightseers [and] ended as a floating circus.'

45. Mrs Paton died when James Paton was ten. At the age of thirteen James ran away from home and shipped aboard the barque *Craigmullen*. Later he set up as a tin-smith in Bootle, Liverpool, but was ruined by an uncle who, as his biggest customer, refused to do business with a minor. The younger Paton became the Liverpool port agent for Cayzer Irvine's Clan Line. He also developed a paint-washing solution less unkind to seamen than the caustic *soojee-moojee* they were accustomed to. This led to the founding of Paton, Calvert & Co., a business that throve, manufacturing polish and packaging. An opera patron, he became Mayor of Southport and was knighted.

46. The *Great Eastern* was in fact more than forty years ahead of her time, her tonnage not being exceeded until 1901.

47. The *Scotia* was commanded by Captain Judkins, who could do little to help, and since there was no risk to life and a penalty – not to mention Samuel Cunard's disapprobation – awaited his ship if the mails were delayed, he left the *Great Eastern* to her fate.

48. Joseph Conrad's semi-fictional Captain Lingard was engaged in this lucrative trade, as was his inspiration, as mentioned in Chapter Three.

49. The eventual success of the *Great Eastern* led to the abandonment of another attempt being made to link Europe and America across the Bering Strait by the Great Northern Telegraph Co. and the Anglo-American Telegraph Co. with their small steamer *Egmont*, which was recalled from the Pacific.

50. Robert Halpin married a Newfoundland woman whose father owned a large whaling enterprise.

51. In 1890 the figures were: steam, 5,042,517, and sail, 2,936,021. Shortly after the turn of the twentieth century the figure for steam reached 10 million, and is consistent up until the outbreak of the First World War in 1914. But there is also a consistency in the tonnage of cargo capacity under sail which, having fallen to 1.7 million in 1905, remained 1.1 million in 1910.

52. The Imperial Lighthouse Service maintained tenders in the Persian Gulf, Ceylon and the West Indies.

53. The term 'Indian Mutiny' is much resented in India today where it is referred to as the First War for Independence.

54. Thus wrote W.S. Lindsay in his monumental *History of Merchant Shipping*, which covers national mercantile fleets other than the British. Lindsay was the same ship-owner whose vessels unsuccessfully challenged Arthur Anderson's Union steamers on the Capetown mail route. He was MP for Whitby in 1854 when he built the *Tynemouth* for this service.

55. See Murray, M., *Union–Castle Chronicle, 1853–1953*, p10.

56. See Crutchley, W.J., *My Life at Sea*, Collins, 1912, p128.

57. The Shetland mail-contract was lost to the Aberdeen, Leith & Clyde Shipping Co.

58. See *Britannia's Realm*. The Admiralty wished to retain the old, armed sailing-brigs which departed weekly, 'wind and weather permitting', as a nursery for seamen and for the placement of naval officers redundant to the fleet's retirement who were nevertheless retained on half-pay.

59. These six steam-vessels were *Don Juan, Iberia, Braganza, Iberia, Manchester* and *Liverpool*.

60. The Royal Navy did not abandon its squadronal colours of red, white and blue until 1864, so the senior British naval ensign in 1840 remained – confusingly – the red. Only in 1864 did the white ensign become exclusive to British men-of-war and yachts of the Royal Yacht Squadron, the blue was allocated to naval auxiliaries and vessels in Government service, leaving the plain red ensign to be born by all other British ships and vessels, namely those in private hands.

61. After extensive modifications, the *Great Liverpool* carried the Indian mails not between Suez and Bombay but between London, Southampton, Falmouth and Alexandria, suffering a major power-failure in 1842 when her crank-shaft fractured and she had to complete her voyage home under sail. Four years later, in 1846, she was wrecked off Cape Finisterre with a small loss of life, but that of all the passengers' baggage and the mails, for she took three days to break up and much was plundered by the Galician Spaniards.

62. The most popular explanation of the etymology of 'posh' is that it was an acronym derived from the stamp made on passengers' ticket documentation which meant that they had booked a cabin on the cooler side of a ship passing down the Red Sea and across the Arabian Sea: 'Port Outwards, Starboard Home'. Inevitably that privilege became associated with social aspiration.

63. The tompion had been left in the gun, and its other fragments narrowly missed striking some seamen on the forecastle.

64. These were the *Hannibal* and *England*. Bibby himself was the majority shareholder in these two vessels, and, of the sailing ships, only the newest, the *Pizarro*, this showed the sagacity of such men. The ownership of coal-hulks was not as daft as it might appear, given the high value of coal at the time. The Bibby family holding in sailing-vessels at this time was £11,888, compared to £135,091 in steamers, with the *Pizarro's* building costing only £7,950 against £35,800 for the steamer *Danube*.

65. The *Arno's* sister, the *Tiber*, was wrecked in 1871 but was afterwards salved and turned into a sailing-vessel.

66. These were the *Calpe, Danube* and *Rhone* of 1852-1853. Bibby also ordered tonnage elsewhere, from Reid and other Clyde yards, as well as Bristol and South Shields, eighteen in all between 1854 and 1859 when he began the long association with Harland.

67. Forwood, p71.

68. Quoted by Gomer Williams, *The Liverpool Privateers and the Liverpool Slave Trade*, William Heinemann, 1897, p204.

FIVE

'DAILY STEAMERS AND HOURLY TELEGRAMS'

Tea, Sugar, Sail and Steam, 1867–1884

Since the acquisition of Hong Kong, the growth of British shipping in the Far East had been astonishing. Besides China, the vast archipelago south and east of Singapore attracted men like Captain Lingard in their quest for rattans and *gutta percha*. Most of these islands were nominally under Dutch rule, its shipping under the Netherland flag, but the great forested littoral of Borneo, populated by fiercely independent and piratical 'sea-people', beckoned the most adventurous spirits. In the 1840s the son of a judge in the East India Company's Bengal civil administration, James Brooke, achieved the position of hereditary rajah of Sarawak. Brooke had served in the Company's army and been severely wounded in action.[1] After long convalescence he resigned his commission and conceived the romantic plan of trading in the eastern archipelago in his brig, the *Findlay*. This proved disastrous, but the death of his father enabled him to buy a large schooner, the *Royalist*, which in wearing the white ensign of the Royal Yacht Squadron and mounting six 6-pounder guns, had all the appearance of a small man-of-war. Brooke and the *Royalist* arrived at Kuching on the Rejang River in Sarawak on 15 August 1839 with the declared intention of collecting botanical specimens and surveying the Borneo coast. Brooke, however, became embroiled in war, supporting the Sultan of Brunei against a rebellion, and was consequently appointed Rajah of the province of Sarawak. Here he raised the status of the Dyak people, who he conceived to be poorly treated by their Malay overlords, established an economy which threatened the traditional way of life of a section of the coastal population and, following a visit by Captain Henry Keppel of HMS *Dido*, secured the Royal Navy's assistance in extirpating the *orang laut* – or 'sea-people' – who had preyed on trade, both indigenous and foreign, for generations. Brooke and Keppel's actions drew

Sarawak and northern Borneo closer under the British wing, opened up trade and enhanced Singapore's already formidable economical position in the region, Keppel's name being remembered in the long quayside later constructed as the island's port at Telok Blanga.

Following the Treaty of Nanking and the acquisition of Hong Kong, mercantile agitations for greater trade along the Chinese coast continued. Despite the access to China conceded by the treaty ports established in 1842 and the prosperity thereof, European and American traders were still excluded from the markets of North China, ever the objective of the British with their traditional woollen manufactures to dispose of. Opium remained the defining profitable commodity, but the quantity of manufactured goods for which perceived markets existed in the north fomented an unrelenting pressure on the Chinese to supplement the concessions of 1842 by something more. Several factors now conspired to bring this about, the first of which had been the weakening of Imperial Manchu authority consequent upon the events of the conflict of 1839–42, which had actually delivered all the demands which Lord Macartney had presented to Peking in 1797. The shock of armed intervention by the British had literally shaken the foundations of the Peacock Throne, and this was further troubled by the Taiping Rebellion of 1856, which led directly to its fall in 1911.[2]

While in Macartney's day Britain had been quite unable to press its will upon the Chinese state, half a century later she was not merely demonstrably capable of, but increasingly minded to do so, thanks to her own growing sense of imperial mission and national self-confidence. There were several subsidiary influences, one of which was the accession of a new Emperor, Hien-Feng, who, while supressing the Taiping rebels, wished to reassert Manchu pre-eminence over the *fan kwai*.

To this explosive mixture two further changes introduced at the local level the oxygen to which only ignition was required. These were, firstly, the removal by the Treaty of Nanking of the intermediary lubrications of the Co-Hong merchants hitherto essential to the transactions of Sino-European trade; and secondly, a supplementary treaty of 1844 which had guaranteed British seafarers from arrest. Thus, when on 8 October 1856 a small Chinese *lorcha*[3] named the *Arrow*, which by virtue of coming from Hong Kong flew the British red ensign and was commanded by a young Briton called Thomas Kennedy, was boarded by an armed party of Manchu soldiers who tore down the British flag, the spark was provided. The incident, minor in itself, was to start what history knows either as The Arrow War or the Second Opium War, which is a complete misnomer as the conflict that followed was not about opium at all but about the opening of markets. As J.M. Scott points out, European and American:

> merchants wanted to be able to go out and sell direct to the people, instead of being restricted… Opium, being small in bulk and high in value, and with a continually growing circle of ever faithful clients, never suffered in this way. Legal or not, it could look after itself.[4]

Nor was the incident of the *Arrow* of sufficient moment to have occasioned a single death, other than it produced a clash of such disparate civilisations that if the *Arrow* had not been the *casus belli* another would have arisen. Wrongs existed on both sides, but, since they intimately involve a British-flagged merchantman, the circumstances require a mention. The *Arrow* was a small coasting vessel owned by a Chinese Hong merchant and was in all respects Chinese, except that she had been registered at Hong Kong for a year under arrangements pertaining at the time. She therefore carried a British master, wore the British ensign and was, ostensibly, British. Kennedy had taken her to Canton to load a cargo and had gone ashore to arrange this when the armed Chinese boarded. Their pretext for doing so was to arrest a member of the *Arrow*'s Chinese crew who had been recognised as a pirate. The Manchu soldiers carried the entire crew into captivity and, although both Kennedy and the British consul at Canton, Harry Parkes, attempted to obtain their release, they failed.

Parkes, who disliked the Imperial Commissioner, Yeh Ming-ch'en, for the obstructions placed in the way of his consular duties, pressed the matter on Hong Kong where the British governor, Sir John Bowring, took up the case with Yeh. The Chinese crew were under the protection of the British flag, Bowring maintained, and the Chinese had no right to seize the *lorcha*, in all of which particulars Bowring was right in principle. The trouble was that the *Arrow*'s temporary British registry had expired on 27 September, and while Commissioner Yeh was wrong to detain innocent Chinese, he was not wrong to do so in the sense that Bowring insinuated. Moreover, Yeh had a well-known prejudice against the tricks foreigners got up to, and politely informed Bowring that 'when Chinese subjects build for themselves vessels, foreigners should not sell registers to them, for if this be done it will occasion confusion...' Bowring, however, defensively argued that since Yeh 'had no knowledge of the expiry of the license', he had been guilty of an act of provocation. An apology was demanded, making, in J.M. Scott's phrase, 'a major issue of it none the less'. Unfortunately Bowring had an eager accomplice in the person of Rear Admiral Sir Michael Seymour, commander-in-chief of the British naval forces in the China station. The two men conceived in consequence that the British nation had been insulted and launched an attack upon Canton.

Beyond observing that Seymour's force was eventually joined by the French, attacked the Taku forts in North China, occupied Peking and burned the Imperial Summer Palace in an act of reprehensible vandalism, the dreadful details of The Arrow War need not detain us further. Neither need the outcry raised against 'Sir John Bowring's War' at home, though it was vociferous. It was in its outcome that it was of immense commercial importance.

Although Britain assisted in the suppression of the Taiping rebels, Emperor Hien-Feng died soon after this further dynastic humiliation and China began her long and painful disintegration. During the hostilities there were hundreds of innocent casualties, almost all of whom, in such a one-sided conflict, were Chinese. However, there were a few civilians caught up from the other side, most notably aboard the British coastal steamer *Thistle* whose Chinese crew mutinied while on a passage from

Canton to Hong Kong. Eleven Europeans, passengers and crew were decapitated by mutineers who wore the badge of Commissioner Yeh.

By the Treaty of Tientsin (Tianjan), signed on 26 June 1858, Peking was obliged to pay huge sums in reparation and accept foreign ambassadors, but China was at last brought into the international pale, ending centuries of isolation. At a more pragmatic level, the Kowloon Peninsula opposite Hong Kong island was ceded on a lease to Great Britain, while eleven further Treaty Ports were obtained, of which Chefoo lay on the north coast of the Shantung peninsula and Newchwang on the Gulf of Liotang, while Tientsin itself, at the head of Gulf of Pech-hli, was only fifty miles from Peking. Furthermore, the Chinese Government removed its prohibition on the importation of opium and agreed to set up a Maritime Customs Service under a British Inspector–General.

Hostilities were not quite over, however, for when in June 1859 the first foreign diplomats arrived off Tientsin to take up their duties in the Chinese capital, the Chinese refused them permission to land, seizing one of them. It was this provocation that led to the bombardment of the Taku forts and the appalling looting of Peking. Matters were brought to a close in 1860, by which time the important reform of the Chinese customs, insofar as they affected shipping, were under way. The Inspector-General was Robert Hart, a former Chinese-speaking British consular official who had served in several ports including Canton and Ningpo. Hart's administration is generally and genuinely regarded as a model of efficiency and probity. Hart recruited many merchant officers as inspectors partly because a subsidiary responsibility of the Imperial Customs was the Chinese lighthouse and buoyage service, which improved coastal navigation and increased the safety of shipping on the China coast. The Imperial Customs Service itself contributed hugely to the imperial revenues and to the approbation of Peking. Hart eradicated corruption at a stroke, doing much to erode the endemic suspicion of foreigners infecting the mandarins with whom he came into contact. He was much respected by everyone, and he set very high standards for himself and his staff. Following his acting appointment in 1859 he was confirmed Inspector-General of Foreign Customs in 1863, retaining this position until his retirement in 1907, loaded with British and Chinese honours in spite of the xenophobic sentiment manifested by the Boxer Rebellion of 1900.[5]

This was largely attributable to the inroads made by the Western powers, Russia and Japan, all of which had an increasing interest in what Britain had prised from the Manchu grasp. In the following fifty years they were all to secure more extra-territorial Treaty Ports upon each of which they stamped their own national characteristics – the British at Wei-Hai-Wai, the Germans at Kiaochow and Tsingtao, and the Russians on Port Arthur (Dairen). Apart from Hong Kong, which remained a British Crown colony to the end, the most important of these acquisitions was Shanghai. Here international extra-territorial concessions supported several Westernised settlements with their own legislature, judiciary and police.

Although Shanghai lies some miles up its tributary, the Huang-pu, the great city dominates the trade of the lower Yangtze-Kiang. Here commerce flourished and, even before the arrival of Alfred Holt's first steamer *Agamemnon* in 1866, both American and British paddle-steamers were operating on these rivers. These shoal-draught craft with their smart, uniformed Chinese crews and immaculate paintwork, penetrated 500 miles up the Yangtze to Hankow, the Treaty Port set most deeply in China's heartland. Full of shifting shoals and variable channels through which the great river raced when in spate, these tortuous waters required powerful little ships, and skill and local knowledge in their handling. The traffic benefited enormously from the paralysis caused by the Taiping Rebellion as there was, for some years, scarcely a junk or *lorcha* trading on the water. Instead, with the national ensign of their flag-state conspicuously displayed on their topsides, the powerful foreign steamers ploughed the yellow *loëss*-bearing rivers on their regular services. Commanded by Westerners, all business was conducted by Chinese *schroffs*, *chinchews* and compradors who, like the Hong merchants before them, acted as intermediaries, but without the power, wealth or status of their predecessors.

There were three principal steam-ship operators, the same three great merchant houses that had operated from Macao and Canton: the American firm of Russell & Co., and the two British firms of Dent and Jardine, Matheson.[6] Released from their long dependence upon the Chinese merchants of the Co-Hong, all three seized every opportunity to expand their businesses, gradually eschewing the carriage of opium in all but small — and now entirely legitimate — consignments. As related, in May 1866 the failure of their bankers, Overend, Gurney, brought down the house of Dent, and for a brief period it looked as though Russell's Shanghai Steam Navigation Co. was going to dominate the river. The Jardine, Matheson operation was less well funded (though both rival companies welcomed and received Chinese investment), owning only two steamers though chartering several others. Then, in 1872, following the move of his business as a forwarding agent from Liverpool to London, John Swire founded a new company called the China Navigation Co., raising all the necessary capital in Britain. Swire had visited Shanghai in early 1867 and realised that his business forwarding woollen and cotton goods would benefit from his own agency in the Far East. To undertake this he went into partnership with Richard Butterfield, a Yorkshire woollen manufacturer, and the partners also took on the agency business of Alfred Holt's new blue-funnelled Ocean Steam Ship Co. Swire shrewdly suggested to Holt that, 'having been immediately struck by the prospects of river shipping,' that 'a Yangtze company might be set up as a branch and feeder of the Blue Funnel Line.' The idea found favour with Alfred Holt who, with his brother Philip, signed up with other investors including Harrison & Crosfield, Ismay, Imrie & Co. and John Scott of Greenock, the builder of Holt's first steamers. Swire's man-on-the-spot, William Lang, recruited two experienced river masters, Captains Martin and MacQueen, with Henry Endicott, a Chinese-speaking American, as his shipping-clerk and comprador, the last two poached from Russell's service.

Jardine, Matheson, meanwhile, reorganised their steamers, relying on their own comprador, Tong King-sing, who, having been educated at Hong Kong's Morrison Institute, spoke English 'like a Briton'. Before joining Jardine, Matheson, Tong had served as interpreter for the Hong Kong police and Hart's Customs Service. He was later to head the China Merchant's Steam Navigation Co. which shared the river and coastal services, but he never relinquished his shares in Jardine, Matheson. The combined effect of the British companies, both of which possessed more able cargo-acquiring compradors than Russell & Co., saw off the Americans in a fiercely competitive price-war. In 1873 twenty-seven steamers operated on these river and coastal services, which extended beyond the Yangtze basin, from the Gulf of Pech-hli in the north to Ningpo and Foochow in the south. This traffic greatly benefited Chinese trade.[7] In the decade ending in 1874 China's imports rose by 39.3 per cent, her exports by 37.1 per cent. Both Butterfield & Swire's China Navigation Co. and Jardine, Matheson's China Coast Steam Navigation Co. would develop an ocean-going fleet to complement their coastal services along the littoral of China, with Butterfield & Swire's coastal steamers dominating commerce south of Shanghai towards Hong Kong and beyond. Here they would load bean-cake for Chinese ports, thereby acquiring the nickname 'bean-cakers', while Jardine's plied north of Shanghai up to Tientsin. The China Navigation Co. also showed an early interest in carrying Muslims returning from the *Haj* and the *Newchang*, picking up pilgrims returning from Mecca on her way out to the Orient from her builders in 1877 before settling into the bean-cake trade. Both companies also benefited from acting as commission agents and loading-brokers, Jardine, Matheson from acting for John Willis, MacGregor, Gow, and others, and Butterfield & Swire from the thriving agency business with Alfred Holt's rapidly expanding line of steamers.

Indeed, such was the energy of Holt's remarkable company that in the summer of 1869, a few months *before* the opening of the Suez Canal, six steamers had seized the palm from the tea-clippers, and four of them bore those distinctive blue funnels. Captain Isaac Middleton had taken the *Agamemnon* all the way up the treacherous Yangtze-Kiang to Hangow to load the first of the season's clip, leaving on 9 June and passing Gravesend on 25 August after a passage of seventy-seven days. This not only beat the steamer *Erl King*'s eighty-five days from the same port but doubled her lading, while the *Achilles*'s sixty-two days from Foochow was convincingly better than the West India & Pacific Steam Navigation Co.'s *West Indian*, which made the run in seventy-eight.[8] Two Holt steamers, the *Ajax* and the brand new *Nestor*, left from Shanghai, enabling Holt to write on 13 October that 'A very great pride and pleasure to me this year has been the almost perfect performance of four of our China steamers with new tea.' This achievement of Holt's steamers has been entirely eclipsed by the idea that it was the opening of the Suez Canal in November 1869, which terminated the glorious but brief era of the China tea-clipper.

The arrival of the American clipper *Oriental* in the Thames with a cargo of China tea in 1850 — which concluded Chapter One — provoked the construction over the next twenty years of a number of fast ships for the sole purpose of carrying tea, producing the so-called 'extreme-clipper', which enjoyed a short hey-day in the 1860s. Apart from its vogue as a favoured beverage of the worthy and necessary Temperance League, tea increased in popularity as a drink among all classes of the British public

— in part due to its more accessible price, a slow increase in general prosperity, better distribution and the quantities in which it now arrived in London. In short, tea was a cargo of some distinction; but it was a difficult commodity to carry over 14,000 miles of indifferent sea, for it was not only ruined by mould if dampened but was easily tainted if brought into contact with other strong-smelling cargoes. Moreover, while it was capable of commanding good freight-rates, its high market-value depended entirely upon its quality on discharge, and more than one cargo, rushed home to capture a high price, was found to have been adulterated by last year's crop. To ensure that they had a first-class product to market — for to do otherwise would wreck their reputations and their businesses — the London tea-merchants offered a premium on the first cargoes arriving in London after the annual harvest. This was often sold using a clipper's name as a brand, if she had become well known thanks to a series of fast passages, and while at one end of the market tea was widely drunk among the poor, to be drinking the first tea of the season became a mark of fashionable distinction.

In the days of the East Indiaman the carrier held all the cards, thanks to the East India Company's monopoly. Curiously, tea matures in flavour when properly stored for some time, and it was customary to maintain a large stock just in case 'the China fleet' was delayed and the supply-chain disrupted. Thirty years later matters were quite otherwise, and, in order to satisfy the complexities of these demands, including that of fashion, the fast sailing ship underwent refinement. Apart from her speed, which demanded a lofty sail plan and adequate stability with a light cargo, she had to be tight, and not admit water. She did not need to be large for any delay in loading was not to be borne, and her place in the queue of waiting ships depended upon her reputation for speed. For this she needed a crack commander and crew, of which the former was the more difficult to find. She had to be capable of sailing well in the light breezes of the tropics and of enduring typhoon and cyclone. Since the tea harvest dictated the time of her departure, she must go to windward well when working against the prevailing monsoon in the South China Sea, and when confronting the strong westerlies homeward-bound off the Cape. Clearly, much was demanded of ship and crew.

Tea-clippers were designed by the most distinguished naval architects of the day and built in the most advanced shipyards. Some were owned by firms whose names are familiar to us: Joseph Somes; George Thompson; Killick, Martin; T. & W. Smith, and Henderson, but there were others, including single ship owners, at least one Parsee house and one London bank, Baring Brothers. One name associated closely with tea-clippers was that of John Willis & Son. Although we have remarked Willis's acquisition of *The Tweed* and her employment on the Australian run, the firm's investment in the tea-trade is of interest.

The founder of the firm, John Willis senior, was born about 1788 in Eyemouth to parents 'only able to endow their son with an iron constitution and an indomitable will'. On the early death of his indigent father and an altercation with his guardian, John Willis went to sea in a coaster and was soon engaged in the West India trade. He made himself useful and indulged in a little private speculation, as was usual, rising in rank until he was made mate. Coming up Channel, his ship ran ashore and her master and crew abandoned her; Willis, however, remained on board, prevented plundering, sent a message to her owners and saved her cargo once the weather had moderated. Receiving a sum of money from the underwriters and the offer of a command from his owners, Willis invested the cash in his new ship, married, and soon afterwards settled in Wapping where he was one of a small community of north-Britons connected with the shipping industry. He rapidly gained a reputation as a hard-driving ship-master and was famous for a voyage to Demerara made in 1835 where he disdained anchoring in The Downs during a strong westerly gale but stretched across to France and then caught a slant of wind that carried him down Channel. Having loaded sugar, Willis headed home only to find in the North Atlantic that a series of depressions had kept westerly winds blowing for days on end. Willis headed up Channel, doubled the South Foreland and found the anchorage full of vessels, several of which he had left there weeks before.[9] By the 1850s he was a ship-owner in his own right, owning the _John Willis_, the _Borderer_, _Janet Willis_ and the _St Abbs_, of which his eldest son, also named John, was in command. He was also building the _Merse_ at Sunderland and, most unusual for the time, he 'never gave an order for a new ship until he was able to pay for her', nor would he 'allow any of his captains to have a share in their ships'. Willis avoided 'all entangling alliances with ship-brokers, merchants and tradesmen'. When his homeward ships arrived at Gravesend, Willis met them himself to take over from the master who was sent to enter them inwards at the Customs House so that bulk could be broken as soon as the ship had berthed. Here Willis would act as his own ship's husband, being particularly attentive to his favourite and newest ship, the _Lammermuir_ of 1856. He died sitting in his garden in Clapton Square on 10 July 1862. 'Almost at the same time his beloved _Lammermuir_ was wrecked in the Gaspar Strait.'[10]

Tea was grown on peasant small-holdings, and picking began in April, the first crop consisting of 'two leaves and a bud'. The second harvesting of leaves was gathered in July, and it was only these two prime pickings that supplied China's foreign trade, the two subsequent harvests being reserved for home consumption. Drying was done locally, and whether the tea was 'black' or 'green' depended upon the method used. The former was largely shipped to Britain, Pekoe being among the most expensive of the _show-chun_ or first spring harvest, but Kaisow and Bohea were also prime products, with Congou and Souchong teas among the cheaper second crops. The green teas were mostly exported to the United States, Gunpowder being the best, with Hyson a green tea of the second picking.

Tea exports centred on Hangkow, which was largely inaccessible to sailing-vessels as it required a long upstream tow — hence Middleton's triumph in taking the _Agamemnon_ there in 1869 — and much of the distribution from the drying areas to the ports was by way of China's vast, neglected system of inland waterways. This made Shanghai a centre for both loading tea and for importing the British manufactures brought out in the clippers. It was also possible at Shanghai to 'top-off' a tea cargo with another high-value cargo: silk. Equally suitable for both imports and exports,

Canton still laboured under some of the old restrictions, and while Congou in particular – being the most widely sold of the teas in Britain owing to its price – tended
to be shipped out of Canton, sampans and junks easily brought it down the Pearl
River to the free-port of Hong Kong. However, since the best black teas were grown
in Fukien province and could be transported to the waiting clippers a month earlier
than deliveries to Canton, Hangkow or Shanghai, the Pagoda anchorage at Foochow
on the Min River became the focus for the most competitive aspect of the tea-trade.
During the 1860s Foochow was exporting over half of China's tea, the total having
doubled between 1853 and 1863, and it is worth noting that it trebled once steam-
vessels had taken over the trade.

Once the tea had arrived for storage at the ports, a lengthy process of negotiating began. The commission agencies – of which Jardine, Matheson & Co. was the
chief – bought on behalf of consignees from whom they took instructions, but they
would also buy and ship cargoes on their own account. Bargaining was carried out
by compradors and *schroffs*, but, increasingly, direct contact between Europeans and
Chinese was necessary, since the indigenous traffickers were less able to dispose of
goods coming from the West. These dealings relied upon the *chaa-szes*, or tea-tasters,
to determine the quality of the individual shipments, and upon their recommendations depended the wholesale price of the tea and the closure of the deal. Even before
the Suez Canal was opened, but after Holt's steamers were on the scene and the
riverine paddlers could speed deliveries to Shanghai and Hong Kong, the telegraph
that aided communication also facilitated long-distance interference, so that Phineas
Ryrie, an employee of the commission agent Turner & Co. at Hong Kong, described
being tired of his day's work which consisted of 'daily steamers and hourly telegrams'.

But this was only part of the problem, for it was then necessary to select a ship and
negotiate a favourable freight-rate, and much of this was conducted by the masters
of the ships, one reason why the selection of a good clipper-commander was such a
tricky business. The faster a ship was reputed to be, or the better a master was known
for safe, rapid passages, the more favourable a rate he and his agent could secure. As
an inducement, on top of the premium, some owners would add a *douceur* of £100
to the master bringing home the 'first clip'. Despite being a very cut-throat business,
clippers were often kept waiting months, particularly after steamers had made inroads
into the trade. The one evil of these transactions insofar as a ship's owners were concerned was that, as of old, the outward traffic was less profitable than the homeward.
This imbalance now had to be borne by the individual owner, so a master was pressed
to maximise his ship's earning ability, and he accomplished this by making intermediate coasting passages between discharging an outward general cargo and loading tea
for home. Thus the complaint of Apprentice Symondson aboard Captain Ferguson's
full-rigged ship *Inverness* at Foochow in August 1873 is not unusual:

> Over five weeks has passed since our arrival, and we still remain without a freight…
> we began to speculate freely upon our destination, aided by the customary unfath-
> omable rumours. One day it was reported that we were going to Formosa to load

coals for Borneo; then that the captain had accepted a charter of tea back to Sydney. At last it transpired that he had arranged to take a native cargo of 'poles' [tree trunks] to Shanghai, in the hopes of securing a tea-freight there for London. The owners [Grant & Co.] had written to him, attacking him severely for his want of success; and being a thoroughly conscientous (sic) man, he seemed to feel it.

But fast ships, anticipating an early cargo and generally known as 'going-ships', often staked everything upon this and arrived at Foochow flying light.[11] Many carried permanent ballast, up to 100 tons of iron kentledge, upon which another 200-250 tons of clean, impermeable shingle was spread, 'porous sandstone or anything approaching it being inadmissable'.[12] Overlaid with a dunnage floor to enable the maximum number of tea-chests to be stowed, the first tiers consisted of old or green tea, shipped at a low freight-rate and intended to act as a barrier between the main cargo and the shingle ballast. Elsewhere the pump-wells were well protected with dunnage and the loading proceeded with great care in the hands of Chinese stevedores. Aboard the *Inverness* Symondson recalled:

> We had cleared up the hold, levelled the ballast, and already had some two hundred half-chests of Oolong stowed away, I being made tallyman. As the chests leave the lighter or 'chop', a small bamboo stick is wedged in between the cane lashings [lifting the sling of chests]. This the tallyman withdraws just before they slide into the hold, and when he has collected one hundred he makes an entry in his tally-book, and returns the bamboos whence they came.

The holds and 'tween decks were filled to capacity, the last chests in each tier being jammed in tightly. 'Each gang of stowers included an enormously fat man whose job it was to get in the "key" chest in each tier' by jumping heavily on it, after which canvas was spread so that any water leaking through the deck ran off down the ship's side into the bilge from where a regular routine of pumping was maintained by the duty-watch at sea. Delivery in lighters and sampans, which secured alongside the anchored ships often in considerable numbers, could be tortuously slow, particularly in vessels loading late, like the *Inverness*:

> One day would see perhaps 200 to 250 half-chests stowed away in the hold, while the following day and the next…would pass away without any 'chop' coming alongside. Each 'chop' carries the flag of its shipping house, so that whenever one hove in sight with its huge mat sail, we could tell at once to what vessel she was bound. The time occupied in loading a ship with tea in Foochow ranges from a fortnight to two months and even more.

Such delays in loading less than 1,000 tons deadweight were clearly frustrating to the masters and crews eager to get away for London. The time was used for the benefit of the ship, all the clippers being titivated to an extraordinary degree, vying with each other in their polished brass, varnished brightwork and, in several cases, the extravagance of their painted bulwark panelling. The smartness of a ship's boats, invariably conveying the master ashore and pulled by the apprentices, along with other inter-ship competitiveness, made Foochow in particular a lively place. For the slower ships, the long wait seemed endless, and in Symondson's case the *Inverness* lost her chance of a homeward cargo altogether.

Matters could, however, be differently arranged. *Cumshaw*, that semi-licit oiling of the works of commerce, could produce startling results and records exist of clippers being loaded at speed, one in Shanghai stowing 8,000 chests of tea and 1,141 bales of silk in two days, the actual cargo-time being seventeen hours. The ballasting and stowage, and consequent trim of a clipper upon which the speed of the voyage depended, were closely supervised by the master and mate. In 1869 Joseph Somes's very fine-lined *Leander* was loaded as deep as Captain Petherick could allow, yet space remained in her hold. Despite this she took 103 days to reach London, leaving Foochow on 1 July and arriving on 12 October. However, she was home with her cargo before the fastest ship that year, the *Sir Lancelot* under Captain R. Robinson, which, although taking only eighty-nine days and making a record passage, did not arrive until 14 October, having left Foochow on 17 July. The earliest clipper to arrive that year was Captain W.H. Burgoyne's *Titania*, which was under way from Shanghai on 16 June and in London by 22 September, taking ninety-eight days on the slightly longer passage from the Huang-pu, while Captain Kemball's famous *Thermopylae*, also from Foochow, took ninety-one days, arriving in the Thames on 2 October. Unfortunately Captain Middleton's steamer *Agamemnon* had beaten them all, coming by way of the Cape of Good Hope, as the clippers had done, having left Hangkow on 9 June.

With the first tea arriving at Foochow in sampans around mid-June, the clippers leaving in the summer months had the south-west monsoon to contend with in the South China Sea; by the time the last of the harvest arrived in November, the favourable north-east monsoon had arrived. Added to these reliable considerations, the months of July to October were the unpredictable typhoon season. Curiously, one of the last ships to arrive with the 1869 crop was the *Solent*, which did not sail until 2 March 1870 and arrived on 3 June, two days before the *Taeping* left Canton with the new year's crop. Unlike the clippers leaving in the summer months of the previous year, Captain Meldrum had the favourable north-east monsoon and the *Solent*'s passage time was only ninety-three days. By way of counter-point, the longest passage times taken to bring the 1869 crop to London were those of the *Lennox Castle* with 136 days and the *Corea*, though there were many others between 120 and 130 days. Captain Carr had the advantage of the favourable monsoon when he headed homeward from Shanghai in the *Corea*, and Captain Talbot had struggled all the way up to Hangkow with the *Lennox Castle* under tow, but his passage time against the south-west monsoon was not reckoned until he was passing Woosung at the confluence of the Huang-pu and the Yangtze-Kiang. One other clipper that was towed up to Hangkow that year, Captain G.Gaye's *Eliza Shaw*, took 123 days from Woosung.

The following year Captain Burgoyne took *Titania* up to Hangkow, leaving on 18 June, passing Woosung on 13th and taking 112 days against the monsoon, all of which gives one some idea of the vagaries of the tea-trade and the unpredictability of the vital homeward passage.

This was not merely complicated by the prevailing monsoon and the possibility of being overtaken by a typhoon, but by the choice of homeward route. Captain Kemball's homeward track of the *Thermopylae* in 1869, when no less than fifty-three first-class clippers left Chinese ports for London, was against the south-west monsoon. Kemball made a series of enormous tacks down the South China Sea, leaving the Min River on 3 July heading eastwards, to the north of Taiwan until south of Okinawa. He then put about onto the port tack and, passing north of the Philippines by way of the Bashi Channel on a heading of WSW, passed south of the feared Pratas Reef and north of the Paracel Islands to fetch the coast of Annam (Vietnam) near Tourane (Da Nang) in eight days. It was the practice of the skilled clipper commanders, when close in to a coast, to work the day, land and nocturnal sea breezes to keep their ships moving. As the land fell away to the west towards the Mekong Delta, the *Thermopylae* came offshore on the starboard tack and headed south, dodging east of the extensive Natuna Islands and raising Tanjung Datu on the Borneo coast after a further eight days. Kemball then had lighter and fluctuating winds and, having passed safely through the hazardous Gaspar Strait, he passed Anjer on 28 July and rapidly cleared Java Head to enter the Indian Ocean.

There was another route, known as 'the Eastern Passage' favoured by the old East Indiamen, which was to head east from the China coast and run east of the Philippines as far south as the Gilolo Strait or the Pitt Passage, thread through the islands west of Ceram and then turn south-west along the north coast of Timor and so into the Indian Ocean. This was the route used by Gaye in *Eliza Shaw* that same year to avoid the south-west monsoon, but equally it might be used as an outward route against the north-easterly monsoon, and was taken by Captain George Moodie bound for Shanghai in the *Cutty Sark* on her maiden voyage. Once in the Indian Ocean the south-east trades were sought and it was on the long 'flying-fish' leg to the vicinity of Mauritius that a ship like *Thermopylae* flew with every sail that her spars could support.

On this homeward voyage a hard-driving master would hardly sleep. Many catnapped in a 'hammock-chair' triced up in the mizzen rigging from where they kept an eye on wind and weather. Apart from tending the sails, one obsession was with trim, and Captain John Keay of the *Ariel* kept a large, wooden box filled with lengths of chain snotters and other iron gear. This was dragged about *Ariel*'s flush main-deck, adjusting her trim to capitalise on the prevailing conditions.

In contrast to the sluggish pace of loading, the demanding market caused speedy discharging, especially when a clipper berthed close to the tea-merchants' premises in Mincing Lane. An extreme example of this was the unloading of the *Fiery Cross* in St Katherine's Dock in 1864. The energetic Captain Richard Robinson brought his ship into the dock after a passage of 114 days from Foochow at 04.00 on 20 September.

The hatches were opened and by 10.00 the following morning the *Fiery Cross* had been emptied of all 14,000 chests of tea.

The *Fiery Cross* was the second clipper so-named, both being designed by William Rennie. The first had stranded on an uncharted reef near Investigator Shoals in the South China Sea on 4 March 1860. Captain Duncan and his crew took to the boats and reached Labuan on the Borneo coast. The second *Fiery Cross*, of 702 tons, was under construction at Liverpool for John Campbell of Glasgow when the first was wrecked. Fitted with old-fashioned stern windows reminiscent of a Blackwaller, her hull was long and slender and proved one of the fastest and most successful British tea-clippers. She had steel lower masts and Cunningham's roller reefing on her deep, three-reefed topsails, later extended to her topgallants in 1864 when her main top-sail was doubled. On her first voyage under Captain John Dallas who had left her older namesake to supervise her building, *Fiery Cross* loaded 870,000lb of tea from Foochow at £5 per ton, plus an extra 10s if she arrived home first. This she accomplished with ease, and the following year under Captain Richard Robinson she trumped the *Flying Spur* to earn the 1862 premium when Robinson accepted a tow for £100 which Captain Ryrie of the *Flying Spur* had refused. In 1863 the premium rose to £1 and Robinson repeated his success.

Richard Robinson, like Kemball, Enright and Keay, was among the handful of crack clipper commanders, and Campbell had lured him from the Brocklebanks' employ, where he had commanded their *Veronica*. To Robinson's chagrin, he was beaten in the 'great race of 1866', which we shall come to shortly, and leaving the *Fiery Cross*, took command of *Sir Lancelot*, having been persuaded to change employment again by her owner, James MacCunn. MacCunn paid him handsomely, regarding him as 'the best man I ever had in any ship, and I knew he had got the best racing results out of *Sir Lancelot*'.[13] Unfortunately Robinson suffered a dismasting outward bound in December 1866, and was fortunate not to lose the ship on the island of Ushant to leeward, but he struggled in to Falmouth where his ship was re-rigged with new spars of Oregon pine in only six weeks, fully justifying MacCunn's assessment of Robinson as 'a fine fellow in every way with dash, daring and energy quite exceptional'. The *Sir Lancelot* picked up a cargo at Shanghai and, despite coming home by way of the Eastern Passage, Robinson managed to overhaul every ship that had left ahead of him except *Taeping* under Captain Dowdy – which arrived nine days earlier than the *Sir Lancelot* - *Ariel*, Captain John Keay, and *Fiery Cross* under Kirkup, both of which arrived the same day.

As she overtook other ships, the *Sir Lancelot* was an impressive sight, as Apprentice Frederick Paton recalled of 11 August 1867, as she passed Ryrie's *Flying Spur* off Algoa Bay, South Africa:

[I]t was a stormy day and we were carrying what was thought by us to be a heavy press of sail…whole topsails and courses with outer jib, whilst other ships in company were close-reefed, when we sighted a clipper ship on the other tack carrying three topgallant sails and flying jib. This was an enormous amount of sail considering the wind and she could not have possibly done so but the swell was running abaft her beam whilst it was right ahead with us…as soon as she got near enough, we began signalling; she proved to be the *Sir Lancelot* from Hangkow, Capt. Robinson… She crossed our bows and just then, when the signalling was going on, her helmsman, paying too much attention to us, allowed her to come up into the wind and get [taken] aback. We thought that she would have been dismasted, she heeling right over and getting sternway. However, they managed to get some sail off her and she righted, but it was a close thing. As the ships were fairly close we could see all that took place on board of her; we saw Capt. Robinson knock down the man at the wheel and jump on him!

And well he might, for to have dismasted his new command twice in one voyage would have strained the quality of MacCunn's mercy beyond tolerance. Richard Robinson left the *Sir Lancelot* at the end of this voyage upon the sudden death of his wife. The ship continued to do well under subsequent masters, though the opening of the Suez Canal greatly altered her trading pattern and in the 1874–75 season, the year that the steamer *Glenartney* carried the tea home in forty-four days, the *Sir Lancelot* brought two tea-cargoes home from China under Captain Felgate. In 1880 MacCunn chartered her to the Indian house of Visram Ibrahim who bought her outright in 1886 and put her in the hands of Captain C. W. Brebner. Of Eurasian stock, Brebner ran her in the Indian Ocean maintained 'like a yacht'. He survived four cyclones in the little ship but she did not survive the fifth and was reported to have foundered off the Sandheads on 1 October 1895 after sale to Persian owners when deeply laden with a cargo of salt from the Red Sea.

The remarkable homeward 'race' of 1866 came to epitomise the era. Its remarkable finish involved just four ships, the *Ariel*, *Taeping*, *Fiery Cross* and *Serica*, though there were fifty-six British clippers loading tea that season for London. All but the *Ellen Rodger* came home safely and none of the passages of the majority were exceptional.[14] Among those loading were the cream of the masters, including Keay, Robinson, Innes and Mackinnon, of which we shall hear more, but also Kemball of the *Yang-tsze*, though better known as master of the *Thermopylae* – which had yet to be built – Ryrie of the *Flying Spur*, Nutsford of the *Taitsing* and McDougall in *Sir Lancelot*.

That year the tea arrived on 24 May, early enough to obviate the usual bargaining. Surrounded by sampans and lighters, the *Ariel* took in her flooring of 391 chests and 220 half-chests, her coolies working night and day to get all 1,230,900lb of it inboard. The other 'going-ships' worked likewise. The handful of first-class clippers that would make so exciting a race of it left Foochow before the month was out: the *Ariel* on 28 May, the *Fiery Cross* on the 29th, the *Taeping* and *Serica* on the 30th, and the *Taitsing* on the 31st. Robinson in the *Fiery Cross*, with his customary energy, had overtaken the *Serica* on the outward passage and had put in an intermediate voyage to Rangoon and back before loading in haste among the cracks. It was customary for the masters to engage in private bets, usually a beaver hat, and occasionally the crews would follow suit. On this occasion the companies of the *Serica* and *Fiery Cross*, long locked in rivalry, are supposed to have bet a month's wages on the outcome.

Captain Keay got the *Ariel* away first, to drop down the Min River under the tow of the tug *Island Queen*. Notorious for her lack of power, the tug caused Keay several problems and he was obliged to anchor inside the bar of the Min, having missed the high-water. So anxious was Robinson to leave that the minute the last chest of tea was under hatches, he threw off the *Fiery Cross*'s moorings and, in David MacGregor's phrase, 'bolted without his papers and without signing bills of lading'. This action, which stole a march on the competition, was supposed to have infuri-ated Captain Innes of the *Serica* as *Fiery Cross* disappeared downstream towards the gorges behind a very taut tow-rope. That same evening, the 29th, the *Fiery Cross* passed the *Ariel* at anchor, crossed the bar, cast off her tug and was away under all possible sail. Keay, meanwhile, retrimmed the *Ariel* and finally crossed the bar fol-lowed by the *Serica* and *Taeping* under MacKinnon on the morning of the 30th. Even now Keay's evil luck held, for in taking off the *Ariel*'s pilot, the *Island Queen*'s boat capsized and the recovery of her crew and disembarkation of the pilot delayed *Ariel* so that both the *Serica* and *Taeping* were an hour ahead. Worse, Keay was fourteen hours behind Robinson. The others followed, led by *Taitsing*, and including Ryrie's *Flying Spur* and Kemball's *Yang-tsze*.

Having made the fastest run down the South China Sea, the *Fiery Cross* passed Anjer on 18 June and headed towards Mauritius. With the leading ships making days' runs in excess of 320 miles, *Fiery Cross* led past the Mascarene archipelago followed by *Ariel*, *Taeping*, *Serica* and *Taitsing*. Robinson ran in along the Natal coast to pick up the favourable Agulhas current but the others held offshore in the stronger winds which, although contrary, gave them legs. Here they encountered other ships: *Ariel* passed the *City of Bombay* and then Currie's *Tantallon Castle*. While *Fiery Cross* was still in the lead at the Cape, Keay's *Ariel* had clipped almost three days off Robinson's lead. *Taeping* passed the Cape next day — 16 July — with *Serica* following on the 19th and *Taitsing* on the 24th. By St Helena, *Taeping* was in the lead, with *Serica* catching-up *Fiery Cross*, and *Ariel* and *Taitsing* trailing, but shortly afterwards Keay found a fine wind and rapidly made ground with *Taitsing* also benefiting. By Ascension the order had changed again. The *Taeping* led, passing the island on 31 July, *Fiery Cross* and *Ariel* following next day with the *Serica* on 2 August. The *Taitsing* had dropped back, pass-ing Ascension on the 8th.

On 9 August *Taeping* and *Fiery Cross* were in sight of one other. Exchanging signals, they remained in distant company in light and failing winds until the 17th when, to the mortification of Robinson and his crew who wallowed in a calm, they watched a breeze fill the sails of the *Taeping* and waft her over the horizon. Carrying a wind further west, Keay's *Ariel* was in the lead as they approached the Cape Verde Islands, followed by *Taeping*, *Fiery Cross*, *Serica* and *Taitsing*, the last two having closed the dis-tance. On 29 August all of the first four — *Ariel*, *Fiery Cross*, *Taeping* and *Serica* — passed Flores, in the Azores. But Captain Nutsford of the *Taitsing* had further reduced the distance, proving — if proof were necessary — there was little to choose between any of these first-class ships and their crews: all depended upon nature, for *Taitsing* swept past Flores on 1 September.

Apart from one day of easterlies, the wind steadied from the westward, and at 01.30 on 5 September, Keay's lookouts caught the loom of the Bishop Rock light, westernmost reef of the Isles of Scilly. Then, at daybreak, Keay saw a vessel under a press of canvas on *Ariel's* starboard quarter. 'Instinct told me that it was *Taeping*,' Keay recalled to Basil Lubbock years later. In a strong WSW breeze the two ships ran up-Channel at 14 knots with studding sails set to the royals. They swept past the Lizard at 08.00, making their numbers to the Lloyd's signal station so that within minutes London was aware. At noon they passed Start Point; at 18.00 the crews swung the anchors over the side with Portland Bill abeam. The *Ariel* was close inshore, carrying the flood tide off St Catherine's lighthouse at 19.25, and midnight found her five miles south of Beachy Head. While the wind held strong, *Ariel* kept her lead, *Taeping* gaining in any slight lull. Coming up with the pilot station off Dungeness at 03.00, Keay hove *Ariel* to and burned the night signals for a pilot, watching anxiously as Captain Mackinnon in *Taeping* appeared to dodge inshore to reach the pilot first. At 05.30 the pilot-cutters approached and Keay at once bore away to pick up his pilot: twenty-five minutes later the pilot told him his was the first ship home.

The two clippers still vied with each other, however, as they sped round the South Foreland and headed up for The Downs. Shortly afterwards they were both compelled to signal for tugs, and here a march was stolen on Keay so that *Taeping* reached Gravesend just under an hour ahead of *Ariel*. Even now matters were not resolved, for they had to await the flood tide. *Ariel* arrived at Blackwall off the East India Dock lock at 21.00, while *Taeping*, heading upstream towards St Katherine's Dock, did not reach the locks until 22.00. But *Ariel* drew more water than her rival and had to wait, so that *Taeping* finally passed into her dock twenty minutes before *Ariel*.

Both masters having repeated their reports through Lloyd's at Deal, their owners agreed to prevent the tea-merchants reneging on the premium by arguing that there had been no clear winner. In the event the extra 10s per ton premium went to *Taeping* as the first vessel to berth, but the monies involved were split between the two owners and the two masters. As the tea-samples were being tossed ashore from *Ariel* and *Taeping* at midnight, *Serica* was being hauled into the West India Dock. Innes had brought her storming up the French coast, passed Deal at noon, caught the flood tide and scraped over the sill of the West India lock at 23.30 that same evening.

As for *Fiery Cross*, her luck had not quite deserted either her or Richard Robinson. She passed the Isle of Wight at 10.00 on 7 September. Then, with a westerly gale blowing by the time she passed Dover, Robinson was compelled to anchor in The Downs. Consequently *Fiery Cross* did not follow the *Taeping* into dock until 08.00 on Saturday the 8th. Twenty-four hours later Nutsford docked the *Taitsing*, all five home well ahead of any other clipper that season.

Despite this exciting climax, the total passage times were unremarkable, at ninety-nine days for the *Taeping* and *Serica*. The *Ariel* and *Taitsing* took 101, the *Fiery Cross* a day longer. Of the other cracks, the *Flying Spur* got away on 5 June and John Ryrie brought her in 122 days later; McDougall left Shanghai in *Sir Lancelot* on 2 July and made London on 5 November after 126 days, while Kemball left Foochow on 12

June and docked the *Yang-tsze* 127 days later.[15] Even this is not the end of the tale for already the steamers had the upper hand. Lost amid the hype was the sobering fact that A. & J. Inglis's auxiliary steam-vessel *Erl King*, having loaded at no less than £12 per ton – twice the rate of the clippers – left Foochow on 5 June, several days after the leaders. She was to berth on 25 August, fifteen days ahead of *Ariel*, *Taeping* and *Serica*.[16] The following year Holt's two steamers *Agamemnon* and *Ajax* loaded in Shanghai, *Ajax* with tea and silk, *Agamemnon* with over 2,000,000lb of tea. Although *Agamemnon's* propeller shaft broke when she was south of Hong Kong and Middleton had to sail back to the colony for repairs, *Ajax* arrived in the Thames three weeks before *Sir Lancelot*. Thus before the canal, the steamer had proved her speed, reliability and capacity to earn a greater return than the tea-clipper on her own turf.

However, typical of the quintet of first-class tea-clippers that caught the public imagination in 1866, the history of the composite ship *Ariel* also testifies to their vulnerability. She had been built by Robert Steele & Co. at Greenock in 1865 to a design by William Rennie, and was very similar to *Sir Lancelot*. While the *Sir Lancelot* was built for MacCunn, the *Ariel* was ordered by Shaw, Maxton & Co. Captain Keay was an exceptionally fine seaman and could get 16 knots out of her with a beam wind and no less than 12 when going to windward. For a vessel with a waterline length of less than 180ft, these speeds are remarkable.[17] She was capable of setting an immense press of canvas, carrying a main skysail above her royal, royal staysails and studding sails from waterline to royal yard, with a 'Jimmie Green' under her bowsprit and a 'Ringtail' added to the spread of her spanker. But to get high speeds much depended upon a hull's after-body, and it was said that while any fool could design a hollow entranced bow, it took genius to design the after-body, or 'run', the importance of which we have already noted. The *Ariel* and her sisters had a long, tapering run and a relatively narrow stern so that there was little reserve buoyancy in their after parts: if the stern fell into the trough of a hollow sea and the ship was not running fast enough, a following and curling wave could break over the stern. It was not unusual for a sailing-vessel to be 'pooped', particularly when running their easting down as we noted with the emigrant ship *Sobraon*, and extreme hull-lines only increased their vulnerability.

John Keay left the *Ariel* after bringing her home from Foochow in the autumn of 1868, taking command of the new *Oberon*. As was customary the chief mate, Courtenay, took over. In 1870, earning an intermediate freight on a run up to Yokohama, the *Ariel* was dismasted. Following a refit, Captain Courtenay left Yokohama bound for New York by way of Cape Horn, which he doubled on 15 January 1871. Crossing to London, the *Ariel* made a passage out to China and home again under a Captain Talbot. Finally, on 31 January 1872, she left London for Sydney under a Captain Cachenaille. She was never heard of again. Contemporary opinion held her to have been pooped, though she may have struck an iceberg, an end considered less likely at the time.[18] So slender was her after-body that when going about, the slightest check to her turning would give her sternway 'so instantly and at such a rate that she was apt to scoop the water over the taffrail, and, being flush-decked, would wash the ropes lying upon the deck into confusion, and so prevent the men standing at the braces from getting the yards trimmed'. She was, therefore 'a very dangerous ship to manage when contending with heavy seas' and, as a consequence, she was more often worn-round, passing her stern rather than her bow through the wind, a far safer manoeuvre discussed earlier. Furthermore, with a favourable but strong wind, 'the *Ariel* would be hove-to when most other clippers would be scudding before the gale' and she had a bad reputation for being wet and suffering damage in heavy weather. Captain Andrew Shewan was in no doubt that she had been destroyed by a pooping; 'She had,' he concluded, 'been designed as a superlative flyer in light weather – other considerations were subordinate to that'. It is a tribute to Keay's skill that he managed her so well.

Despite the conspicuous digging of the Suez Canal, the ultra-conservatism and natural Francophobia of the British ship-owner conditioned him to ignore it. This, in the short-term, was justified by events because the tea-clippers had yet several years of useful life. In the late 1860s a new form of leaner 'extreme-clipper' emerged in which the hull's entrance and run 'were exceptionally long and fine without any dead-flats amidships; there was great dead-rise and the floors curved right up through the bilges into the topsides and then tumbled home.' Thus does David MacGregor describe the composite ship *Thermopylae* which was designed by Bernard Waymouth, a superlative naval architect and secretary of Lloyd's Register. She was built, like all George Thompson's lovely Aberdeen White Star liners, at Walter Hood & Co.'s Aberdeen Yard, and immediately gained a reputation for standing up to her canvas in a blow as well as performing remarkably well to windward, always the square-rigged ship's weak point. Importantly, in view of the foregoing, when running before a heavy following sea she kept her poop dry. In her sail plan Waymouth abandoned the notion of skysails, giving her powerful royals, and adopted the doubled topsail then coming into vogue. At her building she had single topgallants, though later in her career these were doubled on the fore and mainmasts.

On the *Thermopylae*'s maiden voyage, which was to Melbourne, she equalled the *James Baines*'s sixty-three-day record. Having coasted to Sydney for coal, she ran this up to Shanghai before proceeding to Foochow to load tea for home, arriving with a golden cock at her main masthead. She fully justified this *braggadocio*, for she arrived in the Thames ninety-one days after leaving the Min River. The *Thermopylae* was to make eleven voyages to China for tea before making a further eleven voyages out to Australia with a general cargo, coming home with wool. Her first master was Captain Robert Kemball; her second, Charles Matheson, who claimed a day's run of 348 miles. Her third, Captain Jenkins, claimed 350. In 1890 she was sold to a Canadian owner, Mr Reford of Montreal, who reduced her to a barque and put her in the trans-Pacific trade between Hong Kong and Victoria, British Colombia, under a master who sold everything moveable including one boat, her studding sail gear and the Tower muskets in her armoury. Her next commander was over-fond of the bottle, but redeemed himself with some fine ship-handling in a typhoon and landed her cargo of Siamese rice in good condition, though he and his mate were dismissed. In June 1892 under the Nova Scotian Captain Winchester she held her own for three days crossing the Pacific against the Canadian Pacific mail steamer *Empress of India*, but, after some years 'knocking about' the Pacific, she was sold in 1896 to the Portuguese as a training ship and renamed *Pedro Nuñez*. On 13 October 1907 she was towed out to sea and sunk by two Portuguese warships after a far less erratic career than her great rival, the *Cutty Sark*. The *Thermopylae* was believed to have been the better of the two in light airs, though Willis's ship was thought to have had the edge in strong winds.

Captain Robert Kemball was specially selected by Thompson to command the *Thermopylae*. He had made his name in the *Yang-tsze* when in 1867 he had beaten the homeward times of five ships acknowledged to have been faster than his, but his first command had been Redfern & Alexander's *Fairlight*, which he left in 1864 to take over the *Yang-tsze*. He remained in *Thermopylae* until 1876, when Thompson moved him into his newest vessel, the line's flagship, the large *Aristides*.

Robert Kemball was among the finest of the China tea-clipper commanders, and certainly in him *Thermopylae* enjoyed a better bargain than the mixed bag of masters Willis placed on the poop of her rival, the *Cutty Sark,* whilst she was in the tea-trade. Others, however, ran him a close second, men such as John Keay and the others in 'the great race of 1866', but also inlucding Anthony Enright of the *Chrysolite*, Burgoyne and Dowdy, both of whom commanded the *Ariel* in her later life. There were many others, among those commanding the earlier generation of clippers, Killick, Maxton, Willis senior, Shewan senior and John Robertson, who was successively master of the *John o' Gaunt*, *Stornoway* and *Cairngorm*, stand out. But Andrew Shewan junior, himself a distinguished commander of the *Norman Court*, is unequivocal in his identification of, if not the best in any absolute sense, then the *primus inter pares*: Richard Robinson, who was mentioned earlier.

A poor master dishonoured a good ship, and such was the case with the *Black Prince*, part-owned by Baring Bros. Captain William Inglis consistently let his Rennie-designed flyer down by pusillanimity and prevarication, Andrew Shewan devoting an entire chapter in his memoirs to Inglis's timidity.[19] Similarly, the *Cutty Sark* lacked a distinguishing commander until Woodget joined her in the wool-trade, her first master Captain George Moodie being over-cautious rather than timid, and past his prime in 1869. Nevertheless, he proved a fine enough seaman to have rigged a jury rudder when *Cutty Sark* lost hers off the Cape of Good Hope in 1872 during her only straight race with *Thermopylae*. At the time Moodie had a 400-mile lead on his rival, and he recorded speeds of over 17 knots and at least one day's run of 363 miles, but the fine and beneficial combination of master and ship that prevailed on Thompson's *Thermopylae* eluded Willis in *Cutty Sark*.[20] In her early years only Captain Wallace proved a hard driver. A popular, jovial chief mate under the lack-lustre Captain Tiptaft, Wallace took over *Cutty Sark* in 1878. By 1880 *Cutty Sark* was out of the tea-trade and, to Wallace's disgust, under a cut-down sail plan ordered by Willis, loaded a cargo of Welsh coal at Penarth for the United States Navy in the Pacific. But Wallace had trouble finding a crew and was obliged to ship a polyglot bunch which, with an indifferent second mate and a hard-case chief mate named John Anderson, boded ill.

Wallace was instructed to proceed to Anjer for orders; the voyage did not go well as Anderson constantly hazed the seamen with abuse and several grew insolent, one of the three black seamen, John Francis, particularly so. Having acquired his able-seaman's certificate in steamers, Francis proved incompetent aboard a complex clipper, failing to pull his weight. 'This led to a great deal of unpleasantness on board, and … [Francis] was not at all on good terms with the crew.'[21] Notwithstanding their having to carry Francis, the crew conceived a cordial dislike of Anderson. Fearful of mutiny, Wallace mustered and armed the mates and apprentices before calling the crew aft. He then permitted Anderson and Francis to fight out their differences after which, with no advantage to either but the air cleared, an uneasy truce prevailed for a few weeks.

Off the Cape of Good Hope the *Cutty Sark* ran into heavy weather before which Wallace drove her hard, recording 1,050 miles in three days. Once clear of Mauritius, he altered course for Anjer, giving the order at 03.00 on 11 July when Anderson's watch was on deck. Francis happened to be on the forecastle as lookout when his watch took their stations to square-in the yards. Anderson sang out to Francis to let go the fore-tack which was belayed on the forecastle-head, but Francis ignored the command and its repetition. Furious, Anderson ran forward to be met by Francis holding a capstan-bar. In the ensuing struggle Anderson wrenched the capstan-bar from Francis and, bringing it down upon his head, felled him at a stroke. Francis never regained consciousness, died three days later and was buried at sea.

Despite Francis's unpopularity, Anderson's peremptory action was deeply resented by the crew. Guilt-ridden, Anderson locked himself in his cabin while the mood on the ship grew ugly, several seamen swearing Anderson would be brought to justice for murder. When the *Cutty Sark* reached Anjer, Wallace was disappointed not to receive the orders he expected for Yokohama. Instead he was obliged to wait, for neither he nor John Willis had realised that *Cutty Sark*'s reduced sail-plan would make little difference to her speed. Meanwhile Wallace now agreed to turn a blind-eye while Anderson deserted to an American ship, the *Colorado*, anchored close-by. The *Colorado*'s master had declared himself in need of a bucko man-handler, so Wallace doled out some cash for the crew to haggle with the local bum-boats while Anderson slipped over the side into a canoe. Having discovered the deceit, the crew became intransigent: they refused to work, obliging Wallace to take some delegates ashore and make a formal complaint to the Dutch authorities. All the anchored ships were searched for the fugitive, but Anderson had vanished, so it was officially assumed he had gone overboard and been eaten by sharks.

Thus matters stood when Wallace eventually received orders to head for Japan, but again the crew refused duty, so Wallace ordered his faithful petty officers, the boatswain, carpenter and sail-maker, along with his apprentices, to weigh anchor and make sail, at which point the rebels interfered. With his authority challenged, Wallace and his armed afterguard, formally arrested and shackled the four ringleaders before getting the ship under way, whereupon the remainder of the crew returned to a sulky obedience. The *Cutty Sark* now seemed entranced, for after her fast run to Anjer she was beset by calms. The Jeremiahs forward began more agitation and four mornings after leaving Anjer, having been informed that the second mate was about to come on deck at the turn of the watch, Wallace dropped over the taffrail.[22]

The wretched second mate with the material help of the apprentices worked the ship back to Anjer. Here he refused to take command of the ship but, thanks to the telegraph, having informed the ship's owner of Wallace's suicide, received order from Willis to engage a Dutch pilot and take the *Cutty Sark* to Singapore. Here they were met with three items of news, two of which had the waterfront buzzing: the dismasting of the *Bates Family*, and the scandal of the *Jeddah*, both of which we shall refer to later. Of immediate consequence to the *Cutty Sark* was the loss of her charter, followed by the irony of receiving alongside MacGregor, Gow & Co.'s steamer *Glencoe*, into which most of *Cutty Sark*'s coal cargo was transferred. Thus, with her bunkers full, the *Glencoe* departed for London through the Suez Canal with the season's tea.

The unhappy chapter in the *Cutty Sark*'s long life continued, because Willis now cabled Hong Kong where his *Hallowe'en* lay, asking Captain Fowler if his chief mate Bruce was capable of taking command of *Cutty Sark*. The *Hallowe'en*'s master cordially detested his chief officer and enthusiastically replied in the affirmative, so *Cutty Sark*, having lost the competent if misguided Wallace, acquired the incompetent and loathsome Bruce. She went to Calcutta where Bruce discharged her troublesome crew and lay there languishing for a cargo. Finally, she carried the first tea from India to Australia and, a few years later settled into the Australian trade under Richard Woodget, but the tale of Anderson and Francis was not finished.

The vindictive qualities of several of her discharged seamen having been fully aroused, Anderson was afterwards spotted by one of them and, in due course, he was arraigned in the Central Criminal Court before Mr Justice Stephen. The trial did no one credit. It was clear that Wallace had misrepresented Francis's death in the ship's official log book in an attempt to mitigate the consequences, and it was probably this that disturbed the otherwise conscientious Wallace and prompted his suicide. It was admitted that Francis had been both incompetent and provocative but, despite John Willis among others testifying to Anderson's previous good character, the hard-bitten mate unwisely remarked that 'he would do the same thing again given the circumstances'. The jury found Anderson guilty of manslaughter and Stephen, admitting 'that the case was a very painful one…taking into consideration the fact that the deceased had behaved very ill…felt it was his duty to pass a sentence of considerable severity…'

Losing all his certificates of competence, Anderson was sentenced to seven years penal servitude, labouring on the building of Dover Harbour breakwater, every stone of which he afterwards claimed he knew. Upon his eventual release, Anderson called on Willis, who secured him a berth as boatswain and acting second mate on a vessel sailing for Australia. As soon as he arrived in Australia, Anderson went for examination as second mate. Although he was rusty, 'it so happened that both he and his examiner were both Bluecoat boys [i.e. alumni of Christ's Hospital School], and as soon as the latter was told why such an old man was applying for a second mate's ticket, he did his best to help…' Anderson went on to regain his master's certificate and finally worked for the Anglo-American Oil Co. as the master of the naptha-carrying barge _Navahoe_. This strange vessel, built by Harland & Wolff in 1908, though carrying six masts spreading a basic suit of fore-and-aft sails, was regularly towed back and forth across the Atlantic between the Thames and New York by the tanker _Iroquois_, an arrangement that was known as 'The Horse and Cart of the Atlantic'. The _Iroquois_ and the _Navahoe_ were at sea not far from the scene of the sinking _Titanic_ in 1912.[23]

So much for the early career of the troubled _Cutty Sark_, but although a good ship needed a good master to prove herself, there were also faulty ships which required a sensitive hand. Wanting vessels comparable with _The Tweed_ and the _Cutty Sark_, John Willis ordered the _Blackadder_ and _Hallowe'en_ from the Thames-side yard of Maudslay, Son & Field, whose reputation was for engine-building. Some fundamental errors were made in the fittings of the _Blackadder_'s masts and she was dismasted on her maiden voyage in 1870 as well as being involved in a collision, incidents earning her a reputation as a jinxed ship. The ensuing lawsuits delayed the handing-over of the _Hallowe'en_ and, although she was to prove a capable ship, poor _Blackadder_ was dismasted a second time in a typhoon in 1873, though she afterwards enjoyed a creditable career in the Australian wool-trade.

Despite its glamour, a clipper commander's life was tough, though it was possible to put money by and eke out a respectable old age. Andrew Shewan inherited command of the _Norman Court_ when sailing as chief mate to his father. His grandfather had been in command of Peterhead whalers and died in the Arctic ice during the disastrous whaling season of 1830, while his father sailed in the Newfoundland fish-trade, becoming master of a schooner at twenty-one before rising in the service of John Willis's father to command the old man's beloved _Lammermuir_. Shewan senior was then requested by the China tea agents Turner & Co. to commission a clipper in their name. He bought a ship on the stocks at Alexander Hall's Yard at Aberdeen, naming her the _Chaa-sze_.[24] Having meanwhile completed his apprenticeship with Baring Bros, Andrew joined his father who was appointed to command Baring's new clipper, _Norman Court_. Andrew rose to become his father's chief mate and had just passed for master when in February 1873, with the _Norman Court_ outward bound in the English Channel, his 'old man' was attacked by sudden illness. Andrew took the ship into Dartmouth where Baring Bros approved him taking command. The twenty-three-year-old Captain Shewan made a voyage to Foochow, completing it with a fine run home in which he raced neck-and-neck with the much more experienced Captain Alexander Nicholson in the _Argonaut_. Shewan afterwards prospered, married and lived long enough to celebrate his golden wedding.

The anxieties of the job, both at sea and in port, were constant. Even in the 1860s with the presence of a naval guardship at Hong Kong, piracy remained rife on the China coast. Intelligence was gleaned by informers at Hong Kong and elsewhere about the movements of the clippers, particularly those carrying any specie. Even outward-bound ships were vulnerable, and on a bright, moon-lit night in February 1862, Brocklebank's _Veronica_, having picked up her Hong Kong pilot, was assailed by pirate junks. Captain Douglas was warned by the Chinese pilot: 'Captain, one pirate come; suppose he come on board, he kill!' Douglas hailed the steward to hand up a musket from the rack in the saloon and sent a musket-ball through the approaching junk's sail, at which show of resistance the junk sheered off. One of the crew recalled afterwards:

> Our pilot supposed there would be about two hundred pirates on board, and had they boarded us and set fire to the ship great damage would have been done. You can imagine the explosion, as we were loaded with shot and shell for the Government. As soon as we arrived at Hong Kong we reported the case, and the Government sent out a steam gunboat in pursuit. When she came back the authorities told us that twenty-two pirates would be hanged from the bow (sic) of a tree, not more than four hundred yards from where we lay at anchor. Sure enough, next day, when all the ships' bells were ringing noon, up went the first pirate...and as fast as they could be lowered down the noose was put round the neck of the next, till the whole lot were hanged.[25]

It was also widely believed that the fast Hall clipper *The Caliph*, which disappeared in the South China Sea when on her way from New York to China in 1871, had been overwhelmed by pirates. No typhoons were reported, and at the same time MacCunn's *Geraint* went missing.[26]

However, by the 1870s, with the tea-clipper an increasing dead-end for an ambitious master, several took command of steam-vessels where their expertise in the China trade was welcomed. One of these, Captain Robert Thomson, was a hard-driving master who had commanded the *Scawfell* for the Liverpool house of Rathbone Bros from her building in 1858 until 1871 when she was sold to Wilson & Blain of South Shields. He then took over Alfred Holt's auxiliary steam-vessel *Agamemnon* from Isaac Middleton, commanding her for the next ten years. The tea-races under sail were over by 1873, once the Suez Canal was in full use; however, they persisted for the new steamers as they vied for the first of the season's tea and made full use of the new short cut to Europe.

Thanks to the determination of Ferdinand de Lesseps and years of toil by anonymous labourers, the Suez Canal had opened in November 1869. Convinced of the utility of such a canal and after spending four years of investigation following his retirement from the French consular service in 1849, De Lesseps had submitted his proposal for a canal to the imperial Ottoman Sultanate at Constantinople. Although rejected, De Lesseps convinced Mohammed Said that such a canal would be beneficial to Egypt. Said 'had been De Lesseps's great friend for many years', and in 1850 he succeeded as Khedive in Cairo, whereupon he approved De Lesseps surveying a possible route but was obliged to resubmit the proposal to Constantinople for approval by the Sultan. Again the Porte objected, but Said boldly defied his master and De Lesseps proceeded to Paris to raise capital. Finding an encouraging French enthusiasm articulated in the sum of 120 million francs, he went on to London with similar ideas in mind. Although some investors and engineers showed interest, the British in general and their Government in particular opposed the idea. This is traditionally ascribed to Francophobia but, as is so often the case, the reasons were more complex, subtle and weightier; chief among them was the matter of shipping.

British ship-owners were doing well ordering numerous first-class sailing ships which were picking up trade abandoned by the Americans, then sliding into civil war, and there was therefore a consequential benefit to British ship-builders. A canal through the Isthmus would render this investment redundant at a stroke, while there were insufficient reliable British steam-ships to service a long-haul trade 'even though the whole available [British] steam tonnage were run on this new route'.[27] Despite the fact that steamers were already demonstrating the possibilities that lay ahead, many short-sightedly thought that 'steam had yet to prove its efficiency'. There were also technical reservations about the canal itself. It was believed that the levels of the Mediterranean and Red Seas were too disparate to be linked without complex locks, that the sandy environment would make dredging a constant necessity and that, for all these reasons, the enterprise – if successfully accomplished – would prove financially ruinous. Thus vested interest, financial anxiety and technical dubiety, spiced with characteristic anti-Gallicism and xenophobic paranoia over French domination of the route to India, placed British opinion in firm opposition.[28]

De Lesseps persisted, however, assembling a commission of experts who endorsed the project and on 5 January 1856 the Khedive Said authorised him to form a company. On 25 April and without formal consent from Constantinople, work was begun by cutting a fresh-water canal eastwards from the Nile to support the workforce. But both social and diplomatic opposition increased, largely engineered from London by Lord Palmerston. The plight of the wretched *fellahin* labourers, toiling amid the sand of the desert, became a useful weapon, and Palmerston did not scruple to use it. Other complex disputes arose; the whole matter was laid before Napoleon III for arbitration, and mechanical digging equipment replaced forced labour. Following this a new agreement was concluded with the Egyptian Government under Said's successor, Ismail Pasha. This conclusion was followed fifteen months later, in October 1865, by the death of Lord Palmerston, which lifted a last cloud from De Lesseps's horizon. Finally, on 17 November 1869, in the presence of Napoleon III and Empress Eugenie of France, Kaiser Franz Joseph of Austria, the Crown Prince of Prussia, the Khedive Ismail, the Sharif of Mecca and the international diplomatic corps, De Lesseps' dream was realised and the canal between Port Said on the Mediterranean and Port Suez on the Red Sea was open for the transit of shipping.[29]

As noted, the idea that the canal immediately terminated sailing traffic to the Far East is another over-simplification. Even as late as 1876, it was noted that:

> even though largely subsidised, especially to India by way of the Cape, [the P&O steamers] have found it impossible to compete successfully with the sailing ships of Messrs Green of Blackwall, Messrs T. and W. Smith, and other private ship-owners long engaged in the trade.

The canal itself was barely fit for steamers, the inaugural passage of the large French Imperial Yacht *L'Aigle* having been nervously conducted. The narrow and shallow nature of the canal made difficulties for even the comparatively small steamers of the day, so that dredging was necessary to maintain a modest channel. 'Until as late as the year 1883 the history of the canal was somewhat chequered' due to problems arising from vessels grounding and closing the canal until they were removed, administrative delays and the development of passing ships through in 'blocks' controlled by signal stations at intervals along the canal. There was also the general viability of the enterprise which hung in the balance. Shareholders had received a 5 per cent dividend while the canal was under construction, but this ended when it opened. One commentator noted that the canal ran on 'French management, polyglot proprietors, a mixture of French and Egyptian sovereignty, Turkish suzerainty, and British and Anglo-Indian traffic,' a situation which 'formed a commercial, moral, and political chaos as unprecedented as the work itself.'

The crisis arrived in 1875. Following the opening of the canal and in anticipation of steady revenues, Khedive Ismail had adopted a vigorous policy of modernisation in Egypt and was consequently driven into debt by the canal's apparent failure. In 1873 he borrowed £30 million, over twice the cost of the canal. Two years later Egypt confronted bankruptcy with no European banker willing to lend the money Ismail required to service his country's debt. The unfortunate Khedive was close to defaulting. He was expected to sell his only assets, his shares in the canal, to the Société Générale in Paris until the British Prime Minister intervened. Anxious about French imperialist expansion in North Africa and Indo-China, confronted with the spectre of French control over the now shorter route to India, and with the initially sceptical but entirely opportunistic British ship-owner now increasingly relying upon De Lesseps's creation, Benjamin Disraeli secretly purchased Khedive Ismail's shares. Receiving the private sanction of Queen Victoria, Disraeli borrowed from Lionel Rothschild the £4 million necessary to outbid the French. The money was discreetly paid to Ismail who quietly sent his shares to the British consulate in Cairo, enabling Disraeli to write to the Queen, 'You have it, Madam'. The ructions in Paris at the news of the British Government's acquisition of the largest − 44 per cent − shareholding in the Suez Canal, need not detain us but, importantly, 1875 marked the resumption of dividends at 5 per cent.[30]

Despite these tortuous vicissitudes, by 1887 the width of the canal and the introduction of searchlights fitted to a steamer's bow permitted night passages. Transit times began to tumble from the initial fifty-four hours, thus establishing the viability both of the canal and the Suez route itself. To some extent this long delay cushioned the canal's impact upon Britain's large sailing fleet. So too did innate British conservatism, compelling the Peninsular & Oriental Steam Navigation Co. to participate in a farce. The General Post Office was suspicious of the risks attaching to sending Government and private mails via the canal to India and beyond. Moreover, Gladstone's Government and the General Post Office wanted to substantially reduce the subsidy paid to P&O if the much shorter canal route was adopted. Unsurprisingly, the company's board strongly objected, but until 1872 the mail continued to be landed at Alexandria by a P&O steamer, then transported south to Suez and reloaded into the same ship *which had in the interim passed through the canal!* The matter was rationalised by the company relinquishing £20,000 of the annual subsidy, but when in 1886 Gladstone's Liberal Government was back in power following the defeat of Disraeli, tenders were reissued for:

> the whole of the India and China mails, it being made an essential part of the contract that the transit of the mails should be carried on exclusively by the Overland Route from Alexandria and not through the Suez Canal.[31]

It took strong representations from the P&O board, pleading the inefficiencies, the quarantine procedures and the delay inherent in such an antediluvian procedure to convince the Government they were wrong. Finally commonsense prevailed. The company put some larger and faster steam-ships on the service, of which the tactfully named *Khedive* was one. She and her sisters were capable of honouring the contract times of sixteen-and-a-half days to Bombay and thirty-seven-and-a-half to Shanghai. Matters improved rapidly and in 1886, the year after the canal had been deepened, P&O's *Carthage* made the transit in the then record time of eighteen hours.[32] As Lord Brassey pointed out:

> The opening of the Suez Canal, and the recent improvements in steam machinery, which, by reducing the consumption of fuel, have made steam power so much more economical than before, have given a new impulse to the construction of steamers.

Other owners were quick to take advantage of the canal's potential which cut 3,000 miles off the distance round Africa, though it is worth emphasising that steam-ships were still fitted with auxiliary sails. The first British merchantman to pass though the canal was the Anchor Line's steamer *Dido* and by 1882 she and other Henderson steamers had established a regular service to the sub-continent. Benefits were conferred elsewhere, for the opening of the Suez Canal immediately put an end to the woes foretold by many in Singapore's shipping circles who had feared it would end their own valuable entrepôt trade. This proved quite otherwise; in the succeeding decade Singapore's trade more than doubled [33] not least because it was followed by the rapid expansion of steamship routes throughout the Far East. At first sailing-tonnage stagnated, declining after 1876, but steam-tonnage entering and clearing the port escalated rapidly. To this technological change of gear has to be added the almost simultaneous arrival of the telegraph from India. By 1871 this had been extended from Singapore onwards to Hong Kong, Shanghai, Nagasaki and Vladivostok. With global communications extended between Europe, America and Singapore, China and the Far East in general were inexorably drawn closer together. Further British colonial territorial expansion up the Malay Peninsula – Singapore's hinterland – increasing the traffic through the island-city and added new commodities: tin in the mid-1870s, coffee in the following decade and – in 1905 after the transfer of seedlings from Brazil by way of Kew Gardens – rubber.[34]

Like Henderson's Anchor Line, Alfred Holt was quick off the mark. His fleet had grown considerably between 1866 and 1875, by which time his ships were regularly passing through the canal and stopping at Jeddah to embark Muslim pilgrims on their way home after the *Haj*, more of which later. British India's main-line steamers were also passing through, often in company with Holt's, but it was largely the auxiliary steam-ships of Alan Gow which were to wrest the laurels of the high-profile and prestigious China tea-trade from the beautiful tea-clippers.

Alan Gow bought his first sailing ship, the *Estrella de Chile*, in 1867 and employed her serving South America. In 1868 his second full-rigged ship the *Glenavon* sailed for India and she was joined by a third, the *Glenaray*. Almost alone among British owners, the canny Gow had sufficient foresight to anticipate the canal's opening and accordingly ordered a new ship, the barquentine-rigged auxiliary steamer *Glengyle*.[35] On her maiden voyage to China in 1871 the *Glengyle* made a homeward passage of fifty days via Suez, a dramatic saving on time against *Thermopylae's* best passage of ninety-one days. There were risks, however. There was a rise in the consumption of Indian and Ceylonese teas, and this caused the start of a corresponding decline in that of Bohea and other China blooms. To this influential change in consumer-preference had to be added the effect of the canal's opening upon freight-rates, which declined. Nevertheless, as Gow and his partner James McGregor correctly guessed, the China trade remained inviting and they introduced a class of six sisters, the *Glenroy*, *Glenlyon*, *Glenfalloch*, *Glenartney*, *Glenearn* and *Glenfinlas*, to which was added the British-built *Glenorchy*, acquired from Dutch owners. These eight ships established a regular monthly 'liner' schedule of a round voyage every 105 days, and in 1874 the *Glenartney* brought the new season's tea home from Foochow in forty-four days,[36] a record which marked as a crack company what formally became the Glen Line in 1910.

Such passages and increased enterprise on the part of steam-ship owners quickly displaced the tea-clipper, only a dozen of which competed for low freight rates in the final years of 1878 and 1879:

A curious custom then obtained [in China] known as 'circulating'. A vessel would send out a circular stating that she was prepared to accept freight at a certain rate; should she, however, be compelled to drop her rate towards the end of her loading, the lower rate governed the whole of her cargo; it was therefore sometimes advantageous to sail a few hundred tons short in preference to dropping the rate. The fastest ships naturally obtained the highest rates; the first two ships £8 per ton, then in a descending scale until it reached the slowest ship at £3 per ton.

Such curious circumstances produced fierce competition. 'There was great rivalry' between the Gow's 'Glens' and Skinner's 'Castles'. Both built fast steamers which raced against one another in order to get the highest rate. In 1880 the rivals were the *Glencoe* and *Loudon Castle*; then in 1882 Gow brought out his 'finest vessel', the *Glenogle*, only to have her 'entirely eclipsed by the 18 knot *Stirling Castle*...[which] made the passage from Hankow to London in 30 days' the following year. Her master was 'a shrewd Scotsman, a fine ship-master, but somewhat bombastic and "harum-scarun".The ship was visited on her arrival in London by the Prince of Wales, a visit he[r master] much embellished on his return to China.'

Alfred Holt tended to discourage his masters from racing. Instead, as Thomas Golding recalled, a:

> fine fleet of steamers of moderate speed was built up and while other lines were building fast expensive vessels, which made one paying voyage in the year, and whose sailing dates could not always be depended upon, the "Blue Funnel" line gained the confidence of shippers by their regularity and dependability; they were also assisted by an arrangement of subsidiary [coasting lines provided by Butterfield & Swire's China Navigation Co. By this means Holt's]…homeward freights were very high, reaching £16 per ton… In 1880, there were nearly 20 ocean going steamers at Hangkow; the previous year saw the last of the sailing clippers at that port, the *Cutty Sark, Lothair, Windhover*, and *Coriolanus* having towed up, but were unable to obtain cargoes.

These ships were far from worn-out, being built of the finest materials, so much so in the case of the *Cutty Sark* that her construction bankrupted her builders Scott & Linton, and she had to be completed by Denny Brothers. In the last years of the China trade many clippers had failed to find cargoes and their masters had been driven to make passages in ballast from China and Japan down to Australia to load a paying homeward cargo of wool. Among these were the *Cutty Sark* and *Thermopylae*, the *Blackadder* and the *Salamis*, the last like the *Blackadder* conceived as an 'improvement' on her predecessor, the *Thermopylae*. However, such was the demand for wool that most of these superb ships fully justified their existence in a trade for which they were not designed and for which their capacity was limited. With their deep-luffed courses they were intended for subtle windward work, not the largely down-wind outward passage to Australia by the Cape of Good Hope and the long homeward run across the Southern Ocean to double Cape Horn, but in this they continued to excel.

As for the China tea-trade itself, its days were also numbered. Tea — *Thea assamica* — was actually a native plant of Upper Assam, its Chinese counterpart — *Thea sinensis* — a cultivar allegedly carried thither by a missionary. The first exports of tea from Calcutta to Britain had occurred in 1838, depressing the price of the stocks of China tea held by East India merchants like Stewart Marjoribanks as mentioned earlier. This fore-shadowed what was to come, for this crop was grown largely on the East India Company's Indian tea plantations which, following the ending of the Company's trading monopoly, were taken over in 1840 by The Assam Tea Co. By the 1850s, despite a misguided attempt to introduce Chinese methods to India by the Scots botanist Robert Fortune, Indian tea was gaining a toe-hold on the home market, helped by energetic British management. 'There were no squeezing mandarins in India, there was European supervision of the firing and packing of the leaf, and the plantations were connected to civilisation by the railway and the telegraph.'

After the devastating leaf disease wrecked coffee production in Ceylon, tea was being planted there by 1876 and both India and Ceylon teas found increasing favour among the British on account of preferred flavour and lower price. This brought it well within the purchasing power of the vast numbers of British working people, sucking production into an unprecedented market. Moreover, Indian teas had a 'pungent and penetrating flavour [which in contrast to China teas] never became stale, and Indian teas had greater strengths than the far weaker China growths'.

The inward-looking Chinese were indifferent to these changes until it was too late, regarding 'the rumour of competition from other countries with ridicule'. As Alexander Aiken goes on to explain, the quality of their exports diminished too:

> Trenching, manuring and pruning had all been neglected. No new stock had been planted, and the worn-out trees were being stripped of four, or even five, crops a year instead of three... India and Ceylon teas were beating those from China simply because they were in every way better: better cultivated, better cured, better packed, more honestly sold and cheaper.

Consumption of China tea peaked in 1879 at 56,200 tons. Ten years later this was 20,100 tons against India's export of 45,500 tons and Ceylon's of 18,800 tons, a situation exacerbated for the Chinese by their own export taxes. By the end of that year, despite a plan to establish a Scots-run enterprise in Fukien, five of the English tea-exporting houses at Hangkow went out of business. All this ferment had been materially boosted by the Suez Canal: not only had the canal shortened the distance home from China, it had halved the time, and this was even more applicable when, instead of China, a ship turned-round in India.

Such changes altered the pattern of steam-ship operation in the Far East. Sailing ship-owners had, for some time, operated shipping 'rings' which had been the subject of a Royal Commission, but steamer-operations brought new problems to their owners and in August 1875 the first 'Conference' was established to regulate trade with Calcutta. This was intended to smooth out the costs to both the regular scheduled trading ship-owner – the liner-owner – and his customer, the shipper. Initially the attempt to remove the unpredictable, and in many ways unsupportable, irregularities of raw and open competition to the former was not wholly successful since the system was clearly biased in his favour. Understandably the shipper considered himself a victim of a cartel and, when the average parcel of outward-bound cargo was between 4 and 10 tons, he felt victimised. The ship-owner's dilemma lay in funding the less fluctuating and more constant costs in respect of depreciation, hull and cargo insurance, port and light-dues, to which had to be added a massive hike in running-expenses. Crew-wages and victualling costs had risen with the introduction of engineers, greasers, firemen and trimmers, all of whom required pay, food and accommodation, to which there were added the huge expenses of plant-maintenance and fuel with the concomitant reduction in cargo capacity sacrificed to bunkers, boilers and engines. On top of all this was the consideration that while outward-bound cargoes in cargo-liners (with the exception of coal) usually consisted of manufactured goods – household appurtenances and artefacts, all consigned in relatively modest lots – there were almost no homeward consignments of equivalent value. British imports tended to consist of raw materials: wool, jute, iron-ore and so forth, along with foodstuffs such as grain, sugar and rice. Such cargoes could be far more economically borne in sailing-vessels and the new but slow and low-powered steam bulk-carrying 'tramp-ships' then making an appearance.

The Conference System was made feasible by the 'deferred rebate', first introduced in September 1877 on Manchester exports, which rewarded a shipper for his loyalty. By rebating 'primage', originally a payment deducted from the freight-charge by a ship's master, this tithe of the freight-charge was made available by the change of the ship-master from an owning partner to a paid employee of a shipping company. Primage had survived on the pretext that it was a fee paid for the use of the ship's derricks, winches and general cargo-handling facilities, but it was now used to fund a form of bonus. The shipper's loyalty was purchased by deferring any rebate for six months, inducing him to stay loyal to a shipping-line beyond the current term of rebate, or else forfeit that for the previous period.

Following the example of the Calcutta owners, a Far East Conference of shipowners trading to China and Japan was set up under the aegis of John Swire of the China Navigation Co. in 1879. This cartel among cargo-liner owners was intended in particular to smooth out the effects of the fluctuating freight rates for tea which varied from port to port and could be severely undercut even while a vessel was actually loading a cargo, because the final rate was not set until the ship was full and was ready to depart. This compromised any voyage-forecast and could have a disastrous effect upon voyage profits. The Conference members included McGregor, Gow's Glen Line; Jenkins's (Welsh) Shire Line and Thomas Skinner's Castle Line.[37] On Swire's advice Alfred Holt's Ocean Steam Ship Co. also joined but Holt's ships were becoming obsolescent in an era of rapid change while the faster ships of the Castle, Glen and Shire Lines, a general over-tonnaging[38] in the Far East trade and a fall in freight rates, all now posed a threat to Holt. How this affected the fortunes of the various shipping companies running steamers to China we must leave to a subsequent volume for, while the British transferred their allegiance from Suchong to Assam tea, there had been a similar revolution in tea's complimentary commodity: sugar.

In the half-century following the end of the Napoleonic War the entire Caribbean basin had been in ferment. The wars of independence fought by the colonies of Spain had been followed by the secession of Texas, the emancipation of black slaves, the Jamaican rebellion and political and social turbulence in the colonial islands of the Greater and Lesser Antilles. Insofar as the British colonies were concerned:

> The period...which followed emancipation was like the death and rebirth of the
> cassia tree. It was the best and worst of times. One disaster followed another; bank-
> ruptcy and financial chaos in the eighteen forties, droughts and epidemics in the
> eighteen fifties, rioting and bloodshed in the eighteen sixties...[39]

Yet the disintegration of slavery created the conditions for the slow growth of 'a new and dynamic society' which began to thrive and by 1840 all the mixed peoples of the British West Indies possessed equal rights before the law. Shipping continued to serve the interests of the colonies and the mother-country throughout the period, much as it had done before the war. The breaking up of the triangular trade, while it had eliminated the slaver, had given a renewed dignity to the West Indiaman. Many of these, as we have noted, were former East Indiaman, since the rather unspectacular steadiness of the trade in sugar, rum and molasses, created no innovation in ships operating in the West India and associated trades to South America or the Gulf ports comparable with those engaged in commerce with India and the Far East. Though in the immediate post-war world there were crack West Indiamen such as the *Thetis* that caught Edward Cooke's artistic eye and the command of which William Pixley declined. Commenting on the breed in the 1840s, Captain Andrew Shewan remarked that they were 'notoriously unwieldy'. Moreover:

> Many of that class of ships were of almost rectangular construction, so built that the sugar hogsheads might stow well. They were so sluggish and clumsy, and withal so slow, that it was said they could push a floating cocoanut ahead for miles, and carry a bunch of bananas from Port Royal to the Downs in the dead water under the vessel's lee quarter. One of them, the *Spheroid*, achieved fame by carrying away her topmasts when she was driven up to the speed of six knots.

They had no need to be fast. The domestic and re-export market for sugar was assured, as was that for molasses and rum. Although the Royal Navy was the most obvious and reliable purchaser of rum, its use was widespread, for early Victorian society was characterised as much as the Georgian Age for its insobriety. Afloat, grog was used on board merchant ships as a panacea for difficult work in trying conditions, doled out by the mates on the authority of the master. It was also often part of a ship's routine, being issued on Sundays, but it was also liberally splashed-out upon occasions such as ship-launches, even *before* the tricky operation of sending a new hull into its element! Although the temperance movement had so influenced shipping that by the 1880s many British ships were officially 'dry', no self-respecting master would sail without a quantity of rum with which to reward the crew, 'thank' a pilot, or soften the attitude of port officials – even to the extent of buying them off when necessary.

With the mails, without which business could not flourish, in the hands of the Royal Mail Steam Packet Co., there was no need for others to invest in new tonnage, since what was made redundant from 'the first-class trades' to Australia and the Far East was available on the second-hand market. Even the threat of American shipping had been conveniently auto-neutralised by the Civil War, and by the time that the United States' mercantile marine had revived, British steamers had virtually taken over all but coastal and inter-island commerce. Despite the fact that the Royal Mail Steam Packet Co.'s tonnage was well-built and capable of being converted to carrying guns as steam-frigates in a national emergency, the question of the mail subsidy remained a sore point with the Exchequer. The House of Commons insisted on the mail service being opened to competition and public tender, which was a blow to Royal Mail's board, having just built new ships, the 15-knot *Tagus* and *Moselle*, and added the *Tasmanian*, purchased from the failed European and Australian Steam Navigation Co.[40] The directors bowed to pressure and in 1874 accepted a severely reduced subsidy of £86,750, a level at which it remained until the end of the century when freight rates had fallen to £1.50 per ton from a £7-8 high in 1850.

In addition to cargo and the mails, the company's passengers included emigrants from the Iberian Peninsula going to Brazil and the River Plate, an important source of revenue, particularly as the carriage of specie had fallen off. In 1860 one of the company's ships arrived from the West Indies with £1.25 million in silver, a treasure which filled thirty-six wagons drawn by 113 horses as it was carted from Nine Elms to the Bank of England. The freight rate for this was 1 per cent, but by the end of the century this too had reduced by half. Besides, much of the bullion was going to San Francisco, China and Japan. From 1858 until 1909, when it relinquished the task, the Royal Mail Steam Packet Co. also carried the trans-Panama Australian mails, extending its services to Colon and Buenos Aires by 1872. Almost from its inception the company operated in close co-operation in the Pacific with the Pacific Steam Navigation Co. which maintained its passenger and cargo service along the Andean coast of the South American continent.

In the 1860s, although the shipyards of the Clyde were building steamers and sailing-vessels, Sunderland was the greatest constructor in the land, out-building London and Aberdeen. The Clyde, however, was increasing its importance on the West Indian sugar trade through the Port of Greenock near its mouth. John Rennie had overseen the digging of the East India Harbour in 1805 and at first cotton textiles had been the staple export commodity of the port. Coal was shipped out in huge quantities, while linen, hardware and cutlery were also exported; timber and whale-oil were imported from Canada, along with West Indian sugar which, once refined, was also re-exported. Sugar slowly superseded another West Indian import, tobacco, during the first three decades of the nineteenth century.

Besides commodity trading, the environs of Greenock, downstream to Gourock and upstream to Port Glasgow and across the Clyde at Dumbarton, were a mass of smoky industry. All along this riverine littoral the ship-building and repair yards mentioned in the previous chapter, together with their associated canvas-mills, roperies, brass and iron-foundries, engine-making works and — most significantly here — cooperages, flourished. Earlier, around 1830, sugar-refining had been the principal processing industry. Apart from employing 'an immense tonnage in carrying both raw and refined sugar', its associated supporting craft of coopering hogsheads carried out 'a most extensive trade'.

The profits to be made from the manufacture of hogsheads, barrels and their smaller cousins had attracted the Lyle family, who also dabbled in coastal ship-owning, weaving and general merchandising. They had a number of associates who included several 'mariners'. Such were the profits from coopering that the Lyle brothers abandoned ship-owning for a few years until Gideon Lyle acquired a third share of the brigantine *Commerce* in 1816, adding shares in the *Maria* in 1825, while his brother Abram obtained a small interest in the *Belmont*. In 1827, in partnership with William MacDonald and Duncan Gibb of Liverpool, Abram bought the new New Brunswick-built brig *Helen MacGregor*. Putting a Robert Shedden in command, the brig was advertised as bound for Trinidad, and offered as both 'excellent accommodation for passengers' and 'a most eligible conveyance for dry goods'. The *Helen MacGregor* returned a year later with 496 casks of molasses and one barrel of rum actually consigned to Lyle; part of this cargo was trans-shipped to Liverpool. Abram Lyle's business did not thrive and he died in 1849 leaving 'seven thousand pounds less than nothing'. His son, also named Abram, was accordingly possessed of 'a desire to make money' to which he added a fortunate 'a passion for work', giving up a career as advocate to engage in trade. 'Intolerant of all sport and amusement,' Abram Lyle junior was formidable and he served at sea for a few years. His sea-going appears to have been terminated on 28 March 1847 when the *Consort*, of which he was master, was lost. He survived to take over, with his brother Robert, the ailing cooperage on the death of their father. The business was saved by the lowering of import duties on raw sugar which were a spin-off from the Anti-Corn Law agitation and the growing conviction in the rightness of free trade. This first initiative was taken in 1844 and thirty years later had been eroded to nothing, by which time the Lyle family fortunes had been transformed. Abram Lyle became increasingly involved with Robert Kerr and the two unofficial partners complemented each other in their dealings so that by 1851 Kerr owned six ships, most elderly and second-hand, and although several were lost through misadventure, the losses could be made good. Quite modest sugar cargoes could realise profits as the duties fell, so small vessels could maintain the supply-chain, unlike the Quebec timber trade which by 1860 was employing vessels in excess of 1,000 tons.

Using Lyle's barrels for their homeward cargoes, Kerr's Diamond 'K' Line grew. By 1860 the second-hand tonnage had almost all been replaced by new vessels from the shipyard of Archibald MacMillan & Son of Dumbarton, and Kerr had become the largest of Greenock's eighty-six ship-owners. Although Kerr favoured outright ownership, Lyle among others assisted in financing the acquisition of new tonnage. In 1864 Kerr purchased the composite full-rigged ship *Isabel Kerr*, named after his wife, at 1,415 tons the largest ship registered at Greenock. In the two years following she was joined by the *Queen of the Lakes* and *Ceylon*. Before the decade was out seven more ships had been added to the fleet, the largest being the 1,572-ton *Culzean*. Taking advantage of a depression in steam-ship construction, Kerr built in iron, owning two dozen ships by 1872. Although a few of these were despatched elsewhere – the *Varna* being lost in Tasmanian waters, the *Madras* in the South China Sea and the *Ceylon* on her way to Bombay – most were committed to the West Indies and the import of raw *muscovado*, though one voyage was made to Mauritius for Mascarene sugar. Consignments of cotton, rum and coconuts were kept to a minimum.

Outward cargoes were typically 37,000 yards of plain and coloured cotton, linen, hardware, hosiery, stationery, barley, cheese, oats, ale, wrought iron and coal. Kerr and

A charming watercolour of the barque-rigged auxiliary screw steamer *Madras* off Cape
Guardafui, 'the N.E. Point of Africa'. The artist, identified only by the initials W.B.E., was
probably a ship's officer as the image is intended to show the lie of the land as well as the
Madras, her propeller working hard and under a press of sail, including studding sails, with her
ensign and house-flag prominent. (© Courtesy of The British Mercantile Marine Memorial
Collection)

Lyle both invested in their cargoes, often in their entirety, and so successful were they
that they also exported in others' ships, only occasionally resorting to raising loans to
fund such consignments. Against such credits must be set the debits; the Diamond 'K'
Line was not exempt from the charges of over-loading and mismanagement which
formed the core of the agitation by Samuel Plimsoll and others:

> Between 1845 and 1872, twenty-nine of the seventy-five ships operated by Kerr
> and Lyle were lost, wrecked, abandoned or burnt out. Poor maintenance, over load-
> ing and bad seamanship were most frequently to blame. In 1865 James MacDonald,
> captain of the *Margaret Kerr*, appeared before the Greenock Marine Board charged
> with drunkenness while in command and was held to be partly responsible for the
> loss of his ship in the Gulf of Florida. Another master, J.F. Parker of the *Barbadian*,
> was charged by Kerr with 'habitual drunkenness and great neglect' during a voyage
> to Belize.[41]

Kerr's own intervention in the case of Parker does him some credit, and conditions
aboard Kerr's ships were probably as conducive of engendering loyalty as those of
other owners, so the voyage of the *Lephenstrath* in 1865 may not stray far from the

norm. It is, nevertheless, dismal. As John Orbell points out, two men died from disease, two deserted to American ships where wages were higher, two were sent to gaol for violence, one having bitten off part of the ear of Able-Seaman Boyle 'without provocation' when drunk, while another was sent to hospital affected by alcoholic poisoning. The *Lephenstrath* returned to Greenock by way of New York where more of the crew were either discharged by 'mutual agreement' or simply deserted. While excuses may be made over delays at Havana, the climate and the ease with which raw spirits were cheaply available, better regulation on board might have prevented the two deaths, seven discharges and seven desertions that affected the twenty seamen who had signed articles at Greenock in the preceding June.

Lyle, meanwhile, had become, besides an investor in ships, cargoes and barrels, an importing agent for barrel-staves from North America, Scandinavia and Russia. He therewith supplied not only his own firm's needs, but others' too. In 1865 he and Kerr joined a partnership to acquire the Greenock Sugar Refinery from the shipbuilding family of Steele, and this soon accommodated the majority of the *muscovado* then being imported. Lyle's interest in the Diamond 'K' Line ended when Kerr died in 1872 and he acquired Kerr's half-shares in the iron ships *Queen of the Lakes, Java, Zanzibar* and *Colmonell*, but relinquished all other interests in favour of Kerr's heirs. To distinguish his ships and his new enterprise, Lyle, retaining the name of the *Queen of the Lakes*, resolved to establish a distinct identity as the Cape Line. He renamed his other ships *Cape Comorin, Cape Horn* and *Cape Wrath*, though in ordering a new 1,782-ton full-rigged ship from John Reid & Co. at Port Glasgow, Lyle memorialised his friend, naming her *John Kerr*. Three other large cargo-carriers followed; the *Cape Sable, Cape Verde* and *Cape Finisterre*, all built in 1874 by Thomas Wingate & Co. of Glasgow. Full bodied, these vessels made no attempt at being flyers, for it was by this time abundantly clear that fast passages could be better relied upon under steam. Instead they offered the low-cost, low-overhead benefits that would characterise the final phase of British sailing-vessel ownership for which a single commodity, low-freighted cargo like raw sugar, was ideal. In pursuit of this, Lyle switched his loading ports from the West Indies to Java and also began to diversify, carrying other homogeneous cargoes, initiating a tramping trade which ranged worldwide. By 1880 Lyle had added the *Cape of Good Hope, Cape Breton* and *Cape St Vincent*, all of around 1,400 tons and built by J. & G. Thomson of Clydebank. Bringing his fleet to ten vessels, he added his first steamer, the *Cape Clear* of 1,051 tons, in 1881. She was a plain-headed auxiliary steam-vessel built by Robert Steele & Co. of Greenock very similar to Holt's ships in design and power-plant, though she was not a success and quickly disposed of to the Union Steamship Co. of New Zealand.

Lyle continued to suffer losses: the *Queen of the Lakes'* cargo shifted in 1875 and she was abandoned; between 1879 and 1882 the *John Kerr, Cape Sable* and *Cape Comorin* all went missing. This was a sorry tale and the customary outward cargoes of coal were probably to blame. Not only could coal spontaneously combust, as witness the fate of the *Palestine*, but if fine enough — and shipped as 'slurry' — might also shift. Nevertheless, Lyle's partial conversion of his sugar-carriers to world traders went on;

his ships carried both coolies and emigrants, as in the case of the *Cape Sable* which the New Zealand Government chartered in 1874. The growing markets of London and Liverpool drew sugar imports south, while an influx of European beet sugar depressed the price of the cane variety, simultaneously destroying the re-export trade. Isolated from these changes, Greenock declined and Lyle proposed a new and modern plant to be erected alongside the new James Watt Dock, then undergoing construction at a cost of £500,000, so that a berth could be allocated to his sugar-ships. The proposal was rejected outright by the Harbour Trustees and a snubbed Lyle decided to build his new refinery — which would process beet sugar — at Plaistow, on the Thames, an enterprise taken over by his two sons who moved south to establish Silvertown.

The importation of beet sugar into Britain had a major effect upon the West Indies which relied heavily upon exporting cane sugar, rum and molasses, but by the end of our period a new trade was emerging from the Antilles and the Caribbean littoral. From about 1880 onwards, the masters of American ships trading between New England and Jamaica 'sometimes carried home with them small parcels of wild bananas as presents for their friends. The journey was just long enough to ripen the fruit.' Bananas caught on and quickly became a commercial operation run by numerous small companies. In 1899 these drew together and pooled their resources to become the United Fruit Co. of Boston which eventually established a near global demand, relieving Jamaica of its earlier dependence on sugar. The new commodity and the market it created in Britain and Europe would engender a new form of speedy fruit-carrier, no longer the fast little schooners and cutters that served Iberia and the Atlantic Islands but a smart steamer, the tale of which is related in the following volume.

By the time that Holt's *Agamemnon* had reached China in 1866 to threaten the tea-clipper, the North Atlantic passenger, mail and cargo service of Cunard was again subject to competition. By now, of course, the company were employing screw steamers on the North Atlantic, as were their competitors, chiefly the Inman Line. Several of Cunard's old paddlers were converted to sailing ships — as we have seen, a by no means unusual or contemptible practice — and a few like the *Scotia* to screw steamships. As already noted, between 1862 and 1865 Cunard had built their first iron screw steamers for the North Atlantic, the *China*, *Cuba* and *Java*, which were followed by the magnificent *Russia* of 1867.[42] Capable of 14.4 knots, the *Russia* managed the crossing in just over eight days and, under the command of Captain T. Cook, subsequently steamed 630,000 miles and carried 26,000 passengers without a single accident or breakdown.

Theodore Cook, a small man with a quiet voice, was among the Cunard commanders who cultivated a remote distance from their passengers and developed a taciturnity that dissuaded their officers from over-familiarity. This over-done British reserve became something of a company hallmark and stung more than one passenger. A gentleman travelling in the *Persia* during Cook's tenure of command, seeing the heavy wrack overhead and Cook standing upon the bridge cradling his sextant and vainly awaiting a break in the overcast, remarked that the cloud had prevented the captain from making his observation. 'Yes, sir,' Cook is supposed to have replied, 'but it did not prevent you from making yours!' Cook commanded twenty-eight Cunarders, spent forty-seven years at sea and only retired because his health failed. Captain Charles Judkins – he of the *Columbia* that had so entranced Fanny Appleton in the early '40s – served Cunard until 1871 and rose to be the line's commodore. He was said to read divine service in a voice rivalling God's, and in his case the notion of being 'Master under God' seemed particularly apt.

Cunard adopted the compound steam engine in the *Batavia* of 1870, and their subsequent liners gradually increased in size, speed and the luxury of their appointments. The *Calabria*, *Algeria*, *Abyssinia* and *Gallia* carried around 300 first- and 800 third-class passengers as well as a substantial quantity of cargo. In the *Servia* of 3,900 tons, the company built its first steel liner with internal subdivision and double-bottom tanks capable of holding 800 tons of water ballast. In addition to staterooms, she could carry 730 emigrants and was lighted by electricity but to make 17.25 knots it was necessary to carry bunkers of 1,800 tons of coal. The *Umbria* and *Etruria* of 1884 were followed by the then huge *Campania* and *Lucania* whose tonnage of around 13,000 tons was exceeded only by Brunel's monstrous *Great Eastern*. Both were built at the Govan Yard of the Fairfield Shipbuilding Co., the latter being launched on 2 February 1893, and they reduced the passage time to around five days and nine hours at speeds in excess of 20 knots; both made use of wireless telegraphy.

Although the company suffered some casualties, the routine and discipline of their ships' crews was rigidly enforced.[43] Cunard's standing orders laid rigorous strictures on their ship-masters, particularly in poor visibility, inveighing against the peer-pressure applied by 'other captains who may venture to sail their vessels in such weather'. No master overtaken by thick weather at sea was to be:

> actuated by any desire to complete your voyage: your sole consideration being the safety of your ship, and those under your charge; and we caution and instruct you... to make constant use of the lead [when making a landfall], and to enter in your log the fact of your having done so.

Cunard's Mediterranean routes were served by smaller vessels, many of which took part in the vast movement of troops caused by the Crimean War, but its primary source of business lay in the Western Ocean where blue-nosed Samuel Cunard had begun it all in the first place. Here, however, the competition for the huge numbers of people wishing to emigrate added to those for whom trade, family or duty required them to cross to the New World. Not all of this came from the Americans, making up for lost ground after the disasters of the Civil War; some of the shipping companies appearing in the grey waters of the North Atlantic were not new but had their beginnings elsewhere.

The Liverpool White Star Line which had been founded to serve the Australian gold rush of 1851 by H.T. Wilson was, by the end of the 1860s, bankrupt. The company, owned by this time by a small consortium, was on the point of total failure when it was purchased at a knock-down price reputed to have been £2,000 by Thomas Ismay. Ismay had had experience of steamers when on the board of the National Line and had introduced iron hulls on the emigrant run to Australia in 1867. In 1870, Ismay took over the company together with Mr Imrie and backed by Gustav Schwabe (the uncle of Gustav Wolff, Edward Harland's chief draughtsman with whom he had gone into formal partnership in 1862). As noted earlier, Schwabe had invested in Bibby's Mediterranean Line but 'much to his annoyance' had been told he could no longer have an interest in the Bibby operation. While playing billiards with Imrie, Schwabe suggested that Imrie start a new line to New York in which, if he ordered his new tonnage from Sir Edward Harland, Schwabe and his friends would invest. Imrie and his partner Ismay agreed and, in 1870, set up the Oceanic Steam Navigation Co., retaining the red flag with the five-pointed white star of the old emigrant firm. The new company ordered its new tonnage, the appropriately named *Oceanic*, from the Belfast Yard of Harland & Wolff, remaining loyal to these builders throughout the following decades. In their new ship, Ismay, Imrie and Harland created a new standard in ocean travel.

Allusion was made in the previous chapter to Harland's innovations on behalf of Bibby in 1860 which, in compensating for the occupation of the hull's capacity for bunkers and consequent loss of stowage space, produced a steamer with a full-bodied hull that came into its own after the introduction of iron construction. Harland maintained that hulls based upon 'the old-fashioned wave line theory had produced bad sea-boats and poor cargo-carriers', perceiving 'that long, easy convex waterlines with full sections, gave buoyancy at every point, were more easily propelled, and had large deadweight and…capacity.' On beginning his long association with the resuscitated White Star Line, Harland 'built up' the passengers' saloon and accommodation 'citadel fashion in the middle of the ship' creating what became the classic configuration of the ocean liner with the passenger accommodation lifted out of the dark confines of the after hull and abandoning the tradition of sailing ships. With such distinctive modern vessels the Oceanic S.N.C. began to expand. In 1874 a trans-Pacific service between San Francisco and Hong Kong was inaugurated and further new tonnage – the *Majestic* and *Teutonic* – incorporated strengthening to Admiralty specifications for the carriage of guns in wartime.

With the fierce national and international competition prevalent upon the North Atlantic, lines vied for prestige, and this manifested itself in a number of ways: speed, luxury of accommodation, catering, and even – preposterously – the number of funnels. Much of these qualities relied upon a constant increase in size and in 1899 the Oceanic S.N.C. – by now universally known as the White Star Line from its stellar house-flag – ordered the second *Oceanic* from Belfast. This was the first vessel to exceed in length and tonnage the dimensions of Brunel's ground-breaking *Great Eastern*, and as the Australian emigrant trade under sail gave way to the steamer, the White Star Line was increasingly active on the North Atlantic.[44]

The ship-owner and philanthropist, Charles Booth. (Private Collection)

The men running these increasingly powerful companies acquired great power and influence. They also gained reputations that were soon widespread among the seafaring classes. Charles MacIver who ran the Cunard Line in the third-quarter of the century was an uncompromising figure. When one of his masters requested permission for his wife to accompany him to sea, as was common in sailing ships, MacIver gave his permission, but sent a bill for two passenger tickets and relieved the poor man of his command. His marine superintendent at Liverpool was a Captain Watson, 'a remarkable man, with great knowledge of a ship, but a very narrow outlook'. Such men were to be familiar to generations of British merchant seafarers.

Some of the rising steam-ship-owners of Liverpool were mentioned in the previous chapter, but others emerged in the 1860s. Near neighbours and contemporaries of Alfred Holt were Alfred and Charles Booth, who also founded a steamer service in 1866. For a while the Booths were accommodated in India Buildings, a name later inextricably linked with Holts as their headquarters. Like the Holts, the Booths were Unitarians. They were also corn-merchants, and Alfred Booth like Alfred Holt had gained early experience in the firm of Lamport & Holt and the New York agency of Rathbone & Co., entering business on his own account in 1860 with a partner named Walden. Upon Walden's retirement from ill-health, Alfred recruited his brother Charles from the office of Lamport and Holt and in 1866 the Booth brothers inaugurated their steamship service between Northern Europe and Brazil.

Purchasing two steamers, the *Jerome* and *Augustine*, matters got off to a bad start when, after the former was in a collision, she was found to have been at fault, incurred heavy damages and almost ruined the venture at its outset. The brothers persisted, even fighting off fierce competition later from the great German ship-owner Alfred Ballin who sought to drive the Booth Line off the River Amazon. Charles, who took over the business entirely when his older brother retired, lost £250,000 of his own money before he triumphed. An ascetic man, with 'a head like Van Dyck', according to Sir William Rothenstein, Charles Booth was 'the ideal…man of commerce, coura-geous, adventurous, far-seeing, large-minded, and above all, a man of vision'. Poor health forced him to convalesce in Switzerland before making a trip to the Amazon during which he developed ideas on fuel consumption. In addition to being a ship-owner, Charles Booth − who was related to the Webbs − was also a philanthropist with a genuine interest in bettering the lot of the common man. Having observed the London poor he wrote copious papers on social subjects but, although in sympathy with Socialism and the Trade Union movement, he did not agree that their objectives could provide a general betterment in society. Booth argued that under Socialism enterprise and leadership would be squandered and the conduct of business itself would no longer be 'tried in the inexorable Court of profit and loss'. History proved this opinion correct, confirming Rothenstein's opinion of Booth's judgement.

Nevertheless, Charles Booth served on a number of committees working to allevi-ate the suffering of the poor and the introduction of pensions. He became a member of the Royal Society, the recipient of honourary degrees from both Oxford and Cambridge, finally being made a Privy Councillor. He died in 1916 and is unique among British ship-owners in having a memorial in St Paul's Cathedral. Few who today pass Holman Hunt's copy of his own painting, *The Light of the World*, are aware that it was presented by Charles Booth.

The Booth Line itself, whose new ships continued to use the saints' names adopted for the original two vessels, was particularly noted for penetrating 1,000 miles into the Amazonian rain forest and establishing the route up the great river to Manaus. In 1882 the company opened a service between North Brazil and New York and was poised for further expansion in the years to come.

Although P&O had secured the Government mail contract to India, along with its lucrative and useful subsidy, it was the well-known firm of Calcutta merchants, Mackinnon, Mackenzie & Co. founded by another brace of Scotsmen in December 1847 who, in 1856, secured the carriage of the East India Company's own coastal mails between Calcutta and the Burmese Port of Moulmein. In consequence of this *coup*, William Mackinnon − who had lost his partner, Robert Mackenzie, in a shipwreck in 1853 − purchased two small brig-rigged second-hand screw-steamers, the *Baltic* and *Cape of Good Hope* and founded the Calcutta & Burma Steam Navigation Co. He soon afterwards attracted notice by landing the first troops sent out from Britain to suppress the Indian Mutiny.

Mackinnon was 'a shrewd little man who loved to pore over maps and perceive where a ship might carry, or take up, a profitable cargo'. By 1862 the company had extended its mail services to the Straits Settlements, Singapore and the Persian Gulf, and had changed its name to the British India Steam Navigation Co., a handle almost as cumbersome as P&O's and afterwards almost as well-known by its own initials, 'B.I.'.

Further mail contracts were secured that year from the Dutch Government for carrying the mails to the Dutch East India Company. Trading with the Dutch East Indies required ships being registered in Netherlands' territories and a subsidiary, the Netherlands Steam Navigation Co., existed for some years under the Dutch flag until The Hague's colonial policy changed. With the opening of the Suez Canal 'a huge field of operations was opened up' and shortly thereafter the B.I. steamer *India* arrived in London with a full cargo from the Indian sub-continent. This initiated a new building programme, and by 1876 the B.I. mainline service between London, Colombo, Madras and Calcutta embedded the company as a vital component in the dynamics of the Imperial-Indian economy.

In 1872 B.I. began a mail service to Aden and Zanzibar which, in due course, became a 'through-service' from London and Marseilles to East Africa; as with all mail services, express cargo facilities were automatically on offer. The opening up of Zanzibar improved the revenues of the Sultan and settled an increasing number of Indian immigrants on the coast. Stirred by the muscular Christian conviction that commerce would accomplish the collapse of the ancient slave-trade maintained between the African littoral and Arabia, Mackinnon became absorbed in the development of East Africa. According to one of his associates and a man equally interested in opening the region, the explorer H.M. Stanley, 'East Africa had become Mackinnon's love…and the one important object in his life'. In addition to establishing a branch line to Aden he undertook the construction of a road from Lake Nyassa to Dar-es-Salaam, the only good natural harbour on the coast. Less meritoriously he was peripherally involved with the machinations of Leopold, King of the Belgians, in that monarch's assumed fiefdom of the Congo. In 1874 David Livingstone's body was brought from Zanzibar to Aden by B.I.'s *Calcutta* and transferred to P&O's *Malwa* for carriage home.

As well as with P&O, Mackinnon's steamers were now operating in conjunction with the Union Line's service from South Africa to Zanzibar and on 7 May 1879 Captain J.R. Gavin began a direct India–East Africa service in the *Chinsura*. Although she carried a mere handful of passengers and was soon replaced on the route, she was swiftly followed by the *Burmah*, *Punjaub* and *Java*, by which time the Union route with its brisk traffic had been taken over as far south as Lourenço Marques in Portuguese Mozambique. By 1880 Mackinnon's initiative had increased the Sultan of Zanzibar's revenues and some seventy British ships cleared the port annually. Four years later more B.I. ships were operating on the coast, coming from Bombay via Aden – to meet the B.I. 'Home Service' and the P&O mail steamers – and linking with the Castle Line steamers that had by then displaced their rivals the Union Line. The route was not without risk and on 31 March 1886 the *Abyssinia*, Captain M. Macfarlane, was wrecked – though without loss of life – on the Pinda Shoal. Some competition was experienced from the Sultan's own ex-P&O and Castle Line steamers which ran directly between Zanzibar and Bombay, and Bullard King's Natal Line which was running coolies from Bombay to Natal, as mentioned elsewhere.

The British India S.N. Co. regularly modified or extended its services. In 1872 the London–Zanizibar route had offered insufficient homeward lading, though ample cargoes of railway lines, locomotives, rolling stock and industrial machinery filled the outward-bound ships, a circumstance counter to the received orthodoxy of imperial exploitation. As a consequence the service was abandoned and the outward cargoes were trans-shipped. On the other hand, from 1881 B.I. steamers, trading by way of the Torres Strait to Brisbane, formed an association which by 1886 had added control of the Australian Steam Navigation Co. Thus, in conjunction with the Queensland Shipping Co., the Australasian United Steam Navigation Co. was formed. By these means the network of B.I. services, like those of P&O, was inextricably woven into the very fabric of the British Empire and Commonwealth. In times of imperial emergency it was automatically a strategic asset and as such readily available for government service. Troops, stores, artillery, horses, munitions and supplies of all sorts were carried in B.I. ships to trouble-spots, bush-wars and colonial adventures. During the Abyssinian Campaign of 1857-63 three of the company's ships were anchored offshore to provide 30,000 gallons of fresh water for the expeditionary force. The company's vessels were involved in the Russo-Turkish War of 1878, the Zulu War of 1879 and the Transvaal War of 1881. Mackinnon personally provided the *Madura* to transport an expedition from Zanzibar round South Africa to the mouth of the Congo in 1887 to extricate the beleaguered Emin Pasha, and his ships were involved in suppressing the Uganda Rising of 1897 and supplying the Sudan War of 1898. During the major crisis of the Boer War at the end of the century no less than forty British India ships were involved, mostly in the transport of Indian troops to the Cape. But it was operating commercial services radiating from India itself that had provided the dynamic for the company's expansion, along with its associate, P&O, and others.

No better example of the power of trade, nor of the fact that the flag followed and did not precede it, is exceeded by that of the British India S.N.Co. which, for some time, owned more ships than P&O. Eventually these two companies would find common cause and between them own an enormous fleet in which they would employ vast numbers of Indians in their ships, an army of smartly turned-out *sea-cunnies, serangs, tindals, cassabs* and lascars. Their British officers – *malim sahibs* to a man – would adopt Indian habits, speak Hindi and regard themselves as the elite of the British mercantile marine. Notwithstanding other British shipping companies adopted identical practices, as heirs to John Company it was P&O and B.I. who between them considered the Indian Seas their own.

The cultivation of tea in India was just one of many factors that increased Anglo-Indian trade. Following a steady development of trunk roads, it was during Lord Dalhousie's Governor-Generalship between 1847 and 1856 that the railway network began to spread across the sub-continent. Coupled with restoration and then improvements in the existing ancient but neglected irrigation channels, these arterial systems reduced the prevalence of famine across India. Dalhousie's:

period of office...[was] based upon the principle of improving the welfare of the peasants... He believed that, if the well-being of the masses were improved, benefits to trade would inevitably be bound up with it, and events abundantly proved that he was right.

Such major civil works sucked in investment from British capitalists and provided employment for thousands of labourers and a demand for an immense amount of plant. This provided cargoes for hundreds of ships, but the expensive transit of the Suez Canal — excellent for passengers, mails and tea — inhibited more mundane cargoes carrying lower freight-rates. Nevertheless, the cargoes came: ships floored their holds with railway lines, topped off with general cargo, and carried rolling stock and locomotives upon their decks. One company that specialised in the heavy-lifting of locomotives in particular was Cayzer-Irvine's Clan Line.

This was founded in 1878 when Captain William Irvine joined C. W. Cayzer & Co. of Liverpool, a small ship-owning concern which had two sailing-vessels. One, the *Jalawar*, foundered off Java the year Irvine joined Cayzer, while the other, the *North Star*, went missing two years later. In 1881, however, Glaswegian interests bought into the company and the business was transferred to Hope Street, Glasgow, where the Clan Line Association of Steamers was established. This rapidly acquired a sizeable fleet which short thereafter included the passenger and cargo steamers *Clan Monroe, Clan Murray, Clan Buchanan, Clan Cameron, Clan Campbell, Clan Drummond, Clan Forbes, Clan Graham, Clan MacDonald, Clan MacGregor, Clan Mackenzie, Clan Ogilvie* and the *Clan Sinclair*. The *Clan Campbell* was wrecked that same year and replaced by a ship of the same name two years later. Although much of this tonnage was soon sold on, its expansion was due to a diversity of investors, with Cayzer managing the whole fleet and retaining ownership of six vessels. By 1890 he held a majority interest, and the firm changed its name to The Clan Line of Steamers and confined itself to routes from the Clyde and Mersey to South Africa, Bombay and Calcutta.

Dominating the Hughli with its several anchorages and roads at which ships of all classes and sizes could moor and work cargo, Calcutta remained the seat of British commercial power in India.

In 1877 the Port of Calcutta presented a wonderful sight. There were only a few steamers, the P. & O and French Mail Steamers were at Garden Reach and only the then comparatively small fleet of the British India Co were at the upper end towards Howrah bridge; from that point to Kidderpore were several hundred of the finest ships in the world, moored in tiers four deep. The Esplanade moorings, opposite Eden Gardens, were usually reserved for the aristocrats such as the 'Brocklebank', 'Donald Currie', 'City', 'Star' and 'Bay' lines, the Hastings moorings for the poor relations and Kidderpore moorings for vessels engaged in local trade or owned by natives.

Thomas Golding's reference to the 'natives' – typical of his time – touches upon the moral questions raised by imperial domination. While this much later led to independence, a subject outside the scope of this work, the point must be made that alliances with Indian merchants and commodity producers, Parsee ship-owners and ship-builders who backed British maritime expertise had been mutually beneficial to both British *and* Indian interests. It was, of course, this commercial alliance which created that other enormous Anglo-Indian but British-flagged merchant fleet so frequently featured in this work.

Yet this visible mass of shipping could mask misfortune, for between 1877 and 1879 there was a 'depression in the shipping trade, no freights offering for homeward loading [from India] and some [vessels] languished for over two years waiting for cargoes'. Fortunately on his next visit Golding:

> found a very different state of affairs…in 1897 – the trade was entirely in the hands of steamers who were berthed in the new docks; one solitary sailing ship, Messrs Brocklebank's *Zemindar* was moored in the river. The foreshore along the Esplanade had been reclaimed, Princeps Ghat (where we used to land) stood a long way inland…in forlorn and solitary grandeur, similar to the position now occupied by Marble Arch.

While a mercantile officer might be related by blood to members of the colonial services his place in the imperial pecking-order was lowly. The old opportunities to transfer into the Indian Marine, formed at this time from an amalgamation of the Bombay and Bengal Marines, were gone; vacancies were now reserved for naval officers. However, one remaining opportunity offered British merchant officers all the privileges of the *Raj* as a *pukkah sahib*:

> The Bengal Pilot Service, a branch of the Indian Civil Service, was the finest pilot service in the world. The appointments were made by the India Office, usually to cadets from the *Worcester* and *Conway*. They joined as 'Leadsmen' and after a five year probationship became officers of the Pilot Brigs, and eventually Junior Pilots. The Pilot Brigs cruised off the Sand Heads, and the object of this particular rig was to give the Leadsmen experience in handling square rigged vessels… Boarding a vessel during the SW Monsoon was sometimes a ticklish job, a whip [and canvas hammock-chair] from the main yard having occasionally to be brought into play. The Pilot came on board accompanied by [his] Leadsman, servant and sufficient luggage to take an ordinary person round the world. Under ordinary conditions he presented the appearance of a lackadaisical individual, too tired to do anything and having to be dressed by his servant. But the moment that anything called for action, he sprang to life and became a seaman of the highest competence.

It was said that '[t]he river had its own method of selection and would weed-out those unfit for the work' and certainly its practitioners considered themselves an elite as they rose from the humble and over-worked leadsman through the ranks until reaching the illustrious post of a branch pilot.

At the request of early East India Company commanders, the Hughli Pilot Service had been founded in 1669 by six Cinque Port pilots who undertook a survey of the river. One, George Herron, had produced a chart and instructions for navigating its complex waters. They turned out in uniform and had originally enjoyed the status of a Company commander. By the time Golding contemplated their doings they had become the highest paid pilots in the world, headed by Captain F. Warden who was supported by a small Hindu staff of clerks to administer the service. As the captain-superintendent who 'ruled' the service, Walden controlled a string of Tidal Stations manned by *serangs* from which variations in the predicted water levels were signalled to approaching vessels. He was also responsible for several lightvessels and a large number of buoys which marked the often fluctuating channels and required constant attention. In addition, there was a small fleet of pilot-brigs, commanded by semi-retired branch pilots, two of which constantly cruised off the Sandheads with a number of available pilots on board. During the south-west monsoon these were kept continually under sail, each flying a large flag denoting whether they were the inward or outward pilot-vessel. In 1905 the first steam pilot-vessel, the *Fraser*, arrived, to be joined three years later by the *Lady Fraser*, whereupon the last two brigs, *Alice* and *Fame*, were converted as required to lightvessels.

Complementary to the subsidiary merchant service under the British red ensign in the Indian seas, Canada was to add another major merchant fleet to the tonnage of the British Empire. The Nova Scotian Samuel Cunard had migrated his business to Liverpool, but others travelled the other way, among them Benjamin Bowring who had emigrated to Newfoundland after the Napoleonic War. By 1823 Bowring owned a small fleet of sailing-vessels trading across the North Atlantic. His son Charles diversified into sealing on the Labrador coast and increased his fleet so that by the mid-1860s his ships were carrying cargoes to and from India, Australia, New Zealand, and to Chile and Peru by way of the Horn. From 1880, Bowring went into steam, forming the English & American Steamship Co. which ran cargo and passenger services between Liverpool, New York and St John's, Newfoundland. Another subsidiary was the New York, Newfoundland and Halifax Steamship Co., better known as the Red Cross Line, not to be confused with the Yankee packet company of similar name and distinguished from it by a red diagonal saltire as its device. Bowring's steamers ran a coastal passenger service from Newfoundland, along the Canadian Maritime Provinces and Gulf of Maine to New York.

While Bowring's cargo-carrying operations remained coastal and the company also specialised in sealing in the Canadian Arctic, the Allan Line was home-grown, founded in 1808 by a master-mariner, Captain Alexander Allan of Glasgow who had began running stores and supplies to the British Army then embarking upon the early campaigns of the Peninsular War. At the end of hostilities Allan acquired a new vessel, the *Jean*, and took a cargo to Quebec where, convinced of the future of Canada, he set up two of his five sons with commands, sent two to look after the Montreal business and supervised activities in Glasgow himself until his youngest son could take over. Until 1854 the Allan Line ran emigrants west and brought timber east, providing the settlers and loggers on their farms and encampments with the paraphernalia necessary for daily existence as well as the saws and axes needed to clear the virgin forest. Allan also managed sawmills, carried sugar and rum from the Caribbean, and pork from Boston. Most significant were his Scottish passengers who arrived in Canada in considerable numbers. In 1841 Captain Bryce Allan's *Caledonia* had among his charges MacDonalds, McLeods, Duncans, Campbells, Reids and Weirs. Most Atlantic crossings took about three weeks but in 1847 Captain Bryce Allan recorded in the brand-new *Albion*'s log her arrival in Quebec on Friday 4 June 'after a passage of 70 days, including 46 days in which we were detained by ice'.

Following the success of screw-steamers on the Atlantic, Hugh Allan proposed to his brothers from Montreal that they invest in steamers. Four were ordered from William Denny's Dumbarton Yard and in 1854 – the year old Alexander Allan died – the company, known as the Montreal Ocean Steamship Co. gained the Government contract for the mails to the St Lawrence, undertaking to provide a weekly service to Quebec in summer and a fortnightly run to Portland, Maine, in winter, all for an annual subsidy of £24,000. However, before the contract could be taken up, the steam-vessels were chartered for trooping to the Crimea and the mail service was delayed until the spring of 1854, by which time the company was better known as the Allan Line. Services rapidly expanded, the Quebec mail service became weekly throughout the year, with additional fortnightly mail sailings from Liverpool to Halifax, Nova Scotia, extending to St John's, Newfoundland, during the summer. As new routes were introduced between Liverpool and Baltimore, with a summer service between Glasgow and Quebec, the line acquired more ships. Switching to iron hulls Allan steamers were soon running south from ports on the eastern seaboard of the United States to the Rio de la Plata. In this expansion Allan had absorbed the State Line of Glasgow, the Royal Exchange Steam Ship Co. and the Hill Line.

The company was quietly innovative. One of its first four screw-steamers, the *Anglo–Saxon*, crossed from Quebec to Liverpool in the unprecedented time of nine days and five hours, and a decade later the *Peruvian* left Moville on Lough Foyle near Londonderry on 16 December, proceeded to Portland, discharged her cargo, loaded for home and was discharging at Moville on the morning of 10 January 1865. In 1861 Allan had had the *Hibernian* built with a 'spar-deck' forming a dry and safe promenade deck, the unproductive spaces under which were exempt from tonnage measurement. Following Sir Henry Bessemer's new steel-making process introduced in 1875, the Allan Line went on to lead the field in the introduction of steel to the North Atlantic steam-ship in the Denny-built *Buenos Ayrean* of 1879. The company also pioneered in the adoption of twin screws and bilge-keels, fitted first in the *Parisian* to reduce rolling and, in 1905 launched the *Virginian* and the *Victorian* as the first North Atlantic liners to be powered by steam turbines. However, in September 1909, the Allan Line which had been so much a part of the opening of Canada, was absorbed in the great Canadian Pacific Railway Co., of which we shall hear more.

The development of colonial life, fed by a mass emigration whose multiple wants were carried in British ships, required an ever increasing quantity of wares and commodities, among which was kerosene. This had been first produced by a Canadian geologist named Abraham Gesner who refined oil from bitumen, patenting the process under US Law in 1854 for the making of an illuminant. Hitherto – apart from whale-oil – oil lighting had been provided by paraffin, a product of coal or shale discovered by the Scots chemist James Young. Paraffin production brought Young success, for it sold well throughout the British Empire and was used in America until 27 August 1859 when a drilling rig at Titusville, Pennsylvania, turned the world upside down with a strike of mineral oil that created a fever as intemperate as a gold rush. Wells proliferated in the region and in 1861 production had risen to 3 million barrels with fifteen refineries producing kerosene from crude-oil. With an expanding world eager for a cheap lighting-oil and the only comparable source, Russia, subject to monopolistic controls and minimal output, the problem of exporting the massive surplus arose.

Much feared in wooden ships, oil was always a dangerous cargo. It was originally shipped in barrels as part of a general cargo and in 1861 the little brig *Elizabeth Watts* carried the first cargo of kerosene across the Atlantic from Philadelphia to London. Her master, Captain Charles Bryant, is alleged to have got his seamen drunk and shanghaied them on board to get her to sea, such was the fear of an oil cargo. She discharged 901 barrels of 'rock-oil', or petroleum, and 428 barrels of coal-oil. However, it was 1863 before the first bespoke oil-carriers were constructed. Two 416-ton sisters, the sailing-vessels *Atlantic* and *Great Western* – not to be confused with Brunel's ship of the same name – were built for the Petroleum Trading Co. of Newcastle-upon-Tyne. Of iron construction, their lower holds were in fact cargo tanks which could be voided by a steam-pump in twenty-four hours. To minimise the sloshing 'free-surface effect' which could wreak havoc both transversely and longitudinally to any ship working in a seaway, the tanks were subdivided by both fore-and-aft and athwartships bulkheads. The same practice was adopted in the larger full-rigged ship *Ramsay*, built on the Isle of Man for a Mr Gibson. Capable of loading 1,400 tons in her deep-tanks and filling her 'tween decks with barreled or case-oil, she was by this time one of an estimated thousand ships – mostly small wooden vessels – carrying oil across the North Atlantic. Although some wooden sailing-vessels were also fitted with oil tanks, the carriage of oil in barrels in sailing-vessels persisted. However, barrels often – and notoriously in the case of the American brigantine *Mary Celeste* – leaked badly and oil and oil-products were soon being shipped in tinned-steel five-gallon cans, paired in a wooden framework 'case', giving it the colloquial name of 'case-oil'. Such cargoes would grow during the 1880s and, like grain, wool and other bulk cargoes, provide employment for sailing-vessels.

This new source of oil threatened the old whaling fleets of Britain's north-east ports. Although it was to continue for another half-century from Dundee and Peterhead, Arctic whaling and sealing went into decline. By 1860 the Aberdeen fleet was reduced to three vessels, 'the very ancient full-rigged ship *Pacific*', of about 350

tons, and two brigs, the *Lady Franklin* and the *Sophia*, both of which had been built
years earlier to search for Sir John Franklin's failed attempt to discover the North-
West Passage:

> Though the three ships that put out to sea were only a poor remnant of the
> once-flourishing fleet…they still kept up in a minor degree the peculiar customs
> attending their departure. For some days before they left the figureheads of all three
> ships had been adorned with fluttering ribbons. As they got under way the old tubs
> presented a very quaint appearance. At the fore topgallant mastheads the 'crow's
> nests' had been hoisted aloft; from the old time wooden davits the whaleboats hung;
> and under the tops were slung a number of carcases of beef – soon to be frozen hard
> and so to keep for months. It was the fashion in which Greenlanders carried their
> perishable provisions; and it sometimes happened that a joint would be brought
> back in perfect condition from a voyage several months in duration… Festivities
> prevailed in the town for several days prior to the departure… It carried the for-
> tunes of not a few of those left behind; and should disaster overtake it, or a part of
> it, would result in a mournful echo ashore… [T]he symbol of departure which was
> anciently hung aloft on all whaleships…took the form of a 'garland' and was simply
> an iron hoop, covered in and decorated with ribbons of gay colours. In addition to
> being displayed on departure it was also hoisted on 1st May, by which date the ships
> were in Greenland and which was always kept as a holiday there. On that day the
> 'greenhorns'…were initiated…in much the same way as those on board a southern
> going ship were introduced to Neptune when crossing the line.

Whalers and sealers would yet achieve immortality as the age of Polar exploration
reached its climax, but after 1900 the old auxiliary steam-whaler with its whale-boats
would be transformed first by the Norwegian Svend Foyn's invention of the high-
velocity harpoon-gun, and then by the factory-ship which reduced the business to an
industrial process.

By the late 1860s, with the United States still recovering from the Civil War, British
merchantmen were the world's carriers. However, this was not something regarded
everywhere with approval, particularly in America where British practice had its critics. Not without reason, for the incidence of wrecked ships, drowned seafarers and
passengers was rising alarmingly, while losses of cargo affected both the shippers' and
the consignees' pockets. The combined losses, not of seamen, but that of fare-paying
passengers and cargo, attracted public attention. Such tragic wrecks as the *Royal Charter*
aroused public indignation, notwithstanding that it was caused largely by the weather.

While he was to receive little credit for it, it was a wealthy Newcastle ship-owner
and a director of two marine insurance companies who began the campaign for
reform. In November 1867 James Hall wrote to the *Shipping Gazette* calling for
'urgently required' legislation to end 'the unseaworthy conditions in which many
vessels, frequently overladen besides, are sent on their voyages'. Hall recommended
a fixed load-line to define the deepest draught a vessel might load to, Government

inspectors with powers to certificate a vessel's seaworthiness, and local Marine Boards to investigate all ship losses not readily accounted for. Sadly, despite wide national press advocacy and rising insurance rates, Hall's initiative foundered. He could not, he wrote in *The Times* on 15 December 1869, discover 'any disposition whatever to put a stop to such a state of things' despite the fact that: 'Every practical authority I have consulted admits that a vessel should have a certain [height of] side or freeboard' to give her sufficient reserve buoyancy to survive heavy weather, and that it was the duty of the state to enforce a sensible precaution that was set aside by an unscrupulous pursuit of profit. Hall concluded that: 'The first duty of a Government is to protect the lives of its subjects, and to every other class of workmen, excepting sailors, this duty is discharged.' Matters began to change the following March when Hall's initiative was supported by a petition from the Chambers of Commerce of fourteen ports.

Elsewhere William Leng, editor of the *Sheffield Daily Telegraph* and a man who campaigned relentlessly for the under-dog, had employed his pen in raising public concern about loss of life at sea. His article was read by Eliza Plimsoll whose husband Samuel was the Liberal Member of Parliament for Derby. Plimsoll, Leng and Hall were soon in contact, Plimsoll becoming the front-man in the great agitation that history associates with his name alone. Leng bore him no ill-will. Plimsoll, Leng declared:

> chafed at heart that such things should be and no man interfere. With all his heart and soul and strength, he flung himself into the tremendous task – the task of securing justice for our sailors. Nothing daunted him. His life, his fortune, his whole being were henceforth dedicated to the material salvation of our sailors.

Urged on by his remarkable and equally dedicated wife Eliza, Plimsoll assumed the prominent leadership of the reforming movement. His detractors point out his self-promotion amid the myth-making heroic-celebrity culture of the late Victorian age as having usurped the truth. Plimsoll was regarded as a trouble-maker, even by his own party, and his famous outburst on 22 July 1875 in the House of Commons which shook Disraeli's Government and led to *The Times* describing the errant MP as an 'inspired idiot', did nothing for his reputation among many influential people. They also claimed that the steady advance of state regulation, which gradually reformed merchant shipping in the last quarter of the nineteenth century, was the fundamental cause of increasing safety at sea. However, the Merchant Shipping and Navigation Bill of 1871 failed to answer the problem of over-loading until some thirty years after Plimsoll espoused the cause, and the fact was that the legislature never grasped the bullet speeding towards it.

It was with the publication of *Our Seamen* in 1873 that Plimsoll finally drew the nation's attention to the shocking truth of what were called 'coffin ships'.[45] To set Plimsoll's campaign in context, it is important to identify the nature of these vessels. Unlike men-of-war, merchant ships of the era were not usually broken-up after a useful life. They tended to descend the scale of maritime status, ending up in the worldwide tramping, 'timber-droughing' or coastal trades. While on the one hand

Plimsoll was thundering against an annual loss of some hundreds of seamen, the public was beguiled by the excitement of the tea 'races', news of fast steamers, or stories of emigrant-ships that smacked more of adventurous high-endeavour than culpable danger. Was Plimsoll crying wolf too often as the shipping lobby alleged, at least that part of it which owned elderly vessels and made most of their profits in what they regarded as the margins of business? It was the bestselling *Our Seamen* that finally persuaded the public at large that the red ensign flew above a great evil, though there is little doubt that Plimsoll exaggerated it.

The tortuous ramifications of Plimsoll's long and arduous campaign to have a fixed load-line, which prevented a ship being loaded too deeply, took many years. In the interval several Merchant Shipping Bills had been passed but the Board of Trade, under a succession of lack-lustre and time-serving senior civil servants, failed in its duty to confront the most reactionary ship-owners, several of whom had parliamentary seats. Chichester Fortescue, afterwards Lord Carlingford, and Sir Charles Adderley who was said to have been 'always a day behind the world', were obstructionist Presidents of the Board of Trade, while Edward, later Sir Edward, Bates was Plimsoll's chief ship-owning enemy in Parliament. 'Bully' Bates's' Liverpudlian company was notorious for the losses and misadventures of its ships, such as the dismasting of the *Bates Family* mentioned earlier. It was not part of the Government's business, it was argued by Bates and his supporters, to interfere between a ship-owner and the extent to which he loaded his own property. It was not for the state to keep an eye out for Poor Jack, who signed-on a ship of his own free-will.

It was entirely owing to this indifference that Plimsoll, riding the full tide of Victorian moralising sentimentality, assumed the near beatified status he did. And to be fair to him he lost money, property and his health to the cause, believing in the inherent good in the common working-man, especially that of the maligned merchant sailor. In this he was misguided, as some of his co-agitators were to notice, but while his often histrionic outbursts outraged the dignity of the House of Commons, he touched an essential goodness in the aspirations of the wider national psyche. It was a disgrace that – in the world's pre-eminent power – a power moreover which rested its laurels upon a dominion over the sea, those very waves should annually drown a significant portion of its citizens simply because their ships were overloaded. Arguments that by not overloading their own vessels, foreign ships could undercut British freight-rates were refuted by those suggesting the prevention of foreign ships from entering British ports unless they too conformed to the practice of adopting a fixed load-line. This, after prolonged and titanic efforts, was introduced in 1876.

Nevertheless, between 1867 and 1882, 5,987 passengers were drowned at sea while 10,827 British seamen had been lost in the period 1873–80. Since no fewer than 2,779 of them had been aboard ships carrying coal, the *New York Herald* of 18 September 1880 commented that 'a bare recital of the facts alone must fill the mind with wonder and dread'. But the caprice of misfortune and bad weather, as much as faulty navigation in poorly charted waters were also influential, so that even well-run companies had their problems.

Typical among these was the Blue Funnel Line. Capitalizing upon the success of his ships and the prudence of his masters and mates, Alfred Holt & Co. decided to carry their own insurance. However, the bold move was followed by a series of losses, three of which occurred within a year. The *Hector* was wrecked on a reef off Amoy on 4 October 1875; the *Orestes* was also lost to grounding off Galle, Sri Lanka, on 7 March 1876; and the first *Sarpedon* sank after a collision in fog off Ushant on 4 September. This cost Holts £120,000 plus the valuation of the cargoes, that of the *Orestes* alone being worth £300,000. These were followed by 'an "epidemic of broken shafts" in 1877...several quite serious collisions, some of them involving costly delays, salvage operations, and expensive and tedious legal battles.'[46]

There was no lack of acts of God elsewhere, for, in August 1873, a highly destructive hurricane in the North Atlantic destroyed or stranded over 1,000 vessels. It passed east of Sombrero, west of Bermuda and then struck continental North America between Nova Scotia, Cape Breton Island, Newfoundland and Labrador. Amid major structural damage, some 500 people were killed. Then 1880 proved to be an exceptional year for gales. On 3 November the London *Shipping and Mercantile Gazette* stated that:

> We do not know that it has been our lot to record such a list of maritime disasters as have resulted from the violence of the late gales. Our impression of Tuesday contained upwards of 300 casualties, the details...extending over no less than six columns – a terrific list to contemplate. At Lloyd's as many as 130 [total] losses were posted in one day.

Long before he became a British seafarer, Conrad recalled seeing the steamer *James Westo*:

> [S]he hoisted her flag... I saw it suddenly flicker and stream out on the flagstaff. The Red Ensign! ...the symbolic, protecting warm bit of bunting flung wide upon the seas, and destined for so many years to be the only roof over my head'. It was for many seamen, a fragile covering.

Just how fragile, Conrad could not – at that Damascene moment – have possibly imagined. Plimsoll's great agitation opened other matters to parliamentary scrutiny, much of it led by Thomas Brassey MP who chaired or was present at the later among a series of enquiries arising from Parliamentary Commissions, the deliberations of Chambers of Commerce, ship-owners' trade associations and so forth, which were held between about 1830 and 1875. These ran in tandem to the Commission on Unseaworthy Ships during the progress of which Plimsoll made his reputation.

The wealthy Brassey, who we met earlier, was a lawyer who served as MP for Hastings between 1868 and 1886, becoming a civil lord of the Admiralty in Gladstone's second administration from 1880, when he was knighted, until 1884 when he was appointed secretary. Two years later he received a barony. A noted author on marine and naval matters who was also President of the Institute of Naval Architects, Brassey was appointed governor of the colony of Victoria from 1895 to 1900, later continuing his interest in maritime matters in the House of Lords. From 1908 to 1913 he was Lord Warden of the Cinque Ports and in 1911 was granted an earldom. He made several voyages in his yacht *Sunbeam*, including a circumnavigation, an account of which by Lady Brassey was a bestseller.

From his investigations Brassey wrote of the evidence garnered from concern over the state of the British mercantile marine. The question of manning the navy, avoiding impressments of merchant seamen and the general quality of this perceived pool of man-power available to the state had preoccupied naval thinkers for some time. In 1873 Admiral the Hon Sir F.W. Grey had published a pamphlet on *Suggestions for Improving the Character of Our Merchant Seamen and for Providing an Efficient Naval Reserve*. The following year a Commander G.H. Forster had written *The Mercantile Marine Reserve. How to Man the War Fleets of England Without Imprisonment or Conscription*, and there were other similar pamphlets penned by other naval gentlemen.[47]

> During the Commission on Unseaworthy Ships the ship-owners gave forceful evidence that British seamen had deteriorated, a contention borne out by Brassey's enquiry. A poll was taken from thirty-one sailing ship-masters, thirteen masters of auxiliary steamers, four masters of steamships, fourteen late masters who were now owners or 'over-lookers' (ship's husbands or superintendents), thirty-nine sailing ship owners, three steam-ship owners and seven 'others'. Of these worthies, 89% said that seafarers had deteriorated as professionals, 65% that they had deteriorated in physical condition and 71% that they had deteriorated in subordination.

A further meeting of owners with officials of the Board of Trade was held in Liverpool in 1872. In a speech delivered by the Duke of Edinburgh, an experienced naval officer, His Royal Highness said that 'so long as the system of crimping and advance notes existed, they would have no certainty as to how many ships might be lost before they had gone their first day's voyage'. A report was finally delivered in 1874 adducing evidence from a number of British consuls overseas following a general consular circular of 1872. These gentlemen almost universally agreed with Brassey's witnesses, but it has to be recalled that these men only came into contact with merchant seamen when they were in trouble, usually with the local police. Moreover, the almost unanimous opinion condemned the seamen in sailing ships, largely because it was in these ships that the feckless and rootless now increasingly found a living, steadier men going into the more predictable steamers. Consul Newnham of Amsterdam stated that:

> the general condition of seamen *that come under my notice* [my italics] is indifferent, foreign seamen being as a rule a more sober and respectable class of men. The crews of steamships give far less trouble than those of sailing-vessels.

While Consul Cumberbatch from Smyrna confirmed that:

seamen on board sailing ships [had] much deteriorated during the last ten years... Numbers have never been to sea before sixteen or eighteen years of age, and are undersized men, quite unfit for serious navigation. The crews of steamers belonging to the opulent companies give little or no trouble, as they are all picked men, and are much better provided for than the seamen belonging to sailing-vessels, which appear to be obliged to take what is refused by the steamers.

Consul Cridland from Mobile goes further:

The general condition of the seamen who come under the notice of this consulate is a very bad one. In eight cases out of ten their health is very bad, they are generally affected with severe syphilis, they are badly clad, have little effects of any value, and no means of purchasing the same. Many cannot read or write, and they are generally discontented with their condition on board, and further, they seldom tell the truth regarding any matter they complain of. British steamships have only visited this port since the end of the...[American Civil] war, and the crews have never given any trouble to this office, and consequently they are preferable to sailing ships in every respect.

The consul at Trieste considered 'the crews of steamships give much less trouble than the crews of sailing-vessels, who are generally speaking a superior class of men, for the most part married men, and careful for the interest of their families.' Consul Blackwell at Stettin added: 'British seamen...are sadly too much addicted to drink... In this respect the Scotch are the worst, and quite the reverse for the Welsh, who are remarkable for their orderly conduct and sobriety.' From Riga, Consul Grignon reported that compared to seamen from Scandinavia and Germany 'the contrast... is most striking, and entirely to the disadvantage of the [British]'. Grignon ascribes this to gross and widespread indiscipline, though in contradiction to Blackwell he vigorously excepts 'from the above remarks the crews of steamships and those of the regular Scotch traders frequenting this port – no fault can be found with the conduct of either masters or seamen.'

At Philadelphia, Consul Kortright stated the 'British sailor...is often intemperate; seldom provides himself with sufficient clothing for sea service; neglects attacks of venereal and other diseases; spends his wages before he has earned them', all of which was reinforced by Capel de Crowe at Copenhagen who said: 'The wages paid in England are higher than those of most other countries, and the value the British seaman gives in return is as a rule less.' But Crowe, perhaps aware that the better men are not brought to his notice, adds:

When of temperate habits and under a good master he is probably the best sailor in the world, both as regards seamanship and labour capacity, but, unfortunately, temperance appears to have become the exception, insobriety the rule, and when under the influence of drink he is brutal and insubordinate, and acts totally regardless of consequences.

To this dolorous tale the penultimate word comes from Montevideo where Consul-Major St James St John Munro claimed:

> the standard of British seamen seems to deteriorate every year; those that come to this port, with the exception of the wholly Scotch crews, are mostly picked up at Liverpool and Cardiff, and appear to be the refuse of the class, the Cardiff crews being especially bad, and the larger the ship the greater appears to be the insubordinate character of the crew.

No doubt the wretched Captain Wallace would have agreed with this. Almost the only note approaching approbation comes from a port notorious for crimping and shanghaiing, San Francisco, where in 1872 Consul Booker wrote that:

> The seamen shipped at this port are generally men of good physique, and make excellent sailors. During the nineteen years I have been at this Consulate, I have observed no falling off in their physical condition or capacity; they do not appear to me to have morally advanced to any perceptible extent, and I have been surprised at their stationary condition as regards education. [But he then adds] the seaman of the present day is, on the whole, less amenable to discipline than formerly.

One sailing ship master entered a plea for those charged with the management of these reprobates, writing of the generality of steam-ship crews that the:

> ordinary crews of our magnificent ocean steamers are probably the worst afloat… totally ignorant of the ordinary duties of their profession, being unable to hand, reef or steer. In bad weather, and in cases of great emergency, they entail an amount of anxiety on the captain and officers which cannot be estimated by those who are not conversant with the responsibility of a sea life.

The men to whom this anonymous master referred were those manning the emigrant and passenger ships of the North Atlantic who thought nothing, given the opportunity, of rifling the passengers' baggage lockers, and were known to other seamen as 'packet-rats'. As an example of the kind of incident that was regrettably commonplace in British sailing ships is this, which occurred aboard the *Whittington* of Lancaster, owned by the Lancaster Shipowners Co., and is related by her master, Captain Jocelyn Ruthven. It was Ruthven's first command and he had risen quickly, being taken direct from his training in the *Conway* – see below – as an uncertificated officer in the large Liverpool White Star liner *White Star*, Captain John Kerr. Ruthven was well connected and from the Anglo-Irish Ascendancy. His training had been completed under Kerr in several ships; it was full of incident and included the wrecking of the *Victoria Tower*, for which Kerr's master's certificate was suspended for six months. Ruthven's quasi-naval training in *Conway* conditioned him and, like many from the same or the similar stable of the *Worcester*, led him to expect a standard of obedience and discipline which, while it might pertain in some first-class White Star emigrant ships, was usually absent from the generality of British merchantmen. Nevertheless, despite his youth, as may be deduced from the use of the personal pronoun, Ruthven was in no doubt but that he was Master under God, and the excerpt demonstrates how much depended solely on the moral force of a commander's personality:

A few days before my arrival at Port Louis there was a mild attempt at mutiny amongst my crew. Two men that I shipped in Calcutta to replace sailors left in hospital turned out badly and one of them was impertinent to the second mate whilst taking in a topmast stunsail (sic) just before midnight. When brought before me he was defiant, and when I told the Chief Mate to put him in irons, he ran away forward. We soon followed him and found him in the forecastle apparently ready to show fight with the rest of the watch behind him. The sight of my revolver was, however, sufficient, and we fetched him out, put him in irons and solitary confinement and on biscuit and water. The following noon all the seamen, led by his friend came aft and said they would not do any more work unless the culprit was released. After a brief lecture on discipline I told them that I gave them quarter of an hour to choose between [a] return to duty, and [b] starvation. The weather was fine and the wind fair and I told them I could take the ship to Mauritius without them, with the Officers, tradesmen [boatswain, carpenter, sail-maker and cook] and apprentices. 'In that case,' I added, 'everyone of you will go to penal servitude for mutiny on the high seas.' Before the time was up, they had returned unconditionally to duty and the man was not released until the following day, after he had apologized and expressed contrition for his conduct. In Port Louis they [the two men Ruthven had engaged in Calcutta] thought to force my hand to discharge them by kicking up a row on the morning of the day I was sailing. I did discharge them, but not the way they expected, but by putting them in gaol. Their shipmates were quite pleased to part with them and told the Chief Mate that the man I put in irons had been drummed out of the Navy and that the other boasted that he had been a professional thief in London and been in gaol more than once. It is truly extraordinary how good men will allow themselves to be led astray by others that they know to be wrong 'uns, and that they do not even like.

Thomas Golding recalled a more serious mutiny aboard the tea-clipper *Flowery Land*, manned by Filipinos 'who murdered their officers under conditions of great brutality and who were eventually brought to justice. Seven of them were condemned to be hanged. Executions at that time took place in public outside Newgate. Two of the seven were reprieved but...the reprieves were not read out until after all the seven were placed on the scaffold.'

Another young master, Captain Thomas Fraser, was twenty-three in 1873 when he took command of the 678-ton iron barque *Doriga*, owned by Johnston Churchill & Co. of Liverpool. Fraser was possessed of a keen sense of rectitude whose experiences in the tea-clipper *Corea* had given him little love for the ship-owner, but who had proved willing to use his fists to control a crew. He maintained that:

> The seamen in their ignorance, and misled by the universal sympathy for the way they were fed and exploited, and the loud cry of 'coffin ships', assured (sic) a licence and conduct that was most trying and vexatious to the Masters and officers who had to do with them.

The link Fraser makes between the seamen's bad conduct and coffin ships is telling and might contribute some mitigation, but what is the more remarkable is not so much the excuse offered for the crew but the almost purblind resolution of many masters and mates. Summarising the climb to command of a British sailing-vessel, Fraser called it 'a rough hard fight – against the elements and controlling the roughest and most dissolute men of all colours and nations. A life of great personal discomfort and deprivation'.

The truth was that the system of pay and regulation in British merchant ships was imperfect, not only allowing seamen excessive licence in port, but actively encouraging desertion, intemperance and wild behaviour among a class of men who had no stake whatsoever in the society they purported to serve. One has to consider the method of remuneration applied to merchant seamen, when they had to work off their cash-advances, often taken by the crimps – the world's most dubious personnel agents. They also often signed-on for an outward passage only if their destination had the attraction of an adjacent gold-field to which they would desert *en masse*, leaving the master to rustle up a crew from whatever the crimps could muster on sailing-day. Although pay might be superior to that of other nations, it was relatively poor, though not entirely bad. However, no incentives were given to bind a man to his ship, let alone her owners, and while a crew, once shaken down after a day or two, would almost invariably give competent service, the attractions of the shore would be compulsively indulged in after a long and often tedious passage.

Comparisons were frequently made between the mercantile seafarer and his naval cousin. Such studies generally ignored the necessity of Government to invest in the trained blue-jacket on a long-term basis to encourage competent service and loyalty. Such imperatives were entirely absent from the market-forces of the merchant sailors' world, where the British ship-owner was universally known for his desire to cut costs and save money at every opportunity. Moreover, Brassey, in considering the pool of seamen necessary to Great Britain in the event of war, looked back to the 'Great War' with France and her Allies between 1793 and 1815, adducing evidence that even in this allegedly golden age things below decks in a man-of-war had been very far from perfect. The system of impressment, which poached merchant seamen for service in the Royal Navy and did not pick unfortunate landsmen off the streets as popularly imagined, 'having been in force for eighteen years...became so odious to the seamen, that they were arrayed in unnatural hostility to their native country,' a subject aired in *Britannia's Realm*. During the brief period of peace which occurred in 1802, many seamen 'actually embarked for foreign countries without setting foot on their native shore' while some 'went direct from Portsmouth to join the French fleet to fit out their ships at Brest'. Brassey further reports that:

> The reckless and undisciplined men of our time are the successors of men as reckless as themselves. 'An experience,' wrote Captain Pierce, 'of upwards of half a century with these men leads me to believe that the habit of wasting their substance remains unaltered. They are not now guilty of the same extravagant follies as formerly; but they are still plundered, robbed and ruined, and as little careful of the morrow, or of what is to become of them in old age, as formerly.'

The difference was that in the weak and piping years of peace there was not that need for courage required of seamen in war-time, nor that catharsis inherent in the excitement of action for which only men with such a selfless disregard of personal safety were prepared and – importantly – by which means the British tar had triumphed. In short, as the British consul at Vera Cruz had summarised as early as 1847: 'The British seaman…is generally overworked, hardly used, and therefore discouraged, unhappy, and ready to fly to other countries for employment.'

Many seamen gave exemplary service and, in the natural manner of such things, it was a case of giving a dog a bad name. Although indiscipline was in part attributable to woefully weak support of a master's authority, it was by no means endemic. In fact the success of British merchant shipping during the nineteenth century was largely due to the character and stature of British ship-masters, and to the corps of officers from which they were drawn and who in turn reinforced their commanders. Another important feature was the employment of 'foreign' crews, not those men drawn from British colonies but from China and other places such as the Filipinos, aboard the *Flowery Land*. This required a relaxation of the regulations insisting on British nationals being employed under the British flag, since the mercantile marine was still regarded as a wartime poaching-ground for the Royal Navy. The chairman of the influential Liverpool Shipowners' Association argued that 'Permission to man our ships with foreign seamen would be productive of great good, by establishing a wholesale competition with our own at present demoralised race'.

Although impressment remained on the statute book, the more enlightened governments of the day encouraged merchant seamen to join the naval reserve – with only moderate success – but their value to the British Admiralty, unlike that of their officers, was of less consequence than formerly. The steam-ship was acknowledged not to breed seamen of such consummate skills as the best able-seamen who excelled as the top-men in a sailing man-of-war, and in due course the increasing technology of a warship became so sophisticated that the skills acquired by a merchant seaman were of diminishing value to Their Lordships. In 1858, Rear Admiral George Elliott told the Manning Commission that:

> His experience with regard to merchant seamen had been enlarged from having been eighteen months captain of the Port of Gibraltar, a magistrate on shore and

on the water, and shipping master. He considered that a man-of-war's man was as superior to a merchant sailor now in point of seamanship, as they used to consider, whether rightly or wrongly, a merchant sailor was to a man-of-war's man.

The fact was that while Plimsoll pointed out the poor quality of many ships and the careless disregard of their owners for the safety and well-being of their employees, Brassey's evidence paralleled this with the unsurprising evidence that only men of inferior character, sobriety and reliability could be found to man them. This was a world of crimps, cash advance notes and the seamen's suspicion of the missioners trying to ameliorate their lot; the world of shanghaiing, of pier-head jumps, refitting by purchasing expensive slops from the master and flogging the dead-horse after a month at sea.

That the shipping industry felt less concerned with the issue is attested to by the evidence of:

> Another most experienced and impartial witness, Captain Furnell, for twenty-one years the superintendent of a shipping office in London, [who] said that he did not believe that our seamen had deteriorated. In 1873, there were shipped at his office 17,000 seamen, 1,800 mates and 1,100 apprentices… [though Furnell admitted] when in command himself he had had the greatest difficulties to get his men on board. He had gone down [the Thames] to Gravesend with few sober on board.

From which we deduce — and indeed, have noted in the case of even a Blackwall frigate — that this was quite the norm (and we should recall the vast allowance of grog afforded naval ratings at an earlier period, though the matter is seldom admitted by naval authorities). Perhaps more importantly: 'The conduct of the British seaman in tempestuous weather at sea has rarely furnished cause of complaint to ship-masters and ship-owners.' However, as Brassey sagely puts it, 'I think it is true that the character of the British seaman, whether better or worse than formerly, is open to improvement'.

As for the numbers of seamen employed at this time, in 1874 there were 203,606, excluding masters, of which about one-third, 74,843, were employed in steam-ships, a number which was steadily growing. By comparison, in 1792 the merchant service employed 118,000 men, increasing to 173,000 at the end of the Napoleonic War in 1814 and remaining roughly constant thereafter, up until 1861. The corresponding increase in tonnage was from 2,681,000 tons in 1814, rising to 5,895,000 tons in 1861. This growth, even allowing for changes in measurement, was remarkable. 'The economy of labour' had been 'obtained by improved mechanical appliances' because British yards were increasing their building capacity from 90,600 tons in 1873 to 206,000 tons in 1874.

In order to produce boys fit for the merchant service there were a number of training ships, hulked and moored in various locations. Two, *Conway* and *Worcester* on the Mersey and Thames respectively, were for officer-cadets and run like men-of-war; there were eight floating 'Industrial schools': the *Cumberland* in the Gareloch, the *Formidable* at Bristol, *Gibraltar* at Belfast, *Havannah* at Cardiff, *Mars* at Dundee, *Southampton* at Hull, *Wellesley* on the Tyne and the *Endeavour*, a 'land-training-brig', near Hounslow, west of London. There were also three so-called 'Reformatories' for under-age criminals, the *Akbar* and *Clarence* on the Mersey and the *Cornwall* at Purfleet on the Thames. There were also four 'Independent Ships,' three on the Thames: the *Chichester* at Greenhithe, the *Goliath* at Grays and the *Warspite* at Woolwich; the *Indefatigable* lay moored in the Mersey. Not all sent boys to sea, the Reformatories in particular being places of correction. The *Warspite* was maintained by The Marine Society, a philanthropical institution aiming to give poor, truant, destitute, disadvantaged and orphaned boys a skill, most of whom joined one or other of the sea-services, as did the lads from the *Indefatigable*, owned by The Liverpool Sea Training School for Boys, established in 1864.

But there was resistance against the wholesale import of boys of dubious origin and ambiguous character into the ranks of the mercantile marine. The double-edged expedience of, on the one hand, ridding mainstream society of potential nuisances, and on the other, filling berths at a low wage-rate, was opposed by the more altruistic social engineers of the day. Brassey declared:

> Desirable as it is to make an effort to reclaim the unfortunate children of the pauper or criminal classes, it must be admitted that, in introducing boys of this class in large numbers into the merchant service, we incur a serious risk. The calling of the seaman must inevitably be lowered in the estimation of the honest and independent working population, if we allow it to become a general and recognised refuge for the destitute…it is a grave error to suppose that the dregs of society can be educated for a sea life.

Finally, he added the critical factor: 'A sailor, to be worth anything, must be physically strong and healthy.' He concluded that 'we must begin by attracting boys to the sea from pure and untainted sources'.

Misperceptions flourished, the most remarkable of which was articulated by the then eminent Liverpool ship-owner Mr Lamport, who made the remarkable statement that:

> there is so much leisure in a sea life, that I am almost afraid that in many instances it will be found that the boys are not kept sufficiently hard at work to prevent their minds from falling back upon evil thoughts.

Fortunately, a former registrar-general of seamen considered that although:

> not more than 200,000 persons of all conditions are actually employed on British registered ships, and that little more than a moiety of these are seamen [in the specific rather than the generic sense] there can be no reason why all the boys reared

up to maintain this — an insignificant fraction of our population — should not be derived from a *good* source instead of the outcasts of society.

The financing of sea-training institutions became a bone of contention, though one suggestion was to part-fund them as general educational establishments, partly as training-ships for the merchant service and in part as naval gunnery schools. Prominent and socially well-disposed ship-owners in Liverpool were broadly in favour of making a contribution, though an exemption claimed by hard-pressed sailing ship-owners caused problems. In London matters were different, commerce overruling philanthropy: 'There is no place in the world where the ship-owners act so entirely by themselves. They are a rope of sand. In Liverpool, if any public measure were about to be carried out, the shipowners would combine to carry it.' This 'want of unanimity' scuppered the project and matters continued in a piecemeal fashion. The complexities of the numbers of boys under sea-going training as apprentices, and any naval support, being conditional upon the binding of young men to service in the Royal Naval Reserve, only muddied the murky waters of capitalist enterprise. Ship-owners' philanthropy though particular, was not unanimous.

As for the officers, we have already remarked Ruthven's training in the *Conway*, moored then off Rock Ferry on the Mersey. A contemporary, Thomas Golding, had attended the *Conway*'s great rival, 'the Thames Marine Officers' training ship *Worcester*, an old 50-gun frigate moored off Greenhithe…' with its:

> competent staff of scholastic instructors, and an equally competent staff of seaman-ship instructors who were ex-Petty Officers, RN, and a fine type of seamen of the old Sailing Navy…the training given the cadets in sail drill and everything appertaining to seamanship was A1. The same may be said of navigation, although I fear we allowed ourselves to get rather rusty…before we came to be examined for Board of Trade certificates of Competency a few years later [post apprenticeships] and required a certain amount of coaching.

Conditions aboard *Worcester* were spartan, though generally not unacceptable, except in the matter of food, which was appalling, and the one thing former cadets rarely forgave their mentors for. 'Real old Navy cocoa, with the cocoa-butter floating on top [was] the only thing in the way of food I ever enjoyed in the *Worcester*,' recalled Golding.

Despite the provision of chronometers by the 1870s, the cadets were still obliged to work out longitude by lunar observations, a protracted and by then obsolescent method which 'was hard going…' On the other hand, 'our life in the *Worcester* was sensibly designed to put us through the hardening process required to fit us for our coming careers in sailing ships' in which certificated time was necessary before trans-ferring to steamers. The *Worcester* was cleaned daily, the brass work polished, the ropes Flemish-coiled. On Wednesdays and Saturdays the:

decks were scrubbed with sand and water and afterwards dried with squee-gees and swabs. [This] gave a foretaste of joys to come… Topgallant yards were sent down every night at sunset and crossed again at 8 am next morning. The great occasions were in the autumn when we 'unrigged-ship' in readiness for bad weather – unbending all sails, unreeving all running gear and sending down the top-gallant masts; and again in the Spring when we 'rigged-ship' ready for the fine weather. When we left the *Worcester* to join sailing ships we were certainly fully qualified for any work aloft. We were also proficient in boat-work generally, having had constant practice rowing and boat-sailing.[48]

In 1875 Golding went to sea where he found:

There still remained wide differences in the conditions usual in ships sailing from Liverpool and from London, owing a good deal to old tradition and the association of Liverpool with the North Atlantic trade. In this there was still an atmosphere of the old hard-case 'Wooden Ships and Iron Men' hailing from American and Nova Scotian ports where discipline was maintained by the strong arm. Work was accelerated by liberal doses of 'belaying pin soup' and one of the first qualifications in an officer was an ability to 'lay out cold' any refractory member of the crew. A modified form of the old bucko mate could still frequently be met in Liverpool ships, and the crews were ready enough to model themselves on the 'packet rats' of the Atlantic if given any hint of an opportunity by weak officers. By comparison, the seamen who manned the London ships were disciplined and steady going…

In July he joined the 1,200-ton *Zelica* of Liverpool, built of Nova Scotian pine:

She carried the sailor's bug-bear – stuns'ls… Whatever use these sails might have had in light winds with the yacht like tea-clippers, they never paid in an ordinary vessel for the wear and tear on gear and the crew's tempers. The wily old salt, going round the docks looking for a ship, would first look aloft to see if there were [studding sail] boom-irons on the yards, and then in a wooden vessel, look closely whether the pump bolts were bright and worn. The former meant stuns'ls and the latter a leaky vessel and much pumping. Being signed on as an Apprentice merely meant that one paid (or one's parents paid) for the privilege of working just as hard as any of the seamen and living on the same Board of Trade allowance of hard bread and salt provisions which never varied during a four month's passage. If there was any difference in the work the Apprentices did, it was that more than a fair share of the most unpleasant and dirty jobs fell to them. The average sailing ship carried the barest minimum of men, so that even in fine weather there was always work and to spare, and on any job out of the ordinary… like tacking or wearing ship or handling the heavier sails, the call had to be for 'all hands'.

The work was endless, making nonsense of William Lamport's ill-judged assessment; on a voyage to India the entire suit of sails might be shifted at least six times. Guarding against chafe, repairing rigging, varnishing wood, chipping rust and painting steel-work kept the watches busy when they were not attending to the sails:

> There were Shanties for quick pulls, for long dry pulls, for heaving up the anchor and for working the pumps…Their object was to lighten the work… They also acted as a safety valve…enabling the singer to work off his growls against the food, etc and of which no one took any notice… [A]s late as 1881 I saw the tanks filled at Hankow (sic) from the river Yang-tse-kiang with no more than a rough filtering. Powdered alum was put into the water which was allowed to settle before it was run into the tanks, but the alum had only a purely mechanical effect of causing the sediment to settle, and had no chemical value at all.

The *Zelica* loaded a cargo of steam-coal for the P&O steamers and took it to Bombay. She then proceeded to Bassein and loaded rice to Cork for orders, and ultimately Liverpool:

> There was then no tug boat at Bassein, so that we had to make our way up river by 'backing and filling' and painfully dredging our big and heavy ship for 70 miles up stream. [It was] back-breaking work. It consisted of driving up with the tide and alternately paying out and heaving in cable with the old-fashioned hand-windlass, and of bracing the yards round to back, or fill the sails to keep the ship in mid-channel… An officer or apprentice in these days had a certain amount of time ashore between voyages, but I wonder if people understand how amazingly little of shore life was known by the average seaman. I don't exaggerate when I say that it was normal for a man to spend more years at sea in his lifetime than he spent weeks ashore. Too often he came home after one, two, or even three years away, drew his pay for those years of toil, set off to spend it gaily – and in two or three days was penniless, signed on and outward bound on another year-long voyage… The seaman of that day was of a race apart – a race that is now [in 1935] extinct. He lived hard and died hard, and whatever his faults may have been on shore, none who knew him at sea will deny that he was a good seaman who in the tightest jamb [sic] would stand by his shipmates.

But not all masters and mates behaved with the mid-Victorian manliness inculcated in the Goldings and Ruthvens of the maritime world. Reference was made earlier to the scandal of the steamer *Jeddah* when describing the arrival of the *Cutty Sark* in Singapore after the suicide of Captain Wallace in 1880. The affair was regarded as a serious blot on national honour, particularly as it caused a great loss of 'face' to the white man, a serious matter in the Far East at this time. The *Jeddah* was engaged in the *haji* run which took Muslims from the Straits Settlements to Jeddah for the annual pilgrimage to Mecca. British ships picked up pilgrims at a variety of ports as far apart as Basra and Singapore. Where 'the Indian and Malay pilgrims… [were] well behaved…,' wrote Golding, now a junior officer in Gellatly, Hankey & Co.'s steamship *Afghan*. Those from the Persian Gulf ports:

> came aboard armed to the teeth, the weak and sickly were driven below, while the strong and lusty encamped with their belongings on the upper deck whence they refused to budge and the wash deck hose was cut through in twenty places the first time we tried to wash down…At Bushire (Būshehr), they nearly capsized the ship while engaged in a free fight with the other pilgrims who were joining at that port. At Lingah they prevented any more pilgrims coming on board. The latter, in revenge for losing their passage to Jeddah, burned down the Agent's house. They were deterred from similar games at Muscat as HMS *Seagull* was in port and we anchored close to her. The pilgrims taken on board at Muscat brought our total up to 1,500. At Bussorah, we had taken on board El Beggi, chief of the Baktiari Clan, who brought with him 100 armed retainers. At Bushire we were joined by the Persian Governor of Shiraz, who brought with him a large retinue which included several members of his harem; for [whom]…several fist-class cabins had been engaged. Hardly a day passed without a fight between the Shiraz and Baktiari men…

It was a lucrative but unpopular business, a clash of cultures in an age in which pejorations and prejudice were freely expressed:

> I cannot describe the filthy habits of these people, we were all relieved when we arrived at Jeddah without an epidemic breaking out. We remained at Jeddah for six weeks, awaiting the returning pilgrims from Mecca, who had by this time become *Hadjis* (sic). There was a marked difference in the demeanour of these men returning home; those who had embarked full of bounce and truculence, re-embarked in a much chastened mood.

Golding does not attribute this to any spiritual reformation, but to having been 'fleeced and bullied by the boarding-house keepers at Jeddah and Mecca, both on their arrival and return…' and on their trek across the desert to Mecca where 'they were liable to interference at the hands of predatory Bedouin.' Whatever the absolute truth of these assertions, the setting is clear. It was in this business, in which the pilgrim was considered as a human cargo, in which the steamer *Jeddah* was engaged, though it was from Singapore and the Straits Settlements that she embarked her pilgrims.

The *Jeddah* was a medium-sized auxiliary steamer owned by the Singapore Steamship Co. whose proprietor was a certain Syed Mohamed Alsagoff. She sailed from Singapore on 18 July, stopped at Penang before heading across the Indian Ocean carrying 953 pilgrims. The south-west monsoon was blowing and she was labouring in heavy weather as she approached Cape Guardafui. In the gale the engines failed and as the ship rolled in the trough of the sea, she began taking in water. Both seamen and passengers pumped or formed bucket-chains, but uncertainty began to affect the pilgrims. At this point, worried about the mood of the passengers and believing them increasingly hostile, Captain Joseph Clark lost his nerve and ordered the ship abandoned by the officers. Clark had his wife with him and was influenced by the mate, George Augustine Podmore Williams, who was convinced the ship was sinking. The panic – all on the officers' side – was infectious. Two boats were lowered and Clark, Podmore Williams and their colleagues escaped in one in poor conditions, deserting their crew and passengers and confident they had only a few hours more to live. The other boat, under the second mate, contained some of the pilgrims, but to prevent chaos the falls were wisely cut by the pilgrims' headmen and, with the Malay crew of the *Jeddah*, they all resumed pumping.

On 8 August Holt's *Antenor*, Captain J.T. Bragg, was on her way to London from Shanghai. She herself had 680 pilgrims bound for Mecca when she sighted the drifting derelict. Bragg sent his chief officer, Mr Randolph Campbell, away in a boat to make an assessment. Campbell reported the *Jeddah*'s boilers extinguished and 8ft of water sloshing round inside the ship. The difficulties of transferring so large a number of pilgrims were too great, so Bragg decided to take the stricken pilgrim-ship in tow. Aboard the *Jeddah*, Campbell and a small salvage-party managed to connect a towline streamed by the *Antenor*'s second officer. Campbell then persuaded the *Jeddah*'s crew and the pilgrims to resume their pumping, taking the helm himself until sufficient confidence had been gained to hand-over to the *Jeddah*'s own *sea–cunnies*. In due course the *Jeddah* was brought safely in to Aden with no loss of life beyond those of the ship's own second mate and the ten pilgrims lost in his boat.

At the enquiry held at Aden on 20 August 1880 Captain Clark was found guilty of gross misconduct, his certificate being suspended for three years. Having 'more than aided and abetted the master', twenty-eight-year-old Williams was found guilty of 'officious and unseamanlike conduct'. He was severely reprimanded and returned to Singapore a disgraced man. He served briefly on Syed Moshin bin Salleh Al Jofree's *Vidar* before becoming a runner, or 'water-clerk', for the ship-chandlers McAlister & Co. In 1883 he married a Eurasian, Elizabeth Jane Robinson, by whom he had several children, but his own venture into a broking business failed and he took employment offered by Dawood & Co. He redeemed himself somewhat by becoming the Singapore representative of the Imperial Merchant Service Guild, an officers' trade association, and was often referred to as 'Daddy' Williams. He died aged sixty-four of Bulbar Paralysis in 1916, and lies buried at Singapore, but his cowardice was immortalised by his successor as mate of the little *Vidar*, for 'Daddy' Podmore Williams was the model for Joseph Conrad's *Lord Jim*. [49]

By 1882 British ship-owners possessed 71 per cent of the world's carrying capacity and the iron tramp-steamer was encroaching directly upon the sailing-vessel's traditional trades. Some 30,870,000 tons of exports were being carried in British steamers of over 1,500 tons and, quite apart from the steam-ships being used by the 'liner companies', steamers were moving bulk cargoes from the West Indies, Baltic and the Black Sea where Ukranian grain was a regular lading. In addition to Australian wool and grain, sailing-vessels were hauling cargoes of coal, timber, asphalt and phosphates, guano and copper ore. At its inception, at least, the British tramp-steamer was 'a good wholesome ship, a large carrier, with sufficient power to take care of herself in all weathers'.[50] Shipyards began to turn out steamers 'on speculation', which caused a recession in 1884.

By this time steamer-communications were well established across the globe. Until 1882 the monthly mail was carried to Melbourne via Ceylon by P&O, who kept the small steamer *Avoca* on the coast to forward the mail-bags to Sydney, but in that year a direct service to Sydney was established by the P&O steamer *Indus*. The Orient Line had also moved into steam, purchasing three ageing steam-vessels, the *Cuzco*, *Chimborazo* and *Lusitania*, from the Pacific Steam Navigation Co., who also provided masters and mates. Later this company also carried mails, which were picked up at Naples before making the outward transit of the Suez Canal and the tradition of announcing the arrival of the mails by gun-fire dating from the days of the Admiralty packets was maintained for a while. Aboard the *Chimborazo*, 'We had two small brass carronades and used to fire blank shot from one of them when entering port with mails, a practice which a little later fell into disuse'. The Orient Line surveyed and established at their own expense a coaling-station on Diego Garcia in the Chagos Archipelago, lying on the direct track between Cape Guardafui and Cape Leeuwin. Two redundant sailing ships were moored there to act as coal hulks.

Other auxiliary steamers appearing in Australian waters were those of Messrs Wigram & Co., the *Kent*, *Durham*, *Hampshire*, *Northumberland* and *Somersetshire*, which would in time metamorphose into the Federal Steam Navigation Co., but a considerable portion of the passenger trade remained in the hands of sailing-vessels. Messrs Green's *Melbourne*, later renamed and better known as *Macquarie*, the *Superb*, *Carlisle Castle*, *Shannon* and *Lord Warden*, joined Devitt and Moore's fleet, and although George Thompson & Co. had pioneered the steamer service with the *Aberdeen*, mentioned previously, the Aberdeen White Star Line retained some sailing-vessels. The Loch Line and several other companies carried passengers, and when the trade was brisk the Colonial Line put on steamers with temporary accommodation which was rudimentary, dreadfully primitive and disposable. This firm was in due course taken over by Messrs Tyser & Co.

It was not only mail contracts that underwrote such enterprises. Other Government charters and contracts were available. There was a trade in cavalry remounts, sent from Australia to India, and in addition to the spot-charters that distributed bunker coal throughout the Empire for both warships and steam-merchantmen, a company of brokers like Houlder Brothers could become ship-owners by securing a steady contract to supply coal on a regular basis, in their case Cape Colony. By such means cross connections from South Africa to South America were made so that, in due course, like other British companies, Houlder Brothers' business would be best known for its regular services there.

Where one company was successful another often followed, to increase competition and open it still further in the quest for shippers and consignees. The founding of Singapore had created a destination for cargo and in 1859 the first of William Thomson's ships to venture into eastern waters arrived there. What would become known as the Ben Line had been begun in 1839 by the Thomson Brothers of Leith who imported Italian marble into the Firth of Forth in a vessel named the *Carrara*. Eight years later Alexander retired, leaving the firm to his brother William who busied himself shipping coal to Canada and importing timber on the homeward run. The company extended its routes to the Baltic and Mediterranean but by 1884 had abandoned timber-droughing across the Atlantic and entered the expanding trade with China, so much so that its first steamer, the *Benledi* of 1871 – lost near Swatow in 1887 – was followed by the *Bengloe* in 1878, the larger *Benalder* in 1880, the *Benlarig* in 1881, the *Benvenue* in 1883, and others. These handsome steamers, well regulated and beautifully maintained, earned the nickname of 'the Leith yachts', and the conditions aboard them and the ships of B.I., P&O, the Orient Line, Holt's Blue Funnel liners and MacGregor, Gow's Glens offered far better prospects than the anxious, wearying business of managing sailing-vessels.

By the 1880s many ambitious young officers, having served their time in sail, were only too happy to transfer to the regular steamers of the liner companies. 'The contrast between service in a steamer and that in a sailing ship had to be experienced in order to be appreciated,' wrote Thomas Golding:

> We were no longer known as 'Mates', but were classified as 'Officers'. Neat uniforms took the place of any old clothes worn at sea in sailing ships. The three watch system (four hours on and 8 hours off) replaced the old 'Watch and Watch'. The dinner at noon and scanty supper at 6 pm disappeared in favour of lunch and late dinner, at a generous table with trained stewards in attendance… What we appreciated as much as anything was the unlimited supply of fresh water. Instead of having to provide our own beds and blankets (we never ran to sheets), beds and bed linen were supplied. Gone were the long monotonous four months passages and leisurely stay in harbour of the sailing ship; we had a reasonably long stay at our final port of destination but, at all ports of call, cargo work proceeded day and night and often on Sundays. I think the only thing of which we disapproved, was the dirt caused by coal and smoke, after having experienced the spotless cleanliness of the sailing ship.

The tedious and filthy chore of coaling ship was made as tolerable as possible, and even passengers were invited to assist, for which voluntary work they were paid 1*s* per hour and – inevitably – grog at stated intervals during the operation. This task brought to light a serious deficiency in the training of masters and mates, an ignorance of the physics of ship-stability. In November 1882 the Orient liner *Austral* was coaling in Sydney where a method by which alternative colliers bore coal to each side of the ship in turn was in use:

When coaling in this way at night into the forward bunker on the starboard side they continued too long, and with the ship several feet by the stern put the after coal ports in the water, when she filled and sank, sitting quite upright with the promenade deck covered at high water.

The *Austral* was raised, refitted and put back into service, but at the consequent Board of Trade Inquiry the Orient Line directors were anxious to dispel rumours that their ship had turned-turtle. Captain Ruthven, now himself an Orient Line master, commented that having:

> got the highest expert evidence in the world to prove that she could not have capsized…it was quite evident that the Nautical Assessors sitting with the Wreck Commissioner knew nothing about the theory of stability, which was then a closed book to my profession. It had never been investigated by mathematicians until after the loss of HMS *Captain*, which capsized off Cape Finisterre in a gale whilst under steam and a pressure of canvas in September 1870. As we walked away from the Court, Mr Anderson [the Orient Line Chairman] asked me if I understood the theory which had been so much commented on by our expert witness, Dr Francis Elgar. I had to confess that I did not, when he asked if I did not think that the Captain of a modern ship ought to understand it. I quite agreed…

Following work by Ruthven and his chief officer, Mr E.A. Veale, the subject was soon afterwards included in the syllabus for examinations of competence, evidence of one hazard – albeit a surprising one at this late juncture – to which seafaring was exposed, over and above the evils which had been adumbrated by Plimsoll and Brassey. However, not all ignorance could be attributed to the deficiencies of the officers' training. Poor charts lacking much essential information could easily mislead navigators and were still much in evidence, while ignorance of the ocean's currents was widespread, many ship-masters who were aware of them keeping the information a trade-secret in order to steal a march upon rivals.

Although the nineteenth century was the great era of hydrographic surveying, particularly by the Royal Navy, to its great credit, ship losses remained huge. To some extent the auxiliary steam-vessel contributed to maintaining a high level of casualties for she made more landfalls, touched ports more frequently with her bags of mail and was often being pushed at high speeds in defiance of poor visibility or darkness. It was for these reasons that masters like Ruthven, who had a series of groundings in his career, one of which was on the coast of Somalia near Ras Hafun from which he, as chief officer, was lucky to extricate the ship, took a greater interest in determining his position:[51]

> [T]he old practice of fixing the position once a day at noon, which was good enough for sailing ships that as a rule kept clear of the land except at the end of [their] voyages, required supplementing for steamers…

There was therefore a marked and increasing technical competence by well-educated and mathematically minded masters like Ruthven, who not only assured Anderson that he would attend to the matter of his ignorance of stability forthwith, but introduced the taking of stellar sights at morning and evening twilight. The results were more accurate and were helped by the introduction of stellar telescopes for fitting to a sextant.

Great Britain's assumption of the imperial mantle was a somewhat erratic and gradual process. Her entanglement with the administration of India has been followed from the inception of the first East India Company in 1600 and the era of commercial companies being incorporated by royal charter was not finally ended until 1874. From henceforth the Imperial Government in London put in its own colonial service to run colonies. Among such oddities as the exchange of German Zanzibar for British Helgoland, on the other side of Africa the Dutch relinquished their rights to maintain a trading post at Accra, and the port became entirely British-run. Elsewhere, matters were less gently and serendipitously managed, but wherever British power extended, it was merchant shipping that encouraged it in the first place and then afterwards maintained it.

Imperial communications provided ship-owners with rich opportunities as we have noted in several quarters, not least the securing of the mail contract to Capetown in 1857 which gave the Union Steamship Company *its* opportunity. Having been granted several five-year extensions, in 1873 the Commons refused to ratify the Chancellor of the Exchequer's automatic renewal, and upon the expiry of the contract in 1876 it was subsequently split between the Union Line and the newcomer on the Cape route, the Castle Line.

What in 1881 would become the Castle Mail Packet Co. had been founded under the chairmanship of Donald Currie. Scottish-born and Ulster-educated, Currie left school and returned to Greenock aged fourteen, working for an uncle until in 1844, at the age of eighteen, he and his elder brother James moved to Liverpool where they worked for Cunard.[52] Then, in 1862, Currie set up his own shipping company, running crack sailing packets from Liverpool to Calcutta. Named after castles, these had a high reputation for smartness and reliability, but in 1866 he began a change to steam, founding the Liverpool & Hamburg Steamship Co., favouring the best officers he had in his sailing ships and thus building up loyalty and *esprit de corps*. In 1872, on the advice of others, Currie established the Castle Line — not to be confused with that of Thomas Skinner — aimed at challenging the Union Line's domination of the Cape route with two ships, the *Iceland* and the *Gothland*. Despite faster passages than the Union ships and the carriage of 'private mails', returns were poor and Currie was on the verge of pulling out when in 1876 the Prime Minister of Cape Colony, Sir John Molteno, impressed by the superior despatch of Currie's ships, was instrumental in the offer of half the mail contract.

As we have seen, the other half was retained by the Union Line, and the rivalry between the two became intense, particularly when fuelled by the lust for riches caused by the speculations in the gold and diamonds of the Witwatersrand. The

The ship-owner, plutocrat and statesman, Donald Currie. (Private Collection)

Although the Belfast-built *Goth* of 1893 retains her Union Line name, she is in the livery of the new Union-Castle Line following the amalgamation under Donald Currie of the Union Line and the Castle Mail Packet Co. in 1900. Attributed to the Maltese artist Gaetano D'Esposito. (© Courtesy of The British Mercantile Marine Memorial Collection)

Union Co. suffered some problems among which a broken propeller shaft delayed Captain H.E. Draper's *Syrian* and necessitated a further delay for Captain Baynton, whose homeward sailing from the Cape in the *American* was interrupted as she diverted to Ascension, whither Draper had gone for refuge. The tow home was full of incident, most according to one of the *Syrian's* officers, William Crutchley, of little credit to those concerned, and culminating in a collision in which a sailing-vessel, the *Aracan*, drove into the hampered *American* and consequently foundered. Ironically, on another occasion the *American* – this time under a Captain Wait – also suffered from an identical defect.

By 1891 Currie's Castle Line, its ships by now all named after castles just as his former sailing-fleet had been, suddenly lost its record of fast passages to the Cape to the Union Line. In 1893 the Union Line's *Scot* made an outstandingly fast passage that stood as a record for forty years, but the fierce rivalry it engendered and maintained could not continue indefinitely, particularly under the constraints imposed by increased Government control after the Boer War broke out, and required a vast uptake of private merchant ships as war transports. For some time the Union Co.'s board had been seeking to cut costs, and in 1883 had forced a reduction in salary upon their masters, driving senior officers and ratings out of an employment that they had hitherto regarded as second-to-none. In 1900 the two lines merged under the leadership of Currie as the Union-Castle Line. All Currie's new tonnage would be named after castles, dropping the old racial names of the Union Co. It was 'the greatest of all pities…', lamented Captain Crutchley, who was by then regarding the amalgamation from the bridge of a New Zealand steamer.

Currie's rise had been spectacular. While working for Cunard, which was then the only British company offering a regular transatlantic service with a mere handful of ships, Currie had headed the cargo-department when still only in his twenties. Here he learned the value of a Government mail contract and, upon the abolition of the Navigation Laws in 1849, it was Currie who established a Cunard presence at Le Havre, afterwards moving on to Bremen and Antwerp. He was therefore instrumental in founding a link between France and America by way of Liverpool. In branching out on his own in 1844 Currie drew backing from friends in Liverpool and his energies extended beyond his seizure of the service to South Africa. In 1875 he had been elected the chairman of a ship-owners committee to advise Government on amendments to the regulation of the mercantile marine eventually enshrined in the Merchant Shipping Act of 1876.

News of the outbreak of war with the Zulus sparked by the crushing defeat of Lord Chelmsford's force at Isandlwana in January 1879 was brought by a Castle Liner from the Cape to São Vincente in the Cape Verdes – then the nearest telegraph station – and from there transmitted to London. Within forty-eight hours Disraeli's Government had put troops aboard the *Dublin Castle*. In this crisis, however, the palm belonged to the Castle Line's rival, one of whose masters displayed initiative. Hearing of the disaster of Isandlwana while at Capetown, Captain William Crutchley went immediately to the authorities, placing the Union Steamship Co.'s steamer *African* at their disposal. The day following Cetewayo's victory, the *African* embarked the 2nd Battalion, the King's Own Regiment, and conveyed them to Natal. In addition to landing the infantry, Crutchley put ashore one of the *African*'s 12-pounder guns to defend 'the Pynetown peninsula' and support the levies hurriedly being raised from the male settlers there.

Gold had first been discovered in the Transvaal in 1866, and Currie backed gold and diamond mines in South Africa, deriving a fortune from these investments with which he endowed several institutions as diverse as the Universities of London and Edinburgh, Queen's College and the Royal Academy in Belfast, and a nurses' home for University College Hospital, London. Entering politics as a Liberal he was elected to the Commons in 1880, but differed with Gladstone over Irish Home Rule. Although he retained his seat as a Liberal Unionist, he left Parliament in 1900 when the twin preoccupations of the amalgamated Union-Castle Line and the Boer War returned his attention to South Africa. He was by now seventy-five years of age, but undiminished in energy. His ships carried large numbers of troops and supplies to the Cape and at the crisis of the war when Lords Kitchener and Roberts were ordered to the war-zone, Currie arranged for the Castle liner carrying Roberts out from Britain to meet the P&O liner bringing Kitchener from Egypt at Gibraltar so that both might travel and confer on the voyage south. Currie himself, having some sympathy with the Boer cause, attempted reconciliation, which sadly failed, but his public service earned him a knighthood.

By this time Currie's standing was high. In September 1883 he had entertained the Prince of Wales, the Kings of Denmark and Greece and the Tsar of all the Russias aboard the *Pembroke Castle* in Copenhagen. At this international gathering no less than twenty-nine members of the royal houses of Europe boarded the ship, wearying the bands of the accompanying men-of-war who were obliged to play all the national anthems. In June 1895 Currie had detached the *Tantallon Castle* to attend the opening of the Kiel Canal and with the ship anchored in the Kielerfiord he dined his old political master Gladstone, who was by then out of office. Currie was a forceful speaker and a great advocate of South Africa, but he was also passionate about the mercantile marine, lecturing at the Royal United Service Institution on maritime warfare, urging the adoption of an integrated policy that would enlarge the network of coaling stations, deep-sea telegraphy, graving docks and ship-repair facilities across the Empire. He also suggested that closer links should exist between the merchant service and the Royal Navy, over and above the Royal Naval Reserve, which then excluded engineers and firemen. It was, Currie pointed out, 'as important for a steam-vessel to have competent engineers as it is to have good officers'.

At leisure Currie, like many other super-rich Victorian ship-owners, had his estates, his art collection, his shooting and his yacht, the beautiful steamer *Iolaire*. In that deferential age he appears to have been genuinely esteemed by his officers and crews, but particularly by his ship-masters, of whom it was said that they 'thought much of him'. He did not entirely neglect the underdog and was fond of remarking that, 'I always feel sorry for the stewards'. He died on 13 April 1909 and was buried in

Fortingal, Perthshire. From modest beginnings and an attachment with one of the earliest steam-vessel enterprises, Donald Currie had risen to bestride the age, a shipping magnate such as the world — even the world of the East India Company — had not previously seen. His story, beginning in the North Atlantic and ending with domination of the Cape route, links the era with which we began this volume, with what was to come. While Currie enjoyed his art, his castle and his cruises in the *Iolaire*, the toiling workforces he and his fellow shipping grandees employed scraped a bare existence under the simple philosophy of 'more days, more dollars'.

CHAPTER NOTES:

1. Brooke acquired his wound at the battle of Rangpur in January 1825 during the First Burma War. He was left for dead on the field but was eventually rescued and patched up. It was considered too risky to remove the ball reputed to have affected his genitalia, though it was sometime afterwards extracted from his back having migrated through his body. Although Brooke carried out a passionate love affair with the fabulously wealthy heiress Angela Burdett-Coutts, this was probably platonic; the union was never made 'for the best of reasons' and he never subsequently married.

2. The rebellion arose from a combination of quasi-Christian religious mysticism and a desire for agrarian reform led by Hung Hsiu-chuan who wished to establish a Heavenly Kingdom of Peace and was remarkably successful, acquiring territory and establishing a capital at Nanking. However, Hung failed to secure an administrative legitimacy and the Chinese dynasty was assisted in the rebellion's suppression by the British, largely in the person of General Gordon who, before his assassination at Khartoum, was better known by his nickname, 'Chinese' Gordon.

3. A *lorcha* was a Chinese-built craft constructed under European — chiefly Portuguese — influence, but retaining the junk-rig characteristic of wholly indigenous Chinese craft. They were used for coastal trading.

4. See J.M. Scott's *The White Poppy, The History of Opium*.

5. The anti-Western Society of the Harmonious Fists was one of many Chinese 'secret' societies dedicated to remove Western influence and trade. The Government of the Dowager Empress Tzu Hsi tacitly supported the Boxers' objectives, which included attacks on trade and traders, workers on the foreign-owned railways and ships, Christian proselytising, missionaries and converts, and culminated in a fifty-five-day siege of the foreign legations at Peking. It was put down by another international expeditionary force landing at Taku.

6. The American company, Russell & Co. — known to the Chinese as Kee-chong — whose Shanghai Steam Navigation Co. was the most successful of the three firms on the coast, obtained a great advantage from the manner in which the original river berths were allocated. In February 1861 the British admiral, Sir James Hope, led an investigating party of British companies whose representatives selected river-frontages east of Soochow Creek at Hong Kew that seemed beneficial. When Russell & Co.'s agents arrived they were obliged to purchase land adjacent to the Chinese city further upstream at Kin-Lee-Yuen, However, this decision, forced upon them by circumstance, placed them amid their customers and greatly enhanced their take-up of a brisk business.

7. Of these twenty-seven foreign steamers, Russell owned seventeen, Swire four (*Glengyle, Pekin, Shanghai* and *Tunsin*), Jardine's six (*Haining, Appin, Nanzing, Sin Nanzing, Taku* and

Yuentsefei).There were also six vessels owned by the China Merchant's Co. which was supported by the Chinese Government.The *Glengyle* was owned by both of the British companies at various stages of her life. See Kwang-Ching Liu's *Anglo-American Steamship Rivalry in China, 1862–1874*, for a full analysis of this fascinating trade.

8. The *Erl King*, owned by John Wade of London, loaded 1,223,342lb of tea, compared with *Agamemnon*'s 2,516,000lb. *Achilles* and *Ajax* both loaded about 1.12 million-lb and the Nestor 1.8 million, against the *West Indian*'s 1.2 million.

9. Andrew Shewan who knew both Willises, maintained that John Willis, senior, was the inspiration for the shanty 'Stormalong', largely on the strength of this accomplishment.

10. Shewan's recollection of the year of Willis's death may be adrift here, for the *Lammermuir* was lost on 31 December 1863. See David MacGregor, *The Tea-clippers*, p104.

11. This was not always the case. Prior to making his record homeward run in *Sir Lancelot* in 1869, Captain Richard Robinson discharged at Hong Kong then ran down to Bangkok in nine days for rice.Taking a month to load, *Sir Lancelot* returned to Hong Kong in twenty-one days, discharged in seventeen and sailed for Saigon on a passage of ten days. Another cargo of rice was taken up in two weeks and Robinson left for Yokohama on a passage which took him another three weeks, running back to Foochow in six days.This had occupied the time between 10 January when the *Sir Lancelot* first arrived at Hong Kong – she sailed for Bangkok on the 27th – and 20 June, but she had missed the first clip and did not get away until 17 July.

12. It was absolutely essential to keep the cargo dry, one of the reasons that composite-built ships were so suited to this trade, giving the internal capacity and strength of an iron frame, but without the problems of condensation inherent with an iron shell.

13. The *Fiery Cross* was taken over from Robinson by Captain George Kirkup in late 1866 but in 1868 he was poisoned by his Chinese steward, dying at Hong Kong.

14. Reckoned by Shewan to be a very fast clipper, the *Ellen Rodger* was lost by stranding in the Gaspar Strait on 20 September 1866. She was commanded by Captain E. Corbett.

15. There were other crack clippers in the 1866 season such as the *Falcon, Ziba, Belted Will, Min, Highflyer* – whose master, Captain Shutter, died at Shanghai – *Eliza Shaw, Challenger, Scaufell* and Brocklebanks' *Veronica*, to name but some.

16. I am indebted to Alexander Aiken's privately published monograph, *The Steamer Tea Races*, 1996. Mr Aiken, writing of 1866 when the *Erl King* had no other British challenger – the *Agamemnon* then being outward bound – points out that: 'As a matter of record, prior to the regular opening of the market, 2,868 chests of Congou and 500 half-chests of Oolong had been shipped to Hankow; for eventual transmission to England by the French mail steamer which left Shanghai on 23rd May.'

17. The maximum speed a hull can be driven depends upon the resistance its forward motion builds up in smooth water.The theoretical maximum is 1.15 $\sqrt{\text{waterline length}}$, which of course depends upon loaded draught. Later, longer and heavier-built sailing-vessels would exceed these speeds, as did the large American-built clippers used by James Baines's Black Ball Line, but the near-perfection of the best of the China tea-clippers rested on them making fairly consistent speeds irrespective of the wind-strength so that good all-round performance served best.The flyers like *Sir Lancelot, Thermopylae* and *Cutty Sark*, were capable – more-or-less – of this consistency.

18. The *Ariel* was not the only clipper thought to have been lost by pooping – *Omba*, being another – and many came to sad ends, that of *Sir Lancelot* probably being due to over-loading with salt.The handling of these thoroughbreds was not easy and in their dotage they were often under-manned or carrying cargoes for which they were unsuited, or which shifted easily.The superb *Kaisow*, built in 1868 by Steele at Greenock, was knocked down in a storm, only hours after leaving Valparaiso in 1891 with a cargo of manganese ore for Britain. Sold by Killick, Martin & Co. to William Bowen of South

Wales she had a crew of only sixteen when her cargo shifted and she sank. The *Eliza Shaw* foundered off the Cape of Good Hope with a crew of nineteen, Duncan Dunbar's last ship, the clipper *Fychow*, went missing in the North Atlantic with a crew of twenty and the *Chaa-tsze* stranded with a crew of only twelve! Most, however, were lost by striking uncharted or erroneously charted reefs, sometimes through faulty navigation attributable to a lack of sights, and the South China Sea, the Gaspar and Sunda Straits is littered with their bones. Such were the fates of the *Yang-tsze*, *Taeping* and *Serica* among others.

19. Andrew Shewan's delightfully evocative memoir, *The Great Days of Sail*, is full of insights and details. His chapter condemning Inglis, whom he clearly did not dislike, is entitled: *How It Was Not Done*.

20. The shipping of a temporary rudder in heavy seas was a truly amazing feat of ingenuity and seamanship, and Moodie and his men, including two stowaways one of whom proved to be a carpenter and the other a blacksmith materially assisted, deserve every possible credit for the feat. John Willis's brother, who was aboard for his health, tried to order Moodie to make for the nearest port, but Moodie was having none of it. With his apprentice son plying the bellows to the forge and at one point being severely burned, the contrivance was manufactured and got over the counter. Not without several setbacks and considerable difficulties, during which Moodie showed his mettle as a seaman by making a stern board to secure the jury-rig in place, they were triumphant and sailed all the way home under home-made steering. However, their achievement was not unique and several sailing ships, including the *City of Adelaide* under Captain Edward Alsdton in 1877, lost their rudders and had a substitute shipped at sea fabricated from materials on board, so much so that the 'shipping of a jury rudder' was for a long time a subject raised at Board of Trade examinations for masters and mates.

21. From the trial report quoted by Lubbock in his appendix to *The Log of the* Cutty Sark.

22. Like the *Jeddah* incident which furnished Joseph Conrad with the basis of his plot for *Lord Jim*, the manslaughter incident in *Cutty Sark* provided the inspiration for *The Secret Sharer*, while his command of the *Otago* provided the imaginative vehicle.

23. There is an inference in Basil Lubbock's writing that, but for the bad blood that existed between the *Navahoe*'s master and radio-officer, the 'Horse and Cart' might have gone to the assistance of the *Titanic* but the careful Lubbock does not make it explicit that Anderson was the fractious man in charge of the ugly great sailing barge at the time. Anderson died in February 1922 when undergoing surgery for cancer. See also *More Days, More Dollars*.

24. The hull on the stocks had actually been laid down as an auxiliary steam-whaler but her intended owners went bankrupt. Although never comparable with the extreme-clippers, the *Chaa-sze* made some competent passages and like *The Tweed* was one of a number of conversion of steamers which proved able sailing-vessels. Although Turner & Co. requested the ship be obtained, her actual owner was John W. Dudgeon who owned her from 1860 until selling her to Baring Bros in 1867. She was afterwards sold to Devitt & Moore for their Australian trade and then, in 1874 passed to Delaney of London who employed her in the West Indian sugar trade. She was lost off French Guiana later that year.

25. Quoted by Shewan, p160 *et seq*. Piracy was to continue in the region and has not yet been suppressed in 2009.

26. The *Caliph* was owned by Alexander Hector, a cousin of John Willis, and was intended as an improvement on the *Thermopylae*. It was supposed that the ship had touched bottom and had not got off before being surrounded by pirate-cum-fishing junks which, having looted the vessel, set her on fire. Shewan believed her to have been carrying explosives among her general cargo, which ensured her complete destruction. Given the mysterious

disappearances of ships in the South China Sea in the last years of the twentieth century, nothing seems beyond possibility in these waters.

27. See Kirkaldy, A.W., *British Shipping*, p324 *et seq*. This shows the grip that sailing ships maintained on world trade and the slow development and relatively small numbers of steamers involved in global terms.

28. French threats to India and the route to the east had emerged in the Napoleonic War and were only ended by Nelson's victory at Aboukir Bay. When in Egypt Napoleon had had his engineers consider a possible canal, which they did positively. In 1869 France was ruled by Napoleon's nephew, though Napoleon III did not long outlast the canal's opening.

29. The grand opening passage of ships was led by the French Imperial Yacht *L'Aigle* and the Khedivial yacht *Mahroussah*. Although a small British naval vessel attempted to force her way ahead of *L'Aigle*, she was quickly hustled out of the procession and there were otherwise few British present. Sir Frederick Arrow, who was a master-mariner and Elder Brother of Trinity House, wrote an evocative account of the event.

30. See Karabell, Z., *Parting the Desert, The Creation of the Suez Canal*, p262 *et seq*. The act marked increasing British interest and involvement in Egypt which in due course became a puppet-state within the wider embrace of the British Empire – a good example of the flag following trade. The Anglo-French Suez Canal Co. ran the canal until its takeover in 1956 by Colonel Nasser (who had been part of a military *coup d'etât* which deposed the Egyptian puppet, King Farouk, in 1952). Nasser's action provoked 'the Suez Crisis' and an invasion disastrous for their prestige by the two western powers condemned by the United States Government of President Eisenhower.

31. See Cornewall-Jones, R.J., *The British Merchant Service*, p156.

32. At its beginning the canal was 70ft wide at its bottom and 150ft at the surface, allowing for the angle of repose of sand. Its nominal depth was 26ft, though in several places it scarcely reached 20. By 1914 5,000 vessels a year were passing through a very much improved canal – most of its dangerous bends have been eliminated over the succeeding years – with a depth of over 34ft with a bottom width of 147ft and a surface width of 240ft.

33. Falkus, M., *The Blue Funnel Legend*, Macmillan, 1990, p77.

34. For an account of the transplanting of rubber from Brazil, see *More Days, More Dollars*, Vol. 4 of this work, Chapter 3.

35. Not to be confused with the paddle-steamer of the same name operated by Jardine, Matheson and Butterfield & Swire on the China coast.

36. Some time later *Glenartney* was to reduce this to forty-one days, but by then the record was down to thirty-one days.

37. Thomas Skinner's Castle Line should not be confused with Donald Currie's later steamship company. Skinner was said to have been 'a great moving spirit in building clippers on spec and selling as well as owning… [He was] a very clear, level headed practical man'. Skinner owned a number of tea-clippers, none built on extreme lines and which have therefore been largely forgotten. See MacGregor's *The Tea-clippers*.

38. The fall in freight rates and over-tonnaging were in a sense a circulatory circumstance. In 1866 freight rates were about £6 6s per ton but after the canal was opened they dropped to £4 10s and then, by 1877 to £1 10s. This did not reflect a fall in the volume of trade; on the contrary the trade boomed and this attracted over-tonnage which, with the fluctuating rates attached to tea, made a difficult situation worse. This naturally drove the established China traders to form a mutually beneficial but protective cartel in the form of the Far East Conference.

39. Parry, J.H., and Sherlock, P.M., *A Short History of the West Indies*, p188 *et seq*.

40. The Crimean War which put an unprecedented demand on shipping also seriously disrupted schedules, particularly those carrying the mails. The Cape-routed Australian

mail contract was open to tender in 1856 and, lost to P&O, went to the new European & Australian Steam Packet Co. The company owned only two ships and tried to pass the contract to P&O on condition they bought the two ships. The P&O board turned this down, leaving the E&ASP Co. to charter additional tonnage, the Cunarder *Etna*. This was not enough to fulfil the contract and despite overtures to Royal Mail, the company went into liquidation and P&O resumed its carriage of the Australia mails.

41. See Orbell, J., *From Cape to Cape, The History of Lyle Shipping Company*, p24 *et seq.*

42. The Limited Liabilities Act of 1862 freed up capital and revolutionised the financing of shipping which in part explains the increase in steam tonnage in the 1860s.

43. Most notable among these was the loss of the *Oregon* which was in collision with an unidentified vessel in fog near New York in 1885. She was believed to have been struck by a large, laden American schooner which pierced two large forward compartments either side of a water-tight bulkhead. The proximity of other vessels saved the *Oregon's* crew and passengers but the schooner is supposed to have sunk with all hands.

44. It is a point worth noting that shipping companies increasingly tended to market their 'brands' by adopting in addition to a distinctive house-flag, funnel colours and painted livery for their ships' hulls, distinctive names. With a few exceptions, like their two later 'Queens', Cunard ships' names ended with the suffix *-ia*, White Star liners *-ic*; while Brocklebanks began with *M*, Canadian Pacific *Empress of -*, Hains the prefix *Tre-* and J. and C. Harrison of London *Har-*. Other companies adopted themes: castles, glens, rivers, birds, professions, counties, lochs, artists and philosophers. P&O took up oriental names; British India, Indian names; PSNC, South American names; while Alfred Holt's Blue Funnel Line recalled the heroes and heroines of Homer's *Iliad* and *Odyssey* (not all were heroes, the author sailed in the *Elpenor*, named after a swine-herd who fell into a drunken stupor while on a roof and fell to his death as a consequence!).

45. There were many other influential persons in this grand agitation, including the writer Charles Reade whose brother William was a seaman. For the full story see *The Plimsoll Sensation* by Nicolette Jones. Not all owners were opposed to a load line or hostile to reform. In September of that year Thompson's Aberdeen White Star Line launched a full-rigged ship named *Samuel Plimsoll* in the reformer's honour.

46. Falkus, *The Blue Funnel Legend*, p108.

47. For example Major W.T. Johnson's *Gunboats for Volunteers Containing Particulars on the Above Subject Collected by the Author During a Tour Round the Coast*.

48. Among the cadets at this time was a Japanese youth, Togo Hehachero, a future admiral in the Imperial Japanese Navy and the victor of Tsu-shima.

49. When in recent years the graveyard was cleared, Williams's gravestone was removed to his birthplace of Porthleven, Cornwall, largely thanks to Captain Joshua Garner.

50. Forwood, p71.

51. This was the *Garonne* which was approaching the Gulf of Aden and well ahead of her reckoning and the master's and second officer's longitude. Ras Hafun is some ninety miles south of Cape Guardafui, so she was also well south, the cape marking the southern entrance to the gulf. At this time the Orient steamers sailed outwards to Australia by way of Capetown and came home through the Suez Canal.

52. Donald Currie's brother James had also left Cunard employment at the same time as his younger sibling, moving to Leith where, in due course, he founded the Currie Line, linking Leith and Liverpool with Europe.

BIBLIOGRAPHY

PUBLISHED MATERIAL
All published in London unless otherwise stated

Aiken, A., *The Steamer Tea Races*, published by the Author, Glasgow, 1996

Allen, J., *The Sea Years of Joseph Conrad*, Methuen, London, 1967

Allison, R.S., *Sea Diseases*, John Bale Medical Publications, 1943

Ballinghall, J., *The Mercantile Navy Improved or A Plan for the Greater Safety of Lives and Property in Steam Vessels, Packets, Smacks and Yachts*, W. Morrison, 1832

Barnes, H.C.B., *Troopships and Their History*, Seeley, Service, 1963

Barrett, C.R.B. (Editor) *The Trinity House*, Lawrence and Bullen, 1893

Barrow, T., *The Whaling Trade of North–East England, 1750–1850*, University of Sunderland Press, Sunderland, 2001

Bateson, C., *The Convict Ships*, Brown, Son & Ferguson, Glasgow, 1969

Bell, R.C. (Editor) *Diaries from the Days of Sail*, Holt, Rinehart & Winston, New York, 1974

Biden, C., *Naval Discipline in the Merchant Service*, J.M. Richardson, 1830

Blackmore, E., *The British Mercantile marine: A Short Historical Review*, Charles Griffin, 1897

Blake, G., *The Ben Line*, Thomas Nelson, Edinburgh, 1956

    B.I. Centenary, 1856–1956, Collins, 1956

    Gellatly's, 1862–1962, Blackie, Glasgow, 1962

Blake, R., *Jardine Matheson – Traders of the Far East*, Weidenfeld and Nicolson, 1999

Bott, A., *The Sailing Ships of the New Zealand Shipping Company, 1873–1900*, B.T. Batsford, 1972

Bouquet, M., *South Eastern Sail, from the Medway to the Solent, 1840–1940*, David and Charles, Newton Abbot, 1972

Bowditch, N., *American Practical Navigator*, Defense Mapping Agency Hydrographic/Topographic Center, Washington, 1984

Bowen, F.T., *The Men of the Merchant Service*, Macmillian, 1900

Brooks, L., and Ducé, R.H. (Editors), *Seafarers, Ships and Cargoes*, University of London Press, 1951

Brown, C.H., *Nicholls's Seamanship and Nautical Knowledge*, Brown, Son & Ferguson, Glasgow, 1958

Brown, R.D. *The Port of London*, Terence Dalton, Lavenham, 1978

Bullen, F.T., *The Men of the Merchant Service*, Macmillan, 1900

Bulley, A., *The Bombay Country Ships, 1790–1833*, Curzon, Richmond, 2000

Bushell, T.A. *'Royal Mail', A Centenary History of the Royal Mail Line, 1839–1939*, Trade and Travel Publications, 1939

Cable, B., *A Hundred Year History of the P & O*, Ivor Nicholson and Watson, 1937

Cameron, V.L., *The Log of a Jack Tar; or, the Life of James Choyce, Master Mariner*, Fisher Unwin, 1891

Carnegie, H., *Harnessing the Wind, Captain Thomas Mitchell of the Aberdeen White Star Line*, University of Aberdeen, Aberdeen, 1991

Carson, R., *The Sea Around Us*, Readers Union, 1953

Chandler, G., *Liverpool Shipping*, Phoenix House, 1960

Charton, B., and Tietjen, J., *Seas and Oceans*, Collins, 1989

Chatterton, E.K., *Valiant Sailormen*, Hurst and Blackett, 1936

    The Mercantile Marine, Heinemann, 1923

    Windjammers and Shellbacks, Fisher Unwin, 1926

    Ventures and Voyages, Rich and Cowan, 1935

    The Old East Indiamen, Conway Maritime, 1971

    Seamen All, Philip Allan & Co. Ltd, 1928

Clark, A.H., *The Clipper Ship Era, 1843–1869*, 7 C's Press, Riverside, 1970

Coates, W.H, *The Good Old Days of Shipping*, The 'Times of India' Press, Bombay, 1900

    The Old 'Country Trade' of the East Indies, Imray, Laurie, Norie & Wilson, 1911

Cole, S., *Our Home Ports*, Effingham Wilson, 1923

Collis, M., *British Merchant Adventurers*, Collins, 1942

Raffles, Faber and Faber, 1966

Conrad, J., *The Mirror of the Sea, Memories and Impressions*, Methuen, 1935

Cope, L.C., *A Century of Sea Trading, the General Steam Navigation Company Ltd, 1824–1924*, A. & C. Black, 1924

    The Sea Carriers, 1825 – 1925, The Aberdeen Line, Published by the Company, 1925

Cornewall-Jones, R.J., *The British Merchant Service*, Sampson Low, Marston, 1898

Cotton, Sir E., *East Indiamen*, The Batchworth Press, 1949

Course, A.G., *Painted Ports, The Story of the Ships of Messrs Devitt and Moore*, Hollis and Carter, 1961

    The Merchant Navy, A Social History, Frederick Muller, 1963

Cowen, R.C., *Frontiers of the Sea*, Gollancz, 1960

Cree, E. (Edited by Lieven, M.) *The Cree Journals*, Webb & Bower, Exeter, 1981

Crutchley, W.C., *My Life at Sea*, Collins, 1912

Cunliffe, T. (Editor and Principal Author), *Pilots – The World of Pilotage Under Sail and Oars*: Volume 1, *Pilot Schooners of Great Britain and North America*, Le Chasse-Marée/Maritime Life and Traditions, Douarnenez, France, 2001

    Volume 2, *Schooners and Open Boats of the European Pilots and Watermen*, Le Chasse-Marée/Maritime Life and Traditions, Douarnenez, France and Chatham Publishing, Rochester, 2002

Cubbin, G., *Harrisons of Liverpool, A Chronicle of Ships and Men, 1830–2002*, World Ships Society and Ships in Focus, Preston and Gravesend, 2003

Dickens, C., *American Notes*, Caxton (The London Edition), undated

    The Marine Shop from Sketches by 'Boz', Caxton (The London Edition), undated

Downie, W.I., *Reminscences of a Blackwall Midshipman*, W.J. Ham-Smith, 1912

Druett, J., *Rough Medicine, Surgeons at Sea in the Age of Sail*, Routledge, New York, 2000

Dugan, J., *The Great Iron Ship*, Harper and Brothers, New York, 1953

Dulles, F.R., *The Old China Trade*, Houghton Miflin, Boston, 1930

Eames, A., *Ship Master, The Life and Letters of Capt. Robert Thomas, 1843–1903*, Gwyedd Archive Service, 1980

Ellacott, S.E., *The Seaman*, two volumes, Abelard-Schuman, 1970

Ericson, D.B., and Wollin, G., *The Ever-Changing Sea*, Paladin, 1968

Falkus, M., *The Blue Funnel Legend, A History of the Ocean Steamship Co, 1865–1973*, Macmillan, 1990

Farrington, A., *A Biographical Index of East India Company Maritime Service Officers, 1600–1834*, The British Library, 1999

Fayle, C.E., *Seaborne Trade*, Three Volumes, John Murray, 1922-1924

Foreman, S., *Shoes and Ships and Sealing Wax, An Illustrated History of the Board of Trade, 1786–1986*, HMSO, 1986

Forwood, W.B., *Reminiscences of a Liverpool Shipowner, 1850–1920*, Henry Young, Liverpool, 1920

Fox, S., *The Ocean Railway*, HarperCollins, 2003

Fox-Smith, C., *Ocean Racers*, Philip Allan, 1931

Gee, M., *Captain Fraser's Voyages*, Stanford Maritime, 1979

Gibson, J.F. *Brocklebanks, 1770–1950* (Two Volumes), Henry Young, Liverpool, 1953

Gibb, D.E.W., *Lloyd's of London, A Study in Individualism*, Lloyd's, 1972

Golding, T. (Editor), *Trinity House from Within*, Trinity House, 1929

Greenhill, B. and Stonham, D., *Seafaring Under Sail, The Life of the Merchant Seaman*, Patrick Stephens, Cambridge

Gurney, A., *Compass, A Story of Exploration and Innovation*, W.W. Norton, New York, 2004

Hackman, R., *Ships of the East India Company*, World Ship Society, Gravesend, 2001

Haigh, K.R., *Cableships and Submarine Cables*, Adlard Coles, 1968

Haines, R., *Life & Death in the Age of Sail, The Passage to Australia*, National Maritime Museum, Greenwich, 2005

Hall, A., and Heywood, F., *Shipping, A Guide to the Routine in Connection with the Importation and Exportation of Goods and the Clearance of Vessels Inwards and Outwards*, Pitman, 1921

Hardy, C., *A Register of Ships Employed in the Service of the United East India Company from the Year 1760 to the Conclusion of the Commercial Charter*, Parbury Allen & Co., 1835

Haws, D., and Hurst, A.A., *The Maritime History of the World*, Two Volumes, Teredo Books, Brighton, 1985

Hay, K.M. and Roberts, J., *The Sea Voyages of Edward Beck in the 1820s*, Pentland Press, Durham, 1996

Heaton, P.M., *Booth Line*, P.M. Heaton Publishing, Abergavenny, 1987, *Lamport and Holt*, P.M. Heaton Publishing, Abergavenny, 2004

Hernon, I., *Britain's Forgotten Wars, Colonial Campaigns of the 19th Century*, Sutton Publishing, Stroud, 2003

Hollett, D., *Passage to the New World, Packet Ships and Irish Famine Emigrants, 1845–1851*, P.M. Heaton Publishing, Abergavenny, 1995

HMSO, *The Mariner's Handbook*, Sixth Edition, 1989
    Ocean Passages for the World, Third Edition, 1973
    Seafarers and Their Ships, 1955

Home, W.E., *Merchant Seamen, Their Diseases and Their Welfare Needs*, John Murray, 1922

Hope, R., *A New History of British Shipping*, John Murray, 1990
    Poor Jack, Chatham, 2001
    The Merchant Navy, Stanford Maritime, 1980

Horder, M., *On Their Own, Shipwrecks and Survivals*, Duckworth, 1988

Howarth, D., and Howarth, S., *The Story of P & O*, Weidenfeld and Nicolson, 1986

Hughes, R., *The Fatal Shore*, Collins Harvill, 1987

Hughill, S., *Shanties from the Seven Seas, Shipboard Work-Songs*, Routledge and Kegan Paul, 1984

Hurd, A., *Britain's Merchant Navy*, Odhams, 1943
    The Sea Traders, Cassell, 1921

Hurd, D., *The Arrow War*, Collins, 1967

Hyde, F.E., *Blue Funnel*, Liverpool University Press, 1956
  Shipping Enterprise and Management, Harrisons of Liverpool, 1830–1939, Liverpool University Press, Liverpool, 1967
Jones, C., *Sea Trading and Sea Training*, Edward Arnold, 1936
Pioneer Shipowners, Journal of Commerce and Shipping, Liverpool, 1934
Chief Officer in China, 1840–1853, Charles Birchall, Liverpool, 1955
Jones, N., *The Plimsoll Sensation, The Great Campaign to Save Lives at Sea*, Little Brown, 2006
Karabell, Z., *Parting the Desert, The Creation of the Suez Canal*, Alfred A. Knopf, New York, 2003
Keay, J., *The Honourable Company, A History of the English East India Company*, Harper Collins, 1991
Kemp, P. (Editor), *The Oxford Companion to Ships and the Sea*, OUP, Oxford, 1988
Kennedy, G. (Editor), *The Merchant Marine in International Affairs, 1850–1950*, Frank Cass, 2001
Kirkaldy, A.W., *British Shipping, its History, Organisation and Importance*, Kegan Paul, Trench, Trübner & Co. Ltd, 1914
Kwang-Ching, L., *Anglo–American Steamship Rivalry in China, 1862–1874*, Harvard University Press, Cambridge, Massachusetts, 1962
Lawson, W., *Pacific Steamers*, Brown, Son & Ferguson, Glasgow, 1927
Laird, D., *Paddy Henderson*, George Outram, Glasgow, 1961
Lee, A. (Editor), *The Voyage of the* Caroline*, 1827–28*, by Rosalie Hare, with chapters on the Early History of Northern Tasmania, Java, Mauritius and St Helena, Longmans, Green, 1927
Lindsay, W.S., *History of Merchant Shipping, 1816–1874*, Two Volumes, Sampson Low & Co., Undated (*circa* 1890)
Lovett Cameron, V. (Editor), *The Log of a Jack Tar*, Fisher Unwin, 1891
Lubbock, B., *The Log of the* Cutty Sark, James Brown, Glasgow, 1924
  The Western Ocean Packets, Brown, Son & Ferguson, Glasgow, 1977
  The China Clippers, Brown, Son & Ferguson, Glasgow, 1929
  The Blackwall Frigates, Brown, Son & Ferguson, Glasgow, 1922
  The Opium-clippers, Brown, Son & Ferguson, Glasgow, 1953
  Coolie Ships and Oil Sailers, Brown, Son & Ferguson, Glasgow, 1955
  The Colonial Clippers, Brown, Son & Ferguson, Glasgow, 1975
  The Arctic Whalers, Glasgow, Brown, Son & Ferguson, Glasgow, 1978
Lubbock, B., and Spurling, J., *Sail*, Volume 1, Blue Peter Publications, 1927
  Sail, Volume 2, Blue Peter Publications, 1929
  Sail, Volume 3, Blue Peter Publications, 1936
MacGregor, D., *The China Bird*, Chatto and Windus, 1961
  Clipper Ships, Argus Books, Watford, 1979
  Merchant Sailing Ships, 1815–1850, Conway, 1984
  Merchant Sailing Ships, 1850–1875, Conway, 1988
  The Tea-clippers, Their History and Development, 1833–1875, Conway, 1983
  Fast Sailing Ships, Their Design and Construction, 1775–1875, Conway, 1988
  Schooners in Four Centuries, Argus Books, Hemel Hempstead, 1982
Marquand, H., *Memoirs of a Victorian Master Mariner*, Merton Priory Press, Cardiff, 1996
Mason, M., Greenhill, B. and Craig, R., *The British Seafarer*, Hutchinson/BBC/National Maritime Museum, 1980
Mathews, B., *The Ships of Peace*, London Missionary Society, 1919
Mathias, P., and Pearsall, A.W.H., *Shipping: A Survey of Historical Records*, David & Charles, Newton Abbot, 1971
McLellan, *Anchor Line, 1856–1956*, Anchor Line Ltd, Glasgow, 1956
McLuskie, T., *Harland and Wolff, Designs from the Shipbuilding Empire*, Conway, 1998

Mill, H.R., *Siege of the South Pole*, Alston Rivers, 1905

Moffat, H.Y., *From Ship's Boy to Skipper*, Alexander Gardner, Paisley, 1911

Morse, H.B., *The East India Company Trading to China, 1635–1834*, Five Volumes, Oxford University Press, Undated (*c.*1860)

Moyse-Bartlett, H., *A History of the Merchant Navy*, Harrap, 1937

Mould, D.D.C.P. *Captain Roberts of The* Sirius, *Sirius* Commemoration Committee, Cork, 1988

Murray, M., *Union–Castle Chronicle, 1853–1953*, Longmans, Green & Co., 1953

Newton, A.P., *A Hundred Years of the British Empire*, Duckworth, 1940

Newton, J., *A Century of Tankers*, Intertanko, 2002

Norie, J.W., *A Complete Epitome of Navigation*, Charles Wilson, 1864

Norway, A.H., *History of the Post Office Packet Service*, Macmillan & Co., 1895

Orbell, J., *From Cape to Cape, The History of Lyle Shipping*, Paul Harris Publishing, Edinburgh, 1978

P&O, *The P&O, Pocket Book*, A. & C. Black, 1926

Palmer, S., *Politics, Shipping and the Repeal of the Navigation Laws*, Manchester University Press, 1990

Paterson, N., *The China Run; Being the Biography of a Great–Grandmother*, Hodder & Stoughton, 1949

Pixley, W., *Short Autobiography of Captain William Pixley*, W.H. Smith & Son, 1916

Plimsoll, S., *Our Seamen, An Appeal*, Virtue & Co., 1873

Read, A., *The Coastwise Trade of the United Kingdom*, George Thompson, 1925

Rice, A.L., *British Oceanographic Vessels, 1800–1950*, The Ray Society, 1986

Rinman, T., and Brodefors, R., *The Commercial History of Shipping*, Rinman & Lindén AB, Gothenburg, 1983

Ritchie, G.S., *The Admiralty Chart, British Naval Hydrography in the Nineteenth Century*, The Pentland Press, 1995

Robinson, A.H.W., *Marine Cartography in Britain*, Leicester University Press, Leicester, 1962

Rosser, W.H., *The Law of Storms Considered Practically*, Charles Wilson, 1876

Runciman, W., *Collier Brigs and Their Sailors*, Fisher Unwin, 1926

Ruthven, J.F., *Memoirs of Jocelyn Fitzgerald Ruthven, Master Mariner, 1849–1943*, Norman Adlard, Ipswich, 1949

Rutter, O., *Red Ensign, A History of Convoy*, Robert Hale, 1942

Sargent, A.J., *Seaways of the Empire, Notes on the Geography of Transport*, A. & C. Black, 1930

Scoresby, W., *Journal of a Voyage to the Northern Whale–Fishery*, Archibald Constable, Edinburgh, 1823

Scott, J.M., *The White Poppy*, Heinemann, 1969

Shaw, F.H., *Splendour of the Seas*, Edward Stanford, 1953

Shewan, A., *The Great Days of Sail; Some Reminiscences of a Tea–Clipper Captain*, Heath Cranton, 1927

Simpson, G., *The Naval Constructor*, Kegan Paul, Trench & Trübner, 1904

Smith, K., Wattes, C.T. and Watts, M.J., *Records of Merchant Shipping and Seamen*, Public Records Office Guide No.20, PRO Publications, 1998

Stamp, D., *The World, A General Geography*, Longmans, 1966

Starkey, D.J., and Jamieson, A.G., *Exploiting the Sea, Aspects of Britain's Maritime Economy Since 1870*, University of Exeter Press, 1998

Stevens, E.F., *One Hundred Years of Houlders,* Houlder Bros & Co. Ltd, 1950

Sturmey, S.G., *British Shipping and World Competition*, Athlone Press, 1962

Stewart, J.C., *The Sea Our Heritage*, Rowan Press, Rowan Press, Keith, 1995

Strachan, M., *The Ben Line, 1825–1982, An Anecdotal History*, Michael Russell, Norwich, 1992

Sutton, J., *Lords of the East, the East India Company and its Ships*, Conway, 1981

Thomas, R.E., *Stowage: The Properties and Stowage of Cargoes*, Revised Edition, Brown, Son & Ferguson Ltd, Glasgow, 1963

Thornton, R.H., *British Shipping*, Cambridge University Press, 1939

Todd, J., and Whall, W.B., *Practical Seamanship for use in the Merchant Service*, George Philip & Son, 1898

Villiers, A., *Monsoon Seas, The Story of the Indian Ocean*, McGraw-Hill, New York, 1952
Voyaging with the Wind, HMSO, 1975

Walthew, K., *From Rock and Tempest, The Life of Captain George William Manby*, Geoffrey Bles, 1971

Watson, L., *Heaven's Breath, A Natural History of the Wind*, Coronet, 1985

Watson, N., *The Bibby Line, 1807–1990*, James & James, 1990

Wedge, P.L., *Brown's Flag and Funnels*, Brown, Son & Ferguson, 1958

Were, T. N., *Memoir of Thomas Narramore Were*, Griffith, Farran and Welsh, 1887

Williamson, J.A., *The Ocean in English History*, Clarendon, Oxford, 1941

Wilson, C., *Seamanship; Both in Theory and Practice*, Norie and Wilson, 1841

Woodman, R.M., *The History of the Ship*, Conway, 1997
Keepers of the Sea, Revised Edition, Chaffcutter, Ware, 2005
with Wilson, J., *The Lighthouses of Trinity House*, Thomas Reed, Bradford on Avon, 2002

Young, G., *In Search of Conrad*, Hutchinson, 1991

UNPUBLISHED MATERIAL

Baker, John, *Log Book No 1, July 1838 to July 1851*, comprising service from Midshipman to Chief Officer in the ships *Duke of Bedford, John Line, George the Fourth, John Bibby, Zenobia, Earl Grey* and *Mary Ann* (with thanks to the Honourable Company of Master Mariners).

Fairplay, P., *The Pacific Telegraph Cable, 1902, Technological, Commercial and Political Effects*, MA Thesis, University of Greenwich, 2003 (with grateful acknowledgement to Captain Patrick Fairplay).

Singleton, C., *The Competence, Training and Education of the British Nineteenth–Century Master–Mariner, with particular reference to the years from 1815 to 1873*, PhD Thesis, University of London, 1996 (with grateful acknowledgement to Colin Singleton).

OTHER SOURCES

Information has also been culled over a period of many years from a variety of magazines and periodicals, many of them now sadly defunct. These included *The Geographical Journal, The Scottish Geographical Magazine, Great Circle, Polar Record, The Windsor Magazine, The Marine Magazine, The Blue Peter Magazine, The Marine Observer, Sea Breezes* and Sea Breezes Publications, *Ships Monthly, The NUMAST Telegraph, The Mariner's Mirror, Maritime Heritage, Maritime Life and Times, The Seafarer* (now just plain *Seafarer*), and *The Journal of the Honourable Company of Master Mariners*. Other information has been sourced from the publications of The World Ship Trust, The World Ship Society and a number of the 'Ships in Focus' books, and reference has been made to the *Oxford Dictionary of National Biography*. To the producers of these, past and present, I acknowledge my debt.

INDEX

INDEX OF SELECTED SHIPS

Visit our website and discover thousands of other History Press books.
www.thehistorypress.co.uk